Meet the *Southern Living* Foods Staff

On these pages we present the *Southern Living* Foods Staff (left to right in each photograph).

Diane Hogan, Test Kitchens Home Economist; Peggy Smith, Marketing Manager

Susan J. Reynolds, Foods Editor

Leslie Byars, Photo Stylist; Charles Walton IV, Senior Foods Photographer; J. Savage Gibson, Photographer; Tina Evans, Photographer

Patty Vann, Assistant Test Kitchens Director; Kaye Mabry Adams, Test Kitchens Director and Recipe Editor

Susan Dosier, Associate Foods Editor; Dana Adkins Campbell, Associate Foods Editor

Karen Brechin, Editorial Assistant; Jodi Jackson Loe, Editorial Assistant

Elle Barrett, Assistant Foods Editor; Susan Hawthorne Nash, Assistant Foods Editor

Jane Cairns, Test Kitchen Home Economist; Julia Dowling, Test Kitchen Home Economist; Judy Feagin, Test Kitchen Home Economist

Southern Living

1993 ANNUAL RECIPES

Oxmoor
House

Library of Congress Catalog Number: 79-88364
ISBN: 0-8487-1142-4
ISSN: 0272-2003

Manufactured in the United States of America
First printing 1993

Southern Living®
    Foods Editor: Susan J. Reynolds
    Associate Foods Editors: Dana Adkins Campbell,
        Susan Dosier
    Assistant Foods Editors: Elle Barrett,
        Susan Hawthorne Nash
    Editorial Assistants: Karen Brechin, Jodi Jackson Loe
    Test Kitchens Director and Recipe Editor: Kaye Adams
    Assistant Test Kitchens Director: Patty Vann
    Test Kitchens Staff: Jane Cairns, Julia Dowling,
        Judy Feagin, Diane Hogan, Peggy Smith
    Senior Foods Photographer: Charles E. Walton IV
    Photographers: Tina Evans, J. Savage Gibson
    Additional photography by Jim Bathie, page 148; Colleen
        Duffley, page 152; Sylvia Martin, pages 37, 40, 73, 109,
        111, 145, 297; Howard L. Puckett, cover, pages 185 and 333
    Photo Stylist: Leslie Byars
    Additional styling by Bob Gager, pages 37, 40, 73, 109, 145;
        Marjorie Johnston, pages 111 and 185
    Production Manager: Kay Fuston
    Assistant Production Manager: Vicki Weathers

Oxmoor House, Inc.
    Editor-in-Chief: Nancy J. Fitzpatrick
    Senior Foods Editor: Susan Carlisle Payne
    Director of Manufacturing: Jerry R. Higdon
    Art Director: James Boone

Southern Living® 1993 Annual Recipes

    Senior Editor: Olivia Kindig Wells
    Copy Editor: Donna Baldone
    Editorial Assistant: Whitney Wheeler

    Production Manager: Rick Litton
    Associate Production Manager: Theresa L. Beste
    Production Assistant: Marianne Jordan

    Editorial Consultant: Jean Wickstrom Liles
    Indexer: Mary Ann Laurens
    Designer and Illustrator: Carol Middleton

Cover: *Compose a sweet memory for the chocolate lover at
your dinner table, and serve White Chocolate Mousse
in a showstopper Small Chocolate Sack. (Recipes begin
on page 314.)*

Back cover: *Refrigerated piecrusts and commercial lemon curd
make Bowl-Me-Over Fresh Fruit Tarts (page 200) easy.*

Page 1: *Ice cream and cake become a heavenly confection in
Triple Mint Ice-Cream Angel Dessert (page 86).*

Page 4: *Reel in the compliments with Grilled Herbed Salmon
Steaks with Fresh Tomato Sauce Over Basil Pasta (recipes,
page 176) and your favorite summer salad.*

Table of Contents

**Our Year
at *Southern Living***   **10**

January   **11**

Football, Feasting, And Fun   12
Quick & Easy: Start With Chicken   14
On The Light Side: Marinade Magic
   For Beef   15
Light Menu: Wake Up Breakfast
   For A Change   16
Light Favorite: Cream Of
   Broccoli Soup   17
A Cook's Guide To
   Weeknight Survival   18
Put The Freeze On Winter Blues   20
Salads Bloom With Citrus   21
Dive Into Belgian Endive   22
From Our Kitchen To Yours   23
Layer On The Flavor   24
Southern Living Hall Of Fame:
   Southern Sideboards   26

February   **27**

South Florida Sampler   28
Cast Iron: Well Seasoned And Timeless   32
From Our Kitchen To Yours   33
On The Light Side: The Unexpected
   Side Of Chocolate   34

Light Menu: Serve A Relaxing Dinner
   For Two   35
Light Favorite: Dip Into Mock
   Guacamole   36
Anise Flavors The Bread   36
Quick & Easy: Cook Valentine's
   Dinner For Dad   41
Winter Shortcakes   42
Batter Up For These Vegetable
   Pancakes   43
Spruced Up Vegetables   44
Homesick? Try A Pot Pie   45
Weeknight Family Fare   46
Come Home To Breakfast   47
Ginger And Pears—Wow!   47
Begin With A White Sauce   48
A Taste Of Tradition: Arnaud's 75th   49
Not Just Plain Pralines   50
Proof Of The Pudding   51
Baked With You In Mind   52
A Touch Of Almond Flavor   53
Potatoes Are Versatile Vegetables   54
Try Fresh Parmesan Cheese   55
Surprise Yourself With Fennel   56

March   **57**

Mamma Mia! Pizza With Pizzazz   58
Grits To Write Home About   60
Quick & Easy: Wrapping Up A Meal   62

Beef Up Weeknight Meals   63
An Italian-Inspired Terrine   64
Toss A Spring Medley Of Vegetables   65
On The Light Side: Healthful Dieting
   With Flair   66
Light Menu: Add A Fresh Accent
   To Fish   67
Light Favorite: Make Room For
   Eggs Benedict   68
Cumin: A Worldly Spice Comes Home   68
Keep Your Cool With Pepper Soup   69
Easy But Impressive Spring Fare   70
Pasta Toppers   70
Eatin' O' The Green   71
Southern Living Hall Of Fame:
   The Gasparilla Cookbook   72
Exercising The Need To Knead   77
Hot Dog! Supper's Ready   78
So Glad You Dropped By   79
Treats That Travel   80
Sunshine In Every Bite   81
Amazingly Gracious: Luncheon
   Is Served   82
From Our Kitchen To Yours   83

April   **85**

Angel Food Spectacular   86
Devilish Ideas For All Those Eggs   87
Easter At The White House   88

Light & Easy Special Section 89
   Weed Out Menus For Spring 89
   Don't Be Stingy With Starch 90
   Light Entrées In A Flash 91
   Is It A "Butter" Substitute? 92
   Snack Smart 93
   Beef Up Lean Red Meat 94
   What's New In The Dairy Case? 95
   Tour De John 97
   Simple Ways To Lighten
      Recipes 100

The New Flavors Of Grilling 101
From Our Kitchen To Yours 103
Forecast: Expecting Showers 104
Oil + Vinegar + Flavoring =
   Vinaigrette 106
Chicken Dinners With Real Pluck 107
Olé! Soups 108
Well-Seasoned Lamb 113
Bring On The Breadsticks 114
Observe Passover With Tzimmes 114
Quick & Easy: Let Them Eat Pie 114
Asparagus: A Delicacy Of Spring 115

May 117

Picnic At Wolf Trap 118
Breakfast—B&B Style 120
Sweet Onions To Cry For 124
On The Light Side: Help! The Boss Is
   Coming To Dinner 125
Light Favorite: Cookies For The
   Health Conscious 127
Quick & Easy: A Little Dab
   Will Do You 128
Southern Living Hall Of Fame:
   Mountain Measures 129
Shake Up A Cereal Snack 129

Classy Cooking Comes Easy 130
From Our Kitchen To Yours 132

June 133

The Jewels Of Summer 134
Preserve Earth's Bounty 135
From Our Kitchen To Yours 136
When The Time Is Ripe For
   Green Tomatoes 138
Eat The Peas *And* The Pod 138
Enjoy Summer's Easy Rhythm 139
Shortcuts To Make Summer
   Living Easy 142
Hooked On Salads 143
Bake A Batch Of Savory
   Muffins 144
Sorbets—Frozen To Perfection 153
On The Light Side: Have Your Cake
   And Eat It, Too 154
Light Menu: Enchant Guests With
   A Meatless Feast 155
Light Favorite: With
   Mexican Appeal 156
Add Flavor With Smoked Vegetable
   Puree 156
Chicken Takes Wing 157
Quick & Easy: Worldly BLTs 158
Come To Tea 159
Newfangled Biscuits 159
The Mighty Okra 160
Made-In-The-Shade Soups 161
Toppings For A Sweet Tooth 162

July 163

It's A Southern Affair 164
Quick & Easy: Lip-Smacking
   Peanut Butter Treats 166

Summer Suppers® Special Section 167
   20,000 Ideas Under The Sea 167
   Dinner On The Deck 170
   Going The Distance For Friends 171
   Ladies' Night Out 172
   Been Around The Block? 174
   Southern Hospitality Isn't
      Gone With The Wind 175
   Cool Off By The Pool 176

Revamping Camping 178
Southern Living Hall Of Fame:
   A Taste Of Oregon 179
On The Light Side: Scrap The Bacon,
   Taste The Vegetables 180
Light Favorite: Cornbread
   With Zip 182
From Our Kitchen To Yours 182
Fruits And Vegetables—Healthy
   Choices 183

August 189

Light Salads Dressed To Chill 190
Restaurant Brisket,
   Backyard Style 192

For The Kids Special Section 193
   Pets On Parade 193
   The Bus Stops Here 195
   Back-To-School Lunch Bunch 196
   Backyard Bravery 198

Have A Tart 200
Savor Summer's Best Sauces 201
Inventory Your Herb Rack 201
Quick & Easy: New Twists On
   Tostadas 203
Relax—Eat Outdoors 204

Garden-Fresh Fare	206
From Our Kitchen To Yours	207
You Bring The Entrée, I'll Do	
The Rest	208

September 209

The Whole Fruit	210
Praise The Peanut	211
Drink To Your Health	212
Labor Day Easy Grillin'	213
Railgating & Tailgating: USC Style	214
Quick & Easy: Seasoning Shortcuts	
Come In Packets	216
Hold The Pickles, Hold The Onion	217
Infuse Vinegar With Basil	218
Southern Living Hall Of Fame:	
Recipes And Reminiscences	
Of New Orleans	219
From Our Kitchen To Yours	220
On The Light Side: Beans Go Upscale	229
Light Favorite: Cozy Up To Fruit	
Cobbler	230
See The Light With Black Beans	231
Bread Also Rises—In A Machine	231

October 233

Where's The Pumpkin?	234
From Our Kitchen To Yours	235
Smoky Mountain Reunion	236
A Victorian Victory Feast	238
Recipes That Cut The Mustard	239
A Plate Tailored For Fall	241
Frozen Assets	242
On The Light Side: A Halloween	
Party You'll Love At First Bite	244
Light Favorite: Indulge In French	
Onion Soup	246

A New Slant On Slaw	246
These Rings Lighten Up	247
Mega Meat Loaves	247
Let's Do The Twist: Macaroni,	
That Is	248
Spinach With A Flourish	249
A Passion For Pecans	250
Quick & Easy: Jammin' It Up	251
Give Napkins A Ring	252

November 253

Sweet Little Endings	254
Gobblers For Gobbling	256
Holiday Dinners® Special Section	257
Wine & Dine The Wives	257
A Foreign Affair	265
Bah Humbug—A Crabby	
Christmas!	268
Tropical Holiday Elegance	271
Feliz Navidad	273
A Plantation Christmas	277
Christmas For The Birds	283
Old Friends Cheer The New Year	287
Dinners From The Diners	290
Gift Wrap From The Pantry	291
Quick & Easy: Saucy Secrets	292
Southern Living Hall Of Fame:	
A Taste Of Aloha	293
Never Too Much Citrus	294
Simply Chocolate	296
Holiday Nuts	301
On The Light Side: Make It Easy;	
Make A Casserole	301
Light Favorite: Old-Fashioned Chicken	
And Dumplings	302
Light Menu: Ward Off Holiday Pounds	303

Celebrate Earth's Bounty	304
Please Pass The Dressing	305
Time-Saver Turkey	306
From Our Kitchen To Yours	306
Basting Instincts	307
Well-Bred Breads	308
Buenos Días Brunch	309

December 311

Menu Fit For A Crowd	312
Sweet Dreams	314
From Our Kitchen To Yours	316
On The Light Side: Light Velvet	318
Light Menu: Watch the Fat,	
Not the Pot	318
Quick & Easy: Vegetarian	
Entrées	319
Let The Salad Be The Star	320
Go For The Bold!	321
Six Courses Made Simple	322
Homespun Hospitality	324
Chili From The Pantry	326
On Your Mark . . . Get Set . . . Eat	327
Oh! Gratins	328
Goodies To Give	329
Ornaments And Hors D'Oeuvres	330
Very Merry Cranberries	332
Cake Fit For A King	337
The Plate As Canvas	337
An Apple Treat A Day	338
Recipes With "A-Peel"	339
Cheers For The Holidays	340
Make A Quick Jelly	341
Share The Season's Spirit	341

Glossary 342

Recipe Index Section 344

Our Year
At
Southern Living®

It's hard to believe that this is the 15th edition of the *Southern Living® Annual Recipes* cookbook. Think about the changes that have occurred in your life and in the world during the last 15 years. And, when we stop to think about it, the recipes in our *Southern Living® Annual Recipes* books also have changed.

That's because the favorite recipes that you, our readers, send us today are lower in fat, sugar, and salt. Of course, you still send in those delicious, not-so-light recipes, but you also tell us you aren't eating them every day. So this cookbook is filled with what you want—some light recipes and others to indulge in on special occasions.

Many of you need quick and easy recipes that allow you to prepare dinner for your family or get ready for company, in a hurry. At other times, you may enjoy cooking a more elaborate recipe that family and friends describe as spectacular. Again, in this book we give you many recipes to meet both your needs.

Whether the recipe is light or rich, quick or involved, the emphasis is on flavor. We know you want food that tastes terrific and looks beautiful.

As we look back with pride on another year of testing, tasting, photographing, researching, and writing, we hope you'll derive as much pleasure from using *Southern Living® Annual Recipes* as we had preparing it.

Susan J. Reynolds

JANUARY

There's no better time than winter to enjoy warming soups and stews. Curl up in front of a fire with a bowl of our light yet luscious creamy broccoli soup. Or try a hearty stew to chase away the winter chill. Make a batch to serve now, and freeze the rest for later. With a little advance preparation, you can enjoy the garden-fresh flavor of tomatoes on a winter's eve. Add a flavor boost to appetizers, salads, and main dishes with preserved cherry tomatoes dried in a food dehydrator. To end a meal on a sweet note, try crowd-pleasing Orange-Pecan Pound Cake or Zucchini-Carrot Cake.

Football, Feasting, And Fun

Most of this easy-to-tackle Super Bowl appetizer menu can be made a few days—or even a month—ahead. So come kickoff time, you can kick back and relax in front of the TV.

And so can your guests. These finger foods are meant for munching in the family room, from pregame commentary to the last seconds of play.

Use our fumble-free Game Plan (on facing page) to coach you through these simple recipes, and your party (and hopefully your team) is sure to be a winner.

SUPER BOWL SPREAD FOR TWELVE

Hot Vegetable Punch
Pickled Carrots
Sage-Pecan Cheese Wafers
Chicken Almondette Fingers
Artichoke Dip in a Bread Basket
or
Cottage Cheese Sun-Dried Tomato Dip
Orange-Pecan Pound Cake

HOT VEGETABLE PUNCH

2 (46-ounce) cans tomato juice
4 (10½-ounce) cans condensed beef broth, undiluted
5⅓ cups water
12 stalks celery, coarsely chopped
4 onions, sliced
2 carrots, sliced
2 bay leaves
½ teaspoon black peppercorns
2 tablespoons minced fresh parsley
3 tablespoons lemon juice
Garnish: fresh green beans, blanched

Combine first 9 ingredients in a large Dutch oven or stockpot. Bring to a boil; reduce heat, and simmer 35 minutes or until vegetables are tender. Remove from heat, and stir in lemon juice. Pour mixture through a large wire-mesh strainer into a pitcher, discarding vegetables and spices. Serve warm, and garnish, if desired. Yield: 4 quarts.

Note: To blanch fresh green beans, wash, trim ends, and remove strings. Place beans in boiling water 3 minutes; drain. Plunge into ice water 3 minutes; drain. *Mrs. H. W. Walker*
Richmond, Virginia

PICKLED CARROTS

1½ cups cider vinegar
1½ cups water
1 cup sugar
2 tablespoons dillseeds
3 to 4 cloves garlic
2 pounds carrots, scraped and cut into strips

Combine vinegar, water, and sugar in a large saucepan, and bring mixture to a boil, stirring until sugar dissolves. Add dillseeds and remaining ingredients, and bring mixture to a boil over medium heat. Cover, reduce heat, and simmer 6 to 8 minutes. Remove mixture from heat, and chill 8 hours. To serve, pour mixture through a large wire-mesh strainer, discarding liquid. Remove and discard dillseeds and garlic, if desired. Yield: 14 to 16 appetizer servings.

SAGE-PECAN CHEESE WAFERS

1 cup (4 ounces) shredded sharp Cheddar cheese
¾ cup all-purpose flour
¼ cup chopped pecans
1 teaspoon rubbed sage
¼ teaspoon salt
⅛ teaspoon ground red pepper
⅓ cup butter or margarine, cut into small pieces

Position knife blade in food processor bowl, and add first 6 ingredients. Process mixture about 10 seconds or until blended. With processor running, slowly drop butter, one piece at a time, through food chute until mixture forms a ball.

Roll dough to ¼-inch thickness on a lightly floured surface. Cut with a 1½-inch round cutter, and place on ungreased baking sheets. Bake at 350° for 12 to 14 minutes or until edges turn golden. Remove to wire racks to cool. Yield: 3 dozen.
Mrs. Harland J. Stone
Ocala, Florida

CHICKEN ALMONDETTE FINGERS

1 (8-ounce) package tempura batter mix
1 (12-ounce) can beer
1 cup flaked coconut
½ cup sliced almonds
6 skinned and boned chicken breast halves, cut into 24 strips
Vegetable oil
Honey-Poppy Seed Sauce

Combine tempura batter mix and beer; pour mixture into a shallow dish, and set aside. Combine coconut and almonds. Dip each chicken strip into batter mixture, and dredge in coconut mixture.

Pour oil to depth of 1½ inches into a Dutch oven; heat to 350°. Fry chicken strips 2 minutes on each side or until golden brown. Drain on paper towels. Serve chicken fingers with Honey-Poppy Seed Sauce. Yield: 12 appetizer servings.

Honey-Poppy Seed Sauce

½ cup honey
½ cup mayonnaise or salad
  dressing
1 teaspoon poppy seeds

Combine all ingredients in a small
bowl. Yield: 1 cup.   *Betty Beske*
Arlington, Virginia

ARTICHOKE DIP
IN A BREAD BASKET

1 (20-ounce) round loaf
  pumpernickel bread
2 (12-ounce) jars marinated
  artichoke hearts, drained and
  chopped
1 cup grated Parmesan cheese
¾ cup mayonnaise or salad
  dressing
1 cup (4 ounces) shredded Swiss
  cheese
3 green onions, sliced
1 (4-ounce) can diced green chiles,
  drained
1 pickled jalapeño pepper, seeded
  and chopped

Cut top from loaf; scoop out center,
leaving a ½-inch shell. Set shell aside.
Cut remaining bread into 1- to 1½-
inch cubes; place on a 15- x 10- x
1-inch jellyroll pan. Broil 6 inches from
heat (with electric oven door partially
opened) 2 to 3 minutes or until
golden, stirring once. Set aside.
  Combine artichoke hearts and remaining ingredients. Place bread shell
on jellyroll pan; fill with artichoke mixture, and bake at 350° for 15 to 20
minutes or until thoroughly heated.
Serve with toasted bread cubes.
Yield: 4 cups.   *Ferne McClintock*
Birmingham, Alabama

COTTAGE CHEESE
SUN-DRIED TOMATO DIP

2 cups cream-style cottage cheese
1 green onion, cut into 4 pieces
¼ cup finely chopped green pepper
2 tablespoons finely chopped oil-
  packed sun-dried tomatoes
2 tablespoons fresh basil or 2
  teaspoons dried basil
2 teaspoons lemon juice
⅛ teaspoon cracked pepper

Combine all ingredients in container of
an electric blender; process until
smooth, stopping once to scrape down
sides. To serve, spoon into peppers
cut in half, if desired. Serve with
green, sweet red, and sweet yellow
pepper squares or other fresh vegetables. Yield: 2 cups.   *Patsy Bell Hobson*
Liberty, Missouri

ORANGE-PECAN POUND CAKE

1 cup butter or margarine, softened
1 cup sugar
3 large eggs
1½ teaspoons grated orange rind
½ teaspoon grated lemon rind
¼ teaspoon orange extract
½ cup finely chopped pecans
2 cups all-purpose flour, divided
½ teaspoon baking powder
⅛ teaspoon salt
⅓ cup milk
Garnishes: orange and lemon rind
  strips, pecan halves

Beat butter at medium speed with an
electric mixer about 2 minutes or until
soft and creamy. Gradually add sugar,
beating at medium speed 5 to 7 minutes. Add eggs, one at a time, beating
just until yellow disappears. Stir in
rinds and orange extract.
  Combine pecans and ¼ cup flour;
set aside. Combine remaining 1¾
cups flour, baking powder, and salt;
add to butter mixture alternately with
milk, beginning and ending with flour
mixture. Mix at low speed just until
blended after each addition; stir in
floured pecans.
  Pour batter into a greased and
floured 9- x 5- x 3-inch loafpan. Bake

at 325° for 1 hour and 5 minutes or
until a wooden pick inserted in center
comes out clean. Cool in pan on a wire
rack 10 to 15 minutes; remove from
pan, and let cool completely on wire
rack. Garnish, if desired. Yield: 1 loaf.
Gayle Nicholas Scott
Chesapeake, Virginia

Game Plan

A month or two ahead:

■ Bake and freeze Sage-Pecan
Cheese Wafers and Orange-Pecan
Pound Cake.

Up to two days ahead:

■ Make Pickled Carrots and Hot
Vegetable Punch, and refrigerate.

The day before:

■ Make Honey-Poppy Seed Sauce
for Chicken Almondette Fingers.
■ Make cottage cheese dip, and
cut sweet peppers into squares
for dipping; chill both. Or make
artichoke dip, and chill.

The morning of the party:

■ Hollow out loaf of bread and
toast bread cubes for Artichoke
Dip in a Bread Basket.
■ Thaw Sage-Pecan Cheese Wa-
fers and Orange-Pecan Pound
Cake at room temperature.

A half hour before:

■ Batter and fry Chicken Almondette Fingers.
■ Spoon cottage cheese dip into
peppers cut in half or artichoke
dip into hollowed loaf.
■ Reheat Hot Vegetable Punch.
■ Bake artichoke dip in loaf.
■ Set out cheese wafers, carrots,
and pound cake. (Don't slice
pound cake until ready to serve to
keep it from drying out.)

Start With Chicken

Our recipe for Roast Chicken—which you can make start to finish in about an hour—calls for cooking two chickens in one oven so you can serve one at dinner and use the leftovers for these quick recipes. Singles, couples, or families can take advantage of this timesaving, cost-effective technique.

Roasting Chicken: It's Easy

Roasting is a simple cooking technique in which food is cooked by dry heat in an oven. You can roast chicken two ways: either on a vertical roasting rack or on the rack of a broiler pan.

With vertical roasting racks, the chicken "stands up," allowing the fat to drip into a roasting pan. The best roasters are coated with a nonstick finish.

If you don't have a vertical roasting rack, use a broiler pan. Simply place a chicken on the rack in the pan, brush with seasonings, and roast. The drippings will fall into the pan, away from the chicken. Spray the pan and rack with vegetable cooking spray to make cleanup easier.

Flavor Chicken Your Way

Rub chicken with olive oil, soy sauce, or other seasonings for extra flavor. If you like herbs, sprinkle dried or fresh herbs (you'll need three times more fresh than dried) underneath the skin for extra flavor and aroma while cooking. Experiment with other sauces, mustards, or salad dressings, too. Roast as instructed in the Roast Chicken recipe.

ROAST CHICKEN

¼ cup olive oil
¼ cup soy sauce
½ teaspoon garlic powder
2 (3- to 4-pound) broiler-fryers

Combine first 3 ingredients; set aside. Carefully separate skin from body of chickens at neck area, working down to breast and thigh area. Evenly pour half of olive oil mixture between skin and meat of both chickens; brush remaining mixture on outer skin. Place chickens on two vertical roasting racks; set in a lightly greased roasting pan. Bake at 400° on lowest rack of oven 55 to 60 minutes. Yield: 2 broiler-fryers.

Note: Broiler-fryers may be roasted, without vertical roasting racks, on a lightly greased rack in a broiler pan at 400° for 55 to 60 minutes.

ROASTED CHICKEN SALAD

2 cups chopped cooked chicken
½ cup seedless grapes, halved
½ cup chopped pecans, toasted
¼ cup mayonnaise or salad dressing
2 tablespoons sour cream
1 tablespoon fresh lime juice
Lettuce leaves
Pita bread rounds

Combine first 3 ingredients in a medium bowl. Combine mayonnaise, sour cream, and lime juice; stir into chicken mixture. Serve on lettuce or stuff in lettuce-lined pita bread rounds. Yield: 3 to 4 servings.
Sandy Crain
Anderson, South Carolina

EASY CHICKEN À LA KING

1 cup chopped cooked chicken
1 (10¾-ounce) can cream of chicken soup, undiluted
¼ cup milk
1 (2-ounce) jar diced pimiento, drained
1 (4-ounce) can whole mushrooms, drained
½ teaspoon salt
⅛ teaspoon pepper
Chow mein noodles or hot cooked rice

Combine first 7 ingredients in a heavy saucepan; cook over low heat 10 minutes, stirring often. Serve over chow mein noodles or rice. Yield: 2 servings.
Mrs. Gilmer Jefferson
Danville, Virginia

QUICK CHICKEN AND PASTA

2 quarts water
½ teaspoon salt
4 ounces vermicelli, uncooked
¾ cup frozen English peas
⅓ cup Italian salad dressing
1 cup chopped cooked chicken
¼ teaspoon sweet red pepper flakes
2 tablespoons grated Parmesan cheese

Combine water and salt in a large saucepan; bring to a boil. Add vermicelli and peas. Return to a boil; reduce heat, and cook 10 minutes. Drain and set aside.

Heat salad dressing in saucepan. Add chopped chicken and red pepper flakes, and cook, stirring constantly, 2 minutes. Add reserved pasta mixture, and cook until thoroughly heated. Sprinkle with Parmesan cheese, tossing mixture well. Yield: 2 servings.

Jennifer Shupe
Raleigh, North Carolina

ON THE LIGHT SIDE

Marinade Magic For Beef

Beef is finally shedding its fatty reputation and showing its healthful side. And thanks to altered feeding and breeding practices, today's cattle are leaner.

To help you select the leanest cuts at the meat counter, the National Live Stock and Meat Board has identified the 10 "skinniest."

A look at the chart on this page shows that the eye round, top round, and shank cross cuts have fewer than 30% of their total calories from fat—the limit currently recommended by health professionals. The rest of the cuts of beef rate a little higher, but if eaten in moderation, they shouldn't overtax your fat budget.

Just because beef is lean doesn't mean it has to be tough. Marinating it in an acidic mixture such as citrus juice, wine, or vinegar before cooking tenderizes it and adds flavor. Remember to refrigerate meat while it marinates to avoid harmful bacterial growth.

If you want to use the marinade for basting, set some aside before adding the meat.

DELI-STYLE ROAST BEEF

1 (4-pound) eye round roast, trimmed
5 cloves garlic, halved
1 (8-ounce) can tomato sauce
1 cup Burgundy or other dry red wine
¼ cup Worcestershire sauce
¼ cup lemon juice
¼ cup Creole mustard
2 tablespoons hot sauce
2 tablespoons prepared horseradish
2 teaspoons onion powder
2 bay leaves
Vegetable cooking spray

Cut 10 small, deep slits in roast; insert garlic halves into slits. Place in a heavy-duty, zip-top plastic bag. Combine tomato sauce and next 8 ingredients; reserve ⅓ cup marinade. Pour remaining marinade over roast; seal bag. Refrigerate roast and reserved marinade 8 hours.

Remove roast from marinade, discarding marinade. Place on a rack in a shallow roasting pan coated with cooking spray, and insert meat thermometer. Bake at 325° for 1 hour and 30 minutes or until thermometer reaches 140° (rare), basting 3 times with ⅓ cup reserved marinade. Remove from oven; wrap roast securely in plastic wrap to retain moisture. Chill several hours before slicing. Yield: 15 servings (171 calories [29% from fat] per 3-ounce serving).

□ *24.5g protein, 5.6g fat (2.1g saturated), 1.9g carbohydrate, 0.2g fiber, 57mg cholesterol, 169mg sodium, and 8mg calcium.*

AMERICAN STEAKHOUSE BEEF

1 (1½-pound) trimmed lean boneless top sirloin steak
⅓ cup low-sodium soy sauce
⅓ cup unsweetened pineapple juice
⅓ cup dry sherry
¼ cup cider vinegar

Place steak in a large, shallow dish. Combine soy sauce and remaining ingredients; pour over steak. Cover and chill 4 hours, turning steak occasionally. Drain, discarding marinade. Grill over hot coals (400° to 500°) 10 to 15 minutes on each side or to desired degree of doneness. To serve, slice across the grain into thin slices. Yield: 7 servings (210 calories [33% from fat] per 3-ounce serving).

□ *27.4g protein, 7.8g fat (3.2g saturated), 0.3g carbohydrate, 0g fiber, 80mg cholesterol, 96mg sodium, and 10mg calcium.*

The 10 Leanest Cuts of Beef				
Beef Cut (3 ounces cooked)	Calories	Fat (g)	% of Calories From Fat	Cholesterol (mg)
Eye round	143	4.2	26	59
Top round	153	4.2	25	71
Shank cross cuts	171	5.4	28	66
Round tip	157	5.9	34	69
Top sirloin	165	6.1	33	76
Bottom round	178	7.0	35	82
Chuck arm	183	7.0	34	86
Top loin	176	8.0	41	65
Tenderloin	179	8.5	43	71
Flank	176	8.6	44	57

MARINATED SAUERBRATEN BEEF

1 pound trimmed top round roast
Vegetable cooking spray
2 cups water
1 cup Burgundy or other dry red wine
2 small onions, thinly sliced
2 tablespoons pickling spice
2 tablespoons brown sugar
1 teaspoon salt
10 black peppercorns, crushed
2 bay leaves
Sauerbraten Sauce

Brown roast in a nonaluminum Dutch oven coated with cooking spray. Combine water and next 7 ingredients; reserve 1 cup mixture for sauce. Pour remaining mixture over roast. Cover and refrigerate at least 8 hours.

Remove Dutch oven from refrigerator; uncover and place over medium heat. Bring to a boil; cover, reduce heat, and simmer 45 minutes or until tender. Drain. Remove and discard bay leaves. Slice roast, and serve with Sauerbraten Sauce. Yield: 3 servings (319 calories [24% from fat] per 3 ounces of meat and 7 tablespoons sauce).

□ 33.3g protein, 8.6g fat (2.6g saturated), 19.3g carbohydrate, 1.2g fiber, 84mg cholesterol, 563mg sodium, and 89mg calcium.

Sauerbraten Sauce

1 cup reserved marinade
¼ cup gingersnap crumbs
¼ cup nonfat sour cream alternative

Combine first 2 ingredients in a heavy saucepan; cook over medium heat, stirring constantly, until thickened. Reduce heat; stir in sour cream alternative, and cook over low heat until thoroughly heated. (Do not boil.) Yield: about 1 cup (60 calories [18% from fat] per 7 tablespoons).

□ 1.5g protein, 1.2g fat (0.3g saturated), 8.3g carbohydrate, 0.5g fiber, 2mg cholesterol, 20mg sodium, and 35mg calcium.

Meat Tips

■ At the grocery store, look for meat cuts that have the most lean meat for the money. When you buy less expensive cuts, make sure you are not paying for large amounts of gristle, fat, and bone.

■ Buy meat such as ham or pot roast in bulk; cut and freeze it in serving-size portions.

■ Packaged meat from the market should be rewrapped before freezing. Tape the store label on the freezer wrapper to retain a description as to cut, weight, cost, and date.

■ Baste a roast with wine or wine vinegar for a wonderfully distinctive flavor.

LIGHT MENU

Wake Up Breakfast For A Change

Don't shortchange the most important meal of the day—wake up to breakfast. Long noted for its ability to keep you performing at peak capacity through the morning, a substantial breakfast deserves to be celebrated, not avoided.

WIDE-EYED BREAKFAST FOR FOUR

Whole Wheat-Oat Pancakes
Maple Syrup
Canadian bacon
Fresh Fruit With Lemon-Yogurt Dressing

WHOLE WHEAT-OAT PANCAKES
(pictured on page 40)

⅔ cup regular oats, uncooked
½ cup whole wheat flour
½ cup all-purpose flour
1 tablespoon baking powder
¼ teaspoon salt
1 cup skim milk
¼ cup egg substitute
2 tablespoons vegetable oil
Vegetable cooking spray

Place oats in container of an electric blender, and process until finely ground. Transfer to a large bowl, and add whole wheat flour and next 3 ingredients. Combine milk, egg substitute, and oil; add to dry ingredients, stirring just until moistened.

Coat a griddle or nonstick skillet with cooking spray; place over medium heat until hot. Pour ¼ cup batter onto hot griddle. Turn pancake when top is covered with bubbles and edges look cooked. Repeat procedure with remaining batter. Yield: 4 servings (248 calories [30% from fat] per 2 [4-inch] pancakes).

□ 9.3g protein, 8.4g fat (1.5g saturated), 34.7g carbohydrate, 3.7g fiber, 1mg cholesterol, 428mg sodium, and 237mg calcium.   *Kitty Sheehan Montgomery, Alabama*

MAPLE SYRUP
(pictured on page 40)

1 cup firmly packed brown sugar
½ cup water
¼ teaspoon maple flavoring

Combine sugar and water in a small saucepan; bring to a boil, stirring until sugar dissolves. Remove mixture from heat, and stir in flavoring. Yield: 1⅓ cups (39 calories [0% from fat] per tablespoon).

☐ *0g protein, 0g fat (0g saturated), 10.1g carbohydrate, 0g fiber, 0mg cholesterol, 3mg sodium, and 9mg calcium.*

FRESH FRUIT WITH LEMON-YOGURT DRESSING
(pictured on page 40)

2 oranges, peeled and sectioned
1 grapefruit, peeled and sectioned
1 banana, sliced
1 cup fresh or unsweetened frozen sliced strawberries
2 kiwifruit, peeled and sliced
Lemon-Yogurt Dressing
Garnish: fresh mint sprigs

Combine fruit, tossing gently. Serve with Lemon-Yogurt Dressing, and garnish, if desired. Yield: 4 servings (151 calories [5% from fat] per 1 cup fruit and ¼ cup dressing).

☐ *5.3g protein, 0.8g fat (0.2g saturated), 32.9mg carbohydrate, 6.5g fiber, 1mg cholesterol, 44mg sodium, and 164mg calcium.*

Lemon-Yogurt Dressing

1 cup plain nonfat yogurt
1½ tablespoons sugar
1 teaspoon lemon juice

Combine all ingredients in a small bowl. Yield: 1 cup (50 calories [0% from fat] per ¼-cup serving).

☐ *3.3g protein, 0.1g fat (0.1g saturated), 9.1g carbohydrate, 0g fiber, 1mg cholesterol, 43mg sodium, and 113mg calcium.*   *Peggy C. Brown*
Winston-Salem, North Carolina

Cream Of Broccoli Soup

Cut winter's chill with a lightened version of the cold-weather favorite, creamy broccoli soup. Nonfat dry milk and cornstarch thicken the base and give it a creamy consistency without all the fat. Herbs, low-sodium, fat-free chicken broth, and reduced-fat Cheddar cheese add flavor.

LIGHT
CREAM OF BROCCOLI SOUP
(pictured on page 37)

1 (16-ounce) can ready-to-serve, low-sodium, fat-free chicken broth
⅓ cup instant nonfat dry milk powder
3 tablespoons cornstarch
½ teaspoon dried onion flakes
¼ teaspoon salt
¼ teaspoon dried basil
¼ teaspoon dried thyme
¼ teaspoon pepper
1 (10-ounce) package frozen chopped broccoli, thawed and drained
1½ cups skim milk
⅓ cup (1.3 ounces) shredded reduced-fat Cheddar cheese
1 tablespoon butter-flavored granules
Garnish: shredded reduced-fat Cheddar cheese

Combine first 8 ingredients in a large saucepan; bring to a boil, stirring constantly. Cook, stirring constantly, 1 minute. Add broccoli and next 3 ingredients; cook until cheese melts and mixture is thoroughly heated. Garnish individual servings with ½ teaspoon shredded Cheddar cheese. Yield: 4 servings (166 calories [17% from fat] per 1-cup serving).

☐ *14.5g protein, 3.1g fat (1.8g saturated), 20.3g carbohydrate, 2g fiber, 14mg cholesterol, 687mg sodium, and 395mg calcium.*

COMPARE THE NUTRIENTS (per serving)		
	Traditional	Light
Calories	318	166
Fat	24g	3.1g
Cholesterol	58mg	14mg

A Cook's Guide To Weeknight Survival

Every night it's the same story—no matter how hectic the day has been, the family needs to eat. And most of the time, they don't want to wait. Using our weeknight survival kit of easy-to-prepare meals, you'll be finished in a flash.

To help you put together your kit, we've selected main dishes that include canned items and foods that can be chopped or measured in advance. We also suggest menus to go with each recipe. Choose dinners for the week, and buy the groceries. When you find an extra minute, decide what can be done ahead.

Beef Stroganoff
English peas, carrots, and
onions
Whole wheat rolls

BEEF STROGANOFF

1 pound boneless top round steak
2 tablespoons all-purpose flour, divided
⅔ cup water, divided
1 tablespoon vegetable oil
1 (1-ounce) envelope onion soup mix
1 (4-ounce) can sliced mushrooms, undrained
1 (8-ounce) carton sour cream
Hot cooked noodles

Slice steak diagonally across grain into thin strips; dredge in 1 tablespoon flour, and set aside. Combine remaining 1 tablespoon flour and ⅓ cup water; set aside.

Cook steak in oil in a large skillet over medium-high heat 5 minutes or until browned. Add remaining ⅓ cup water, soup mix, and mushrooms; cover, reduce heat, and simmer 10 minutes. Add flour mixture to skillet; cook, stirring constantly, until thickened. Stir in sour cream; heat thoroughly (do not boil). Serve immediately over hot cooked noodles. Yield: 4 servings.

Note: To save additional time, you can substitute 1 pound stir-fry beef strips for boneless top round steak.
Catherine Nixon
Tulsa, Oklahoma

Family-Style Meat Loaf
Green beans and new potatoes
Steamed carrots

FAMILY-STYLE MEAT LOAF

1 pound lean ground beef
½ pound lean ground pork
½ cup chopped onion
½ cup chopped green pepper
1 large egg, beaten
½ cup uncooked regular oats or cracker crumbs
1 tablespoon chili powder
½ teaspoon salt
¼ teaspoon pepper
Tomato Gravy

Combine first 9 ingredients; shape into an 8-inch loaf, and place in a 9- x 5- x 3-inch loafpan. Pour Tomato Gravy over meat loaf, and bake at 350° for 1 hour or until done. Yield: 6 servings.

Tomato Gravy

½ cup chopped onion
½ cup chopped green pepper
2 tablespoons vegetable oil
1 tablespoon all-purpose flour
1 (16-ounce) can whole tomatoes, undrained and chopped
1 teaspoon chili powder
¼ teaspoon salt
¼ teaspoon pepper
Pinch of sugar

Cook onion and green pepper in oil in a saucepan over medium heat, stirring constantly; add flour, stirring until smooth. Cook, stirring constantly, 1 minute. Add tomatoes and remaining ingredients; bring to a boil. Remove from heat. Yield: about 2 cups.
Lovena Owen
Lockhart, Texas

Taco-Topped Potatoes
Spinach salad
Commercial salad dressing

TACO-TOPPED POTATOES

4 large baking potatoes (about 2¾ pounds)
1 pound ground beef
½ cup chopped onion
1 (1¼-ounce) package taco seasoning mix
¾ cup water
1 cup commercial taco sauce
½ cup (2 ounces) shredded Monterey Jack cheese with peppers

Scrub potatoes; prick several times with a fork. Place potatoes 1 inch apart on a microwave-safe rack or paper towels. Microwave at HIGH 14 to 17 minutes, turning and rearranging once; let stand 2 minutes.

Brown ground beef and onion in a skillet, stirring until beef crumbles; drain. Stir in seasoning mix and water; bring to a boil. Reduce heat, and simmer, stirring occasionally, 15 minutes or until liquid evaporates. Stir in taco sauce; cook until thoroughly heated.

Cut an X to within ½ inch of bottom of each potato. Squeeze potatoes from opposite sides and ends to open; fluff potato pulp with a fork. Spoon meat mixture on potatoes, and sprinkle with cheese. Yield: 4 servings.

Pork Chops With Baked Beans
Coleslaw
Whole wheat breadsticks

PORK CHOPS
WITH BAKED BEANS

1 (16-ounce) can pork and beans
½ cup chopped onion
¼ cup firmly packed brown sugar
¼ cup catsup
1 teaspoon prepared mustard
4 (½-inch-thick) boneless pork chops (about 1 pound)
¼ cup catsup
1 tablespoon brown sugar
1 teaspoon Worcestershire sauce

Combine first 5 ingredients in a lightly greased 2-quart baking dish. Place pork chops on beans. Combine ¼ cup catsup and remaining ingredients; spread on pork chops. Cover and bake at 350° for 25 minutes. Uncover and bake an additional 10 minutes. Yield: 4 servings.
Sandra Barnett
Birmingham, Alabama

Spaghetti-Ham Pie
Broccoli spears
Fresh fruit salad

SPAGHETTI-HAM PIE

6 ounces spaghetti, uncooked
4 cloves garlic, minced
2½ tablespoons olive oil
¼ cup all-purpose flour
¼ teaspoon salt
⅛ teaspoon freshly ground pepper
¾ cup half-and-half
1½ cups milk
¼ to ½ cup chopped cooked ham
¼ cup grated Parmesan cheese, divided

Cook spaghetti according to package directions; drain. Set aside.

Cook garlic in olive oil in a Dutch oven over medium heat, stirring constantly, 5 minutes. Stir in flour, salt, and pepper. Cook, stirring constantly, 1 minute. Gradually add half-and-half and milk; cook over medium heat, stirring constantly, until thickened and bubbly. Stir in spaghetti.

Spoon half of spaghetti mixture into a lightly greased 9-inch pieplate; sprinkle with ham and 2 tablespoons Parmesan cheese. Top with remaining spaghetti mixture, and sprinkle with remaining 2 tablespoons Parmesan cheese. Bake at 425° for 15 to 20 minutes or until lightly browned. Yield: 6 servings.
W. Kevin Bales
Tulsa, Oklahoma

Creamy Turkey Sauté
Tossed green salad
Commercial vinaigrette dressing
Whole wheat rolls

CREAMY TURKEY SAUTÉ

8 turkey cutlets (about 1 pound)
2 tablespoons vegetable oil
1 pound fresh mushrooms, sliced
2 large green onions, sliced
2 (3-ounce) packages cream cheese, cut into cubes
¼ cup plus 2 tablespoons milk
1 teaspoon salt
½ teaspoon pepper
Hot cooked rice

Cook turkey cutlets in oil in a large nonstick skillet over medium heat 3 to 4 minutes on each side or until browned. Remove from skillet; keep warm. Add mushrooms and green onions to skillet; cook 2 minutes or until tender. Add cream cheese and next 3 ingredients, stirring until cream cheese melts. To serve, place turkey over rice, and top with mushroom mixture. Yield: 4 servings.
Carol Y. Chastain
San Antonio, Texas

Lemon-Dill Chicken
Brussels sprouts
Broiled tomatoes

LEMON-DILL CHICKEN

2 to 3 tablespoons butter or margarine
1 (4-ounce) can sliced mushrooms, drained
1 tablespoon dried dillweed
2 tablespoons lemon juice
1 teaspoon salt
½ teaspoon paprika
Dash of pepper
1 clove garlic, minced
1 (3-pound) broiler-fryer, cut up and skinned
Hot cooked rice

Melt butter in a large skillet over medium heat. Add mushrooms, dillweed, lemon juice, salt, paprika, pepper, and garlic, and bring to a boil. Add chicken in a single layer, and return to a boil. Cover, reduce heat, and simmer 30 minutes or until chicken is tender, turning once. Serve over rice. Yield: 4 to 6 servings.
Trenda Leigh
Richmond, Virginia

Survival Skills

■ Shred, grate, or cube and measure cheeses on the weekend for the upcoming week. Store cheeses in an airtight container in the refrigerator.

■ Measure spices and other dry ingredients; combine those added to a recipe at the same time in one storage container.

■ Chop vegetables, such as onions and peppers, and store them in the refrigerator. (Because the quality and nutrient content of cut vegetables decreases with time, don't store them for more than two days.)

■ Brown ground meats in advance; cut poultry and meats into pieces as specified in the recipe, and refrigerate. (If storing meat longer than two days, freeze it.) Fresh fish is best when cooked the day of purchase.

■ Prepare pasta or rice in advance, and refrigerate; reheat as needed.

Put The Freeze On Winter Blues

It's miserably cold outside, and you're feeling as bleak as the day. Have no fear—winter blues therapy is here. Head to the kitchen, and perk up your spirit with a little bit of stirring. Pick one (or all) of these recipes to cook now and freeze for later. You'll have a warm kitchen today and an entrée or dessert on hand for a hectic day down the road.

BEEF BRISKET POT ROAST

1 tablespoon vegetable oil
1 (3-to 4-pound) beef brisket, trimmed
2 large onions, cut into quarters
1 clove garlic, crushed
¾ cup beef broth
¼ cup catsup
1 teaspoon salt
1 teaspoon Worcestershire sauce
½ teaspoon pepper

Heat oil in a Dutch oven. Add brisket, and brown on both sides; remove brisket. Add onion and garlic; cook over medium heat, stirring constantly, until tender. Add broth and remaining ingredients. Return brisket to pan; bring to a boil. Cover, reduce heat, and simmer 2 hours. Remove brisket, reserving broth mixture, and cut brisket into ¼-inch slices. Carefully spoon reserved broth mixture into container of an electric blender; process until smooth, stopping once to scrape down sides. Return sliced brisket and broth mixture to pan. Bring to a boil; cover, reduce heat, and simmer 1 hour or until beef is tender.

Place desired portions of brisket and broth mixture in heavy-duty, zip-top plastic bags or airtight containers. Freeze up to 3 months. To serve, thaw in refrigerator; place in a saucepan, and bring to a boil. Reduce heat, and simmer 5 minutes. Yield: 8 servings.
Alice McRae
De Funiak Springs, Florida

HAM-AND-BLACK-EYED PEA STEW

1 ham hock
1 pound dried black-eyed peas
8 cups water
1 large onion, chopped
1 medium-size green pepper, chopped
3 stalks celery, chopped
1½ pounds cooked ham, cut into 1½-inch cubes
1 bay leaf
2 tablespoons catsup
1 tablespoon Worcestershire sauce
¼ teaspoon pepper
¼ teaspoon hot sauce
½ cup chopped fresh parsley
1 bunch green onions, thinly sliced

Place ham hock in a small saucepan; cover with water. Bring to a boil, and cook 2 minutes. Drain.

Sort and wash peas; place in a large Dutch oven. Add ham hock, 8 cups water, and next 5 ingredients. Bring to a boil; reduce heat, and simmer, uncovered, 30 minutes, stirring occasionally. Stir in catsup and next 3 ingredients. Simmer, uncovered, 15 minutes or until tender, stirring occasionally. Stir in parsley and green onions; remove and discard bay leaf. Cool; spoon desired portions into airtight containers, and freeze 1 to 2 months. To serve, thaw in refrigerator, and cook over low heat, stirring occasionally, until thoroughly heated. Yield: 3 quarts.
Edith Askins
Greenville, Texas

ZUCCHINI-CARROT CAKE

1¼ cups all-purpose flour
1 teaspoon baking powder
1 teaspoon baking soda
½ teaspoon salt
1 cup sugar
1 teaspoon ground cinnamon
1 cup grated carrots
1 cup grated zucchini
⅔ cup vegetable oil
2 large eggs
Cream Cheese Frosting

Combine first 6 ingredients in a large mixing bowl; set aside.

Combine carrots and next 3 ingredients; add to dry ingredients, and beat at high speed with an electric mixer 4 minutes. Pour into a greased 9-inch square pan. Bake at 350° for 40 minutes or until a wooden pick inserted in center comes out clean. Let cool in pan on a wire rack.

Spread with Cream Cheese Frosting; cut into squares. Remove squares, and place in an airtight container; freeze up to 3 months. Yield: 9 servings.

Cream Cheese Frosting

1 (3-ounce) package cream cheese, softened
3 tablespoons butter or margarine, softened
2 cups sifted powdered sugar
1 teaspoon vanilla extract

Beat cream cheese and butter at medium speed with an electric mixer until fluffy; gradually add powdered sugar, beating mixture well. Stir in vanilla. Yield: 1 cup.

Note: Batter may be baked in paper-lined muffin pans at 350° for 25 minutes. Yield: 15 cupcakes.

Therese Reid
Rhodesdale, Maryland

CHOCOLATE CHIP-PUDDING COOKIES

1 cup butter or margarine, softened
¾ cup firmly packed brown sugar
¼ cup sugar
1 (3.9-ounce) package chocolate instant pudding mix *
2 large eggs
1 teaspoon vanilla extract
2¼ cups all-purpose flour
1 teaspoon baking soda
1 (12-ounce) package semisweet chocolate morsels
1 cup chopped pecans

Beat butter at medium speed with an electric mixer until creamy; gradually add brown sugar, sugar, and pudding mix, beating well. Add eggs and vanilla, mixing well.

Combine flour and soda; gradually add to butter mixture, mixing well. Stir in chocolate morsels and pecans; drop by rounded teaspoonfuls onto ungreased cookie sheets. Bake at 375° for 8 to 10 minutes. Cool on cookie sheets 3 minutes. Remove to wire racks to cool completely. Place in an airtight container, and freeze up to 8 months. Yield: 10 dozen.

* 1 (3.9-ounce) package vanilla instant pudding mix may be substituted for chocolate instant pudding mix.

Mary Anna Roquemore
Opp, Alabama

Salads Bloom With Citrus

Capture the sharp, clean flavor of oranges and grapefruit in crisp salads and salad dressings.

For attractive orange sections without membranes, begin with a sharp knife and chilled fruit. Peel in a spiral motion to remove rind. Cut off any remaining white peel, slicing from top to bottom. To section the fruit, work over a bowl to collect the juice. Slip knife between section membrane and orange section. At the center, continue up the other side of the section, releasing it. (Squeeze the leftover pulpy membrane over the bowl to extract all the juice.)

Rather than sectioning citrus fruit, you can cut it into slices—but do this before peeling. Then, working with one slice at a time on a flat surface, cut away a small section of the rind. Rotate the slice, and continue until all the rind has been removed.

FRUIT SALAD WITH HONEY-LEMON DRESSING

2 bananas, sliced
2 tablespoons fresh lemon juice
1 grapefruit, peeled and sectioned
3 oranges, peeled and sectioned
1 Red Delicious apple, cored and cubed
1 Golden Delicious apple, cored and cubed
¼ cup honey
1 (3-ounce) package cream cheese, softened
¼ teaspoon grated lemon rind
2½ tablespoons fresh lemon juice
3 tablespoons honey
1 tablespoon water
Lettuce leaves
¼ cup flaked coconut, toasted

Toss banana slices in 2 tablespoons lemon juice; drain and reserve lemon juice. Layer banana and remaining fruit in a bowl. Combine ¼ cup honey and reserved lemon juice; drizzle over fruit. Cover and chill at least 3 hours.

Beat cream cheese at medium speed with an electric mixer until creamy. Add lemon rind and next 3 ingredients, beating until blended. Using a slotted spoon, spoon fruit mixture evenly onto lettuce-lined salad plates. Drizzle with cream cheese mixture, and sprinkle with coconut. Yield: 4 to 6 servings.

TURKEY-IN-THE-ORANGE SALAD

½ cup lemon yogurt
3 tablespoons mayonnaise or salad dressing
2 tablespoons frozen orange juice concentrate, thawed
Dash of salt
4 oranges, peeled and sliced
½ pound thinly sliced smoked turkey, cut into ¼-inch strips
1 purple onion, sliced and separated into rings
Fresh spinach
Cracked black pepper

Combine first 4 ingredients; cover and chill.

Arrange orange slices, turkey, and onion on spinach-lined salad plates. Drizzle with dressing, and sprinkle with pepper. Yield: 6 servings.

An Orange of A Different Color

The peels of Florida oranges range in color from orange to yellow-orange to even greenish-yellow. Since oranges from the Sunshine State grow in a subtropical climate, the warm night temperatures prevent development of the deep-orange color. Not to worry though. The thin-skinned fruit is still juicy and ripe inside. Don't forget, when shopping for oranges, as well as grapefruit, choose firm, heavy fruit with no soft spots.

ORANGE-STRAWBERRY SALAD WITH ORANGE-CURD DRESSING

4 large oranges, peeled and
   sectioned
3 cups fresh strawberries, halved
Boston lettuce leaves
Orange-Curd Dressing
4 tablespoons sliced almonds,
   toasted
Garnish: orange rind strips

Arrange fruit on lettuce-lined salad plates. Drizzle with Orange-Curd Dressing, and sprinkle with toasted almonds. Garnish, if desired. Yield: 10 servings.

Orange-Curd Dressing

½ cup sugar
¼ teaspoon cornstarch
3 tablespoons orange juice
1 large egg
1 egg yolk
1 teaspoon grated lemon rind
1 tablespoon lemon juice
2 tablespoons butter or margarine

Combine sugar and cornstarch in a small saucepan; stir in orange juice and remaining ingredients. Cook over low heat 4 minutes, stirring constantly, until slightly thickened. Transfer to a small bowl; cover and chill. Yield: ⅔ cup.

Dive Into Belgian Endive

Perhaps you've heard of Belgian endive, but could you identify it?

This pricey green is no iceberg, so don't even think of shredding it for tacos. Belgian endive is for special occasions, and not just for salads. Try it braised as a side dish with English peas, or pipe your favorite party spread onto individual leaves for impressive hors d'oeuvres.

Now that we've whetted your appetite, here's a shopping hint: the paler,

the better. That's the point of Belgian endive *and* the reason for its expense. The delicacy is planted by hand and grown in the dark to prevent photosynthesis, which causes greening. It's often shipped and displayed wrapped in blue tissue paper to further protect it from light.

MARINATED CRAB-AND-ENDIVE SALAD

½ pound fresh lump crabmeat
¼ cup chopped purple onion
¼ cup sweet red pepper strips
¼ cup chopped sweet yellow
   pepper
¼ cup olive oil
2 tablespoons white vinegar
1 tablespoon Dijon mustard
¼ teaspoon dried thyme
Lettuce leaves
2 small heads Belgian endive
2 green onions, thinly sliced

Combine first 8 ingredients; cover and chill 3 hours. Line salad plates with lettuce leaves; arrange endive over lettuce. Top with crabmeat mixture, and sprinkle with green onions. Yield: 2 servings.
Alberta Pinkston
Corryton, Tennessee

ENDIVE-WATERCRESS SALAD

¼ cup olive oil
3 tablespoons white wine vinegar
1 teaspoon Dijon mustard
½ teaspoon salt
¼ teaspoon freshly ground pepper
3 heads Belgian endive
2 bunches watercress, rinsed and
   torn
½ cup chopped walnuts, toasted

Combine first 5 ingredients in a jar; cover tightly, and shake vigorously. Rinse endive lightly; pat dry, and trim ends. Arrange on salad plates; top with watercress. Drizzle dressing over top, and sprinkle with toasted walnuts. Yield: 6 to 8 servings.
Barbara Buell
Richmond, Virginia

BRAISED BELGIAN ENDIVE AND PEAS

4 small heads Belgian endive
2 cloves garlic, halved
2 tablespoons butter, melted
¼ cup chicken broth
¼ teaspoon salt
⅛ teaspoon freshly ground pepper
1 (10-ounce) package frozen
   English peas

Rinse endive lightly; pat dry, and trim ends. Cook endive and garlic in butter in a large skillet (not cast iron) over medium-high heat about 4 minutes or until endive is lightly browned, turning once; drain. Add chicken broth, salt, and pepper; cover, reduce heat, and simmer 5 minutes. Add peas; cover and simmer 4 minutes. Serve immediately. Yield: 4 servings.

Belgian Endive Basics

Yes, this pleasantly bitter green comes from Belgium, but the preparation need not be foreign. Follow these easy steps.

■ Rinse gently and immediately pat dry or wipe with a damp paper towel, and remove a couple of outer leaves. (Soaking the greens in water turns the delicate bitter flavor into too much of a good thing.)

■ Slice off the bottom ¼ inch of each head with a paring knife.

■ Separate the leaves by hand, cutting off more of the core, if necessary, as you go.

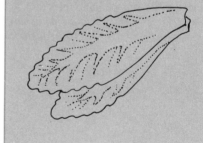

From Our Kitchen To Yours

If you want to preserve the fruits of your labor without taking up too much storage space, consider an electric food dehydrator. With a little advance preparation, you can add a garden-fresh flavor to dishes all year long.

Drying Cherry Tomatoes

Wash cherry tomatoes, and cut in half. Arrange tomato halves on the plastic trays of an electric food dehydrator. (Three quarts will fill four racks.) Drying will take 10 to 12 hours at 140°. Drying times can vary, however, depending on the size of the cherry tomato halves and the efficiency of the dehydrator.

When properly dried, the halves will shrivel into deep-red morsels with a concentrated tomato taste. They should be crisp and tough, but pliable.

Examine each batch of tomatoes, removing halves as they dry. Let halves cool, and store in airtight containers in a cool, dry place up to a month. (Dried tomatoes reabsorb moisture readily, causing color and flavor changes. Their color may also turn black due to long storage, but the dried tomato halves are still safe to eat.) To lengthen freshness, freeze.

MARINATED DRIED CHERRY TOMATOES

1 cup dried cherry tomato
  halves
¼ cup white wine vinegar
¼ cup water
⅓ cup olive oil
2 cloves garlic, crushed
4 black peppercorns
¾ teaspoon dried basil
½ teaspoon dried oregano
½ teaspoon dried parsley
¼ teaspoon dried thyme

Combine tomato halves, vinegar, and water; let stand 1 hour, stirring occasionally. Drain, discarding vinegar mixture.

Combine tomato halves, olive oil, garlic, peppercorns, basil, oregano, parsley, and thyme; let mixture stand 1 hour, stirring occasionally. Cover mixture, and store in refrigerator up to 1 week. Yield: 1 cup.

Note: Cherry tomatoes will be lightly coated with olive oil. Do not add more olive oil. For safety reasons, home-dried tomatoes should not be immersed in oil.

Uses for Marinated Dried Cherry Tomatoes

■ Top cream cheese or goat cheese with marinated tomatoes, and serve with crackers.
■ Process with cream cheese, shape into a ball, and roll in toasted pine nuts. Serve with bagel chips.
■ Spread over a round of Brie, and wrap in a commercial puff pastry sheet; bake until golden.
■ Combine with quartered artichoke hearts, and serve as a relish with grilled steak, or toss with pasta and a little cream.
■ Split French baguettes in half. Top each half with goat cheese and marinated tomatoes; bake until warm.
■ Serve on an antipasto tray.

Uses for Dried Cherry Tomatoes

■ Cut dried tomato halves into pieces with kitchen shears to substitute in recipes calling for commercial dried tomato bits, or add them to recipes (omelets and salsa) as you would spices or other seasonings.
■ Use dried cherry tomato halves on pizzas, sandwiches, salads, or vegetable dishes. Reconstitute (return to original consistency) by pouring boiling water over tomatoes and letting them stand for 5 minutes. When adding to stew, chili, or a recipe with liquid that boils or simmers, the halves do not need to be reconstituted.

Why to Dry

Dried foods are low in calories, high in nutrients, convenient, and lightweight—ideal for snacks and backpacking.

Considered the oldest method of food preservation, dehydrating removes the natural moisture from food by slowly drying it, preventing the growth of bacteria, yeasts, and molds. Food that is placed on the plastic stackable trays of an electric food dehydrator dries without the use of preservatives, additives, or salt. A fan circulates air and a thermostat maintains the optimum temperature of 140°; higher temperatures cook the food instead of drying it.

Electric food dehydrators are sold at most major retail outlets, including department, specialty, and hardware stores.

Layer On The Flavor

If lasagna sounds good, but you're tired of the same old recipe, try one of these variations.

Lasagna is a good choice for freezing because the ingredients don't get mushy after being frozen.

LASAGNA SUPREME

12 lasagna noodles, uncooked
1 pound ground beef
1 clove garlic, minced
1 small onion, chopped
2 (6-ounce) cans tomato paste
1 (16-ounce) can whole tomatoes, undrained and chopped
1½ cups water
1 tablespoon dried basil
1 teaspoon salt
½ teaspoon dried rosemary
2 bay leaves
2 large eggs, lightly beaten
2 cups ricotta cheese
1 (8-ounce) carton sour cream
2 tablespoons dried parsley or
    ¼ cup chopped fresh parsley
½ teaspoon salt
¼ teaspoon pepper
1 cup (4 ounces) shredded Cheddar cheese, divided
½ cup grated Parmesan cheese, divided
½ cup grated Romano cheese, divided
2 (8-ounce) packages mozzarella cheese slices

Cook lasagna noodles according to package directions. Drain; set aside.

Cook ground beef, garlic, and onion in a large skillet over medium heat until meat is browned, stirring until meat crumbles. Drain well. Wipe pan drippings from skillet with a paper towel. Combine tomato paste and next 6 ingredients in skillet; stir in meat. Bring to a boil, stirring occasionally; reduce heat and simmer, uncovered, 1 hour and 15 minutes, stirring often. Remove and discard bay leaves.

Combine eggs and next 5 ingredients; set aside.

Arrange 4 lasagna noodles in bottom of a lightly greased 13- x 9- x 2-inch baking dish. Layer with one-third each of meat mixture, egg mixture, and Cheddar, Parmesan, and Romano cheeses. Repeat layers twice. Bake at 375° for 30 to 35 minutes or until bubbly. Arrange mozzarella cheese slices over top; bake an additional 5 minutes. Let stand 10 minutes. Yield: 8 to 10 servings.

Note: To make an extra one to freeze, prepare half of lasagna in an 8-inch square baking dish, and bake as directed above. Prepare remaining lasagna in an 8-inch square aluminum pan; freeze, unbaked, up to 2 months. To bake, thaw in refrigerator 24 hours; let stand at room temperature 30 minutes. Bake at 375° for 35 to 40 minutes; add mozzarella cheese slices, and bake an additional 5 minutes.
Betty Beske
Arlington, Virginia

EASY LASAGNA

½ pound lean ground beef or turkey
1 (30-ounce) jar spaghetti sauce
½ cup water
8 lasagna noodles, uncooked and divided
1 (15-ounce) container ricotta cheese
1 large egg, beaten
½ teaspoon ground white pepper
8 (1-ounce) slices mozzarella cheese, divided
½ cup grated Parmesan cheese

Crumble beef into a microwave-safe colander; place in a 9-inch pieplate, and cover with wax paper. Microwave at HIGH 3 to 5 minutes or until meat is no longer pink, stirring after 1½ minutes; drain well.

Combine spaghetti sauce and water. Spread ½ cup of sauce in a lightly greased 11- x 7- x 1½-inch baking dish. Arrange 4 uncooked lasagna noodles on sauce. Combine ricotta cheese, egg, and pepper; spread one-half over noodles. Layer with half each of mozzarella cheese, remaining sauce, and beef. Repeat layers. Cover tightly with heavy-duty plastic wrap. Fold back a small corner of wrap to allow steam to escape.

Microwave at MEDIUM (50% power) 30 to 40 minutes, giving a half-turn at 15-minute intervals. Sprinkle with Parmesan cheese; cover and let stand 10 minutes before serving. Yield: 8 servings.

Note: To bake in a conventional oven, prepare as directed. Cover with aluminum foil, and bake at 350° for 50 minutes. Sprinkle with Parmesan cheese, and bake, uncovered, 10 minutes. Let stand 10 minutes before serving.
Brenda Rogers
Durham, North Carolina

If You Get the Urge To Experiment . . .

■ Substitute cottage cheese for ricotta. Cottage cheese yields a more moist product, while ricotta cheese is cheesier in taste and more traditional.

■ Sprinkle on a variety of cheeses. Experiment with Cheddar, American, and Romano. You might also try Gouda, Swiss, or—for a little spicy heat—Monterey Jack with hot peppers.

■ Substitute spicy sausage when the recipe calls for ground beef. For a lower-fat choice, use the same amount of ground turkey or chicken.

■ Use precooked noodles available at the grocery store. Follow the directions on the package to eliminate cooking the noodles before placing them in the baking dish. (In Easy Lasagna, you can use the regular noodles without cooking them.)

CHICKEN LASAGNA

1 (2½- to 3-pound) broiler-fryer
6 cups water
1 teaspoon salt
1 clove garlic, minced
2 tablespoons butter or margarine,
  melted
1 (10¾-ounce) can cream of celery
  soup, undiluted
½ teaspoon dried oregano
¼ teaspoon pepper
8 lasagna noodles, uncooked
1 (8-ounce) loaf process American
  cheese, cut in ¼-inch slices,
  divided
2 cups (8 ounces) shredded
  mozzarella cheese, divided
2 tablespoons grated Parmesan
  cheese

Place chicken in a Dutch oven; add water and salt. Bring to a boil; cover, reduce heat, and simmer 45 minutes or until tender. Drain, reserving broth, and let cool slightly. Bone chicken, cutting meat into bite-size pieces; set aside.

Cook garlic in butter in a large skillet over medium-high heat, stirring mixture constantly, 2 minutes. Add ¾ cup reserved broth, soup, oregano and pepper.

Cook lasagna noodles according to package directions in remaining reserved chicken broth, adding more water, if necessary; drain. Spoon a small amount of sauce into a lightly greased 11- x 7- x 1½-inch baking dish. Layer with half each of lasagna noodles, sauce, chicken, and American and mozzarella cheeses. Repeat procedure with noodles, sauce, and chicken, reserving remaining cheeses to add later. Bake at 350° for 25 minutes; top with remaining cheeses, and bake an additional 5 minutes. Let stand 10 minutes. Yield: 6 servings.

Note: To save time, cook chicken in a pressure speed cooker; follow manufacturer's instructions. *Grace Scott*
Houston, Texas

VEGETABLE LASAGNA CASSEROLE

3 quarts water
2 teaspoons salt
1 teaspoon olive oil
9 lasagna noodles, uncooked
4 medium carrots, scraped and
  thinly sliced
4 medium zucchini, thinly sliced
¼ cup reduced-calorie margarine
¼ cup all-purpose flour
2 cups skim milk
1 tablespoon dried basil or ¼ cup
  chopped fresh basil
¾ teaspoon salt
¾ teaspoon freshly ground pepper
Vegetable cooking spray
½ cup (2 ounces) shredded
  mozzarella cheese
Basil-Tomato Sauce

Bring water, salt, and olive oil to a boil in a large Dutch oven; add lasagna noodles, and return to a boil. Cook 15 minutes or just until tender. Drain and set aside.

Arrange carrot and zucchini in a vegetable steamer over boiling water. Cover and steam 8 minutes or until crisp-tender; set aside.

Melt margarine in a heavy saucepan over low heat, and add flour, stirring until smooth. Cook 1 minute, stirring constantly. Gradually add milk; cook over medium heat, stirring constantly, until mixture is thickened and bubbly. Stir in basil, salt, and pepper.

Spread ½ cup white sauce in an 11- x 7- x 1½-inch baking dish coated with cooking spray. Arrange one-third of noodles on sauce; top with one-third of vegetables and ½ cup white sauce. Repeat noodle, vegetable, and sauce layers twice. Cover and bake at 350° for 45 minutes. Uncover and sprinkle with cheese; bake an additional 5 minutes. Serve Basil-Tomato Sauce over individual servings. Yield: 6 servings.

Basil-Tomato Sauce

1 (28-ounce) can whole tomatoes,
  drained and coarsely chopped
1½ teaspoons dried basil or 4
  teaspoons chopped fresh basil
1 tablespoon lemon juice
⅛ teaspoon freshly ground
  pepper

Combine all ingredients in container of an electric blender; process until smooth. Pour into a medium saucepan; bring to a boil, stirring occasionally. Cover, reduce heat, and simmer 5 minutes. Yield: 1⅓ cups.
Doris Garton
Shenandoah, Virginia

Herb Tips

■ Crush dried herbs gently with a mortar and pestle to enhance their flavor. Slightly bruising fresh plants will increase their effectiveness.

■ Use finely chopped fresh herbs whenever possible. Dried whole herbs are usually the next best choice since they maintain their strength longer than the commercially ground form. Use three times more fresh herbs in a recipe if it calls for the more potent dried form.

■ Avoid combining two strong-flavored herbs, such as bay leaf, rosemary, or sage; the flavors will compete with each other. Instead, use a strong herb with a milder one. The accent herbs are slightly milder than the strong herbs and include basil, tarragon, and oregano. Medium-flavored herbs are dillweed, marjoram, winter savory, fennel, mint, and lemon thyme. The group of delicate herbs includes chervil, chives, parsley, and summer savory.

Since *Southern Sideboards* was first published in 1978, more than 280,000 copies of this 415-page book have been sold. As a result, the Junior League of Jackson, Mississippi, has shared their Southern heritage and donated more than $1 million to local community projects.

■ This recipe is slightly different from the *Southern Sideboards* original. For a thicker product, we thoroughly drained the ingredients and changed the recipe procedure.

CREAMED CRABMEAT WITH ARTICHOKE HEARTS

½ pound fresh mushrooms, sliced
½ cup sliced green onions
¼ cup finely chopped onion
1 tablespoon butter or margarine, melted
2 pounds fresh lump crabmeat, drained
1 (14-ounce) can artichoke hearts, quartered
½ cup butter or margarine
½ cup all-purpose flour
2 cups whipping cream
¾ cup dry white wine
2 tablespoons chopped fresh parsley
2 tablespoons lemon juice
2 teaspoons salt
½ teaspoon ground white pepper
¼ teaspoon ground red pepper

Cook first 3 ingredients in 1 tablespoon butter in a heavy saucepan over medium heat, stirring constantly, until tender; drain. Press mushroom mixture, crabmeat, and artichoke hearts between paper towels to remove excess moisture; set aside.

Melt ½ cup butter in a saucepan over low heat; add flour, stirring until smooth. Cook 1 minute, stirring constantly. Gradually add whipping cream; cook over medium heat, stirring constantly, until mixture is thickened and bubbly. Stir in white wine and remaining ingredients.

Layer half of crabmeat, artichoke hearts, and mushroom mixture in a lightly greased 13- x 9- x 2-inch baking dish; top with half of sauce. Repeat procedure with remaining ingredients and sauce. Bake, uncovered, at 350° for 40 minutes or until thoroughly heated. Yield: 10 servings.

Tip: *When frozen, crabmeat becomes tough and watery, losing flavor. You will achieve a better product by using fresh crabmeat in a recipe and then freezing it. To serve, thaw the crabmeat dish in the refrigerator and then follow the recipe cooking instructions.*

APRICOT-ALMOND COFFEE CAKE

1 cup butter or margarine, softened
2 cups sugar
2 large eggs
1 teaspoon almond extract
2 cups all-purpose flour
1 teaspoon baking powder
¼ teaspoon salt
1 (8-ounce) carton sour cream
1 cup sliced almonds
1 (10-ounce) jar apricot preserves

Beat butter at medium speed with an electric mixer about 2 minutes or until creamy. Gradually add sugar, beating at medium speed 5 to 7 minutes. Add eggs, one at a time, beating mixture just until yellow disappears. Stir in almond extract.

Combine flour, baking powder, and salt; add to butter mixture alternately with sour cream, beginning and ending with flour mixture. Mix at low speed just until blended after each addition.

Place about one-third of batter into a greased and floured 12-cup Bundt pan. Sprinkle with half of almonds, and dot with half of apricot preserves. Top with remaining batter; sprinkle with remaining almonds, and dot with remaining preserves. Bake at 350° for 50 to 55 minutes, or until a wooden pick inserted in center comes out clean. Cool in pan on a wire rack 10 to 15 minutes; remove from pan, and let cool completely on wire rack. Yield: one 10-inch coffee cake.

Note: You may substitute vanilla extract for almond extract, ½ cup chopped pecans for almonds, and 3 tablespoons brown sugar and 2 teaspoons ground cinnamon for apricot preserves.

FEBRUARY

Take a culinary tour of this chapter, and sample Cuban-inspired recipes that make the most of the exotic vegetables, tropical fruits, and seafood of South Florida. In addition, we suggest classic Creole dishes that made New Orleans world famous. Throughout the South, chocolate remains a Valentine mainstay; here it makes a delicious pairing with orange or almond. But for a flavor adventure, discover the unexpected side of chocolate in chili, chicken, and pork dishes. Chocolate's not reserved just for desserts anymore.

South Florida Sampler

The traditional dishes and creative new tastes of South Florida will have you eager to sample the local flavor. It may take you awhile to fly south for the winter, but a tropical dining experience is as close as your kitchen.

Cuban Cuisine

■ The literal translation of Ropa Vieja, a traditional Cuban dish, is indeed "old clothes." The flank steak is boiled until tender, then shredded with two forks to resemble tattered clothing.

ROPA VIEJA

2 pounds flank steak, trimmed and
  cut into 1-inch strips
1 large onion, quartered
3 cups water
2 whole pimientos
2 large green peppers, cut into
  strips
2 large onions, cut into strips
4 cloves garlic, crushed
2 tablespoons vegetable oil
1 (10¾-ounce) can tomato puree
2 bay leaves
½ cup dry white wine
Vegetable oil
French or Cuban bread, cut into
  ½-inch slices
Garnishes: pimiento strips, canned
  English peas

Combine steak, onion quarters, and water in a large Dutch oven; bring to a boil. Cover, reduce heat, and simmer 1 hour or until meat is tender. Drain, reserving 1½ cups of liquid; cool. Shred meat mixture with two forks, and set aside.

Place 2 whole pimientos in container of an electric blender; process until smooth. Set aside.

Cook green peppers, onion strips, and garlic in 2 tablespoons vegetable oil in a large skillet over medium-high heat, stirring constantly, 3 minutes. Add reserved pureed pimientos, tomato puree, bay leaves and white wine; cook 3 minutes. Stir in shredded meat and 1½ cups reserved liquid; cook 10 minutes. Remove and discard bay leaves.

Pour oil to depth of ¼ inch into a large skillet. Fry bread slices in hot oil over medium heat until lightly browned on each side. Place meat mixture on a platter, and surround with bread slices. Garnish, if desired. Yield: 8 servings.

■ Juanita Plano of Coral Gables, Florida, serves this well-known side dish with rice. Much of the characteristic flavor of the dish comes from sofrito—a sautéed mixture of onion, green pepper, garlic, herbs, and spices. (Sofrito typically contains tomatoes, but hers does not.)

BLACK BEANS

1 (16-ounce) package dried black
  beans
5 cups water
¼ pound bacon, chopped
2 green peppers, chopped
2 medium onions, chopped
4 cloves garlic, minced
1 teaspoon ground cumin
1 teaspoon dried oregano
3 bay leaves
¾ teaspoon salt
¼ teaspoon pepper
1 tablespoon red wine vinegar
¼ cup olive oil (optional)
Garnishes: chopped onion, chopped
  fresh cilantro

Sort and wash beans; place in a Dutch oven. Add 5 cups water, and soak 2 to 3 hours. (Do not drain.) Bring to a boil; cover, reduce heat, and simmer 30 minutes, stirring occasionally.

Cook chopped bacon in a large skillet over medium heat, stirring constantly, until crisp; remove bacon with a slotted spoon, reserving drippings in skillet. Drain bacon on a paper towel, and set aside. Cook green pepper, onion, and garlic in drippings over medium-high heat, stirring constantly, 10 to 15 minutes.

Add cumin, oregano, and bay leaves; cook 1 minute. Add vegetable mixture to beans; cover and simmer 1 hour or until beans are tender. Remove and discard bay leaves; stir in salt and next 3 ingredients. Sprinkle with bacon, and garnish, if desired. Yield: 8 servings.

■ This Cuban version of a typical Spanish fritter contains cooked, mashed yuca and malanga (root vegetables) and anise extract (from a licorice-flavored seed). A cinnamon stick and a piece of fresh lime rind lend flavor to the sugar syrup served with the Buñuelos.

BUÑUELOS

1 pound yuca, peeled and cut into 1-inch pieces
1 pound malanga, peeled and cut into 1-inch pieces
1 large egg, lightly beaten
¼ teaspoon anise extract
½ to ¾ cup all-purpose flour
Vegetable oil
Sugar Syrup
Garnish: lime wedges

Cook yuca in boiling water to cover 12 to 15 minutes or until tender; drain and set aside. Cook malanga in boiling water to cover 10 to 12 minutes or until tender. (Cook separately to avoid overcooking malanga.) Position knife blade in food processor bowl; add half of yuca. Pulse 5 or 6 times or until finely chopped. Repeat procedure several times with remaining yuca and malanga.

Combine yuca, malanga, egg, and anise extract in a large bowl; gradually add enough flour to make a soft dough. Divide into 24 balls. Roll each ball into an 8-inch rope; cross ends, shaping each rope into a loop.

Pour oil to depth of 2 inches into a Dutch oven; heat to 375°. Fry buñuelos, a few at a time, about 1 minute on each side or until lightly browned. Drain on paper towels. Place on a serving plate; serve with syrup. Garnish, if desired. Yield: 24 buñuelos.

Sugar Syrup

2 cups sugar
¼ teaspoon salt
1 cup water
1 (3-inch) stick cinnamon
1 lime rind strip (about 2 inches)
1 teaspoon vanilla extract

Combine first 5 ingredients in a heavy saucepan, and cook over medium heat, stirring constantly, until sugar dissolves. Cook, without stirring, until mixture reaches 220° (about 2 minutes). Remove cinnamon stick and lime rind; stir in vanilla. Yield: 1½ cups.

■ Yuca, also called cassava, is a potato-like root vegetable common in Cuban cooking. (Check the produce section of your grocery store for yuca, which looks like a large, dark sweet potato with a thick, barklike skin.) Juanita Plano crushes the garlic for her mojo (a garlic sauce made with citrus juices) with a wooden mortar and pestle she has had for years. If you don't have a mortar and pestle, use a garlic press or the flat side of a chef's knife.

YUCA CON MOJO

1 pound fresh yuca
1 quart water
1 tablespoon salt
1 small onion, thinly sliced and separated into rings
4 cloves garlic, crushed
⅓ cup vegetable oil
¼ cup fresh lime juice
¼ cup orange juice
1 teaspoon cider vinegar
¼ teaspoon salt
⅛ teaspoon pepper
Garnish: chopped fried pork cracklings

Peel yuca and cut into 2-inch chunks. Combine water and 1 tablespoon salt in a Dutch oven; bring to a boil. Add yuca; cover, reduce heat, and cook 25 to 30 minutes or until tender. Drain and keep warm.

Cook onion and garlic in oil in a large skillet over medium heat, stirring constantly, until tender. Add lime juice and next 4 ingredients; cook over low heat 2 to 3 minutes, stirring often. Pour garlic mixture (mojo) over yuca. Garnish, if desired. Yield: 4 servings.

Tip: *Save lemon and lime rinds. Store in the freezer, and grate as needed for pies, cakes, and cookies. Or the rinds can be candied for holiday uses.*

■ This one means "bacon from heaven" even though it doesn't contain any bacon. But the sweet, creamy flan (Spanish baked custard) does have a heavenly flavor. You bake it in a "water bath," which means to place the pan holding the custard mixture in a larger shallow pan of water. The water comes only part of the way up (not over) the sides of the custard pan, delicately cooking the custard in moist heat until custard is set.

TOCINO DEL CIELO

1½ cups sugar
1 cup water
1¼ teaspoons grated lime rind
1 (3-inch) stick cinnamon
¾ cup sugar
6 large eggs, lightly beaten
1 (14-ounce) can sweetened condensed milk
1 teaspoon vanilla extract

Combine 1½ cups sugar, water, lime rind, and cinnamon in a small saucepan. Cook over medium heat, stirring constantly, until mixture comes to a boil. Cook, without stirring, until mixture reaches 230° (about 10 minutes). Pour through a wire-mesh strainer into a small bowl, discarding lime rind and cinnamon; set syrup mixture aside.

Sprinkle ¾ cup sugar in a heavy saucepan; place over medium heat. Cook, stirring constantly, until sugar melts and turns a light golden brown. Pour into an 8½- x 4½- x 3-inch loafpan; set aside.

Combine eggs and condensed milk; gradually stir in syrup mixture and vanilla. Pour mixture over caramelized sugar in loafpan; cover with aluminum foil, and place in a large shallow baking pan. Add hot water to pan to depth of 1 inch.

Bake at 350° for 1 hour and 50 minutes. Remove pan from water; uncover and let cool on a wire rack. Cover and chill 8 hours. Loosen edges with a spatula, and invert onto a platter. Yield: 8 to 10 servings.

What's Cooking in The Keys

■ Louie's Backyard, a scenic restaurant in the Florida Keys, calls for "croutons" and "croûtes" in this unusual salad. These are simply fancy terms for French or Italian bread cut into shapes. Croutons are cubes, while croûtes, in this case, are slices meant to hold a white bean spread.

CAESAR SALAD WITH WHITE BEANS

¾ cup extra-virgin olive oil
¼ cup vegetable oil
¼ cup red wine vinegar
1½ teaspoons minced garlic
6 anchovy fillets, rinsed and finely chopped
2 tablespoons lemon juice
1 teaspoon cracked black pepper
1 teaspoon Dijon mustard
¼ cup grated Parmesan cheese
2 large heads romaine lettuce, torn into pieces
Croutons and croûtes
White Bean Spread
Garnishes: sun-dried tomato strips, fresh sage leaves

Combine first 9 ingredients in a jar. Cover tightly, and shake vigorously. Chill dressing mixture.

Combine romaine lettuce and croutons (cubes) in a large bowl; gradually add dressing mixture, tossing gently. Arrange on individual plates. Spoon White Bean Spread onto croûtes (slices), arranging 2 around edge of each salad. Garnish, if desired. Yield: 12 servings.

Croutons and Croûtes

3 cups French or Italian bread cubes
6 tablespoons extra-virgin olive oil, divided
24 (¼-inch-thick) slices French or Italian bread

Toss bread cubes with 3 tablespoons olive oil; place on a baking sheet. Brush bread slices with remaining 3 tablespoons olive oil; place on baking sheet. Bake at 350° for 12 to 15 minutes or until lightly browned and crisp.

White Bean Spread

1 cup dried white beans
5 cups water
3 cloves garlic
1 tablespoon chopped fresh sage or 1 teaspoon dried rubbed sage
1¼ teaspoons salt, divided
½ teaspoon ground white pepper, divided
½ cup extra-virgin olive oil
1 (7-ounce) jar oil-packed sun-dried tomatoes, drained and chopped
½ cup chopped fresh parsley

Sort and wash beans; place in a Dutch oven. Cover with water 2 inches above beans; let soak 8 hours. Drain beans, and return to Dutch oven. Add 5 cups water, garlic, sage, 1 teaspoon salt, and ¼ teaspoon pepper. Bring to a boil; cover, reduce heat, and simmer 1½ hours or until tender. Drain, reserving bean liquid.

Position knife blade in food processor bowl; add one-fourth of bean mixture. Set remaining bean mixture aside. Slowly pour olive oil through food chute with processor running, blending just until bean mixture is smooth. (If necessary, add enough reserved bean liquid to make a smooth paste; discard remaining bean liquid.) Fold bean paste, sun-dried tomatoes, parsley, remaining ¼ teaspoon salt and ¼ teaspoon pepper into remaining whole bean mixture. Keep warm. Yield: 2½ cups.

Coming to Terms with Florida Foods

Here's a quick lesson on tropical fruits and vegetables.

■ **Boniato**—Cuban version of the sweet potato, but it has a white flesh, and is not as sweet; may be substituted for a sweet potato although flavor and cooking times will differ
■ **Calabaza**—Cuban squash
■ **Guava**—small round or pear-shaped tropical fruit with intense flavor; often made into a paste for cooking and baking; popular in Cuban pastries
■ **Malanga**—Cuban root vegetable; shaggy brown skin and pinkish flesh; nutty taste
■ **Mamey**—large fruit with rough brown skin and pinkish flesh; sweet pumpkin taste; texture of avocado
■ **Mango**—sweet-tart fruit with fragrant, juicy, yellow flesh; green skin when unripe; yellow skin with a red blush when ripe
■ **Plantain**—looks like a large banana; green when unripe, black when ripe; used in dishes from appetizers to desserts; starchy flavor, not sweet
■ **Scotch bonnet pepper**—small, hot, fruity pepper common in Caribbean cooking
■ **Yuca**—(also called cassava) Cuban root vegetable with a hard, white flesh and brown barklike skin; may be substituted for a potato although flavor and cooking times will vary

■ Head to the produce section for many of these ingredients. Cilantro is a cousin to parsley, and fresh ginger looks like a root with its knotty form and thin, barklike skin. Just peel it with a sharp knife; then chop for this dish. A fresh jalapeño pepper adds zip to the tropical taste.

FRIED MARINATED SHRIMP WITH MANGO SLAW

32 unpeeled large fresh shrimp
1 medium-sized yellow onion, coarsely chopped
2 jalapeño peppers, seeded and chopped
¼ cup chopped fresh ginger
6 cloves garlic, coarsely chopped
¼ cup chopped fresh cilantro
⅓ cup lemon juice
1½ teaspoons salt
¼ teaspoon freshly ground pepper
2 tablespoons water
2 large eggs, lightly beaten
3 cups soft breadcrumbs
Vegetable oil
Mango Slaw
Garnishes: lime wedges, edible tropical flowers

Peel and devein shrimp; place in a shallow dish or a heavy-duty, zip-top plastic bag.

Position knife blade in food processor bowl; add onion, jalapeño pepper, ginger, garlic, cilantro, lemon juice, salt, pepper, and water. Process 20 seconds or until onion mixture forms a smooth paste, stopping once to scrape down sides. Pour over shrimp. Cover or seal, and refrigerate 2 hours, turning occasionally.

Remove shrimp from marinade, and discard marinade. Dip shrimp in beaten eggs, and dredge in breadcrumbs. Let stand 10 minutes.

Pour vegetable oil to depth of 2 to 3 inches in a Dutch oven, and heat to 350°. Fry shrimp, a few at a time, in hot oil until golden, turning once. Drain shrimp on paper towels. Serve with Mango Slaw, and garnish, if desired. Yield: 8 appetizer or 4 main-dish servings.

Mango Slaw

2 firm mangoes
1 sweet red pepper, cut into thin strips
1 purple onion, cut into thin strips
1 poblano chile pepper
6 green onions, sliced
¼ cup chopped fresh cilantro
¼ cup fresh lime juice
1 to 2 teaspoons dried crushed red pepper
½ teaspoon salt
½ teaspoon freshly ground black pepper

To peel mangoes, score skin lengthwise in 4 to 6 places using a sharp knife. Pull skin off, and discard. Cut pulp away from sides of long pit in 2 large sections. Slice into thin strips.

Combine mango, red pepper, and onion strips in a large bowl; set aside. Cut poblano chile pepper into quarters; remove seeds and membranes. Cut into thin strips; add to mango mixture. Add green onions and remaining ingredients, tossing to coat. Cover and chill. Yield: 5 cups.

■ You may not be familiar with yellowtail snapper, but it's popular in Key West, Florida. You can substitute red snapper, which, like yellowtail, usually comes with the skin on one side; leave it on for cooking.

YELLOWTAIL SNAPPER WITH JULIENNE VEGETABLES

½ cup Dijon mustard
2 egg yolks
4 (6- to 8-ounce) yellowtail snapper fillets
1½ cups coarsely chopped cashews
1 tablespoon unsalted butter
1 tablespoon olive oil
Julienne Vegetables
2 tablespoons chopped shallots
½ cup orange juice
1 tablespoon fresh lime juice
¼ cup unsalted butter, melted
1 tablespoon chopped fresh parsley
Garnishes: lime and lemon wedges, fresh basil sprigs, edible tropical flowers

Combine mustard and egg yolks; brush generously over skinless side of fillets. Dredge coated sides in cashews; refrigerate 10 minutes.

Heat 1 tablespoon butter and oil in a large nonstick skillet; place fillets, nut side down, in skillet. Cook over medium heat 5 to 8 minutes; carefully turn and cook 5 to 8 minutes or until fish flakes easily when tested with a fork. Arrange Julienne Vegetables on a large platter; place fillets, nut side up, on vegetables. Keep warm.

Wipe skillet with a paper towel; add shallots, and cook over medium heat, stirring constantly, until tender. Add juices, and bring to a boil. Cook until mixture is reduced to about 3 tablespoons. Stir in ¼ cup melted butter, 1 teaspoon at a time, using a wire whisk. Stir in parsley, and pour over fillets; garnish, if desired. Serve immediately. Yield: 4 to 6 servings.

Julienne Vegetables

1 clove garlic, minced
2 tablespoons olive oil
1 medium-size sweet potato, peeled and cut into thin strips
1 large carrot, scraped and cut into thin strips
1 small jicama, peeled and cut into thin strips
3 leeks (bulb ends only), cut into thin strips
½ teaspoon salt
¼ teaspoon pepper

Cook garlic in olive oil in a large skillet over medium heat, stirring constantly, until golden. Add vegetables, and cook, stirring constantly, 3 to 5 minutes or until crisp-tender. Sprinkle with salt and pepper. Yield: 4 to 6 servings.

Cast Iron: Well Seasoned And Timeless

Cast iron is the original energy-saving, nonstick cookware. It's durable, affordable, and healthful to use. Cast iron's density conducts heat evenly, virtually eliminating hot spots that plague lighter utensils. The natural nonstick surface of a seasoned piece of cast-iron cookware gets very hot and cooks food quickly. The disadvantages? It's heavy, and you can't put it in the dishwasher.

(For tips on seasoning cast-iron cookware, see "From Our Kitchen To Yours" on facing page.) We tested these recipes in cast iron; however, you may use any heavy cookware.

MOGUMBO

2 cups mixed dried beans
1 large onion, coarsely chopped
5 cloves garlic, crushed
¼ cup olive oil
6 cups water, divided
1 cup brown rice, uncooked
1 tablespoon olive oil
⅛ teaspoon salt
1 to 2 dried cayenne peppers
1 (6-ounce) can tomato paste
2 teaspoons salt
1 teaspoon dried crushed red
  pepper
½ teaspoon hickory-smoked salt
½ teaspoon dried thyme
¼ teaspoon celery seeds
⅛ teaspoon dried tarragon
20 black peppercorns

Sort and wash beans, rinsing 3 or 4 times; place in a bowl. Cover with water 2 inches above beans; let soak 8 hours. Drain.

Cook onion and garlic in ¼ cup olive oil in a 5-quart, cast-iron, flat-bottomed Dutch oven over medium-high heat until tender; add beans and 3 cups water. Bring to a boil; cover, reduce heat, and simmer 1½ hours, stirring occasionally.

Bring 2 cups water to a boil in a cast-iron saucepan; stir in rice, 1 tablespoon olive oil, ⅛ teaspoon salt, and cayenne peppers. Cover, reduce heat, and simmer 20 minutes or until tender. Remove and discard peppers.

Add cooked rice, tomato paste, and remaining 1 cup water to bean mixture. Combine 2 teaspoons salt and remaining ingredients in a mortar or small bowl, and grind with a pestle or crush with the back of a spoon; stir into bean mixture. Cover and simmer 15 minutes, stirring occasionally. Remove from heat; cover and let stand 15 minutes. Yield: 9 cups

Note: To make Mogumbo Dip, position a knife blade in food processor bowl; add 2 cups Mogumbo and ¼ cup white wine vinegar. Process until smooth. Transfer to a wok or saucepan; cook over low heat, stirring constantly, until thoroughly heated. Yield: about 2 cups. *Dana Barnes*
Birmingham, Alabama

BEEF-AND-SHRIMP STIR-FRY
(pictured on pages 38 and 39)

1 cup beef broth
1 cup chicken broth
1 tablespoon chopped green onions
1 tablespoon soy sauce
1 bay leaf
3 black peppercorns
½ teaspoon dried thyme
⅛ teaspoon dried oregano
1 tablespoon cornstarch
1½ tablespoons water
½ pound unpeeled medium-size
  fresh shrimp
1 tablespoon olive oil
½ pound beef tenderloin, cut into
  1-inch strips
¾ cup fresh broccoli flowerets
½ cup sliced zucchini
½ sweet red pepper, cut into thin
  strips
½ cup snow pea pods
½ cup sliced fresh mushrooms
Hot cooked rice

Combine first 8 ingredients in a medium saucepan, and bring to a boil; reduce heat, and simmer 30 minutes.

Remove from heat, and pour liquid through a wire-mesh strainer into a 2-cup liquid measuring cup, discarding solids. Return broth mixture to saucepan. Combine cornstarch and water, stirring until smooth; stir into broth mixture, and bring to a boil. Cook 1 minute; remove from heat. Set aside.

Peel and devein shrimp; set aside.

Heat olive oil in a cast-iron wok 10 to 15 minutes or until hot. Add shrimp, beef, and broccoli; cook, stirring constantly, 1 to 2 minutes. Add zucchini and remaining vegetables; cook, stirring constantly, 2 minutes. Add broth mixture, and cook until thoroughly heated. Serve over rice. Yield: 4 servings. *Sue-Sue Hartstern*
Louisville, Kentucky

POLENTA WITH SAUSAGE

2 quarts water
1 tablespoon salt
2 cups yellow cornmeal
1 pound sweet or hot Italian
  sausage, sliced
1 (15-ounce) can tomato paste
2 (14½-ounce) cans ready-to-serve
  beef broth
½ teaspoon rubbed sage
½ cup freshly grated Parmesan
  cheese

Combine water and salt in a 4-quart, cast-iron saucepan; bring to a boil. Gradually add cornmeal, stirring constantly. Cook over medium heat, stirring frequently, about 30 minutes or until consistency of mashed potatoes. Remove from heat; keep warm.

Cook sausage in a 10-inch cast-iron skillet, stirring occasionally; drain well. Add tomato paste and next 2 ingredients; cook over low heat 30 minutes.

Spoon polenta onto a serving platter; top with sausage mixture, and sprinkle with cheese. Yield: 4 servings. *Caroline W. Kennedy*
Newborn, Georgia

SAVORY CORN STICKS
(pictured on pages 38 and 39)

2 jalapeño peppers, seeded and
  chopped
2 cloves garlic, minced
⅓ cup vegetable oil
½ cup yellow cornmeal
½ cup all-purpose flour
2 teaspoons baking powder
¾ teaspoon salt
1 tablespoon sugar
1 tablespoon chopped fresh cilantro
  or 1 teaspoon dried cilantro
1 large egg, lightly beaten
½ cup milk
Vegetable cooking spray

Cook jalapeño peppers and garlic in oil in a small saucepan over medium heat, stirring constantly, until tender; set aside. Combine cornmeal and next 5 ingredients; add jalapeño pepper mixture, egg, and milk, stirring until smooth.

Coat a cast-iron breadstick or corn stick pan with cooking spray; heat in a 425° oven 3 minutes or until hot. Remove pan from oven; spoon batter into pan. Bake at 425° for 15 to 20 minutes or until lightly browned. Yield: 8 breadsticks or 6 corn sticks.

From Our Kitchen To Yours

Most cooks who have long used cast iron know that tender loving care turns the pieces into cherished heirlooms. Following are some tips on how to season and care for your cast-iron cookware.

Seasoning Secrets

New silver-colored cast-iron cookware earns its black sheen only after becoming well seasoned. Because cast iron is a porous material, it absorbs oil, forming a protective coating that keeps food from sticking and prevents rust. A drop of water dances on the hot surface of a properly seasoned cast-iron pan.

For new pieces, scrub off the pre-seasoning coat of wax with steel-wool soap pads and hot water; handwash with a mild detergent and dry cookware thoroughly. Iron left uncoated will rust; immediately spread solid vegetable shortening on the inside, including the underside of the lid (do not use butter or margarine). Place in a 250° to 300° oven for 15 minutes; remove from the oven, and wipe any excess grease around the interior to keep the surface evenly coated. Return to oven, and bake for 1½ to 2 hours. Remove from oven, and let cool to room temperature. Repeat this procedure two or three times.

To continue the seasoning process, cook foods that are high in fat—bacon, sausage, hamburgers—the first few times. Avoid any foods with high moisture and acid content in the beginning; certain recipes, such as soups and stews, have a tendency to remove the seasoning. All pieces eventually need reseasoning. It's time when food begins to stick, rust appears, or you experience a metallic taste. Treat all used pieces as you would a new one—scrub, dry, and reseason.

Handle with Care

■ Remove food from cast-iron cookware after cooking; do not use for storing leftovers.
■ Clean while the cast iron is still warm yet cool enough to handle.
■ Use a mild dishwashing liquid. Soak in water for just a minute or two; longer soaking damages the seasoning.
■ Rub with a nonabrasive scouring cloth, if necessary.
■ Run a heavily caked piece through a regular cycle in a self-cleaning oven; scrub off iron oxide flakes, and reseason.
■ *Never* place in a dishwasher. The harsh detergent, water jet, and humid, hot environment are damaging.
■ Towel dry cookware after each washing, or place in a warm oven just until dry.
■ Place a coffee filter in cast-iron cookware to absorb any excess moisture.
■ Store cookware and lids separately, especially in humid climates where condensation could occur, causing cookware to rust.
■ Be aware that steaming or poaching can be damaging to a cast-iron lid.
■ *Never* marinate in cast iron; acidic mixtures will damage the seasoning.

Note: For recipes using cast-iron cookware, see "Cast Iron: Well Seasoned And Timeless," on facing page.

Sharing Traditions

Dana Barnes's kitchen is a "cultural parlor." He travels the world just sitting at his table. By teaching the true meaning of Southern hospitality, he has a friend on nearly every continent. His friends live or have lived in the small apartment complex not far from the campus of the University of Alabama in Birmingham, Alabama, where he works.

The small kitchen is comforting with his collection of shiny, black cast-iron cookware hanging from a wrought-iron rack.

As a bean-and-lentil dish slowly cooks in a 15-year-old Dutch oven, Dana grinds herbs and spices in a 110-year-old lava stone mortar. The spicy mixture—named Mogumbo (an East African term meaning passion) by his friends—lends itself to stimulating conversations. For his recipe, see facing page.

The Unexpected Side Of Chocolate

Although most chocolate is enjoyed in sweet beverages or confections, there is a savory side to it that shouldn't be overlooked. Chocolate adds distinct character to many lower-fat main dishes and sauces.

Nancy Porter of Winston-Salem, North Carolina, adds cocoa powder to her Firestarter Chili for leaner Southwestern flair. Tomatoes, Hungarian paprika, beer, and a touch of peanut butter set this chili on fire with flavors that mingle well with cocoa.

BARBECUED PORK LOIN ROAST

1 (2¼-pound) boneless pork loin
  roast, trimmed
¾ cup no-salt-added catsup
¾ cup finely chopped onion
1 clove garlic, minced
1 tablespoon honey
1½ teaspoons unsweetened cocoa
1½ teaspoons brown sugar
2¼ teaspoons lemon juice
1½ teaspoons liquid smoke
⅛ teaspoon pepper
Dash of mace
Vegetable cooking spray

Butterfly roast by making a lengthwise cut in center, cutting to within ½ inch of other side, and open roast. Place in a shallow dish; set aside.

Combine catsup and next 9 ingredients; spread half of marinade mixture on roast, reserving remaining marinade. Cover roast, and refrigerate 8 hours. Cover and refrigerate reserved marinade.

Remove roast from marinade, discarding marinade. Coat a grill rack with cooking spray, and place rack over medium-hot coals (350° to 400°).

Place roast on rack, and cook, turning once, 20 minutes or until meat thermometer inserted in thickest portion of roast registers 160°. Remove roast from grill, and wrap in heavy-duty plastic wrap.

Cook reserved marinade in a heavy saucepan over medium-low heat 15 minutes, stirring often. Cut meat into thin slices, and serve with sauce. Yield: 9 servings (178 calories [21% from fat] per 3-ounce serving with 1½ tablespoons sauce).

□ *24.8g protein, 4.2g fat (1.4g saturated), 9.4g carbohydrate, 0.3g fiber, 79mg cholesterol, 66mg sodium, and 12mg calcium.*

CHICKEN WITH MOLE SAUCE

2½ cups no-salt-added chicken
  broth, divided
½ cup onion slices, separated into
  rings
1 clove garlic, sliced
½ cup raisins
¼ cup slivered almonds
3 tablespoons chili powder
2 tablespoons sesame seeds
1 tablespoon unsweetened cocoa
1 tablespoon sugar
½ teaspoon ground allspice
¼ teaspoon salt
¼ teaspoon pepper
1 tablespoon cornmeal
Vegetable cooking spray
8 (4-ounce) skinned, boned chicken
  breast halves

Combine 2 cups chicken broth, onion, and garlic in a small saucepan; cook over medium heat 10 minutes or until onion is tender. Pour into container of an electric blender; add raisins and next 8 ingredients. Process until smooth, stopping once to scrape down sides. Return mixture to saucepan; stir in cornmeal. Cook over medium heat, stirring constantly, until thickened and bubbly. Remove from heat, and keep Mole Sauce warm.

Coat a nonstick skillet with cooking spray; place over high heat until hot. Add chicken breasts; brown quickly on both sides. Reduce heat; add remaining ½ cup chicken broth, and cook 15 minutes, or until chicken is tender.

Spoon ¼ cup Mole Sauce onto each plate; place a chicken breast over sauce. Yield: 8 servings (232 calories [25% from fat] per 3 ounces of chicken and ¼ cup sauce).

□ *28.6g protein, 6.5g fat (1.3g saturated), 14.1g carbohydrate, 2.1g fiber, 72mg cholesterol, 169mg sodium, and 61mg calcium.*

FIRESTARTER CHILI

2 pounds top round steak,
  trimmed
Vegetable cooking spray
1 cup chopped onion
½ cup chopped green pepper
½ cup chopped sweet red pepper
1 jalapeño pepper, seeded and
  chopped
2 cloves garlic, minced
1 (13¾-ounce) can ready-to-serve,
  fat-free, no-salt-added beef broth
1 (10-ounce) can tomatoes with
  green chiles
1 (8-ounce) can tomato sauce
¼ cup light beer
2 tablespoons chili powder
1 tablespoon ground cumin
1 tablespoon unsweetened cocoa
1 tablespoon creamy peanut butter
1 tablespoon reduced-sodium soy
  sauce
1 tablespoon hot sauce
1 teaspoon dried oregano
1 teaspoon reduced-sodium
  Worcestershire sauce
½ teaspoon Hungarian paprika
¼ teaspoon ground ginger
¼ teaspoon ground white pepper
⅛ teaspoon ground coriander

Partially freeze steak; cut into ½-inch cubes, and set aside.

Coat a Dutch oven with cooking spray; place over medium heat until hot. Add steak, onion, and next 4 ingredients, and cook until meat browns, stirring often. Stir in beef broth and remaining ingredients; bring to a boil. Cover, reduce heat, and simmer 1½ hours, stirring occasionally. Yield: 6 servings (302 calories [28% from fat] per ⅔-cup serving).

☐ *39g protein, 9.5g fat (2.9g saturated), 13g carbohydrate, 2.7g fiber, 95mg cholesterol, 662mg sodium, and 46mg calcium.*

LIGHT MENU

Serve A Relaxing Dinner For Two

Reserve some time for just the two of you to unwind from the pressures of the day. As you talk things over, you'll have time to prepare a special dinner together.

DELUXE MENU FOR TWO

Lemon Veal with rice
Garlic Broccoli
Ginger-Marmalade Glazed Beets

LEMON VEAL

1 tablespoon all-purpose flour
1 teaspoon beef-flavored bouillon granules
½ teaspoon paprika
½ teaspoon chopped fresh parsley
¼ teaspoon dried rosemary
⅛ teaspoon pepper
½ pound boneless round rump veal, trimmed and cut into 1-inch cubes
Vegetable cooking spray
2 medium carrots, scraped and cut into thin strips
¼ cup dry white wine
¼ cup water
1 tablespoon lemon juice
2 cups hot cooked rice (cooked without salt or fat)

Combine first 6 ingredients in a heavy-duty zip-top plastic bag; add veal, seal bag, and shake to coat.

Coat a nonstick skillet with cooking spray; place over medium heat until hot. Add veal, and cook, stirring constantly, until lightly browned. Add carrots and next 3 ingredients; bring to a boil, stirring constantly. Cover, reduce heat, and simmer 40 minutes. Serve over rice. Yield: 2 servings (472 calories [14% from fat] per ¾ cup meat mixture and 1 cup rice).

☐ *32.5g protein, 7.3g fat (1.8g saturated), 61.3g carbohydrate, 3.7g fiber, 100mg cholesterol, 577mg sodium, and 69mg calcium.* Terri Cohen
North Potomac, Maryland

GARLIC BROCCOLI

1 clove garlic, minced
¾ teaspoon olive oil
2 cups fresh broccoli flowerets
2 tablespoons sliced green onions
¼ cup ready-to-serve, no-salt-added chicken broth
⅛ teaspoon salt
⅛ teaspoon coarsely ground pepper
1 tablespoon grated Parmesan cheese

Cook garlic in oil in a large nonstick skillet over medium-high heat, stirring constantly, until tender. Add broccoli and next 4 ingredients; cover and cook 5 minutes or until crisp-tender. Sprinkle with Parmesan cheese. Yield: 2 servings (58 calories [43% from fat] per 1-cup serving).

☐ *4g protein, 2.8g fat (0.8g saturated), 6g carbohydrate, 3g fiber, 2mg cholesterol, 219mg sodium, and 86mg calcium.*

GINGER-MARMALADE GLAZED BEETS

¾ pound fresh beets
3 tablespoons reduced-calorie orange marmalade
1 tablespoon unsweetened apple juice
1 tablespoon lemon juice
1 teaspoon minced crystallized ginger

Leave root and 1 inch of stem on beets; scrub with a vegetable brush. Cook beets in boiling water to cover 30 minutes or until tender. Drain. Pour cold water over beets, and drain. Trim off roots and stems, and rub off skins. Cut cooked beets into ¼-inch slices.

Combine marmalade and remaining ingredients in a saucepan; add beets, stirring to coat. Cook over low heat until thoroughly heated. Yield: 2 servings (98 calories [0% from fat] per ½-cup serving).

☐ *2.7g protein, 0.3g fat (0g saturated), 23g carbohydrate, 1.7g fiber, 0mg cholesterol, 129mg sodium, and 48mg calcium.* Margaret Ellen Holmes
Jackson, Tennessee

Produce Pointers

■ When buying fresh produce for two, select small sizes. Produce is one type of food in which small items usually don't cost more per serving than large ones.

■ Remember that overcooking destroys nutrients in vegetables. Warm leftovers carefully in a double boiler or a microwave. Even better, just mix them cold in a salad.

■ Steaming fresh vegetables over boiling water preserves more vitamins than cooking them in boiling water.

Dip Into Mock Guacamole

What fruit is easily transformed into a dip? The avocado of course—as guacamole. But with its buttery texture, it comes as no surprise that at 306 calories per medium avocado, 88% (30 grams) comes from fat.

By replacing the avocado with asparagus in Mock Guacamole, the recipe's fat content is reduced by about 25 grams. Only a small amount of reduced-calorie mayonnaise is added to the recipe for spreadability.

MOCK GUACAMOLE

2 (10½-ounce) cans cut asparagus, drained
1 cup finely chopped tomato
¼ cup finely chopped onion
2 tablespoons lemon juice
1 tablespoon reduced-calorie mayonnaise
½ teaspoon garlic salt
½ teaspoon chili powder
¼ teaspoon hot sauce

Position knife blade in food processor bowl, and add asparagus. Process until smooth, and transfer to a large mixing bowl. Stir in tomato and remaining ingredients. Place in a paper towel-lined wire-mesh strainer or colander, and let drain 1 hour. Cover and chill at least 3 hours. Yield: 2 cups (10 calories [4% from fat] per 2 tablespoons).

□ *0.5g protein, 0.4g fat (0g saturated), 1.5g carbohydrate, 0.3g fiber, 0mg cholesterol, 79mg sodium, and 4mg calcium.* Sandra Tyner
College Station, Texas

COMPARE THE NUTRIENTS (per serving)		
	Traditional	Light
Calories	30	10
Fat	2.6g	0.4g
Cholesterol	0mg	0mg

Anise Flavors The Bread

Licorice-flavored anise was one of the first herbs mentioned in history. The Greeks, Romans, and Egyptians believed it possessed medicinal powers. Today, it's popular in Italian liqueurs and Scandinavian or German breads.

ANISE-WHOLE WHEAT BREAD

2 packages active dry yeast
2 cups warm water (105° to 115°)
3 cups all-purpose flour, divided
1½ cups whole wheat flour
2¼ teaspoons salt
3 tablespoons butter or margarine, softened
3 tablespoons honey
1 tablespoon anise seeds, crushed and divided

Combine yeast and warm water in a 2-cup liquid measuring cup; let stand 5 minutes. Combine yeast mixture, 1½ cups all-purpose flour, and next 4 ingredients in a large mixing bowl. Beat at low speed with an electric mixer until blended; beat at medium speed 2 minutes. Stir in remaining 1½ cups all-purpose flour. Cover and let rise in a warm place (85°), free from drafts, 50 minutes or until doubled in bulk.

Lightly butter a 2-quart soufflé dish; sprinkle with 2 teaspoons anise seeds. Set aside. Vigorously stir dough 30 seconds; pour into prepared soufflé dish, and sprinkle with remaining seeds. Bake at 375° for 50 to 55 minutes or until lightly browned. Remove from soufflé dish, and let cool completely on a wire rack. Yield: 1 loaf.
Mary Belle Purvis
Greeneville, Tennessee

Light Cream of Broccoli Soup (page 17) doesn't lack creamy texture or rich taste—only fat and calories.

Above: *Cutting chilled margarine into the flour makes these lower-fat Herbed Biscuits (page 67) tender and flaky enough for any biscuit lover.*

Left: *Cast a spell with cast iron when you stir up colorful Beef-and-Shrimp Stir-Fry accompanied by Savory Corn Sticks. (Recipes, pages 32 and 33.)*

Get a jump on the day with Whole Wheat-Oat Pancakes, Maple Syrup, Canadian bacon, and Fresh Fruit With Lemon-Yogurt Dressing. (Recipes, pages 16 and 17.)

Cook Valentine's Dinner For Dad

Parents get a lot of loving hugs and kisses on February 14—not to mention homemade cards and treasures. But a supper especially for Dad, prepared by his favorite little hands, can create a special memory. This quick Valentine's menu is easy enough for children to prepare with a little help from an adult.

Both the Éclair Cake and the Turtle Candies must be made a day ahead or first thing in the morning. An older child or adult should be in charge, as both recipes involve working with hot sugar mixtures.

Because the steaks are browned in hot oil, an older person will also need to supervise the preparation of Steak Parmesan. After the meat is browned, young helpers can assemble the dish.

Everyone can pitch in to prepare Quick-and-Easy Mashed Potatoes, steamed broccoli, and a green salad with Vinaigrette Dressing.

DAD'S VALENTINE DINNER

Steak Parmesan
Quick-and-Easy Mashed Potatoes
Green salad with Vinaigrette Dressing
Steamed broccoli
Turtle Candies
or
Éclair Cake

STEAK PARMESAN

½ cup fine, dry breadcrumbs
½ cup grated Parmesan cheese, divided
1 large egg, lightly beaten
1 tablespoon water
⅛ teaspoon pepper
4 cubed sirloin steaks (about 1 pound)
¼ cup vegetable oil
1 cup commercial pizza sauce

Combine breadcrumbs and ¼ cup cheese; set aside. Combine egg, water, and pepper. Dip steaks in egg mixture; dredge in breadcrumb mixture. Brown steaks in hot oil in a skillet over medium heat 3 minutes on each side. Arrange in an 8-inch square baking dish. Top with pizza sauce; bake at 325° for 20 minutes. Sprinkle with remaining ¼ cup cheese. Yield: 4 servings.
Marge Killmon
Annandale, Virginia

QUICK-AND-EASY MASHED POTATOES

2¾ cups water
1 cup milk
1 (6.5-ounce) package instant mashed potato flakes
1 (8-ounce) package cream cheese, softened
3 green onions, chopped
1 (2-ounce) jar diced pimiento, drained (optional)
1 teaspoon fresh or frozen chopped chives
1 teaspoon salt
¼ teaspoon pepper

Combine water and milk in a heavy saucepan, and bring to a boil. Remove from heat, and stir in potato flakes. Add cream cheese and remaining ingredients, stirring mixture until blended. Cover and keep warm. Yield: 4 servings.
Bebe May
Pensacola, Florida

VINAIGRETTE DRESSING

⅓ cup white wine vinegar
2 tablespoons lemon juice
⅛ teaspoon garlic powder or 1 clove garlic, minced
½ teaspoon Dijon mustard
⅛ teaspoon salt
¼ cup olive oil

Combine first 5 ingredients; slowly add olive oil, stirring constantly with a wire whisk until blended. Serve over a green salad. Yield: ⅔ cup.
Marion Hall
Knoxville, Tennessee

TURTLE CANDIES

1 (12-ounce) package semisweet chocolate morsels
1¼ cups pecan halves
28 caramels, unwrapped
2 tablespoons whipping cream

Microwave chocolate morsels in a glass bowl at HIGH for 1½ minutes, stirring after 1 minute. Stir until smooth; cool until slightly thickened. Drop chocolate by tablespoonfuls onto a wax paper-lined baking sheet, shaping into 16 (1½-inch) circles. Reserve remaining chocolate. Arrange 4 pecans over each circle; chill until firm.

Place caramels and whipping cream in a glass bowl. Microwave at HIGH 2 minutes or until caramels melt; stir after 1 minute. Let stand 4 minutes or until slightly thickened. Spoon caramel mixture evenly over pecans. Microwave remaining chocolate at HIGH 1 minute, stirring after 30 seconds; quickly spread chocolate over caramel mixture. Refrigerate until firm. Yield: 16 candies.

ÉCLAIR CAKE

1 (16-ounce) package graham
    crackers, divided
2 (3.4-ounce) packages vanilla
    instant pudding mix
3 cups milk
1 (8-ounce) carton frozen whipped
    topping, thawed
1 cup sugar
½ cup butter or margarine
⅓ cup milk
½ cup semisweet chocolate morsels
½ cup chopped pecans

Layer one-third of graham crackers in
a 13- x 9- x 2-inch dish.

Combine pudding mix and 3 cups
milk in a large mixing bowl. Beat at
low speed with an electric mixer until
blended (about 2 minutes). Fold in
whipped topping; spoon half of mixture on graham crackers. Repeat layers ending with graham crackers.

Combine sugar, butter, and ⅓ cup
milk in a saucepan. Bring to a boil,
stirring constantly. Boil 1 minute, stirring often. Remove from heat; stir in
chocolate morsels. Spoon over graham crackers, and top with pecans.
Cover and chill 8 hours. Yield: 12 to
15 servings.   *Peggy H. Amos*
                          Martinsville, Virginia

a ball. Roll dough to ⅛-inch thickness
on a lightly floured surface; sprinkle
with sugar. Cut into 24 rounds using a
2½-inch biscuit cutter, and place on a
lightly greased baking sheet. Bake at
425° for 10 minutes. Remove to wire
racks to cool.

Spoon half of strawberries evenly
over 12 pastry rounds; top with remaining pastry rounds and strawberries. Pipe or dollop with sweetened
whipped cream. Garnish, if desired.
Yield: 12 servings.   *Cindie Hackney*
                              Longview, Texas

Winter Shortcakes

Try a fresh approach to dessert. For
Banana-Pecan Shortcake, layer shortbread rounds, brown sugar-flavored
cream, sliced bananas, and chopped
pecans. Quick Apple Shortcake starts
conveniently with a mix. Prepare the
muffin-textured cake; then top cake
wedges with Apple-Cinnamon Sauce
made from commercial fried apple
slices, raisins, and cinnamon. Add a
scoop of vanilla ice cream for dessert
à la mode.

STRAWBERRY
CRISPY SHORTCAKES

2 cups all-purpose flour
1 teaspoon baking powder
¼ teaspoon salt
½ cup shortening
3 tablespoons butter
¼ cup cold water
Sugar
2 (10-ounce) packages frozen
    strawberries in syrup, thawed
Sweetened whipped cream
Garnish: fresh mint sprigs

Combine first 3 ingredients; cut in
shortening and butter with a pastry
blender until crumbly. Sprinkle cold
water (1 tablespoon at a time) evenly
over surface; stir with a fork until dry
ingredients are moistened. Shape into

QUICK APPLE SHORTCAKE

1 (7-ounce) package apple-cinnamon
    muffin mix
½ cup milk
¼ cup sour cream
¼ cup chopped pecans
Apple-Cinnamon Sauce

Combine first 4 ingredients, stirring
just until blended. Pour into a greased
and floured 9-inch round cakepan.
Bake at 450° for 8 to 10 minutes or
until a wooden pick inserted in center
comes out clean. Cool in pan on a wire
rack 10 minutes; remove from pan,
and let cool completely on wire rack.
To serve, cut into wedges, and top
with Apple-Cinnamon Sauce. Yield: 8
servings.

Apple-Cinnamon Sauce

1 (28-ounce) jar fried apple slices,
    undrained
¼ cup raisins
¼ teaspoon ground cinnamon

Combine all ingredients in a small
saucepan; bring to a boil. Reduce heat
to low; simmer 5 minutes. Cool.
Yield: about 2½ cups.   *Shellie Smith*
                    Oklahoma City, Oklahoma

Kitchen Safety for Kids
Of All Ages

■ Tie long hair back. Roll up long
or floppy sleeves.
■ Turn saucepan and skillet handles to the side or back of the
range to avoid accidental spills.
■ Unplug mixers before putting
the beaters in or taking them out.
■ Never handle a knife by the
blade. Watch what you are cutting
and never cut toward yourself.
■ To prevent burns, keep clothing
and hands away from gas or electric burners.
■ Use thick, dry pot holders.
■ When removing lids from pans,
always tilt the lid away from you
to prevent the steam from burning
your face.
■ Be careful when draining foods
cooked in boiling water; the steam
can burn you.
■ When washing dishes, don't add
knives or appliance blades to dish-
pan. Someone reaching into dish-
pan could get cut.
■ Turn off all appliances immediately after using them.

BANANA-PECAN SHORTCAKE

1 cup butter or margarine,
   softened
¾ cup firmly packed brown sugar
1 teaspoon vanilla extract
2 cups all-purpose flour
1 cup ground pecans
⅛ teaspoon ground cinnamon
3 bananas, peeled and thinly sliced
2 tablespoons lemon juice
½ cup whipping cream
2 tablespoons firmly packed brown
   sugar
1 cup sour cream
¼ cup coarsely chopped pecans,
   toasted

Beat butter at medium speed with an electric mixer until creamy; gradually add ¾ cup brown sugar, beating well. Stir in vanilla. Combine flour and next 2 ingredients; add to butter mixture, mixing until blended.

Divide dough in half. Place each portion of dough on a lightly greased baking sheet; roll to ¼-inch thickness, and trim each into a 10-inch circle. Bake at 350° for 15 to 20 minutes. Cool 10 minutes on baking sheets; gently remove to wire racks, and cool completely.

Combine banana slices and lemon juice; set aside. Beat whipping cream and 2 tablespoons sugar until stiff peaks form; fold in sour cream. To serve, place a shortbread round on a serving plate; spread with half of whipped cream mixture, and arrange banana slices on top. Place remaining shortbread round over banana slices, and spread with remaining whipped cream mixture. Sprinkle with pecans. Yield: one 2-layer shortcake.

Batter Up For These Vegetable Pancakes

We can't say who first added diced or pureed vegetables to pancake batter. However they began, vegetable pancakes have evolved from down-home potato cakes to patties of ground corn, squash, carrots, and rice, to name a few. They are easy to prepare. Serve them with grilled or roasted meats, poultry, or seafood and a salad for a well-rounded meal.

VEGETABLE-RICE PANCAKES

3 cups cooked brown rice
1 cup grated carrots
2 large eggs, lightly beaten
½ cup finely chopped onion
¼ cup whole wheat flour
¼ cup all-purpose flour
¼ cup chopped fresh parsley
1 clove garlic, minced
1 teaspoon salt
¼ teaspoon ground pepper
Vegetable cooking spray

Combine first 10 ingredients, stirring just until blended. Coat a large skillet with cooking spray. For each pancake, spoon ¼ cup batter into hot skillet, pressing into thin patties. Cook until browned; turn and cook other side. Yield: 15 pancakes. *Valerie Stutsman*
Norfolk, Virginia

CORN PANCAKES

2 large eggs
2 cups frozen whole kernel corn,
   thawed
¼ cup all-purpose flour
½ teaspoon baking powder
½ teaspoon salt
¼ teaspoon pepper
¼ cup butter or margarine, divided
Sour cream
Salsa
Garnish: fresh cilantro sprigs

Position knife blade in food processor bowl; add first 6 ingredients. Pulse ingredients until corn is coarsely chopped.

Melt 2 tablespoons butter in a large skillet, adding remaining butter as needed. For each pancake, spoon about 2 tablespoons batter into hot skillet. Cook until tops are covered with bubbles and edges look cooked; turn and cook other side. Serve with sour cream and salsa. Garnish, if desired. Yield: 8 pancakes.
Nora Henshaw
Okemah, Oklahoma

ZUCCHINI PANCAKES

1 pound zucchini, shredded
¾ cup pancake mix
½ cup (2 ounces) shredded Swiss
   cheese
½ cup milk
1 large egg, lightly beaten
¼ cup chopped onion
¼ cup butter or margarine, divided

Squeeze zucchini between layers of paper towels until very dry; set aside.

Combine pancake mix and next 3 ingredients, stirring just until dry ingredients are moistened. Gently stir in zucchini and onion. Melt 2 tablespoons butter in a large skillet, adding remaining butter as needed. For each pancake, spoon ¼ cup batter into hot skillet. Cook until tops are covered with bubbles and edges look cooked; turn and cook other side. Yield: 8 pancakes.
Erma Jackson
Huntsville, Alabama

What About the Syrup?

Of course, a sweet syrup wouldn't be right for these pancakes, so try our suggested toppings:

Corn relish	Mayonnaise
Crumbled goat	Pesto
cheese	Pizza sauce
Guacamole	Ricotta cheese
Herb butter	Salsa
Honey mustard	Sour cream
Spaghetti sauce	

Spruced Up Vegetables

These vegetable dishes are easy to make for family dinners yet dressed up enough for company. Add an entrée and salad to complete the meal.

With the exception of Potatoes Moussaka, the casseroles can be assembled and refrigerated up to six hours before baking. The sauce for Potatoes Moussaka can be prepared up to an hour ahead; assemble the casserole just before baking.

EGGPLANT CASSEROLE

1 large eggplant, peeled and cubed
1 (8-ounce) package mozzarella
  cheese, cubed
1 (15-ounce) jar marinara sauce
⅓ cup grated Parmesan cheese

Cook eggplant in boiling water 5 minutes; drain well. Place in a lightly greased 1½-quart casserole; add mozzarella cheese, and top with marinara sauce. Cover and bake at 350° for 30 minutes. Sprinkle with Parmesan cheese, and bake an additional 5 minutes. Yield: 6 servings.

Nora Henshaw
Okemah, Oklahoma

SPINACH-ARTICHOKE CASSEROLE

2 (10-ounce) packages frozen
  chopped spinach, thawed and well
  drained
1 (6-ounce) jar marinated artichoke
  hearts, drained
2 (3-ounce) packages cream cheese,
  softened
2 tablespoons butter or margarine,
  softened
¼ cup milk
¼ teaspoon freshly ground
  pepper
2 tablespoons grated Parmesan
  cheese

Combine spinach and artichokes in a large bowl. Combine cream cheese and next 3 ingredients; stir into spinach mixture. Spoon mixture into a lightly greased 1½-quart casserole. Sprinkle with Parmesan cheese. Bake, covered, at 350° for 30 minutes; uncover and bake an additional 10 minutes. Yield: 6 servings.

Carole Drennan
Abilene, Texas

POTATOES MOUSSAKA

2 pounds red potatoes, thinly sliced
  (about 6 medium)
¾ teaspoon salt
½ cup butter or margarine,
  divided
1 large onion, chopped
3 cloves garlic, minced
1 small eggplant, peeled and
  cubed
1 cup peeled, chopped tomato
½ teaspoon dried basil
½ teaspoon dried oregano
½ teaspoon ground cinnamon
2 tablespoons all-purpose flour
2 cups milk
½ cup grated Parmesan cheese

Layer potatoes in a 13- x 9- x 2-inch baking dish; sprinkle with salt, and set aside.

Melt 2 tablespoons butter in a large skillet; add onion and garlic. Cook over medium heat, stirring constantly, 5 minutes. Add eggplant, tomato, basil, oregano, and cinnamon; cook 5 minutes, stirring often. Spoon eggplant mixture over potatoes. Melt remaining 6 tablespoons butter in a small saucepan over low heat; add flour, stirring until smooth. Cook, stirring constantly, 1 minute. Gradually add milk; cook over medium heat, stirring constantly, until mixture is thickened and bubbly. Pour over eggplant mixture; sprinkle with Parmesan cheese. Bake, uncovered, at 350° for 35 minutes or until potatoes are tender. Yield: 8 servings.

Leslie Genszler
Roswell, Georgia

CARROT-PECAN CASSEROLE

3 pounds carrots, sliced
⅔ cup sugar
½ cup butter or margarine,
  softened
½ cup chopped pecans, toasted
¼ cup milk
2 large eggs, lightly beaten
3 tablespoons all-purpose flour
1 tablespoon vanilla extract
1 teaspoon grated orange rind
¼ teaspoon ground nutmeg
Garnishes: carrot curl, fresh parsley
  sprigs

Cook carrots in a small amount of boiling water in a medium saucepan 12 to 15 minutes or until tender.

Drain carrots, and mash. Stir in sugar and next 8 ingredients. Spoon into a lightly greased 2-quart casserole. Bake at 350° for 40 minutes. Garnish, if desired. Yield: 10 to 12 servings.

Erma Jackson
Huntsville, Alabama

Vegetable Savvy

■ Use a stiff vegetable brush to scrub vegetables rather than peel them. Peeling causes a loss of vitamins found in and just under the skin. For many vegetables, such as squash, peeling is not necessary.

■ Always store potatoes and onions in a cool, dark place with air circulation to prevent sprouting.

■ The darker the orange color of carrots, the greater the content of vitamin A.

■ Eggplant flesh darkens rapidly when cut, so don't peel until just before cooking. Rub cut surfaces with lemon or lime juice to prevent darkening.

Homesick?
Try A Pot Pie

There is something comforting about a pot pie with its thickened mixture of vegetables and meat and its rich pastry topping.

If you're leery of making your own pot pies because of preparing the pastry, fear not. Both of these recipes have easy toppings.

BEEF POT PIES WITH YORKSHIRE PUDDING TOPPING

2 large eggs
1 cup all-purpose flour
¼ teaspoon salt
⅛ teaspoon pepper
1 cup milk
2 small potatoes, peeled and cubed (about ½ pound)
½ cup chopped onion
1 clove garlic, minced
1 tablespoon butter or margarine, melted
¾ cup whipping cream
1 tablespoon Worcestershire sauce
1½ teaspoons prepared horseradish
2½ cups cubed rare roast beef
1 cup frozen English peas, thawed
¼ teaspoon salt
⅛ teaspoon pepper
2 tablespoons butter or margarine, melted
1 egg white

Combine first 5 ingredients in container of an electric blender; process until smooth, stopping once to scrape down sides. Cover batter, and chill 30 minutes.

Cook potatoes in boiling salted water to cover in a small saucepan 10 minutes or until tender; drain well, and set aside.

Cook onion and garlic in 1 tablespoon butter in a large skillet over medium heat, stirring mixture constantly, until tender; add whipping cream, Worcestershire sauce, and horseradish. Cook over medium heat, stirring constantly, until mixture is thickened (about 8 minutes).

Combine reserved potatoes, roast beef, English peas, ¼ teaspoon salt, and ⅛ teaspoon pepper in a large bowl, and add whipping cream mixture, tossing to coat. Spoon potato mixture evenly into four lightly greased 2-cup baking dishes. Pour 2 tablespoons butter evenly around inside top edges of baking dishes; place on a baking sheet, and set aside.

Beat egg white at high speed with an electric mixer until stiff peaks form; fold into batter.

Bake pies at 450° for 2 minutes. Remove from oven, and pour about ½ cup batter over top of each pie. Bake at 450° for 15 minutes; reduce temperature to 400°, and continue baking an additional 10 to 15 minutes or until pies are puffed and golden. Yield: 4 servings.
Mike Singleton
Memphis, Tennessee

TURKEY POT PIE

½ cup mayonnaise or salad dressing
2 tablespoons all-purpose flour
1 cup milk
1½ cups chopped cooked turkey
1 (10-ounce) package frozen mixed vegetables, thawed and drained
1 teaspoon chicken-flavored bouillon granules
⅛ teaspoon pepper
1 (4-ounce) package refrigerated crescent rolls

Melt mayonnaise in a heavy saucepan over low heat; add flour, stirring until smooth. Cook, stirring constantly, 1 minute. Gradually add milk; cook over medium heat, stirring constantly, until mixture is thickened and bubbly. Stir in turkey and next 3 ingredients; cook over medium heat until thoroughly heated. Spoon into a 9-inch quiche dish or pieplate.

Unroll crescent rolls, and place rectangular pieces side by side on a lightly floured surface, firmly pressing perforations to seal. Roll dough into a 10-inch square; cut into 1-inch strips, and arrange in a lattice design over turkey mixture. Bake at 375° for 15 to 20 minutes or until golden brown. Let stand 10 minutes before serving. Yield: 4 servings.
Rita Williams
Mount Juliet, Tennessee

Lots of Leftovers?

■ Extend the storage life of your turkey leftovers by freezing them. Slice, chop, or cube the meat, and package it in meal-size portions, making it easy to use in recipes.

■ When you have small portions of meat or poultry left over, cut them up into bite-size pieces; then freeze the pieces until you have enough to add to a pot pie or casserole.

Weeknight Family Fare

Are you on the lookout for a streamlined menu for your famished family? Your search may end here. Follow our game plan to have supper on the table in about an hour.

The recipe for All-American Meat Loaf makes two loaves. Simply freeze the additional loaf for another meal. Recruit younger family members to perform easy jobs such as making the salad and setting the table.

ALL-AMERICAN MEAT LOAF

2 pounds ground chuck
¾ cup quick-cooking oats, uncooked
1 medium onion, chopped
½ cup catsup
¼ cup milk
2 large eggs, lightly beaten
1 tablespoon prepared horseradish
1 teaspoon salt
¼ teaspoon pepper
½ cup catsup
1 tablespoon prepared horseradish
3 tablespoons brown sugar
2 teaspoons prepared mustard

Combine ground chuck, oats, onion, catsup, milk, eggs, 1 tablespoon horseradish, salt, and pepper in a large bowl; shape into 2 (7½- x 4-inch) loaves. Place on a lightly greased rack of a broiler pan; bake at 350° for 40 minutes.

Combine ½ cup catsup and remaining ingredients; spoon over meat loaf, and bake an additional 5 minutes. Yield: 2 loaves or 8 servings.

Note: To freeze one meat loaf after cooking, cool and wrap in heavy-duty aluminum foil. Seal, label, and freeze up to three months. To reheat, thaw in refrigerator eight hours. Bake, in foil, at 350° for 45 minutes or until thoroughly heated.

Sabrina McFarling
Hawesville, Kentucky

PARMESAN POTATOES

2 tablespoons butter or margarine
½ cup chopped green pepper
⅓ cup chopped onion
¼ cup grated Parmesan cheese
½ teaspoon seasoned salt
½ teaspoon seasoned pepper
¼ teaspoon garlic powder
2 pounds potatoes, peeled and cut into ¼-inch slices
Paprika

Place butter in a 2-quart baking dish; microwave at HIGH 30 seconds or until butter melts. Add green pepper, onion, Parmesan cheese, salt, pepper, and garlic powder, stirring well. Stir in potatoes. Cover tightly with heavy-duty plastic wrap; fold back a small corner of wrap to allow steam to escape. Microwave at HIGH 12 to 14 minutes or until tender, uncovering and stirring every 5 minutes. Sprinkle with paprika. Yield: 4 servings.
Mrs. Charles DeHaven
Owensboro, Kentucky

SPINACH SALAD

1 pound fresh spinach
1 (11-ounce) can mandarin oranges, drained
1 medium-size purple onion, thinly sliced and separated into rings
Tangy Orange Vinaigrette Dressing

Remove stems from spinach; wash leaves thoroughly, and pat dry. Tear leaves into bite-size pieces. Combine spinach, oranges, and onion rings; toss with Tangy Orange Vinaigrette Dressing. Serve immediately. Yield: 4 to 6 servings.

Tangy Orange Vinaigrette Dressing

1½ teaspoons grated orange rind
1½ teaspoons Dijon mustard
½ teaspoon minced garlic
¼ teaspoon hot sauce
¼ cup cider vinegar
½ cup vegetable oil

Position knife blade in food processor bowl. Add first 5 ingredients, and pulse 2 or 3 times or until blended. With food processor running, pour vegetable oil through food chute in a slow, steady stream; process until blended. Yield: ¾ cup. *Trudy Dunn*
Dallas, Texas

LEMON FLUFF PIE

1 (3-ounce) package lemon-flavored gelatin
1 cup boiling water
½ cup cold water
1 (8-ounce) carton lemon yogurt
1 (8-ounce) container frozen whipped topping, thawed
1 (9-ounce) graham cracker crust

Combine gelatin and 1 cup boiling water, stirring 2 minutes or until gelatin dissolves. Add ½ cup cold water. Chill until the consistency of unbeaten egg white. Fold in yogurt and whipped topping; pour into graham cracker crust. Refrigerate until firm. Yield: one 9-inch pie.

Game Plan For a Timely Meal

■ Dissolve flavored gelatin for lemon pie, and place in refrigerator to chill.
■ Prepare meat loaf, and place in oven to bake.
■ Assemble pie, and place it in refrigerator to set.
■ Prepare Parmesan Potatoes; put in the microwave to cook.
■ Combine spinach, fruit, and onion for salad; make dressing.

Come Home To Breakfast

The next time you need a dinner idea, try breakfast foods as a soothing hot meal to end a cold winter's day. Or you may want to serve one of these recipes the next time you have guests for breakfast or brunch.

EGGS BAKED IN MUSHROOM SAUCE

1 pound fresh mushrooms, sliced
¼ cup butter or margarine, melted
3 tablespoons all-purpose flour
2 cups whipping cream
1 egg yolk, lightly beaten
1 teaspoon beef-flavored bouillon granules
1 tablespoon grated onion
2 tablespoons chopped fresh parsley
¼ teaspoon salt
¼ teaspoon pepper
⅛ teaspoon dried thyme
8 large eggs
Grated Parmesan cheese
4 English muffins, halved and toasted

Cook mushrooms in butter in a large saucepan over medium heat, stirring constantly, 5 minutes; remove mushrooms with a slotted spoon, and set aside. Add flour to drippings, stirring until smooth. Cook, stirring constantly, 1 minute. Combine whipping cream and next 3 ingredients. Gradually add to flour mixture; cook over medium heat, stirring constantly, until mixture is thickened and bubbly. Stir in reserved mushrooms, parsley, and next 3 ingredients.

Pour into a lightly greased 13- x 9- x 2-inch dish. Make 8 indentations in mushroom mixture, and break an egg into each. Sprinkle each with Parmesan cheese, and bake at 350° for 7 to 8 minutes. Serve over English muffin halves. Yield: 8 servings.

Sally B. Harris
Tarboro, North Carolina

HAM-AND-EGGS CRESCENT PIZZA

1 (8-ounce) package refrigerated crescent rolls
¼ cup chopped onion
1 tablespoon butter or margarine, melted
1 cup finely chopped cooked ham
1 cup (4 ounces) shredded Swiss cheese
4 large eggs, lightly beaten
½ cup milk
½ teaspoon salt
¼ teaspoon pepper
1 tablespoon chopped fresh or frozen chives

Unroll crescent rolls, and place in an ungreased 13- x 9- x 2-inch pan. Press ½ inch up sides to form a crust; seal perforations. Bake at 375° for 5 minutes on lower rack of oven; set aside.

Cook onion in butter in a small skillet over medium heat, stirring constantly, until crisp-tender; stir in ham, and spoon evenly over dough. Sprinkle with cheese. Combine eggs and next 3 ingredients; pour over cheese. Sprinkle with chives. Bake at 350° for 25 to 30 minutes or until set. Serve immediately. Yield: 6 to 8 servings.

Mrs. Ezra Sanders
Obion, Tennessee

HERBED CHEESE OMELET

1 (3-ounce) package cream cheese, softened
1½ teaspoons sour cream
¼ teaspoon lemon juice
¼ teaspoon dried parsley flakes
⅛ teaspoon salt
⅛ teaspoon garlic powder
⅛ teaspoon ground white pepper
⅛ teaspoon dried dillweed
8 large eggs
2 tablespoons water
½ teaspoon ground white pepper
1 tablespoon olive oil
1 tablespoon butter or margarine
2 tablespoons chopped green onions

Combine first 3 ingredients in a large bowl; add parsley flakes and next 4 ingredients, mixing well.

Combine eggs, water, and ½ teaspoon ground white pepper; stir with a wire whisk or fork until blended.

Heat a 10-inch heavy skillet over medium heat until hot enough to sizzle a drop of water. Add olive oil and butter, and rotate pan to coat bottom. Pour egg mixture into skillet. As mixture starts to cook, gently lift edges of omelet with a spatula, and tilt pan so uncooked portion flows underneath. Spoon cream cheese mixture in center, and fold sides over filling. Sprinkle with green onions, and serve immediately. Yield: 4 servings.

Heather Riggins
Nashville, Tennessee

Ginger And Pears — Wow!

Ginger is one of the world's most widely used spices. Known for its ability to round out the flavor of many foods, it works especially well with pears.

Cooking time for pears may vary depending on their variety, size, shape, and texture. For best results, choose firm-to-ripe Bosc, Bartlett, or Anjou pears for preparing recipes.

HONEY-BAKED PEARS

6 medium pears, cored and halved lengthwise
¾ cup honey
2 tablespoons crystallized ginger
¾ cup water

Arrange pear halves, cut side down, in a lightly greased 13- x 9- x 2-inch pan. Drizzle with honey, and sprinkle with ginger; add water. Cover and bake at 350° for 45 minutes or until tender. Yield: 4 to 6 servings. *Dorsella Utter*
Louisville, Kentucky

GINGER-PEAR PIE

1 unbaked 9-inch pastry shell
1 cup gingersnap crumbs
¼ cup firmly packed brown sugar
1 tablespoon all-purpose flour
½ teaspoon ground cinnamon
⅛ teaspoon salt
¼ cup butter or margarine,
    softened
5 medium pears, peeled, cored, and
    thinly sliced (about 2½ pounds)
1 medium pear (optional)
1 tablespoon finely chopped pecans
    (optional)

Bake pastry shell at 450° for 9 to 11 minutes; set aside.

Combine gingersnap crumbs and next 5 ingredients. Layer half of pear slices in pastry shell; spread half of gingersnap mixture over pears. Repeat procedure with remaining pears and gingersnap mixture. Cover loosely with aluminum foil, and bake at 375° for 40 minutes. Uncover and bake an additional 10 minutes, if you do not plan to garnish.

To garnish, peel optional pear; cut in half, leaving stem intact in one half. Remove core and thinly slice half with stem, cutting to, but not through, stem end. Reserve half without stem for other use. After baking pie 40 minutes, fan and arrange pear half with stem on pie; sprinkle with pecans. Bake, uncovered, an additional 10 minutes. Yield: one 9-inch pie.

La Juan Coward
Jasper, Texas

Spice Tips

■ To freshen air throughout the house, boil 1 tablespoon of whole cloves in a pan of water.

■ Store spices in a cool place and away from any direct source of heat, because the heat will destroy their flavor. Red-colored spices will maintain flavor and retain color longer if they are stored in the refrigerator.

Begin With A White Sauce

Take a basic white sauce, and add flavorful ingredients to jazz up vegetables, meats, rice, and pasta. Dress broiled chicken with Lemon-Parsley Sauce. Top potatoes or steamed vegetables with Florentine Sauce. Or try Basil-Tomato Sauce for a chicken or pasta dinner.

If you're a novice cook or hesitant about making a white sauce, follow our easy instructions. A heavy saucepan, wire whisk (or spoon), and constant stirring help ensure a successful, smooth sauce.

We tried microwaving the sauce but found that it doesn't really save time. Leftover sauce can be refrigerated and reheated using a medium setting on the range or medium power in the microwave.

MEDIUM WHITE SAUCE

2 tablespoons butter or margarine
2 tablespoons all-purpose flour
1 cup milk
½ teaspoon salt
Dash of ground white pepper

Melt butter in a heavy saucepan over low heat; add flour, stirring until smooth. Cook, stirring constantly, 1 minute. Gradually add milk; cook over medium heat, stirring constantly, until thickened and bubbly (about 3 minutes). Stir in salt and ground white pepper. Yield: 1 cup.

Florentine Sauce: Melt butter in a heavy saucepan over low heat; add ¼ cup sliced green onions. Cook 1 minute. Add flour, and proceed as directed for Medium White Sauce on this page. Stir in 1 cup finely chopped fresh spinach and ⅛ teaspoon ground nutmeg; cook just until heated. Serve over pasta, chicken, fish, or tomatoes. Yield: about 1¾ cups.

Basil-Tomato Sauce: Melt butter in a heavy saucepan over low heat; add 2 tablespoons chopped shallots. Cook 1 minute. Add flour and proceed as directed for Medium White Sauce, reducing salt to ¼ teaspoon. Stir in 2 tablespoons commercial pesto sauce and 1 cup chopped tomato, and cook mixture just until heated. Serve over pasta, chicken, fish, or squash. Yield: 1⅔ cups.

Lemon-Parsley Sauce: Prepare Medium White Sauce as directed. Stir in 1 teaspoon grated lemon rind, 1 tablespoon lemon juice, and ¼ cup chopped fresh parsley. Serve over chicken, fish, or green vegetables. Yield: 1 cup.

Cheese Sauce: Prepare Medium White Sauce as directed. Stir in 1 cup (4 ounces) shredded Cheddar or Swiss cheese, stirring until cheese melts. For a zippy Mexican-style sauce, substitute Monterey Jack or Pepper Jack. Serve over pasta, chicken, fish, ham, potatoes, or vegetables. Yield: 1⅓ cups.

A Taste Of Tradition: Arnaud's 75th

New Orleanians know a good thing when they see it, and they hang on to it. Take Arnaud's. This French Quarter member of the culinary old guard is still serving up tradition in grand style 75 years after it first opened.

Cutting-edge cuisine it's not, but that's the point. Those who dine *want* to step back in time and experience what Arnaud's does best—classic Creole. And the atmosphere? Classic New Orleans.

From the moment you arrive, festivity fizzes in the air. You'll be seated in one of six public dining rooms where the light of chandeliers glimmers in beveled glass windows fronting Bienville Street.

More of the past unfolds on Arnaud's second floor in the Mardi Gras Museum with an astonishing display of exquisite jeweled ball gowns and other memorabilia belonging to the restaurant's former owner, who was queen of 22 Mardi Gras balls. (You don't want to miss this. The exhibit is free, and you're welcome to view it whether or not you're having a meal.)

Tracing her royalty from 1937 to 1968, Germaine Cazenave Wells was the daughter of the restaurant's founder, Arnaud Cazenave. He's credited with creating the facility and its reputation, but Germaine took her father's dramatic flair a step further with a personality as colorful as her Mardi Gras fashions.

She took over the restaurant following her father's death in 1948 and operated Arnaud's for nearly 30 years until her own health declined. Unfortunately, so did the restaurant—until Germaine handed over the reins to her chosen successor, Archie Casbarian in 1978.

A visit to the restaurant today is a wonderful blend of the past and present. The menu indicates which dishes are Arnaud's specialties. Shrimp Arnaud has been served here since the beginning, in 1918. Frenchman Arnaud Cazenave created this signature dish using a traditional remoulade sauce (with a mayonnaise base) adapted with spicy Creole mustard and paprika.

On your first visit to Arnaud's, you might consider Oysters Stewed in Cream for a soup course, Crabmeat Karen as an entrée, and Strawberries Arnaud for dessert. We like all three recipes so well, we are passing them along to you.

CRABMEAT KAREN

1 cup finely chopped fresh
   mushrooms
¾ cup finely chopped green onions
1 large egg, lightly beaten
¼ cup whipping cream
½ teaspoon salt
¼ teaspoon ground white pepper
¼ teaspoon ground red pepper
1 pound fresh lump crabmeat,
   drained
1 cup soft breadcrumbs
White Wine Sauce
3 (17¼-ounce) packages frozen puff
   pastry sheets, thawed
2 large eggs, lightly beaten
Garnishes: cherry tomatoes, fresh
   parsley sprigs

Combine first 7 ingredients; add crabmeat and breadcrumbs, tossing gently. Set aside.

Begin preparing White Wine Sauce. While it is simmering, roll puff pastry to ⅛-inch thickness. Cut 12 "crabs" from pastry with a 7- x 4-inch crab-shaped cookie cutter, if available. If not, make separate paper pattern pieces, cutting the body portion about 7 x 4 inches. Cut two patterns for the claws, one about 5 x 2 inches and the other about 2 x 1 inches.

Placing pattern pieces separately on the pastry, cut 12 body portions and 24 of each claw section with a pastry wheel or knife. Spoon reserved crabmeat mixture evenly onto 6 body portions, leaving a ½-inch border on all sides. Brush edges with beaten eggs; top with remaining 6 body portions, pinching edges to seal. Place on a baking sheet, brushing with beaten eggs; set aside.

Attach one longer claw section to each shorter claw section, pressing edges to seal. Brush edges of 12 "claws" with beaten eggs; top with remaining claws, pressing edges to seal. Place on a baking sheet; brush with beaten eggs. Bake "crabs" and "claws" at 375° for 20 minutes or until golden.

Spoon 3 tablespoons White Wine Sauce into center of each plate. Place a hot "crab" in the center, and arrange a "claw" on each side. Garnish, if desired, and serve immediately. Yield: 6 servings.

White Wine Sauce

¼ cup chopped shallots
½ cup dry white wine
2 teaspoons fish-flavored bouillon
2 cups boiling water
½ bunch fresh parsley
3 bay leaves
1 sprig fresh thyme
1 stalk celery, cut into pieces
2 black peppercorns
½ cup whipping cream
1½ tablespoons cornstarch
1 tablespoon water
⅛ teaspoon salt
⅛ teaspoon ground white pepper

Combine shallots and wine in a small saucepan; bring to a boil. Reduce heat, and simmer 5 minutes or until reduced by one-third. Dissolve bouillon in boiling water; set aside. Cut a 14-inch square of cheesecloth; place parsley and next 3 ingredients in center. Tie with string. Add to wine mixture with bouillon and peppercorns. Bring to a boil, reduce heat, and simmer 20 minutes.

Pour liquid through a large wire-mesh strainer into a bowl, reserving broth. Discard vegetables and herbs. Combine broth and whipping cream in saucepan; bring to a boil, reduce heat, and simmer 10 minutes. Combine cornstarch and water, stirring until smooth. Gradually stir into whipping cream mixture; cook, stirring constantly, 1 minute. Stir in salt and white pepper. Yield: 1¼ cups.

Note: Check gourmet kitchen shops for a crab-shaped cookie cutter.

OYSTERS STEWED IN CREAM

3½ cups water
2 (10-ounce) containers Standard
  oysters, drained
½ cup chopped celery
½ cup chopped green onions
½ cup chopped onion
1 tablespoon butter, melted
½ teaspoon finely chopped
  garlic
⅛ teaspoon dried thyme
⅛ teaspoon ground red pepper
1 bay leaf
¾ cup whipping cream
2 cups milk
¼ cup butter
½ cup all-purpose flour
1 teaspoon salt
¼ teaspoon ground white pepper

Bring water to a boil in a medium saucepan; add oysters, and cook 3 minutes. Remove oysters with a slotted spoon, reserving 3 cups liquid; set both aside.

Cook celery, green onions, and onion in 1 tablespoon butter in a Dutch oven over medium heat, stirring constantly, until tender. Stir in 2½ cups reserved liquid, garlic, and next 3 ingredients; bring to a boil. Stir in whipping cream; reduce heat, and simmer 5 minutes. Stir in milk, and return to a simmer.

Melt ¼ cup butter in a small saucepan over low heat; add flour, stirring until smooth. Cook, stirring constantly, 1 minute (mixture will form a ball). Gradually stir in remaining ½ cup reserved liquid; cook over medium heat, stirring constantly, about 3 minutes or until smooth (mixture will be very thick). Gradually add flour mixture to milk mixture, stirring with a wire whisk until blended. Add oysters, salt, and white pepper; cook until thoroughly heated. Remove and discard bay leaf. Yield: 6⅓ cups.

STRAWBERRIES ARNAUD

3 cups vanilla ice cream
3 cups sliced fresh strawberries
Strawberries Arnaud Sauce
Whipped cream
Garnish: fresh mint

Place 1 scoop (½ cup) ice cream into each champagne or dessert glass; add ½ cup strawberries to each serving. Top with about ¼ cup Strawberries Arnaud Sauce and a dollop of whipped cream. Garnish, if desired. Yield: 6 servings.

Strawberries Arnaud Sauce

2 cups Burgundy or other dry red
  wine
½ cup sugar
1 lime, sliced
½ orange, sliced
1 whole clove
1 (3-inch) stick cinnamon

Bring wine to a boil in a saucepan; add remaining ingredients, stirring until sugar dissolves. Return to a boil, and boil 1 minute. Remove from heat, and let stand 30 minutes. Pour liquid through a large wire-mesh strainer into a bowl, discarding fruits and spices. Cover and refrigerate up to 2 weeks. Yield: 1¾ cups.

Not Just Plain Pralines

Let's get this straight: Is that "pray-leen" or "praw-leen"? Just utter "prayleen" to many a New Orleanian and their shuddering cringe will quickly let you know you've goofed. Cooking instructor and humorist Joe Cahn of the New Orleans School of Cooking and Louisiana General Store in Jax Brewery knows a good praline when he makes one. He advises students, "If it's smooth and creamy, it's a 'praw-leen'; if it's coarse and gritty, then it's a 'pray-leen.'"

Here, he shares 10 variations of the pecan candy, each calling for just one or two extra ingredients tossed into the pot for a new twist.

BASIC PRALINES

Vegetable cooking spray
1½ cups sugar
¾ cup firmly packed brown sugar
¼ cup plus 2 tablespoons butter
½ cup milk
1½ cups chopped pecans

Lightly coat a few sheets of wax paper with vegetable cooking spray; set aside. Combine 1½ cups sugar and remaining ingredients in a heavy 3-quart saucepan. Bring to a boil over medium heat, stirring constantly. Boil, uncovered, stirring constantly, 1 to 2 minutes or until a candy thermometer reaches 220°. (You may need to lower the heat with a thinner saucepan, and rely on a candy thermometer instead of a timer.)

Remove from heat, and beat with a wooden spoon 4 to 6 minutes or just until mixture begins to thicken. Working rapidly, drop by tablespoonfuls

Quick Fixes For Praline Problems

■ If pralines don't harden as they should, fold them into softened vanilla ice cream for **Praline Ice Cream**. Or scrape the soft mixture up, chill, and roll it into 1-inch balls. Dip balls into melted semisweet chocolate to make **Praline-Chocolate Truffles**.
■ If the candy mixture hardens in the saucepan, break into pieces and fold into softened vanilla ice cream, and you have **Praline Crunch Ice Cream**, or sprinkle the crumbled candy mixture over a commercial cheesecake and serve **Praline Cheesecake**.

onto prepared wax paper; let stand until firm. Yield: 2½ dozen.

Orange Pralines: Add 2½ to 3 tablespoons Cointreau or other orange-flavored liqueur before cooking.

Café au Lait Pralines: Add 1½ tablespoons instant coffee granules before cooking.

Mocha Pralines: Add 1½ to 2 tablespoons instant coffee granules and ½ cup semisweet chocolate morsels before cooking.

Chocolate-Peanut Butter Pralines: Add ½ cup semisweet chocolate morsels and ¼ cup creamy peanut butter before cooking.

Peanut Butter Pralines: Add 2 tablespoons creamy peanut butter before cooking and 1 teaspoon vanilla to cooked mixture before beating.

Chocolate-Mint Pralines: Add 5 (½-ounce) chocolate-covered peppermint patties before cooking.

Hot Spicy Pralines: Add ½ teaspoon ground red pepper to mixture before cooking.

Bourbon Pralines: Add 3 tablespoons bourbon before cooking.

Chocolate Pralines: Add 2 (1-ounce) squares unsweetened chocolate before cooking.

Vanilla Pralines: Stir 1 teaspoon vanilla extract into cooked mixture before beating.

Proof Of The Pudding

To make a good bread pudding, crumble not-so-fresh bread into a shallow casserole, pour in an uncooked custard mixture, and bake until the pudding is puffed and golden.

If you decide to experiment with different types of bread, keep this tip in mind: When substituting another bread for the usual sliced white variety, make sure it is dry because while the pudding bakes, the bread acts as a sponge, soaking up the custard.

TENNESSEE BREAD PUDDING WITH BOURBON SAUCE

2 cups hot water
1½ cups sugar
1 (12-ounce) can evaporated milk
4 large eggs
1 cup flaked coconut
½ cup crushed pineapple, drained
½ cup raisins
⅓ cup butter or margarine, melted
1 teaspoon vanilla extract
½ teaspoon ground nutmeg
9 slices white bread with crust, cut into ½-inch cubes
Bourbon Sauce

Combine water and sugar in a bowl, stirring until sugar dissolves. Add milk and eggs, stirring with a wire whisk until blended. Stir in coconut and next 5 ingredients. Add bread cubes; let stand 30 minutes, stirring occasionally. Pour into a greased 13- x 9- x 2-inch pan; bake at 350° for 45 minutes or until a knife inserted in center comes out clean. Serve warm with Bourbon Sauce. Yield: 12 servings.

Bourbon Sauce

1 cup light corn syrup
¼ cup butter or margarine
¼ cup bourbon
½ teaspoon vanilla extract

Bring corn syrup to a boil in a saucepan. Remove from heat, and cool slightly. Using a wire whisk, stir in butter, bourbon, and vanilla. Serve warm. Yield: 1½ cups. *Mary Colley Donelson, Tennessee*

BISCUIT PUDDING

2 large eggs, lightly beaten
2 cups milk
1 cup sugar
1 teaspoon ground cinnamon
¼ teaspoon ground nutmeg
½ teaspoon vanilla extract
3 cups crumbled biscuits *
½ cup raisins (optional)

Combine first 6 ingredients; add crumbled biscuits and, if desired, raisins, stirring well. Spoon into a lightly greased 9-inch square pan. Bake at 350° for 40 minutes or until a knife inserted in center comes out clean. Yield: 9 servings.

* 1 (10-count) can refrigerated biscuits, baked according to package directions and crumbled, may be used for crumbled biscuits.

Note: ½ cup apple jelly may be spread on bottom of pan before adding biscuit mixture. *Ruby G. Tomlin Andalusia, Alabama*

Egg Safety Tips

■ Refrigerate eggs in their original carton at a temperature that is below 40°.

■ Do not purchase eggs that are unrefrigerated. Discard any cracked ones.

■ Cook yolks thoroughly until there is no visible liquid; for hard-cooked eggs, cook 7 minutes; poach eggs 5 minutes; and fry eggs 3 minutes on each side.

■ Promptly refrigerate foods containing eggs, such as cream pies, custards, and puddings; use within three to four days.

■ When making homemade ice cream, heat milk-and-egg mixture to 160°, or use a cooked custard as the ice-cream base.

SPICED BREAD PUDDING

6 large eggs, lightly beaten
2 cups sugar
2 tablespoons pumpkin pie spice
1 (12-ounce) can evaporated milk
2 cups milk
1 teaspoon vanilla extract
8 hamburger buns
½ cup raisins (optional)
Spicy Sauce

Combine first 3 ingredients in a large bowl; stir in evaporated milk, milk, and vanilla. Break buns into small chunks; stir into egg mixture, and let stand 5 minutes. Add raisins, if desired. Pour into a greased 13- x 9- x 2-inch baking dish. Bake at 325° for 45 minutes or until golden brown. Remove from oven, and spoon Spicy Sauce over top. Yield: 15 servings.

Spicy Sauce

¾ cup sugar
1½ tablespoons cornstarch
½ teaspoon pumpkin pie spice
½ cup evaporated milk
½ cup milk
1 tablespoon butter or margarine
1 teaspoon vanilla extract

Combine first 3 ingredients in a heavy saucepan; stir in evaporated milk and milk. Cook over low heat, stirring constantly, until thickened and bubbly. Remove from heat; stir in butter and vanilla. Yield: 1¼ cups.   *Patti Price*
Madison, West Virginia

Tip: *Read labels to learn the weight, quality, and size of food products. Don't be afraid to experiment with new brands. Store brands can be equally good in quality and nutritional value, yet lower in price than well-known brands. Lower grades of canned fruit and vegetables are as nutritious as higher grades. Whenever possible, buy most foods by weight or cost per serving rather than by volume or package size.*

Baked With You In Mind

Remember when a neighbor left a box of brownies at your door when she knew you'd had a hard day? And when your office buddy brought a package of fresh-baked cookies to say congratulations on your promotion? They both knew that there's something loving about home-baked goodies. These yummy treats are just right for those times when you want to let someone know you care.

CHERRY BONBON COOKIES

24 maraschino cherries, undrained
½ cup butter or margarine, softened
¾ cup sifted powdered sugar
1½ cups all-purpose flour
⅛ teaspoon salt
2 tablespoons half-and-half
1 teaspoon vanilla extract
Powdered sugar
Cherry Glaze

Drain cherries, reserving ¼ cup juice for glaze; set aside.
 Beat butter at medium speed with an electric mixer until creamy; gradually add ¾ cup sugar, beating well. Stir in flour and next 3 ingredients. Shape into 24 balls. Press each ball around a cherry, covering completely; place on ungreased cookie sheets. Bake at 350° for 18 to 20 minutes. Remove to wire racks to cool completely. Sprinkle with powdered sugar, and drizzle with Cherry Glaze. Yield: 2 dozen.

Cherry Glaze

2 tablespoons butter or margarine, melted
1 cup sifted powdered sugar
¼ cup reserved cherry juice
Red food coloring (optional)

Combine first 3 ingredients; add food coloring, if desired. Place in a small heavy-duty, zip-top plastic bag; seal. To drizzle, snip a tiny hole at one corner of bag, and gently squeeze bag. Yield: ½ cup.   *Phyllis Keeney*
Elkton, Maryland

CHOCOLATE-ORANGE DELIGHTS

¼ cup butter or margarine, softened
1 cup sugar
1 cup firmly packed brown sugar
2 large eggs
3 (1-ounce) squares unsweetened chocolate, melted
½ cup sour cream
2 teaspoons grated orange rind
2 cups all-purpose flour
1 teaspoon baking soda
½ teaspoon salt
1 cup chopped walnuts or pecans
1 (12-ounce) package semisweet chocolate morsels
Chocolate Glaze

Beat butter at medium speed with an electric mixer until creamy; gradually add sugars, beating well. Add eggs, one at a time, beating after each addition. Add unsweetened chocolate, sour cream, and orange rind, mixing well. Combine flour, soda, and salt; add to creamed mixture. Stir in walnuts and chocolate morsels.
 Drop dough by rounded teaspoonfuls onto lightly greased cookie sheets. Bake at 350° for 8 to 10 minutes. Cool on cookie sheet 1 minute; remove to wire racks to cool completely. Drizzle with Chocolate Glaze. Yield: 7 dozen.

Chocolate Glaze

3 (1-ounce) squares semisweet chocolate
3 tablespoons butter or margarine
½ teaspoon orange extract

Place chocolate and butter in a small heavy-duty, zip-top plastic bag; seal. Submerge in hot water until chocolate melts. Add orange extract, and knead into chocolate mixture. To drizzle, snip a tiny hole at one corner of bag, and gently squeeze bag. Yield: ½ cup.

Mrs. A. Mayer
Richmond, Virginia

SWEETHEART COOKIES

1 cup butter or margarine, softened
1½ cups sugar
2 large eggs
1 teaspoon almond extract
4 cups all-purpose flour
1 teaspoon baking soda
Buttercream Frosting

Beat butter at medium speed with an electric mixer until creamy; gradually add sugar, beating well. Add eggs and almond extract, beating well. Combine flour and soda; add to creamed mixture, mixing well. Roll to ¼-inch thickness on a floured surface. Cut with a 2½-inch heart-shaped or round cookie cutter; place on lightly greased cookie sheets. Bake at 375° for 10 to 12 minutes. Remove to wire racks to cool. Spread with Buttercream Frosting. Yield: 4 dozen.

Buttercream Frosting

⅓ cup butter or margarine, softened
3 cups sifted powdered sugar
2 tablespoons milk
½ teaspoon almond extract

Beat butter at medium speed with an electric mixer; add sugar and remaining ingredients; beating until blended. Yield: 1 cup.

Rose Alleman
St. Amant, Louisiana

A Touch Of Almond Flavor

Most people recognize amaretto as the rich almond-flavored liqueur that enhances almost anything chocolate— from rich, creamy cheesecakes to warming beverages.

But they're surprised at how amaretto boosts the flavor of entrées. The sauce of Amaretto-Lime Veal on page 54 may remind you of an island cocktail.

CHOCOLATE-ALMOND CHEESECAKE

1½ cups chocolate wafer crumbs
1 cup slivered almonds, toasted and chopped
⅓ cup sugar
⅓ cup butter or margarine, softened
3 (8-ounce) packages cream cheese, softened
1 cup sugar
¼ cup amaretto or other almond-flavored liqueur
1 teaspoon almond extract
1 teaspoon vanilla extract
4 large eggs
1 (16-ounce) carton sour cream
1 tablespoon sugar
1 teaspoon vanilla extract
½ cup slivered almonds, toasted

Combine first 4 ingredients; firmly press onto bottom and 1 inch up sides of a 9-inch springform pan. Set aside.

Beat cream cheese at medium speed with an electric mixer until creamy; gradually add 1 cup sugar, beating well. Add liqueur, almond extract, and 1 teaspoon vanilla; beat well. Add eggs, one at a time, beating after each addition. Pour into prepared crust. Bake at 375° for 50 minutes; remove from oven, and let stand 5 minutes (center will be soft).

Combine sour cream, 1 tablespoon sugar, and 1 teaspoon vanilla; spread evenly on cheesecake. Bake at 500° for 5 minutes. Remove to a wire rack;

let cool completely. Cover and chill 8 hours. Before serving, remove sides of pan, and press ½ cup slivered almonds around top edge of cheesecake. Yield: 10 to 12 servings.

Sharon Kay Johnston
Fort Worth, Texas

HOT LACED MARSHMALLOW CHOCOLATE

⅓ cup cocoa
3 tablespoons sugar
2 cups milk
⅔ cup marshmallow cream
¼ cup amaretto or other almond-flavored liqueur

Combine cocoa and sugar in a medium saucepan; gradually stir in milk. Add marshmallow cream, and cook over medium-high heat, stirring constantly with a wire whisk until smooth and just below boiling point. Stir in liqueur. Serve with marshmallows or whipped cream. Yield: 3¾ cups.

POTS DE CRÈME AU CHOCOLATE

2 cups half-and-half
2 large eggs, lightly beaten
2 tablespoons sugar
3⅓ cups semisweet chocolate morsels
3 tablespoons amaretto or other almond-flavored liqueur
2 teaspoons vanilla extract
Pinch of salt
Garnishes: whipped cream, chocolate shavings

Combine first 3 ingredients in a heavy saucepan; cook over medium heat 12 minutes or until temperature reaches 160°. Add chocolate morsels and next 3 ingredients, stirring until smooth. Spoon into individual serving containers; cover and chill. Garnish, if desired. Yield: 5 to 6 servings.

Robert W. Nolen
Falls Church, Virginia

AMARETTO-LIME VEAL

4 slices bacon, chopped
⅓ cup sliced almonds
Vegetable oil
1 pound (¼-inch-thick) veal cutlets
¼ teaspoon salt
½ teaspoon coarsely ground pepper
½ cup all-purpose flour
½ cup amaretto or other almond-
  flavored liqueur
1½ tablespoons fresh lime juice
½ cup sliced green onions
¼ cup butter or margarine, divided

Cook bacon in a large skillet until browned; remove and drain on paper towels, reserving drippings in skillet. Add almonds to drippings, and cook over medium heat, stirring constantly, until lightly browned; remove and drain on paper towels, reserving drippings. Add oil to drippings to make ¼ cup; set aside.

Sprinkle cutlets evenly with salt and pepper; dredge in flour. Heat 2 tablespoons drippings mixture in skillet; add half of cutlets, and cook 1 minute on each side or until lightly browned. Remove to a serving dish; keep warm. Repeat procedure with remaining 2 tablespoons drippings mixture and cutlets. Drain excess drippings from skillet.

Add liqueur, lime juice, and green onions to skillet; bring to a boil, scraping bottom of skillet to loosen browned particles. Boil 2 minutes, stirring often. Remove from heat; add butter, 1 tablespoon at a time, stirring until butter melts. Stir in almonds, and spoon over cutlets. Sprinkle with bacon. Yield: 4 servings.

Potatoes Are Versatile Vegetables

No matter how you say it—po-TAY-to or po-TAH-to—this versatile staple of many diets doesn't have to translate into boring predictability.

Use "new" potatoes or round "all-purpose whites" to simmer or sauté. "Long whites," such as russet Burbank (or Idaho) and White Rose, and long "all purpose" are best for baking, broiling, deep-fat frying, or mashing.

OREGANO-AND-LEMON SKILLET POTATOES

6 small potatoes (about 1½
  pounds)
1 large onion, chopped
2 tablespoons olive oil
1 teaspoon salt
1 teaspoon dried oregano
¼ teaspoon freshly ground pepper
2 tablespoons lemon juice

Peel potatoes, and cut into ¼-inch cubes. Place in cold water; let stand 1 hour. Drain well, and pat dry. Set aside.

Cook onion in olive oil in a large skillet over medium-high heat, stirring constantly, 1 minute. Add potato cubes, and cook, stirring constantly, 8 minutes. Stir in salt and remaining ingredients; cover, reduce heat, and simmer 5 minutes or until potatoes are tender. Yield: 4 to 6 servings.
Peggy Fowler Revels
Woodruff, South Carolina

BAKED PLEATED POTATOES

6 small baking potatoes (about 1½
  pounds)
¼ cup butter or margarine, melted
1 tablespoon dried chives
1 teaspoon dried tarragon
1 teaspoon dried chervil
¾ teaspoon salt
½ teaspoon pepper

Wash potatoes, and pat dry. Cut each potato crosswise into ⅛-inch slices, cutting to, but not through, bottom of potato. Place on a baking sheet. Combine butter and remaining ingredients; brush over potatoes. Bake at 400° for 1 hour or until done. Yield: 6 servings.
Sharon Avinger
Lexington, South Carolina

FRIED POTATO PATTIES

2 cups cooked, mashed potatoes
1 cup (4 ounces) shredded
  mozzarella cheese
1 large egg, lightly beaten
½ teaspoon salt
½ teaspoon garlic powder
½ teaspoon onion powder
¼ teaspoon pepper
1 large egg, lightly beaten
1 cup soft breadcrumbs
¼ to ½ cup vegetable oil

Combine first 7 ingredients; shape into 6 patties. Dip each patty in lightly beaten egg, and lightly coat with breadcrumbs. Pour oil into a large, heavy skillet. Fry in hot oil over medium heat until lightly browned, turning once. Drain on paper towels. Yield: 6 servings.
Beverly Garver
Anderson, South Carolina

BROILED MARINATED POTATOES

4 large baking potatoes (about 1¾
  pounds)
Vegetable oil
½ cup red wine vinegar
¼ cup olive oil
3 cloves garlic, minced
2 tablespoons finely chopped onion
1 tablespoon Dijon mustard
¼ teaspoon pepper
¼ teaspoon dried oregano
⅛ teaspoon salt

Wash potatoes, and rub skins with vegetable oil. Bake at 450° for 45 minutes. (Potatoes will not be thoroughly cooked.) Let cool. Cut each potato in half lengthwise. Cut each half lengthwise and crosswise into 4 wedges. Place in a large bowl; set aside.

Combine red wine vinegar and remaining ingredients; pour over potato wedges, and let stand 2 hours, stirring occasionally. Remove from marinade, and place on a lightly greased rack; place rack in a broiler pan. Broil 5½ inches from heat (with electric oven door partially opened) 7 minutes on each side or until golden brown. Yield: 6 servings.

Try Fresh Parmesan Cheese

Most people try grated Parmesan cheese from the green can before they ever taste it fresh, and that well-known product will always be a favorite at family meals. But grating the fresh cheese takes the Parmesan experience just one step further.

Parmesan's reputation comes from the cheese produced in several areas of Italy, including Parma (the root of its name), Reggio Emilia, Modena, and Bologna. In Italy, *grana* refers to cheeses that are distinguished by their grainy texture when properly aged. Two major types of grana cheese, Parmigiano-Reggiano and Grana Padano, are produced there. In the United States, both are called Parmesan cheese.

Aging gives the product its tangy flavor. Older cheeses have a yellow cast; younger ones are whitish and have a smoother texture. You can carve younger cheeses into paper-thin strips with a cheese plane. Older ones are best suited for grating. The texture of grated cheese will vary, depending on the kind of grater used and hole size.

A real connoisseur will detect distinct flavor differences between old and young versions and those made in Italy and elsewhere. Wisconsin produces the most American-made Parmesan, and its cheese gives the Italian ones a good run for their money. (Try not to confuse Parmesan cheese with Romano, another grainy cheese with a black rind; Romano is stronger and more pungent.)

If you've never tried freshly grated Parmesan cheese, buy a wedge the next time you visit the grocery store. It's more expensive than commercially grated Parmesan, but you'll appreciate the difference.

FRESH SPINACH SAUTÉ

1 pound fresh spinach
2 tablespoons olive oil
2 tablespoons Chablis or other dry white wine
¼ cup freshly grated Parmesan cheese

Remove stems from spinach; wash leaves thoroughly, and pat dry. Cook spinach in olive oil in a large skillet over high heat, stirring constantly, about 30 seconds or until spinach wilts. Add wine to skillet, and cook 30 seconds or until all liquid is absorbed. Sprinkle spinach with grated Parmesan cheese, and serve immediately. Yield: 4 servings.

BROCCOLI-PARMESAN FETTUCCINE

2 cups broccoli flowerets
8 ounces fettuccine, uncooked
2 tablespoons butter or margarine
1 (6-ounce) package Canadian bacon, cut in thin strips
⅓ cup whipping cream
1½ cups freshly grated Parmesan cheese
½ teaspoon salt
½ teaspoon freshly ground pepper

Cook broccoli in boiling water to cover 3 minutes; drain, and plunge into ice water. Drain and set aside.

Cook fettuccine according to package directions; drain and place in a large bowl. Set aside.

Melt butter in a large skillet over medium-high heat. Add Canadian bacon, and cook, stirring constantly, 2 minutes. Stir in broccoli, and cook 1 minute or until thoroughly heated. Add broccoli mixture, whipping cream, and remaining ingredients to fettuccine; toss gently. Serve immediately. Yield: 4 servings. *Mary Pappas*
Richmond, Virginia

PARMESAN-SPINACH SPREAD

1 (10-ounce) package frozen chopped spinach, thawed
1¼ cups freshly grated Parmesan cheese, divided
¼ cup finely chopped onion
1 (3-ounce) package cream cheese, softened
¾ cup mayonnaise or salad dressing
1 teaspoon hot sauce
1 teaspoon dried Italian seasoning
½ teaspoon garlic powder
¼ teaspoon freshly ground pepper
1 teaspoon paprika

Press spinach between paper towels to remove excess moisture. Combine spinach, 1 cup Parmesan cheese, and next 7 ingredients. Spoon into a greased 1-quart baking dish. Bake at 350° for 10 minutes. Sprinkle with remaining ¼ cup Parmesan cheese and paprika; bake an additional 10 minutes. Serve with crackers or party rye. Yield: 2½ cups.
Mrs. J. Russell Buchanan
Dunwoody, Georgia

HERBS-AND-CHEESE BREAD

½ cup mayonnaise or salad
  dressing
1½ teaspoons dried Italian
  seasoning
½ teaspoon freshly ground pepper
1 (16-ounce) loaf unsliced French
  bread
1 cup freshly grated Parmesan
  cheese

Combine first 3 ingredients; set aside. Cut bread in half lengthwise, and place on a baking sheet. Spread mayonnaise mixture on cut side of each bread half; sprinkle with cheese. Bake at 400° for 10 minutes or until cheese melts. Cut into slices, and serve immediately. Yield: 1 loaf.

Surprise Yourself With Fennel

Having the crispness of celery and a flavor reminiscent of licorice, fennel makes itself at home in many dishes. Serve it raw, parboiled, steamed, baked, marinated, or drizzled with herbed butter.

MARINATED FENNEL SALAD

2 heads fennel (about 2 pounds)
⅓ cup olive oil
2 tablespoons white wine vinegar
1 tablespoon lemon juice
½ clove garlic, minced
⅛ teaspoon salt
¼ teaspoon pepper
Red leaf lettuce
1 tablespoon chopped fennel leaves
½ cup crumbled blue cheese

Rinse fennel thoroughly. Trim and discard bulb bases. Trim stalks from the bulb; discard hard outside stalks, and reserve leaves for another use. Cut bulbs in half lengthwise, and cut crosswise into thin slices. Cook in boiling water 2 minutes; drain and rinse with cold water.

Combine olive oil and next 5 ingredients in a large bowl; stir in fennel. Cover and refrigerate 8 hours.

Serve on a lettuce-lined plate, and sprinkle with fennel leaves and blue cheese. Yield: 4 servings.

ITALIAN-STYLE BRAISED FENNEL

3 heads fennel (about 3 pounds)
3 tablespoons butter or margarine,
  melted
¼ teaspoon salt
¼ teaspoon pepper
1 cup (4 ounces) shredded sharp
  Cheddar cheese
2 large tomatoes, chopped
½ teaspoon sugar
¼ teaspoon dried savory
¼ teaspoon celery seeds
⅛ teaspoon garlic powder
2 slices bacon, cut in half

Rinse fennel thoroughly. Trim and discard bulb bases. Trim stalks from the bulb; discard hard outside stalks, and reserve leaves for another use. Cut bulbs lengthwise into quarters; pat dry. Cook in butter in a large skillet over medium heat until golden, stirring occasionally. Transfer to a 2-quart casserole; sprinkle with salt and pepper, and top with cheese.

Combine tomato and next 4 ingredients; spoon over cheese. Top with bacon; cover and bake at 350° for 45 to 50 minutes. Uncover and bake 5 minutes or until bacon is crisp. Yield: 6 servings.
Margaret Ellen Holmes
Jackson, Tennessee

STEAMED FENNEL WITH GARLIC BUTTER

¼ cup butter or margarine,
  softened
2 cloves garlic, minced
2 heads fennel (about 2 pounds)
Pepper
Lemon wedges

Combine butter and garlic; set aside.
Rinse fennel thoroughly. Trim and discard bulb bases. Trim stalks from the bulb; discard hard outside stalks, and reserve leaves for another use. Starting at one side, cut bulbs lengthwise into ¼-inch slices. Arrange in a vegetable steamer over boiling water. Cover and steam 10 minutes; transfer to a serving dish. Sprinkle lightly with pepper; serve with lemon wedges and garlic butter. Yield: 4 to 6 servings.

Fennel Facts

■ Fennel is an aromatic plant with pale green, celerylike stalks and bright green, feathery foliage. It originated in the Mediterranean and is also grown in the United States.

■ Fennel has a large bulb base that can be prepared like a vegetable. Both the base and stalks can be eaten raw in salads or cooked in a variety of methods such as braising or sautéing. The fragrant, graceful greenery can be used as a garnish or snipped like fresh dillweed.

■ The flavor is described as "sweet anise" or licorice flavored. Fennel is sweeter and more delicate than anise, and when cooked, fennel becomes even lighter in taste than in its raw state. It must be used with a light touch, however, or it will impart a bitter flavor.

MARCH

Grits, that staple of Southern life, just got better. In this chapter, we share some old-fashioned cooking secrets along with new flavor variations for grits. We add pizzazz to pizza by trying different types of crust and topping combinations. As a special breakfast treat or to highlight a meal, try our recipes for homemade breads, from sweet to savory. No one will be able to resist the tantalizing taste of fresh-baked bread right out of the oven. Always a top vote-getter, pasta is a big winner with our easy-to-prepare shellfish and vegetable toppings. As a bonus, try Luscious Lemon Cake. There's a little bit of sunshine in every bite.

Mamma Mia! Pizza With Pizzazz

Unlike most pizzas, which are about as exciting as the music piped into an elevator, these soar with the pleasure and power of an Italian opera.

And these homemade pizzas, whether made with a single or double crust, are so convenient to make. Simply prepare the crust and sauce recipes, divide into portions, and freeze. Then the next time you crave a pizza, all you have to do is thaw the ingredients, assemble the pizza, and pop it into the oven.

The Parmesan Pizza Crust recipe can be doubled, making enough dough for four pizzas. You can refrigerate the dough overnight or freeze it for later use.

For a flavor twist, warm 3 tablespoons of chopped fresh basil in 1 teaspoon of olive oil and knead it into the dough.

For a snack or as an accompaniment to soup or salad, try focaccia—a seasoned Italian flatbread pronounced foh-CAH-chee-ah—from one portion of the refrigerated dough. Brush the flattened pizza dough with olive oil, sprinkle with fresh herbs and garlic, and bake according to the directions for a single-crust pizza; add cheese, if desired.

PARMESAN PIZZA CRUST
(pictured on page 76)

2 packages active dry yeast
2 cups warm water (105° to 115°)
6 to 7 cups all-purpose flour, divided
2 teaspoons salt
2 teaspoons sugar
½ cup grated Parmesan cheese
½ cup vegetable oil
Vegetable cooking spray
Cornmeal
Olive oil

Combine yeast and water; let stand 5 minutes. Combine yeast mixture, 3 cups flour, and next 4 ingredients in a large mixing bowl; beat at low speed with an electric mixer until blended. Stir in enough remaining flour to make a medium-stiff dough. Cover and let rise in a warm place (85°), free from drafts, 45 minutes or until dough is doubled in bulk.

Turn dough out onto a lightly floured surface, and knead 4 or 5 times. Coat two 12-inch pizza pans with cooking spray; sprinkle with cornmeal. Divide dough in half, and pat each portion evenly into pans; brush with olive oil, and prick with a fork. Bake at 425° for 10 minutes. Add desired sauce and toppings, and bake at 425° for 15 to 20 minutes; sprinkle with desired cheeses, and bake an additional 5 minutes. Yield: two 12-inch pizzas.

Note: For a double-crust pizza, pat half of dough into bottom and up sides of a 14-inch, deep-dish pizza pan; set remaining half of dough aside. Bake at 425° for 10 minutes; add desired sauce, toppings, and cheese. Roll out remaining dough, and place over toppings. Fold edges together, and seal. Bake at 425° for 20 to 25 minutes or until golden. Yield: one 14-inch double-crust pizza.

Note: To freeze, divide risen dough in half before kneading, wrap in plastic wrap, and place in heavy-duty, zip-top plastic bags; freeze up to three months. Thaw in refrigerator overnight.
Debbie Huffman
Woodland, Mississippi

WHOLE WHEAT PIZZA CRUST

2 packages active dry yeast
1 tablespoon honey
1¼ cups warm water (105° to 115°)
2¼ cups all-purpose flour
1¼ cups whole wheat flour
1 teaspoon salt
2 tablespoons vegetable oil
Vegetable cooking spray
Cornmeal
Olive oil

Combine first 3 ingredients; let stand 5 minutes. Combine yeast mixture, flours, salt, and oil in a large mixing bowl; beat at low speed with an electric mixer until blended. Cover and let rise in a warm place (85°), free from drafts, 1½ hours or until dough is doubled in bulk.

Turn dough out onto a lightly floured surface, and knead 4 or 5 times. Coat two 12-inch pizza pans with cooking spray; sprinkle with cornmeal. Divide dough in half, and pat each portion evenly into pizza pans; brush with olive oil, and prick with a fork. Bake at 450° for 8 to 9 minutes. Add desired sauce and toppings, and bake 10 minutes; sprinkle with desired cheeses, and bake an additional 5 minutes. Yield: two 12-inch pizzas.

Note: For a double-crust pizza, pat half of dough into bottom and up sides of a 14-inch deep-dish pizza pan; set remaining half of dough aside. Bake at 450° for 8 to 9 minutes; add desired sauce, toppings, and cheese. Roll out remaining dough, and place over toppings. Fold edges together, and seal. Bake at 450° on lowest oven rack 15 minutes. Yield: one 14-inch double-crust pizza.

Note: To freeze, divide risen dough in half before kneading, wrap in plastic wrap, and place in heavy-duty, zip-top plastic bags; freeze up to three months. Thaw in refrigerator overnight.   *Cynda Spoon*
Broken Arrow, Oklahoma

RED PEPPER-TOMATO SAUCE

1 (14-ounce) jar roasted red
  peppers, drained
1 cup commercial pizza sauce

Place peppers in container of an electric blender or food processor; process until smooth. Add sauce; process until blended. Refrigerate sauce up to one week. Yield: 2½ cups.

Note: Red Pepper-Tomato Sauce can be divided into portions and frozen up to three months. Thaw frozen sauce in refrigerator.

SPINACH PESTO SAUCE
(pictured on page 76)

1 (10-ounce) package frozen
  chopped spinach, thawed and well
  drained
¾ cup grated Parmesan cheese
¼ cup chopped walnuts
2 cloves garlic, pressed
1 tablespoon dried basil
½ teaspoon salt
⅓ cup olive oil
2 tablespoons butter, softened
¼ cup hot water

Position knife blade in food processor bowl; add all ingredients, and process until smooth. Refrigerate up to 1 week. Yield: 1¾ cups.

Note: Spinach Pesto Sauce can be divided into portions and frozen up to three months. Thaw in refrigerator.

BLACK BEAN SAUCE

1 (16-ounce) can black beans,
  drained
1 (4-ounce) can chopped green
  chiles, undrained
1 teaspoon chicken-flavored
  bouillon granules
½ teaspoon garlic powder
½ teaspoon dried cilantro

Combine beans and chiles in container of an electric blender or food processor; process until smooth. Add bouillon, garlic powder, and cilantro, processing until blended. Refrigerate up to 1 week. Yield: 1½ cups.

Note: Black Bean Sauce can be divided into portions and frozen up to three months. Thaw in refrigerator.

Pizza Pointers

■ Sprinkle a lightly greased pizza pan with cornmeal.
■ Press dough to ½-inch or less thickness into pan with hands.
■ Brush dough with olive oil, and prick bottom and sides of dough with a fork.
■ Let shaped dough stand at room temperature 10 minutes.
■ Bake dough in a preheated oven about 10 minutes before adding toppings.
■ Drain vegetables well before placing on crust.
■ Place slightly less sauce and toppings in the center to allow the crust to cook evenly.
■ Cool slightly before cutting; kitchen shears cut neat slices and don't scratch pans.

Topping Combinations For Single-Crust Pizza

■ Spinach Pesto Sauce; chopped or sliced fresh vegetables; Cheddar, mozzarella, and provolone cheeses
■ Spinach Pesto Sauce; chopped roasted red peppers; chopped marinated artichokes; sliced ripe olives; Cheddar and Monterey Jack cheeses
■ Spinach Pesto Sauce; crumbled cooked bacon; sliced roasted red peppers; fontina (semifirm cheese with a nutty flavor) and Gruyère cheeses

■ Red Pepper-Tomato Sauce; sautéed minced shallots and garlic; Romano, feta, and mozzarella cheeses
■ Red Pepper-Tomato Sauce; Cheddar, mozzarella, provolone, and Swiss cheeses
■ Caramelized onions; toasted walnuts; fontina and Gruyère cheeses
■ Cooked shrimp; oil-packed sun-dried tomatoes, chopped; chopped fresh basil; fontina and mozzarella cheeses
■ Black Bean Sauce; sliced mushrooms; sliced green onions; chopped fresh tomatoes; Monterey Jack and Cheddar cheeses

Note: Mix and match these toppings and sauces. Some pizzas will work without a sauce.

Filling Combinations For Double-Crust Pizza

■ Black Bean Sauce; chopped, cooked shrimp; Havarti and crumbled blue cheeses
■ Red Pepper-Tomato Sauce; sliced, cooked Italian sausage, oil-packed sun-dried tomatoes, chopped; sliced mushrooms; Gorgonzola (semisoft blue cheese) and mozzarella cheeses

Note: Our double-crust fillings may also be used on a single-crust pizza; however, the ingredients make enough filling to support a top crust.

Grits To Write Home About

A classic Southern breakfast just would not be right without grits. But no one eats them plain.

Breakfast in Charleston, South Carolina, and the South Carolina-Georgia Lowcountry often includes shrimp and grits.

Why Are Grits Southern?

Grits, made from coarsely ground corn, have long been a staple in Southern kitchens.

In the era preceding the Civil War, Southerners were more interested in growing cash crops, such as tobacco and cotton, and grew corn mainly to sustain the people and animals on their plantations and farms. During the Civil War, most of the wheat products were sent to the soldiers, while families back home depended more on corn for their food.

Another theory speculates that migration to the United States brought new preferences to the industrialized North while the South welcomed smaller numbers of immigrants. Wheat soon became the grain of choice in the North while Southerners still ate corn. No matter which theory holds true, our love for corn and grits remains today.

■ Shrimp and grits is a Lowcountry classic. Those from the area will tell you they grew up eating just such a dish for breakfast.

CLASSIC CHARLESTON BREAKFAST SHRIMP
(pictured on page 74)

1 pound unpeeled medium-size
  fresh shrimp
2 tablespoons lemon juice
¼ teaspoon salt
⅛ teaspoon ground red pepper
¼ cup finely chopped onion
⅓ cup finely chopped green pepper
3 tablespoons melted bacon
  drippings
2 tablespoons all-purpose flour
¾ cup Shrimp Stock or chicken
  broth
Creamy Grits
Garnishes: green pepper strips,
  fresh lemon slices

Peel and devein shrimp. Combine shrimp and next 3 ingredients in a small bowl; set aside.

Cook onion and green pepper in bacon drippings in a large skillet over medium-high heat, stirring constantly, about 10 minutes. Sprinkle flour over vegetables; cook, stirring constantly, about 2 minutes or until flour begins to brown. Add shrimp and Shrimp Stock; cook, stirring constantly, 2 to 3 minutes or until shrimp turn pink and gravy is smooth. Add water or additional stock, if gravy is too thick. Serve immediately over Creamy Grits. Garnish, if desired. Yield: 2 servings.

Note: If you make the Shrimp Stock, use the fresh shrimp leftover from the stock to make Classic Charleston Breakfast Shrimp.

Shrimp Stock

2 pounds unpeeled medium-size
  fresh shrimp with heads
3 quarts water
1 large carrot
2 stalks celery, quartered
1 medium onion, quartered
½ cup fresh thyme with stems
½ cup fresh parsley sprigs
½ cup fresh basil leaves
½ cup fresh oregano with
  stems
1 tablespoon dried savory

Remove heads and peel shrimp; place heads and shells in a large Dutch oven. Reserve shrimp for another use. Add water and remaining ingredients; bring to a boil. Reduce heat, and simmer, uncovered, 45 minutes. Pour mixture through a wire-mesh strainer into a container, discarding solids. Reserve desired amount of stock, and freeze remaining stock for another use. Yield: 2 quarts.

Creamy Grits

2 cups water
2 tablespoons butter or margarine
½ cup regular or stone-ground
  grits, uncooked
1 cup half-and-half or whipping
  cream, divided

Down to the Nitty-Gritty

Grits can be very different, depending on whether they are ground at a gristmill or purchased at the supermarket. This guide to the types of grits available will help you with the differences.

■ **Instant grits**—Some say eating instant grits is comparable to drinking instant coffee—you be the judge. These grits have been precooked and dehydrated. To prepare, simply add boiling water.

■ **Quick and regular grits**—These are both made from dried corn usually with the hull and germ removed. The difference between the two is a matter of granulation. Quick grits cook in 5 minutes; regular grits cook in 10 minutes.

■ **Whole-ground or stone-ground grits**—These grits are ground from dried corn. You'll find these grits at a gristmill.

Bring water and butter to a boil in a heavy saucepan. Stir in grits; return to a boil over medium heat. Reduce heat, and cook, stirring occasionally, 10 minutes or until thickened. Stir in ½ cup half-and-half; simmer 10 minutes, stirring occasionally. Add remaining ½ cup half-and-half; simmer 10 minutes, stirring occasionally. Serve immediately. Yield: 2 servings.

Adapted from Hoppin' John's Lowcountry Cooking, *Bantam Books, 1992*

■ The grits cakes need to chill 3 to 4 hours before you make this dish; in fact, you can mix the black beans and picante sauce ahead of time, too. To serve, cook the grits cakes (like making hash browns), heat the bean mixture, and assemble.

SOUTHWESTERN GRITS CAKES

4 cups water
1 teaspoon salt
1 cup quick-cooking grits, uncooked
½ cup chopped green onions
1 (4-ounce) can chopped green chiles, drained
2 tablespoons diced pimiento, drained
⅛ teaspoon hot sauce
2 tablespoons butter or margarine, divided
1 (15-ounce) can black beans, rinsed and drained
1 (8-ounce) jar picante sauce
1 medium tomato, seeded and chopped
2 tablespoons chopped fresh cilantro

Bring water and salt to a boil in a medium saucepan. Stir in grits; return to a boil over medium heat, stirring constantly. Cover, reduce heat, and simmer 5 minutes. Remove from heat; stir in green onions and next 3 ingredients. Pour into a buttered 9-inch square pan; cover and chill 3 to 4 hours or until firm. Invert pan to remove grits; cut grits into 4 squares. Cut each square into 2 triangles.

Heat 1 tablespoon butter over medium heat; add 4 triangles, and cook 5 to 7 minutes on each side or until lightly browned. Gently remove to a serving platter; keep warm. Repeat with remaining butter and triangles.

Combine black beans and picante sauce in a small saucepan; cook over medium heat, stirring often, until thoroughly heated. Spoon over grits cakes; sprinkle with chopped tomato and cilantro. Serve immediately. Yield: 4 servings.

Note: Grits cakes (or triangles) can also be baked at 350° for 7 minutes or broiled (with electric oven door partially opened) 7 minutes on one side. (Do not turn.)   *Janice Elder*
Charlotte, North Carolina

If You're New to These Parts

■ Grits are made from coarsely ground corn. When the corn is ground even more finely, the product becomes cornmeal. Corn was first introduced to colonists by American Indians. They served the newcomers a steaming bowl of cracked maize (corn) that had been cooked into a stew. The Indians called it *ustatahamen;* it is believed that the word hominy is derived from their word.
■ Hominy grits are the same as grits. In Charleston, South Carolina, old cookbooks use hominy as the word for cooked grits. Today, most people just call them grits.
■ The markets consuming the most grits are, in descending order: New Orleans; Birmingham/ Montgomery; New York City; Charleston/Savannah; Charlotte; Jacksonville/Tampa; Shreveport/ Jackson, Mississippi. Almost 95% of grits in the U.S. are made from white corn. Florida consumes the most grits made from yellow corn, but that's only about 2% of the state's total grits consumption.

Grits Go Uptown

Chef Jeff Tuttle of Pawleys Plantation Golf and Country Club in South Carolina, grew up in Upstate New York, so it's not surprising he shied away from traditional grits upon his arrival in the South. But the beautiful scenery of Pawleys Island, South Carolina, slowly seduced him. And like many chefs today, Tuttle uses ingredients native to the region— grits included.

Eating a creamy polenta in California inspired Jeff to develop his recipe for Pan-Fried Grits on page 62. He tops grits with fresh leeks and oysters, providing an intriguing mix of texture and flavors.

It's a restaurant recipe, so it's more involved. But this one is worth the extra effort.

PAN-FRIED GRITS WITH CREAMED OYSTERS

3 cups whipping cream
¼ teaspoon salt
⅛ teaspoon pepper
2 medium leeks
2 (10-ounce) containers Standard oysters, undrained
1 clove garlic, minced
1 shallot, finely chopped
3 tablespoons butter or margarine, melted
8 shiitake mushroom caps, thinly sliced
Pan-Fried Grits
Garnish: thin strips of fresh spinach leaves

Combine first 3 ingredients in a heavy saucepan; bring to a boil over medium heat. Reduce heat to low, and simmer, stirring occasionally, 35 to 40 minutes or until mixture is reduced to 1½ cups. Cover and set aside.

Wash leeks, and cut white part into thin strips, reserving green tops for another use; set aside.

Drain oysters, reserving ½ cup liquid; set aside. Cook garlic and shallot in butter in a large skillet over medium-high heat, stirring constantly, until tender.

Add leeks and mushrooms; cook 2 to 3 minutes or until tender, stirring frequently. Add oysters and reserved liquid; cook 3 to 5 minutes or until oysters begin to curl. Add whipping cream mixture; cook until thoroughly heated, stirring occasionally. To serve, place 2 triangles of Pan-Fried Grits on each plate; top with oyster mixture. Garnish, if desired. Yield: 6 servings.

Pan-Fried Grits

8 cups water
2 teaspoons salt
¼ cup butter or margarine
2 cups quick-cooking yellow grits, uncooked
2 large eggs, divided
⅓ to ½ cup butter or margarine, divided

Combine first 3 ingredients in a Dutch oven; bring to a boil. Stir in grits;

bring to a boil over medium heat. Reduce heat, and cook 4 to 5 minutes, stirring occasionally.

Beat 1 egg with a fork. Gradually stir about one-fourth of hot mixture into beaten egg; add to remaining hot mixture, stirring constantly. Pour into a buttered 15- x 10- x 1-inch jellyroll pan; cover and chill 8 hours. Cut grits into 6 (5-inch) squares; cut each square into 2 triangles.

Beat remaining egg in a shallow dish. Dip each triangle in egg. Melt half of remaining butter in a large skillet. Add as many triangles as will fit, and cook on each side until golden brown. Repeat procedure with remaining triangles and butter. Yield: 12 triangles.   *Jeff Tuttle*
Pawleys Island, South Carolina

■ Grillades (gree-YAHDS) and grits —like salt and pepper or bread and butter—are an assumed pair in New Orleans. A Louisiana twist on smothered steak, grillades are thinly pounded squares of beef or veal round served in a tomato gravy over grits. It sounds like dinner, and sometimes it is, but brunch is the most popular menu spot for this dish.

GRILLADES AND GRITS
(pictured on page 75)

2 (½-inch-thick) slices top round steak (about 1½ pounds)
1½ teaspoons salt
¾ teaspoon black pepper
⅛ teaspoon ground red pepper
4 cloves garlic, minced
2 tablespoons all-purpose flour
2 tablespoons butter or margarine, melted
1 cup chopped onion
½ cup chopped celery
½ cup chopped green pepper
1 (16-ounce) can tomatoes, undrained
1 cup water
2 cups regular grits, uncooked
Garnish: celery leaves

Pound steak to ¼-inch thickness with a meat mallet or rolling pin. Cut steak into 2-inch squares; set aside.

Combine salt and next 3 ingredients. Rub into meat; sprinkle meat with flour. Brown one-third of meat at a time on both sides in butter in a Dutch oven; remove meat from Dutch oven, and set aside.

Add onion, celery, and green pepper to Dutch oven. Cook over medium heat, stirring constantly, 5 minutes or until vegetables are tender. Add tomatoes and 1 cup water; return steak to Dutch oven. Cover, reduce heat, and simmer 30 minutes. Turn meat, and simmer, covered, an additional 15 minutes or until meat is tender.

Cook grits according to package directions just before serving. Spoon grillades over grits, and garnish, if desired. Yield: 4 servings.

QUICK & EASY

Wrapping Up A Meal

"That's a wrap," the movie director says. You can say the same to your family with these recipes featuring foods that are wrapped.

PEPPERY CHICKEN IN PITA

6 skinned and boned chicken breast halves (about 1½ pounds)
¼ cup teriyaki sauce
1 teaspoon dried thyme
1 teaspoon ground white pepper
1 teaspoon black pepper
½ teaspoon garlic powder
½ teaspoon ground red pepper
2 tablespoons olive oil
⅓ cup mayonnaise or salad dressing
1 tablespoon prepared horseradish
6 (8-inch) pita bread rounds
2 cups shredded lettuce

Cut chicken lengthwise into ½-inch-wide strips, and place in a shallow dish. Pour teriyaki sauce over chicken; cover and chill 2 hours.

Remove chicken from marinade, discarding marinade. Combine thyme and next 4 ingredients; sprinkle evenly over chicken. Heat 1 tablespoon olive oil in a large skillet over medium-high heat. Cook half of chicken 5 to 7 minutes, turning once. Drain on paper towels. Repeat procedure with remaining chicken.

Combine mayonnaise and horseradish. Spread each pita round with about 1 tablespoon mayonnaise mixture; sprinkle evenly with lettuce, and top with chicken. Fold two sides over chicken, and secure with a wooden pick. Yield: 6 servings.

Note: To prevent bread from cracking when folding, wrap pita rounds in heavy-duty plastic wrap, and microwave at HIGH 45 seconds or until thoroughly heated.

HAM-AND-CHEESE BUNDLES

1 cup finely chopped cooked ham
½ cup (2 ounces) shredded Swiss cheese
1½ tablespoons spicy brown mustard
⅛ teaspoon garlic powder
1 (8-ounce) can refrigerated crescent dinner rolls

Combine first 4 ingredients; set aside. Unroll dough, and separate into 4 rectangles; press perforations to seal. Spoon ham mixture evenly in center of each rectangle. Bring corners to the center over filling; twist to close top, pinching dough together to seal. Place on a lightly greased baking sheet. Bake at 350° for 15 to 18 minutes or until golden brown. Yield: 4 servings.

HAM APPETILLAS

2 (8-ounce) packages cream cheese, softened
⅓ cup mayonnaise or salad dressing
2 tablespoons chopped green onions
¼ cup chopped black olives
8 (8½-inch) flour tortillas
3 (2½-ounce) packages thinly sliced ham

Combine cream cheese, mayonnaise, green onions, and olives; spread evenly on tortillas. Arrange 4 ham slices over each tortilla; roll up tightly, and wrap each individually in plastic wrap. Refrigerate at least 3 hours. Cut tortillas into ½-inch slices. Yield: 8½ dozen.
Michelle King
Duluth, Georgia

WEEKNIGHT ENCHILADAS

1 pound ground beef
1 small onion, chopped
1 (10¾-ounce) can tomato soup, undiluted
1 (10-ounce) can mild enchilada sauce
8 (7-inch) flour tortillas
2 cups (8 ounces) shredded Cheddar cheese, divided
Sour cream (optional)

Cook ground beef and onion in a large skillet over medium heat until meat is browned, stirring until meat crumbles; drain. Return to skillet; stir in tomato soup and enchilada sauce. Spread about ¼ cup meat mixture on each tortilla; sprinkle tortillas evenly with 1 cup cheese. Roll up, and place, seam side down, in a 13- x 9- x 2-inch baking dish.

Pour remaining meat mixture over tortillas. Cover and bake at 350° for 20 minutes. Uncover and sprinkle evenly with remaining 1 cup cheese; bake an additional 5 minutes or until cheese melts. Serve with sour cream, if desired. Yield: 4 servings.
Lynn Barber
Siler City, North Carolina

Beef Up Weeknight Meals

When you think of ground beef, no-fuss family dishes come to mind. But what about larger beef cuts? They can make meal planning easy, too. The secret is to season them simply, add vegetables if you like, and cook for a few hours until the meat is tender.

■ For dinner, serve the brisket with gravy (it makes its own—you just add flour). Save the leftover meat, add barbecue sauce, and make sandwiches for lunch the next day.
Prep time: 10 minutes
Cooking time: 2½ hours

BEEF BRISKET IN BEER

1 (3½- to 4-pound) beef brisket
½ teaspoon salt
¼ teaspoon pepper
1 onion, thinly sliced
2 tablespoons brown sugar
1 (12-ounce) can beer
¼ cup commercial chili sauce
2 tablespoons all-purpose flour
½ cup water
Salt and pepper to taste

Trim excess fat from brisket, and place in a lightly greased 13- x 9- x 2-inch baking dish. Sprinkle with ½ teaspoon salt and ¼ teaspoon pepper; top with onion slices. Combine brown sugar, beer, and chili sauce; pour over meat. Cover with aluminum foil, and bake at 350° for 2 hours. Remove foil, and bake an additional 30 minutes or until tender. Remove meat to a serving platter; keep warm. Skim and discard fat from pan juices; reserve 1 cup pan juices.

Combine flour and water; slowly stir into reserved pan juices in a saucepan. Cook over medium heat, stirring constantly, until gravy is smooth and thickened. Add salt and pepper, and serve with brisket. Yield: 8 servings.
Joan Grimmett
Ravenswood, West Virginia

■ Chuck roast is an economical choice for families. If you're more concerned with fat than cost, try a sirloin roast.
Prep time: 10 minutes
Cooking time: 2 hours

EASY OVEN ROAST

1 (3- to 3½-pound) chuck roast
2 tablespoons steak sauce
2 tablespoons dry onion soup mix
1 (10¾-ounce) can golden
  mushroom soup, undiluted

Place roast on heavy-duty aluminum foil; brush with steak sauce, and sprinkle with onion soup mix. Spoon mushroom soup on top; wrap loosely with foil. Place in a 13- x 9- x 2-inch pan. Bake at 350° for 2 hours. Yield: 6 servings.
Edith Amburn
Mount Airy, North Carolina

■ If you're using regular rice, start it first, and then begin the stir-fry recipe. Regular rice takes 20 minutes to cook and will be ready just in time to serve with the stir-fry.
Prep time: 10 to 15 minutes
Cooking time: 12 to 14 minutes

HUNGARIAN STIR-FRY

1 pound boneless top round steak
1 tablespoon cornstarch
¼ cup Burgundy or other dry red
  wine
2 tablespoons vegetable oil, divided
1 large sweet onion, sliced and
  separated into rings
1 cup sliced fresh mushrooms
1 tablespoon sweet Hungarian
  paprika
½ cup beef broth
Hot cooked rice

Slice steak diagonally across grain into thin strips; place in a shallow dish. Combine cornstarch and wine; pour over steak, and set aside.

Pour 1 tablespoon oil around top of preheated wok or skillet, coating sides; heat at medium-high (375°) 2 minutes. Add onion and mushrooms; stir-fry 3 to 4 minutes or until onion is tender. Remove from wok; set aside.

Pour remaining 1 tablespoon oil into wok; heat 2 minutes. Remove steak from marinade, reserving marinade. Add steak to wok, and stir-fry 3 minutes or until browned. Return vegetables to wok. Combine reserved marinade, paprika, and beef broth; add to wok, and cook, stirring constantly, until thickened. Serve over rice. Yield: 4 servings.

■ Serve cornbread with this one-dish corned beef meal.
Prep time: 15 to 20 minutes; leave the potatoes unpeeled to save time.
Cooking time: 3 hours

CORNED BEEF AND CABBAGE

1 (4-pound) corned beef brisket
4 cups water
6 medium potatoes
6 medium carrots, scraped and
  quartered
6 small onions
1 small turnip, cubed
1 small head cabbage, cut into
  wedges
½ teaspoon pepper

Place brisket in a large Dutch oven; add water, and bring to a boil. Cover, reduce heat, and simmer 2 hours. Add potatoes and next 3 ingredients; cover and cook 30 minutes. Add cabbage and pepper; cover and cook an additional 30 minutes. Yield: 8 to 10 servings.
Christiana Courtenay
Adrian, Georgia

An Italian-Inspired Terrine

Many of us have a love affair with the signature flavors of Italy—basil, garlic, Parmesan cheese, and tomatoes.

We've used these ingredients to give our Italian Cheese Terrine authentic flavor.

This dish is streaked with the colors of its homeland—red, white, and green. The red Basil-Tomato Sauce is loaded with intensely flavored sun-dried tomatoes, which are packed in olive oil and found in the specialty food section of most supermarkets. Pesto—a blend of fresh basil, pine nuts, Parmesan cheese, garlic, and olive oil—gives the cream cheese layer its pale-green color. Pesto is commercially prepared and available year-round canned, fresh, or frozen.

To serve the terrine, invert it onto a cheese board or serving platter, and cut into thin wedges. Serve with crackers or baguette slices.

ITALIAN CHEESE TERRINE

1 (8-ounce) package cream cheese,
  softened
2 tablespoons butter or margarine,
  softened
½ cup grated Parmesan cheese
2 tablespoons commercial pesto
9 (1-ounce) slices Muenster or
  mozzarella cheese, divided
Basil-Tomato Sauce
Garnish: fresh herb sprig

Beat cream cheese and butter at medium speed with an electric mixer until creamy. Add Parmesan cheese and pesto; beat until smooth. Set aside.

Line a 3-cup bowl or mold with plastic wrap, allowing edges to hang over 6 to 7 inches. Diagonally cut 5 slices Muenster cheese in half; arrange cheese triangles in bowl pinwheel fashion, slightly overlapping to line bowl. Spread half of cream cheese mixture over cheese; top with half of Basil-Tomato Sauce. Cut 2 slices Muenster cheese in half crosswise; arrange cheese rectangles over tomato mixture. Repeat with remaining cream cheese mixture, Basil-Tomato Sauce, and 2 slices Muenster cheese cut into rectangles. Fold plastic wrap over layers, sealing securely; place a heavy object, such as a small cast-iron skillet, on top to compact layers. Chill at least 8 hours or up to 3 days.

Invert terrine onto a cheese board or serving platter, and peel off plastic wrap; garnish, if desired. Serve terrine with crackers or baguette slices. Yield: 3 cups.

Basil-Tomato Sauce

1 (14½-ounce) can whole tomatoes, undrained
¾ cup chopped onion
1 tablespoon minced fresh garlic
2 tablespoons olive oil
2 bay leaves
½ teaspoon sugar
¼ teaspoon dried basil
1 (7-ounce) jar oil-packed sun-dried tomatoes, drained and chopped

Drain whole tomatoes, reserving ¼ cup juice. Chop tomatoes; set aside.

Cook onion and garlic in olive oil in a large skillet over medium heat, stirring constantly, until tender. Stir in chopped tomato, ¼ cup reserved juice, bay leaves, sugar, and basil; bring to a boil. Reduce heat, and simmer, stirring often, 3 to 5 minutes or until thickened; remove from heat. Remove and discard bay leaves; stir in sun-dried tomatoes. Cover and chill at least 2 hours. Yield: 1¼ cups.

Toss A Spring Medley Of Vegetables

Be sure greens are fresh, and gently but thoroughly wash and dry them before serving. It's customary to tear rather than cut greens to prevent bruising. But due to its sturdiness, iceberg lettuce remains the exception; it can be either sliced or shredded.

If you don't grow your own herbs, retain the freshness of those you purchase by first rinsing them in cold running water, and then shaking off the excess. Wrap in a dry cloth or paper towel, and refrigerate in a plastic bag up to four days.

BOSTON LETTUCE AND WATERCRESS SALAD

1 head Boston lettuce, rinsed and torn
1 bunch watercress, rinsed and torn
1 tablespoon red wine vinegar
1 tablespoon Dijon mustard
⅛ teaspoon salt
⅛ teaspoon freshly ground pepper
1 to 2 cloves garlic, minced
2 tablespoons vegetable oil

Combine lettuce and watercress in a large bowl; set aside. Combine red wine vinegar and next 4 ingredients, using a wire whisk. Gradually add oil, whisking briskly until well blended. Pour over greens, tossing well. Yield: 6 servings.
Helen Maurer
Christmas, Florida

SPINACH SALAD

1 pound fresh spinach
1 cup strawberries, halved
1 cup pecan halves, toasted
Poppy Seed Dressing

Remove stems from spinach; wash leaves thoroughly, and pat dry. Tear into bite-size pieces. Combine spinach, strawberries, and pecans; drizzle with Poppy Seed Dressing. Serve immediately. Yield: 6 servings.

Poppy Seed Dressing

⅓ cup cider vinegar
⅓ cup vegetable oil
¼ cup sugar
1 tablespoon Dijon mustard
1 teaspoon salt
½ teaspoon pepper
1 small onion, chopped
2 teaspoons poppy seeds

Combine first 7 ingredients in container of an electric blender; process until smooth, stopping once to scrape down sides. Stir in poppy seeds. Yield: 1 cup.
Anita Hensley
Grandview, Missouri

FRESH MUSHROOM SALAD

1 pound fresh mushrooms, sliced
⅓ cup lemon juice
1 tablespoon chopped fresh or frozen chives
1 tablespoon chopped fresh parsley
1 teaspoon dried tarragon
Dressing
1 bunch watercress, rinsed and torn

Combine first 5 ingredients in a large bowl, tossing to coat. Cover and refrigerate 1 hour. Drain and return to bowl; add Dressing, tossing to coat. Serve on a bed of watercress. Yield: 6 to 8 servings.

Dressing

½ cup commercial Italian salad dressing
1 (2-ounce) jar diced pimiento, undrained
1½ teaspoons sugar
½ teaspoon salt
⅛ teaspoon pepper
2 teaspoons prepared mustard

Combine all ingredients in a small bowl; cover dressing, and refrigerate 1 hour. Yield: ¾ cup.
Barbara Wagner
Gainesville, Florida

DILLED CUCUMBER SALAD

2 medium cucumbers, unpeeled and thinly sliced
⅓ cup thinly sliced green onions
1 tablespoon fresh dillweed or 1 teaspoon dried dillweed
½ teaspoon salt
⅛ teaspoon ground white pepper
¾ cup sour cream
Lettuce leaves

Pat cucumber slices between paper towels. Combine cucumber slices and next 4 ingredients in a medium bowl; toss gently. Fold in sour cream; chill. Serve on lettuce leaves. Yield: 6 servings.
Evelyn Snellings
Richmond, Virginia

ON THE LIGHT SIDE

Healthful Dieting With Flair

If you're trying to be health-conscious and tired of preparing the same old foods, try an unusual source for inspiration—a menu designed for people with diabetes.

The American Diabetes Association's and the American Dietetic Association's cookbook, *Family Cookbook, Volume IV: The American Tradition,* features recipes that will add flair and flavor to your plate. Though it's chock-full of exciting dishes from all around the country, we chose to test and share a few of the cookbook's Southern selections.

These recipes demonstrate how traditional regional foods can be presented with a healthful twist. (In addition to a nutrition analysis, exchange values follow each recipe to aid in meal planning without calculating calories or balancing nutrients. If you have diabetes and are confused about how to fit these into your prescribed meal plan, consult your physician or registered dietitian.)

GAME HENS WITH CHUTNEY-MUSTARD GLAZE

1 (1¼-pound) Cornish hen, skinned and split
Vegetable cooking spray
2 tablespoons chopped mango chutney
2 teaspoons Dijon mustard

Place hen halves, cut side down, on a rack coated with cooking spray; place rack in a broiler pan. Combine chutney and mustard, and brush about one-third of chutney mixture over hen. Bake, uncovered, at 325° for 50 to 60 minutes, brushing twice with chutney mixture. Yield: 2 servings (288 calories [30% from fat] per hen half). Exchanges per serving: 4 Lean Meat and 1 Fruit.

□ *37g protein, 9.6g fat (4.3g saturated), 11g carbohydrate, 0g fiber, 113mg cholesterol, 209mg sodium, and 22mg calcium.*

RICE WITH BLACK-EYED PEAS

2 teaspoons olive oil
1 cup chopped onion
2 cloves garlic, minced
1 cup long-grain rice, uncooked
½ teaspoon dried crushed red pepper
2 cups no-salt-added chicken broth
¼ cup Chablis or other dry white wine
1 (15.8-ounce) can black-eyed peas, rinsed and drained
1 cup chopped tomato
¼ cup chopped fresh cilantro or parsley
¼ teaspoon freshly ground pepper

Heat olive oil in a large skillet over medium heat. Add onion and garlic; cook 3 minutes, stirring often. Stir in rice and red pepper; cook, stirring constantly, 1 minute. Add chicken broth and wine; bring to a boil. Cover, reduce heat, and simmer 18 minutes.

Stir in peas and tomato; cook 1 minute or until thoroughly heated. Remove from heat; stir in cilantro, and sprinkle with pepper. Yield: 6 servings (207 calories [11% from fat] per ¾ cup serving).
Exchanges per serving: 2½ Starch/Bread.

□ *7g protein, 2.5g fat (0.4g saturated), 39g carbohydrate, 6g fiber, 0mg cholesterol, 104mg sodium, and 48mg calcium.*

SUGAR SNAP PEAS WITH BASIL AND LEMON

1 teaspoon olive oil
¾ pound Sugar Snap peas
¼ cup coarsely chopped fresh basil
½ teaspoon grated lemon rind
¼ teaspoon salt
¼ teaspoon ground white pepper
Lemon wedges

Heat oil in a nonstick skillet over medium heat. Add peas; stir-fry 3 minutes or until crisp-tender. Sprinkle with basil and next 3 ingredients; stir-fry 1 minute. Serve immediately with lemon wedges. Yield: 2 servings (95 calories [25% from fat] per serving).
Exchanges per serving: 2 Vegetable and 2 Fat.

□ *4.8g protein, 2.6g fat (0.4g saturated), 13.8g carbohydrate, 4.5g fiber, 0mg cholesterol, 300mg sodium, and 85mg calcium.*

HERBED BISCUITS
(pictured on page 39)

2 cups all-purpose flour
1 tablespoon baking powder
½ teaspoon baking soda
¼ teaspoon salt
¼ teaspoon dried thyme, crushed
¼ teaspoon dried rosemary, crushed
¼ teaspoon dried basil, crushed
¼ cup margarine
¾ cup low-fat buttermilk

Combine first 7 ingredients in large bowl; cut in margarine with a pastry blender until mixture is crumbly. Add buttermilk, stirring with a fork just until dry ingredients are moistened. Turn dough out onto a lightly floured surface, and knead lightly 5 times. Roll to ½-inch thickness; cut with a 2-inch round cutter. Place on an ungreased baking sheet, and bake at 400° for 10 to 12 minutes or until golden brown. Serve warm. Yield: 1 dozen (125 calories [30% from fat] per biscuit).
Exchanges per serving: 1 Starch/Bread and 1 Fat.

□ *3g protein, 4.2g fat (0.8g saturated), 18g carbohydrate, 0.8g fiber, 1mg cholesterol, 217mg sodium, and 79mg calcium.*

LIGHT MENU

Add A Fresh Accent To Fish

Break out of the winter dinner doldrums and awaken your palate with a fresh spring menu. A cascading topping of mixed vegetables brightens the flavor and appearance of baked orange roughy. Cornbread Supreme, a cornbread hybrid with a thick spoonbread consistency, makes an attractive addition to the plate. Assorted baby lettuces, also known as mesclun, serve as the bed for zesty Mustard Vinaigrette. You can find mesclun prepackaged at some supermarkets, or simply select the young greens by hand in the produce section.

SPRING MENU FOR FOUR

**Vegetable-Topped Orange Roughy
Baby Lettuces With
Mustard Vinaigrette
Cornbread Supreme**

VEGETABLE-TOPPED ORANGE ROUGHY
(pictured on page 73)

4 (4-ounce) orange roughy fillets
¼ cup lemon juice
¼ cup Chablis or other dry white wine
½ teaspoon salt
¼ teaspoon pepper
⅛ teaspoon garlic powder
1 cup chopped tomato
1 cup sliced carrot
¼ cup sliced green onions
¼ cup chopped fresh parsley

Place orange roughy in an 11- x 7- x 1½-inch baking dish. Combine lemon juice and wine; pour over fish. Combine salt, pepper, and garlic powder; sprinkle about half of mixture over fish, reserving remaining mixture. Combine tomato and next 3 ingredients; spoon over fish, and sprinkle with remaining salt mixture. Cover and bake at 350° for 25 to 30 minutes or until fish flakes easily when tested with a fork. To serve, use a slotted spoon. Yield: 4 servings (113 calories [8% from fat] per serving).

□ *17.6g protein, 5.1g fat (0.5g saturated), 6.2g carbohydrate, 1.5g fiber, 23mg cholesterol, 379mg sodium, and 22mg calcium.*
*Mrs. R. L. McKeithan
Hamlet, North Carolina*

BABY LETTUCES WITH MUSTARD VINAIGRETTE
(pictured on page 73)

¼ cup rice wine vinegar
1 tablespoon water
1 tablespoon Dijon mustard
2 teaspoons low-sodium soy sauce
½ teaspoon sugar
¼ teaspoon lemon juice
⅛ teaspoon pepper
⅛ teaspoon hot sauce
4 cups mixed baby lettuces or other mixed greens

Combine first 8 ingredients in a jar. Cover tightly, and shake vigorously; chill. To serve, shake dressing, and drizzle over lettuces, tossing to coat. Yield: 4 servings (18 calories [20% from fat] per 1-cup serving).

□ *1.2g protein, 0.4g fat (0.1g saturated), 2.3g carbohydrate, 0.7g fiber, 0mg cholesterol, 144mg sodium, and 16mg calcium.*

CORNBREAD SUPREME
(pictured on page 73)

1 cup yellow cornmeal
½ teaspoon baking soda
½ teaspoon salt
1 (8-ounce) carton plain nonfat yogurt
1 (8¾-ounce) can cream-style corn
¼ cup evaporated skim milk
¼ cup egg substitute
2 tablespoons vegetable oil
Vegetable cooking spray

Combine first 3 ingredients; add yogurt and next 4 ingredients, stirring just until moistened. Spoon into 6 (6-ounce) custard or soufflé cups coated with cooking spray. Bake at 350° for 30 minutes or until a knife inserted in center comes out clean. Serve immediately. Yield: 6 servings (180 calories [28% from fat] per serving).

□ *6.3g protein, 5.7g fat (1g saturated), 27.4g carbohydrate, 2.7g fiber, 1mg cholesterol, 445mg sodium, and 128mg calcium.*
*Mary Anne Dekle
Staunton, Virginia*

Make Room For Eggs Benedict

Now even the health-conscious can enjoy Eggs Benedict with our version, which is low in fat and cholesterol, yet filled with the same dignified flavor of the original.

A combination of reduced-calorie mayonnaise, plain nonfat yogurt, and lemon juice matches the consistency and flavor of traditional hollandaise sauce. And egg substitute, baked in custard cups, mimics poached eggs.

LIGHT EGGS BENEDICT

Vegetable cooking spray
4 slices lean Canadian bacon
1 cup egg substitute
2 whole wheat English muffins, split and toasted
Mock Hollandaise Sauce
Paprika
Garnish: fresh parsley sprigs

Coat a large nonstick skillet with cooking spray; place over medium heat until hot. Add bacon, and cook until thoroughly heated, turning once. Remove from heat; keep warm.

Place ¼ cup egg substitute in each of 4 (6-ounce) custard cups coated with cooking spray. Cover cups loosely with wax paper, and microwave at HIGH 2 to 3 minutes, giving cups a half-turn after 1 minute. Let stand 2 minutes.

Place 1 bacon slice on each muffin half; top each with cooked egg substitute and 3 tablespoons Mock Hollandaise Sauce. Sprinkle with paprika. Garnish, if desired, and serve immediately. Yield: 4 servings (219 calories [27% from fat] per serving).

□ 16.3g protein, 6.7g fat (0.7g saturated), 22.3g carbohydrate, 0g fiber, 20mg cholesterol, 789mg sodium, and 132mg calcium.

Mock Hollandaise Sauce

½ cup plain nonfat yogurt
¼ cup reduced-calorie mayonnaise
2 teaspoons lemon juice
⅛ teaspoon ground red pepper

Combine all ingredients in a small bowl, stirring until well blended. Yield: ¾ cup (19 calories [66% from fat] per tablespoon).

□ 0.6g protein, 1.4g fat (0g saturated), 1.2g carbohydrate, 0g fiber, 2mg cholesterol, 44mg sodium, and 19mg calcium.

COMPARE THE NUTRIENTS (per serving)		
	Traditional	Light
Calories	473	219
Fat	38.3g	6.7g
Cholesterol	450mg	20mg

Cumin: A Worldly Spice Comes Home

Cooks from Mexico to India use cumin seeds like a fireman uses a hose—to cool down the heat.

The earthy-tasting cumin seeds balance the fire of chiles and curry, making them palatable for even the most tentative tasters.

Cumin's pungent smell and musty taste are frequently paired with oregano, cilantro, red pepper, and chili powder in Tex-Mex dishes.

Because of its distinctive taste, cumin should be used sparingly until you are comfortable with its aromatic, nutty flavor.

CARNE GUISADA

3 pounds round steak, trimmed and cubed
2 tablespoons vegetable oil
1 tablespoon all-purpose flour
2 tablespoons chopped onion
2 tablespoons chopped green pepper
2 tablespoons chopped tomato
1 to 2 cloves garlic, minced
1 (10-ounce) can tomatoes with green chiles, undrained
1 (8-ounce) can tomato sauce
¼ cup water
1 to 1½ teaspoons ground cumin
1 teaspoon salt
⅛ teaspoon pepper
Flour tortillas (optional)
Hot cooked rice (optional)

Cook steak in oil in a heavy skillet over medium-high heat, stirring constantly, until browned. Sprinkle with flour, and stir well. Add onion and remaining ingredients. Bring to a boil over medium heat; reduce heat, and simmer, uncovered, 40 minutes or until meat is tender and sauce is thick. Serve in flour tortillas or over hot cooked rice. Yield: 4 cups.

Barbara Anderson
Conroe, Texas

CHICKEN CHIMICHANGAS

3 (5-ounce) cans 98% fat-free chicken, drained
⅓ cup sliced green onions
¾ teaspoon ground cumin
½ teaspoon dried oregano
¼ teaspoon salt
1 (16-ounce) jar salsa or picante sauce, divided
8 (8-inch) flour tortillas
1 (8-ounce) package shredded Monterey Jack or Cheddar cheese, divided
Vegetable cooking spray
Nonfat sour cream alternative

Combine first 5 ingredients in a large saucepan; stir in ⅔ cup salsa. Cook over medium heat 5 minutes, stirring often. Spoon about 2 tablespoons of chicken mixture just below center of each tortilla; sprinkle tortillas evenly with half of cheese.

Fold left and right sides of tortilla to partially enclose filling. Fold up top and bottom edges of tortilla (making a square). Place folded side down in a lightly greased 13- x 9- x 2-inch baking dish, coated with cooking spray. Repeat procedure with remaining tortillas. Bake at 475° for 13 minutes.

Heat remaining salsa in a small saucepan; pour over tortillas, and sprinkle evenly with remaining cheese. Top each serving with a dollop of sour cream alternative. Yield: 8 servings.
Sharla Sparhawk
Knoxville, Tennessee

MEXI-CHICKEN CASSEROLE

1 large onion, chopped
1 tablespoon vegetable oil
3 medium tomatoes, peeled and chopped
2 cups chopped cooked chicken
½ cup chicken broth
2 teaspoons chili powder
1 teaspoon salt
1 teaspoon ground cumin
1 teaspoon dried oregano
6 corn tortillas, cut into fourths and divided
1 cup (4 ounces) shredded sharp Cheddar cheese, divided

Cook onion in oil in a Dutch oven over medium-high heat, stirring constantly, until tender; add tomato and next 6 ingredients. Bring to a boil; reduce heat, and simmer 5 minutes. Layer

---

Roasting Cumin

You can buy cumin seeds whole or ground. Roasting enhances the flavor of whole seeds. To roast, heat in a dry skillet until the seeds are more fragrant and lightly browned. After cooking, use whole or grind using a mortar and pestle, spice mill, electric blender, or coffee grinder.

---

half each of chicken mixture, tortillas, and cheese in a lightly greased 11- x 7- x 1½-inch baking dish. Repeat procedure with remaining chicken mixture and tortillas. Cover and bake at 350° for 25 minutes. Uncover and sprinkle evenly with remaining ½ cup cheese, and bake an additional 5 minutes. Yield: 6 to 8 servings.
Barbara Nibling
San Angelo, Texas

MEXICAN PINTO BEANS

1 pound dried pinto beans
5 cups water
6 slices bacon, finely chopped
1 large onion, chopped
½ green pepper, chopped
1½ tablespoons ground cumin
1 tablespoon chili powder
1½ teaspoons salt
1 teaspoon pepper

Sort and wash beans; place in a Dutch oven. Cover with water 2 inches above beans; bring to a boil. Boil 1 minute. Cover, remove from heat, and let stand 1 hour. Drain and return beans to Dutch oven. Add 5 cups water and remaining ingredients. Bring to a boil; cover, reduce heat, and simmer 1½ hours or until beans are tender. Serve with a slotted spoon. Yield: 7 cups.
Nancy Sloan
Lake Village, Arkansas

TACO SAUCE

½ teaspoon cumin seeds
1 (16-ounce) can whole tomatoes, undrained
2 jalapeño peppers, seeded
1 small onion, sliced
1 clove garlic, peeled
1 teaspoon salt
1 teaspoon pepper
Garnish: seeded jalapeño pepper slices

Place a small skillet over medium-high heat until hot; add cumin seeds, and cook, stirring constantly, until seeds

---

are more fragrant and lightly browned. Let cool.

Combine seeds and next 6 ingredients in container of an electric blender or food processor; process until blended. Pour mixture into a medium saucepan, and bring to a boil. Reduce heat, and simmer 5 minutes. Garnish, if desired. Yield: 2 cups.
Becky Holzhaus
Castroville, Texas

Keep Your Cool With Pepper Soup

If you love the idea of soup as an appetizer course, but hate the last-minute fuss, Chilled Sweet Red Pepper Soup solves the dilemma.

CHILLED SWEET RED PEPPER SOUP

½ cup butter or margarine
3 large sweet red peppers, sliced
2 cups chopped leeks
1½ cups chicken broth
3 cups buttermilk
⅛ teaspoon ground white pepper
Sweet yellow peppers, halved and seeded
Garnish: fresh chives

Melt butter in a large saucepan. Add sweet red pepper slices, leeks, and broth; bring to a boil. Cover, reduce heat, and simmer, stirring occasionally, 30 minutes or until vegetables are tender.

Pour mixture into container of an electric blender or food processor; process until smooth, stopping once to scrape down sides. Pour through a wire-mesh strainer into a large bowl, making sure to get 3 cups liquid. Stir in buttermilk and white pepper. Cover and chill at least 2 hours. Serve in seeded sweet pepper halves, and garnish, if desired. Yield: 6 cups.
W. N. Cottrell, II
New Orleans, Louisiana

Easy But Impressive Spring Fare

Usher in warmer weather with a menu with a Middle-Eastern flavor. The aroma of lamb cooking on the grill should whet the appetite for these tasty kabobs. Tabbouleh, a perfect accompaniment, is a salad of chopped vegetables and bulgur wheat seasoned with hefty amounts of parsley and mint. And for a finale, there's orange-flavored custard with fresh strawberries and kiwifruit.

EASY SPRING MENU FOR EIGHT

Tabbouleh
Lamb Shish Kabobs
Cheesy Pita Triangles
Citrus Custard With Fresh Fruit

TABBOULEH

11 medium tomatoes, divided
1 cup bulgur wheat
2 cups hot water
1 cup peeled, seeded, and chopped cucumber (optional)
1½ cups finely chopped fresh parsley
½ cup finely chopped fresh mint
½ cup chopped green onions
½ cup fresh lemon juice
2 tablespoons olive oil
½ teaspoon salt
¼ teaspoon pepper
8 lettuce leaves

Core tomatoes; cut 8 into 6 wedges each, cutting to, but not through, base. Carefully spread wedges apart; scoop out pulp, and chop. Set tomato shells aside. Finely chop remaining 3 tomatoes; combine chopped tomato, and measure 3 cups; set aside.

Combine wheat and water; let stand 1 hour. Squeeze excess water from wheat with hands. Combine wheat, chopped tomato, and cucumber, if desired, and next 7 ingredients. Cover and chill at least 1 hour. Spoon mixture into tomato shells; serve on lettuce leaves. Yield: 8 servings.

Beppy Hassey
Montgomery, Alabama

LAMB SHISH KABOBS

3 (1-pound) lamb steaks
⅓ cup lemon juice
¼ cup olive oil
¼ cup finely chopped onion
1 teaspoon salt
2 purple onions, quartered
24 Sugar Snap peas or snow pea pods
½ pound fresh mushrooms
1 (15¼-ounce) can spear pineapple, drained

Trim fat from lamb; bone and cut into 1-inch cubes. Place in a large shallow dish or heavy-duty, zip-top plastic bag. Combine lemon juice and next 3 ingredients; pour over lamb. Cover or seal; marinate in refrigerator 3 hours, turning occasionally. Drain, discarding marinade.

Alternate lamb, onion, Sugar Snap peas, mushrooms, and pineapple on 8 skewers. Grill, covered, over medium coals (300° to 350°) 5 minutes on each side or to desired degree of doneness. Yield: 8 servings.

Suzanne Braunstein
Brooksville, Florida

CHEESY PITA TRIANGLES

4 (8-inch) white or whole wheat pita bread rounds
1½ cups (6 ounces) shredded Swiss cheese

Cut each pita bread round into 6 triangles; sprinkle cheese inside each triangle. Place on a baking sheet, and bake at 350° for 10 minutes. Serve immediately. Yield: 8 servings.

CITRUS CUSTARD WITH FRESH FRUIT

5 egg yolks, well beaten
½ cup sugar
2 tablespoons lemon juice
1 tablespoon grated orange rind
½ cup whipping cream, whipped
1 (11-ounce) can mandarin oranges, drained and divided
2 kiwifruit, peeled and sliced
1 cup strawberries, sliced
Garnish: fresh mint sprigs

Combine first 4 ingredients in a small nonaluminum heavy saucepan. Cook over medium heat, stirring constantly, until mixture thickens (about 4 minutes). Let cool. Fold in whipped cream and ½ cup oranges. Spoon into 8 compotes, and chill. Just before serving, top with remaining oranges, kiwifruit, and strawberries. Garnish, if desired. Yield: 8 servings.

Pasta Toppers

If you've always liked the ease, speed, and taste of pasta but get bored with run-of-the-mill meat sauce, try these toppers for pasta. They create unusual one-dish meals when they're drizzled over strands of fettuccine, spaghetti, egg noodles, or vermicelli. Each recipe is easy and can be prepared in one skillet or saucepan.

SHRIMP SCAMPI

2 pounds unpeeled jumbo fresh shrimp
1 medium onion, finely chopped
4 cloves garlic, minced
½ cup butter or margarine, melted
½ teaspoon dried tarragon
2 tablespoons fresh lemon juice
½ teaspoon steak sauce
½ teaspoon Worcestershire sauce
¼ teaspoon hot sauce
2 tablespoons chopped fresh parsley
Hot cooked fettuccine

Peel and devein shrimp, and set shrimp aside.

Cook onion and garlic in butter in a large skillet over medium heat, stirring constantly, 3 to 4 minutes; add tarragon and next 4 ingredients. Bring to a boil; add shrimp, and cook, stirring constantly, 5 to 6 minutes or until shrimp turn pink. Sprinkle with parsley. Serve over fettuccine. Yield: 4 to 6 servings.

Sue P. Wilson
Etowah, North Carolina

ZUCCHINI-MUSHROOM SAUCE

2 medium onions, chopped
1 cup chopped celery with leaves
3 tablespoons olive oil
2 cloves garlic, minced
1 tablespoon dried oregano
1 teaspoon dried basil
1 teaspoon dried thyme
1 teaspoon dried parsley flakes
2 medium zucchini, cut into ¾-inch slices and quartered
1 medium-size green pepper, cut into ½-inch squares
1 (15-ounce) can tomato sauce
1 (8-ounce) can tomato sauce
¼ cup brandy (optional)
½ pound fresh mushrooms, sliced
Hot cooked egg noodles

Cook onion and celery in olive oil in a large Dutch oven over medium heat, stirring constantly, 3 to 4 minutes; add garlic and next 4 ingredients, and cook, stirring constantly, 3 minutes. Add zucchini and green pepper; cook, stirring constantly, 5 minutes or until crisp-tender.

Add tomato sauce and, if desired, brandy; cover and simmer 25 minutes. Add mushrooms; cover and simmer 25 minutes. Serve over egg noodles. Yield: 12 servings.

Frank Weisel
Gaithersburg, Maryland

SPINACH PASTA SAUCE

2 cloves garlic, sliced
2 tablespoons butter or margarine, melted
2 (9.5-ounce) packages frozen creamed spinach, thawed
1 cup half-and-half
⅓ cup grated Parmesan cheese
Hot cooked spaghetti
4 slices bacon, cooked and crumbled

Cook garlic in butter in a medium saucepan over medium heat, stirring constantly, until lightly browned; remove and discard garlic. Add spinach and half-and-half. Bring to a boil, stirring constantly; reduce heat, and add Parmesan cheese. Cook over low heat, 8 to 10 minutes, stirring occasionally. Serve over spaghetti; sprinkle with crumbled bacon. Yield: 4 to 6 servings.

Judith Hafner
Murray, Kentucky

CREAMY TOMATO SAUCE

2 cloves garlic, minced
2 tablespoons butter or margarine, melted
6 large tomatoes, peeled, seeded, and chopped (about 2 pounds)
½ teaspoon salt
¼ teaspoon freshly ground pepper
½ cup whipping cream
2 tablespoons chopped fresh basil or 2 teaspoons dried basil
Hot cooked vermicelli

Cook garlic in butter in a large skillet over medium heat, stirring constantly, 1 minute. Add tomato, salt, and pepper; cook 12 to 15 minutes or until sauce is thickened. Gradually stir in whipping cream and basil, and cook sauce an additional 10 minutes. Serve over vermicelli. Yield: 4 to 6 servings.

Alicia Pettineo
Coral Springs, Florida

Eatin' O' The Green

Like a box of crayons—all green crayons, that is—our pretty salad paints a portrait of spring. The rich color of kiwifruit, the yellow-green of pears, and the whispered shade of Granny Smith apples and seedless grapes combine for a beautiful, delicious green-on-green treat. And—begorra!—it's just in time for St. Patrick's Day.

GREEN FRUIT SALAD WITH HONEY-LIME DRESSING

4 kiwifruit, peeled and cut into slices
2 Granny Smith apples, unpeeled, cored, and sliced
2 pears, unpeeled, cored, and sliced
1 cup seedless green grapes
Lettuce leaves
Honey-Lime Dressing
1 (2-ounce) package slivered almonds, toasted
Garnish: lime rind

Arrange fruit on lettuce leaves; drizzle with Honey-Lime Dressing. Sprinkle with almonds, and garnish, if desired. Yield: 4 servings.

Honey-Lime Dressing

1 (16-ounce) carton plain yogurt
2 tablespoons honey
2 teaspoons grated lime rind

Combine all ingredients in a small bowl, stirring to blend. Yield: 2 cups.

Margaret Gangler
Longboat Key, Florida

Tip: *To prepare kiwifruit, first chill the fruit; then peel and thinly slice crosswise for use in recipes or as an eye-catching garnish.*

The Gasparilla Cookbook

First printed in 1961, *The Gasparilla Cookbook* is the oldest in our *Southern Living* Hall of Fame series. Today, with more than 250,000 copies sold, the Junior League of Tampa, Florida, has donated profits in excess of $300,000 to numerous community projects.

PICADILLO II

1 pound ground beef
1 pound ground pork
2 medium onions, chopped
1 large green pepper, chopped
3 large tomatoes, peeled and chopped
½ cup raisins
½ cup Burgundy or other dry red wine
¼ cup pimiento-stuffed olives, chopped
¼ cup white vinegar
1 tablespoon capers
1 tablespoon brown sugar
2 teaspoons salt
1 teaspoon garlic powder
⅛ teaspoon pepper

Combine first 4 ingredients in a large Dutch oven; cook over medium-high heat until meat browns, stirring until it crumbles. Drain well. Return to Dutch oven; add tomato and remaining ingredients. Bring to a boil; cover, reduce heat, and simmer 1 hour, stirring occasionally. Serve over hamburger buns or hot cooked rice. Yield: 6 cups.

■ This fruit tray can be served year-round. Simply choose fruits that are in season.

TROPICAL FRUIT TRAY

2 cups cream-style cottage cheese
1 (3-ounce) package cream cheese, softened
¼ cup crumbled blue cheese
¼ cup sour cream
¼ cup chopped walnuts
2 large bananas, cut into 2-inch slices
2 tablespoons lime juice
½ cup flaked coconut
1 (20-ounce) can pineapple slices, drained
3 cups whole strawberries, halved
1 small honeydew, cut into wedges
1 cantaloupe or papaya, sliced
Garnishes: lime wedges, fresh mint sprigs

Combine first 4 ingredients in a small mixing bowl; beat at medium speed with an electric mixer until creamy. Spoon into a bowl, and sprinkle with walnuts; place in center of a large serving platter.

Dip banana slices in lime juice; roll in coconut. Arrange banana slices, pineapple, and next 3 ingredients on platter. Garnish, if desired. Yield: 12 servings.

CLARET LEMONADE

⅓ cup sugar
Juice of 3 lemons (about ⅔ cup)
½ cup claret or other dry red wine
3 cups sparkling mineral water, chilled

Combine sugar and lemon juice, stirring until sugar dissolves. Add wine and sparkling water, and serve over ice. Yield: 4 cups.

■ We tried to make this recipe quicker for busy cooks. However, we weren't satisfied with the results when we used frozen spinach instead of fresh.

SPINACH PARMESAN

4 pounds fresh spinach
½ cup water
½ cup grated Parmesan cheese
½ cup whipping cream
⅓ cup butter or margarine, melted
⅓ cup finely chopped onion
⅛ teaspoon pepper
⅓ cup fine, dry breadcrumbs

Remove stems from spinach; wash leaves thoroughly. Combine spinach and water in a Dutch oven; cover and cook over medium heat 8 minutes or until tender. Drain well. Combine spinach, Parmesan cheese, and next 4 ingredients; spoon into a lightly greased 11- x 7- x 1½-inch baking dish. Top with breadcrumbs. Bake at 450° for 10 to 15 minutes or until thoroughly heated. Yield: 6 servings.

Right: *Catch the fresh flavor of Vegetable-Topped Orange Roughy complemented by Cornbread Supreme and Baby Lettuces With Mustard Vinaigrette in this light menu. (Recipes, page 67.)*

Classic Charleston Breakfast Shrimp (page 60), a Lowcountry grits specialty, can be enjoyed any time of day.

A Creole favorite, Grillades and Grits (page 62), features squares of round steak braised in tomato gravy.

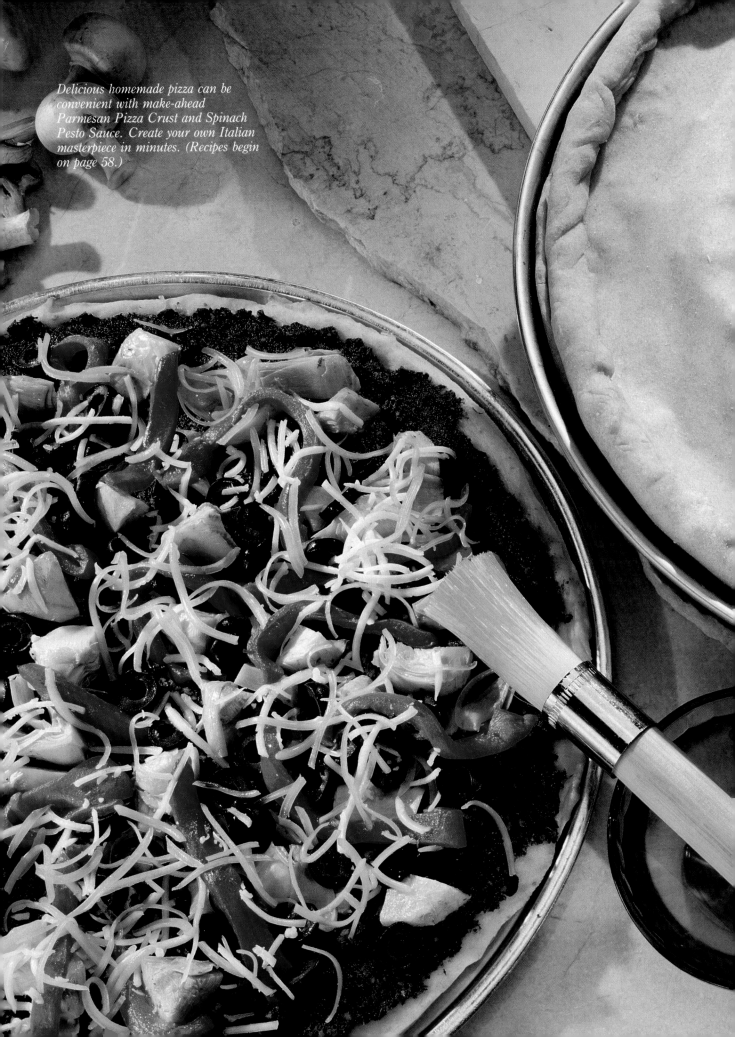

Delicious homemade pizza can be convenient with make-ahead Parmesan Pizza Crust and Spinach Pesto Sauce. Create your own Italian masterpiece in minutes. (Recipes begin on page 58.)

Exercising The Need To Knead

Orthopedic surgeon Harold Cannon, of Birmingham, Alabama, loves to bake bread several times a week. He's even planned family vacations around visits to European bakeries.

He has difficulty deciding which recipes are his favorites—there are so many. However, he shares a few family favorites.

■ Unbleached flour is all-purpose flour that has not had any bleaching agents added during processing. It is used interchangeably with all-purpose flour and is available at your local grocery store.

WALNUT BREAD

2 packages active dry yeast
¼ cup warm water (105° to 115°)
1½ cups milk
2 tablespoons olive oil
2 tablespoons honey
2 teaspoons salt
2 cups unbleached flour, divided
2 cups whole wheat flour
1 cup rye flour
1 cup coarsely chopped walnuts

Combine yeast and warm water in a 1-cup liquid measuring cup; let stand 5 minutes. Combine yeast mixture, milk, and next 3 ingredients in a large mixing bowl; beat at medium speed with an electric mixer until well blended. Combine 1½ cups unbleached flour and next 3 ingredients; gradually add to yeast mixture, beating after each addition.

Turn dough out onto a lightly floured surface; knead in remaining ½ cup unbleached flour, and continue kneading until smooth and elastic (about 5 minutes). Place in a well-greased bowl, turning to grease top. Cover and let rise in a warm place (85°), free from drafts, 1 hour or until doubled in bulk.

Punch dough down, and divide in half; shape each portion into a 6-inch ball, and place on a lightly greased baking sheet. Cover and let rise in a warm place (85°), free from drafts, 45 minutes or until doubled in bulk.

Using a sharp knife or razor blade, gently make a ¼-inch-deep cut in the shape of an X in the top of each loaf; bake at 375° for 20 to 25 minutes or until loaves sound hollow when tapped. Remove to wire racks to cool. Yield: 2 loaves.

RAISIN-WHOLE WHEAT BREAD

1½ cups raisins
2 packages active dry yeast
1¾ cups warm water
   (105° to 115°)
3 tablespoons honey
2 tablespoons vegetable oil
2 teaspoons salt
3 cups whole wheat flour
2 to 2½ cups unbleached flour,
   divided

Place raisins in a small saucepan; cover with water. Bring to a boil; cover, remove from heat, and let stand 15 minutes. Drain and pat dry. Set aside.

Combine yeast and 1¾ cups warm water in a 2-cup liquid measuring cup; let stand 5 minutes. Combine yeast mixture, honey, oil, and salt in a large bowl. Gradually add 3 cups whole wheat flour, mixing until blended. Gradually stir in 2¼ cups unbleached flour, stirring to make a soft dough. Stir in raisins.

Turn dough out onto a lightly floured surface, and knead until smooth and elastic (about 8 minutes), adding enough remaining ¼ cup unbleached flour to prevent dough from sticking to hands. Place in a well-greased bowl, turning to grease top. Cover and let rise in a warm place (85°), free from drafts, 1 hour or until doubled in bulk.

Punch dough down; turn out onto a lightly floured surface, and knead lightly 8 to 10 times. Divide dough in half. Shape each portion into a loaf. Place into 2 well-greased 8½- x 4½- x 3-inch loafpans.

Cover and let rise in a warm place (85°), free from drafts, 30 minutes or until doubled in bulk. Bake at 350° for 35 to 40 minutes or until loaves sound hollow when tapped. Remove from pans immediately; cool on wire racks. Yield: 2 loaves.

ONION FOCACCIA

3 packages active dry yeast
2 cups warm water (105° to 115°)
3 tablespoons olive oil
2 teaspoons salt
6 cups unbleached flour, divided
1 large purple onion, chopped
1 tablespoon olive oil

Combine yeast and warm water in a 2-cup liquid measuring cup; let stand 5 minutes. Combine yeast mixture, olive oil, and salt in a large bowl. Stir in 5 cups unbleached flour to make a stiff dough.

Turn dough out onto a lightly floured surface, and knead in enough remaining flour to make a firm dough.

Place in a well-greased bowl, turning to grease top. Cover and let rise in a warm place (85°), 45 minutes or until doubled in bulk.

Cook onion in olive oil in a large skillet over medium-high heat, stirring constantly, until tender. Set aside.

Punch dough down, and divide in half. Roll each half into a 12-inch circle, and place in a lightly greased 12-inch pizza pan.

Arrange onion evenly on each round; gently press into dough. Cover and let rise in a warm place (85°), free from drafts, 20 minutes. Using fingertips, press small indentations into dough; let rise an additional 10 minutes. Bake at 400° for 20 to 25 minutes or until golden. Remove to wire racks to cool.

Serve with antipasto meats, olive oil for dipping, and mustards. Yield: 2 (12-inch) bread rounds.

OLIVE BREAD

1 package active dry yeast
½ cup warm water (105° to 115°)
2 teaspoons sugar
1½ cups warm milk (105° to 115°)
½ cup cornmeal
1½ teaspoons salt
1 (6-ounce) can sliced ripe olives, drained
2 tablespoons olive oil
2 cups whole wheat flour
2 to 2½ cups unbleached flour, divided

Combine first 3 ingredients in a 1-cup liquid measuring cup; let stand 5 minutes. Combine yeast mixture, milk, and next 5 ingredients in a large bowl. Stir in 1 cup unbleached flour. Gradually stir in enough remaining unbleached flour to make a firm dough.

Turn dough out onto a lightly floured surface, and knead until smooth and elastic (about 3 minutes). Place dough in a well-greased bowl, turning to grease top. Cover and let rise in a warm place (85°), free from drafts, 1 hour or until dough is doubled in bulk.

Punch dough down, and divide in half; shape each portion into a 6-inch ball, and place on lightly greased baking sheets. (If desired, use a sharp knife or razor blade to make a ¼-inch-deep cut in the shape of an X in the top of each loaf.)

Cover and let rise in a warm place (85°), free from drafts, 30 minutes or until doubled in bulk. Bake at 350° for 35 to 40 minutes or until loaves sound hollow when tapped; remove to wire racks to cool. Yield: 2 loaves.

Hot Dog! Supper's Ready

Who says you can't teach an old dog new tricks? Taking that most humble (and popular) of foods, readers have come up with some terrific new ideas for serving hot dogs to the family.

MEXICAN FRANKS

10 (6-inch) corn tortillas
Vegetable oil
1 (15-ounce) can chili without beans
1 (8-ounce) can tomato sauce, divided
1 tablespoon minced onion
¼ teaspoon hot sauce
10 frankfurters
1 (4-ounce) can chopped green chiles, drained
1 cup (4 ounces) shredded Cheddar cheese

Fry tortillas, one at a time, in ¼-inch hot oil 3 to 5 seconds on each side or just until softened. Drain on paper towels. Set aside.

Combine chili, ¼ cup tomato sauce, onion, and hot sauce in a small bowl.

Place a frankfurter in center of each tortilla; top with 2 tablespoons chili mixture. Roll up, and place seam side down in a lightly greased 11- x 7- x 1½-inch baking dish. Repeat procedure with remaining tortillas; set aside. Combine remaining tomato sauce and remaining chili mixture; pour over tortillas.

Sprinkle with chiles. Cover and bake at 350° for 25 minutes. Uncover and sprinkle evenly with cheese; bake an additional 5 minutes. Yield: 10 servings.

HOT DOG PIZZAS

1 (11-ounce) can refrigerated buttermilk biscuits
¼ cup mayonnaise
¼ teaspoon garlic powder
1¼ cups (5 ounces) shredded mozzarella cheese, divided
3 frankfurters, sliced
⅓ cup sliced pimiento-stuffed olives (optional)

Separate biscuits, and press each into a 4-inch circle on lightly greased baking sheets. Combine mayonnaise and garlic powder; brush evenly over biscuit rounds. Sprinkle ¾ cup cheese evenly over mayonnaise mixture, and top with frankfurter slices and, if desired, olives. Bake at 400° for 5 minutes; sprinkle with remaining ½ cup cheese, and bake an additional 5 minutes or until lightly browned and cheese melts. Serve immediately. Yield: 10 servings.

HOT DOG SUPPER

8 frankfurters
8 hot dog buns
Vegetable cooking spray
Mustard
Catsup
1 small onion, chopped
1 (15.5-ounce) can chili with beans
½ cup (2 ounces) shredded Cheddar cheese

Cook frankfurters 5 minutes in boiling water to cover; drain. Place in buns, and arrange in a 13- x 9- x 2-inch baking dish coated with cooking spray. Top each with mustard and catsup, and sprinkle evenly with onion. Spoon on chili, spreading to cover frankfurters. Bake at 350° for 20 minutes or until thoroughly heated. Sprinkle with cheese, and bake an additional 5 minutes. Yield: 8 servings.

Jennifer Cairns
Birmingham, Alabama

CORN DOG BITES

1 cup self-rising flour
⅔ cup cornmeal
1 tablespoon sugar
2 tablespoons vegetable oil
1 large egg, lightly beaten
1 cup buttermilk
1 (16-ounce) package frankfurters
Vegetable oil
Mustard (optional)
Catsup (optional)

Combine first 3 ingredients in a large bowl. Combine 2 tablespoons oil, egg, and buttermilk; stir into flour mixture, mixing well. Cut each frankfurter into 5 pieces. Dip each piece into batter, coating completely. (Use wooden picks to aid in dipping.)

Frank Facts

■ Whether labeled hot dogs, frankfurters, franks, or weiners, the products are basically the same—precooked, smoked sausage made of chopped meat or poultry and seasonings.
■ You have a choice—hot dogs are now made from chicken, turkey, beef, or pork, as well as a combination of these. Specialty stores in some areas even sell vegetable hot dogs.
■ Read the label—hot dogs vary greatly in fat content.

Pour oil to depth of 3 to 4 inches into a Dutch oven; heat to 375°. Fry pieces until golden, turning once; drain on paper towels. Serve immediately with mustard or catsup, if desired. Yield: 8 to 10 servings.

Frances Christopher
Iron Station, North Carolina

So Glad You Dropped By

Don't be caught off guard again without goodies to serve unexpected guests. With these easy recipes, you can stock your kitchen by tomorrow afternoon for unexpected company. Each recipe uses five or fewer ingredients, and some of the recipes can be made ahead and frozen up to two months. Others can be mixed together at the last second using items you keep on hand.

■ You can keep this savory appetizer at room temperature in an airtight container up to two weeks, and pull it out for company at a moment's notice.

PEPPER PECANS

¼ cup golden Worcestershire sauce
2 tablespoons butter or margarine, melted
¼ teaspoon hot sauce
⅛ teaspoon pepper
2 cups pecan halves

Combine first 4 ingredients in a medium bowl. Stir in pecans, and let stand 30 minutes; drain. Spread pecans in a single layer in a 13- x 9- x 2-inch pan. Bake at 250° for 35 minutes, stirring every 10 minutes. (You may store pecans up to 2 weeks in an airtight container.) Yield: 2 cups.

Romanza O. Johnson
Bowling Green, Kentucky

■ Keep Cream Cheese Mints in the freezer; thaw and serve on a crystal platter or silver tray for a traditional treat with a twist. This version of party mints is soft, creamy, and lightly coated with sugar.

CREAM CHEESE MINTS

½ (8-ounce) package cream cheese, softened
1 (16-ounce) package powdered sugar, sifted
⅛ teaspoon peppermint oil or
  ½ teaspoon peppermint extract
2 or 3 drops of green food coloring (optional)
Granulated sugar

Beat cream cheese and powdered sugar at medium speed with an electric mixer until smooth. Add peppermint oil and, if desired, food coloring. Shape into ½-inch balls; roll in granulated sugar. Chill 1 to 2 hours or until firm. (You may press them into candy molds before chilling, if desired.) Yield: 6 dozen.

Note: Mints may be frozen in an airtight container up to two months. Peppermint oil is available at drugstores and cake decorating supply stores.

Nancy P. Chawk
St. Petersburg, Florida

■ Served with bagels or gingersnaps, this last-minute treat is great for a midmorning snack or in the afternoon with hot tea.

FRUITED CREAM CHEESE SPREAD

1 (8-ounce) container soft cream cheese
1 (8-ounce) can crushed pineapple, drained
½ cup sliced fresh strawberries

Combine all ingredients in a small bowl, stirring well until blended. Serve with bagels or gingersnaps. Yield: 2 cups.

■ Place these confections in a single layer on a cookie sheet and freeze just until firm. Transfer to an airtight container or a heavy-duty, zip-top plastic bag. To serve, thaw fudge balls, and place in miniature paper liners. (You can also make a day ahead and simply chill until serving.)

STRAWBERRY FUDGE BALLS

1 (8-ounce) package cream cheese, softened
1 (6-ounce) package semisweet chocolate morsels, melted
¾ cup vanilla wafer crumbs
¼ cup strawberry preserves
½ cup almonds, toasted and finely chopped

Beat cream cheese at medium speed with an electric mixer until creamy. Add melted chocolate, beating until smooth. Stir in vanilla wafer crumbs and strawberry preserves; cover and chill 1 hour.

Shape cream cheese mixture into 1-inch balls. Roll fudge balls in chopped almonds. Store fudge balls in the refrigerator. (You may freeze fudge balls up to 2 months.) Yield: 4 dozen.   *Erma Jackson*
Huntsville, Alabama

■ Containing just three ingredients, this sweet fruit-and-cheese appetizer spread can go from cupboard to coffee table in less than five minutes.

PEAR-CREAM CHEESE SPREAD

¼ cup pear preserves
1½ teaspoons prepared horseradish
1 (3-ounce) package cream cheese, softened

Combine pear preserves and horseradish in a small bowl; stir well. Spoon preserves mixture over cream cheese. Serve with date-nut bread, gingersnaps, or crackers. Yield: 4 appetizer servings.

Treats That Travel

Building sand castles, hiking through the woods, or just playing outdoors makes kids—and adults—hungrier. For spring-break excursions, we've selected some take-along treats.

For traveling, pack goodies in a sturdy container that won't crush easily, such as a tin, heavy cardboard box, or plastic container.

TOFFEE CRUNCH COOKIES

½ cup butter or margarine, softened
1 (18.25-ounce) package butter recipe yellow cake mix with pudding
2 large eggs
1 tablespoon water
1 (6-ounce) package almond brickle chips
½ to 1 cup chopped pecans

Beat butter at medium speed with an electric mixer until creamy; add cake mix, eggs, and water, beating mixture until blended. Stir in brickle chips and pecans.

Drop cookie dough by tablepoonfuls onto ungreased cookie sheets. Bake at 350° for 8 to 10 minutes or until edges are browned. (Top will look moist.) Remove to wire racks to cool. Yield: 4 dozen.   *Kay Franklin*
Hoover, Alabama

CHOCOLATE-PEANUT CRISPIES

½ cup sugar
½ cup light corn syrup
1 cup chunky peanut butter
6 cups crisp corn, rice, and wheat cereal
½ cup chopped dry-roasted peanuts
1 cup semisweet chocolate mini-morsels

Combine sugar and corn syrup in a Dutch oven; cook over medium heat,

stirring constantly, until sugar dissolves and mixture begins to boil. Remove from heat, and add peanut butter, stirring until smooth. Gradually stir in cereal and peanuts. Stir in chocolate mini-morsels, and press into a lightly greased 15- x 10- x 1-inch jelly-roll pan. Let cool, and cut into 1½-inch squares. Yield: 5 dozen.
Marilyn Darby
Tunica, Mississippi

CRISPY COCONUT-OATMEAL COOKIES

1 cup shortening
1 cup sugar
1 cup firmly packed brown sugar
2 large eggs
1 teaspoon vanilla extract
2 cups all-purpose flour
1 teaspoon baking soda
½ teaspoon baking powder
½ teaspoon salt
2 cups regular oats, uncooked
2 cups crisp rice cereal
1 cup flaked coconut

Beat shortening and sugars at medium speed with an electric mixer until blended; add eggs and vanilla, beating well. Combine flour and next 3 ingredients; add to shortening mixture, mixing well. Stir in oats and remaining ingredients. Shape into 1-inch balls, and place 2 inches apart on lightly greased cookie sheets; flatten slightly with a fork. Bake at 350° for 12 minutes. Transfer to wire racks to cool. Yield: 7 dozen.   *Mildred Matthews*
Bartlesville, Oklahoma

Tip: *To loosen cookies left on a cookie sheet too long, return to 350° oven for 2 minutes, and remove the cookies from cookie sheet immediately.*

Sunshine In Every Bite

Maybe it was the first time you had real lemonade made from fresh lemon juice. Or maybe it was when you first squeezed a wedge of lemon over grilled, fresh-from-the-ocean fish and tasted the difference. Somewhere along the way, you fell in love with the flavor of sunshine in this fruit.

Not only are lemons great in dishes from appetizers to desserts, they also make quick, easy garnishes for meals (see box on this page).

LEMON-EGG DROP SOUP

6 cups water
6 teaspoons chicken-flavored
  bouillon granules
1 teaspoon grated lemon rind
⅓ cup fresh lemon juice
½ cup sliced fresh mushrooms
2 cloves garlic
2 teaspoons soy sauce
⅛ teaspoon ground white pepper
2 large eggs, lightly beaten
Garnishes: sliced lemons, chopped
  green onions

Combine first 7 ingredients in a large saucepan; bring to a boil. Cover, reduce heat, and simmer 15 minutes. Stir in white pepper. Slowly pour in beaten eggs, stirring constantly, until eggs form lacy strands. Immediately remove from heat; remove and discard garlic. Ladle soup into bowls, and garnish, if desired. Yield: 5¾ cups.

LUSCIOUS LEMON CAKE

8 egg yolks
¾ cup butter or margarine,
  softened
1¼ cups sugar
2½ cups sifted cake flour
1 tablespoon baking powder
¼ teaspoon salt
¾ cup milk
1 teaspoon grated lemon rind
1 teaspoon fresh lemon juice
1 teaspoon vanilla extract
Lemon Frosting
Garnishes: lemon wedges, fresh
  mint leaves

Beat egg yolks at high speed with an electric mixer 4 minutes or until thick and pale. Set aside.

Beat butter at medium speed with an electric mixer until creamy; gradually add sugar, beating well. Add egg yolks, beating well.

Combine flour, baking powder, and salt; add to butter mixture alternately with milk, beginning and ending with flour mixture. Mix after each addition. Stir in lemon rind, juice, and vanilla.

Spoon batter into 3 greased and floured 8-inch round cakepans. Bake at 375° for 18 to 20 minutes or until a wooden pick inserted in center comes out clean. Cool in pans on wire racks 10 minutes; remove from pans, and cool completely on wire racks.

Spoon about 1 cup Lemon Frosting into a decorating bag fitted with a large tip; set aside. Spread remaining frosting between layers and on top and sides of cake. Pipe 8 frosting rosettes around top edge of cake, and garnish, if desired. Chill until serving time. Yield: one 3-layer cake.

Lemon Frosting

1 cup butter or margarine,
  softened
2 teaspoons grated lemon rind
⅓ cup lemon juice
8 cups sifted powdered sugar
1 to 2 tablespoons half-and-half
  (optional)

Beat butter at medium speed with an electric mixer until creamy; stir in lemon rind and juice. (Mixture will appear curdled.) Gradually add sugar; beat at high speed 4 minutes or until spreading consistency. Gradually add half-and-half, if needed. Yield: 4 cups.
Shelby W. Adkins
Penhook, Virginia

Great Looks for Lemons

For an easy, inexpensive garnish, try lemons. Look in kitchen shops for a **citrus zester** or a **citrus peeler.** Pull the zester lengthwise down lemons or other citrus fruits, and you get fine, lacy strands of rind to sprinkle decoratively on foods. Pull the peeler around the fruit to make continuous strips of rind to loop or drape over dishes or tie around vegetables, such as green beans or carrots, making individual "bundles."

With an ordinary **paring knife,** you can make wedges and slices quickly. Cut slices in halves or fourths for smaller garnishes, or serve lemon halves wrapped in cheesecloth and tied with ribbon or kitchen twine for squeezing juice on fish or vegetables. (Cheesecloth holds the seeds in while letting the lemon juice out.)

LEMON MERINGUE TORTE WITH RASPBERRY SAUCE

4 large eggs, separated
1 cup sugar
½ teaspoon vanilla extract
½ cup sugar
1 tablespoon lemon rind
3 tablespoons lemon juice
⅔ cup whipping cream
2 tablespoons sugar
1 teaspoon vanilla extract (optional)
Raspberry Sauce

Cover 2 baking sheets with unglazed brown paper (not recycled paper). Draw 3 (8-inch) circles on paper, and set aside.

Beat egg whites at high speed with an electric mixer until foamy. Gradually add 1 cup sugar, 1 tablespoon at a time, beating until stiff peaks form and sugar dissolves (2 to 4 minutes). Stir in ½ teaspoon vanilla. Spread meringue on brown paper circles. Bake at 250° for 1 hour; turn off heat, and leave meringues in oven with door closed at least 1 hour. Carefully peel off meringues from brown paper; let cool completely on wire racks.

Combine egg yolks, ½ cup sugar, lemon rind, and juice in a small non-aluminum heavy saucepan. Cook over medium heat, stirring constantly, until mixture thickens (about 6 minutes). Set aside to cool.

Beat whipping cream at high speed with an electric mixer until foamy; gradually add 2 tablespoons sugar, beating until soft peaks form. Stir in 1 teaspoon vanilla, if desired. Fold into egg yolk mixture; spread between meringue layers. Refrigerate 1 hour, and serve with Raspberry Sauce. Yield: one 8-inch torte.

Raspberry Sauce

2 (10-ounce) packages frozen raspberries, thawed
¼ cup sugar
2 tablespoons cornstarch

Place raspberries in container of an electric blender; process until smooth. Pour through a wire-mesh strainer into a bowl, pressing raspberries against sides of strainer with back of a spoon to squeeze out juice. Discard pulp and seeds. Combine raspberry juice, sugar, and cornstarch in a saucepan. Cook over medium heat, stirring constantly, until mixture comes to a boil. Boil, stirring constantly, 1 minute. Yield: 1¾ cups.

Joan Curd
Memphis, Tennessee

Citrus Savvy

■ When buying any type of fresh citrus, always look for fruits that have smooth and blemish-free skins. Indications of a high juice content are that the fruits feel firm and are heavy for their size.

■ When you use fresh lemons for cooking, remember that one medium lemon will yield 2 to 4 tablespoons juice and 1 tablespoon grated rind.

■ Whenever a recipe calls for both the rind and the juice of citrus fruit, wash and grate the fruit before juicing.

■ Submerge an unpeeled lemon or orange in hot water for 15 minutes before squeezing to yield more juice.

Amazingly Gracious: Luncheon Is Served

Easy and elegant, that's our springtime menu. From the make-ahead chicken rolls to the nose-tickling champagne oranges, our menu is perfect for a bridesmaids' luncheon or any gathering of friends. Keep in mind, too, that the recipes all double easily if you're planning on serving more than six guests.

A MAKE-AHEAD LUNCHEON FOR SIX

Pesto-Stuffed Chicken Rolls
Lemon Vegetables
Green salad with vinaigrette
Champagne Oranges
or
Daiquiri Pound Cake
Coffee

PESTO-STUFFED CHICKEN ROLLS

6 large skinned and boned chicken breast halves
¼ teaspoon salt
¼ teaspoon pepper
1 (3-ounce) package cream cheese, softened
¼ cup commercial pesto
½ cup finely chopped sweet red pepper
¾ cup corn flake crumbs
½ teaspoon paprika
Vegetable cooking spray
Garnish: fresh basil sprigs

Place each piece of chicken between 2 sheets of plastic wrap; flatten to ¼-inch thickness, using a meat mallet or rolling pin. Sprinkle with salt and pepper; set aside.

Combine cream cheese, pesto, and sweet red pepper in a small bowl, stirring with a fork until smooth. Spread 2 tablespoons over each chicken breast; roll up lengthwise, securing with wooden picks.

Combine corn flake crumbs and paprika; dredge chicken rolls in crumb mixture. Place in an 11- x 7- x 1½-inch baking dish coated with cooking spray. Cover and refrigerate 8 hours.

Remove from refrigerator, and let stand at room temperature 30 minutes. Bake, uncovered, at 350° for 35 minutes; let stand 10 minutes. Remove wooden picks, and slice into 1-inch rounds. (An electric knife works best.) Garnish, if desired. Yield: 6 servings.

Note: To make and bake on the same day, prepare according to above directions, omitting the 8-hour refrigeration time.

LEMON VEGETABLES

4 small new potatoes, unpeeled and sliced
2 carrots, cut into thin strips
2 yellow squash, cut into thin strips
1 zucchini, sliced
⅓ cup butter or margarine, melted
1 tablespoon grated lemon rind
3 tablespoons lemon juice
¼ teaspoon salt
⅛ teaspoon pepper

Arrange potato and carrot in a vegetable steamer over boiling water; cover and steam 8 minutes. Add yellow squash and zucchini; cover and steam 2 minutes or until crisp-tender. Place vegetables in a serving bowl. Combine butter and remaining ingredients; pour over vegetables, tossing gently. Yield: 6 servings.

CHAMPAGNE ORANGES

½ cup sugar
½ cup orange marmalade
1½ cups champagne *
8 large navel oranges, peeled and sectioned
½ cup slivered almonds, toasted

Combine sugar and orange marmalade in a small saucepan; cook over medium heat until sugar dissolves. Cool slightly. Combine sugar mixture, champagne, and orange sections, stirring gently. Cover and refrigerate 8 hours. To serve, spoon orange sections into individual compotes or dishes, and sprinkle with almonds. Yield: 7 cups.

* 1½ cups sparkling white grape juice may be substituted for champagne.
Louise Bainter
Grove, Oklahoma

DAIQUIRI POUND CAKE

1 cup butter or margarine, softened
½ cup shortening
3 cups sugar
5 large eggs
3 cups all-purpose flour
½ teaspoon baking powder
1 cup milk
2 tablespoons rum
1 tablespoon grated lime rind
2 teaspoons lime juice
1½ teaspoons vanilla extract
½ teaspoon lemon juice
Daiquiri Glaze

Beat butter and shortening at medium speed with an electric mixer about 2 minutes or until soft and creamy. Gradually add sugar, beating at medium speed 5 to 7 minutes. Add eggs, one at a time, beating just until yellow disappears.

Combine flour and baking powder; add to creamed mixture alternately with milk, beginning and ending with flour mixture. Mix at lowest speed just until blended after each addition. Stir in rum and next 4 ingredients.

Spoon batter into a greased and floured 10-inch tube pan. Bake at 325° for 1 hour and 30 minutes or until a wooden pick inserted in center comes out clean. Cool in pan on a wire rack 10 to 15 minutes; remove from pan. While warm, prick top of cake with a wooden pick; pour Daiquiri Glaze over cake. Let cool completely on a wire rack. Yield: one 10-inch cake.

Daiquiri Glaze

¼ cup sugar
¼ cup butter or margarine
2 tablespoons lime juice
3 tablespoons rum

Combine sugar, butter, and lime juice in a small saucepan; bring to a boil. Boil, stirring constantly, 1 minute. Remove from heat, and stir in rum. Yield: ½ cup.
Rosa M. Hinton
Augusta, Georgia

From Our Kitchen To Yours

How do you determine if food that you planned to cook tonight thawing in the refrigerator can be safely refrozen?

According to the USDA, if food feels very cold and has not been held longer than two days at refrigerator temperatures, it is usually safe to refreeze (see chart on page 84). Because partial thawing and refreezing reduce quality, label containers "refrozen," and use within eight weeks.

It's simple enough to refreeze a package or two of partially thawed foods, but what steps can be taken when the gusting winds of a spring storm drop limbs on power lines, cutting electricity for days? Everything in the freezer slowly begins to thaw, and the foods in the refrigerator warm up. Do they have to be thrown out? There's no need for frustration when you follow these guidelines.

Emergency Guidelines

Keep the door closed.

A full upright or chest freezer keeps items frozen about 48 hours; each frozen package acts like a block of ice, keeping the items around it cool. With fewer blocks to retain the cold, a half-full freezer keeps foods frozen about 24 hours. Provide extra insulation by covering the freezer with blankets or quilts, making sure the air vents on the outside of the freezer aren't blocked.

After a power failure, foods stored in the refrigerator will remain cool four to six hours, depending on your kitchen's temperature.

Move food to another freezer or refrigerator.

If power can't be returned before foods warm up, store items in a friend's freezer or refrigerator. Transport food in ice chests, insulated cardboard boxes, or wrapped in thick layers of newspapers and blankets.

Add dry ice to the freezer.

To locate a source in your community, check the Yellow Pages under "Ice—Dry" or "Carbonic Gas." Twenty-five pounds of dry ice keeps a full 10-cubic-foot freezer cold for three to four days and a half-full freezer cold for two to three days. Place heavy cardboard on top of frozen packages, and put the dry ice on top of the cardboard. (Never touch dry ice with bare hands, and don't try to cut or chip it yourself. Ask the dry ice company to cut the ice, if necessary, and to wrap each piece in newspaper.) Don't open the freezer again unless it's necessary to move food or to add more dry ice.

To help keep refrigerated foods cold longer, add bags or blocks of regular ice to the refrigerator shelves.

Keep or Discard?

Appearance and odor are never reliable indicators of safety. Food may look and smell fine, but if it's been at room temperature too long, food poisoning bacteria may have multiplied in the food. Also never taste food to determine if it's okay.

Instead, use the guidelines in the food safety chart below. Foods such as meats, poultry, seafood, eggs, dairy products, and vegetables (or any dishes made with these products) are most likely to spoil.

Hooray—Power Is ON

When power is restored, turn the adjustable temperature control of the freezer and refrigerator to the coldest positions. The appliances will run continuously, and foods will refreeze or chill more quickly. Place warmer packages against the refrigerated surface, leaving room for air to circulate around them. Don't open the refrigerator or freezer unless necessary. After food is well frozen (or chilled), turn the temperature controls to their normal settings.

Quick Reference for Food Safety

Freezer Food	What to Do
Beef, veal, lamb, pork, poultry, ground meats, meat casseroles, pizzas, cheesecakes, vegetables, cooked foods, custard pies, cream-filled pastries	Refreeze if it contains ice crystals or feels very cold. Throw out if thawed and has been above 40° for two hours.
Breads, doughnuts, cookies, cakes, nuts	Refreeze if no signs of mold growth.
Fruits, fruit juices	Refreeze if no sour odor or signs of mold growth.
Raw seafood	Throw out if thawed and above 40° for two hours or more. Do not refreeze; cook immediately if very cold.

Refrigerated Food	What to Do
Milk, cream, sour cream, eggs, egg substitute, custard, yogurt, pudding, cottage cheese, soft cheeses, casseroles, soups, stews, seafood, poultry, ham, lunchmeat, pasta salads, frankfurters, meat pizzas, vegetables, vegetable juices, refrigerated cookie dough, cream-filled pastries	Keep if cold or held above 40° less than two hours. Throw out if held above 40° more than two hours.
Butter, margarine, hard or processed cheeses, fruit juices, fresh fruit, herbs, fruit pies, peanut butter, jelly, vinegar-based salad dressings, taco and barbecue sauces, mustard, catsup, pickles, olives, relish, coconut, dried fruit	Keep if quality hasn't been affected.
Mayonnaise, mayonnaise-based salad dressing, tartar sauce, prepared horseradish	Throw out if above 50° for more than eight hours.

APRIL

To celebrate spring, invite the neighbors over and fire up the grill! Add a new flavor sensation to grilled meat, poultry, and seafood with our marinades and herb and spice rubs. In the "Light & Easy" special section, we offer recipes and cooking tips for the health- and calorie-conscious. As for sweets, try angel food cake with a new twist. This heavenly confection goes from simple to spectacular when it's layered with fruit, filled with ice cream, or floated in a pool of minty chocolate sauce.

Angel Food Spectacular

Ahhh . . . angel food. With light-as-a-cloud texture and delicately sweet flavor, it's certainly one of our most heavenly cakes. And with our new ideas, it's easy to make. Just use a commercially prepared cake or a mix; then pair it with one of our suggestions to make a spectacular dessert.

Add a fluffy fruit custard for Pineapple Angel Food Trifle. And who wouldn't be delighted with Triple Mint Ice-Cream Angel Dessert, which boasts colorful layers of cool mint.

Share these celestial confections with family and friends. Even Gabriel will sing your praises.

TRIPLE MINT ICE-CREAM ANGEL DESSERT
(pictured on page 1)

1 (10-inch) angel food cake
4 cups chocolate-mint ice cream, softened and divided
2 cups pink peppermint ice cream, softened
Whipped Cream Frosting
Chocolate-Mint Sauce

Split cake horizontally into 4 equal layers. Place bottom cake layer on a serving plate; spread top of layer with half of chocolate-mint ice cream to within ½ inch from edge. Top with second cake layer; cover and freeze 45 minutes or until firm. Spread second cake layer with pink peppermint ice cream. Add third cake layer; cover and freeze 45 minutes or until firm. Spread third layer with remaining chocolate-mint ice cream, and top with remaining cake layer; cover and freeze until firm.
 Spread Whipped Cream Frosting on top and sides of cake. Cover and freeze up to 12 hours, if desired; let stand at room temperature 15 to 20 minutes before serving. Serve with Chocolate-Mint Sauce. Yield: one 10-inch cake.

Whipped Cream Frosting

3 cups whipping cream
3 tablespoons powdered sugar
1½ teaspoons vanilla extract

Beat whipping cream at low speed with an electric mixer until thickened; add sugar and vanilla, beating until firm peaks form. Yield: 6 cups.

Chocolate-Mint Sauce

¾ cup half-and-half
1 (10-ounce) package mint chocolate morsels
1½ cups miniature marshmallows
¼ teaspoon salt
1 teaspoon vanilla extract

Heat half-and-half in a heavy saucepan over low heat. Stir in chocolate morsels, marshmallows, and salt; cook, stirring constantly, until chocolate and marshmallows melt. Remove from heat; stir in vanilla. Yield: 1½ cups.

Note: Dip knife in hot water to make cutting cake easier.   *Jan Carlton Virginia Beach, Virginia*

ANGEL CAKE SURPRISE

1 (10-inch) angel food cake
½ cup semisweet chocolate morsels
3 cups whipping cream, divided
1 tablespoon Chambord or other raspberry-flavored liqueur *
¼ cup sifted powdered sugar
Garnishes: grated chocolate, fresh raspberries

Slice off top one-third of cake; set aside. Using a sharp knife, hollow out center of remaining cake, leaving a 1-inch shell; reserve cake pieces for another use. Place cake shell on serving plate, and set aside.
 Melt chocolate morsels in a heavy saucepan over low heat, stirring occasionally, until smooth; remove from heat, and cool.
 Beat 1 cup whipping cream until firm peaks form; fold in liqueur and melted chocolate. Spoon into cake shell; place top one-third of cake over filling, pressing firmly.
 Beat remaining 2 cups whipping cream until foamy; add powdered sugar, beating until firm peaks form. Spread over top and sides of cake; chill up to 8 hours. Garnish, if desired. Yield: one 10-inch cake.

* 1 tablespoon Cointreau or other orange-flavored liqueur may be substituted for Chambord.   *Louise Jackson Shreveport, Louisiana*

PINEAPPLE ANGEL FOOD TRIFLE

1 (16-ounce) can pineapple tidbits, undrained
2 (3.4-ounce) packages vanilla instant pudding mix
3 cups milk
1 (8-ounce) carton sour cream
1 (10-inch) angel food cake, cut into 1-inch cubes
1 (8-ounce) carton frozen whipped topping, thawed
Garnishes: mint leaves, canned pineapple slices

Drain pineapple tidbits, reserving 1 cup juice; set aside. Combine instant pudding mix, ½ cup reserved juice, and milk in a large mixing bowl; beat at low speed with an electric mixer 2 minutes or until thickened. Fold in sour cream and pineapple tidbits.

Place one-third of cake cubes in bottom of a 16-cup glass bowl; drizzle with 2 to 3 tablespoons remaining reserved pineapple juice. Spoon one-third of pudding mixture over cake. Repeat procedure twice, ending with pudding mixture. Cover and chill at least 3 hours.

Just before serving, spread top with whipped topping. Garnish, if desired. Yield: 12 servings.

Devilish Ideas For All Those Eggs

Once the children's Easter festivities subside, parents are left holding the basket, wondering what to do with all those dyed eggs. Why not make deviled eggs?

Just add a few ingredients to the yolks, and pipe them back into the whites with a pastry bag if you're feeling fancy. (If the filling has hot and spicy ingredients, the eggs are "deviled"; if not, they're "stuffed.")

EASY STUFFED EGGS

6 large hard-cooked eggs
3 tablespoons sandwich spread
1½ tablespoons mayonnaise or salad dressing
¼ teaspoon salt
⅛ teaspoon pepper
Paprika

Slice eggs in half lengthwise, and carefully remove yolks. Mash yolks; add sandwich spread and next 3 ingredients, stirring until smooth. Spoon or pipe into egg whites. Sprinkle with paprika. Yield: 12 servings.
Mary Pappas
Richmond, Virginia

CURRIED DEVILED EGGS

6 large hard-cooked eggs
3 tablespoons mayonnaise or salad dressing
1 teaspoon Worcestershire sauce
½ teaspoon curry powder
½ teaspoon ground red pepper
⅛ teaspoon salt
Paprika
Garnish: sliced pimiento-stuffed olives

Slice eggs in half lengthwise, and carefully remove yolks. Mash yolks; add mayonnaise and next 4 ingredients, stirring until smooth. Spoon or pipe into egg whites. Sprinkle with paprika, and garnish, if desired. Yield: 12 servings.
Sandi Pichon
Slidell, Louisiana

CHILE-CHEESE DEVILED EGGS

12 large hard-cooked eggs
1 (3-ounce) package cream cheese, softened
1 (4-ounce) can chopped green chiles, undrained
2 to 3 tablespoons milk
¼ teaspoon salt

Slice eggs in half lengthwise, and carefully remove yolks. Position knife blade in food processor bowl; add yolks, cream cheese, and remaining ingredients. Process until smooth, stopping once to scrape down sides. Spoon or pipe into egg whites. Yield: 24 servings.

BLUE CHEESE STUFFED EGGS

12 large hard-cooked eggs
½ cup crumbled blue cheese
½ cup sour cream
1 tablespoon white vinegar
¼ teaspoon salt (optional)

Slice eggs in half lengthwise, and carefully remove yolks. Position knife

blade in food processor bowl; add yolks, blue cheese, and remaining ingredients. Process until smooth, stopping once to scrape down sides. Spoon or pipe into egg whites. Yield: 24 servings.
Frances Christopher
Iron Station, North Carolina

HERB-SOUR CREAM STUFFED EGGS

8 large hard-cooked eggs
⅓ to ½ cup sour cream
2 to 3 tablespoons finely chopped fresh or 2 to 3 teaspoons freeze-dried chives
1 to 2 tablespoons finely chopped fresh or 1 to 2 teaspoons dried dillweed
2 teaspoons white wine vinegar
¼ teaspoon salt
⅛ teaspoon ground white pepper
Garnish: fresh parsley

Slice eggs in half lengthwise, and carefully remove yolks. Mash yolks; add sour cream and remaining ingredients, stirring until smooth. Spoon or pipe into egg whites. Garnish, if desired. Yield: 16 servings.

It's All in the Timing

Here's how to make perfect hard-cooked eggs:

Place eggs in a single layer in a saucepan. Add enough cold water to measure at least one inch over eggs. Cover and bring just to a boil. Remove from heat. Let stand, covered, 15 to 17 minutes. Pour off water, and run cold water over eggs to stop cooking, thus preventing darkening of the yolks.

To remove shell, gently tap egg all over, roll between hands to loosen shell, and hold under cold running water as you peel.

HAM DEVILS

6 large hard-cooked eggs
2 tablespoons mayonnaise or salad dressing
2 tablespoons cream cheese, softened
1 teaspoon prepared mustard
1 teaspoon lemon juice
3 tablespoons finely chopped cooked ham
2¼ teaspoons chopped fresh or ¾ teaspoon dried dillweed
½ teaspoon caraway seeds
⅛ teaspoon salt
Garnish: fresh dillweed sprigs

Slice eggs in half lengthwise, and carefully remove yolks. Mash yolks; add mayonnaise and next 3 ingredients, stirring until smooth. Stir in ham and next 3 ingredients. Spoon into egg whites; garnish, if desired. Yield: 12 servings.

Trenda Leigh
Richmond, Virginia

SWEET DEVILED EGGS

8 large hard-cooked eggs
1 tablespoon sugar
2 tablespoons prepared mustard
2 tablespoons half-and-half
1 tablespoon white vinegar
½ teaspoon salt
Paprika
Garnish: fresh parsley

Slice eggs in half lengthwise, and carefully remove yolks. Mash yolks; add sugar and next 4 ingredients, stirring until smooth. Spoon or pipe into egg whites. Sprinkle with paprika, and garnish, if desired. Yield: 16 servings.

Adelyne Smith
Dunnville, Kentucky

Note: Can't find an egg-dyeing kit? Just mix 1 cup water, ¼ cup white vinegar, and a few drops of food coloring for a homemade version.

Easter At The White House

On the Monday after Easter, lots of parents carefully tuck baskets into closets until next year. But in Washington, D.C., the largest Southern celebration of bunnies, eggs, and pastels is just hopping to life. And it's at the nation's home— 1600 Pennsylvania Avenue.

Children eight years old and under (and up to two adults per child) are welcome to roam the South Lawn of the White House, enjoying a colorful palette of Easter characters and activities. Everyone looks forward to the main attraction—the Easter Egg Roll.

First Lady Dolley Madison introduced the game during her husband's presidency. After learning that Egyptian youngsters playfully rolled colored eggs along the ground near the Pyramids, she adapted the idea for American children. And so began a grand tradition.

At the finish line, players turn in their hard-cooked eggs (White House chefs dye more than 25,000 for the day) for a souvenir wooden egg signed by the President and First Lady.

Easter at Your House

If you can't visit the White House, these ideas will come in handy for your own Easter party for children.

■ **Egg Roll:** Create a few racing "lanes" by laying rope or twine on the grass, and mark start and finish lines. Brighten the finish line with festive helium-filled balloons and an Easter basket filled with inexpensive prizes. Give each child a dyed Easter egg and a kitchen spoon, and blow a whistle to start the race. Declare each child in the race a winner with a prize at the finish line.

■ **Egg Race:** Using the same lanes created for the Egg Roll, place a dyed egg on the starting line in each lane. Have children kneel at the starting line, hands clasped behind their back, and push the egg to the finish with their nose.

■ **Egg Hunt:** The White House version of Easter egg hunting confines the activity to a small area, making supervising children easier. Section off a small spot in your yard, and spread fresh pine straw (or hay) over the area. Conceal dyed or filled plastic eggs in the straw. Let children in, a few at a time, for two or three minutes of hunting. Hide more eggs between groups.

■ **Storytelling:** After children have played games, serve them refreshments and read them a story about Easter.

Light & Easy

Weed Out Menus For Spring

Spring is the season of new beginnings, so break the cycle of repetitious recipes—clean out heavyweight standbys from your menus, and replace them with healthier variations your family will enjoy.

The following is a collection of favorite recipes with a new twist on ingredients or preparation techniques that reduce both calories and fat. Don't be surprised if these are better than the traditional versions.

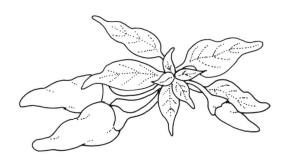

CHILI

Vegetable cooking spray
1 pound 93% or 96% low-fat ground beef
1 cup chopped onion
1 cup chopped green pepper
6 cloves garlic, minced
2 (14½-ounce) cans no-salt-added stewed tomatoes, undrained and chopped
1 (16-ounce) can no-salt-added kidney beans, drained
1 (8-ounce) can no-salt-added tomato sauce
1 (1-ounce) envelope onion soup mix
1 cup water
3 tablespoons chili powder
1 tablespoon paprika
1¼ teaspoons hot sauce

Coat a Dutch oven with cooking spray; place over medium-high heat until hot. Add ground beef; brown, stirring until it crumbles. Drain and pat dry with paper towels. Wipe drippings from Dutch oven; recoat Dutch oven with cooking spray. Add onion, green pepper, and garlic; cook over medium heat, stirring constantly, until tender. Add ground beef, stewed tomatoes, and remaining ingredients. Bring to a boil; cover, reduce heat, and simmer 30 minutes, stirring occasionally. Yield: 9 servings (278 calories [24% from fat] per 1-cup serving).

□ 18.8g protein, 7.4g fat (2.6g saturated), 38g carbohydrate, 3.7g fiber, 31mg cholesterol, 468mg sodium, and 137mg calcium. *Joan A. Lee Ocean Springs, Mississippi*

GREEN BEANS WITH MUSHROOMS

1 pound fresh green beans
Vegetable cooking spray
1 teaspoon reduced-calorie margarine
1 cup sliced fresh mushrooms
2 cloves garlic, minced
¼ teaspoon onion powder
¼ teaspoon salt
⅛ teaspoon pepper

Wash beans; trim ends, and remove strings. Arrange beans in a steaming rack placed over boiling water; cover and cook 8 to 10 minutes. Plunge into cold water; drain and set aside.

Coat a nonstick skillet with cooking spray, and melt margarine in skillet over medium heat. Add mushrooms and garlic; cook, stirring constantly, 3 minutes or until mushrooms are tender. Add green beans, onion powder, salt, and pepper, and cook 3 minutes or until heated. Yield: 4 servings (93 calories [10% from fat] per ¾-cup serving).

□ 4.5g protein, 1g fat (0.2g saturated), 19.6g carbohydrate, 3.1g fiber, 0mg cholesterol, 171mg sodium, and 103mg calcium. *Mrs. H. W. Haynes Lafayette, Louisiana*

OVEN-FRIED CHICKEN

½ cup crisp rice cereal crumbs
½ teaspoon pepper
½ teaspoon paprika
¼ teaspoon salt
4 (6-ounce) skinned chicken breast
  halves
Butter-flavored cooking spray

Combine first 4 ingredients in a shallow dish. Coat chicken with cooking spray; dredge in cereal mixture. Place on a baking sheet coated with cooking spray, and coat chicken again with cooking spray. Bake at 350° for 50 minutes or until done. Yield: 4 servings (170 calories [21% from fat] per chicken breast half).

□ 28.3g protein, 3.9g fat (0.9g saturated), 3.4g carbohydrate, 0.1g fiber, 77mg cholesterol, 256mg sodium, and 17mg calcium.   Dorcas Moncer
Huntington, West Virginia

POTATOES AU GRATIN

3½ cups peeled, finely chopped
  potato
½ cup low-fat cottage cheese
½ cup nonfat buttermilk
1 tablespoon chopped fresh or
  frozen chives
2 teaspoons cornstarch
½ teaspoon salt
⅛ teaspoon pepper
Vegetable cooking spray
¼ cup (1 ounce) shredded part-skim
  mozzarella cheese
⅛ teaspoon paprika

Cook potato in boiling water to cover 8 minutes or until tender (do not overcook). Drain and set aside.
  Combine cottage cheese and buttermilk in container of an electric blender or food processor; process until smooth. Transfer to a large bowl;

stir in potato, chives, and next 3 ingredients. Spoon into a 1-quart casserole coated with cooking spray. Bake at 350° for 20 minutes; sprinkle with cheese and paprika, and bake an additional 5 minutes. Yield: 6 servings (116 calories [10% from fat] per ½-cup serving).

□ 6.3g protein, 1.2g fat (0.7g saturated), 20.4g carbohydrate, 1.6g fiber, 4mg cholesterol, 516mg sodium, and 76mg calcium.   Betty DeLee
Dallas, Texas

Don't Be Stingy With Starch

The next time you reject a baked potato, reconsider. It's not the potato (containing only 90 fat-free calories) that's to blame, but the butter and sour cream avalanche that covers it. So stick with starches—like dried beans and peas, grain products and dry cereals, potatoes and yeast breads. These food items are low in fat and rich in carbohydrates.

SPICY MEXICAN CORN

1 (8-ounce) jar picante sauce
1 (16-ounce) package frozen whole
  kernel corn
½ cup (2 ounces) shredded part-
  skim mozzarella cheese

Drain picante sauce, reserving liquid; set vegetable mixture aside. Measure reserved liquid, adding water if necessary to measure ½ cup. Combine reserved liquid and corn in a small saucepan. Cook, uncovered, over medium heat about 5 minutes or until

tender, stirring occasionally. Add vegetable mixture, and bring to a boil. Reduce heat, and simmer 1 minute. Spoon into a serving bowl; sprinkle with cheese, covering until cheese melts. Yield: 2½ cups (153 calories [18% from fat] per ⅔-cup serving).

□ 7.4g protein, 3.1g fat (1.6g saturated), 27.7g carbohydrate, 2.8g fiber, 8mg cholesterol, 708mg sodium, and 107mg calcium.   Narita Roady
Elmore City, Oklahoma

HOT-AND-LIGHT
POTATO SALAD

4 cups unpeeled thinly sliced red
  potato
1 tablespoon reduced-calorie
  margarine
1 cup chopped onion
½ cup fat-free mayonnaise
⅓ cup apple cider vinegar
1 tablespoon sugar
½ teaspoon salt
¼ teaspoon pepper
1 tablespoon chopped fresh parsley

Cook potato in boiling water to cover 8 to 10 minutes or until tender (do not overcook). Drain and set aside.
  Melt margarine in a heavy nonstick skillet over medium heat; add onion, and cook, stirring occasionally, 2 to 3 minutes. Combine mayonnaise and next 4 ingredients; stir into onion mixture. Add potatoes; cook, stirring constantly, 2 minutes or until thoroughly heated. Sprinkle with parsley. Yield: 6 servings (156 calories [6% from fat] per ¾-cup serving).

□ 3.5g protein, 1.1g fat (0.2g saturated), 34.4g carbohydrate, 3g fiber, 0mg cholesterol, 356mg sodium, and 19mg calcium.   Ganet Marsden
Canton, Texas

VEGETABLES AND RICE

1 cup brown rice, uncooked
1 cup ready-to-serve,
  reduced-sodium, fat-free chicken
  broth
1²⁄₃ cups water
2 teaspoons reduced-calorie
  margarine
1 cup chopped onion
1 cup chopped green pepper
1 (8-ounce) can sliced water
  chestnuts, drained
1 (4-ounce) can sliced mushrooms,
  drained
1 tablespoon low-sodium soy sauce
⅛ teaspoon salt
⅛ teaspoon pepper

Combine first 3 ingredients in a large saucepan; bring to a boil. Cover, reduce heat, and simmer 50 minutes or until moisture is absorbed and rice is tender.

Melt margarine in a heavy skillet; add onion and green pepper, and cook over medium-high heat, stirring constantly, 5 minutes. Add water chestnuts and mushrooms; cover and simmer 5 minutes. Add soy sauce, salt, and pepper, and stir into rice. Yield: 6 servings (158 calories [10% from fat] per 1-cup serving).

□ *3.6g protein, 1.7g fat (0.3g saturated), 31.8g carbohydrate, 2.1g fiber, 0mg cholesterol, 134mg sodium, and 16mg calcium.* Kim Bahr
Durham, North Carolina

Light Entrées In A Flash

In the same time it takes to battle traffic and long lines at fast-food restaurants, you can put an appealing,

healthful, and usually less expensive meal on the table at home. It just takes a little planning.

Reserve time once a week to map out meals and snacks, and make a grocery list. Many recipes can be doubled or made in advance and frozen to use later. Little more than thawing and/or reheating makes them ready in a flash. Cooking methods such as grilling, sautéing, and microwaving can hasten cooking time.

Before starting to cook, review all recipes to become familiar with procedures. Then formulate a mental or written game plan and assemble needed equipment. As a rule, start with the recipe that takes the longest to prepare, and while it's cooking or chilling, finish the rest of the meal.

PARMESAN-CRUSTED PERCH

2 tablespoons grated Parmesan
  cheese, divided
⅓ cup plain low-fat yogurt
2 tablespoons prepared horseradish
2 tablespoons Dijon mustard
2 tablespoons lemon juice
1 teaspoon margarine, melted
8 (4-ounce) perch fillets
Vegetable cooking spray

Combine 1 tablespoon cheese and next 5 ingredients; spread evenly on 1 side of fillets. Place fillets, coated side up, on a rack coated with cooking spray; place rack in broiler pan. Sprinkle with remaining cheese.

Broil 6 inches from heat (with electric oven door partially opened) 18 minutes or until golden and fish flakes easily when tested with a fork. Yield: 8 servings (127 calories [17% from fat] per fillet).

□ *23.1g protein, 2.4g fat (0.6g saturated), 1.7g carbohydrate, 0g fiber, 104mg cholesterol, 221mg sodium, and 128mg calcium.*

SUNBURST CHICKEN-AND-WALNUT SALAD
(pictured on page 110)

1½ cups water
1 medium onion, halved
1 stalk celery, halved
4 black peppercorns
4 (4-ounce) skinned and boned
  chicken breast halves
2 tablespoons cider vinegar
1½ tablespoons vegetable oil
2 teaspoons honey
½ teaspoon dry mustard
½ teaspoon dried tarragon
½ teaspoon grated orange rind
2 oranges, peeled and sectioned
8 lettuce leaves
2 tablespoons chopped walnuts,
  toasted

Combine first 4 ingredients in a large skillet, and bring to a boil. Cover, reduce heat, and simmer 10 minutes. Place chicken in skillet; cover and simmer 10 minutes or until tender. Remove chicken, and let cool (discard vegetables and reserve broth for another use). Cut chicken into strips; set aside.

Combine vinegar and next 5 ingredients, stirring with a wire whisk. Add orange sections; set aside.

Line each salad plate with 2 lettuce leaves. Remove orange sections from dressing, and divide evenly among plates. Place chicken strips in dressing, and toss gently; divide strips evenly among plates. Drizzle remaining dressing evenly over salads; sprinkle each with ½ tablespoon walnuts. Yield: 4 servings (277 calories [35% from fat] per serving).

□ *29.1g protein, 10.7g fat (1.9g saturated), 16.6g carbohydrate, 4.5g fiber, 72mg cholesterol, 77mg sodium, and 73mg calcium.* Kimberly J. Orr
Fort Worth, Texas

Light & Easy

SPICY HOT EGGPLANT CASSEROLE

1 medium eggplant (about 1½ pounds), peeled and cut into ¼-inch-thick slices
1 (10-ounce) can tomatoes with green chiles, drained, chopped, and divided
¼ cup soft breadcrumbs, divided
¼ teaspoon dried oregano, divided
½ cup no-salt-added tomato sauce, divided
2 tablespoons grated Parmesan cheese, divided
½ cup (2 ounces) shredded reduced-fat Cheddar cheese, divided
Vegetable cooking spray

Cook eggplant in a small amount of boiling water 5 minutes; drain well. Layer half each of eggplant, tomatoes, and next 5 ingredients in a 1½-quart casserole coated with cooking spray. Repeat layers, omitting top layer of Cheddar cheese. Bake at 350° for 15 minutes; sprinkle with remaining Cheddar cheese, and bake 5 minutes. Yield: 3 servings (153 calories [29% from fat] per 1-cup serving).

□ 9.1g protein, 5g fat (2.8g saturated), 16.6g carbohydrate, 1.9g fiber, 15mg cholesterol, 631mg sodium, and 243mg calcium. *Mrs. Fred L. Myers*
Rockport, Texas

Tip: *Refrigerate cheese in its original wrap until opened. After opening, rewrap the cheese tightly in plastic wrap, plastic bags, or aluminum foil, or place in airtight containers and refrigerate.*

Is It A "Butter" Substitute?

How will you take your fat-free butter? Sprinkled or poured? Flavored with a hint of sour cream or chives, bacon, or Cheddar cheese? First introduced to the market in 1979, butter substitutes have diversified. But are they really better than butter or margarine? In terms of savings in fat and calories, yes. About ¾ teaspoon of butter substitute sprinkles or 1 tablespoon of reconstituted mix has the same flavoring power as 1 tablespoon of butter or margarine, and boasts zero grams of fat. However, the three leading brands of plain butter flavoring are a questionable savings in sodium, with 98 to 135 milligrams per ¾-teaspoon serving, compared to 1 tablespoon of butter at 123 milligrams or margarine at 100 milligrams. Sodium values also vary among flavored varieties of sprinkles.

BASIL-BROWN BUTTER SAUCE
(pictured on page 111)

1 (½-ounce) envelope butter-flavored mix
¼ cup all-purpose flour
2 cups ready-to-serve, low-sodium chicken broth
⅓ cup balsamic vinegar
2 tablespoons chopped fresh basil
2 tablespoons tomato paste

Combine butter-flavored mix and flour in a small saucepan; gradually stir in chicken broth and balsamic vinegar. Cook over medium heat, stirring constantly, until thickened and bubbly. Stir in basil and tomato paste; reduce heat to low, and cook, stirring constantly, until sauce is thoroughly heated. Yield: 2⅓ cups (7 calories [0% from fat] per 1 tablespoon).

□ 0.2g protein, 0g fat (0g saturated), 1.3g carbohydrate, 0.1g fiber, 0mg cholesterol, 25mg sodium, and 1mg calcium. *Joyce Witherington*
Kinston, North Carolina

COTTAGE POTATOES

4 (4-ounce) potatoes
Vegetable cooking spray
3 tablespoons butter-flavored sprinkles

Scrub potatoes, and prick several times with a fork. Place potatoes 1 inch apart on a microwave-safe rack or paper towels. Microwave at HIGH 10 minutes, turning and rearranging once. Let cool to touch. Cut crosswise into ¼-inch slices. Place on a baking sheet coated with cooking spray. Coat potato slices lightly with cooking spray, and sprinkle with butter-flavored sprinkles.

Bake at 400° for 25 to 30 minutes or until potato slices are crisp. Yield: 4 servings (204 calories [0% from fat] per potato).

□ 5.5g protein, 0.9g fat (0.2g saturated), 43.7g carbohydrate, 4g fiber, 1mg cholesterol, 265mg sodium, and 33mg calcium. *Peggy Brown*
Winston-Salem, North Carolina

LAZY DAY TURKEY

1½ tablespoons butter-flavored
 mix
¼ cup water
½ cup chopped onion
½ cup chopped green pepper
½ cup sliced fresh mushrooms
1 clove garlic, minced
2 cups cubed, cooked turkey
 breast
1 (10¾-ounce) can ready-to-serve,
 reduced-fat cream of chicken soup
½ cup skim milk
2 tablespoons no-sugar-added
 apricot spread
1 tablespoon dry white wine
¼ teaspoon salt
¼ teaspoon ground nutmeg
¼ teaspoon pepper
4 cups hot cooked rice or pasta
 (cooked without salt or fat)

Combine butter-flavored mix and water, stirring until mix dissolves. Pour
into a large skillet; add chopped onion
and next 3 ingredients. Cook over medium heat, stirring constantly, until
tender. Stir in turkey and next 7 ingredients; bring to a boil over medium
heat. Reduce heat, and simmer, uncovered, 10 to 15 minutes, stirring occasionally. Serve over rice or pasta.
Yield: 4 servings (386 calories [6%
from fat] per ¾ cup meat mixture and
1 cup rice).

☐ *27.6g protein, 2.6g fat (0.3g saturated), 58.7g carbohydrate, 1.7g fiber,
63mg cholesterol, 660mg sodium, and
89mg calcium.* Shirley Gasparini
Cape Coral, Florida

Snack Smart

These snack recipes are low in fat,
but not in nutrients. They are quick to
fix and call for ingredients you probably already have.

If you don't have the ingredients,
add them to your grocery list to have
on hand when you need a quick nutritious nibble.

Portable Power Snacks

Keeping snacks in your purse,
briefcase, gym bag, car, desk
drawer, or home or office refrigerator will ensure a convenient
and powerful energy boost when
you need it the most. Below are
quick snack suggestions catego-
rized by food groups.

Breads and Cereals
Bagels
Breadsticks
Dry cereal
Fat-free or low-fat crackers
Fig bars
Gingersnaps
Graham crackers
Granola bars (choose those with
 less than 3 grams of fat per 100
 calories)
Pita bread
Popcorn cakes
Pretzels
Vanilla wafers
Whole grain rolls
Whole wheat bread

Vegetables
Raw vegetables
Vegetable juice

Fruits
Fresh fruit
Dried fruit
Juice and frozen juice bars

Milk, Yogurt, and Cheese
Fat-free ice cream
Fat-free or low-fat frozen yogurt
Frozen fudge pops
Ice milk
Nonfat or low-fat yogurt
String cheese or cheese with 5
 or fewer grams of fat per ounce
Skim or low-fat, plain or
 chocolate milk

Meats and Poultry
Lunch meat (95% to
 98% fat-free)
Water-packed tuna
Turkey breast meat

CRUNCHY SNACK MIX

2 cups corn-and-rice cereal
2 cups crispy wheat cereal squares
1½ cups bite-size pretzels
½ cup dry-roasted peanuts,
  unsalted
2 tablespoons reduced-calorie
  margarine, melted
2 teaspoons low-sodium
  Worcestershire sauce
½ teaspoon salt-free, extra spicy
  herb-and-spice blend
1 cup raisins

Combine first 4 ingredients in a large roasting pan. Combine margarine and Worcestershire sauce; pour over cereal mixture, tossing gently. Sprinkle with herb-and-spice blend. Bake at 250° for 30 to 35 minutes, stirring every 10 minutes. Remove from oven; stir in raisins, and cool. Store in an airtight container. Yield: 11 cups (151 calories [30% from fat] per 1-cup serving).

□ *3.5g protein, 5g fat (0.6g saturated), 25g carbohydrate, 1.7g fiber, 0mg cholesterol, 217mg sodium, and 25mg calcium.*

PIZZA ON A BAGEL

⅓ cup sliced fresh mushrooms
¼ cup finely chopped onion
¼ cup chopped green pepper
⅓ cup commercial pizza sauce
2 whole wheat bagels, halved and
  toasted
2 tablespoons (½ ounce) shredded
  part-skim mozzarella cheese
1 tablespoon grated Parmesan
  cheese

Combine first 3 ingredients in a 9-inch pieplate; microwave on HIGH 2 to 3 minutes. Stir in pizza sauce, and microwave 1 minute. Spread sauce evenly on bagel halves; top with mozzarella and Parmesan cheese. Broil 6 inches from heat (with electric oven door partially opened) until cheeses melt. Serve immediately. Yield: 4 servings (85 calories [19% from fat] per serving).

□ *6g protein, 1.8g fat (0g saturated), 22.2g carbohydrate, 1g fiber, 1mg cholesterol, 318mg sodium, and 85mg calcium.*

GARBANZO DIP

1 (19-ounce) can chick-peas
  (garbanzo beans), drained
½ cup commercial oil-free Italian
  dressing
1 clove garlic
1 tablespoon fresh lemon juice
Assorted raw vegetables

Combine first 4 ingredients in container of an electric blender; process until smooth, stopping once to scrape down sides. Chill. Serve with vegetables. Yield: 1¾ cups (64 calories [13% from fat] per 2 tablespoons and ½ cup vegetables).

□ *3g protein, 1.9g fat (0.1g saturated), 11.6g carbohydrate, 1.8g fiber, 0mg cholesterol, 151mg sodium, and 18mg calcium.*
                              Dorie Cochran
                              Rockville, Maryland

Beef Up
Lean Red Meat

Anyone on a cholesterol-lowering diet may find the doctor quick to advise "no red meat." But that's not necessary. Averaging 24mg of cholesterol per ounce, today's leaner beef rivals dark meat turkey or chicken. Cattle are now bred to carry less fat. Also, butchers are trimming the fat on cuts of meat to ⅒ to ⅛ inch versus the former ½ inch.

It's easy to identify the leanest cuts of beef: They're the ones coming from the parts of the animal that are exercised the most. The round cuts from the back of the leg or the loin (upper back) are the leanest.

BEEF AND CAULIFLOWER
OVER RICE

1 pound boneless top round steak
3 tablespoons reduced-sodium soy
  sauce
Vegetable cooking spray
3 cups cauliflower flowerets
¾ cup coarsely chopped sweet red
  pepper
2 cloves garlic, minced
1 tablespoon cornstarch
⅓ teaspoon beef-flavored bouillon
  granules
½ to 1 teaspoon dried crushed red
  pepper
½ teaspoon sugar
1 cup water
1 cup sliced green onions
2 cups hot cooked rice (cooked
  without salt or fat)

Trim fat from steak; slice diagonally across grain into thin strips; place in a shallow dish. Sprinkle with soy sauce, stirring gently to coat; cover and chill 30 minutes.

Coat a Dutch oven with cooking spray; place over medium heat until hot. Add meat and cook, stirring until browned. Reduce heat; cover and cook 10 minutes. Stir in cauliflower, sweet red pepper, and garlic; cover and cook 5 minutes.

Combine cornstarch and next 4 ingredients in a small bowl, stirring until smooth; stir into meat mixture. Add green onions; bring to a boil. Cook,

Light & Easy

stirring constantly, 1 minute. Serve over rice. Yield: 4 servings (296 calories [24% from fat] per 1¼ cups meat mixture and ½ cup rice).

□ *21.1g protein, 7.9g fat (2.7g saturated), 35g carbohydrate, 3.6g fiber, 68mg cholesterol, 908mg sodium, and 60mg calcium.* Delana Pearce
Mulberry, Florida

STEAK KABOBS

1½ pounds sirloin tip, trimmed
¼ cup low-sodium soy sauce
2 tablespoons brown sugar
½ teaspoon ground ginger
2 teaspoons dry sherry
1½ teaspoons vegetable oil
1 (15¼-ounce) can unsweetened pineapple chunks
6 cups hot cooked rice (cooked without salt or fat)

Cut meat into ½-inch cubes; place in a shallow dish or a heavy-duty, zip-top plastic bag, and set aside. Combine soy sauce and next 4 ingredients; pour over meat, and cover or seal. Refrigerate at least 3 hours. Drain meat, discarding marinade.

Alternate meat and pineapple on 14-inch skewers. Grill over medium-hot coals (350° to 400°) 8 minutes or until desired degree of doneness, turning often. Serve with rice. Yield: 6 servings (460 calories [17% from fat] per 1 kabob and 1 cup rice).

□ *30.4g protein, 8.8g fat (3.2g saturated), 61.5g carbohydrate, 1g fiber, 76mg cholesterol, 380mg sodium, and 40mg calcium.* Kathie Rupert-Wayne
Houston, Texas

Note: If wooden skewers are used, soak 30 minutes in water before using to prevent burning.

What's New In The Dairy Case?

Dairy products have gone on a diet. A casual stroll past the dairy case reveals many new product labels boldly proclaiming "low-fat," "reduced-fat," "light," or "fat-free."

Sadly, less milk fat usually means some flavor loss. To correct this, extra salt is often added, so anyone needing to control sodium should check product labels.

Also, the elimination of fat changes cooking character, so you may have to do a little experimenting to see how these new products perform. The Wisconsin Milk Marketing Board offers these tips for cooking with reduced-fat and fat-free cheeses.

■ Avoid cooking with direct heat, such as broiling or toasting, to prevent the cheese from toughening. Also, fat-free cheese will burn or brown quicker and must be watched carefully.

■ Slice fat-free cheese very thin to enable it to melt quickly.

■ Melt cheese over low heat while stirring in the same direction to prevent lumpiness, and expect a 25% longer melting time due to the lower cooking temperature.

■ Blend shredded reduced-fat cheeses with flour, cornstarch, or arrowroot for a smoother consistency in sauces.

According to many dairy companies, fat-free sour cream alternative can be used in all baking and cooking applications with only a slight loss of tenderness in baked goods. In uncooked dishes, fat-free sour cream alternative works well in dips, uncooked salad dressings, cold desserts, and toppings.

For information comparing the lightened version of dairy products with its heavier counterpart, see the chart on page 96.

BANANA SMOOTHIE

1 medium banana
1 cup skim milk
1 cup fat-free vanilla ice cream
2 tablespoons sugar

Combine all ingredients in an electric blender; process until smooth. Serve immediately. Yield: 2 cups (161 calories [2% from fat] per ⅔-cup serving).

□ *4.3g protein, 0.3g fat (0g saturated), 35.8g carbohydrate, 1.2g fiber, 2mg cholesterol, 70mg sodium, and 162mg calcium.* Barbara G. Oneto
Lafayette, Louisiana

GUILT-FREE CHEESE SAUCE

1 tablespoon reduced-calorie margarine
1 tablespoon all-purpose flour
1 cup skim milk
½ cup (2 ounces) shredded fat-free Cheddar cheese
¼ teaspoon ground white pepper
⅛ teaspoon salt
⅛ teaspoon ground red pepper

Place margarine in a 1-quart glass bowl; microwave at HIGH 30 seconds. Stir in flour with a wire whisk; gradually add milk, whisking until smooth. Microwave at HIGH 6 minutes, stirring at 2-minute intervals, until mixture is smooth and thickened. Add cheese and remaining ingredients, stirring until cheese melts. Serve over steamed vegetables. Yield: 1 cup (10 calories [34% from fat] per tablespoon).

□ *0.6g protein, 0.4g fat (0g saturated), 1.2g carbohydrate, 0g fiber, 0mg cholesterol, 34mg sodium, and 19mg calcium.* Leslie Byars
Birmingham, Alabama

Compare the Difference

Product	Amount	Calories	Fat (g)	Cholesterol (mg)	Sodium (mg)	Calcium (mg)
Regular vanilla ice cream	½ cup	175	11.8	44	54	99
Fat-free vanilla ice cream	½ cup	100	0	0	45	100
Regular sour cream	½ cup	246	24.1	51	61	133
Fat-free sour cream alternative	½ cup	80	0	0	80	160
Regular shredded Cheddar cheese	1 ounce	114	9.4	30	176	204
Fat-free shredded Cheddar cheese	1 ounce	40	0	5	200	250
Regular cream cheese	1 ounce	99	9.9	31	84	23
Fat-free cream cheese	1 ounce	25	0	5	170	100
Regular cottage cheese	½ cup	108	4.7	30	176	204
Nonfat cottage cheese	½ cup	70	0	5	419	60

FRESH FRUIT TARTLETS

1 cup wheat bran cereal
10 gingersnaps
½ teaspoon ground cinnamon
2 tablespoons reduced-calorie margarine, melted
Vegetable cooking spray
½ cup fat-free sour cream alternative
1 tablespoon unsweetened frozen orange juice concentrate, thawed and undiluted
1 cup fresh strawberries, halved
1 kiwifruit, sliced
½ cup fresh blueberries
2 tablespoons apple jelly

Position knife blade in food processor bowl; add cereal and gingersnaps. Process until finely ground. Add cinnamon and margarine; process until blended. Press about ¼ cup into each of 4 (4-inch) tart pans (with removable bottoms) coated with cooking spray. Bake at 350° for 7 to 8 minutes; remove from oven, and let cool.

Combine sour cream alternative and orange juice concentrate; spread over crusts, and arrange fresh fruit evenly on top of crusts.

Place apple jelly in a heavy saucepan; cook over medium heat until melted. Brush over fruit. Yield: 4 servings (223 calories [27% from fat] per tartlet).

□ 4.2g protein, 6.8g fat (1.4g saturated), 38.1g carbohydrate, 3.9g fiber, 7mg cholesterol, 200mg sodium, and 59mg calcium.

SKINNY RANCH DIP

1 (24-ounce) carton nonfat cottage cheese
1 (1.1-ounce) envelope reduced-calorie Ranch-style salad dressing mix
½ cup skim milk
1 tablespoon white vinegar

Combine all ingredients in an electric blender; process until smooth. Serve with assorted fresh vegetables. Yield: 3 cups (12 calories [0% from fat] per tablespoon).

□ 1.9g protein, 0g fat (0g saturated), 1.2g carbohydrate, 0g fiber, 1mg cholesterol, 117mg sodium, and 11mg calcium.

Tip: When selecting blueberries, look for berries that are plump, firm, clean, and deep blue with a silvery frost. A reddish tinge indicates immature berries.

Light & Easy

CHOCOLATE-AMARETTO CHEESECAKE

½ cup teddy bear-shaped chocolate graham cookie crumbs, divided
Vegetable cooking spray
4 (8-ounce) packages fat-free cream cheese
2 cups sugar
⅔ cup unsweetened cocoa
⅔ cup all-purpose flour
3 tablespoons amaretto
2 tablespoons vanilla extract
½ cup egg substitute
Reduced-calorie refrigerated instant whipped cream
2 tablespoons sliced almonds, toasted

Sprinkle ¼ cup crumbs on bottom of a 9-inch springform pan coated with cooking spray. Set remaining ¼ cup crumbs aside.

Position knife blade in food processor bowl; add cream cheese and next 5 ingredients. Process until smooth. Add egg substitute, and process just until blended. Pour mixture into pan. Bake at 300° for 45 to 50 minutes, or until center is almost set. Sprinkle with remaining ¼ cup crumbs. Let cool completely on a wire rack. Cover and refrigerate 8 hours. Top each slice with a small amount of reduced-calorie whipped cream and sprinkle with almonds. Yield: 16 servings (226 calories [8% from fat] per slice).

□ 10.7g protein, 2.1g fat (0.4g saturated), 37.8g carbohydrate, 0.4g fiber, 10mg cholesterol, 378mg sodium, and 211mg calcium.   Joyce Mattox
St. Simons Island, Georgia

Tour De John

Since 1990, Winnie and John Smoot have organized a group of their closest cycling companions to participate in the annual "Tour de John" bicycling event. Starting at their Bethany Beach, Delaware, townhouse, they embark on a 12-mile ride along Route 1 to Rehoboth Beach, Delaware, and a post-race feast.

Each year Winnie proudly salutes the team with a different menu. This year, she felt a lighter meal would be a nice complement to the event.

Winnie sent us her proposed post-race feast menu, and we modified three of the recipes to reflect current health guidelines of no more than 30% of total calories from fat and less than 10% saturated fat.

POST-RACE FEAST FOR SIXTEEN

Black-Eyed Pea Pâté with Garlic Pita Wedges *
Spicy Pepper Soup
Seafood Salad Sussex Shores
Seasoned Toast Strips
Chocolate-Kahlúa Brownies *
Assorted fresh fruit
With Raspberry Sauce
Citrus Punch
Sparkling water

* On this page and the next two pages, you'll see how the recipe modifications in Black-Eyed Pea Pâté, Garlic Pita Wedges, and Chocolate-Kahlúa Brownies evolved into lighter fare. For more tips on how to lighten recipes, turn to page 100.

BLACK-EYED PEA PÂTÉ

1 cup dried black-eyed peas
2¾ cups no-salt-added chicken broth
1 tablespoon canned jalapeño pepper liquid
3 canned jalapeño peppers, seeded and coarsely chopped
⅓ cup chopped onion
1 clove garlic
¼ cup (1 ounce) shredded reduced-fat Cheddar cheese
1½ teaspoons margarine
1 (4-ounce) can diced green chiles, drained
¾ teaspoon salt
½ teaspoon ground cumin
½ teaspoon hot sauce

Combine peas and broth in a saucepan; bring to a boil. Cover, reduce heat, and simmer 50 to 55 minutes or until tender; drain well. Position knife blade in food processor bowl; add peas, jalapeño pepper liquid, and next 3 ingredients. Process until smooth; set aside.

Combine cheese and margarine in a small saucepan; cook over low heat until cheese melts. Stir in pea mixture, chiles, and remaining ingredients. Spoon into a large paper towel-lined wire-mesh strainer or colander; let stand 1 hour or until excess liquid has drained. Shape as desired, and chill 8 hours. Serve with pita wedges. Yield: 2¼ cups (28 calories [26% from fat] per 2 tablespoons).

□ 1.6g protein, 0.8 fat (0.3g saturated), 3.4g carbohydrate, 0.3g fiber, 1mg cholesterol, 264mg sodium, and 21mg calcium.

Changes made: Replaced water with no-salt-added chicken broth to add flavor; reduced margarine from 1 cup to 1½ teaspoons; and Cheddar cheese from 2 cups regular to ¼ cup reduced-fat. The savings are 142 calories and 13 grams of fat per serving.

GARLIC PITA WEDGES

3 (6-inch) whole wheat pita bread
   rounds
¼ cup commercial oil-free
   Italian salad dressing
1 teaspoon garlic powder
2 tablespoons chopped parsley

Separate each pita bread into 2 rounds; cut each into 8 wedges to make 48 triangles. Brush rough side of each triangle with dressing, and place on ungreased baking sheets, dressing side up. Sprinkle garlic powder and parsley evenly over triangles. Bake at 425° for 10 minutes or until lightly browned. Cool on wire racks. Store in an airtight container. Yield: 16 servings (30 calories [9% from fat] per 3 chips).

☐ *0.2g protein, 0.1g fat (0g saturated), 2.0g carbohydrate, 0.3g fiber, 0mg cholesterol, 14mg sodium, and 3mg calcium.*

Changes made: Reduced serving size from 4 to 3 pita wedges; replaced regular Italian salad dressing with a fat-free variety, and eliminated margarine. The savings are 41 calories and 4 grams of fat per serving.

SPICY PEPPER SOUP

4 cups chopped sweet red pepper
   (1¾ pounds)
4 cups peeled and cubed potato
   (1½ pounds)
1½ cups chopped purple onion
4 cups water
2 (16-ounce) cans tomato
   sauce
1 cup dry, white vermouth
½ cup chopped fresh cilantro
¾ teaspoon ground cumin
¾ teaspoon ground red pepper
¼ teaspoon ground cinnamon
Garnish: fresh cilantro sprigs

Combine first 4 ingredients in a Dutch oven; bring to a boil. Cover, reduce heat, and simmer 20 minutes or until vegetables are tender. Stir in tomato sauce and next 5 ingredients. Bring to a boil; reduce heat, and simmer 10 minutes. Place half of soup mixture in container of an electric blender; process until smooth. Repeat. Garnish, if desired. Yield: 12 cups (76 calories [3% from fat] per ¾-cup serving).

☐ *1.9g protein, 0.3g fat (0.1g saturated), 14.1g carbohydrate, 2.2g fiber, 0mg cholesterol, 180mg sodium, and 18mg calcium.*

SEAFOOD SALAD SUSSEX SHORES

3 pounds lump crabmeat, drained
2 cups finely chopped celery
⅓ cup chopped green onions
¾ cup fat-free mayonnaise
1 (7-ounce) jar diced pimiento,
   drained
3 tablespoons lemon juice
½ teaspoon salt
¼ teaspoon garlic powder
¼ teaspoon ground red pepper
Red leaf lettuce
Marinated Potato Slices
1½ cups cucumber slices
2 cups tomato wedges

Combine first 9 ingredients. Serve on lettuce leaves with Marinated Potato Slices, cucumber slices, and tomato wedges. Yield: 16 servings (136 calories [34% from fat] per ¾ cup salad and about ½ cup vegetables).

Marinated Potato Slices

8 red potatoes (1¼ pounds)
1 cup olive oil
⅓ cup red wine vinegar
2 tablespoons Dijon mustard
½ teaspoon salt
¼ teaspoon ground white pepper

Cook potatoes in boiling water to cover 8 minutes or just until tender. Cool, and cut into thin slices. Combine oil and remaining ingredients; pour over potato slices. Cover and refrigerate 8 hours. Yield: 16 servings (136 calories [34% from fat] per serving).

☐ *17.8g protein, 5.1g fat (0.8g saturated), 3.9g carbohydrate, 0.4g fiber, 76mg cholesterol, 432mg sodium, and 98mg calcium.*

SEASONED TOAST STRIPS

16 slices thin-sliced white bread
Butter-flavored cooking spray
1 tablespoon salad seasoning

Remove crust from bread; coat one side with cooking spray. Lightly sprinkle coated side of each slice with salad seasoning, and cut into 4 strips.

Place strips on baking sheets; bake at 325° for 12 to 15 minutes or until lightly browned. Yield: 16 servings (73 calories [16% from fat] per 4 toast strips).

☐ *2.2g protein, 1.3g fat (0.2g saturated), 12.6g carbohydrate, 0.5g fiber, 1mg cholesterol, 181mg sodium, and 18mg calcium.*

Note: The nutritional analysis of this recipe is more accurately calculated by cutting bread into strips.

Light & Easy

CHOCOLATE-KAHLÚA BROWNIES

1½ cups sugar
½ cup egg substitute
3 tablespoons Kahlúa or other coffee-flavored liqueur
¼ cup margarine, melted
1¼ cups sifted cake flour
½ cup cocoa
1 teaspoon baking powder
½ cup finely chopped walnuts
Vegetable cooking spray
Garnishes: whole strawberries and fresh mint sprigs

Combine first 4 ingredients in a large mixing bowl, stirring well. Combine flour and next 2 ingredients; stir into sugar mixture. Fold in walnuts. Spoon batter into a 9-inch square pan coated with cooking spray. Bake at 325° for 30 to 35 minutes or until a wooden pick inserted in center comes out clean. Cool in pan on a wire rack; cut into squares. Garnish, if desired. Yield: 16 brownies (173 calories [29% from fat] per brownie).

□ *3.1g protein, 5.5g fat (1.0g saturated), 27.2g carbohydrate, 0.3g fiber, 0mg cholesterol, 65mg sodium, and 23mg calcium.*

Changes made: Reduced saturated fat by replacing butter with margarine and reducing quantity from 1 cup to ¼ cup; kept the sugar content high to produce a chewier product that would mimic the consistency of higher-fat brownies; replaced 1 cup chopped pecans with lower-fat walnuts. The savings are 174 calories and 15 grams of fat per serving.

RASPBERRY SAUCE

1 (10-ounce) package frozen raspberries in light syrup, thawed
Garnish: fresh mint sprigs

Position knife blade in food processor bowl; add raspberries. Process until smooth. Pour through a large wire-mesh strainer into a bowl, discarding seeds. Chill. Serve with fresh fruit. Yield: 1 cup (18 calories [0% from fat] per tablespoon).

□ *0.1g protein, 0g fat (0g saturated), 4.6g carbohydrate, 1.2g fiber, 0mg cholesterol, 0mg sodium, and 3mg calcium.*

CITRUS PUNCH

1 cup water
¼ cup sugar
3 cups unsweetened pineapple juice
3 cups water
1 (6-ounce) can frozen orange juice concentrate, thawed and undiluted
½ cup lemon juice
3 (12-ounce) cans lemon-lime carbonated beverage, chilled
Garnish: lemon slices

Combine 1 cup water and sugar in a small saucepan; cook over low heat, stirring constantly, until sugar dissolves. Remove from heat; cool. Stir in pineapple juice and next 3 ingredients; cover and chill. Just before serving, stir in carbonated beverage; serve over ice cubes. Garnish, if desired. Yield: 3 quarts (85 calories [0% from fat] per 6-ounce serving).

□ *0.4g protein, 0.1g fat (0g saturated), 21.4g carbohydrate, 0.2g fiber, 0mg cholesterol, 10mg sodium, and 26mg calcium.*

Light Cooking Tips

■ Watch calories the sensible way by totaling all the calories eaten in a day. Plan a heathful snack as part of your day's total menu plan rather than sneaking candy or an unhealthful snack.

■ By using vegetable cooking spray instead of margarine or oils to grease baking pans and skillets, you'll save fat calories.

■ Look for nontraditional ways to include a variety of foods in your diet. If you don't care for milk as a beverage, consider trying a milk-based soup as part of your milk allowance for the day.

■ Instead of serving sauces or creams over vegetables, use seasonings such as bouillon, lemon juice, herbs, spices, or butter substitutes.

■ Try a little calorie-free club soda in grape or apple juice to add a bubbly sparkle and to make the fruit juice calories go further.

■ Satisfy your craving for sweets by choosing low-fat foods. For example, have a slice of low-fat angel food cake for dessert rather than cheesecake. Or opt for plain low-fat gingersnaps for a snack instead of a fat-laden doughnut.

Light & Easy

Simple Ways To Lighten Recipes

When we lighten recipes in our Test Kitchens, our primary goal is to reduce fat, cholesterol, and calories. The tips below will help you prepare healthful foods, and make good-tasting changes in your favorite dishes. Not all substitutions work for all recipes, so some experimenting may be required.

Instead of . . .	Try . . .	And save . . . Fat (g)	Chol (mg)	Cal
Baking chocolate (1 ounce)	3 tablespoons dry cocoa plus 2 teaspoons sugar and 1 tablespoon water	13	0	70
Butter, margarine, shortening, or vegetable oil (1 tablespoon)	½ the amount called for in recipe;	6	15	51
	or 1 tablespoon reduced-calorie margarine;	6	31	52
	or an equal amount of unsweetened applesauce (in baked goods only)	95	12	31
Cheese (1 ounce)	½ the amount called for in recipe;	5	15	57
	or 1 ounce reduced-fat or part-skim (with 5 or fewer grams of fat per ounce)	4	12	30
Chicken broth, canned, regular (1 cup)	1 cup ready-to-serve, reduced-sodium, fat-free, canned chicken broth	4	0	19
Cream or half-and-half (1 tablespoon)	1 tablespoon evaporated skimmed milk	3	9	17
Cream of mushroom soup (10¾-ounce can)	10¾-ounce can 99% fat-free cream of mushroom soup	18	0	151
Egg (1 large)	¼ cup egg substitute;	6	258	61
	or 2 large egg whites	6	258	59
Ground beef (1 ounce)	1 ounce 93% or 96% low-fat ground beef;	3	4	11
	or 1 ounce lean ground turkey	4	4	23
Mayonnaise (1 tablespoon)	1 tablespoon reduced-calorie mayonnaise;	6	2	55
	or fat-free mayonnaise;	11	8	86
	or 1½ teaspoons reduced-calorie mayonnaise mixed with 1½ teaspoons plain nonfat yogurt	9	5	73
Pecans, chopped (½ cup)	¼ cup toasted (this works with any type nut)	20	0	199
Sour cream (½ cup)	½ cup plain nonfat yogurt;	24	49	182
	or ½ cup nonfat sour cream alternative (for baked goods, add 1½ teaspoons flour to each ½ cup of yogurt or sour cream alternative)	24	51	166
Whole milk (1 cup)	1 cup skim milk	8	29	63

The New Flavors Of Grilling

Grilling has changed. It's not just sizzling hot dogs and hamburgers anymore. But don't rake yourself over the coals trying to come up with new ideas because we've done it for you.

Select your favorite meat, poultry, or seafood; choose a flavoring; and follow our tips to make grilling easier, more healthful, and more delicious.

Create Your Own Sensations

For subtle flavor, add hardwood chips or chunks (mesquite, hickory, oak, or fruitwoods), or fresh or dried herbs (bay leaves, marjoram, sage, basil, rosemary) to the charcoal. Soak wood chips and herbs 30 minutes and drain; add them directly to the hot coals. For a gas grill, wrap the soaked chips or herbs in foil, leaving the ends open; place on hot lava rocks.

Marinades and rubs also add flavor to grilled foods. Try one of the recipes we offer or experiment with a creation of your own.

Learn the How-to's of Grilling

■ To keep lower-fat foods from sticking, lightly coat cold grill rack with vegetable cooking spray; then place food on the grill.
■ Use long tongs to turn food.
■ Use a grill basket for fish and other foods that tend to break apart easily.
■ Allow 15 to 30 minutes for coals to reach cooking temperature. If you don't have a thermometer, try this simple hand test. Cautiously hold the palm of your hand at cooking height over the coals. Count the number of seconds you can leave it there before the heat forces you to pull away. (The same test will work for gas grills that don't have thermometers.)

Time/Temperature
Two seconds/Hot (400° to 500°)
Three seconds/Medium-hot (350° to 400°)
Four seconds/Medium (300° to 350°)
Five seconds/Low (under 300°)

■ If in doubt about how hot the grill should be for a particular food, try cooking larger cuts, such as pork loin roasts, over medium coals, and smaller cuts, such as steaks or chicken, over medium-hot coals.
■ Grilling time will vary with food choice, outside air temperature, wind velocity, distance of the food from the coals, and whether or not the grill is covered.
■ Use an instant-read meat thermometer to test the doneness of meat and poultry. Insert the thermometer into the thickest part of the meat, avoiding bone or fat. (For smaller cuts, insert thermometer into the side.) Beef and lamb are rare at 140°, medium-rare at 150°, medium at 160°, and well-done at 170°. Lamb is best at 160° or below. Grill pork and veal to 160°. Cook whole poultry to 180° (check temperature in thigh) and poultry parts to 170°. Remove the thermometer after checking the temperature.
■ Remove large cuts of meat from the grill when the internal meat temperature is five degrees lower than desired. Let stand for 10 minutes to allow juices to set and the temperature to increase the last five degrees.
■ Fish, shrimp, and scallops should be cooked just until they are opaque all the way through (a good guideline for fish is 6 to 12 minutes per inch of thickness; for shrimp and scallops, 2 to 6 minutes). Soft-shell crabs should be cooked until lightly browned (12 to 16 minutes). Seafood should be turned once during cooking.
■ Soak wooden skewers for 30 minutes before use, to prevent burning.
■ To easily turn kabobs, use stainless steel, flat-bladed skewers. Round skewers often create large holes, causing food to slip instead of turn.

Rub or Sprinkle on Flavor

A rub is a highly concentrated blend of herbs and spices that flavors the exterior of the meat as it grills. If you're in a hurry, sprinkle rubs on foods instead. They are great for bulky pieces of meat that are difficult to marinate or when you don't have time to marinate. Once prepared, store rubs in empty spice jars for easy sprinkling.

CREOLE RUB

1 tablespoon salt
1½ teaspoons garlic powder
1½ teaspoons onion powder
1½ teaspoons paprika
1¼ teaspoons dried thyme
1 teaspoon ground red pepper
¾ teaspoon black pepper
¾ teaspoon dried oregano
½ teaspoon ground bay leaves
¼ teaspoon chili powder

Combine all ingredients; store in an airtight container. Sprinkle on seafood, chicken, or beef before grilling. Yield: ¼ cup.

JERK RUB

1½ tablespoons sugar
1 tablespoon onion powder
1 tablespoon dried thyme
2 teaspoons ground allspice
2 teaspoons freshly ground pepper
2 teaspoons ground red pepper
1 teaspoon salt
¾ teaspoon ground nutmeg
¼ teaspoon ground cloves

Combine all ingredients; store mixture in an airtight container. Sprinkle on chicken or seafood before grilling. Yield: ⅓ cup.

SEAFOOD SEASONING RUB

1½ teaspoons ground bay leaves
1½ teaspoons dry mustard
1½ teaspoons black pepper
1 teaspoon salt
¾ teaspoon ground nutmeg
½ teaspoon ground celery seeds
½ teaspoon ground cloves
½ teaspoon ground ginger
½ teaspoon paprika
½ teaspoon ground red pepper

Combine all ingredients; store mixture in an airtight container. Sprinkle on seafood or chicken before grilling. Yield: about ¼ cup.

HERB RUB

1 tablespoon dried thyme
1 tablespoon dried oregano
1½ teaspoons poultry seasoning
1 teaspoon dried rosemary
1 teaspoon dried marjoram
1 teaspoon dried basil
1 teaspoon dried parsley flakes
½ teaspoon salt
⅛ teaspoon pepper

Combine all ingredients; store mixture in an airtight container. Sprinkle on fish, poultry, or pork before grilling. Yield: ¼ cup.

MEXICAN RUB

¼ cup chili powder
1 tablespoon onion powder
1 tablespoon ground cumin
2 teaspoons salt
1½ teaspoons dried oregano
1 teaspoon garlic powder
1 teaspoon ground red pepper

Combine all ingredients; store in an airtight container. Sprinkle on chicken, ribs, or fish before grilling. Yield: ½ cup.

For More Healthful Grilling

Research findings suggest that some compounds formed during grilling foods are potentially hazardous. These substances are caused by grilling meat, poultry, or seafood at high temperatures too long or by the excessive smoke from fire flare-ups. To reduce risks, grill foods at a moderate-to-low temperature just until done. Also choose lean cuts of meat, trim all visible fat, use low-fat or nonfat marinades, and avoid charring the food.

Create New Tastes With Marinades

Marinades are highly flavored liquids used to add flavor and, in some cases, tenderize meats. They usually consist of an acidic liquid, such as lemon juice, wine, vinegar, or soy sauce; oil; and seasonings, such as spices and herbs. The more acidic the marinade, the better it tenderizes. Keep the following in mind as you marinate foods:

■ Pierce meats or poultry with a fork before placing in marinade to allow more flavor penetration.
■ Plan on ⅓ to ½ cup marinade per pound of food.
■ Use a covered glass dish for marinating. Or place meat and marinade in a heavy-duty, zip-top plastic bag.
■ Marinate foods in the refrigerator, never at room temperature.
■ Marinating times vary because foods and marinades differ in how they react. Over-marinating can cause foods to become mushy or have a flavor that is too strong.
■ Basting foods during grilling increases the flavor. To baste with marinade, reserve a portion before it comes in contact with the raw food. Discard used marinades because they may contain microorganisms that can cause food poisoning.

ORIENTAL MARINADE

1½ cups unsweetened orange juice
⅓ cup dry sherry
⅓ cup low-sodium soy sauce
3 tablespoons dark brown sugar
2 tablespoons peeled, finely chopped gingerroot
1 tablespoon grated orange rind
2 cloves garlic, minced
1½ teaspoons coriander seeds, crushed
1½ teaspoons freshly ground pepper
¼ teaspoon salt

Combine all ingredients. Pour over flank steak, and refrigerate 8 hours before grilling. Yield: 2¼ cups.

TERIYAKI MARINADE

1 cup soy sauce
1 cup water
¾ cup sugar
¼ cup Worcestershire sauce
3 tablespoons white vinegar
3 tablespoons vegetable oil
⅓ cup freeze-dried chives
2 teaspoons garlic powder

Combine all ingredients, stirring until sugar dissolves. Use to brush on chicken while grilling, to marinate chicken in refrigerator 2 hours before grilling, or to marinate flank steak in refrigerator 8 hours before grilling. Yield: 3 cups.   *Bettie D. Flener*
Bowling Green, Kentucky

SOUTHWESTERN MARINADE

⅓ cup lime juice
⅓ cup olive oil
2 tablespoons tequila
2 tablespoons chopped fresh cilantro
1 clove garlic, minced
1 jalapeño pepper, seeded and chopped
¼ teaspoon salt
¼ teaspoon pepper

Combine all ingredients. Pour over peeled and deveined jumbo shrimp or soft-shell crab, and refrigerate 2 hours before grilling. Or brush on shrimp or soft-shell crab while grilling. Yield: about ¾ cup.

GARLIC-HONEY MARINADE

¼ cup lemon juice
¼ cup honey
2 tablespoons soy sauce
1 tablespoon dry sherry
2 cloves garlic, minced

Combine all ingredients. Pour over boneless pork, and refrigerate 8 hours before grilling. Yield: ¾ cup.
Mary Pappas
Richmond, Virginia

CINNAMON-SOY MARINADE

2 tablespoons soy sauce
2 tablespoons dry sherry
2 tablespoons sugar
¼ to ½ teaspoon ground cinnamon

Combine all ingredients, stirring until sugar dissolves. Pour over flank steak, and refrigerate 8 hours before grilling. Yield: ¼ cup.   *Joan Powell*
Dallas, Texas

CITRUS MARINADE

½ cup orange juice
¼ cup lemon juice
¼ cup lime juice
2 tablespoons vegetable oil
2 teaspoons dried rosemary, crushed
¼ teaspoon salt
⅛ teaspoon ground white pepper

Combine all ingredients. Pour over amberjack or orange roughy fillets, and refrigerate 8 hours before grilling. Yield: 1 cup.

HONEY-MUSTARD MARINADE

½ cup honey
¼ cup Dijon mustard
¼ cup lemon juice
¼ cup soy sauce
2 cloves garlic, crushed

Combine all ingredients. Use to brush on chicken while grilling, to marinate chicken in refrigerator 2 to 8 hours before grilling, or to marinate pork tenderloin in refrigerator 8 hours before grilling. Yield: 1⅓ cups.
Laurie McIntyre
Houston, Texas

From Our Kitchen To Yours

For grilling enthusiasts, these new items—along with a few old standbys—can speed grilling and broaden your outdoor culinary repertoire.

■ Select the chimney-type starter for charcoal grills to help coals heat quickly using a match and a few pieces of newspaper. Or choose an electric charcoal lighter with a heating element similar to the electric element loops in ovens; you'll need an electric outlet nearby. Liquid starters can give an unpleasant flavor to the food.

■ Use a grill thermometer to determine the temperature of the cooking surface. A magnetic back attaches it to metal racks. This gadget is especially helpful when cooking large cuts of meat; by adjusting the airflow or gas burners, a constant temperature can be maintained.

■ Add subtle flavor to grilled foods with aromatic woods. To save time, keep a metal smoker box filled with hardwood chips. Place the covered box on hot charcoal, and wait 15 minutes for the unsoaked chips to begin smoking. For a gas grill, place the box on cold lava rocks and light.

■ Select long-handled tongs and a spatula for turning food without tearing or piercing, which will cause it to lose its natural juices.

■ Choose pastry or basting brushes made of natural bristles, not nylon, for dabbing on sauces and brushing on thin layers of reserved marinade. (Don't use marinade that has touched raw meat because it can cause food poisoning.)

■ Use flat metal skewers to support the weight of meat and other items and to prevent spinning. Foods can spin on round skewers, cooking the same side over and over. Dual-pronged skewers hold pieces securely in place and the easy-slide handle glides food onto a plate.

■ Keep fragile foods, such as fish, seafood, or some types of vegetables, from falling apart when turning and prevent small food from slipping

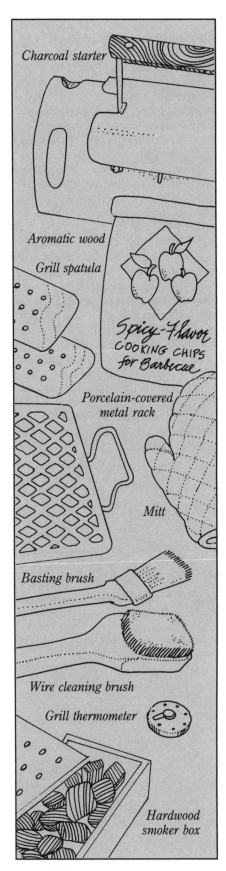

Charcoal starter

Aromatic wood

Grill spatula

Spicy-Flavor COOKING CHIPS for Barbecue

Porcelain-covered metal rack

Mitt

Basting brush

Wire cleaning brush

Grill thermometer

Hardwood smoker box

through the cracks with a grill basket. Oil the racks before use so food won't stick and tear apart.

■ Select porcelain-covered close-meshed metal racks, which fit directly on the grill's rack, to provide maximum support for thick foods while allowing juices to drip through and help prevent smaller pieces of food from falling into the coals. We selected a rack with two handles and a one-inch side, making lifting or turning food easy with its spatula stopping edge. For stir-frying foods, we chose one shaped like a wok.

■ Coat the grill rack with vegetable cooking spray before placing it over hot coals. After each use, make the messy but essential task of cleaning easier by loosening residue on the rack of a charcoal grill with a stiff-wire brush (crumpled aluminum foil may also be used). Then wipe the grill rack with paper towels. For a gas grill, place a sheet of aluminum foil, shiny side down, on the grill rack; close the lid, and turn the gas burner on high for 15 to 20 minutes. Remove the foil, and scrub food off the grill rack with a stiff-wire brush.

■ Use an instant-read thermometer to gauge the doneness of meat.
■ Buy disposable heavy-gauge foil pans; they make good drip pans for indirect grilling.

To Cook Directly or Indirectly?

How you prepare the fire depends on the food. Fast-cooking flat meats, such as steaks, chops, kabobs, and hamburgers, should be cooked directly over hot coals or lava rocks. Direct heat results in quick cooking with more surface browning.

Turkeys, roasts, and other large cuts require slow, even cooking without the food being directly over the heat source. In gas grills, light one burner, and place the food over a drip pan on the opposite side, away from the heat source. With the lid closed, the heat from the burner warms the grill like an oven, helping to prevent flare-ups. For a charcoal grill, arrange hot coals at the sides of the grill or around a drip pan, making sure the drip pan is slightly larger than the food. Place meat over the drip pan, and close the lid.

Forecast: Expecting Showers

A shower for parents-to-be—what better reason for celebration and sharing than an anticipated beginning.

To start planning, consult your calendar, and pick a date for friends to assemble. Next, decide what you'll serve. Each buffet menu includes a refreshing beverage and a hearty main dish. All recipes are quick and easy with an eye toward economy. If you're expecting a large group, let others bring complementing side dishes. Plan to serve favorites of the expectant parents, including a dessert that will satisfy even the strongest cravings.

Traditional gifts—not this time. Invite guests to help build a culinary "layette" by bringing their favorite casseroles, frozen. During the party store the entrées in a disposable, plastic foam cooler. Cap the festivities by sending the soon-to-be mom and dad home with meals they can enjoy after the baby comes.

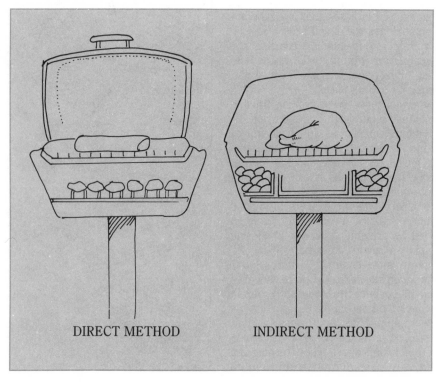

DIRECT METHOD   INDIRECT METHOD

**PARENTS-TO-BE PICNIC
FOR EIGHT**

Apple-Berry Sparkler
Commercial dip with assorted
fresh vegetables
Grilled chicken quarters
Baked Beans Quintet
Dill-and-Sour Cream
Potato Salad
Herbed French bread
Chocolate Chip Pound Cake

APPLE-BERRY SPARKLER

1 (6-ounce) can frozen apple juice concentrate, thawed and undiluted
1 (12-ounce) can frozen cranberry juice concentrate, thawed and undiluted
6 cups sparkling mineral water, chilled
Garnish: lemon slices

Combine juice concentrates; chill. Just before serving, stir in mineral water. Serve over ice, and garnish, if desired. Yield: 2 quarts.

BAKED BEANS QUINTET

6 slices bacon
1 cup chopped onion
1 clove garlic, minced
1 (16-ounce) can butterbeans, drained
1 (17-ounce) can lima beans, drained
1 (15-ounce) can pork and beans
1 (15-ounce) can red kidney beans, drained
1 (19-ounce) can chick-peas, drained
¾ cup catsup
½ cup molasses
¼ cup firmly packed brown sugar
1 tablespoon Worcestershire sauce
1 tablespoon prepared mustard
¼ teaspoon pepper

Cook bacon in a large skillet until crisp; remove bacon, reserving drippings in skillet. Crumble bacon, and set aside. Cook onion and garlic in drippings, stirring constantly, until tender; drain. Combine bacon, onion mixture, butterbeans, and next 4 ingredients in a large bowl. Stir in catsup and remaining ingredients. Spoon into a lightly greased 2½-quart bean pot or baking dish. Cover and bake at 375° for 1 hour. Yield: 8 to 10 servings.   *Carolyne M. Carnevale*
Ormond Beach, Florida

DILL-AND-SOUR CREAM POTATO SALAD

3 pounds unpeeled new potatoes
⅔ cup mayonnaise or salad dressing
1 (8-ounce) carton sour cream
1 tablespoon chopped fresh dill
2 teaspoons chopped fresh parsley
½ teaspoon salt
½ teaspoon pepper
Garnish: fresh dillweed sprig

Cook unpeeled potatoes in boiling, salted water to cover 15 minutes or until tender; drain and let cool to touch. Leaving skins on, cut potatoes into eighths. Place in a large bowl. Combine mayonnaise and next 5 ingredients; add to potatoes, tossing gently. Cover and chill 8 hours. Garnish, if desired. Yield: 8 servings.
Prissy Grozinger
Shreveport, Louisiana

CHOCOLATE CHIP POUND CAKE

1 (18.25-ounce) yellow cake mix with pudding
1 (3.9-ounce) package chocolate instant pudding mix
½ cup sugar
¾ cup vegetable oil
¾ cup water
4 large eggs
1 (8-ounce) carton sour cream
1 (6-ounce) package semisweet chocolate morsels
Sifted powdered sugar

Combine first 3 ingredients, stirring with a wire whisk to remove large lumps. Add oil and next 3 ingredients, stirring until smooth. Stir in chocolate morsels. Pour batter into a greased and floured 12-cup Bundt pan. Bake at 350° for 1 hour or until a wooden pick inserted in center comes out clean. Cool in pan on a wire rack 10 minutes; remove from pan, and cool completely on wire rack. Sprinkle with powdered sugar. Yield: one 10-inch cake.
Becky DeWare
Houston, Texas

FIESTA MENU FOR EIGHT

**Citrus Cooler
Tortilla chips with salsa
Meatless Enchiladas
Spanish rice
Marinated Tex-Mex Salad
Cinnamon Crisps with
Vanilla frozen yogurt
(topped with Kahlúa, if desired)**

CITRUS COOLER

6¼ cups pink grapefruit juice, divided
2 cups pineapple juice
½ cup frozen orange juice concentrate or tangerine juice concentrate, thawed and undiluted
2 cups lime-flavored sparkling mineral water, chilled
Garnish: lime slices

Pour 2¼ cups grapefruit juice into ice trays, filling 24 sections; freeze. Combine remaining 4 cups grapefruit juice and next 2 ingredients; cover and chill 3 to 4 hours. Just before serving, stir in mineral water. Place 3 frozen grapefruit juice cubes in each of 8 glasses; fill evenly with fruit juice mixture. Garnish, if desired. Serve immediately. Yield: 8½ cups. *Julie Zadeck*
Shreveport, Louisiana

Fresh Fruits

■ Fresh pineapple does not ripen further after it's picked. Choose one that is firm and fresh looking and use within five days.
■ For a delicious and simple dessert, pour cream sherry over chilled grapefruit.
■ If stored at room temperature, grapefruit will keep for a day or two; when refrigerated, the fruit will keep up to four months.

MEATLESS ENCHILADAS

1 large onion, chopped
3 cloves garlic, minced
2 tablespoons olive oil
1 (16-ounce) can diced tomatoes, undrained
1 (15-ounce) can tomato sauce
1½ tablespoons chili powder
½ teaspoon dried oregano
½ teaspoon ground cumin
1 (15-ounce) can black beans, drained
1 (12-ounce) can whole kernel corn, drained
½ cup sliced ripe olives
1 cup small-curd cottage cheese
1 (4-ounce) can chopped green chiles, drained
2 cups (8 ounces) shredded Cheddar cheese, divided
10 (6-inch) corn tortillas
¼ cup olive oil

Cook onion and garlic in 2 tablespoons olive oil in a large Dutch oven over medium-high heat, stirring constantly, until tender; add tomatoes and next 4 ingredients. Bring sauce to a boil; reduce heat, and simmer, uncovered, 25 minutes. Spoon about 1 cup sauce into a lightly greased 13- x 9- x 2-inch baking dish; set aside. Add black beans, corn, and olives to remaining sauce; set aside.

Combine cottage cheese, green chiles, and ¾ cup Cheddar cheese; set aside.

Fry tortillas, one at a time, in ¼ cup oil in a medium skillet 5 seconds on each side or just until softened. Drain on paper towels. Spoon about 2 tablespoons cottage cheese mixture down center of each tortilla; roll up, and place, seam side down, in baking dish. Spoon remaining sauce over tortillas. Cover and bake at 350° for 20 minutes. Uncover and sprinkle with remaining Cheddar cheese; bake an additional 5 minutes. Yield: 6 to 8 servings.
Donna Kirchman
Newberry, Florida

Tip: *When using cheese in a recipe, do not overcook it as cheese will become stringy.*

MARINATED TEX-MEX SALAD

1 large jicama, cut into thin strips
1 large sweet red pepper, cut into thin strips
1 large green pepper, cut into thin strips
1 Anaheim chile pepper, cut into thin strips
3 medium carrots, cut into thin strips
1 medium zucchini, cut into thin strips
¾ cup water
⅓ cup lime juice
¼ cup olive oil
¼ cup chopped fresh cilantro
1 tablespoon sugar
¼ teaspoon salt
¼ teaspoon ground red pepper

Combine first 6 ingredients in a large bowl. Combine water and remaining ingredients; pour over vegetables, tossing gently. Cover and refrigerate 8 hours. Yield: 8 servings.
Eileen Wehling
Austin, Texas

CINNAMON CRISPS

6 (6-inch) flour tortillas, cut into quarters
1 teaspoon reduced-calorie margarine, melted
¼ cup sugar
1 teaspoon ground cinnamon

Place tortillas on lightly greased baking sheets; brush with margarine. Combine sugar and cinnamon; sprinkle on tortillas. Bake at 350° for 10 minutes. Cool and store in an airtight container. Serve with vanilla frozen yogurt and Kahlúa, if desired. Yield: 2 dozen.
Edith Askins
Greenville, Texas

Oil + Vinegar + Flavoring = Vinaigrette

Oil plus vinegar plus flavoring equals vinaigrette—that's all there is to it. The types and amounts of oil, vinegar, and flavorings may change, but vinaigrette's basic components stay the same. The classic vinaigrette has three parts oil to one part vinegar.

BASIL VINAIGRETTE

1⅓ cups olive oil
⅔ cup white wine vinegar
¼ cup finely chopped fresh basil
2 green onions, finely chopped
1 teaspoon salt
½ teaspoon pepper

Combine all ingredients in a jar. Cover tightly, and shake vigorously; chill. Just before serving, shake well, and toss dressing with torn romaine, Bibb, and red leaf lettuces. Yield: 1½ cups.
Nora Henshaw
Okemah, Oklahoma

SESAME-SOY DRESSING

⅓ cup sugar
⅓ cup white wine vinegar
¼ cup soy sauce
¼ cup chopped onion
1 clove garlic
2 teaspoons sesame seeds
1½ teaspoons sesame oil
⅛ teaspoon salt
1½ cups vegetable oil

Combine first 8 ingredients in container of an electric blender; process until smooth, stopping once to scrape down sides. With blender running, gradually add oil in a slow, steady stream; cover and chill. Just before serving, toss with torn fresh spinach and Belgian endive. Yield: 2⅓ cups.
Mary J. Ealey
Smithfield, Virginia

WARM CURRY VINAIGRETTE

¼ cup chopped green onions
2 tablespoons red wine vinegar
1 teaspoon curry powder
2 teaspoons Dijon mustard
2 tablespoons olive oil
2 tablespoons vegetable oil
¼ cup chopped fresh basil
¼ teaspoon salt
¼ teaspoon pepper

Combine first 4 ingredients in a small saucepan with a wire whisk. Cook over low heat, stirring constantly, until blended. Whisk in oils. Remove from heat, and whisk in basil, salt, and pepper. Just before serving, toss with torn red leaf and green leaf lettuces. Yield: ¼ cup.   *Mrs. E. W. Hanley*
Palm Harbor, Florida

HONEY-WALNUT DRESSING

⅓ cup vegetable oil
2½ tablespoons Dijon mustard
2½ tablespoons red wine vinegar
2½ tablespoons water
½ cup honey
⅓ cup walnuts, toasted and
   chopped
Crumbled cooked bacon (optional)

Combine oil and mustard with a wire whisk, and stir in vinegar and water. Add honey, whisking until blended.

Add walnuts; cover and chill. Just before serving, toss with torn fresh spinach, radicchio, and watercress; add crumbled cooked bacon, if desired. Yield: 1¼ cups.   *Rita W. Cook*
Corpus Christi, Texas

Chicken Dinners With Real Pluck

These chicken dinners won't ruffle your feathers. The whole meal is cooked in a pot or dish; all you add is a salad or bread, and dinner is served.

Great chicken dinners start with basic ingredients imaginatively seasoned. For this idea, an old favorite, chicken and rice, has been paired with tomatoes and canned chiles to make Chicken-and-Chiles Casserole. In Vegetable-Chicken Bake With Sweet Bacon Dressing, a full-flavored dressing transforms a basic casserole into a sweet-sour dish fancy enough to serve at a casual get-together.

CHICKEN-AND-CHILES CASSEROLE

8 skinned and boned chicken breast
   halves
¼ teaspoon salt
¼ teaspoon pepper
1 (8-ounce) package shredded
   mozzarella cheese
1 (4-ounce) can sliced mushrooms,
   drained
1 (10¾-ounce) can cream of
   chicken soup, undiluted
2 tomatoes, peeled and diced
1 (4-ounce) can chopped green
   chiles
Hot cooked rice

Sprinkle chicken breasts evenly with salt and pepper, and place in a lightly greased 11- x 7- x 1½-inch baking

dish. Combine cheese and next 3 ingredients, and pour over chicken. Sprinkle with chiles. Bake, uncovered, at 350° for 35 minutes. Serve over rice. Yield: 8 servings.

CHICKEN FLORENTINE

1 (10-ounce) package frozen
   chopped spinach, thawed
¼ cup Italian-seasoned
   breadcrumbs
2 tablespoons grated Parmesan
   cheese
6 skinned and boned chicken breast
   halves
¼ teaspoon salt
¼ teaspoon pepper
½ cup chopped onion
2 cloves garlic, minced
2 tablespoons butter or margarine,
   melted
2 tablespoons all-purpose flour
1¼ cups milk
1 (4-ounce) package boiled ham,
   finely chopped
¼ teaspoon salt
¼ teaspoon pepper

Drain spinach well, pressing between layers of paper towels; set aside.

Combine breadcrumbs and cheese; set aside. Sprinkle chicken breasts evenly with ¼ teaspoon salt and ¼ teaspoon pepper; dredge in breadcrumb mixture, reserving remaining breadcrumb mixture. Place chicken in a lightly greased 11- x 7- x 1½-inch baking dish.

Cook onion and garlic in butter in a large skillet over medium heat, stirring constantly, until onion is tender. Add flour, stirring until blended. Cook, stirring constantly, 1 minute. Gradually add milk; cook over medium heat, stirring constantly, until mixture is thickened and bubbly.

Stir in spinach, ham, and next 2 ingredients; cook 3 minutes or until thoroughly heated. Spoon over chicken; sprinkle with reserved breadcrumb mixture. Bake, uncovered, at 350° for 45 minutes. Yield: 6 servings.
Grace Underwood
Apopka, Florida

VEGETABLE-CHICKEN BAKE WITH SWEET BACON DRESSING

8 skinned and boned chicken breast halves
½ teaspoon pepper
½ cup all-purpose flour
¼ cup vegetable oil
6 medium-size red potatoes, unpeeled and sliced
1 (9-ounce) package frozen French-cut green beans, thawed and drained
Sweet Bacon Dressing

Sprinkle chicken with pepper, and dredge in flour. Brown on both sides in hot oil in a heavy skillet; drain on paper towels, and set aside.

Place potatoes and green beans in a lightly greased 13- x 9- x 2-inch baking dish. Pour half of Sweet Bacon Dressing over vegetables. Top with chicken breasts, and pour remaining dressing over chicken. Cover and bake at 350° for 1 hour. Yield: 8 servings.

Sweet Bacon Dressing

5 slices bacon
Vegetable oil
⅔ cup balsamic vinegar or red wine vinegar
2½ tablespoons brown sugar
1 teaspoon salt
½ teaspoon ground red pepper
1 clove garlic, crushed

Cook bacon in a large skillet until crisp; remove bacon, reserving drippings. Add enough oil to drippings to measure ¼ cup. Crumble bacon, and set aside. Combine drippings, vinegar, and remaining ingredients in a jar. Cover tightly, and shake well. Add bacon. Yield: 1 cup.

Olé! Soups

Much like the musicians in their beloved mariachi bands, Mexican cooks combine diverse ingredients to create divine results. Our Mexican soup and chili recipes do the same.

SPICY TORTILLA SOUP
(pictured on page 109)

1 large onion, coarsely chopped (about 12 ounces)
3 tablespoons vegetable oil
4 corn tortillas, coarsely chopped
6 cloves garlic, minced
1 tablespoon chopped fresh cilantro or parsley
2 (10¾-ounce) cans tomato puree
2 quarts chicken broth
1 tablespoon ground cumin
2 teaspoons chili powder
2 bay leaves
⅛ teaspoon ground red pepper
3 corn tortillas
Vegetable oil
2 skinned and boned chicken breast halves, cut into strips
1 avocado, peeled, seeded, and cubed
1 cup (4 ounces) shredded Cheddar cheese

Position knife blade in food processor bowl; add chopped onion, and process until smooth. Measure 1 cup onion puree, and set aside; reserve any remaining puree for another use.

Heat 3 tablespoons vegetable oil in a Dutch oven over medium heat; cook 4 chopped tortillas, garlic, and cilantro in hot oil until tortillas are soft. Add 1 cup onion puree, tomato puree, and next 5 ingredients. Bring to a boil; cover, reduce heat, and simmer 30 minutes. Remove and discard bay leaves.

Cut 3 tortillas into thin strips. Pour oil to depth of 1 inch into a large, heavy skillet. Fry strips in hot oil over medium heat until browned. Remove tortillas, reserving ½ tablespoon oil in skillet; drain tortillas on paper towels, and set aside. Add chicken strips to skillet, and cook about 10 minutes or until chicken is done.

Spoon soup into bowls; add chicken strips, avocado, and cheese. Top with tortilla strips. Serve immediately. Yield: 11 cups.
Becky Bradshaw
Bedford, Texas

RED CHILI

1 to 1½ pounds top round steak, cut into ¼-inch pieces
2 tablespoons vegetable oil
1½ tablespoons all-purpose flour
3 cups water
1 clove garlic, crushed
1 (8-ounce) can tomato sauce
⅓ cup chili powder
½ teaspoon salt

Brown steak in hot oil over medium heat in a Dutch oven. Add flour; cook 1 minute, stirring constantly. Add water and remaining ingredients; bring to a boil. Cover, reduce heat, and simmer 30 minutes or until meat is tender. Yield: about 4 cups.

M. De Mello
Hollywood, Florida

CHILLED AVOCADO SOUP

2 ripe avocados, peeled and seeded
1 (14-ounce) can ready-to-serve chicken broth
1 cup plain yogurt
2 tablespoons lemon juice, divided
1 ripe avocado, peeled, seeded, and finely chopped
Coarsely ground pepper

Position knife blade in food processor bowl; add 2 avocados. Process until smooth, scraping down sides once. Combine pureed avocado, chicken broth, yogurt, and 1 tablespoon lemon juice; cover and chill. Toss chopped avocado with remaining 1 tablespoon lemon juice; set aside. Just before serving, stir in chopped avocado and pepper. Yield: 5 cups.

Leslie Genszler
Roswell, Georgia

Discover the sensational taste and look of Southwestern fare in Spicy Tortilla Soup (recipe, page 108).

Above right: *Basil-Brown Butter Sauce (recipe, page 92) for pasta or vegetables boasts zero grams of fat.*

Above left: *Mayonnaise eliminates the need for eggs or a white sauce in Easy Crab Imperial (recipe, page 128). The mayonnaise binds the ingredients and provides a creamy texture.*

Far left: *You can have Sunburst Chicken-and-Walnut Salad (recipe, page 91) on the table in just 30 minutes.*

Left: *Quick-and-easy Sweet Onion Butter (recipe, page 124) adds a peppery-onion flavor to hot breads or baked potatoes.*

*Garnish Garlic-Rolled Lamb Roast
(recipe, page 113) with fresh rosemary
sprigs and blanched sweet red pepper
strips; serve with steamed asparagus.*

Well-Seasoned Lamb

An assortment of fresh lamb cuts claims space in most supermarket meat counters, yet lamb often is approached with uncertainty. For years cookbooks have insisted that lamb be roasted until well done. But anyone who has savored lamb roasted until juicy and pink will testify to its superior taste and texture.

Lamb is as versatile as beef, pork, or poultry. Try cooking Garlic-Rolled Lamb Roast just until the meat thermometer reads 140° to 150° to enjoy it at its juicy best.

GARLIC-ROLLED LAMB ROAST
(pictured on page 112)

1 (4- to 6-pound) boned, rolled, and
   tied leg of lamb
6 to 8 cloves garlic, halved
2 (8-ounce) bottles Dijon
   vinaigrette
2 tablespoons all-purpose flour
¼ cup water
¼ cup dry red wine
⅛ teaspoon pepper
Garnishes: fresh rosemary sprigs,
   sweet red pepper strips

Make several ½-inch slits on outside of lamb and insert garlic. Place lamb in a large shallow dish; pour 1 bottle Dijon vinaigrette over lamb. Cover and marinate 24 hours in refrigerator, turning lamb occasionally. Remove from marinade, discarding marinade.

Place lamb, fat side up, on a rack in a shallow roasting pan; insert meat thermometer, making sure it does not touch fat. Bake at 350° for 1 hour and 45 minutes or until desired degree of doneness (rare 140°, medium 160°, and well-done 170°). Remove to a serving platter, reserving drippings in pan; let stand 10 minutes before carving.

Skim fat from pan drippings. Measure remaining liquid; add remaining bottle Dijon vinaigrette and enough water to measure 1¼ cups. Pour into a saucepan.

Combine flour and ¼ cup water, stirring well; add to pan drippings mixture. Add wine and pepper. Cook over medium heat, stirring constantly, until thickened and bubbly. Serve with lamb. Garnish, if desired. Yield: 8 to 10 servings.   *Mrs. W. M. Alvine*
Winter Springs, Florida

BARBECUED LAMB SHANKS

6 lamb shanks
3 tablespoons all-purpose flour
2 tablespoons vegetable oil
1 cup catsup
½ cup water
¼ cup cider vinegar
¼ cup firmly packed brown sugar
2 tablespoons Worcestershire
   sauce
2 teaspoons salt
2 teaspoons dry mustard
1 medium onion, sliced
Hot cooked rice

Dredge lamb shanks in flour, and brown in oil in a large Dutch oven; set aside. Drain off drippings, and discard.

Combine catsup and next 6 ingredients; pour over lamb in Dutch oven. Add onion; cover and simmer 2 hours, basting occasionally. Uncover; simmer an additional 15 minutes. Serve over hot cooked rice. Yield: 6 servings.   *Nancy Swinney*
Tallahassee, Florida

DESTIN LAMB STEAK

1½ tablespoons Dijon mustard
½ teaspoon dried rosemary
¼ teaspoon dried dillweed
¼ teaspoon ground ginger
⅛ teaspoon garlic powder
1 teaspoon Worcestershire
   sauce
¼ teaspoon prepared horseradish
1 (¾-inch-thick) center cut leg of
   lamb slice (about 12 ounces)
Olive oil

Combine first 7 ingredients; set aside. Brush lamb with olive oil, and place on lightly greased rack of a broiler pan. Broil 4 inches from heat (with electric oven door partially opened) 5 minutes. Turn lamb and spread with half of mustard sauce; broil 5 minutes. Turn lamb and spread with remaining sauce; broil 1 to 2 minutes or until bubbly. Yield: 2 servings.
Frank Jacobson
Destin, Florida

Bring On The Breadsticks

Bread is a standard mealtime accompaniment, so why not make it novel now and then? Serve it as breadsticks.

This recipe uses a versatile, honey-wheat dough with one or more toppings. Best of all, making these slim sticks doesn't require a special pan. By crimping foil to create individual baking grooves, you can obtain sticks with a crispy crust.

SESAME-WHEAT BREADSTICKS

½ cup warm water (105° to 115°)
1 teaspoon active dry yeast
2 teaspoons honey
1 tablespoon butter or margarine, melted
½ teaspoon salt
¾ cup whole wheat flour
¾ cup all-purpose flour
Vegetable cooking spray
1 large egg, lightly beaten
¼ teaspoon salt
2 tablespoons sesame seeds *

Combine first 3 ingredients in a 1-cup liquid measuring cup; let stand 5 minutes. Combine yeast mixture, butter, and salt in a large bowl. Combine flours, and gradually stir 1¼ cups flour mixture into yeast mixture. Set remaining ¼ cup flour mixture aside. Place dough in a well-greased bowl, turning to grease top. Cover and let rise in a warm place (85°), free from drafts, 1½ hours or until dough is doubled in bulk.

Turn dough out onto a surface sprinkled with remaining ¼ cup flour mixture. Divide into 15 equal-size pieces. Roll each piece into a 10-inch stick. Crimp aluminum foil, if desired; place on a baking sheet, and lightly coat with cooking spray. Place sticks on foil; cover and let rise 1 hour.

Combine egg and salt; brush on each breadstick, and sprinkle with sesame seeds. Bake at 400° for 12 minutes or until golden brown. Remove to wire racks to cool. Yield: 15 breadsticks.

* Poppy seeds, caraway seeds, or grated Parmesan cheese may be substituted for sesame seeds.

Note: To crimp foil, fold a 30-inch sheet of foil into dividers ½-inch high and ¾-inch apart.

Observe Passover With Tzimmes

Derived from a Yiddish word, tzimmes (TSIM-ihs) is a stew of fruits and vegetables. Mixed Fruit Tzimmes With Brisket from the Temple Emanuel Sisterhood in Winston-Salem, North Carolina, fits the definition. The added brisket comes out tender and juicy, and lime adds unexpected zip—perfect for Passover.

MIXED FRUIT TZIMMES WITH BRISKET

1 (6-ounce) package dried apricots
1 (8-ounce) package dried apples
1 (12-ounce) package pitted prunes
2 tablespoons vegetable oil
1 (3-pound) beef brisket
2 teaspoons salt
¼ teaspoon pepper
3 carrots, cut into 2-inch pieces
1 lime, cut into ¼-inch slices
2 cups orange juice
2 cups water
¼ cup honey
Garnishes: lime wedges, parsley

Combine fruit in a large bowl; cover with water. Let stand 1 hour; drain. Reserve 6 prunes.

Heat oil in a Dutch oven. Add brisket, and brown on both sides; sprinkle with salt and pepper. Arrange fruit, carrot, and lime slices around brisket.

Combine orange juice and next 2 ingredients; pour over brisket. Bring mixture to a boil. Remove from heat; cover and bake at 350° for 3 hours. Remove brisket, fruit, and carrot to a serving platter. Add 6 reserved prunes. Garnish, if desired. Yield: 8 to 10 servings.

Let Them Eat Pie

The secret of these pies is in the mixing—whipping, stirring, and blending. The ingredient lists are short and simple; you probably have most of the items in your refrigerator or pantry.

NO-BAKE CHERRY CONFETTI PIE

1 (14-ounce) can sweetened condensed milk
1 (8-ounce) can crushed pineapple, undrained
1½ cups miniature marshmallows
½ cup flaked coconut
½ cup chopped pecans
1 (21-ounce) can cherry pie filling
1 (12-ounce) container frozen whipped topping, thawed
2 baked 9-inch pastry shells

Combine first 5 ingredients. Stir in pie filling. Fold in whipped topping. Spoon into pastry shells; chill 1 hour before serving. Yield: two 9-inch pies.

Eleanor K. Brandt
Arlington, Texas

BLUEBERRY-BANANA PIE

1 (8-ounce) package cream cheese, softened
⅓ cup sugar
1 baked 9-inch pastry shell
2 bananas, sliced
1 cup blueberry pie filling
1 cup whipping cream, whipped

Combine cream cheese and sugar; beat at high speed with an electric mixer until light and fluffy. Spread evenly in bottom of cooled pastry shell. Arrange banana slices on cream cheese layer. Spread pie filling over bananas. Top with whipped cream, and chill. Yield: one 9-inch pie.

Carolyn Kornegay
Calypso, North Carolina

"WORKING FOR PEANUTS" PIE

1 (8-ounce) package cream cheese, softened
1 cup sifted powdered sugar
1 cup chunky peanut butter
½ cup milk
1 (8-ounce) container frozen whipped topping, thawed
1 (9-inch) graham cracker crust
¼ cup coarsely chopped peanuts

Combine first 4 ingredients in a large mixing bowl; beat at medium speed with an electric mixer until well blended. Fold in whipped topping; spoon into crust, and sprinkle with peanuts. Chill 8 hours. Yield: one 9-inch pie.

Gwen Louer
Roswell, Georgia

COCONUT PIE

¼ cup sugar
2 large eggs, lightly beaten
½ cup evaporated milk
½ cup canned coconut milk or milk
1 (8½-ounce) can cream of coconut
½ cup flaked coconut
1 (8-inch) graham cracker crust

Combine first 5 ingredients; stir in coconut. Pour into prepared crust. Bake at 350° for 50 to 55 minutes. Yield: one 8-inch pie.

Note: Canned coconut milk is available in supermarkets near other canned milk products.

William Moreno
Richmond, Virginia

For the Fluffiest Pies

Lightly whipped, creamy pies are easy to make, but they're even easier if you know a few tricks and shortcuts. These are the sleights of hand we use:
■ To trim preparation time, rely on commercial refrigerated pie crusts and crumb crusts. Use the size specified in the recipe to prevent overflow.
■ To soften cream cheese, remove the wrapper and microwave at HIGH for 30 seconds.
■ How much do you whip cream to make a fluffy topping? Just past the soft peak stage—if you remove the beaters, they'll leave a soft peak in the whipped cream.
■ Frozen whipped topping is a popular ingredient in our readers' pies. A lower-fat alternative to whipped cream, it boasts more sugar than fat. For best results, thaw in the refrigerator, not on the countertop.
■ Ready to lighten up? "Lite" frozen whipped topping may be substituted for regular frozen whipped topping in these recipes, and the same amount of light cream cheese may be substituted for regular cream cheese.

Asparagus: A Delicacy Of Spring

Asparagus plants take two or more years of care before they produce harvestable spears, and they require lots of hand labor during planting, growing, and gathering. Because asparagus is extra perishable, it must be harvested and processed very rapidly. Within hours of being picked, the asparagus is on the way to the local markets. Care is taken to keep it cool and moist at every step of processing.

Fresh asparagus is in season from February through June. However, canned and frozen asparagus are available year round.

ASPARAGUS-AND-MUSHROOM SAUTÉ

½ pound small fresh asparagus
¼ cup chopped green onions
2 tablespoons olive oil
½ pound fresh mushrooms, cut in half lengthwise
1 tablespoon chopped fresh or 1 teaspoon dried thyme
½ teaspoon salt
¼ teaspoon freshly ground pepper
3 tablespoons Chablis or other dry white wine
1 (3-ounce) package grated Parmesan cheese
1 teaspoon grated lemon rind

Snap off tough ends of asparagus. Remove scales from stalks with a vegetable peeler or knife, if desired. Cut asparagus into 1-inch pieces, and set aside.

Cook green onions in olive oil in a large skillet over high heat, stirring constantly, 1 minute. Reduce heat to medium. Add asparagus, mushrooms, and next 3 ingredients; cook, stirring constantly, 3 minutes. Add wine; cover and cook 2 minutes. Drain. Sprinkle with cheese and lemon rind. Serve immediately. Yield: 4 servings.

CREAMY LEMON-ASPARAGUS SALAD

1 (3-ounce) package lemon-flavored
  gelatin
¾ cup boiling water
2 tablespoons white wine vinegar
2 (3-ounce) packages cream cheese
½ cup commercial creamy
  Parmesan salad dressing
½ pound fresh asparagus
¼ cup finely sliced green onions
¼ cup finely chopped sweet red
  pepper
Lettuce leaves

Combine gelatin and ¾ cup boiling water in a large saucepan, stirring 2 minutes or until gelatin dissolves. Add vinegar and cream cheese; cook over low heat, stirring constantly, until cheese melts. Stir in salad dressing, and chill until the consistency of unbeaten egg white.

Snap off tough ends of asparagus. Remove scales from stalks with a vegetable peeler or knife, if desired. Arrange asparagus in a steamer basket; place over boiling water. Cover and steam 5 to 7 minutes or until crisp-tender; drain. Plunge asparagus into ice water; drain. Cut into ½-inch pieces, reserving tips for garnish.

Fold asparagus, green onions, and red pepper into gelatin mixture. Spoon mixture into 6 lightly oiled ½-cup molds or into a lightly oiled 3-cup mold. Cover and chill 8 hours. Unmold onto lettuce leaves, arranging reserved asparagus tips for garnish. Yield: 6 servings.

ASPARAGUS WITH GOAT CHEESE SAUCE

2 pounds fresh asparagus
1 (3-ounce) package cream
  cheese
1 (3-ounce) package goat cheese
¼ cup mayonnaise or salad
  dressing
¼ to ⅓ cup milk
1 tablespoon chopped fresh or
  frozen chives
Paprika
Garnishes: fresh chives, lemon rind
  strip

Snap off tough ends of asparagus. Remove scales from stalks with a vegetable peeler or knife, if desired. Arrange asparagus in a steamer basket; place over boiling water. Cover and steam 5 to 7 minutes or until crisp-tender. Transfer to a serving plate; keep warm.

Combine cheeses and mayonnaise in a heavy saucepan; cook over medium heat, stirring constantly, until smooth. Stir in milk and chives, and spoon over asparagus. Sprinkle with paprika, and garnish, if desired. Serve immediately. Yield: 8 servings.

Asparagus Tips

When shopping for asparagus, select firm, tall stalks with tightly closed tips. There should be just a light brushing of lavender on the rich green of the vegetable. (Skip spears colored khaki green and those with shriveled skin.) Plump spears are ideal for entrées and casseroles, while the slender ones are best for appetizers and salads. When you bring asparagus home, wrap the cut ends in moist paper towels; then seal in a plastic bag and refrigerate. Try to use within a few days for optimum freshness.

Cooking Tips

Asparagus is grown in sandy soil, so be sure to wash spears thoroughly to remove gritty soil. If stems are tough, use a vegetable peeler to remove the outer layer. Steam asparagus as directed in the recipes above for best flavor and a crisp-tender texture. Steaming also preserves vitamins and nutrients. However, you may boil or microwave spears, if you prefer. Cooking times vary according to the size.
Boiling: Place asparagus and 1 cup water in a skillet. Bring water to a boil; cover, reduce heat, and simmer 2 to 5 minutes. Drain.
Microwave: Place 1 pound asparagus in a round microwave-safe dish with tips pointed toward the center; add 2 tablespoons water. Cover tightly with heavy-duty plastic wrap, and fold back a small edge of wrap to allow steam to escape. Microwave at HIGH 4 to 6 minutes or until asparagus is crisp-tender, giving dish a half-turn after 2 minutes. Drain.

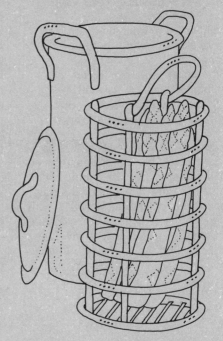

This basket and pan are made especially to keep tender asparagus tips above water, so they don't become mushy and lose flavor during steaming.

MAY

I f breakfast is your favorite meal, pay close attention.
Owners of bed-and-breakfast inns offer some real eye-opener
recipes in this chapter. The aroma of Virginia ham, feathery-
light eggs, spiced apples, and walnut coffee cake will get your
day—and you—started off right. For late afternoon,
plan an elegant picnic and menu to match. Make the outdoor
dining event one to remember with a veal terrine appetizer,
salmon entrée, and pound cake as a finale.

Picnic At Wolf Trap

Imagine the splendor of elegant outdoor dining prior to a sunset concert. Just as the feast winds down, the settling darkness silences the crowd for the evening's final course—music set to the stars.

Nestled in the rolling hills of Vienna, Virginia, Wolf Trap Farm Park for the Performing Arts provides a symphony of food *and* music. Each spring and summer, hundreds of patrons gather there to savor food and nature's beauty, while awaiting the evening's performance.

Carry this picnic menu with you to your next concert in the park, or build your own menu based on one or more of these recipes.

ELEGANT PICNIC
FOR EIGHT

Appetizer Course
Veal Terrine With Mustard Sauce
Endive With Caviar
Baby Squash
Deviled Nuts
Chardonnay

Main Course
Salmon Fillets With Sweet Corn Relish
Miniature Cornmeal Muffins
Red Potato Salad
Green Beans Vinaigrette
Chardonnay

Dessert Course
Old-Fashioned Pound Cake
Fresh Raspberry Sauce
Champagne

VEAL TERRINE
WITH MUSTARD SAUCE

2 apples, cored and quartered
1 medium onion, quartered
2 pounds ground veal
1 large egg, lightly beaten
1 teaspoon salt
¼ teaspoon ground white pepper
¼ teaspoon ground nutmeg
¼ teaspoon paprika
⅛ teaspoon ground cinnamon
2 tablespoons Cognac or other brandy
Vegetable cooking spray
½ cup slivered almonds
Red Delicious apple slices
Mustard Sauce

Position knife blade in food processor bowl; add half of apple and onion quarters. Process 1½ minutes or until smooth, stopping once to scrape down sides; transfer to a large bowl. Repeat procedure with remaining apple and onion quarters. Stir in veal and next 7 ingredients.

Spoon mixture into a 9- x 5- x 3-inch loafpan coated with cooking spray; press into pan. Sprinkle with slivered almonds. Bake at 350° for 1 hour and 15 minutes. Cool in pan on a wire rack (do not drain). Cover and place a weight on top. Refrigerate 8 hours. Remove from pan, and serve with apple slices and Mustard Sauce. Yield: one 9-inch loaf.

Mustard Sauce

¼ cup Dijon mustard
¼ cup fat-free mayonnaise
¼ teaspoon dried dillweed

Combine all ingredients; cover and chill. Yield: ½ cup.

ENDIVE WITH CAVIAR

6 ounces light cream cheese, softened (about ¾ cup)
1¼ teaspoons chopped fresh or frozen chives
1¼ teaspoons finely chopped almonds
1¼ teaspoons fat-free mayonnaise
2 medium heads Belgian endive
2 tablespoons red caviar

Combine first 4 ingredients; beat at medium speed with an electric mixer until smooth. Spread in middle of endive leaves, and lightly sprinkle with caviar. Yield: 8 servings.

BABY SQUASH

1 cup grated Parmesan cheese
1 teaspoon garlic salt
7 baby yellow squash *
7 baby zucchini *

Combine cheese and garlic salt. Wash vegetables, and roll wet vegetables in cheese mixture. Place on a lightly greased baking sheet; bake at 300° for 30 minutes. Yield: 8 servings.

* Substitute 2 small squash and 2 small zucchini for baby yellow squash and zucchini; cut each into quarters, and bake at 300° for 30 minutes.

DEVILED NUTS

1 pound pecan halves
⅓ cup butter or margarine, melted
1 teaspoon Worcestershire sauce
¾ teaspoon salt
½ teaspoon hot sauce

Place pecans in a 13- x 9- x 2-inch pan. Combine butter and remaining ingredients; pour over pecans, stirring to coat. Spread pecans evenly in pan; bake at 300° for 20 minutes, stirring twice. Drain on paper towels; cool. Store pecans in an airtight container. Yield: 4 cups.

SALMON FILLETS WITH SWEET CORN RELISH

2 tablespoons vegetable oil
2 pounds salmon fillets, cut into 8 portions
¼ teaspoon salt
Sweet Corn Relish

Brush oil on skinless side of salmon; sprinkle with salt. Grill over medium-hot coals (350° to 400°) 7 minutes on each side or until fish flakes easily when tested with a fork. Serve with Sweet Corn Relish. Yield: 8 servings.

Sweet Corn Relish

4 to 5 ears fresh yellow corn
1 cup chopped cabbage
⅓ cup chopped onion
⅓ cup chopped green pepper
⅓ cup chopped sweet red pepper
¼ cup sugar
1½ teaspoons dry mustard
¾ teaspoon celery seeds
¾ teaspoon mustard seeds
¾ teaspoon ground turmeric
½ to ¾ teaspoon salt
1 cup white vinegar
¼ cup water

Cook corn 5 minutes in boiling water to cover; drain. Cut kernels from cob. Combine corn, cabbage, and remaining ingredients in a large saucepan; bring mixture to a boil. Cover, reduce heat, and simmer 20 minutes. Chill. Yield: 3 cups.

MINIATURE CORNMEAL MUFFINS

2 cups cornmeal
1 teaspoon baking soda
1 teaspoon salt
2 large eggs, lightly beaten
2 cups buttermilk
2 tablespoons butter or margarine, melted
Vegetable cooking spray

Combine first 3 ingredients in a large bowl; make a well in center of mixture. Combine eggs and next 2 ingredients; add to dry ingredients, stirring just until moistened. Place miniature paper baking cups into miniature (1¾-inch) muffin pans. Coat inside of paper cups with cooking spray; spoon batter into cups, filling three-fourths full. Bake at 400° for 18 minutes or until lightly browned. Yield: 4 dozen.

RED POTATO SALAD

8 to 10 large red potatoes (about 4 pounds)
½ sweet red pepper, cut into thin strips
Watercress Mayonnaise
Watercress
Tomato wedges

Cook potatoes in boiling water to cover 30 minutes or until tender. Drain and cool slightly. Cut into chunks. Combine potatoes and red pepper in a large bowl; stir in Watercress Mayonnaise. Place on a bed of watercress, and arrange tomato wedges around salad. Yield: 8 to 10 servings.

Watercress Mayonnaise

1½ cups mayonnaise
½ cup watercress leaves, chopped
1 tablespoon chopped fresh dill
1 teaspoon lemon juice
½ teaspoon salt
⅛ teaspoon ground white pepper

Combine all ingredients in a food processor or electric blender; process until smooth. Yield: about 1½ cups.

Picnic with a Personal Touch

Try these tips for adding a special flair to your picnic.

■ Preassemble flatware into bundles using your favorite cloth napkins secured with a pretty bow. Insert a flower or greenery from your garden into the bow for a fresh accent. Bundling flatware makes place setting easy, and you can use the bundles to keep lightweight plates from blowing away.

■ Present food on serving pieces having a story or history or on treasured heirlooms.

■ Create a more individual and interesting look by using a variety of styles of eating and serving utensils instead of matched sets. Also, simple baskets or wooden cutting boards often work as serving pieces and nicely accent an outdoor theme.

■ Use fresh fruit and French bread loaves to make attractive centerpieces.

■ Keep cut flowers fresh for decorating by transporting them in a stable container filled with water. Pack fresh herbs for garnishing loosely in a plastic bag.

■ Let the top of your picnic basket double as a cutting, assembling, or serving area.

■ Use a colorful quilt as soft seating for guests and an inviting backdrop for well-dressed plates.

■ Keep insect repellent handy for guests to ensure that you and your party are the only ones feasting.

GREEN BEANS VINAIGRETTE

2 pounds fresh green beans
4 sprigs fresh tarragon
Herbed Vinaigrette

Arrange green beans in a steamer basket; place over boiling water. Add tarragon. Cover and steam 8 to 10 minutes or until crisp-tender. Remove and discard tarragon. Place beans on platter; drizzle with Herbed Vinaigrette. Yield: 8 servings.

Herbed Vinaigrette

¾ cup safflower oil
2 tablespoons olive oil
¼ cup balsamic vinegar
1 clove garlic, crushed
1 teaspoon chopped fresh
   tarragon

Combine all ingredients in a small bowl. Yield: 1 cup.

OLD-FASHIONED POUND CAKE

2 cups butter, softened
2¾ cups sugar
6 large eggs
3¾ cups all-purpose flour
⅛ teaspoon salt
¼ teaspoon ground nutmeg
½ cup milk
1 teaspoon vanilla extract

Beat butter at medium speed with an electric mixer about 2 minutes or until soft and creamy. Gradually add sugar, beating at medium speed 5 to 7 minutes. Add eggs, one at a time, beating just until yellow disappears.

Combine flour, salt, and nutmeg; add to creamed mixture alternately with milk, beginning and ending with flour mixture. Mix at low speed just until blended after each addition. Stir in vanilla.

Pour batter into a greased and floured 10-inch tube pan. Bake at 325° for 1 hour and 15 to 20 minutes or until a wooden pick inserted in center comes out clean. Cool in pan on a wire rack 10 to 15 minutes; remove from pan, and let cool completely on wire rack. Yield: one 10-inch cake.

FRESH RASPBERRY SAUCE

3 cups fresh raspberries, halved
¼ cup sugar
1 teaspoon crème de cassis

Combine all ingredients in a medium bowl, stirring gently until sugar dissolves; cover and chill at least 3 hours. Serve over pound cake or ice cream. Yield: 1½ cups.

Breakfast — B&B Style

In easygoing visits to six B&Bs (bed-and-breakfast inns) across the South, we gathered recipes and flavor from innkeepers who entertain every morning with style. Join us on our journey and enjoy some of their recipes beginning on facing page.

The Colonel's Lady, Gatlinburg, Tennessee

There's no be-here, be-there itinerary or list of rules at The Colonel's Lady owned by John and Lee Mellor in Gatlinburg, Tennessee. All you do is enjoy the easy, one-on-one encounter with this quiet perch atop the Smoky Mountains. Certainly, if the mythical colonel did have a lady, this is surely the way she'd want to be treated.
■ **The Colonel's Lady,** 1120 Tanrac Trail, Gatlinburg, Tennessee 37738

Seven Sisters Inn, Ocala, Florida

Each room of the Victorian home, Seven Sisters Inn in Ocala, Florida, (the rooms are named for the original owner's seven sisters) struts its own charm. "We did it all," Bonnie Morehardt says proudly, referring to the design team consisting of her parents, her brothers, and her B&B co-owner, a full-time pilot named Ken Oden.
■ **Seven Sisters Inn,** 820 S.E. Fort King Street, Ocala, Florida 32671

Stillwater Inn, Jefferson, Texas

Bill Stewart, formerly a chef at such distinguished Dallas restaurants as the French Room, Callaud's, and Cafe Pacific, brought fine dining to this tidy small East Texas town in 1984, and he and wife Sharon later added the B&B accommodations at the Stillwater Inn in Jefferson, Texas.
■ **Stillwater Inn,** 203 East Broadway, Jefferson, Texas 75657

The Manor at Taylor's Store, Smith Mountain Lake, Virginia

The Manor at Taylor's Store, near Roanoke, Virginia, is a country club among B&Bs, a place to arrive early and stay late. Breakfast here is good for you. Mary Lynn Tucker, busy in the kitchen, counts every gram of fat.
■ **The Manor at Taylor's Store,** Route 1, Box 533, Smith Mountain Lake, Virginia 24184

Dairy Hollow House, Eureka Springs, Arkansas

Owned by Ned Shank and his wife (the children's book and cookbook author Crescent Dragonwagon, who took the whimsical name when she was a teenager), Dairy Hollow House in Eureka Springs, Arkansas, has been hosting vacationers for 13 years.

With three rooms in a tucked-away 1888 farmhouse, and three more in the main house, Dairy Hollow House is a favorite of Bill and Hillary Clinton.
■ **Dairy Hollow House,** 515 Spring Street, Eureka Springs, Arkansas 72632

The Lion & The Rose, Asheville, North Carolina

"I pride myself on a different breakfast every day you stay," says Jeanne Donaldson of The Lion & The Rose, a century-old Queen Anne Victorian B&B in Asheville, North Carolina.

"My record was the guest who had 13 nights with us. I did crêpes with various toppings, crab Benedict, asparagus omelets with rarebit sauce, and champagne with raspberries." For grand effect, Jeanne marches out a procession of chinas, goblets, and gold vermeil flatware.

■ **The Lion & The Rose,** 276 Montford Avenue, Asheville, North Carolina 28801

STUFFED RAINBOW TROUT

¼ cup butter or margarine
½ cup finely chopped onion
½ cup finely chopped celery
¼ cup chopped fresh parsley
1 clove garlic, minced
½ teaspoon salt
¼ teaspoon dried tarragon
⅛ teaspoon lemon pepper
3 cups Italian bread cubes
1 large egg, lightly beaten
1 tablespoon Chablis or other dry white wine
4 (8- to 10-ounce) whole farm-raised trout, dressed
½ teaspoon salt
1 tablespoon lemon juice
1 tablespoon soy sauce
½ cup all-purpose flour
2 slices bacon, cut in half
Garnishes: lemon slices, fresh parsley sprigs

Melt butter in a large skillet over medium heat; add onion and celery, and cook, stirring constantly, until tender. Remove from heat; stir in parsley and next 4 ingredients. Add bread cubes; toss gently. Combine egg and white wine; stir into bread mixture. Spread evenly into an 11- x 7- x 1½-inch baking dish; set aside.

Rinse trout; pat dry. Sprinkle inside of fish evenly with ½ teaspoon salt. Combine lemon juice and soy sauce; brush inside of fish, reserving remaining lemon juice mixture. Dredge fish in flour. Place over stuffing, overlapping slightly. Drizzle with reserved lemon juice mixture. Place bacon over trout. Cover and bake at 350° for 45 minutes. Uncover and bake an additional 15 minutes. Yield: 4 servings.

The Colonel's Lady
Gatlinburg, Tennessee

VIRGINIA HAM BREAKFAST SOUFFLÉ

1 pound Virginia ham sausage or turkey sausage
4 green onions, chopped
1 to 2 cloves garlic, minced
2 (8-ounce) cartons egg substitute
1 cup skim milk
¼ teaspoon salt
¼ teaspoon ground red pepper
¾ teaspoon dry mustard
6 slices whole wheat bread, cubed
Vegetable cooking spray

Cook first 3 ingredients in a large skillet until sausage is browned, stirring until it crumbles; drain. Rinse with hot water; drain well, and press between layers of paper towels. Set aside.

Combine egg substitute and next 4 ingredients in a large bowl; stir in sausage mixture and bread cubes. Spoon into 10 (6-ounce) ramekins or custard cups coated with cooking spray; cover and chill 8 hours. Remove from refrigerator 30 minutes before baking. Bake, uncovered, at 350° for 30 minutes or until set. Serve immediately. Yield: 10 servings.

The Manor at Taylor's Store
Smith Mountain Lake, Virginia

LION BENEDICT

1 tablespoon butter or margarine
½ cup sliced green onions
1 pound lump crabmeat, drained
4 sourdough English muffins, split and toasted
Leaf lettuce
Poached Eggs
Lime Hollandaise Sauce
Paprika
Garnish: Roma or plum tomato slices

Melt butter in a large skillet over medium heat; add green onions, and cook, stirring constantly, 1 minute. Add crabmeat, and cook until thoroughly heated; keep warm.

Arrange English muffin halves on individual lettuce-lined plates; spoon crabmeat mixture evenly over halves.

Top with Poached Eggs, and drizzle with Lime Hollandaise Sauce. Sprinkle with paprika, and garnish, if desired. Yield: 4 to 8 servings.

Poached Eggs

8 large eggs

Lightly grease a large saucepan; add water to depth of 2 inches. Bring to a boil; reduce heat, and maintain at a light simmer. Working with 4 eggs at a time, break eggs, one at a time, into a saucer; slip into water, holding saucer close to water. Simmer 5 minutes or until cooked. Remove eggs with a slotted spoon; trim edges of eggs, if desired. Repeat procedure with remaining eggs. Yield: 8 eggs.

Lime Hollandaise Sauce

4 large eggs, lightly beaten
½ teaspoon salt
½ teaspoon grated lime rind
2 tablespoons fresh lime juice
½ cup butter or margarine, divided

Combine first 3 ingredients in top of a double boiler, and place over hot (not boiling) water. Gradually add lime juice, stirring constantly; add butter, 2 tablespoons at a time, stirring constantly after each addition until butter is melted. Cook, stirring constantly, until temperature reaches 160° (about 10 to 15 minutes). Serve immediately. Yield: 1 cup.   *The Lion & The Rose*
Asheville, North Carolina

Tip: *When squeezing fresh lemons, limes, or oranges for juice, first grate the rind by rubbing the washed fruit against surface of grater, taking care to remove only the outer colored portion of the rind. Wrap the rind in plastic in teaspoon portions, and freeze for future use.*

THREE CHEESE STUFFED FRENCH TOAST

8 (2-inch-thick) slices French bread
¾ cup (3 ounces) shredded
  mozzarella cheese
½ (8-ounce) package cream cheese,
  softened
1 tablespoon ricotta cheese
3 tablespoons apricot jam
2 large eggs, lightly beaten
½ cup milk
1 cup corn flake crumbs
2 tablespoons butter or margarine
1 (12-ounce) bottle apricot syrup
¼ cup butter or margarine
2 tablespoons sugar
2 teaspoons ground ginger
16 peach slices
Sifted powdered sugar

Starting from one side, split each bread slice, leaving opposite side attached (so that when open, bread looks like butterfly wings). Using a fork, hollow out a shallow pocket on the inside of each slice, discarding crumbs; set aside. Combine cheeses; stir in apricot jam. Spoon about 2 tablespoons cheese mixture into each bread slice, and place slices in a 13- x 9- x 2-inch baking dish. Cover and refrigerate 8 hours.

Combine eggs and milk; dip bread in mixture, and dredge in corn flake crumbs. Melt 2 tablespoons butter in a large skillet over medium heat; cook bread 2 minutes on each side or until golden brown. Place in a lightly greased 13- x 9- x 2-inch baking dish. Bake at 400° for 15 minutes.

Cook syrup in a saucepan over low heat until thoroughly heated; remove from heat, and keep warm.

Combine ¼ cup butter, sugar, and ginger in a large skillet over medium heat; add peaches, and cook 3 minutes, stirring gently. Arrange French toast on individual plates; top each serving with peach slices, and sprinkle with powdered sugar. Serve with syrup. Yield: 8 servings.

Seven Sisters Inn
Ocala, Florida

FEATHERBED EGGS

¾ cup crumbled Cornbread
Vegetable cooking spray
1½ cups (6 ounces) shredded extra-
  sharp Cheddar cheese
6 large eggs, lightly beaten
1½ cups milk
1 teaspoon hot sauce
1 teaspoon Pickapeppa sauce
¼ teaspoon freshly ground pepper
¼ teaspoon seasoned salt

Place about 2 tablespoons crumbled bread into bottom of each of 6 (6-ounce) ramekins or custard cups coated with cooking spray. Top each with ¼ cup cheese. Combine eggs and remaining ingredients; pour ½ cup into each ramekin. Bake at 375° for 20 to 25 minutes or until golden. Yield: 6 servings.

Cornbread

¼ cup butter or margarine
1 cup yellow cornmeal
1 cup all-purpose flour
1 tablespoon baking powder
¼ teaspoon baking soda
¼ teaspoon salt
2 tablespoons sugar
1¼ cups buttermilk
1 large egg, lightly beaten
¼ cup corn oil

Melt butter in an 8-inch cast-iron skillet in a 375° oven for 5 minutes. Combine cornmeal and next 5 ingredients; make a well in center of mixture. Combine buttermilk, egg, and oil; add to dry ingredients, stirring just until dry ingredients are moistened.

Remove skillet from oven. Pour batter into skillet. Bake at 375° for 25

---

minutes or until golden brown. Yield: about 6 cups crumbled cornbread or 6 servings. *Dairy Hollow House Eureka Springs, Arkansas*

WHOLE GRAIN PANCAKES

1 cup whole wheat flour
2 tablespoons baking powder
2 tablespoons sugar
½ teaspoon ground allspice
¼ teaspoon ground nutmeg
2 egg whites, lightly beaten
1 cup skim milk
2 tablespoons canola or vegetable oil
Vegetable cooking spray
Garnishes: fresh strawberries, thinly sliced ham

Combine first 5 ingredients; make a well in center of mixture. Combine egg whites, milk, and oil; add to dry ingredients, stirring just until dry ingredients are moistened. Let stand 20 minutes.

For each pancake, spoon about 2 tablespoons batter onto a moderately hot griddle coated with cooking spray. Turn when tops are covered with bubbles and edges look cooked. Garnish, if desired. Yield: 8 to 10 pancakes.
The Manor at Taylor's Store Smith Mountain Lake, Virginia

BLUEBERRIES À LA FREDERICK

2 pints fresh blueberries
2 teaspoons grated orange rind
2 teaspoons grated lemon rind
2 tablespoons lemon juice
⅓ cup sugar
1 cup whipping cream

Combine first 5 ingredients, tossing gently; cover and chill. Spoon into individual bowls, and serve with whipping cream. Yield: 4 servings.
The Colonel's Lady Gatlinburg, Tennessee

MIXED FRUIT COMPOTE

½ cup dried pitted prunes
½ cup dried apricots
1 cup apple juice
1 (2-inch) stick cinnamon
1 tablespoon grated orange rind
1 orange, peeled, sectioned, and chopped
1 grapefruit, peeled, sectioned, and chopped
1 Granny Smith apple, peeled, cored, and chopped
1 banana, sliced
⅓ cup orange juice
1 to 2 tablespoons brown sugar
3 tablespoons chopped walnuts, toasted

Combine prunes and apricots in a small bowl; set aside. Cook apple juice and cinnamon stick in a small saucepan over medium heat until hot; pour over fruit mixture. Cover and let stand 8 hours.

Remove cinnamon stick; add orange rind and next 6 ingredients, tossing gently. Sprinkle with walnuts. Yield: 6 to 8 servings. *Dairy Hollow House Eureka Springs, Arkansas*

SPICED APPLES

3 cooking apples, peeled, cored, and thinly sliced
2 tablespoons unsalted butter or unsalted margarine, melted
⅓ cup pecan halves, toasted
1 tablespoon brown sugar
⅛ teaspoon ground cinnamon
⅛ teaspoon ground nutmeg
1 teaspoon vanilla extract

Cook apples in butter in a large skillet over low heat, stirring occasionally, until tender. Add pecans and remaining ingredients, tossing gently. Serve with French toast or waffles. Yield: 6 servings.
Stillwater Inn Jefferson, Texas

FRESH RASPBERRY CRÊPES WITH YOGURT FILLING

1 (16-ounce) carton plain nonfat yogurt
Crêpes
Melted butter
2 cups fresh raspberries
Powdered sugar

Line a large wire-mesh strainer with cheesecloth; place over a bowl. Add yogurt; cover and refrigerate at least 24 hours until yogurt is well drained and thickened, stirring occasionally.

Place a rounded teaspoonful of yogurt in center of each crêpe. Fold left and right sides of crêpe to center; fold remaining edges to form a rectangle. Cover and keep warm. Repeat procedure with remaining crêpes.

To serve, place 3 filled crêpes on each plate. Brush with butter, and sprinkle evenly with raspberries and powdered sugar. Dollop with remaining yogurt. Yield: 8 servings.

Crêpes

1⅓ cups all-purpose flour
½ teaspoon salt
2⅔ cups milk
4 large eggs
3 tablespoons butter, melted
Vegetable cooking spray

Combine first 3 ingredients in a large mixing bowl, beating at medium speed with an electric mixer until smooth. Add eggs, and beat well; stir in butter. Cover and refrigerate at least 3 hours.

Spray bottom of a 6-inch crêpe pan or heavy skillet lightly with cooking spray; place over medium heat until just hot, but not smoking.

Pour ¼ cup batter into pan; quickly tilt pan in all directions so batter covers pan with a thin film. Cook about 1 minute or until crêpe can be shaken loose from pan. Flip crêpe, and cook about 30 seconds. Transfer crêpe to wax paper to cool. Repeat procedure until all batter is used, stacking crêpes between layers of wax paper to prevent sticking. Yield: 24 (6-inch) crêpes.
The Lion & The Rose Asheville, North Carolina

WALNUT COFFEE CAKE

½ cup sugar
1½ teaspoons ground cinnamon
½ cup finely chopped walnuts
¾ cup butter or margarine,
  softened
1 cup sugar
½ cup firmly packed brown sugar
3 large eggs
2 cups all-purpose flour
1 cup whole wheat flour
1 tablespoon baking powder
¾ teaspoon baking soda
½ teaspoon salt
1½ cups sour cream
1 teaspoon vanilla extract
2 tablespoons butter or margarine,
  cut into small pieces
Sifted powdered sugar

Combine first 3 ingredients; spoon about 2 tablespoons nut mixture into a greased and floured 12-cup Bundt pan. Set pan and remaining nut mixture aside.

Beat ¾ cup butter at medium speed with an electric mixer until soft and creamy; gradually add 1 cup sugar and brown sugar, beating mixture well. Add eggs, one at a time, beating after each addition.

Combine flours and next 3 ingredients; add to butter mixture alternately with sour cream, beginning and ending with flour mixture. Mix after each addition. Stir in vanilla.

Spoon half of batter into prepared pan; sprinkle with half of remaining nut mixture. Add remaining batter, spreading evenly, and top with remaining nut mixture. Dot with 2 tablespoons butter. Bake at 350° for 40 to 45 minutes or until a wooden pick inserted in center of cake comes out clean. Cool in pan on a wire rack 10 minutes; remove from pan, and cool on wire rack. Sprinkle with powdered sugar. Yield: one 10-inch cake.

The Colonel's Lady
Gatlinburg, Tennessee

YIA YIA'S HOLLAND RUSK PUDDING

1 (4-ounce) package Holland Rusk
  biscuits
1¼ cups sugar, divided
½ cup unsalted butter or unsalted
  margarine, melted
¼ cup all-purpose flour
2 cups milk
3 large eggs, separated
1 teaspoon vanilla extract
¼ teaspoon almond extract
1 tablespoon sugar
Sweetened whipped cream
Garnish: apple wedges

Place knife blade in food processor bowl; add biscuits. Process until smooth. Combine biscuit crumbs, ½ cup sugar, and butter. Press ⅔ cup mixture into bottom of an 11- x 7- x 1½-inch baking dish; reserve remaining crumb mixture.

Combine remaining ¾ cup sugar and flour in a heavy saucepan; stir in milk and egg yolks. Cook over low heat, stirring often, until mixture begins to thicken; stir in flavorings. Pour mixture through a large wire-mesh strainer into baking dish.

Beat egg whites at high speed with an electric mixer until foamy. Add 1 tablespoon sugar, beating until stiff peaks form. Spread over custard, and sprinkle with reserved crumb mixture. Bake at 325° for 20 to 25 minutes. Cool. Serve with whipped cream, and garnish, if desired. Yield: 8 servings.

Stillwater Inn
Jefferson, Texas

Sweet Onions To Cry For

While sweet onions aren't as likely to cause tears as other onions, some do. So, the next time you chop onions, try one of these tear-drying tips:
■ Cut or trim the root end last, since the sulfuric compounds that cause tears are concentrated at the base of the onion.
■ When possible, peel and cut onions under running water. The sulfuric compounds will react with the water, instead of your eyes.
■ Refrigerate onions for a few hours before cutting.
■ If the recipe calls for several pounds of onions, try chopping them in a food processor.

SWEET ONION RELISH

10 pounds sweet onions, cut into
  quarters
¼ cup salt
2 teaspoons pickling spice
2¼ cups sugar
2 cups apple cider vinegar
  (5% acidity)
2 tablespoons diced pimiento
½ teaspoon ground turmeric

Position knife blade in food processor bowl; add onion quarters, a few at a time. Process until finely chopped. Combine 12 cups onion and salt in a large bowl; let stand 30 minutes. Drain, squeezing all excess juice from mixture. Place pickling spice on a 6-inch square of cheesecloth; tie with string. Combine onion, spice bag, sugar, and remaining ingredients in a large Dutch oven. Bring to a boil; reduce heat, and cook about 30 minutes or until thick. Discard spice bag.

Pack onion mixture into hot jars, filling to ½ inch from top. Remove air bubbles; wipe jar rims. Cover at once with metal lids, and screw on bands. Process in boiling-water bath 10 minutes. Yield: 9 pints.

SWEET ONION BUTTER
(pictured on page 111)

½ cup butter or margarine,
  softened
¼ cup grated sweet onion,
  undrained
1 tablespoon minced fresh parsley
1 teaspoon ground white pepper
½ teaspoon dry mustard

Combine all ingredients in a small mixing bowl; beat at low speed with an electric mixer until blended. Serve with hot bread or baked potatoes. Yield: ¾ cup.

KIWIFRUIT-ONION CHUTNEY

1 cup white vinegar
1 cup firmly packed brown sugar
¾ teaspoon salt
½ teaspoon ground ginger
⅛ teaspoon ground red pepper
1 cup peeled, chopped cooking
  apple
½ cup thinly sliced sweet onion
½ cup raisins
¼ lemon, thinly sliced
1½ cups peeled, chopped kiwifruit

Combine first 5 ingredients in a large saucepan; cook over low heat until mixture is reduced to 1 cup. Add apple and next 3 ingredients; cook 10 minutes. Stir in kiwifruit; bring to a boil. Remove from heat; cool. Cover and chill. Serve with poultry, pork, or ham. Yield: 2½ cups.

Note: To serve as an appetizer, process ¾ cup Kiwifruit-Onion Chutney in container of an electric blender or food processor; pour over 1 (8-ounce) package cream cheese, and serve with crackers.

ON THE LIGHT SIDE

Help! The Boss Is Coming to Dinner

It's 1:30 p.m. on a workday and suddenly you remember that last week you invited your boss and her husband to dinner—tonight! What can you do?

There's hardly enough time to cook—let alone shop—and the dining room's a wreck. To make matters worse, the boss's doctor has her on a low-fat, low-cholesterol diet that she follows *religiously*.

Relax. What seems to be a dilemma is actually an opportunity to impress your supervisor with a great meal, spotlighting your light-cooking savvy. You'll be a whopping success because we've got the game plan, complete with a menu and built-in options for versatility. By 7:30 p.m. you'll have a healthful dinner on the table—worthy of both praise and a raise.

BOSS'S DINNER
FOR FOUR

**Creamy Ham Dip with assorted
fresh vegetables
Wilted Spinach Salad or
Salad Composé
Chicken Cordon Bleu or
Broiled Tuna With Rosemary
Linguine With
Red Pepper Sauce
Commercial fruit sorbet
Sparkling water**

CREAMY HAM DIP

1 (8-ounce) container fat-free cream
  cheese, softened
3 ounces reduced-fat, low-sodium,
  honey-flavored ham slices, finely
  chopped
¼ cup finely chopped celery
2 tablespoons finely chopped
  onion
1 tablespoon sweet pickle relish,
  drained
1 tablespoon chopped fresh parsley

Position knife blade in food processor bowl; add cream cheese and ham. Process until smooth. Stir in celery, onion, and relish.

Spoon mixture into a serving container, and sprinkle with chopped parsley. Serve dip with assorted fresh vegetables. Yield: 1½ cups (14 calories [13% from fat] per tablespoon).

□ *1.9g protein, 0.2g fat (0g saturated), 2.1g carbohydrate, 0g fiber, 3.4mg cholesterol, 90mg sodium, and 34mg calcium.*

Note: Ham and cream cheese may be blended at medium speed with an electric mixer until smooth.

WILTED SPINACH SALAD

Vegetable cooking spray
2 ounces reduced-fat, low-sodium,
  honey-flavored ham slices,
  chopped
12 ounces fresh spinach
2 hard-cooked egg whites, coarsely
  chopped
4 ounces fresh mushrooms, sliced
1 (8-ounce) bottle fat-free sweet-
  and-sour salad dressing

Coat a nonstick skillet with cooking spray. Add ham, and cook over medium heat, stirring constantly, until lightly browned. Drain on paper towels; set aside.

Remove stems from spinach; wash leaves thoroughly, and pat dry. Tear into bite-size pieces; arrange one-fourth of spinach on each of 4 individual salad plates. Top each with one-fourth of egg whites and mushrooms; set aside. Bring salad dressing to a boil in a small saucepan over high heat; pour ¼ cup over each salad. Sprinkle evenly with ham. Yield: 4 servings (78 calories [15% from fat] per serving).

□ *7.3g protein, 1.3g fat (0.g saturated), 11.8g carbohydrate, 3.8g fiber, 7mg cholesterol, 251mg sodium, and 87mg calcium.*

SALAD COMPOSÉ

40 small fresh green beans or snow pea pods
20 Bibb lettuce leaves
1 (14.4-ounce) can hearts of palm, drained and sliced
1 head Belgian endive, sliced crosswise and separated into rings
1 large tomato, thinly sliced
4 large mushrooms, sliced
Wine Vinegar Dressing

Wash green beans; trim ends, if desired. Cook beans in boiling water to cover 30 seconds; drain and plunge into ice water until chilled. Drain and set aside.

Line 4 salad plates evenly with lettuce leaves; arrange green beans, hearts of palm, and next 3 ingredients evenly over lettuce. Serve with Wine Vinegar Dressing. Yield: 4 servings (142 calories [26% from fat] per salad and 2 tablespoons dressing).

□ 4.5g protein, 4.1g fat (0.7g saturated), 26.1g carbohydrate, 3.6g fiber, 0mg cholesterol, 169mg sodium, and 41mg calcium.

Wine Vinegar Dressing

½ cup red wine vinegar
1 tablespoon vegetable oil
½ cup chopped green onions
1 teaspoon dried parsley flakes
½ teaspoon sugar
¼ teaspoon salt
¼ teaspoon pepper

Combine all ingredients in container of an electric blender; process 30 seconds. Yield: about ½ cup (41 calories [75% from fat] per tablespoon).

□ 0.3g protein, 3.4g fat (0.6g saturated), 2.6g carbohydrate, 0.3g fiber, 0mg cholesterol, 149mg sodium, and 11mg calcium.
Nancy Gerard
Chantilly, Virginia

CHICKEN CORDON BLEU

4 (4-ounce) skinned and boned chicken breast halves
3 tablespoons chopped fresh parsley
1 teaspoon dried Italian seasoning, divided
4 (1-ounce) reduced-fat, low-sodium, honey-flavored ham slices
4 (1-ounce) slices part-skim mozzarella cheese
1 tablespoon fat-free mayonnaise
1 teaspoon warm water
⅓ cup soft breadcrumbs
Vegetable cooking spray

Place each piece of chicken between 2 sheets of wax paper; flatten to ¼-inch thickness using a meat mallet or rolling pin. Sprinkle with parsley and ¼ teaspoon Italian seasoning. Place a ham slice and a cheese slice on each chicken breast; roll up from short side, and secure with wooden picks.

Combine mayonnaise and water; brush on chicken, covering all sides. Combine breadcrumbs and remaining ¾ teaspoon Italian seasoning; dredge chicken rolls in mixture. Place on a baking sheet coated with cooking spray. Bake at 425° for 15 minutes or until chicken is done. Remove wooden picks. Yield: 4 servings (264 calories [15% from fat] per serving).

□ *38.8g protein, 9.3g fat (3.8g saturated), 4.5g carbohydrate, 0.3g fiber, 103mg cholesterol, 483mg sodium, and 213mg calcium.*

Mrs. John B. Wright
Greenville, South Carolina

BROILED TUNA WITH ROSEMARY

4 (4-ounce) tuna steaks
½ cup Chablis or other dry white wine
1 tablespoon lemon juice
½ teaspoon garlic powder
1½ teaspoons fresh rosemary
½ teaspoon dried oregano
¼ teaspoon salt
⅛ teaspoon pepper
Vegetable cooking spray
Garnish: fresh rosemary sprigs

Place tuna steaks in a large heavy-duty, zip-top plastic bag. Combine wine and next 6 ingredients; pour over steaks. Seal bag, and refrigerate 1½ hours, turning bag occasionally.

Remove steaks, discarding marinade. Place steaks on a rack coated with cooking spray; place rack in broiler pan. Broil 4 to 5 inches from heat (with electric oven door partially opened) 3 to 4 minutes on each side or until done. Garnish, if desired. Yield: 4 servings (165 calories [30% from fat] per serving).

□ *25.4g protein, 5.5g fat (1.4g saturated), 0.4g carbohydrate, 0g fiber, 42mg cholesterol, 88mg sodium, and 2mg calcium.*

LINGUINE WITH RED PEPPER SAUCE

8 ounces linguine, uncooked
Vegetable cooking spray
2 tablespoons olive oil
6 cups chopped sweet red pepper
3 cloves garlic, crushed
½ cup balsamic vinegar or red wine vinegar
⅔ cup chopped fresh basil
½ teaspoon salt
¼ teaspoon pepper

Cook linguine according to package directions, omitting salt or fat; drain and keep warm. Coat a nonstick skillet with cooking spray; add olive oil, sweet red pepper, and garlic. Cook over low heat, stirring occasionally, 30 minutes.

Place in container of an electric blender or food processor. Add vinegar and remaining ingredients; process until smooth. Spoon over linguine, and serve immediately. Yield: 4 servings (337 calories [24% from fat] per 1 cup pasta and ¼ cup sauce).

□ *9.5g protein, 8.9g fat (1.2g saturated), 56.4g carbohydrate, 5g fiber, 0mg cholesterol, 304mg sodium, and 41mg calcium.*

LIGHT FAVORITE

Cookies For The Health Conscious

Pat Lawler of Waco, Georgia, sent us her recipe for a healthier oatmeal cookie. Using her proportions we developed an even lighter version. To impart a slightly richer flavor, we replaced ¼ cup of vegetable oil in her recipe with margarine. We then

dropped 17.6 grams of fat from the recipe by substituting ½ cup of raisins for ¼ cup of chopped walnuts.

OATMEAL-RAISIN COOKIES

¼ cup margarine, softened
½ cup sugar
½ cup firmly packed brown sugar
½ cup egg substitute
2 teaspoons vanilla extract
¾ cup all-purpose flour
¼ teaspoon baking soda
⅛ teaspoon salt
1½ cups quick-cooking oats, uncooked
½ cup raisins
Vegetable cooking spray

Beat margarine at medium speed with an electric mixer. Gradually add sugars, beating well. Add egg substitute and vanilla; mix well.

Combine flour and next 3 ingredients. Gradually add to margarine mixture, mixing well. Stir in raisins.

Drop dough by 2 teaspoonfuls onto cookie sheets coated with cooking spray. Bake at 350° for 10 to 12 minutes or until lightly browned. Remove to wire racks to cool. Yield: 3 dozen cookies (65 calories [21% from fat] per cookie).

□ *1.2g protein, 1.5g fat (0.3g saturated), 11.7g carbohydrate, 0.5g fiber, 0mg cholesterol, 27mg sodium, and 9mg calcium.*

COMPARE THE NUTRIENTS (per serving)		
	Traditional	Light
Calories	80	65
Fat	3.2g	1.5g
Cholesterol	10mg	0mg

A Little Dab Will Do You

In these recipes, we call for either mayonnaise or salad dressing. If you've ever wondered what the difference between the two is, read on. We have the scoop (or should that be dollop) on the issue.

Mayonnaise is a blend of vegetable oil, vinegar, eggs, salt, lemon juice, and sugar. Salad dressing contains the same ingredients; however, it's made with less oil, and food starch is added.

In each of these recipes, we experimented with light, low-fat, and fat-free mayonnaises and salad dressings to reduce calories and fat. We had excellent results, too.

■ Mayonnaise is the base for the grilling sauce on this tuna. It seals in flavor and cooks with little or no sticking; try the mayonnaise-based sauce on chicken breasts, too.

GRILLED FLORIDA TUNA

½ cup mayonnaise or salad
   dressing
1 tablespoon lime juice
1 clove garlic, pressed
½ teaspoon ground red
   pepper
½ teaspoon ground cumin
4 (½-inch-thick) tuna steaks (about
   1 pound)

Combine first 5 ingredients. Brush on steaks. Grill, covered, over medium coals (300° to 350°) 5 to 7 minutes on each side. Yield: 4 servings.

Tip: *When buying whole fish, don't discard the head and tail; cooked with the fish or by themselves, they make good fish stock for chowders, sauces, or aspics.*

■ The most difficult part of this recipe is picking the crabmeat. The dish has a mild flavor, emphasizing the delicate crabmeat. If you're accustomed to spicier crabmeat dishes, stir in Old Bay seasoning to taste.

EASY CRAB IMPERIAL
(pictured on page 111)

1 pound fresh crabmeat, drained
   and flaked
⅔ cup mayonnaise or salad dressing
1 tablespoon chopped fresh parsley
2 teaspoons lemon juice
3 to 4 tablespoons grated Parmesan
   cheese
Paprika

Combine first 4 ingredients. Spoon about ½ cup mixture into 4 shell-shaped baking dishes; sprinkle with cheese. Bake at 350° for 15 minutes or until thoroughly heated. Sprinkle with paprika. Yield: 4 servings.

Note: Easy Crab Imperial may be baked in 4 baked (3-inch) pastry shells.
Patti Leonard
Pasadena, Maryland

■ Most traditional salad dressings team Roquefort with sour cream. This recipe relies on mayonnaise, which is also a crucial ingredient in homemade Thousand Island dressing.

ROQUEFORT DRESSING

2 (3-ounce) packages Roquefort
   cheese, crumbled
2 cups mayonnaise or salad
   dressing
½ teaspoon garlic powder
1 teaspoon ground white pepper
2 tablespoons white vinegar
¼ cup milk

Combine all ingredients; cover and chill. Serve with mixed greens, drizzle over a baked potato, or use as a dip for vegetables. Yield: 3 cups.
Arlene Cox
Elizabethton, Tennessee

■ Mayonnaise functions as a seasoning and slaw dressing in this recipe. To make coleslaw even quicker and easier, purchase chopped cabbage at the supermarket.

OLD-FASHIONED
SWEET COLESLAW

5 cups finely chopped cabbage
   (about 1 small head)
2 carrots, scraped and shredded
1 to 2 tablespoons sugar
½ teaspoon salt
¼ teaspoon pepper
⅓ cup mayonnaise or salad
   dressing

Combine first 2 ingredients in a large bowl. Sprinkle with sugar, salt, and pepper; toss gently. Stir in mayonnaise. Cover and chill thoroughly. Yield: 6 to 8 servings.
Sue Braley
Pulaski, Tennessee

Mountain Measures

If you've never traveled through the Appalachian Mountains, you can journey there in your kitchen with *Mountain Measures*. This collection of more than 800 tested recipes features numerous heritage recipes, designated throughout the book by quilt-block symbols. A sampling of West Virginia photographs, poetry, and prose helps carry the pioneer and mountain spirit through the book.

First published in 1974 by the Junior League of Charleston, West Virginia, the book has sold more than 100,000 copies. As a result, more than $220,000 has been donated to community projects.

GERMAN CHOCOLATE PIE

1 (4-ounce) package sweet baking
   chocolate
¼ cup butter or margarine
1 (13-ounce) can evaporated
   milk
1½ cups sugar
3 tablespoons cornstarch
⅛ teaspoon salt
2 large eggs
1 teaspoon vanilla extract
2 unbaked 8-inch pastry shells
1⅓ cups flaked coconut
½ cup chopped pecans
Garnishes: whipped cream,
   chocolate shavings

Combine chocolate and butter in a medium saucepan; cook over low heat, stirring until chocolate melts. Remove from heat, and gradually stir in milk; set aside.

Combine sugar, cornstarch, and salt in a large bowl; add eggs and vanilla, mixing well. Gradually stir in chocolate mixture using a wire whisk. Pour into pastry shells, and sprinkle with coconut and pecans. Bake at 375° for 45 minutes. (Pie may appear soft, but will become firm after cooling.) Cool at least 4 hours. Garnish, if desired. Yield: two 8-inch pies.

■ We liked the flavor of the meatballs, but found they fell apart easily when served with party picks as appetizers. Instead, we preferred them on sub rolls or over pasta. To allow some of the fat to drain from the meatballs, we baked them on a lightly greased rack in a broiler pan, instead of on a baking sheet.

CHARLESTON PRESS CLUB MEATBALLS

1 pound lean ground beef
1 large egg, lightly beaten
½ cup finely chopped onion
½ cup finely chopped green
   pepper
½ cup cracker meal
¼ cup catsup
¼ teaspoon salt
¼ teaspoon pepper
Barbecue Sauce

Combine first 8 ingredients in a large bowl, and shape into 20 (2-inch) balls. Place on a lightly greased rack in broiler pan.

Bake meatballs at 350° for 20 minutes. Remove from oven. Add meatballs to Barbecue Sauce, stirring gently to coat all sides. Yield: 4 to 6 servings.

Barbecue Sauce

1 small onion, finely chopped
2 tablespoons olive oil
1¼ cups tomato puree
1 cup water
¼ cup cider vinegar
2 tablespoons prepared mustard
1 teaspoon brown sugar
1 tablespoon Worchestershire
   sauce
½ teaspoon chili powder
½ teaspoon salt
⅛ teaspoon garlic powder
½ teaspoon hot sauce

Cook onion in olive oil in a large saucepan over medium heat, stirring constantly, until tender. Add tomato puree and next 8 ingredients; bring to a boil. Cover, reduce heat, and simmer 45 minutes, stirring occasionally. Stir in hot sauce; cook an additional 15 minutes. Yield: 1⅔ cups.

Shake Up A Cereal Snack

There's a whole lot of shakin' going on with this plentiful snack, which youngsters can help make and share with all the kids on the block. No one owns a bowl that's big enough to mix boxfuls of ingredients, so toss them together in a large plastic bag. It's as easy as open, pour, shake, and then bake.

The fiber-rich medley blends the savory taste of nuts and pretzel chips with a hint of honeyed cereal. But unlike many grab-a-handful snacks, it's healthy, and it's not sticky.

CEREAL SNACK MIX

1 (12-ounce) package honey graham
   cereal
1 (12.3-ounce) package corn-and-
   rice cereal
1 (14-ounce) package O-shaped oat
   and wheat bran cereal
1 (12-ounce) can mixed nuts
1 (8½-ounce) package pretzel chips
1 cup butter or margarine, melted
2 tablespoons Worchestershire
   sauce
1 tablespoon seasoned salt

Combine first 5 ingredients in a large plastic bag; set aside. Combine butter and remaining ingredients; cool slightly, and pour into bag. Close and shake gently until well coated. Divide mixture into 2 large roasting pans; place pans on racks in oven, one above the other. Bake at 225° for 1 hour, stirring every 15 minutes. Remove from oven; spread on paper towels to cool. Store in airtight containers. Yield: 8 quarts.

Linda P. Jones
Mount Airy, North Carolina

Classy Cooking Comes Easy

Those who have attended Margot Hahn's cooking school say she has class . . . several, in fact. But the favorite is "How To Throw a Dinner Party and Take a Nap Before the Guests Arrive." She's not interested in a 10-course culinary production. Chances are, neither are you.

For 15 years, Margot has shared this hobby in her Washington, D.C., home with a dozen or so students at a time. Students are always looking for outstanding recipes, but Margot finds they're even more interested in planning meals and getting all the food on the table at the same time.

■ An avid gardener, Margot ends up with *lots* of fresh zucchini. She doesn't like the look of those oversized ones common in home gardens, so she purees them in the food processor for this wonderful soup.

ZUCCHINI SOUP WITH CILANTRO

1 large onion, chopped
3 tablespoons butter or margarine, melted
3 pounds zucchini, chopped
1 (14½-ounce) can ready-to-serve chicken broth
2 cups buttermilk, divided
1 cup fresh cilantro, chopped and divided
3 tablespoons lemon juice
½ teaspoon salt
¼ to ½ teaspoon pepper
Garnishes: zucchini slices, fresh cilantro sprigs

Cook onion in butter in a 3-quart saucepan over medium heat, stirring constantly, until tender; add zucchini and chicken broth. Bring to a boil; reduce heat, and cook 15 to 20 minutes. Remove from heat; cool.

Combine half of zucchini mixture, ½ cup buttermilk, and ½ cup cilantro in container of an electric blender or food processor; process until smooth, stopping once to scrape down sides. Pour into a large bowl. Repeat procedure with remaining zucchini mixture, ½ cup buttermilk, and remaining cilantro. Add to bowl, and stir in remaining 1 cup buttermilk, lemon juice, salt, and pepper. Chill at least 8 hours. Garnish each serving, if desired. Yield: 8 cups.

SUMMER IN SPRING

Crab Canapés
Zucchini Soup With Cilantro
Spicy New York Strip Roast
Marinated Black Beans
Fresh Mozzarella-Tomato-Basil Salad
Caramel Turtle Truffle Tart

■ This appetizer recipe leaves no last-minute fuss. Both the bread rounds and crabmeat mixture can be made ahead of time.

CRAB CANAPÉS

12 slices white sandwich bread
2 tablespoons mayonnaise
1 tablespoon prepared horseradish
½ teaspoon catsup
½ teaspoon olive oil
3 to 5 drops of hot sauce
1 cup fresh crabmeat, flaked *
Cracked pepper

With a 2-inch cookie cutter, cut 2 rounds out of each bread slice; place on a baking sheet. Broil 5½ inches from heat (with electric oven door partially opened) 1 to 2 minutes or until golden.

Combine mayonnaise, horseradish, catsup, olive oil, and hot sauce in a medium bowl; stir in crabmeat. Spread evenly on unbaked side of bread rounds. Sprinkle with cracked pepper. Yield: 12 appetizer servings.

* 1 (6-ounce) can lump crabmeat, drained, may be substituted for fresh crabmeat.

Note: Crabmeat mixture may be served with 1 (1.4-ounce) package of 24 crispy appetizer shells instead of bread rounds. Spoon mixture evenly into shells.

Tip: *When selecting onions, consider all of the flavor possibilities. The large Spanish or Bermuda onion and the small white onion are usually mild in flavor, while Globe types, such as red, brown, and small yellow onions, are stronger flavored.*

■ Margot calls this a roast because of the size and cooking method, but the butcher will actually label it as a steak.

SPICY NEW YORK STRIP ROAST

1 (1¾-pound) New York strip steak (about 3 inches thick)
1 teaspoon dried thyme
1 teaspoon dried oregano
1 teaspoon dried rosemary
¼ teaspoon salt
¼ teaspoon freshly ground black pepper
¼ teaspoon ground red pepper
1 tablespoon olive oil

Trim excess fat from steak. Combine thyme and next 5 ingredients in a small bowl; crush with back of a spoon. Pat mixture evenly on both sides of steak.

Heat olive oil in a cast-iron or oven-proof heavy skillet over medium-high heat; add steak (chilled), and cook 3 minutes on each side. Bake at 450° for 20 to 25 minutes or until desired degree of doneness. Remove from oven; cover with aluminum foil, and let stand 10 minutes. To serve, cut into thin slices. Yield: 4 to 6 servings.

■ Something from a can never looked—or tasted—so elegant. You can make this easy, colorful side dish the day before, and refrigerate it until serving time.

MARINATED BLACK BEANS

⅓ cup red wine vinegar
⅓ cup olive oil
¾ teaspoon salt
½ teaspoon freshly ground pepper
3 cloves garlic, crushed
3 (15-ounce) cans black beans, rinsed and drained
1 (10-ounce) package frozen cut corn, thawed
1 large sweet red pepper, chopped
1 medium-size green pepper, chopped
1 purple onion, chopped
Garnish: chopped fresh parsley

Combine first 5 ingredients; let stand 30 minutes. Combine black beans and next 4 ingredients in a large bowl; add dressing, tossing to coat. Cover and chill 8 hours. Garnish, if desired. Yield: 10 to 12 servings.

■ Margot grows her own basil, so she has plenty on hand to garnish the plate. She just clips and rinses a small bunch before casually tucking it into the center of the tomato and mozzarella ring.

FRESH MOZZARELLA-TOMATO-BASIL SALAD

½ pound fresh mozzarella cheese *
3 medium tomatoes, sliced
½ teaspoon salt
¼ teaspoon pepper
3 tablespoons olive oil
½ cup chopped fresh basil
Garnish: fresh basil leaves

Remove cheese from brine, and cut into 16 thin slices; sprinkle tomato slices evenly with salt and pepper. Alternate tomato and cheese slices on a serving platter; drizzle with olive oil. Cover and chill 4 hours. Just before serving, sprinkle with chopped basil. Garnish, if desired. Yield: 8 servings.

* Fresh mozzarella is a soft, white cheese available at gourmet grocery stores or cheese shops. It is sometimes packed in a brine, a strong solution of water and salt used for pickling or preserving foods.

■ You make this tart the day before and forget about it. But no one will forget about it once they taste it.

CARAMEL TURTLE TRUFFLE TART

Sugar Cookie Crust
1½ cups semisweet chocolate morsels
¾ cup whipping cream, divided
1 (14-ounce) package caramels
3 cups chopped pecans

Make dough for Sugar Cookie Crust, and press into bottom and up sides of an 11-inch tart pan; prick bottom generously with a fork. Bake at 400° for 10 minutes or until golden; cool.

Combine chocolate morsels and ¼ cup whipping cream in a small microwave-safe bowl; microwave on HIGH 1 to 1½ minutes until chocolate melts, stirring once. Spread 1 cup mixture evenly in bottom of baked pastry, reserving remaining mixture. Chill 30 minutes.

Combine caramels and remaining ½ cup whipping cream in a heavy saucepan; cook over low heat, stirring constantly, until caramels melt and mixture is smooth. Stir in pecans, and spread evenly over chocolate layer. Spoon reserved chocolate mixture into a small, zip-top plastic bag. (If chocolate is firm, microwave on HIGH 30 seconds or until soft.) Cut a small hole in corner of bag; drizzle chocolate over tart. Chill at least 1 hour. Let stand 30 minutes before serving. Yield: one 11-inch tart.

Sugar Cookie Crust

1⅓ cups all-purpose flour
⅓ cup sugar
½ cup butter, cut into slices
1 large egg
1 teaspoon vanilla extract

Position knife blade in food processor bowl; add first 3 ingredients. Process 1 minute or until mixture is crumbly. Remove food pusher. Add egg and vanilla through chute with processor running; process until mixture forms a smooth dough. Yield: enough pastry for one 11-inch tart.

From Our Kitchen To Yours

Mince, chop, cube. What do these often-confusing terms mean? And does it *really* matter if the carrots are cut into large cubes or small, irregular-shaped pieces? Because definitions vary, we give explanations of the terms we use, helping you to understand our techniques.

In our recipes, the size we cut the foods is influenced by appearance, texture, and cooking time. Personal preference makes a difference, too.

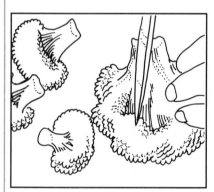

Flowerets: *For flowerets, cut the small buds of broccoli or cauliflower from their stout, edible stems, reserving the stems for another use.*

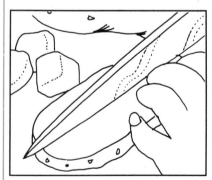

Cube: *To cut into ½-inch or larger square chunks. (Some rounded fruits or vegetables, such as apples or turnips, may be cut into chunks that are not perfectly square.)*

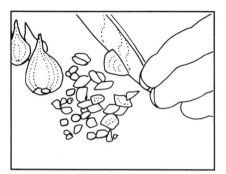

Mince: *To cut food into tiny, irregular-shaped pieces using a chef's knife in a rocking motion. We use this technique primarily for garlic and sometimes fresh herbs and shallots.*

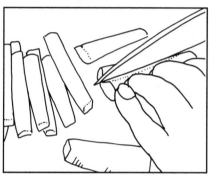

Julienne: *To cut food into thin strips about 2 inches long. Our recipes instruct to cut vegetables into thin strips rather than julienne because the term "thin strips" is easier to understand.*

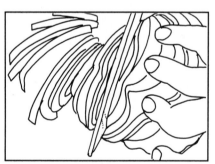

Shred: *To cut into long, narrow strips. Foods like cabbage that grow in concentric layers can be shredded by slicing with a sharp knife or the slicing disc of a food processor. You can rub other types of food, such as cheese, against the coarse side of a hand-held metal grater to shred.*

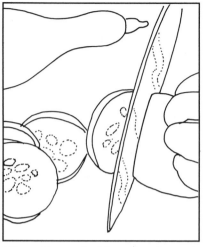

Slice: *To cut food into flat pieces of the same thickness. For most of our recipes, we thinly slice foods crosswise into ¼-inch pieces. When it makes a difference in appearance or cooking time, the recipe directions specify size and whether to slice crosswise or lengthwise.*

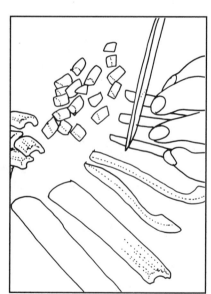

Chop: *To cut into small, irregular-shaped pieces. We use the terms "finely chopped" for ¼-inch pieces and "coarsely chopped" for ¼- to ½-inch pieces. (Some cooks use the term "diced" for "finely chopped.") To speed chopping, cut food into strips the desired width; stack strips, and cut crosswise into pieces.*

JUNE

Make your next picnic, pool party, or cookout memorable and serve that summertime favorite—homemade peach ice cream. And that's just one peachy dessert idea you'll find in this chapter. When the temperature goes up, cool down with fruity sorbets—refreshing frozen treats that are kind to the waistline. For energy-efficient (your energy) summer fare, try our seafood salads. They're quick, easy to prepare, and won't keep you anchored to your kitchen. Preserve your garden bounty and enjoy the fruits of your labor all year long. We tell you how in 10 easy canning steps.

The Jewels Of Summer

Bursting with natural sweetness and an unmistakable fragrance, rosy-skinned peaches often claim a special place in memories and traditions. Maybe you recall snatching the season's first fruit from a neighbor's tree, or savoring the pleasure of a flaky homemade cobbler, bubbling hot from the oven. Peaches are truly the gems of the season.

June through August, peaches fill baskets at roadside stands and produce counters at supermarkets. Select fruit that is a rich yellow or cream color with no tinges of green. Avoid soft, overripe peaches or those with bruises or blemishes.

Remember, peaches bruise easily, so handle them carefully. To test for ripeness, press fruit *gently* between your thumb and finger. The fruit should feel firm, but have a little "give." Peaches that are very firm may be stored on the kitchen counter for a day or two to finish ripening. Once peaches are ripe, refrigerate them and eat within a week.

The easiest way to enjoy a fresh peach is to wash it and eat it. If you want fruit without the skin, dip the peach into rapidly boiling water for 30 seconds, then into cold water. The skin should slip right off. Even better, enjoy the fruit in these peachy recipes.

PEACH MELBA SUNDAE SHAKE
(pictured on page 151)

⅔ cup fresh or frozen raspberries, thawed
2 tablespoons sugar
1 large peach, peeled and sliced *
¾ cup milk
2 cups peach ice cream, softened
Peach ice cream
Garnishes: fresh raspberries, peach slices, fresh mint sprigs

Combine raspberries and sugar in container of an electric blender; process until smooth. Transfer to a small container, and set aside. Wash blender container.

Combine peaches and milk in container of electric blender; process until smooth. Add 2 cups peach ice cream, and process until smooth, stopping once to scrape down sides. Spoon about 2 tablespoons raspberry mixture into bottom of two 16-ounce glasses; add peach mixture. Top each with a scoop of peach ice cream, and drizzle with remaining raspberry mixture. Garnish each serving, if desired. Yield: 2 servings.

* 1 cup frozen peach slices, thawed, may be substituted for fresh peach.
Mrs. Harland J. Stone
Ocala, Florida

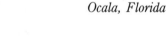

CARAMEL PEACHES

6 large peaches, peeled and sliced *
3 tablespoons sugar
¼ cup butter or margarine, cut into small pieces
1 cup whipping cream

Place peaches in a lightly greased 11- x 7- x 1½-inch baking dish; sprinkle with sugar, and dot with butter.

Bake peaches at 400° for 25 to 30 minutes or until tender and liquid is slightly thickened, stirring once. Stir in whipping cream; bake an additional 15 minutes, stirring every 5 minutes. Cool on a wire rack 15 minutes; serve warm. Yield: 4 to 6 servings.

* 6 cups frozen sliced peaches, thawed, may be substituted for fresh.

PEACH CRISP

4 cups sliced fresh or frozen peaches
¾ cup sugar, divided
½ teaspoon ground cinnamon
1 cup all-purpose flour
½ cup butter or margarine

Toss peaches, ⅓ cup sugar, and cinnamon in a large bowl; spoon into a lightly greased 8-inch square baking dish or a 9-inch deep-dish pieplate, and set aside.

Combine flour and remaining sugar; cut in butter with a pastry blender until mixture is crumbly. Sprinkle on top of peaches. Bake at 375° for 35 to 40 minutes. Yield: 6 to 8 servings.
Betty Mitchell
Little Rock, Arkansas

HONEYED PEACHES 'N' CREAM
(pictured on page 150)

¼ cup Chambord or other raspberry-flavored liqueur
2 tablespoons honey
1 teaspoon lemon juice
½ teaspoon ground ginger
4 cups sliced fresh or frozen peaches, thawed
Crème Fraîche Sauce or vanilla ice cream
2 tablespoons slivered almonds, toasted (optional)

Combine first 4 ingredients in a bowl; add peaches, tossing gently. Cover and chill 2 hours. Spoon into individual dishes; top with Crème Fraîche Sauce or vanilla ice cream. Sprinkle with almonds, if desired, and serve immediately. Yield: 6 servings.

Crème Fraîche Sauce

⅓ cup sour cream
⅓ cup whipping cream
2 tablespoons powdered sugar

Combine all ingredients; cover and chill 8 hours. Yield: ⅔ cup.

Note: Chambord is a black raspberry-flavored liqueur. *Louise Jackson*
Shreveport, Louisiana

FROZEN PEACH TORTE

1½ cups coarsely crumbled almond
  or coconut macaroon cookies,
  divided
2½ cups sliced fresh or frozen
  peaches, thawed
1 cup sugar
1 tablespoon lemon juice
½ teaspoon almond extract
1 cup whipping cream, whipped

Sprinkle half of cookie crumbs evenly in an 8-inch square pan; set aside. Position knife blade in food processor bowl; add peaches and next 3 ingredients. Process 1 minute, stopping once to scrape down sides. Transfer to a large bowl; fold in whipped cream. Pour over crumbs in pan, and top with remaining crumbs. Cover and freeze 8 hours. Remove from freezer 15 minutes before serving. Cut into squares. Yield: 9 servings.
Patty McCoy Horton
Demopolis, Alabama

PEACH ICE CREAM

6 to 8 large peaches, peeled and
  sliced (about 7 cups)
3 cups milk, divided
2 large eggs, lightly beaten
1 (12-ounce) can evaporated milk
2½ cups sugar
1 (12-ounce) can peach nectar

Combine half of peaches and ¼ cup milk in container of an electric blender; process until smooth. Transfer to a medium bowl, and repeat procedure with remaining peaches and ¼ cup milk. Set aside.

Combine remaining 2½ cups milk and next 3 ingredients in a large heavy saucepan; cook over medium heat 8 minutes, stirring occasionally. Remove from heat, and stir in peach mixture and nectar.

Pour into freezer container of a 4-quart hand-turned or electric freezer. Freeze mixture according to manufacturer's instructions. Pack freezer with additional ice and rock salt; let stand 1 hour before serving. Yield: 1 gallon. *Jackie Moon*
Nicholasville, Kentucky

Preserve Earth's Bounty

The next time you want to escape back to the "good old days," try canning. Gather an abundance of garden-fresh vegetables and fruits, and create your own tradition of food preservation. See "From Our Kitchen To Yours" beginning on page 136 for information on boiling-water bath canning equipment and how to use it.

PEACH JAM
(pictured on page 146)

3 pounds fresh peaches
1 (1¾-ounce) package powdered
  pectin
2 tablespoons lemon juice
5 cups sugar
½ teaspoon whole allspice

Peel, pit, and coarsely mash peaches to measure 4 cups. Combine peaches, pectin, and lemon juice in a Dutch oven; bring to a boil over high heat, stirring constantly. Stir in sugar and allspice; return to a boil, and cook, stirring constantly, 1 minute. Remove from heat; skim off foam.

Quickly ladle hot mixture into hot sterilized jars, filling to ¼ inch from top. Remove air bubbles; wipe jar rims. Cover at once with metal lids, and screw on bands. Process in boiling-water bath 5 minutes. Yield: 6 half pints. *Azine G. Rush*
Monroe, Louisiana

ONION JELLY
(pictured on page 147)

2 pounds sweet onions, cut into
  quarters
2 cups water
¾ cup white vinegar (5% acidity)
1 (1¾-ounce) package powdered
  pectin
5½ cups sugar

Position knife blade in food processor bowl; add half of onion quarters. Process 30 seconds. Drop remaining onion quarters through food chute with processor running; process 30 seconds or until finely chopped. Combine onion and water in a large saucepan; bring to a boil. Remove from heat, and let cool. Pour through a large wire-mesh strainer lined with wet cheesecloth into a 4-cup liquid measuring cup, reserving onion juice and discarding onion pulp. Add water to onion juice to equal 3 cups, if necessary.

Combine 3 cups onion juice, vinegar, and pectin in a large saucepan; bring to a boil, stirring constantly. Add sugar, and return to a boil, stirring constantly; boil 2 minutes. Remove from heat, and skim off foam.

Quickly pour hot mixture into hot sterilized jars, filling to ¼ inch from top. Remove air bubbles; wipe jar rims. Cover at once with metal lids, and screw on bands. Process in boiling-water bath 5 minutes. Yield: 7 half pints. *Kathie Godwin*
Athens, Georgia

PICKLED JALAPEÑO PEPPERS

4 pounds fresh jalapeño peppers
6 cups apple cider vinegar (5% acidity)
1½ cups water
¾ cup pickling salt

Prick pointed end of each pepper with a large needle. (Do not cut off stems.) Tightly pack peppers into hot jars, filling to ½ inch from top. Combine vinegar and remaining ingredients; bring to a boil. Reduce heat to low, and simmer 5 minutes. Pour hot mixture over peppers, filling to ½ inch from top. Remove air bubbles; wipe jar rims. Cover at once with metal lids, and screw on bands. Process in boiling-water bath 10 minutes. Yield: 8 pints.

Joan Collins
Hurricane, West Virginia

DILL GREEN BEANS
(pictured on page 146)

3 pounds fresh green beans
10 cloves garlic, divided
10 fresh dill sprigs, divided
5 teaspoons sweet red pepper flakes, divided
5 teaspoons pickling spice, divided
50 black peppercorns, divided
5 (4- x ½-inch) carrot sticks, divided
¼ cup pickling salt
3 cups white vinegar (5% acidity)
3 cups water

Wash beans, and trim ends; cut into lengths ½ inch shorter than jar. Cook beans in boiling water to cover 3 minutes; drain. Plunge into ice water; drain and set aside. Place 2 cloves garlic, 2 dill sprigs, 1 teaspoon red pepper flakes, 1 teaspoon pickling spice, 10 peppercorns, and 1 carrot stick into each of five hot jars. Pack beans tightly into jars, filling to ½ inch from top.
    Combine pickling salt, vinegar, and water; bring to a boil. Cover beans

with boiling mixture, filling to ½ inch from top. Remove air bubbles; wipe jar rims. Cover at once with metal lids, and screw on bands. Process in boiling-water bath 15 minutes. Yield: 5 pints.

Alice Byars
Mayfield, Kentucky

GREEN TOMATO SWEET RELISH
(pictured on page 146)

12 large green tomatoes, quartered
6 green peppers, quartered
2 sweet red peppers, quartered
3 large onions, quartered
2 teaspoons pickling salt
4 cups sugar
3 cups cider vinegar (5% acidity)
2 teaspoons ground turmeric
1 (6-ounce) jar prepared mustard

Position knife blade in food processor bowl; add vegetables, a few at a time. Process until ground. Transfer to a large nonaluminum bowl; sprinkle with pickling salt, and let stand 3 to 4 hours. Drain. Combine sugar, vinegar, and turmeric in a Dutch oven; cook over medium heat, stirring constantly, until sugar dissolves. Add vegetables, and bring to a boil. Stir in mustard, and cook, stirring constantly, until thickened. Pack hot mixture into hot jars, filling to ½ inch from top. Remove air bubbles; wipe jar rims. Cover at once with metal lids, and screw on bands. Process in boiling-water bath 15 minutes. Yield: 7 (12-ounce) jars.

Vara Hitchcock
Birmingham, Alabama

Tip: *If there's any mold, scum, or cloudiness of liquid in a home-canned product when opened, throw it away immediately. Don't try tasting it.*

PICKLED YELLOW SQUASH
(pictured on page 146)

8 cups thinly sliced yellow squash (about 3 pounds)
2 quarts water
⅔ cup pickling salt
3 cups sugar
2 cups white vinegar (5% acidity)
1 tablespoon celery seeds
1 tablespoon mustard seeds
2 cups chopped green pepper (about ½ pound)
2 cups thinly sliced onion (about 2 pounds)
1 (4-ounce) jar diced pimiento, drained

Place squash in a large nonaluminum container. Combine water and pickling salt, stirring until salt dissolves; pour over squash. Cover and let stand 1 hour. Drain well. Combine sugar and next 3 ingredients in a Dutch oven. Add squash, green pepper, and remaining ingredients; bring to a boil. Remove from heat, and pack hot vegetables into hot jars, filling to ½ inch from top; cover with hot vinegar syrup, filling to ½ inch from top. Remove air bubbles; wipe jar rims. Cover at once with metal lids, and screw on bands. Process in boiling-water bath 15 minutes. Yield: 4 pints.

Sonya Headley
Kilgore, Texas

From Our Kitchen To Yours

Canning with bushels of produce from the farmers market may not be cost efficient for you; however, it's worth the effort to make small quantities of pepper jelly and a few other family favorites if you grow vegetables or fruit abundant enough to preserve.
    The tradition of food preservation continues in many homes, but the recipes used in grandmother's steamy

kitchen must be updated. Follow these simple canning steps and specific food safety guidelines to ensure that the food you preserve will be safe. And see our recipes beginning on page 135 for some new ideas.

Can It in a Boiling-Water Bath

To preserve food in jars, we frequently use the boiling-water bath method in the Test Kitchens because it doesn't require as much time or the use of a pressure canner. The boiling-water process is used for high-acid foods, such as fruits, tomatoes, and pickles—as well as jams, jellies, preserves, relishes, conserves, marmalades, honeys, and syrups. (For questions on preserving low-acid foods that must be processed in a pressure canner, such as meats and vegetables, contact your county Extension agent.) The boiling-water bath processes jars of food at 212°, destroying microorganisms that cause spoilage or food poisoning. Air is forced out between the jar and lid, forming a vacuum seal as the food cools and contracts. This vital seal prevents invasion by outside microorganisms, which could cause contamination during storage.

What You'll Need

Regular kitchen equipment is adequate for most boiling-water bath canning; however, if you plan to fill the pantry shelves, you might want to invest in a **water-bath canner.** The round canner is usually made of aluminum or porcelain-covered steel. It has a tight-fitting lid and a metal rack to hold jars off the bottom of the canner, allowing the water to circulate. A large heavy-duty aluminum container, such as a **stockpot,** works well in place of a canner. Place a round cooling rack inside, and cover with a baking sheet if you don't have a lid. (**Tip:** Place old metal screw-on bands under the middle of the rack for added support when the jars are placed on it.)

No matter which container you choose, it must be deep enough to allow at least ½ inch between the rack and the container's bottom, one inch of water above the jars, and one inch from the top of the water to the edge of the container, giving the water room to boil. As a rule of thumb, add at least three inches to the height of the jars to determine the canner depth needed. You'll need a container at least eight inches deep for pints, and 10 inches deep for quarts.

Using special Mason-type home **canning jars** and **lids** with screw-on bands is essential. Breakage and seal failure are much greater with jars and lids not manufactured specifically for home canning.

Jar-lifting tongs are necessary to safely place jars into and remove from a boiling-water bath.

10 Simple Steps

1. Place water-bath canner or large stockpot with a rack inside on cook top; fill halfway with water, and begin heating. (**Tip:** It takes awhile for the water to heat.)
2. Wash jars, screw-on bands, and lids in hot soapy water; rinse well. If recipe calls for "hot" jars, fill or cover jars with hot water, and keep them hot until ready to fill with food. (**Tip:** Place the clean jars in the heating water in the canner.)

If the recipe states to fill "hot, sterilized" jars, place jars right side up on the rack in the canner, making sure they are covered with water, and bring water to a boil; boil 10 minutes. Remove jars from water, and fill immediately, saving the boiling water for processing the filled jars.

Heat the lids, following the manufacturer's directions.
3. Prepare food according to recipe, and pack into prepared jars, filling to within ¼ or ½ inch from top of jar, leaving the amount of the space specified in recipe directions. (**Tip:** The exact headspace between the inside of the lid and the top of the food is **mandatory** for the expansion of food as it processes and forms a vacuum in the cooled jars.)
4. Remove air bubbles by running a plastic spatula down between the food and the inside of the jar, gently shifting the food, so that any trapped air in the jar escapes. Add more liquid, if needed, to fill jars to the level required in the recipe.

5. Wipe off the jar rims with a clean, damp cloth. Place metal lids on the jar rims with sealing compound next to the glass, and screw on the metal bands until tight.
6. Using a jar lifter, carefully lower hot, filled jars into nearly boiling water in the canner, placing jars one inch apart on the rack. (**Tip:** If you're using small jars and the container is deep enough, process two tiers at a time, using a wire cooling rack to hold the upper layer of jars; ensure adequate circulation by staggering the jars so they're not directly above each other.)
7. Add additional hot or boiling water to the canner, if necessary, to bring the water level to at least one inch above the tops of all jars. Cover the canner, and bring water to a full boil. (**Tip:** Bubbles will break the surface and won't disappear when stirred.) Begin counting the processing time when the water boils; let water boil gently and steadily for the time recommended in the recipe. (Check with your county Extension agent annually for updated processing times.)
8. Remove jars at once, and place, right side up, on a rack or a surface padded with a cloth; let cool at room temperature, away from drafts, 12 to 24 hours. Do *not* retighten metal bands after processing. (**Tip:** You may hear "plinking" or "popping" sounds as the lids seal.)

How to Pit Cherries

Before cooking or canning cherries, the tooth-breaking cherry stone is easily removed with a cherry-and-olive pitter.

This spring-loaded gadget resembles a hand-held hole punch with a cupped ring at the end of one blade to hold the fruit. When pressed, the other blade's rod pokes through the cherry, punching out the pit without damaging the fruit. Different styles are available at specialty stores.

9. Check the seals of cooled jars. Remove the bands, and make sure the lids are concave (curved in) and don't move when pressed with a finger.
10. Wipe off jars; label and date. Store in a cool, dry place without metal bands. (**Tip:** For best quality, use jellied products within a few months, other foods within a year.)

Your Questions, Our Answers

Do pickles and jellies have to be processed? No, but the filled jars must be stored in the refrigerator. Prepare the recipes up to the point of processing, packing the food according to recipe directions, and then refrigerate rather than place in the boiling-water bath.

Can jars of pickled beans, squash pickles, and peach preserves be processed at the same time? Yes, place jars in the canner at the same time, removing jars when their specific processing time is up.

What if a jar doesn't seal? Refrigerate an unsealed jar, and use as if it had just been opened. Or if there are several unsealed jars, reprocess them within 24 hours. To reprocess, remove the lid and check the top of the jar for tiny nicks. If any are discovered, change the jar; top with a new, treated lid, and place in a boiling-water bath for the same processing time. Label food that has been recanned, and use those jars first; the texture will be softer.

How long can jars be reused? Use jars over and over as long as they have smooth sealing rims and no chips, cracks, or scratches. Never reuse the metal lids because the sealing compound won't reseal, but you can reuse the screw-on bands unless they are rusted or bent.

When The Time Is Ripe For Green Tomatoes

A bountiful summer garden can take on a life of its own, especially at the peak of tomato season. Maybe you've already filled your refrigerator with red tomatoes and are clearing off kitchen counters to make room for green ones. If so, green tomatoes with their piquant flavor are excellent for frying, broiling, baking, and in salsas and relishes.

THREE TOMATO SALSA
(pictured on page 145)

1 cup chopped red tomato
1 cup chopped yellow tomato
1 cup chopped green tomato
½ cup finely chopped purple onion
2 cloves garlic, minced
⅓ cup olive oil
¼ cup red wine vinegar
2 tablespoons chopped fresh cilantro
1 tablespoon chopped fresh parsley
1 tablespoon chopped fresh chives
⅛ teaspoon salt
⅛ teaspoon ground red pepper
⅛ teaspoon black pepper

Combine all ingredients; cover and chill 3 to 4 hours. Yield: 3 cups.
Jane Maloy
Wilmington, North Carolina

CURRIED GREEN TOMATOES

2 green onions, sliced
2 tablespoons butter or margarine, melted
1 teaspoon curry powder
¼ teaspoon lemon pepper
¼ teaspoon garlic powder
¼ teaspoon seasoned pepper
3 green tomatoes, cut into ¼-inch slices

Cook green onions in butter in a large skillet over medium heat until tender. Stir in curry powder and next 3 ingredients. Add tomato, and cook over low heat until tender. Yield: 4 servings.
Carol Barclay
Portland, Texas

HOT TOMATOES

8 medium-size green tomatoes
1 cup corn cut from cob
1 jalapeño pepper, minced
¼ cup chopped sweet red pepper
¼ cup sliced green onions
3 tablespoons chopped fresh basil
2 tablespoons chopped fresh cilantro
1 cup (4 ounces) shredded Monterey Jack cheese
½ teaspoon salt
¼ teaspoon pepper
1½ tablespoons cornmeal
1½ tablespoons butter or margarine

Cut tops from tomatoes; set tops aside. Scoop out pulp, leaving shells intact; chop pulp, and set aside. Invert shells onto paper towels to drain. Combine pulp, corn, and next 8 ingredients; spoon into tomato shells. Sprinkle evenly with cornmeal, and dot with butter. Place reserved tops, cut sides down, and filled tomatoes on a lightly greased baking sheet. Bake at 400° for 25 minutes or until thoroughly heated. Cover filled tomatoes with tops. Yield: 8 servings.
Peggy H. Amos
Martinsville, Virginia

Eat The Peas And The Pod

These peas are a snap—a Sugar Snap, that is. And like their cousin, the popular snow pea, Sugar Snap peas are eaten shells and all. Sugar Snaps are appreciated for their crisp texture, so don't overcook. Serve them stir-fried, sautéed, simmered, or steamed, or raw or blanched with dips. Use them in any recipe that calls for snow peas or Chinese pea pods.

PEAS AND PASTA

1 (12-ounce) package fettuccine, uncooked
1 cup fresh or frozen English peas
½ pound fresh Sugar Snap peas, trimmed
½ pound fresh mushrooms, sliced
1 (8-ounce) package country ham, cut into ¼-inch strips
3 tablespooons butter or margarine, divided
2 tablespoons all-purpose flour
1 cup chicken broth
1 cup half-and-half
1 tablespoon chopped fresh or 1 teaspoon dried thyme
3 tablespoons chopped fresh or frozen chives
¼ teaspoon salt
½ to ¾ teaspoon pepper
2 tablespoons lemon juice
¼ cup freshly grated Parmesan cheese

Cook fettuccine according to package directions; drain and keep warm.

Arrange peas in a steamer basket; place over boiling water. Cover and steam 5 to 7 minutes or until crisp-tender. Drain and set aside.

Cook mushrooms and ham in 1 tablespoon butter in a large skillet over medium heat, stirring constantly, until mushrooms are tender. Remove from skillet, and set aside.

Melt remaining 2 tablespoons butter in skillet over low heat; add flour, stirring until smooth. Cook, stirring constantly, 1 minute. Gradually add broth and half-and-half; cook over medium heat, stirring constantly, until thickened and bubbly. Stir in thyme and next 4 ingredients. Stir in Parmesan cheese, mushroom mixture, and about half of peas. Pour over fettuccine, tossing gently. Sprinkle with remaining peas, and serve immediately. Yield: 6 to 8 servings.

CREAMED SUGAR SNAPS AND CARROTS

½ pound carrots, thinly sliced
¼ pound pearl onions, peeled
½ cup water
½ teaspoon salt
½ pound fresh Sugar Snap peas, trimmed
½ cup whipping cream
½ teaspoon salt
½ teaspoon pepper
2 tablespoons chopped fresh dill
1 teaspoon lemon juice

Combine first 4 ingredients in a large saucepan; bring to a boil. Cover, reduce heat, and simmer 5 minutes. Add Sugar Snap peas; cook, covered, 3 to 4 minutes or until vegetables are crisp-tender. Drain and set aside.

Add whipping cream to saucepan, and cook over medium heat, stirring constantly, 3 minutes. Stir in vegetables, ½ teaspoon salt, and remaining ingredients; cook until thoroughly heated. Yield: 4 servings.

SUGAR SNAPS AND PEPPERS

1 clove garlic, minced
2 tablespoons olive oil
1 pound fresh Sugar Snap peas, trimmed
½ cup finely chopped sweet red pepper
½ cup finely chopped sweet yellow pepper
¼ teaspoon salt
¼ teaspoon pepper

Cook garlic in olive oil in a large skillet over medium-high heat, stirring constantly, 1 to 2 minutes. Add peas and sweet peppers; cook, stirring constantly, 5 minutes or until vegetables are crisp-tender. Sprinkle with salt and pepper. Yield: 4 to 6 servings.

Enjoy Summer's Easy Rhythm

Whether your weekend destination is a beachfront condominium, a cabin at the lake, or your favorite front-porch rocking chair, these menus and recipes will carry you from dawn to dusk with surprising ease.

BREAKFAST MENU

Sunrise Smoothie
Fresh Vegetable Frittata
Banana-Nut Muffins
Juice   Coffee

■ Bake muffins ahead of time. Cool, pack in zip-top plastic bags, and freeze until serving time.

■ Assemble the frittata the night before, refrigerate, and pop it in the oven early the next day.

SUNRISE SMOOTHIE

1 (8-ounce) carton vanilla or coffee-flavored yogurt
¾ cup orange juice, chilled
⅛ teaspoon ground cinnamon
4 ice cubes

Combine first 3 ingredients in container of an electric blender. With blender on high, add ice cubes, one at a time, processing until smooth after each addition. Serve immediately. Yield: about 2 cups.

Tip: *Fruited and flavored yogurts add a rich texture to desserts, shakes, and snacks with less fat and cholesterol. Use lemon or vanilla yogurt in fruit dishes, sauces, and some salad dressings or as toppings for desserts.*

FRESH VEGETABLE FRITTATA

1 large sweet red pepper, chopped
1 cup sliced fresh mushrooms
1½ cups (6 ounces) shredded Swiss
   cheese, divided
¼ pound asparagus, cut into 1-inch
   pieces
7 large eggs, lightly beaten
½ cup mayonnaise or salad
   dressing
½ teaspoon salt
2 tablespoons chopped fresh or 2
   teaspoons dried basil

Layer pepper, mushrooms, and half of cheese in a lightly greased 9½-inch deep-dish pieplate. Top with asparagus and remaining cheese. Combine eggs and remaining ingredients; pour evenly over cheese. Bake at 375° for 35 minutes or until a knife inserted in center comes out clean. Let stand 5 minutes. Serve hot or at room temperature. Yield: 8 servings.

Note: Fresh Vegetable Frittata may also be baked in an 8½-inch-square aluminum foil pan. *Martha Johnston*
Birmingham, Alabama

BANANA-NUT MUFFINS

1½ cups all-purpose flour
½ cup wheat germ
⅓ cup sugar
1 tablespoon baking powder
½ teaspoon salt
1¼ cups mashed banana (about 3
   medium)
½ cup milk
¼ cup vegetable oil
1 large egg, lightly beaten
Vegetable cooking spray
Topping

Combine first 5 ingredients in a large bowl; make a well in center of mixture. Combine banana and next 3 ingredients; add to dry ingredients, stirring just until moistened. Place paper baking cups in muffin pans, and coat with cooking spray; spoon 3 tablespoons batter into each cup. Bake at 400° for 15 to 20 minutes or until

golden. Remove from oven, and sprinkle 1 teaspoon Topping over each muffin. Return to oven, and bake an additional 5 minutes. Remove from pans immediately. Yield: 15 muffins.

Topping

⅓ cup flaked coconut
⅓ cup chopped pecans
2 tablespoons honey
2 tablespoons butter or margarine,
   melted

Combine all ingredients in a small bowl. Yield: about ½ cup.
Mimi Davis
Little Rock, Arkansas

LUNCH MENU

Primavera Salad
Artichoke Bread
Melon wedges with lime
Commercial cookies
Iced tea with lemon

■ Double the recipe for Versatile Vinaigrette, and use half of it on Primavera Salad. Reserve the remaining half to use in Grilled Marinated Beef Roast in the supper menu.

■ Cook broccoli and pasta ahead, and chill until ready to assemble Primavera Salad. Prepare other salad ingredients, and store in individual plastic containers.

PRIMAVERA SALAD

1 pound broccoli
1 (12-ounce) package bow tie pasta,
   uncooked
Versatile Vinaigrette
1 (10-ounce) package fresh spinach
1 pound smoked turkey breast, cut
   into thin strips
1 pint cherry tomatoes, halved
½ cup chopped fresh basil
¼ cup chopped fresh parsley
⅓ cup pine nuts, toasted

Remove broccoli leaves, and cut off tough ends of stalks; discard. Wash broccoli thoroughly, and cut into 1-inch pieces. Cook in boiling water to cover 1 minute; drain immediately, and plunge into ice water. Drain and pat dry with paper towels; chill.

Cook pasta according to package directions. Drain; rinse with cold water, and drain again. Combine pasta and Versatile Vinaigrette, tossing to coat. Place in a large heavy-duty, zip-top plastic bag. Chill 2 hours or overnight.

Remove stems from spinach; wash leaves thoroughly, and pat dry. Combine spinach, broccoli, pasta, turkey, and remaining ingredients, tossing gently. Yield: 8 to 10 servings.

Versatile Vinaigrette

⅔ cup vegetable oil
¼ cup white wine vinegar
¼ cup water
1½ teaspoons salt
1 tablespoon freshly ground
   pepper
1 clove garlic, pressed

Combine all ingredients in a jar. Cover jar tightly, and shake vigorously. Yield: 1 cup.

ARTICHOKE BREAD

¼ cup butter or margarine
2 to 3 cloves garlic, pressed
2 teaspoons sesame seeds
1 (14-ounce) can artichoke hearts,
   drained and chopped
1 cup (4 ounces) shredded Monterey
   Jack cheese
1 cup grated Parmesan cheese
½ cup sour cream
1 (16-ounce) loaf unsliced French
   bread
½ cup (2 ounces) shredded Cheddar
   cheese

Melt butter in a skillet over medium-high heat. Add garlic and sesame seeds; cook, stirring constantly, until lightly browned. Remove from heat. Stir in artichoke hearts and next 3 ingredients. Cover and refrigerate, if desired. If refrigerated, let artichoke mixture stand at room temperature 10 minutes before assembling.

Cut bread in half lengthwise. Scoop out center of each half, leaving a 1-inch shell; set shells aside. Crumble removed pieces of bread, and stir into artichoke mixture. Spoon evenly into shells, and sprinkle with Cheddar cheese. Place each half on a baking sheet, and cover with aluminum foil. Bake at 350° for 25 minutes; uncover and bake 5 minutes or until cheese melts. Cut into slices. Yield: 12 servings.   *Karin Barro*
Shreveport, Louisiana

SUPPER MENU

**Chilled boiled shrimp with Commercial rémoulade sauce
Grilled Marinated Beef Roast
Tomato-and-Cucumber Summer Salad
Corn Casserole
Fresh dilled green beans
Vanilla ice cream with Chocolate fudge sauce
Wine   Coffee**

■ Begin marinating roast at least eight hours before grilling.

■ Prepare dressing for Tomato-and-Cucumber Summer Salad several days ahead and refrigerate.

GRILLED MARINATED BEEF ROAST
(pictured on page 149)

1 (4-pound) boneless English-cut roast
Versatile Vinaigrette
1 cup soy sauce

Place roast in a large shallow dish or heavy-duty, zip-top plastic bag; set roast aside.

Combine Versatile Vinaigrette and soy sauce. Reserve ½ cup mixture; cover and refrigerate. Pour remaining mixture over roast. Cover or seal,

and marinate in refrigerator 8 hours, turning occasionally.

Drain roast, discarding marinade. Cook, covered with grill lid, over medium-hot coals (350° to 400°) 20 minutes on each side or to desired degree of doneness, basting occasionally with ½ cup reserved mixture. To serve, slice roast into thin slices. Yield: 8 to 10 servings.

Versatile Vinaigrette

⅔ cup vegetable oil
¼ cup white wine vinegar
¼ cup water
1½ teaspoons salt
1 tablespoon freshly ground pepper
1 clove garlic, pressed

Combine all ingredients in a jar. Cover jar tightly, and shake vigorously. Yield: 1 cup.   *John Feagin*
Birmingham, Alabama

TOMATO-AND-CUCUMBER SUMMER SALAD
(pictured on page 149)

¼ cup mayonnaise or salad dressing
3 tablespoons white vinegar
1 green onion, chopped
1 clove garlic, pressed
1 teaspoon sugar
½ to ¾ teaspoon salt
1 teaspoon Worcestershire sauce
½ teaspoon hot sauce
½ cup vegetable oil
1 cup chopped fresh parsley
Leaf lettuce
3 medium tomatoes, thinly sliced
2 cucumbers, thinly sliced

Combine first 8 ingredients in container of an electric blender; process until smooth, stopping once to scrape down sides. With blender on high, gradually add oil in a slow, steady stream. Stir in parsley. Cover dressing and chill.

Arrange lettuce on chilled salad plates. Top with tomato and cucumber slices. Drizzle with dressing. Yield: 6 to 8 servings.

CORN CASSEROLE
(pictured on page 149)

2 (16½-ounce) cans yellow cream-style corn
2 cups (8 ounces) shredded Cheddar cheese
1 (4-ounce) can chopped green chiles, drained
½ cup finely chopped onion
1 cup milk
2 large eggs, lightly beaten
1 cup yellow cornmeal
1½ teaspoons garlic salt
½ teaspoon baking soda

Combine first 6 ingredients in a large bowl. Combine cornmeal and remaining ingredients; stir into corn mixture. Pour into a lightly greased 11- x 7- x 1½-inch baking dish. Bake at 350° for 50 minutes or until a knife inserted in center comes out clean. Yield: 8 servings.   *Mary Ward*
Weatherford, Texas

Cooking Tips

■ When buying garlic, select firm, plump bulbs with dry, unbroken skins. Store in a cool, dry, well-ventilated place. The flavor will remain sharp up to four months.

■ Salad greens should never be cut with a knife because it may discolor and bruise the leaves. Gently tearing the leaves is better and makes a prettier salad.

■ Cooking vegetables such as green peppers and cucumbers briefly in boiling water will make them more digestible.

■ Wash or chop vegetables and open cans before you begin preparing any recipe. It is also a good idea to have most ingredients measured before beginning to cook.

Shortcuts To Make Summer Living Easy

Don't waste summer's warmth and sunshine slaving in the kitchen. Try these ideas for taking the easy way out, and enjoy the lazy days ahead.

Enjoy the Season's Freshest

■ Splash a small amount of liqueur or other alcoholic beverage over fresh fruit for a light dessert. Try champagne over pineapple or Marsala wine with melon.

■ Experiment with lime or orange juice on fish. Fish and lemon juice are natural partners, but other citrus choices will also give a fresh flavor.

■ Freeze any leftovers after a meal of garden-fresh vegetables. When you have 2 cups of vegetables or more, thaw, and puree in blender. Add chicken broth or half-and-half to desired consistency, and season with salt and pepper to taste. This makes a flavorful soup—hot or cold.

■ Puree fresh berries or peaches in a blender with an equal amount of cream or plain yogurt, and serve as a sauce over pound cake or ice cream for a hurry-up dessert.

■ Add summer color to your table. Arrange wildflowers in a pitcher; fill vases with fresh herbs or add clusters of zinnias, petunias, or impatiens to the table for a colorful accent.

■ Fill your favorite assortment of baskets with piles of fresh peaches, plums, or strawberries for an edible and colorful centerpiece.

Fix It Fast

■ Select a full-service supermarket; it can be your best friend when you want to pull a special dinner together in a matter of minutes. Many stores will steam fresh seafood to order. Pick up a salad from the grocer's salad bar and rolls from the in-store bakery. For dessert, select a sorbet or sherbet from the freezer case.

■ Shape patties for burgers in a flash. Shape ground meat or poultry into a log, partially freeze, and cut into slices of preferred thickness. Any unsliced portion may be rolled in plastic wrap and frozen for later use.

■ Brush commercial breadsticks with Italian-style salad dressing and toast breadsticks until golden as a quicker alternative to garlic bread. The dressing also works well as a marinade for grilled meats, poultry, seafood, and vegetables.

■ Keep glasses chilling in the freezer for frosty beverages in a hurry.

■ Give tea a refreshing twist by freezing pink lemonade in ice-cube trays and substituting for ice.

■ Chill white wine, beer, or champagne quickly by adding a cup of salt to the ice. It will lower the temperature of the ice and chill the beverage faster.

Let Common Kitchen Items Do Double Duty

■ Use a leafy stalk of celery to baste foods instead of a basting brush. The celery eliminates brush washing and gives extra flavor to grilled meats, fish, and poultry.

■ Use a coarse grater to grate butter when a pie or casserole needs to be dotted with butter. (Be sure the butter is cold before grating.)

■ Make short work of chopping canned tomatoes. Insert a pair of kitchen shears into the opened can, making snips as needed. Pour chopped tomatoes from can, and use as recipe directs.

■ Place a metal colander upside down over skillet when frying or sautéing to prevent splatters and allow steam to escape.

■ Use a pizza cutter to cut day-old bread into cubes for croutons—it's faster than a knife.

■ Chop hard-cooked eggs for egg salad or avocados for chunky guacamole with a pastry blender.

■ Use a swivel-bladed vegetable peeler—the handiest gadget of all, especially when you need just a little grated cheese to top burgers or garnish a salad. The peeler will also come in handy when you want to remove the strings from celery stalks for vegetable trays or when you'd like a few curls of chocolate for garnish.

Give New Life to Leftovers

■ Team leftover grilled chicken or beef with tortilla chips, lettuce, and salsa mixed with sour cream for a main-dish salad.

■ Combine extra pieces of deboned fish, flaked and stirred with your favorite commercial dressing or mayonnaise, to make a quick sandwich filling.

■ Use your favorite dip as a condiment for sandwiches or as a dressing on cold meat salads.

■ Plan for potluck. Toward the end of a week, serve a meal made from leftovers. Round out the menu with fresh bread, and serve the market's prettiest fruit for dessert.

Make a Quick Kitchen Getaway

■ Soak dirty dishes in hot, soapy water as you are preparing a meal, and you won't have as much scraping to do during final cleanup.

■ Line baking dishes or pans with aluminum foil. After dinner remove the foil; there are no food-encrusted containers to scrub.

■ Heat 1 cup water and 3 tablespoons lemon juice in microwave-safe cup on HIGH for 5 minutes for a quick microwave cleanup. Steam makes spatters easy to wipe up, and odors are replaced with a lemony smell.

■ Try boiling a few drops of liquid dishwashing detergent in several cups of water in a saucepan to loosen and remove cooked-on starchy foods, such as rice or potatoes.

Delegate. Delegate. Delegate.

You may have the bonus of a few extra hands to help out around the house during the slower-paced summer months. Find a task for each person. Then *everyone* can enjoy some vacation fun.

Hooked On Salads

These seafood salads, featuring fish and shellfish, are creative, colorful, and substantial.

Tuna-and-Red Pepper Salad and Caribbean Shrimp-and-Black Bean Salad are light and refreshing for lunch or dinner. Our other recipe serves up warm seafood on crisp greens, a delectable counterpoint in temperature and taste. Perfect summer fare, these salads are sure to net you a generous portion of compliments.

CARIBBEAN SHRIMP-AND-BLACK BEAN SALAD

1 (15-ounce) can black beans, rinsed and drained
1 small green pepper, finely chopped
½ cup sliced celery
½ cup sliced purple onion, separated into rings
2 tablespoons chopped fresh cilantro
⅔ cup picante sauce
¼ cup lime juice
2 tablespoons vegetable oil
2 tablespoons honey
¼ teaspoon salt
3 cups water
2 pounds unpeeled medium-size fresh shrimp
Lettuce leaves
Garnish: cherry tomato halves

Combine first 10 ingredients; toss gently. Cover and refrigerate 8 hours.

Bring water to a boil; add shrimp, and cook 3 to 5 minutes or until shrimp turn pink. Drain well; rinse with cold water. Chill. Peel and devein shrimp.

Arrange shrimp around edge of lettuce-lined plates; spoon black bean mixture in center. Garnish, if desired. Yield: 4 servings.
Carol S. Noble
Burgaw, North Carolina

TUNA-AND-RED PEPPER SALAD

2 (6⅛-ounce) cans solid white tuna packed in water, drained and separated into chunks *
2 large sweet red peppers, cut into thin strips
1 cup chopped fresh parsley
½ cup chopped fresh cilantro
2 tablespoons rice vinegar
1 tablespoon vegetable oil
1 tablespoon sesame oil
¼ teaspoon dried crushed red pepper
¼ teaspoon salt
Radicchio
Leaf lettuce

Combine first 4 ingredients in a large bowl. Combine vinegar and next 4 ingredients; drizzle over tuna mixture, and toss gently. Cover and chill up to 1½ hours, if desired. Arrange on radicchio and leaf lettuce; serve immediately. Yield: 4 servings.

* 1 pound fresh tuna may be substituted for canned tuna. Place tuna in a lightly greased shallow baking pan. Bake at 375° for 10 to 12 minutes or until done.
Jean Wilkinson
Lafayette, Louisiana

SALMON ON MIXED GREENS WITH CREAMY DILL DRESSING

2½ pounds salmon fillets, cut into 6 pieces
2 tablespoons olive oil, divided
⅛ teaspoon salt
⅛ teaspoon pepper
½ cup red wine vinegar
¼ cup olive oil
¼ cup vegetable oil
1½ tablespoons Dijon mustard
1 teaspoon minced garlic
2 teaspoons dried dillweed
⅛ teaspoon salt
⅛ teaspoon pepper
2 cups whipping cream
12 cups mixed greens

Brush salmon pieces evenly with 1 tablespoon olive oil; sprinkle evenly with ⅛ teaspoon salt and ⅛ teaspoon pepper. Cook salmon in remaining 1 tablespoon olive oil in a large skillet over medium-high heat 5 minutes on each side or until done.

Combine vinegar and next 7 ingredients in a medium bowl; slowly add whipping cream, stirring with a wire whisk until blended. Combine greens and half of dressing, tossing to coat. Place on a large platter; top with warm salmon. Serve with remaining dressing, if desired. Yield: 6 servings.
Patti Trippeer
Germantown, Tennessee

Salad Smarts

■ When selecting peppers, size is not an indication of quality. Buy peppers with smooth, slick skin that has not shriveled.

■ Marinate leftover vegetables (beets, carrots, beans, broccoli, cauliflower, corn, and brussels sprouts) in pourable salad dressing for relishes and salads.

■ Don't add salt to green salad until just before serving. Salt wilts and toughens salad greens.

Bake A Batch Of Savory Muffins

Check out these four muffin recipes to determine which fits into your next meal. All feature major ingredients that aren't sweet but are very versatile. Team them with a soup, salad, or main dish, or warm them up to solo as a snack.

CHEESY SAUSAGE MUFFINS

¼ pound ground pork sausage, cooked and drained
1 (3-ounce) package cream cheese, cut into small cubes
½ cup (2 ounces) shredded Cheddar cheese
¼ cup chopped green onions
1 cup biscuit mix
2 large eggs, lightly beaten
⅔ cup milk

Combine first 5 ingredients in a large bowl; make a well in center. Combine eggs and milk; add to sausage mixture, stirring just until moistened. Spoon into greased miniature muffin pans, filling three-fourths full. Bake at 350° for 35 to 40 minutes. Remove from pans immediately. Yield: 2 dozen.
Ginny Whitt
Mount Washington, Kentucky

HAM-AND-CHEESE MUFFINS

1¾ cups all-purpose flour
⅓ cup rye flour
2 teaspoons baking powder
¼ teaspoon salt
1 tablespoon light brown sugar
⅓ cup finely chopped cooked ham
½ cup (2 ounces) shredded Swiss cheese
1 large egg, lightly beaten
1 cup milk
¼ cup vegetable oil
¾ teaspoon spicy brown mustard
½ teaspoon Worcestershire sauce
3 drops of hot sauce

Combine first 5 ingredients in a large bowl; stir in ham and cheese. Make a well in center. Combine egg and remaining ingredients; add to dry ingredients, stirring just until moistened. Spoon into greased muffin pans, filling two-thirds full. Bake at 400° for 22 to 25 minutes. Remove from pans immediately. Yield: 1 dozen.

TEX-MEX CORN MUFFINS

1½ cups yellow cornmeal
½ teaspoon baking soda
½ teaspoon salt
1 (2-ounce) jar diced pimiento, drained
1 cup (4 ounces) shredded Cheddar cheese
½ cup finely chopped onion
¼ cup chopped green chiles
1 clove garlic, minced
2 large eggs, lightly beaten
1 cup milk
1 (8¾-ounce) can yellow cream-style corn

Heat ungreased muffin pans in a 400° oven 10 minutes or until hot.
Combine first 3 ingredients in a large bowl; stir in pimiento and next 4 ingredients. Make a well in center. Combine eggs, milk, and corn; add to dry ingredients, stirring just until moistened. Spoon into muffin pans, filling three-fourths full. Bake at 400° for 30 minutes or until golden. Remove from pans immediately. Yield: 1½ dozen.
Joy Allard
San Antonio, Texas

ONION-DILL MUFFINS

1½ cups wheat bran cereal
1¼ cups milk
2 large eggs, lightly beaten
3 tablespoons vegetable oil
1 cup all-purpose flour
¾ cup whole wheat flour
1 tablespoon baking powder
½ teaspoon salt
2 tablespoons sugar
½ teaspoon dried dillweed
½ teaspoon dry mustard
½ cup finely chopped onion

Combine cereal and milk in a small bowl; let stand 2 minutes or until cereal is softened. Stir in eggs and oil.
Combine flours and next 5 ingredients in a medium bowl; stir in onion. Make a well in center; add cereal mixture, stirring just until moistened. Spoon into a greased muffin pan, filling three-fourths full. Bake at 400° for 18 minutes or until golden. Remove from pan immediately. Yield: 1 dozen.

Muffin-Making Tips

■ Use a shiny muffin pan for best results.
■ Combine dry ingredients in a bowl, forming a well in the center. Combine wet ingredients, and pour into well.
■ Stir batter just until all ingredients are moist. The batter should be lumpy.
■ Grease muffin pans with solid shortening only; do not use oil, butter, or margarine.
■ Spoon batter into pan immediately, and bake as directed.
■ Remove muffins from pan immediately when done.

Right: *Reap the harvest of summer with a trio of fresh tomatoes—green, red, and yellow—in colorful Three Tomato Salsa (recipe, page 138).*

(From top) Dill Green Beans, Peach Jam, Green Tomato Sweet Relish, and Pickled Yellow Squash preserve the tastes of summer. (Recipes begin on page 135.)

Welcome new neighbors with a gift from your kitchen. Give a jar of homemade Onion Jelly (recipe, page 135).

Right: *Set the table with a colorful menu brimming with fresh summer flavors—Grilled Polenta With Black Bean Salsa and Steamed Garden Vegetables (recipes, page 155).*

Far right: *Toast a brilliant sunset with Grilled Marinated Beef Roast, Corn Casserole, Tomato-and-Cucumber Summer Salad, and fresh dilled green beans (recipes, page 141).*

Above: *Corn, chopped green chiles, and sweet red pepper give Mexican Cornbread (recipe, page 182) a unique look and taste.*

Right: *Traveling Linguine With Roasted Vegetables (recipe, page 178)—camp food has never tasted nor looked this good.*

Dressed with liqueur and topped with ice cream, Honeyed Peaches 'n' Cream (recipe, page 134) will satisfy your sweet tooth.

Cool down a steamy summer day with Peach Melba Sundae Shake (recipe, page 134), featuring raspberries and peaches.

Serve Strawberry Sorbet (recipe, page 153) the easy way—freeze a bed of crushed ice in serving dishes, and add scoops of sorbet just before serving. Garnish with sprigs of fresh mint.

Sorbets—Frozen To Perfection

Ices, sorbets, and granitàs—no matter what you call them, these frozen refreshers differ from ice cream and sherbet in that they contain no milk or cream. They're simply frozen mixtures of fruit juice (and/or liquids such as wine), water, and sometimes sweetener.

All these sorbets are frozen in a pan. Several recipes specify freezing the mixture until almost firm, beating it until slushy, and then refreezing. Beating these mixtures gives the sorbets a smooth texture (other recipes are smooth without beating).

STRAWBERRY SORBET
(pictured on page 152)

⅔ cup boiling water
½ cup sugar
4 cups fresh or frozen strawberries, sliced
2 tablespoons orange juice
1 teaspoon grated lemon rind
1 tablespoon lemon juice
Garnish: fresh mint sprigs

Combine boiling water and sugar in a large bowl, stirring until sugar dissolves; let cool. Stir in strawberries and next 3 ingredients. Press into a 13- x 9- x 2-inch pan; freeze until almost firm. Spoon into a large mixing bowl; beat at medium speed with an electric mixer until smooth. Return to pan, and freeze until firm. To serve, let stand at room temperature 10 to 15 minutes; garnish, if desired. Yield: 4 cups.

CRAN-APPLE SPICE SORBET

2 cups apple cider
½ cup sugar
½ teaspoon whole cloves
2 (3-inch) cinnamon sticks
2 cups unsweetened applesauce
1 cup cranberry juice
2 tablespoons lemon juice

Combine first 4 ingredients in a small saucepan; bring to a boil, stirring constantly. Reduce heat, and simmer 5 minutes. Remove and discard cloves and cinnamon sticks. Stir in applesauce and remaining ingredients. Cover and chill 1 hour.

Pour mixture into a 13- x 9- x 2-inch pan, and freeze until almost firm. Spoon into a large mixing bowl; beat at medium speed with an electric mixer until slushy. Return to pan, and freeze 8 hours. To serve, let stand at room temperature 10 minutes. Yield: 6 cups.
Erma Jackson
Huntsville, Alabama

LEMON SORBET

3 cups boiling water
1 cup sugar
2 teaspoons grated lemon rind
½ cup lemon juice

Combine boiling water and sugar in a large bowl, stirring until sugar dissolves; let cool. Add lemon rind and juice. Pour into a 9-inch square pan; freeze until firm. To serve, let stand at room temperature 10 minutes. Yield: 4 cups.
Judi Strange
Trussville, Alabama

GRAPEFRUIT-MINT SORBET

1½ cups boiling water
½ cup sugar
2 cups commercial refrigerated grapefruit juice
1½ teaspoons finely chopped fresh mint

Combine first 2 ingredients, stirring until sugar dissolves; let cool. Add grapefruit juice and mint. Pour into a 9-inch square pan; freeze until almost firm. Spoon into a large mixing bowl; beat at medium speed with an electric mixer until slushy. Return to pan, and freeze 8 hours. To serve, let stand at room temperature 20 minutes. Yield: 3½ cups.
Paul Seery
Birmingham, Alabama

PEACH SORBET

½ cup sugar
¼ cup light corn syrup
2 cups water, divided
1 (16-ounce) package frozen peaches, thawed
3 tablespoons lemon juice
½ cup peach nectar
⅛ teaspoon almond extract

Combine sugar, corn syrup, and 1 cup water in a small saucepan; bring to a boil, stirring constantly. Reduce heat, and simmer 3 minutes; let cool.

Place peaches and remaining 1 cup water in container of an electric blender or food processor; process until smooth, stopping once to scrape down sides. Combine peach mixture, syrup mixture, lemon juice, and remaining ingredients. Pour into a 13- x 9- x 2-inch pan, and freeze until almost firm. Spoon into a large mixing bowl; beat at medium speed with an electric mixer until slushy. Return to pan, and freeze 8 hours. To serve, let stand at room temperature 10 minutes. Yield: 5 cups.

Tip: *During the week, keep a shopping list handy to write down items as you need them. This will eliminate unnecessary trips to the store. Before your weekly shopping trip, make a complete shopping list. If you arrange the list according to the layout of the store, you will save yourself time and steps.*

Have Your Cake And Eat It, Too

Wishing away the urge for a sweet snack isn't fun. Instead, whip up a snack cake for a truly lean between-meal treat that also satisfies your sweet tooth.

LEMON-POPPY SEED CAKE

1 (18.5-ounce) package 97% fat-free yellow cake mix
½ cup sugar
⅓ cup vegetable oil
¼ cup water
1 cup plain nonfat yogurt
1 cup egg substitute
3 tablespoons lemon juice
2 tablespoons poppy seeds
Vegetable cooking spray
Lemon Glaze

Combine cake mix and sugar in a large mixing bowl; add vegetable oil and next 4 ingredients. Beat at medium speed with an electric mixer 6 minutes. Stir in poppy seeds.

Pour into a 10-cup Bundt pan coated with cooking spray. Bake at 350° for 40 minutes or until a wooden pick inserted in center comes out clean. Cool in pan on a wire rack 10 minutes. Remove from pan; drizzle with Lemon Glaze, and cool completely on wire rack. Yield: 24 servings (156 calories [27% from fat] per slice).

□ 2.8g protein, 4.7g fat (1.1g saturated), 25.6g carbohydrate, 0.1g fiber, 0.2mg cholesterol, 168mg sodium, and 44mg calcium.

Lemon Glaze

½ cup sifted powdered sugar
2 tablespoons lemon juice

Combine all ingredients, stirring until smooth. Yield: ¼ cup (60 calories [0% from fat] per tablespoon).

□ 0g protein, 0g fat (0g saturated), 15.6g carbohydrate, 0g fiber, 0mg cholesterol, 0mg sodium, and 1mg calcium.   Dani Chadwich Beasley Nashville, Tennessee

BANANA-COCONUT CAKE

1¾ cups all-purpose flour
½ teaspoon baking soda
¼ teaspoon salt
⅓ cup sugar
1¼ teaspoons cream of tartar
¾ cup mashed ripe banana
¼ cup egg substitute
¼ cup skim milk
¼ cup margarine, melted
1 teaspoon vanilla extract
1 tablespoon flaked coconut
¼ teaspoon ground cinnamon
Vegetable cooking spray

Combine first 5 ingredients in a large bowl; make a well in center of mixture. Combine banana and next 4 ingredients; add to dry mixture, stirring until moistened. Combine coconut and cinnamon; set aside.

Coat an 8-inch square pan with cooking spray. Spoon batter into pan; sprinkle with coconut mixture. Bake at 350° for 20 to 25 minutes or until a wooden pick inserted in center comes out clean. Cool in pan on a wire rack 5 minutes. Remove from pan; let cool on wire rack. Yield: 8 servings (230 calories [25% from fat] per serving).

□ 4.3g protein, 6.5g fat (1.5g saturated), 39.3g carbohydrate, 1.9g fiber, 0mg cholesterol, 241mg sodium, and 34mg calcium.

CHOCOLATE-CINNAMON CAKE

1½ cups all-purpose flour
1 teaspoon baking powder
½ teaspoon baking soda
¼ teaspoon salt
1 cup sugar
⅓ cup unsweetened cocoa
1 teaspoon ground cinnamon
1 cup nonfat buttermilk
¼ cup egg substitute
2 tablespoons margarine, melted
2 teaspoons vanilla extract
Vegetable cooking spray
¼ cup chopped walnuts

Combine first 7 ingredients in a large bowl. Combine buttermilk and next 3 ingredients; add to dry ingredients, stirring until blended. Spoon into an 8-inch square pan coated with cooking spray; sprinkle with walnuts. Bake at 350° for 30 minutes or until a wooden pick inserted in center comes out clean. Cool in pan on a wire rack. Yield: 12 servings (178 calories [20% from fat] per serving).

□ 4.2g protein, 4g fat (0.7g saturated), 31.6g carbohydrate, 0.6g fiber, 1mg cholesterol, 161mg sodium, and 60mg calcium.

SOUR CREAM COFFEE CAKE

½ cup walnuts, chopped
¼ cup reduced-calorie margarine, softened
½ cup sugar
½ cup egg substitute
1½ cups all-purpose flour
1½ teaspoons baking powder
1 teaspoon baking soda
⅛ teaspoon salt
1 cup nonfat sour cream alternative
1 teaspoon vanilla extract
¼ cup sugar
2 teaspoons ground cinnamon
Vegetable cooking spray

Place walnuts in a pan; bake at 350° for 8 to 10 minutes or until lightly toasted. Cool.

Beat margarine at medium speed with an electric mixer until creamy, and gradually add ½ cup sugar, beating well. Add egg substitute, beating mixture well.

Combine flour and next 3 ingredients; add to margarine mixture alternately with sour cream alternative, beginning and ending with flour mixture. Mix after each addition. Stir in vanilla and walnuts.

Combine ¼ cup sugar and cinnamon; fold half of mixture into cake batter. Spoon into a 9-inch square pan coated with cooking spray, and sprinkle with remaining sugar mixture. Bake at 350° for 30 to 35 minutes or until a wooden pick inserted in center comes out clean. Cool in pan on a wire rack 10 minutes. Remove from pan; invert and cool on wire rack. Yield: 9 servings (255 calories [24% from fat] per serving).

□ *7g protein, 6.7g fat (0.7g saturated), 41.6g carbohydrate, 1.1g fiber, 0mg cholesterol, 242mg sodium, and 70mg calcium.* Mrs. E. W. Hanley
Palm Harbor, Florida

LIGHT MENU

Enchant Guests With A Meatless Feast

The beauty of entrées composed of grains, beans, and vegetables is that they furnish substantial protein and carbohydrates with only a minimum of fat. The trick is not to load them down with cream, cheese, or other high-fat toppings.

Grilled Polenta topped with Black Bean Salsa, accompanied by a heaping serving of Steamed Garden Vegetables, makes a satisfying meal. We guarantee that you'll hardly miss the meat. Because it takes a larger volume of vegetables and grains to match the full protein complement of meat, the portions are larger than in traditional meat menus.

GRILLED POLENTA WITH BLACK BEAN SALSA
(pictured on page 148)

4 cups ready-to-serve,
 reduced-sodium, fat-free chicken
 broth
1 cup yellow cornmeal
Vegetable cooking spray
Black Bean Salsa

Bring chicken broth to a boil in a heavy saucepan; gradually add cornmeal, stirring constantly. Reduce heat, and cook 20 minutes or until mixture is thick, stirring often.

Spread cornmeal mixture into a 9-inch square pan coated with cooking spray; refrigerate until firm. Cut polenta into four squares; diagonally cut each square in half. Coat a grill basket with cooking spray; arrange polenta triangles in basket. Cook, covered with grill lid, over hot coals (400° to 500°) 5 minutes on each side or until polenta begins to brown. Serve with Black Bean Salsa. Yield: 4 servings (296 calories [6% from fat] per 2 polenta triangles and 1 cup salsa).

□ *12.3g protein, 1.9g fat (0.2g saturated), 55.9g carbohydrate, 7g fiber, 0mg cholesterol, 263mg sodium, and 40mg calcium.*

Black Bean Salsa

2 cups canned black beans, drained
 and rinsed
¾ cup finely chopped tomato
½ cup finely chopped onion
½ cup finely chopped sweet red
 pepper
¼ cup chopped fresh cilantro
1 teaspoon finely chopped jalapeño
 pepper
⅓ cup red wine vinegar

Combine all ingredients in a large bowl, and toss gently. Cover and chill. Serve with polenta. Yield: 4 cups (144 calories [6% from fat] per 1-cup serving).

□ *8.9g protein, 0.9g fat (0.2g saturated), 27.2g carbohydrate, 5.2g fiber, 0mg cholesterol, 257mg sodium, and 38mg calcium.*

STEAMED GARDEN VEGETABLES
(pictured on page 148)

½ pound carrots with tops,
 trimmed
½ pound broccoli flowerets
¼ pound zucchini, sliced
¼ pound yellow squash, sliced
¼ pound fresh mushrooms
1 medium-size sweet red pepper,
 cut into strips
1 medium-size green pepper, cut
 into strips
1 medium-size sweet yellow
 pepper, cut into strips
1 teaspoon dried Salad Supreme
 seasoning
Garnishes: lemon slices, fresh sage
 sprigs, parsley sprigs

Arrange carrot in a steamer basket, and place over boiling water. Cover and steam 8 minutes or until crisp-tender; remove and keep warm. Arrange broccoli and next 6 ingredients in steamer basket over boiling water. Cover and steam 6 minutes or until crisp-tender.

Evenly arrange the vegetables on dinner plates; sprinkle evenly with Salad Supreme seasoning. Garnish each serving, if desired. Yield: 4 servings (74 calories [12% from fat] per serving).

□ *4.1g protein, 1g fat (0.1g saturated), 14.7g carbohydrate, 3.7g fiber, 0mg cholesterol, 119mg sodium, and 67mg calcium.*

With Mexican Appeal

The name chiles rellenos means "stuffed chiles"—a modest description for this enticing Mexican favorite. Mildly pungent Anaheim or poblano chile peppers, stuffed with Monterey Jack cheese, are coated with an egg mixture and fried.

In our lightened version, we used canned green chiles to save preparation time. They're a bit softer and messier than fresh peppers, but they still capture the dish's characteristic flavor. To reduce the fat in the recipe by about 32 grams, we substituted 6 ounces of ⅓-less-fat Monterey Jack cheese for 8 ounces of regular. Instead of using egg yolk in the coating, we folded an equivalent amount of egg substitute into the beaten egg white. And finally, instead of frying, the coated chiles were browned in a nonstick pan sprayed with vegetable cooking spray and baked in the oven.

LIGHT CHILES RELLENOS

6 ounces ⅓-less-fat Monterey Jack cheese
3 (4-ounce) cans whole green chiles, drained
¼ cup egg substitute
⅛ teaspoon salt
⅛ teaspoon pepper
4 egg whites
Vegetable cooking spray
½ cup all-purpose flour
1 (14½-ounce) can no-salt-added stewed tomatoes, undrained and chopped

Cut cheese into 9 (2- x ½- x ½-inch) pieces; place 1 piece inside each chile. (Cheese pieces may need trimming slightly to fit chiles.) Set aside.

Combine egg substitute, salt, and pepper in a large bowl. Beat egg whites until stiff peaks form; fold into egg substitute mixture.

Place a large nonstick skillet coated with cooking spray over medium heat. Quickly dredge cheese-filled chiles in flour, and coat each generously with egg white mixture. Place coated chiles in skillet, and brown on both sides.

Transfer browned chiles to a 13- x 9- x 2-inch baking dish coated with cooking spray. Pour tomatoes over chiles, and bake at 350° for 30 minutes. Yield: 3 servings (384 calories [30% from fat] per serving).

□ 31.2g protein, 13g fat (7g saturated), 36.5g carbohydrate, 1.9g fiber, 42mg cholesterol, 653mg sodium, and 578mg calcium.

COMPARE THE NUTRIENTS (per serving)		
	Traditional	Light
Calories	714	384
Fat	44.5g	13g
Cholesterol	398mg	42mg

Add Flavor With Smoked Vegetable Puree

From smoker to blender to simple puree, this vegetable mixture—pungent with hickory-smoked flavor—has many uses. Serve it as a sauce or use it as a base for other easy recipes. You'll enjoy its distinctive taste, and if you're watching sodium, there's a bonus. The puree adds a hint of smoky flavor but contains no added salt.

Store the puree in the refrigerator, or simply freeze portions in ice-cube trays. Use the cubes to add flavor to recipes such as mashed potatoes, meat loaf, vegetable soup, chili, and barbecue sauce.

■ Try topping cooked pasta or baked potatoes with this classic soup.

SMOKED VEGETABLE GAZPACHO

2 cups Smoked Vegetable Puree (see recipe)
2 tablespoons olive oil
2 tablespoons white wine vinegar
1 clove garlic, pressed
1 jalapeño pepper, finely chopped
½ teaspoon salt
½ teaspoon dried oregano
½ teaspoon pepper
1 cup chopped cucumber, carrot, or yellow squash
Garnish: cooked shrimp

Combine first 9 ingredients; cover mixture, and chill. Garnish, if desired. Yield: 3 cups.

■ Keep this puree in the refrigerator up to three days or freeze up to six months. Use as a substitute for picante sauce or salsa on enchiladas, tacos, nachos, or fajitas, or serve with grilled meats and steamed vegetables.

SMOKED VEGETABLE PUREE

Hickory chips
6 large tomatoes
3 large sweet red peppers
1 large onion
2 small yellow squash

Soak hickory chips in water 30 minutes. Prepare charcoal fire in smoker;

let burn 20 minutes. Place chips on coals. Place water pan in smoker, and add water to pan. Place vegetables on food rack. Cover with smoker lid; cook 2 to 3 hours or until vegetables are tender, removing vegetables as they become tender.

Core tomatoes, and remove stems from peppers; remove outer skin from onion, and cut in half. Place half of vegetables in container of an electric blender; process until smooth, stopping once to scrape down sides. Repeat procedure with remaining vegetables. Divide into desired portions, and freeze up to 6 months, if desired. Yield: 8 cups.

Cream Sauce: Combine ½ cup Smoked Vegetable Puree; ¼ cup sour cream; 1 clove garlic, pressed; ¼ teaspoon salt; ¼ teaspoon pepper; and a dash of hot sauce. Cover and chill. Serve with grilled meats, fish, steamed vegetables, or omelets. Yield: ¾ cup.

Shortcut Aioli: Combine ⅓ cup Smoked Vegetable Puree; ½ cup mayonnaise; 2 cloves garlic, pressed; ¼ teaspoon salt; ¼ teaspoon pepper; and a dash of hot sauce. Serve mixture as a sandwich spread. Yield: about ¾ cup.

Vegetable Soup: Combine 2 cups Smoked Vegetable Puree; 1 cup ready-to-serve chicken broth or half-and-half; and ⅛ teaspoon pepper. Cook over medium heat until thoroughly heated, stirring occasionally. Yield: 3 cups.

Tip: *Onions offer outstanding nutritive value. At their best, they are a good source of calcium and vitamins A and C, and they contain iron, riboflavin, thiamine, and niacin. Onions have a high percentage of water and supply bulk. They are low in calories and have only a trace of fat.*

Chicken Takes Wing

Ever have one of those days when you want something different to fix for supper that will satisfy any appetite? Or maybe you have an occasion when you need an inexpensive hors d'oeuvre with a different twist?

Each of these main-dish or appetizer favorites calls for chicken wings cut to resemble miniature drumsticks. If you're short on time, the supermarket butcher can do the trimming and, if desired, skinning.

DOWN-HOME CHICKEN DRUMMETTES

1½ pounds chicken drummettes
½ teaspoon garlic powder
¼ teaspoon pepper
¼ cup butter or margarine
1 (1-ounce) envelope onion soup mix
½ to ¾ cup water
1 (8-ounce) carton sour cream
1 (10¾-ounce) can cream of chicken soup
Hot biscuits

Sprinkle drummettes with garlic powder and pepper. Melt butter in a large skillet over medium-low heat. Add drummettes, and cook until done, turning occasionally. Remove drummettes; drain on paper towels, and keep warm. Pour off drippings, reserving ¼ cup in skillet.

Combine onion soup mix and water; stir into reserved drippings, and cook over low heat 5 minutes. Combine sour cream and chicken soup; add to drippings mixture, and simmer 10 minutes, stirring often. Serve over split biscuits with drummettes on the side. Yield: 4 to 5 servings.

Mary Petrilla
Bradenton, Florida

GINGER-GARLIC APPETIZER DRUMMETTES

¼ cup soy sauce
⅓ cup reduced-sodium chicken broth
¼ cup minced fresh gingerroot
4 small cloves garlic, minced
1½ tablespoons sesame seeds, toasted
1½ tablespoons dark sesame oil
¾ teaspoon balsamic or white vinegar
2 pounds chicken drummettes

Combine first 7 ingredients in an 11- x 7- x 1½-inch baking dish. Add drummettes, turning to coat; cover and refrigerate 2 hours, turning occasionally. Remove from marinade.

Place drummettes on a lightly greased rack; place rack in broiler pan. Broil 5 to 6 inches from heat (with electric oven door partially opened) 7 minutes on each side or until done, turning once. Yield: 8 to 10 appetizer servings. *Barbara E. Bach*
Clearwater, Florida

ORANGE-PECAN CHICKEN DRUMMETTES

1 (6-ounce) can frozen orange juice concentrate, thawed and undiluted
3 large eggs, lightly beaten
2 tablespoons water
1 cup all-purpose flour
⅓ cup finely chopped pecans
3 pounds chicken drummettes, skinned
⅓ cup butter or margarine, melted
Red Hot Sauce
Hot cooked rice

Combine first 3 ingredients, and set orange juice mixture aside. Combine flour and pecans, and set aside.

Dip drummettes in orange juice mixture; dredge in flour mixture. Pour butter into a 15- x 10- x 1-inch jellyroll pan; arrange drummettes in a single layer. Bake at 375° for 25 minutes. Spoon Red Hot Sauce over drummettes, and bake an additional 30 minutes. Serve over rice. Yield: 8 to 10 servings.

Red Hot Sauce

2 cups catsup
¾ cup firmly packed brown sugar
3 to 4 tablespoons hot sauce

Combine all ingredients, stirring until smooth. Yield: 2¾ cups.   *June Jones Hudson, Florida*

SOUTHWESTERN CHICKEN DRUMMETTES

⅔ cup fine, dry breadcrumbs
⅔ cup finely crushed corn chips
1 (1¼-ounce) package taco seasoning mix
2 pounds chicken drummettes, skinned
1 (16-ounce) jar taco sauce, divided

Combine breadcrumbs, crushed corn chips, and taco seasoning mix in a small bowl. Dip drummettes, one at a time, into ½ cup taco sauce, and dredge in crumb mixture; place on a lightly greased baking sheet. Bake at 375° for 30 to 35 minutes. Serve with remaining taco sauce. Yield: 8 to 10 appetizer servings.   *Joan Powell Dallas, Texas*

QUICK & EASY

Worldly BLTs

Remember when you first tasted a bacon, lettuce, and tomato sandwich? One bite and grilled cheese moved to second place.

Here's your chance to experience that first taste of a BLT all over again. We've created three new versions of the beloved sandwich, each with an international salute. The basic trio of ingredients remains, but from the countries of Greece, India, and France come some worldly additions.

BLT CROISSANTS

1 (3-ounce) package cream cheese, softened
1 (3-ounce) package goat cheese, softened
¼ cup chopped oil-packed sun-dried tomatoes
1 teaspoon dried basil
4 large croissants, cut in half horizontally *
8 slices bacon, cooked and well drained
1 cup torn Bibb or red leaf lettuce

Combine cream cheese and goat cheese, stirring until smooth; stir in tomatoes and basil. Set aside. (Cover and chill 8 hours, if desired.)

Spread cheese mixture evenly on each croissant half, and place on an ungreased baking sheet. Bake at 325° for 5 minutes or until cheese mixture begins to melt. Remove from oven, and place 2 strips of bacon on bottom halves of croissants. Top evenly with lettuce and tops of croissants. Serve immediately. Yield: 4 servings.

* 2 (6-ounce) packages frozen croissants, thawed, can be substituted. Prepare as directed, placing only 1 strip of bacon on each croissant. Yield: 8 servings.

BLT IN PITA POCKETS

4 pita bread rounds, cut in half
Cucumber Spread
Romaine lettuce
16 slices bacon, cooked and broken into pieces
16 tomato slices
6 ounces feta cheese, crumbled
½ cup Greek olives, pitted and sliced

Spread each pita half with Cucumber Spread. Line each half with romaine lettuce; evenly add bacon and tomato to each. Sprinkle evenly with cheese and olives. Yield: 8 servings.

Cucumber Spread

½ cup plain yogurt
¼ cup finely chopped cucumber
1 tablespoon lemon juice
1 teaspoon dried dillweed
¼ teaspoon salt
⅛ teaspoon pepper

Combine all ingredients; cover and chill 1 hour. Yield: ⅔ cup.

CURRIED BLT SANDWICHES

8 slices oatmeal bread, lightly toasted
Curry Spread
12 slices bacon, cooked and crumbled
¼ cup raisins
¼ cup cashew nuts, coarsely chopped
2 large tomatoes, sliced
Lettuce leaves

Coat one side of each bread slice with Curry Spread. Sprinkle bacon, raisins, and nuts evenly on 4 slices; top each with tomato slices and a lettuce leaf. Cover with remaining 4 bread slices. Yield: 4 servings.

Curry Spread

2 tablespoons mayonnaise or salad dressing
2 tablespoons sour cream
1 tablespoon chutney
1 teaspoon curry powder
½ teaspoon grated orange rind
Pinch of ground ginger
Pinch of ground cumin

Combine all ingredients; cover and chill. Yield: ⅓ cup.

Come To Tea

The Colonel's Lady, a bed-and-breakfast inn in Gatlinburg, Tennessee, owned by Lee and John Mellor, makes these miniature sandwiches for afternoon tea. But serve them anytime, and they'll lend an air of graciousness to the occasion.

DOUBLE-FILLED PARTY SANDWICHES
(pictured on page 185)

18 slices oatmeal bread
Cheese-and-Orange Filling
Tomato-Curry-Orange Butter
Garnishes: orange strips

Remove crust from bread. Spread half of bread slices with Cheese-and-Orange Filling; spread remaining bread slices with Tomato-Curry-Orange Butter. Place spread sides of bread together. Cut into quarters.

Garnish, if desired. Yield: 36 party sandwiches.

Cheese-and-Orange Filling

1 (11-ounce) can mandarin oranges, drained
1 (8-ounce) package cream cheese, softened
½ cup finely chopped walnuts, toasted
½ teaspoon ground cinnamon

Press orange segments between paper towels to remove excess moisture. Combine oranges and remaining ingredients. Yield: 1⅓ cups.

Tomato-Curry-Orange Butter

½ cup butter, softened
¼ teaspoon curry powder
¼ teaspoon grated orange rind
¼ teaspoon catsup
⅛ teaspoon salt

Combine all ingredients in a small bowl. Yield: ½ cup.

Note: To make one day ahead, cover top of prepared sandwiches with wax paper. Top with a slightly dampened lightweight kitchen towel, and store in refrigerator.

Newfangled Biscuits

Biscuits warm up your senses. They look tempting, rest in your hand just so, and taste good. And the tantalizing aroma from the kitchen when these biscuits are baking—it's just like a call from home.

Our newfangled biscuits are fruited, herbed, or spiced, and go from the breakfast tray to the dessert plate. If biscuits recall good times, this batch is certain to create new memories.

CINNAMON-RAISIN BREAKFAST BISCUITS

1⅓ cups corn flakes cereal
2 tablespoons brown sugar
1 teaspoon ground cinnamon
2 tablespoons butter or margarine, melted
2½ cups biscuit mix
2 tablespoons sugar
½ cup raisins
⅓ cup buttermilk
⅓ cup tonic water
½ teaspoon vanilla extract
Frosting

Combine first 3 ingredients in container of an electric blender or food processor; process until mixture resembles fine crumbs. Transfer to a small bowl; add butter, stirring until moistened. Set aside.

Combine biscuit mix, sugar, and raisins in a large bowl; add buttermilk, tonic water, and vanilla, stirring with a fork until dry ingredients are moistened. Turn dough out onto a lightly floured surface, and knead lightly 3 or 4 times. Gradually sprinkle with crumb mixture; knead just until crumb mixture is blended. Shape into 12 balls, and place on a lightly greased baking sheet. Press each into a ½-inch-thick biscuit. Bake at 400° for 15 to 18 minutes or until evenly browned. Transfer immediately to a wire rack, and spread evenly with frosting. Yield: 1 dozen.

Frosting

1½ cups sifted powdered sugar
2 tablespoons butter or margarine, melted
2 tablespoons sour cream
1 teaspoon vanilla extract

Combine all ingredients in a small bowl. Yield: ⅔ cup. *Margaret Cotton Franklin, Virginia*

RASPBERRY-ALMOND BISCUITS

3 cups all-purpose flour
1 tablespoon baking powder
½ teaspoon baking soda
⅛ teaspoon salt
½ cup sugar
¾ cup butter or margarine, cut into pieces
1 cup fresh or frozen raspberries, thawed and well drained
½ cup chopped almonds
1½ teaspoons grated orange rind
¾ cup milk
¾ cup plain yogurt

Combine first 5 ingredients in a large bowl; cut in butter with a pastry blender until butter is the size of peas. Stir in raspberries, almonds, and orange rind. Add milk and yogurt, stirring with a fork until dry ingredients are moistened. (Dough will be very sticky.) Turn dough out onto a heavily floured surface, and knead lightly 5 or 6 times.

Roll to ¾-inch thickness; cut with a 2½-inch round cutter; place on a lightly greased baking sheet. Bake at 400° for 20 to 25 minutes or until lightly browned. Yield: 20 biscuits.

BASIL BISCUITS

1 package active dry yeast
2 tablespoons warm water (105° to 115°)
1 cup buttermilk
2½ cups all-purpose flour
1½ teaspoons baking powder
½ teaspoon baking soda
¼ teaspoon salt
2 tablespoons sugar
½ cup shortening
¼ cup finely chopped fresh basil
2 tablespoons finely chopped oil-packed sundried tomatoes

Combine yeast and warm water in a 2-cup liquid measuring cup, and let stand 5 minutes. Stir in buttermilk, and set aside.

Combine flour and next 4 ingredients in a large bowl; cut in shortening with a pastry blender until shortening is the size of peas. Add buttermilk mixture, basil, and tomatoes, stirring with a fork until dry ingredients are moistened. (Dough will resemble cottage cheese and be sticky.) Turn dough out onto a heavily floured surface, and knead lightly 4 or 5 times.

Roll to ½-inch thickness; cut with a 2½-inch round cutter. Place on a lightly greased baking sheet. Cover and let rise in a warm place (85°), free from drafts, 30 minutes. Bake at 450° for 10 to 12 minutes or until browned. Yield: 1 dozen.

The Mighty Okra

Throughout the South, okra has become synonymous with gumbo. A natural thickener, it is one of our most venerable vegetables—a staple in soups and stews from Shreveport to Savannah.

Okra has more recipe variations than a round slice of it has spokes. The flavor ranges from delicate to tart, and the texture varies from smooth to crisp. It can be stewed, fried, baked, or pickled. Is there any way okra hasn't been prepared? Not anymore. May we offer you a Fresh Okra Muffin?

OKRA GOULASH

4 slices bacon
1 medium onion, chopped
2 cups sliced fresh okra
1½ cups fresh corn, cut from cob (about 3 ears)
4 medium tomatoes, peeled and chopped
½ teaspoon salt
½ teaspoon pepper

Cook bacon in a large skillet until crisp; remove bacon, reserving 2 tablespoons drippings in skillet. Crumble bacon, and set aside. Cook onion in drippings over medium heat, stirring constantly, until tender. Add okra, and cook, stirring constantly, 5 minutes. Add corn and remaining ingredients. Cover and simmer 15 minutes, stirring occasionally. Sprinkle with crumbled bacon. Yield: 6 to 8 servings.
Mary Robinson
Montevallo, Alabama

FRIED OKRA AND GREEN TOMATOES

1 pound fresh okra, cut into ½-inch slices
2 medium-size green tomatoes, coarsely chopped
1 medium onion, coarsely chopped
½ cup white cornmeal
Vegetable oil
Salt

Combine first 3 ingredients in a medium bowl; add cornmeal and toss gently. Pour oil to depth of 2 inches into a large skillet; heat to 375°. Fry half of mixture until golden. Remove with slotted spoon, and drain. Repeat procedure. Sprinkle with salt, and serve immediately. Yield: 6 servings.

OKRA PILAF

4 slices bacon
½ pound fresh okra, cut into 1-inch slices
2½ cups water
¾ teaspoon salt
¼ teaspoon pepper
1 cup long-grain rice, uncooked

Cook bacon in a large skillet until crisp; remove bacon, reserving 2 tablespoons drippings in skillet. Crumble bacon, and set aside. Cook okra in drippings over medium heat, stirring constantly, about 5 minutes or until lightly browned. Add water and remaining ingredients; bring to a boil. Cover, reduce heat, and simmer 20 minutes or until liquid is absorbed and rice is tender. Sprinkle with crumbled bacon. Yield: 4 servings.

Ethel C. Jernegan
Savannah, Georgia

FRESH OKRA MUFFINS

2 cups self-rising cornmeal
1 tablespoon sugar
½ teaspoon salt
1¼ cups milk
2 large eggs, lightly beaten
¼ cup vegetable oil
1 teaspoon Worcestershire sauce
¼ teaspoon hot sauce
2 cups thinly sliced fresh okra
   (about ½ pound)
¼ cup chopped onion

Combine first 3 ingredients in a medium bowl; make a well in center of mixture. Combine milk and next 4 ingredients; add to dry ingredients, stirring just until moistened. Fold in okra and onion.

Grease muffin pans, and place in a 400° oven for 5 minutes. Quickly spoon batter into prepared pans, filling two-thirds full; bake at 400° for 20 minutes or until lightly browned. Remove from pans immediately. Yield: 1½ dozen.

Frances H. Smith
Clanton, Alabama

Made-In-The-Shade Soups

To begin or end a summer meal, nothing is more refreshing than cold soup. Our three recipes make lavish use of bountiful summer fruits and vegetables, and require little or no cooking.

"I only tell my best friends how I make this soup," confesses Louise Jackson of Shreveport, Louisiana. The trick behind her Secret Gazpacho is its base: leftover green salad with vinaigrette dressing.

Cold soups can be presented with elegance or simplicity. If your children think all soups should be steamy, try serving theirs in tall, chilled glasses as "soup smoothies."

BANANA-RASPBERRY BISQUE

1 cup fresh raspberries
4½ cups half-and-half, divided
½ cup whipping cream
3 tablespoons powdered sugar
4 ripe bananas, peeled, sliced,
   and frozen
Cinnamon Pound Cake Croutons

Combine raspberries, ½ cup half-and-half, whipping cream, and powdered sugar in container of an electric blender; process until smooth, stopping once to scrape down sides. Pour through a wire-mesh strainer into a large bowl, discarding seeds. Cover and refrigerate.

Just before serving, combine half of bananas and 2 cups half-and-half in container of an electric blender; process until smooth. Pour banana mixture into a large bowl; repeat procedure with remaining 2 bananas and 2 cups half-and-half.

Pour banana mixture into small bowls. Using a squirt bottle, carefully drizzle raspberry mixture over banana mixture; drag a wooden pick or knife through raspberry mixture to make desired design (do not stir). Top with Cinnamon Pound Cake Croutons. Yield: 6½ cups.

Cinnamon Pound Cake Croutons

4 (½-inch) slices commercial frozen
   pound cake, cut into ½-inch cubes
Butter-flavored cooking spray
3 tablespoons sugar
½ teaspoon ground cinnamon

Coat pound cake cubes with cooking spray. Combine sugar and cinnamon; sprinkle over cubes, tossing gently to coat. Place cubes on a buttered baking sheet, and bake at 300° for 15 minutes or until lightly browned, stirring frequently. Cool. Store in an airtight container. Yield: 2 cups.

SECRET GAZPACHO

4 cups tossed green salad with
   vinaigrette dressing
4 cups cocktail vegetable juice
1 tablespoon lemon juice
½ teaspoon hot sauce
¼ teaspoon salt
¼ teaspoon pepper
Dilled Croutons

Place salad in blender; process until smooth, stopping once to scrape down sides. Combine salad mixture and next 5 ingredients; cover and chill. To serve, top with Dilled Croutons. Yield: 5¾ cups.

Dilled Croutons

3 tablespoons olive oil
½ teaspoon dried dillweed
⅛ teaspoon garlic salt
4 slices white bread, trimmed and
   cut into ½-inch cubes

Combine first 3 ingredients; drizzle over bread cubes, tossing gently. Spread bread cubes evenly on an ungreased baking sheet. Bake at 300° for 25 minutes or until golden, stirring after 10 minutes. Yield: 2 cups.

Louise Jackson
Shreveport, Louisiana

PEA-AND-WATERCRESS SOUP

3 tablespoons butter or margarine
1 small onion, finely chopped
1 bunch watercress, chopped
½ cup fresh or frozen English
   peas
2 tablespoons long-grain rice,
   uncooked
2 cups chicken broth
1 cup skim milk
¼ teaspoon ground white pepper
Garnish: chopped fresh mint

Melt butter in a large saucepan over medium heat; add onion, and cook, stirring constantly, 5 minutes. Add watercress; cook, stirring constantly, 3 minutes. Add peas and rice; cook, stirring constantly, 5 minutes. Stir in chicken broth; bring to a boil. Cover, reduce heat, and simmer 20 minutes. Remove from heat; cool slightly.

   Spoon half of mixture into container of an electric blender; process until smooth. Pour into a large saucepan, and repeat procedure with remaining mixture. Stir in milk and white pepper; bring to a boil. Remove from heat; cool slightly. Cover and chill thoroughly. Garnish, if desired. Yield: 2⅓ cups.
Caroline W. Kennedy
Newton, Georgia

Toppings For A Sweet Tooth

Busy days call for snacks and sweets that can be put together at a moment's notice. These homemade toppings and dips are easy to make. Serve them with fruits and purchased bakery treats.

   Honey-flavored Peanut Butter Lovers' Dip and Sour Cream Sauce go well with assorted fresh fruits—bananas, apples, pears, strawberries,

peaches, and nectarines. Spicy gingersnaps and plain or lemon pound cake complement Apple-Nut Topping. Rum Sundae Sauce tastes just like butter-rum flavored hard candy, and it is thick and rich enough to be a terrific ice cream topping. Prepare the sauce ahead and store it in the refrigerator. When ready to serve, reheat it in the microwave at MEDIUM power, stirring often.

BRANDIED CHOCOLATE FONDUE

2 (6-ounce) packages semisweet
   chocolate morsels
2 tablespoons water
¼ cup whipping cream
¼ cup brandy
1 tablespoon instant coffee granules
Dash of ground cinnamon

Combine chocolate and water in a small saucepan; cook over low heat until chocolate melts and mixture is smooth, stirring often. Add whipping cream and remaining ingredients, stirring until well blended. Serve warm with fresh strawberries. Yield: ⅔ cup.

Note: To keep fondue warm, reheat as needed in a microwave oven on MEDIUM power. Or double the recipe and serve in a fondue pot or small chafing dish.
Karen Etheredge
Newton, Georgia

PEANUT BUTTER LOVERS' DIP

⅔ cup creamy peanut butter
⅔ cup honey
¼ cup lemon juice

Combine all ingredients in a small mixing bowl; beat at low speed with an electric mixer until smooth. Serve with apple slices and banana chunks. Yield: 1⅓ cups.
Edith Askins
Greenville, Texas

RUM SUNDAE SAUCE

¾ cup firmly packed brown sugar
⅓ cup water
⅓ cup light corn syrup
2 tablespoons butter or margarine
⅛ teaspoon salt
½ teaspoon rum extract

Combine first 5 ingredients in a small saucepan; cook over medium heat, stirring until sugar dissolves. Reduce heat to low; cook, without stirring, until a candy thermometer reaches 230°. Remove from heat, and cool slightly. Stir in rum extract. Serve over ice cream. Yield: 1 cup.
Jean Voan
Shepherd, Texas

SOUR CREAM SAUCE

¾ cup sour cream
2 tablespoons frozen orange juice
   concentrate, thawed and
   undiluted
3 tablespoons honey

Combine all ingredients in a small bowl; cover and chill. Serve over fresh fruit. Yield: 1 cup.

APPLE-NUT TOPPING

2 (3-ounce) packages cream cheese,
   softened
½ cup sour cream
2 tablespoons brown sugar
½ teaspoon ground cinnamon
½ apple, grated
½ cup chopped pecans

Combine first 4 ingredients in a small mixing bowl; beat at low speed with an electric mixer until smooth. Stir in apple and pecans. Cover and refrigerate. Serve with gingersnaps, shortbread cookies, or pound cake. Yield: 1½ cups.

JULY

Show your Southern pride and serve our menu of updated
down-home fare at your next gathering. Try two Southern
staples in a new way — black-eyed peas in a tangy salsa
and turnip greens as the base for a hot, cheesy dip.
Delicious food and warm friendships are the main ingredients
for a lively supper club, a Southern style of entertaining. In
this chapter, Southern hostesses share their secrets for
successful entertaining in their homes, on their decks, or at
poolside in our "Summer Suppers" special section.
For more food ideas in outdoor settings, try our recipes for
camp food. Serve up around a campsite and we guarantee
you'll have happy campers.

It's A Southern Affair

If country ham, turnip greens, and black-eyed peas are some of your favorite foods, you're in good company. But if you think these down-home flavors might just be too informal for your next fancy gathering, think again.

After requests for a uniquely Southern reception menu, we decided to give it a try. The result is a feast of finger foods, appetizers, and a beverage fit for even the finest of parties.

For starters, we dressed uniquely Southern foods in their Sunday best, transforming black-eyed peas into a tangy salsa, and using turnip greens as the base for a hot, cheesy dip. The salty tingle of country ham and the straightforward taste of buttermilk inspired us further. So we've used those flavors in a showy shrimp-and-cucumber canapé and in pecan-studded chicken fingers. We kept an eye out for ease of preparation, too.

More than anything, this reception menu captures the excitement of celebrating Southern style. So serve your Southern heritage with pride. These recipes will show you how.

A SOUTHERN RECEPTION MENU

Black-Eyed Pea Salsa with tortilla chips
Hot Turnip Green Dip With Jalapeño-Corn Muffins
Shrimp-and-Cucumber Canapés
Buttermilk-Pecan Chicken Fingers
Mint Julep Brownies
Pineapple Tea

BLACK-EYED PEA SALSA
(pictured on pages 186 and 187)

1 (16-ounce) can black-eyed peas, drained
2 tomatoes, chopped
1 bunch green onions, sliced
1 tablespoon chopped fresh cilantro
3 tablespoons fresh lime juice
1 tablespoon olive oil
1 to 2 cloves garlic, minced
½ teaspoon ground cumin
¼ teaspoon salt
Leaf lettuce

Place peas in a colander; rinse with cold water, and drain. Combine tomatoes and next 7 ingredients in a medium bowl; stir in peas. Cover and refrigerate at least 4 hours. Place in a lettuce-lined compote or bowl; serve with tortilla chips. Yield: 2½ cups.

HOT TURNIP GREEN DIP WITH JALAPEÑO-CORN MUFFINS
(pictured on pages 186 and 187)

1 (10-ounce) package frozen chopped turnip greens, thawed and well drained
¼ teaspoon grated lemon rind
½ cup finely chopped onion
½ cup finely chopped celery
2 tablespoons butter or margarine, melted
1 (2½-ounce) can sliced mushrooms, drained
1 (10¾-ounce) can cream of mushroom soup, undiluted
1 (6-ounce) roll process cheese food with garlic
1 teaspoon Worcestershire sauce
5 drops of hot sauce
Garnishes: cherry tomato slices, fresh parsley sprigs
Jalapeño-Corn Muffins

Position knife blade in food processor bowl; add turnip greens and lemon rind. Process until finely chopped.

Cook onion and celery in butter in a Dutch oven over medium heat, stirring constantly, until tender. Stir in turnip green mixture, mushrooms, and next 4 ingredients. Cook over medium heat until thoroughly heated. Serve from a chafing dish. Garnish, if desired. Serve with Jalapeño-Corn Muffins. Yield: 3 cups.

Jalapeño-Corn Muffins

2 cups jalapeño cornbread mix
1 large egg, lightly beaten
1 cup milk
2 tablespoons vegetable oil

Grease miniature (1¾-inch) muffin pans, and place pans in a 400° oven for 5 minutes.

Place cornbread mix in a bowl; make a well in center. Combine egg and remaining ingredients; add to cornbread mix, stirring just until moistened. Spoon into muffin pans, filling two-thirds full. Bake at 400° for 11 minutes. Yield: 28 muffins.

Carol Barclay
Portland, Texas

SHRIMP-AND-CUCUMBER CANAPÉS
(pictured on pages 186 and 187)

4 cups water
36 unpeeled medium-size fresh shrimp
3 medium cucumbers
1 (8-ounce) package thinly sliced country ham, trimmed
1 (8-ounce) container cream cheese with chives
Garnishes: diced pimiento, fresh parsley sprigs

Bring 4 cups water to a boil; add shrimp, and cook 3 to 5 minutes or until shrimp turn pink. Drain well; rinse with cold water. Peel and devein shrimp; cover and chill.

Wash cucumbers; trim ends. Cut into ½-inch slices. Scoop out center of each slice to, but not through, bottom. Invert cucumbers on paper towels, and let stand 30 minutes.

Place ham in a large skillet; add water to cover. Bring to a boil; reduce heat, and simmer 3 minutes on each side. Drain.

Position knife blade in food processor bowl; add ham. Pulse 10 times or until ham is chopped. Add cream cheese; pulse 10 times or until blended. Spoon into a pastry bag fitted with a No. 5 tip; pipe into each cucumber slice. Top with shrimp; garnish, if desired. Yield: 36 appetizer servings.

A Centerpiece From the Garden

When we asked Laura Dee Wood, of Birmingham, Alabama, if we could use the front porch of her home as the location for our photography, she readily agreed. An enthusiastic floral designer, Laura made our centerpiece. She follows no rules when arranging flowers, and advises, "Just arrange them the way they grow."

Before arranging, Laura Dee clips roses from the garden of her Birmingham friends Marsha and Bob Oliver, and then adds hydrangeas and lilies from her garden along with additional cuttings from a flower shop. For the arrangement on pages 186 and 187, she chooses a silver basket. After soaking florist foam in water, she then places it in the basket. Florist tape anchors the foam to the container. She says a tall arrangement needs a sturdy base.

To begin, she inserts a long, straight-stemmed rose for the center. Next, she adds larger flowers to either side and fills in from there, adding breathy Queen Anne's lace and smaller flowers wherever openings exist to keep the feeling light and airy. Because she is using only flowers with sturdy stems, she doesn't need to reinforce them with wire.

BUTTERMILK-PECAN CHICKEN FINGERS
(pictured on pages 186 and 187)

6 skinned and boned chicken breast halves
1 cup all-purpose flour
1 cup pecans, toasted and ground
¼ cup sesame seeds
1 tablespoon paprika
¾ teaspoon salt
⅛ teaspoon pepper
1 large egg, lightly beaten
1 cup buttermilk
⅓ cup butter or margarine, melted
Garnishes: lettuce, lemon slices

Cut each chicken breast half into 4 strips. Combine flour and next 5 ingredients; set aside.

Combine egg and buttermilk. Dip chicken strips into buttermilk mixture, and dredge in flour mixure.

Pour butter into a 15- x 10- x 1-inch jellyroll pan; add chicken, turning to coat. Bake at 375° for 30 minutes; drain. Garnish, if desired. Yield: 24 appetizer servings.   *Ilene V. Ray*
Huntington, West Virginia

MINT JULEP BROWNIES
(pictured on page 188)

4 (1-ounce) squares unsweetened chocolate
1 cup butter or margarine
4 large eggs
2 cups sugar
1½ cups all-purpose flour
½ teaspoon salt
2 tablespoons bourbon
1 teaspoon peppermint extract
1 tablespoon powdered sugar
Garnish: fresh mint leaves

Combine chocolate and butter in a heavy saucepan; cook over low heat, stirring constantly, until chocolate melts. Let stand 10 minutes.

Beat eggs at medium speed with an electric mixer until thick and pale (about 2 minutes); gradually add sugar, beating well. Add chocolate mixture, flour, and next 3 ingredients; beat at low speed 1 minute. Spoon into a lightly greased and floured 13- x 9- x 2-inch pan. Bake at 350° for 25 to 30 minutes or until a wooden pick inserted in center comes out clean. Cool on a wire rack 10 minutes. Sprinkle with powdered sugar; cut into bars. Garnish, if desired. Yield: 4 dozen.

PINEAPPLE TEA
(pictured on page 188)

¼ cup unsweetened instant tea
2 cups sugar
4 cups boiling water
8 cups unsweetened pineapple juice
3 cups water
1 cup lemon juice
Maraschino cherries
Pineapple chunks
Garnish: fresh mint sprigs

Combine tea and sugar; add 4 cups boiling water, stirring to dissolve. Add pineapple juice, 3 cups water, and lemon juice; chill.

Pour ¼-inch water into each section of two ice cube trays, and freeze until firm. Place a cherry in the center of each cube in one tray; repeat procedure with pineapple chunks in other tray. Pour ¼-inch water into each section over fruit, and freeze until firm. Fill sections with additional water, and freeze until firm. (Freezing in stages prevents fruit from floating to top of ice cube.) Serve tea over fruited ice cubes, and garnish, if desired. Yield: 17 cups.   *Betty Czebotar*
Baltimore, Maryland

Tip: *Ice will be clearer if you first boil the water and allow it to cool before freezing it. Make ice cubes for a party ahead of time and store them in plastic bags in the freezer until needed. Count on 350 cubes for 50 people or 7 cubes per person. Muffin pans can be used to make extra-large ice cubes to float in punch.*

Lip-Smacking Peanut Butter Treats

Entice children to the kitchen with an ingredient they love—peanut butter. It lends razzle-dazzle to all the recipes here, even French toast.

These easy-to-prepare recipes offer a chance to teach your kids how to measure, follow a recipe, and actually use those fractions they learn in math. For additional kid-friendly recipe tips, remember these following ones:

■ Select simple recipes—those with only a few steps that can be finished in less than 30 minutes.
■ Assist children when the recipe calls for baking or using a hot cooking surface. Use the time to teach kitchen safety, as well as cooking.
■ Ask your children what they would like to make. Their answers may surprise (and inspire) you.

PEANUT BUTTER CANDY

½ cup sugar
½ cup light corn syrup
1 cup creamy peanut butter
1 teaspoon vanilla extract
2 cups corn flakes cereal

Combine sugar and corn syrup in a medium saucepan; bring to a boil over medium heat, stirring constantly. Remove from heat; add peanut butter and vanilla, stirring until smooth. Stir in cereal. Drop by rounded teaspoonfuls onto wax paper; let cool. Yield: 3 dozen. *Mrs. E. W. Hanley*
Palm Harbor, Florida

SPIDER COOKIES

1 (6-ounce) package butterscotch morsels
¼ cup creamy peanut butter
1 (3-ounce) can chow mein noodles
Raisins *

Combine butterscotch morsels and peanut butter in a 2-quart glass bowl. Microwave at HIGH 2 minutes, stirring once. Add chow mein noodles, stirring to coat. Drop by rounded teaspoonfuls onto wax paper; top each with 2 raisins. Chill, if desired. Yield: 4½ dozen.

* Halved candied cherries may be substituted for raisins for holiday baking. *Sheila L. Deere*
Mountain Home, Arkansas

PEANUT BUTTER BARS

1 (18.25-ounce) package yellow cake mix
2 large eggs
1 cup chunky peanut butter
½ cup butter or margarine, melted
1 (6-ounce) package semisweet chocolate morsels
1 (14-ounce) can sweetened condensed milk

Combine first 4 ingredients in a large mixing bowl; beat at medium speed with an electric mixer 1 to 2 minutes.

Press half of cake mix mixture into bottom of an ungreased 13- x 9- x 2-inch baking pan. Bake at 350° for 10 minutes. Remove from oven; sprinkle with chocolate morsels, and drizzle with condensed milk. Sprinkle with remaining cake mix mixture. Bake at 350° for 30 minutes. Cool and cut into bars. Yield: 2 dozen. *J. A. Allard*
San Antonio, Texas

PEANUT BUTTER FRENCH TOAST

½ cup creamy peanut butter
8 slices sandwich bread
2 bananas, sliced
4 large eggs, lightly beaten
½ cup milk
2 tablespoons butter or margarine

Spread peanut butter evenly over 4 bread slices; arrange banana slices evenly over peanut butter. Top with remaining bread slices; set aside.

Combine eggs and milk in a shallow dish. Melt butter in a large nonstick skillet over medium heat. Dip each sandwich into egg mixture, turning to coat both sides; place in hot skillet. Cook 3 to 4 minutes on each side or until browned. Serve immediately. Yield: 4 servings. *Shelby W. Adkins*
Penhook, Virginia

summer suppers.

20,000 Ideas Under The Sea

Well, maybe not *that* many. But when Ann Cain and Missy Buchanan of Rockwall, Texas, host their supper club, the creative ideas add up quickly. And when they share their secrets, you'll discover that it's easy, too. These innovative Texas hostesses offer more fun ideas from A to Z in their book, *Bubblin' Over: Simple Ideas for Spectacular Parties.*

On the next 10 pages of our bonus section, we toast more supper clubs. Call them what you will: supper clubs, dinner groups, gourmet groups. Whatever, Southerners gather to celebrate "Summer Suppers."

SEAFOOD CELEBRATION FOR TWELVE

Sea Mist
Crab Spread with
Assorted crackers
Shrimp With Pasta Primavera
Ginger-Cinnamon Carrots
Strawberry-Spinach Salad
Nautical Knots
Surf-and-Sand Parfaits with
Toasted pecans

SEA MIST

1 (46-ounce) can unsweetened pineapple juice
1 (46-ounce) can apricot nectar
3 (6-ounce) cans frozen lemonade concentrate, thawed and undiluted
4 (10-ounce) bottles ginger ale, chilled
1 (750-milliliter) bottle champagne, chilled

Combine first 3 ingredients; chill. Just before serving, stir in ginger ale and champagne. Yield: 5 quarts.

Tip: *Create a refreshing, tempting nonalcoholic bubbly beverage by adding sparkling mineral water to nutritious fruit juice concentrates.*

CRAB SPREAD

2 pounds fresh crabmeat, drained and flaked *
⅔ cup sliced green onions
1 (8-ounce) package cream cheese, softened
¼ to ⅓ cup mayonnaise or salad dressing
2 tablespoons lemon juice
1 teaspoon hot sauce
1 teaspoon Worcestershire sauce
¾ teaspoon salt
¼ teaspoon pepper
Red cabbage leaves
1 bunch fresh parsley
1 lime slice
1 maraschino cherry

Press crabmeat between paper towels to absorb excess moisture. Combine crabmeat and green onions in a large bowl; set aside.

Combine cream cheese and next 6 ingredients; add to crabmeat mixture, tossing to coat. Cover crabmeat mixture, and chill 8 hours.

To serve, mound on a large tray in the shape of a fish's body. Add cabbage leaves for the head and fin, parsley for the tail, and a lime slice and cherry for the eye. Serve spread with assorted crackers. Yield: 4½ cups.

* Crab-flavored seafood product may be substituted for fresh crabmeat.

SHRIMP WITH PASTA PRIMAVERA

3 pounds unpeeled medium-size
  fresh shrimp
1½ cups chopped green onions
3 to 4 cloves garlic, minced
¾ teaspoon salt
¾ teaspoon ground red pepper
¾ teaspoon black pepper
¾ teaspoon dried basil
¾ teaspoon dried oregano
¾ teaspoon dried thyme
1½ cups butter or margarine,
  melted
1½ pounds fresh mushrooms, sliced
1 cup dry white wine
Pasta Primavera
Garnishes: cherry tomatoes, fresh
  parsley sprigs

Peel and devein shrimp; set aside.
Cook green onions and next 7 ingredients in butter in a large skillet over medium heat, stirring often. Add shrimp, mushrooms, and wine; cook 3 to 4 minutes or until shrimp turn pink, stirring occasionally. Remove from skillet with a slotted spoon, and serve over Pasta Primavera. Garnish, if desired. Yield: 12 servings.

Pasta Primavera

2 (12-ounce) packages thin
  spaghetti or vermicelli
1 (8-ounce) bottle red
  wine-and-vinegar salad dressing
3 medium-size green peppers,
  chopped
3 medium-size sweet red peppers,
  chopped
3 medium-size yellow squash, cut
  into thin strips
3 cups sliced fresh mushrooms
  (optional)
1½ cups chopped green onions
¾ cup sliced pitted ripe olives
½ teaspoon salt

Cook spaghetti according to package directions; drain and keep warm.

Combine salad dressing and remaining ingredients in a large skillet; cook over medium heat about 5 minutes or until vegetables are crisp-tender, stirring often. Pour over spaghetti, tossing gently. Yield: 12 servings.

GINGER-CINNAMON CARROTS

3 pounds carrots, scraped and cut
  into thin strips
3 tablespoons butter or margarine
½ cup sugar
¼ cup firmly packed brown sugar
2 to 3 teaspoons ground ginger
2 to 3 teaspoons ground cinnamon
1½ teaspoons almond extract
Garnish: fresh parsley sprigs

Arrange carrots in a steamer basket, and place over boiling water. Cover and steam 10 to 15 minutes or until crisp-tender.
Melt butter in a large saucepan; add sugars and next 3 ingredients. Cook over low heat, stirring constantly, until sugars dissolve. Add carrots, tossing until glazed. Garnish, if desired. Yield: 12 servings.

STRAWBERRY-SPINACH SALAD

2 pounds loose fresh spinach *
1 quart fresh strawberries, halved
1 (2-ounce) package slivered
  almonds, toasted
1 (2.25-ounce) package sliced
  almonds, toasted
Poppy Seed Dressing

Remove stems from spinach; wash leaves thoroughly, and pat dry. Tear into bite-size pieces. Combine spinach, strawberries, and almonds in a large bowl; cover and chill.
Just before serving, pour Poppy Seed Dressing over salad; toss gently. Yield: 12 to 16 servings.

* 2 (10-ounce) packages fresh spinach may be substituted.

Poppy Seed Dressing

¼ to ½ cup sugar
¼ cup apple cider vinegar
1½ teaspoons finely chopped onion
¼ teaspoon paprika
¼ teaspoon Worcestershire sauce
½ cup vegetable oil
1 tablespoon poppy seeds

Combine first 5 ingredients in container of an electric blender. Process about 30 seconds, stopping once to scrape down sides. With blender on high, gradually add oil in a slow, steady stream through opening in lid; stir in poppy seeds. Yield: 1 cup.

NAUTICAL KNOTS

2 (11-ounce) cans refrigerated soft
  breadsticks
2 tablespoons butter or margarine,
  melted
1 teaspoon sesame seeds
1 teaspoon poppy seeds

Separate dough strips, and tie each loosely into a knot; place 1 inch apart on greased baking sheets. Brush dough strips with butter; sprinkle with seeds. Bake at 350° for 15 minutes or until golden. Yield: 16 breadsticks.

Dive into a Seascape

Invitation—Cut fish shapes from clear or tinted transparency sheets, and decorate with paint pens. Wrap in blue tissue paper, put in a Mylar bubble packing envelope, and hand deliver invitations.

Decorations—Find or borrow souvenir seashells, fish posters, and fish or hammock netting. Hang several iridescent Christmas ornaments from the ceiling or trees with fishing line to make "ocean bubbles."

Table setting—Buy inexpensive blue fabric to cover tables (skip hemming for ease) and bright tropical fabric for napkins. Add wooden, fish-shaped napkin rings, and put rolled "messages" into tiny corked bottles. Write guests' names on snorkels and goggles with paint pens for place cards.

Centerpieces—Place goldfish in fishbowls or large, clear vases. Be sure to treat the water to remove chlorine so the fish don't go belly-up. (Check with a pet store for information on chlorine removal.) If desired, you can first add clean seashells to bottom of container.

Arrange cut flowers and greenery in separate containers (or order arrangements from florist). Just before the party, place containers of fish on table and top with floral arrangements.

Music—Play a tape of ocean sounds from a portable tape player placed behind the trunk-turned-treasure chest.

Party games—"Go Fish": Draw fish on cards, making two of each kind for pairs. Shuffle and deal to arriving guests, having them mingle to find their card's mate.

"Fish Tales": Have guests reel in the laughter with their funniest fishing stories.

Party favors—Ladle goldfish and water from centerpieces into heavy-duty, zip top plastic bags, and send them home as party favors. Give a plush beach towel to each couple.

SURF-AND-SAND PARFAITS

1 (16-ounce) package gingersnaps
2 cups pecan pieces
1 tablespoon unflavored gelatin
¼ cup cold water
4 egg yolks, lightly beaten
½ cup fresh lime juice
¾ cup sugar
Pinch of salt
1 tablespoon grated lime rind
4 drops of green food coloring
2 cups whipping cream
½ cup sifted powdered sugar
1 teaspoon light rum
Lime-Rum Cream
Garnish: lime slices
Toasted pecans

Position knife blade in food processor; add gingersnaps and pecan pieces. Process until crumbly; set aside.

Sprinkle gelatin over cold water; stir and let stand 1 minute. Set aside. Combine egg yolks and next 3 ingredients in a heavy saucepan. Cook over medium heat, stirring constantly, 7 to 8 minutes or until a thermometer registers 160°. Remove from heat; add gelatin mixture and lime rind, stirring until gelatin dissolves. Stir in food coloring. Set aside. Beat whipping cream at high speed with an electric mixer until soft peaks form. Gradually add powdered sugar; beat until stiff peaks form. Stir in rum; fold whipped cream mixture into gelatin mixture. Chill 2 hours or until set. Spoon evenly into 12 parfait glasses. Top with reserved crumb mixture and Lime-Rum Cream; garnish, if desired. Serve with toasted pecans. Yield: 12 servings.

Lime-Rum Cream

1 cup whipping cream
3 tablespoons powdered sugar
1 teaspoon grated lime rind
2 teaspoons light rum

Beat whipping cream at high speed with an electric mixer until soft peaks form. Add sugar and remaining ingredients, beating until stiff peaks form. Yield: 2 cups.

Dinner On The Deck

A light summer breeze carries the irresistible aroma of charcoal smoke through a Raleigh, North Carolina, neighborhood. Follow your nose and you'll find a fun supper club on Jesse and Violet Rhinehart's deck. Those aren't burgers *or* chicken—they're turkey steaks.

The hosts buy a whole bone-in turkey breast and have their butcher cut it into "steaks" that look like huge pork chops. Soaked in a tangy, five-ingredient marinade, the steaks are big on flavor and easy to grill.

LET'S TALK TURKEY FOR TWELVE

**Grilled Marinated Turkey Steaks
or Greek-Style Leg of Lamb
Grilled Vegetable Kabobs
Parmesan Onions
Frozen Viennese Torte**

GRILLED MARINATED TURKEY STEAKS

1 (5-pound) bone-in turkey breast *
½ cup soy sauce
¼ cup vegetable oil
1 tablespoon ground ginger
1 teaspoon dry mustard
3 cloves garlic, pressed

Purchase bone-in turkey breast. Ask butcher to cut in half lengthwise, and then cut each half crosswise into 1-inch-thick "steaks" resembling large pork chops.

Combine soy sauce and remaining ingredients; pour over turkey. Cover turkey, and refrigerate 8 hours. Remove turkey from marinade, discarding marinade. Grill turkey, covered with lid, over medium-hot coals (350° to 400°) 8 to 10 minutes on each side. Yield: 12 servings.

* 1 (5-pound) boneless turkey breast may be substituted. Cut turkey in same manner yourself.

GREEK-STYLE LEG OF LAMB

1 (4-pound) boneless leg of lamb
1 cup vegetable oil
½ cup olive oil
½ cup lemon juice
1 tablespoon onion powder
1 tablespoon fresh or 1 teaspoon dried oregano
1 tablespoon fresh or dried rosemary
6 cloves garlic, pressed

Place lamb in a large shallow dish or a heavy-duty, zip-top plastic bag; set aside. Combine vegetable oil and remaining ingredients; reserve ¼ cup marinade mixture. Pour remaining marinade mixture over lamb. Cover or seal, and refrigerate 8 hours, turning occasionally.

Remove lamb from marinade, discarding marinade. Grill, covered with lid, over medium-hot coals (350° to 400°) 40 minutes or until meat thermometer registers 140°(rare), 150°(medium), or 160°(medium-well), turning once and basting with ¼ cup reserved marinade mixture. Yield: 12 servings.

GRILLED VEGETABLE KABOBS

3 medium ears fresh corn
2 cups water
3 medium zucchini, cut into 1-inch-thick slices (about 1½ pounds)
3 medium-size yellow squash, cut into 1-inch-thick slices (about ¾ pound)
12 cherry tomatoes (optional)
½ cup butter or margarine, melted
½ teaspoon dried chervil
½ teaspoon dried basil
¼ teaspoon garlic powder
¼ teaspoon onion powder

Remove husks and silks from corn. Bring water to a boil in a Dutch oven. Add corn, zucchini, and yellow squash; cover and cook 5 minutes. Drain. Plunge into ice water to stop the cooking process; drain. Cut corn into 1-inch-thick slices. Alternate vegetables on 12 (14-inch) skewers, and end each skewer with a cherry tomato, if desired.

Combine butter and remaining ingredients; brush on kabobs. Set remaining butter mixture aside. Grill kabobs, covered with lid, over medium-hot coals (350° to 400°) 15 to 20 minutes, basting with remaining butter mixture and turning occasionally. Yield: 12 servings.

PARMESAN ONIONS

6 (1-pound) Vidalia or other sweet onions, cut in half crosswise
2 tablespoons butter or margarine
½ cup grated Parmesan cheese
½ teaspoon salt
¼ teaspoon pepper
Lettuce leaves (optional)

Cut 12 (12-inch) squares of heavy-duty aluminum foil; place an onion half, cut side up, in center of each. Dot each onion half with butter; sprinkle with cheese, salt, and pepper. Wrap well; place on a baking sheet. Bake at 350° for 40 minutes or until tender. Serve on lettuce leaves, if desired. Yield: 12 servings.

Note: Instead of baking, Parmesan Onions may be grilled, covered with lid, over medium-hot coals (350° to 400°) 40 minutes or until tender.

FROZEN VIENNESE TORTE

18 large cinnamon graham crackers
2 (2-ounce) packages slivered
  almonds
⅓ cup butter or margarine, cut into
  small pieces
1 quart chocolate ice cream,
  softened
1 quart coffee ice cream, softened
1 quart vanilla ice cream, softened
2½ teaspoons ground cinnamon
1 (2-ounce) package slivered
  almonds, toasted
Amaretto-Cinnamon Sauce

Position knife blade in food processor bowl; add graham crackers and 2 packages almonds. Process until crushed. Add butter, processing until blended. Firmly press mixture evenly onto bottom and 1 inch up sides of a 10-inch springform pan. Bake at 375° for 10 minutes. Cool on a wire rack.

Spread chocolate ice cream onto bottom and 1 inch up sides of crust; freeze until firm. Spread coffee ice cream over chocolate ice cream; freeze until firm. Beat vanilla ice cream and cinnamon at low speed with an electric mixer until blended; spread over coffee ice cream, and freeze 8 hours. To serve, sprinkle each slice with toasted almonds, and drizzle with Amaretto-Cinnamon Sauce. Yield: 12 to 14 servings.

Amaretto-Cinnamon Sauce

¾ cup amaretto or other almond-
  flavored liqueur
¾ cup honey
¼ teaspoon ground cinnamon

Combine all ingredients in a small saucepan; cook over medium heat until thoroughly heated, stirring often. Remove from heat, and cool to room temperature. Yield: 1½ cups.

Going The Distance For Friends

It was smooth sailing for Sue Ewing's supper club—until her husband's job transfer rocked the boat. She and Martin had grown attached to their Richmond, Virginia, group, and they hated the thought of living three hours away in Roanoke.

At one of the last gatherings before the move, someone threw a lifesaver: Who says you can drive only a couple of blocks to supper club? Good friends are worth going a few miles. Now this group makes a weekend of their gatherings, taking turns in the two cities.

Each event starts with a Saturday champagne toast and appetizers, and ends with a lazy Sunday morning spent over coffee and breakfast, highlighting a special dinner in between. But the cooking and cleanup doesn't all fall on the hosting couple. "Now that we've got this distance between us and travel to get together, everyone pitches in to help," Sue explains. "It's a very comfortable group."

■ Martin Ewing is from England, so Sue makes this mushroom pâté reminiscent of the cuisine of his homeland especially for him, and it's popular at supper club as well. This recipe has come to be known by the group as simply *"The* Pâté."

PÂTÉ DE CHAMPIGNON

8 slices bacon
1 cup chopped mushrooms
½ cup chopped onion
1 clove garlic, minced
2 tablespoons vegetable oil
¼ cup dry sherry
½ teaspoon cracked pepper
½ teaspoon dried thyme
⅛ teaspoon ground nutmeg
½ pound ground pork
½ pound ground chicken
¼ cup chopped roasted pistachio
  nuts
1 large egg, lightly beaten
2 tablespoons chopped fresh
  parsley

Line bottom and sides of two 5- x 3- x 2-inch loafpans evenly with bacon, letting excess bacon hang over edges of pans. Set aside.

Cook mushrooms, onion, and garlic in oil in a medium skillet over medium heat, stirring constantly, 3 to 4 minutes or until tender; add sherry and next 3 ingredients. Bring to a boil; cover, reduce heat, and simmer 5 minutes. Set aside.

Combine pork and remaining ingredients; stir in vegetable mixture. Spoon evenly into prepared pans, pressing with back of a spoon to firmly pack mixture; cover with overhanging bacon. Bake at 350° for 1 hour and 15 minutes; drain.

Remove from pan, and cool on paper towels. Cover and chill 8 hours. Serve with crackers. Yield: 24 appetizer servings.

■ Meg and Michael Armstrong created this appetizer with a touch of Virginia. They use a pork sausage that contains ground Smithfield ham. You can use regular ground pork sausage as a substitute.

STUFFED MUSHROOMS

42 large fresh mushrooms
1 pound mild ground pork sausage with ham or ground pork sausage
1 (8-ounce) package cream cheese, softened
1 teaspoon dried crushed red pepper

Clean mushrooms with damp paper towels. Remove stems, and reserve for another use. Place rack in a large broiler pan; place mushroom caps, stem side up, on rack. Set aside.

Cook sausage in a large skillet until browned, stirring until it crumbles; drain and return to skillet. Stir in cream cheese and red pepper. Spoon evenly into mushroom caps; bake at 350° for 15 minutes. Serve immediately. Yield: 3½ dozen.

■ One of the best sweet potato rolls our Test Kitchens staff has ever tested, this recipe is definitely worth a try. Surprisingly, it is started in an electric blender.

SWEET POTATO ROLLS

2 packages active dry yeast
1½ cups warm water (105° to 115°)
3 cups whole wheat flour
3 cups all-purpose flour
⅓ cup firmly packed brown sugar
1¼ teaspoons salt
½ cup butter or margarine, softened
2 large eggs
1 (16-ounce) can cut sweet potatoes, drained

Combine yeast and warm water in container of an electric blender; process 30 seconds. Let stand 5 minutes. Combine flours in a large bowl. Add 1 cup flour mixture, sugar, and remaining ingredients to yeast mixture in blender; process until smooth, stopping once to scrape down sides. Gradually stir yeast mixture into remaining flour mixture to make a soft dough.

Turn dough out onto a heavily floured surface, and knead until smooth and elastic (about 5 minutes). Place in a well-greased bowl, turning dough to grease top. Cover and let rise in a warm place (85°), free from drafts, 1 hour or until doubled in bulk.

Punch dough down, and divide in half; shape each portion into a ball. Roll each portion of dough into a 16-inch circle on a floured surface, and cut each circle into 16 wedges. Roll up wedges, beginning at wide end, and place, point side down, on a greased baking sheet. Cover and let rise in a warm place, free from drafts, 30 minutes or until doubled in bulk. Bake at 350° for 15 minutes or until golden. Yield: 32 rolls.

Note: Dough may be made ahead. Knead, place in a greased bowl, and cover securely with plastic wrap. Refrigerate at least 6 hours. Punch dough down; proceed as directed.

Tip: *Read food labels carefully for nutrient information. Nutrition labels give the number of calories and the amount of protein, carbohydrates, and fat in a serving of the product. They also give information on cholesterol, sodium, fiber, sugars, and major vitamins and minerals in the product.*

■ Bill and Cheryl Walker of Richmond, Virginia, have hectic lifestyles, so this fresh, easy salad fits nicely into their schedules. To streamline the recipe even more, buy chilled grapefruit sections in a jar in the produce department of the supermarket instead of cutting them yourself.

AVOCADO-FRUIT SALAD WITH HONEY-YOGURT DRESSING

1 head Boston lettuce, torn
4 avocados, peeled and sliced
1 cup grapefruit sections (1 grapefruit)
¾ cup walnut halves, toasted
½ cup seedless green grapes
Honey-Yogurt Dressing

Arrange first 5 ingredients on salad plates; top with Honey-Yogurt Dressing, and serve immediately. Yield: 8 servings.

Honey-Yogurt Dressing

1 (16-ounce) carton vanilla yogurt
¼ cup honey
3 tablespoons lemon juice
¼ teaspoon salt
⅛ teaspoon ground white pepper

Combine all ingredients in a small bowl; cover and chill. Yield: 1⅔ cups.

Ladies' Night Out

When a group of Nashville, Tennessee, women gather for "Ladies' Night Out," they stir up more than trouble.

They set aside one night a month to forget about jobs, spouses, and children—and focus instead on cooking.

Not the hurry-up-and-get-it-on-the-table type, but the let's-get-in-the-kitchen-and-play kind.

The hostess picks the entrée and other members bring side dishes. While sampling their creations, they evaluate each recipe, discussing possible improvements and garnishes.

"A lot of us entertain, so this is a fun way to try new recipes on people who don't mind," says Renee Hill, one of the supper club's founders. "We've all acquired tastes for new things and learned tips on being better hostesses," she said.

Over the next few days, the hostess makes the suggested changes to the recipes, then gives copies to the other members. They add them to their supper club notebooks, as both a handy reference for entertaining and a reminder of good times.

■ You'll find fresh gingerroot in the produce section. It's a flavorful, short, stubby root. Peel the "bark" off a two-inch piece with a paring knife, and thinly slice the peeled piece to add zing to this marinade.

For easy turning and cleanup, marinate the meat in a large heavy-duty, zip-top plastic bag rather than a dish.

PEKING PORK TENDERLOIN

¼ cup soy sauce
2 cloves garlic, sliced
2 inches gingerroot, peeled and
    sliced
3 (1½-pound) pork tenderloins
¾ cup honey
2 (2⅛-ounce) cans sesame seeds
    (about ¾ cup)

Combine first 3 ingredients in a large, shallow dish or a large heavy-duty, zip-top plastic bag; add tenderloins. Cover or seal; refrigerate 1 hour,

turning occasionally. Remove from marinade, discarding marinade; pat dry. Coat tenderloins with honey; roll in sesame seeds.

Place on a lightly greased rack in a broiler pan. Bake at 375° for 25 to 30 minutes or until a meat thermometer inserted in thickest portion registers 160°. Let stand 5 minutes before slicing. Yield: 12 servings.

Note: To transport, wrap baked pork in plastic wrap, then aluminum foil.

■ Lots of people are insecure working with delicate phyllo pastry, but it's easier than you think. (Be sure the expiration date hasn't passed because old phyllo will be brittle.)

While preparing Brie in phyllo, leave a slightly damp kitchen towel over the unfolded pastry stack to keep it pliable. If it tears, all is not lost. Because you are tightly wrapping the Brie in many layers, a few small tears will hardly be visible.

BRIE WRAPPED IN PHYLLO

12 sheets frozen phyllo pastry,
    thawed
Butter-flavored cooking spray
1 (2-pound) round Brie cheese

Place 1 sheet of phyllo on a baking sheet coated with cooking spray. (Keep remaining phyllo covered with a slightly damp towel to prevent it from drying out.) Coat phyllo sheet evenly with cooking spray. Layer 5 additional sheets on top, coating each with cooking spray. Place Brie on stacked sheets, and bring edges up over cheese. Layer remaining 6 sheets, spraying each; place over Brie, tucking edges under. Bake at 350° for 30 minutes or until golden. Let stand at least 30 minutes before serving. Yield: 24 to 30 servings.

■ Into every gourmet menu, one easy dish must fall. You start with a package mix, but by the time you have added a few interesting ingredients, no one would ever guess. Watch out . . . this one's richer than it looks.

SPINACH FANTASTIC

1 (6-ounce) package long-grain and
    wild rice mix
2 (10-ounce) packages frozen
    chopped spinach, thawed
2 cups (8 ounces) shredded
    Monterey Jack cheese
¼ cup butter or margarine, melted
1 tablespoon chopped onion
¾ teaspoon dry mustard
½ teaspoon salt

Cook rice according to package directions. Press spinach between paper towels to remove excess moisture. Combine rice, spinach, and remaining ingredients; spoon into a lightly greased 2-quart shallow casserole. Bake, uncovered, at 350° for 35 to 40 minutes. Yield: 6 servings.

Note: You may assemble casserole, cover, and chill 8 hours. Remove from refrigerator; let stand at room temperature 30 minutes, and then bake as directed.

Tip: *Most cheeses should be wrapped in moisture-proof airtight wrappers. One exception is "moldy" cheese, such as blue cheese, which needs to breathe and should be kept in a covered container with the top loosened. Store all cheeses in the refrigerator.*

■ Yes, Rosemary-Garlic Yams calls for *20* garlic cloves. For this side dish, leave the peels on, and crush the garlic cloves with a wide knife blade turned on its side. The long baking time mellows garlic's pungency. You may even enjoy squeezing the cooked cloves from their peels and eating them with the yams.

ROSEMARY-GARLIC YAMS

9 yams or sweet potatoes, peeled (about 4½ pounds)
20 unpeeled cloves garlic, crushed
½ cup olive oil
1 tablespoon fresh or dried rosemary
½ teaspoon salt
¼ teaspoon pepper

Cut yams into 1-inch slices; cut each slice into quarters. Place in a large shallow pan; sprinkle with crushed garlic cloves. Add olive oil and remaining ingredients, stirring to coat. Bake at 450° for 25 to 30 minutes or until tender, stirring every 10 minutes. Remove and discard garlic, if desired. Yield: 12 servings.

Sweet Potato Pointers

■ When buying sweet potatoes, select well-shaped, firm potatoes with smooth, bright-colored skins. Avoid any potatoes with cuts and holes.

■ Never store uncooked fresh sweet potatoes in the refrigerator as the coolness will cause them to lose their flavor and turn black.

■ So how do you crush dried tarragon? You can do it the old-fashioned way with a mortar and pestle. Or try using a more available tool—your hands. Just rub the spice between your thumb and forefinger to crumble it directly into the dish.

ASPARAGUS VINAIGRETTE

1 pound fresh asparagus spears
⅓ cup tarragon wine vinegar or white wine vinegar
1 tablespoon lemon juice
1 tablespoon chopped green onions
1 clove garlic, pressed
½ teaspoon dried tarragon, crushed
½ teaspoon Dijon mustard
⅛ teaspoon salt
Garnish: lemon rind rings

Snap off tough ends of asparagus. Remove scales with a vegetable peeler or knife, if desired. Cover and cook asparagus in boiling water 5 minutes. Drain and place in a shallow dish. Combine vinegar and next 6 ingredients; pour over asparagus. Cover and chill 8 hours. Remove from marinade. Serve in "bundles" in lemon rind rings, if desired. Yield: 4 servings.

Been Around The Block?

It can be embarrassing not to know the family just three doors down. Michelle King found a great way to solve that problem in her Duluth, Georgia, neighborhood. She formed a supper club for the whole subdivision, paving an easy way for people to meet each other.

About 40 couples get together every other month in several homes,

and the groups are reshuffled each time so residents can meet new folks.

Sample these international recipes from the neighborhood's "Olympic Celebration" anticipating the '96 summer games in nearby Atlanta, and use the group's gold-medal tips on the facing page to start your own neighborhood supper club.

CREAMY ENCHILADAS

2 medium onions, chopped
2 cloves garlic, minced
2 tablespoons vegetable oil
4 cups chopped cooked chicken
2 (16-ounce) cans tomato puree
4 fresh Anaheim chiles, seeded and finely chopped
½ teaspoon salt
5 cups half-and-half
10 chicken-flavored bouillon cubes
24 (6-inch) flour tortillas
2 cups (8 ounces) shredded Monterey Jack cheese
Garnish: sliced ripe olives

Cook onion and garlic in oil in a Dutch oven over medium heat, stirring constantly, until tender. Add chicken and next 3 ingredients, and bring to a boil. Reduce heat, and simmer, uncovered, 15 minutes, stirring occasionally. Set aside.

Combine half-and-half and bouillon cubes in a large saucepan; cook over low heat until bouillon cubes dissolve. Dip tortillas one at a time in half-and-half mixture to coat. Spoon about ¼ cup chicken mixture down center of each tortilla; roll up tortillas, and place, seam side down, in two lightly greased 13- x 9- x 2-inch baking dishes. Pour remaining half-and-half mixture evenly over tortillas. Cover and bake at 350° for 10 minutes; uncover and bake 10 minutes. Sprinkle with cheese, and bake an additional 5 minutes or until cheese melts. Garnish, if desired. Yield: 12 servings.

TORTELLINI WITH PARSLEY-CAPER SAUCE

1 to 2 cloves garlic
¾ cup finely chopped fresh parsley
¼ cup grated Parmesan cheese
2 tablespoons sunflower kernels
2 tablespoons capers
⅛ teaspoon salt
⅛ teaspoon pepper
½ cup olive oil
1 (9-ounce) package refrigerated cheese-filled tortellini, uncooked
1½ teaspoons olive oil

Position knife blade in food processor bowl. Drop garlic through food chute with processor running; process 5 seconds or until minced. Add parsley and next 5 ingredients; process until smooth, stopping occasionally to scrape down sides. Gradually pour ½ cup olive oil through food chute with processor running, blending just until mixture is smooth. Set aside.

Cook tortellini according to package directions; drain. Add 1½ teaspoons olive oil; toss gently. Pour sauce over tortellini, and toss. Yield: 25 appetizer servings.

A Supper Club Starting Block

On your mark:
■ Hand-deliver or mail invitations to neighbors. Include your phone number for responses.
■ Hold a planning session to pick dates and themes. (Copy and distribute schedule soon afterward.)
■ Assign host homes for the parties for that year. (The Duluth members host only about every 18 months.)

A month before:
■ Hosts/hostesses plan the menu.

A week before:
■ Hosts/hostesses hand-deliver or mail a copy of one recipe from the menu to each couple attending.

The finish line:
■ Couples bring assigned dishes to host's home for the party, and then divide expenses evenly at the end of the evening.

Southern Hospitality Isn't *Gone With The Wind*

Tradition reigns in Lynchburg, Virginia. Meet this formal—but not fussy—supper club that calls itself The Lucullan Society.

The *what*? Now, no true *Gone With the Wind* buff would have to ask, but let author Margaret Mitchell explain. In a passage about a meager supper amid Civil War poverty, she mentions Lucullus, a Roman general known for his lavish banquets. After a dessert of sweet potato pie, Rhett Butler presents coveted bonbons and cigars. Mitchell writes "Everyone agreed it was indeed a Lucullan banquet."

That particular line caught the fancy of Bob Blevins, a member of the gourmet group, and it is their ongoing theme. They've traded hoopskirts for cocktail dresses, and fried chicken for grilled salmon, but the mood comes from a century past.

"There's a touch of the Old South—it's elegance and doing something nice for other people," says this night's hostess, Edie Light. Her husband, Cham, begins the evening by reading Mitchell's passage, then raises his glass in a toast.

HERBED SUMMER DINNER FOR EIGHT

Goat Cheese With Sun-Dried Tomatoes and Rosemary
Frozen Whiskey Sours
Grilled Herbed Salmon Steaks
Fresh Tomato Sauce Over Basil Pasta
Green salad with Parmesan cheese
Amaretto Crème on Fresh Fruit

GOAT CHEESE WITH SUN-DRIED TOMATOES AND ROSEMARY
(pictured on page 221)

6 sun-dried tomato halves
3 cloves garlic, pressed
2 tablespoons olive oil
1 tablespoon chopped fresh or dried rosemary
1 French baguette
Olive oil
1 (10-ounce) package goat cheese
Garnish: fresh rosemary sprigs

Cover tomatoes with boiling water; let stand 5 minutes. Drain and chop. Combine tomatoes and next 3 ingredients; cover and chill up to 4 hours.

Slice baguette thinly; brush rounds with additional olive oil. Place on a baking sheet, and bake at 350° for 8 minutes or until lightly toasted. Just before serving, place goat cheese on a plate, and top with marinated tomatoes. Serve with baguette rounds, and garnish, if desired. Yield: 8 appetizer servings.

Note: Tomatoes should not be marinated more than 4 hours.

FROZEN WHISKEY SOURS

1 (6-ounce) can frozen orange
  juice concentrate, thawed and
  undiluted
1 (6-ounce) can frozen lemonade
  concentrate, thawed and
  undiluted
1 (6-ounce) can frozen limeade
  concentrate, thawed and
  undiluted
4⅓ cups water
2 cups bourbon
1 (1-liter) bottle club soda, chilled

Combine first 5 ingredients in a large
freezer container; cover and freeze.
Remove from freezer 30 minutes before serving. Break into chunks; add
club soda, and stir until slushy. Yield:
about 3 quarts.

GRILLED HERBED
SALMON STEAKS
(pictured on page 4)

8 (¾-inch-thick) salmon steaks
¾ cup dry, white vermouth or dry
  white wine
¾ cup olive oil
1½ tablespoons lemon juice
1 tablespoon chopped fresh thyme
  or 1 teaspoon dried thyme
1 tablespoon chopped fresh
  marjoram or 1 teaspoon dried
  marjoram
1 tablespoon chopped fresh sage or
  1 teaspoon rubbed sage
1 tablespoon chopped fresh parsley
¾ teaspoon salt
⅛ teaspoon freshly ground pepper
Garnish: fresh thyme sprigs

Place salmon in two shallow dishes.
Combine vermouth and next 8 ingredients; reserve ⅓ cup marinade. Pour
remaining marinade over salmon;
cover and refrigerate 1 hour. Remove
from marinade, discarding marinade.

Grill, covered with lid, over medium-
hot coals (350° to 400°) 5 to 6 minutes
on each side or until salmon is done,
brushing frequently with reserved ⅓
cup marinade. Garnish, if desired.
Yield: 8 servings.

Note: Salmon steaks may be broiled
5½ inches from heat (with electric
oven door partially opened) 6 to 8
minutes on each side or until done,
brushing frequently with ⅓ cup reserved marinade.

FRESH TOMATO SAUCE
OVER BASIL PASTA
(pictured on page 4)

6 pounds tomatoes, peeled, seeded,
  and chopped (about 7 large)
16 cloves garlic, minced
1 teaspoon salt
½ teaspoon pepper
1 (16-ounce) package linguine,
  uncooked
¾ cup freshly grated Parmesan
  cheese
½ cup butter or margarine,
  softened
¼ cup chopped fresh basil or
  1 tablespoon dried basil

Combine tomatoes and garlic in a
heavy saucepan; bring to a boil. Reduce heat, and cook 15 to 20 minutes,
stirring occasionally. Stir in salt and
pepper; keep warm.
  Cook linguine according to package
directions; drain. Add Parmesan
cheese and remaining ingredients,
tossing well. To serve, top pasta with
tomato mixture. Yield: 8 servings.

AMARETTO CRÈME
ON FRESH FRUIT

4 egg yolks, lightly beaten
½ cup sugar
2 tablespoons all-purpose flour
1 cup milk
1 tablespoon amaretto or other
  almond-flavored liqueur
¼ teaspoon vanilla extract
Fresh peach slices and
  raspberries

Combine first 3 ingredients in a medium saucepan; gradually add milk,
stirring until smooth. Cook over low
heat, stirring constantly, 6 to 7 minutes or until thermometer registers
160°. Remove mixture from heat, and
stir in amaretto and vanilla. Cover and
chill. Serve over peach slices and
raspberries or other fresh fruit. Yield:
1½ cups.

Cool Off
By The Pool

The Florida sun blazes on through
early evening, but this Rockledge supper club keeps its cool in style. Ross
and Jean Parkhurst, this party's hosting couple, welcome their friends with
ice cold sippers served poolside.
Then, as dusk falls, they enjoy a Spanish feast with tropical touches.
  Fascinated with the cuisine of other
cultures, the group focuses on a different country at each gathering.
  As the menu unfolds, from appetizer to dessert, guests may not remember whether they're on the
Mediterranean or the Atlantic coast.
They've got the best of both worlds.

summer
suppers.

SHRIMP, ORANGE, AND OLIVE SALAD WITH SHERRY VINAIGRETTE

3 tablespoons sherry wine vinegar
  or red wine vinegar
1 clove garlic, pressed
1 teaspoon sugar
1 teaspoon grated orange rind
⅓ cup olive oil
3 cups water
1 pound unpeeled medium-size
  fresh shrimp
2 navel oranges
1 cup sliced pimiento-stuffed olives
5 cups torn Bibb lettuce
5 cups torn leaf lettuce
2 green onions, sliced

Combine first 4 ingredients in a large bowl; gradually add olive oil, beating with a wire whisk. Set aside.

Bring water to a boil; add shrimp, and cook 3 to 5 minutes or until shrimp turn pink. Drain well; rinse with cold water. Peel and devein shrimp; set aside.

Peel oranges, and cut into ½-inch round slices; cut slices into quarters. Add oranges, shrimp, and olives to dressing; cover and chill at least 1 hour. To serve, toss lettuces and green onions with shrimp mixture. Yield: 8 servings.

SCALLOPS WITH CHAMPAGNE-SAFFRON SAUCE

2¼ pounds bay scallops
¼ cup butter or margarine, melted
1½ cups champagne or sparkling
  wine
Pinch of saffron
1 cup whipping cream
1 teaspoon lemon juice
¼ teaspoon salt
¼ teaspoon pepper

Cook scallops in butter in a large skillet over medium heat, stirring constantly, 3 minutes or until tender. Drain, discarding drippings, and set scallops aside.

Add champagne and saffron to skillet. Bring to a boil over medium heat, and cook until reduced by half (about 7 minutes). Add whipping cream and remaining ingredients; cook until mixture thickens (about 10 minutes). Add scallops, and cook over low heat just until thoroughly heated. Yield: 10 to 12 appetizer servings.

TROPICAL PUFF PASTRY BASKETS

3 large ripe mangoes, divided
2 tablespoons honey
1 teaspoon unflavored gelatin
1 tablespoon water
4 egg yolks
¼ cup honey
⅔ cup whipping cream
⅓ cup sour cream
Puff Pastry Baskets
½ fresh pineapple, peeled, cored,
  and sliced
2 kiwifruit, peeled and sliced

Peel, pit, and slice 2 mangoes. Position knife blade in food processor bowl; add mango slices and 2 tablespoons honey. Process 3 to 4 minutes or until smooth, stopping once to scrape down sides. Chill sauce.

Sprinkle gelatin over water; let stand 1 minute. Combine egg yolks and ¼ cup honey in a heavy saucepan; cook over low heat about 3 minutes, beating constantly with a wire whisk. Remove from heat; add gelatin, beating well. Cool and set aside.

Combine whipping cream and sour cream in a large bowl; beat at medium speed with an electric mixer until stiff peaks form. Fold in egg yolk mixture; cover and chill at least 2 hours.

To serve, peel, pit, and slice remaining mango. Spoon whipped cream mixture into Puff Pastry Baskets; top with pineapple, mango slices, and kiwifruit. Spoon mango sauce onto dessert plates, and place pastry baskets on top of sauce. Yield: 8 servings.

Puff Pastry Baskets

3 tablespoons sugar
¼ teaspoon ground allspice
1 (17¼-ounce) package frozen puff
  pastry sheets, thawed

Combine sugar and allspice. Unfold 1 pastry sheet; sprinkle with 1 tablespoon sugar mixture. Roll a sheet into a 13- x 12-inch rectangle on a lightly floured surface. Trim to a 10-inch square, and cut into 4 (5-inch) squares.

Fold each square in half diagonally, forming a triangle. Cut a ½-inch-wide strip on two 5-inch-long sides, cutting to within ½ inch from triangle point. Unfold triangle and attached strips; brush strips with water. Lift up strips, and slip one under the other, pulling points in opposite directions. Place strips on edges of base, gently pulling to match corners. Press edges to seal. Repeat procedure with remaining puff pastry sheet.

Sprinkle remaining sugar mixture over borders; prick each center several times with a fork. Place on ungreased baking sheets; bake at 375° for 20 minutes or until golden. Cool on a wire rack. Yield: 8 baskets.

Revamping Camping

Whatever your definition of "roughing it," you'll find these recipes as enticing as a babbling brook. And even if communing with nature isn't in your plans, you'll enjoy these recipes just as well when they're prepared in the comfort of your kitchen.

BREAKFAST OATMEAL SURPRISE

2 cups quick-cooking oats, uncooked
½ cup chopped dates or chopped dried apples *
⅓ cup chopped pecans
½ cup firmly packed brown sugar
½ teaspoon ground cinnamon
½ cup instant nonfat dry milk powder

Combine all ingredients in a heavy-duty, zip-top plastic bag. To serve, pour boiling water over desired amount of oats mixture, barely covering mixture. Stir and let stand 2 minutes. For thinner oatmeal, add more boiling water; to thicken, add more oatmeal mixture. Yield: 3 cups oatmeal mix.

* 2 (0.9-ounce) packages orchard fruit snack mix may be substituted.

GLAZED BREAKFAST FRUIT SANDWICHES

1 (21-ounce) can cherry pie filling
1 (16-ounce) loaf cinnamon bread
¼ cup butter or margarine, softened
½ cup sifted powdered sugar
2 tablespoons water

Spread about 3 tablespoons pie filling on one side of half of bread slices; top with remaining bread slices. Spread one side of each sandwich with butter. Place each sandwich, buttered side down, in a cast-iron skillet. Cook over medium heat 1 to 2 minutes or until lightly browned. Butter top side of each sandwich; turn and cook 1 to 2 minutes.

Combine powdered sugar and water; drizzle over sandwiches. Serve with remaining pie filling, if desired. Yield: 8 servings.

Note: Sandwiches can also be served as a dessert. *Cindy Kendrick Leawood, Kansas*

TRAVELING LINGUINE WITH ROASTED VEGETABLES
(pictured on page 148)

2 yellow squash, cut into chunks
2 zucchini, cut into chunks
1 purple onion, quartered
1 small eggplant, unpeeled and cut into chunks
1 sweet red pepper, quartered
⅓ cup butter or margarine
2 to 3 teaspoons dried Italian seasoning
½ teaspoon pepper
2 teaspoons chicken-flavored bouillon granules
2 quarts water
8 ounces linguine, uncooked
¼ cup grated Parmesan cheese

Place first 5 ingredients on a lightly greased 24- x 18-inch piece of heavy-duty aluminum foil; dot with butter, and sprinkle with Italian seasoning and pepper. Seal securely. Cook on a grill rack over hot coals (400° to 500°) 20 to 30 minutes or until vegetables are tender. Remove from heat, and keep sealed.

Combine bouillon granules and about 2 quarts water in a stockpot; cover and place in hot coals. Bring to a boil; add linguine, and cook until tender. Drain. Top with vegetables; sprinkle with cheese. Yield: 2 to 3 servings. *C. M. Rodes Louisville, Kentucky*

GRILLED PIZZAS

2¼ cups biscuit mix, divided
½ cup cold water
1 (14½-ounce) squeeze bottle pizza sauce
1 (3½-ounce) package sliced pepperoni
1 (8-ounce) package shredded mozzarella cheese
Vegetable cooking spray

Combine 2 cups biscuit mix and water, stirring to make a soft dough. Turn out onto a surface dusted with remaining biscuit mix; roll dough to coat, and

shape into a ball, kneading gently five times. Divide into 4 equal portions; pat each portion into a 5-inch circle. Cover grill rack with heavy-duty aluminum foil. Place circles on foil, and cook over medium-hot (350° to 400°) coals 8 minutes. Turn over; top with pizza sauce, pepperoni, and cheese. Cover with foil coated with cooking spray. Cook 10 to 12 minutes or until edges are brown and cheese melts. Yield: 4 servings.   *Carol S. Noble*
Burgaw, North Carolina

TRAIL JAMBALAYA

1 cup long-grain rice, uncooked
1 tablespoon dried onion flakes
1 tablespoon dried green pepper flakes
1 tablespoon dried parsley flakes
2 teaspoons beef-flavored bouillon granules
½ teaspoon dried shredded green onions
½ teaspoon black pepper
¼ teaspoon garlic powder
¼ teaspoon dried thyme
⅛ teaspoon ground red pepper
2 cups water
1 (8-ounce) can tomato sauce
1 pound smoked sausage, cut into ¼-inch slices

Combine first 10 ingredients in a heavy-duty, zip-top plastic bag. Combine rice mix, 2 cups water, and tomato sauce in a Dutch oven. Bring to a boil; cover, reduce heat, and simmer 20 minutes. Stir in smoked sausage, and cook until throughly heated. Yield: 4 servings.

Don't Want to Carry An Ice Chest?

Some of the recipes in the camping story on the facing page have ingredients that normally require refrigeration. If it's not convenient to take along an ice chest, make the following recipe changes.

■ **Trail Jambalaya**—Freeze the sausage in its vacuum package, and keep it well insulated with newspaper or clothing. The sausage will thaw slowly and should be safe if you prepare and eat the jambalaya on the first day of your trip. Summer sausage (which doesn't need refrigeration) can be substituted, but will change the flavor slightly.

■ **Traveling Linguine With Roasted Vegetables**—Though the vegetables keep best in an ice chest, they can be left out for a day or two. Depending on the temperature, the vegetables may become limp, but they're still safe to eat; wash thoroughly before grilling. Carry the butter in a container with a tight lid. If it melts, pour the butter over the vegetables instead of dotting it on. Another option: Carry a bottle of liquid margarine.

■ **Grilled Pizzas**—Buy pepperoni that doesn't need refrigeration. Or freeze the pepperoni, and keep it well insulated. It will thaw slowly and should be safe if you prepare and eat the pizza the first day of your trip. Unopened packages of shredded mozzarella cheese should keep up to 24 hours without refrigeration. If desired, 2 cups shredded provolone cheese can be substituted. Because it's a drier cheese, it can be kept two or three days without refrigeration.

A Taste Of Oregon

One of the best-selling community cookbooks of all time is the Junior League of Eugene's *A Taste of Oregon*. One indication of its popularity came from an American woman who wrote to replace the copy she left behind when fleeing Kuwait during the Iraqi occupation. The league happily replaced her book.

Since the book's first printing in 1980, the league has sold more than 272,000 copies, raising over $550,000 for charitable causes.

SUMMER SALAD

6 to 8 cups mixed salad greens, torn into bite-size pieces
1 cucumber, peeled and thinly sliced
1 (11-ounce) can mandarin oranges, drained
3 tablespoons sliced green onions or ½ medium-size sweet onion, sliced and separated into rings
1 ripe avocado, peeled and thinly sliced
Dressing

Combine first 5 ingredients in a large bowl. Just before serving, toss with Dressing. Yield: 8 servings.

Dressing

½ cup vegetable oil
¼ cup frozen orange juice concentrate, thawed and undiluted
2½ tablespoons sugar
2 tablespoons red wine vinegar
1 tablespoon lemon juice
¾ teaspoon grated orange rind
½ teaspoon grated lemon rind
¼ teaspoon salt
¼ teaspoon pepper

Combine all ingredients in a jar. Cover tightly, and shake mixture vigorously. Yield: 1 cup.

■ If you look for this recipe in *A Taste of Oregon*, you'll find it listed as Fresh Salmon With Mushrooms and Scallions because in Oregon, the words scallion and green onion are considered interchangeable. In the South, we use the term scallion to refer to a more expensive cousin of the green onion, so we altered the title of the recipe.

FRESH SALMON WITH MUSHROOMS AND GREEN ONIONS

2½ to 3 pounds fresh salmon fillets
1 tablespoon lemon juice
¼ teaspoon salt
¼ teaspoon pepper
¼ cup butter or margarine
½ pound fresh mushrooms, sliced
1 cup sliced green onions with tops
1 teaspoon grated lemon rind
½ teaspoon dried marjoram
½ teaspoon garlic powder
⅛ teaspoon salt
⅛ teaspoon pepper
Sour cream (optional)
Black caviar (optional)
Garnishes: lemon slices, fresh watercress or fresh parsley sprigs

Line a 15- x 10- x 1-inch jellyroll pan with aluminum foil. Place salmon, dark skin down, on foil; sprinkle with lemon juice, ¼ teaspoon salt, and ¼ teaspoon pepper. Bake at 450° for 10 minutes; cool slightly. Transfer to a lightly greased 13- x 9- x 2-inch baking dish. (Dark skin will stick to foil; remove any remaining dark skin.)

Melt butter in a large skillet over medium-high heat. Add mushrooms and next 6 ingredients, cook, stirring constantly, about 5 minutes or until liquid evaporates. Spoon mushroom mixture over fish. Cover and bake at 350° for 25 to 30 minutes or until fish flakes easily when tested with a fork. If desired, serve with sour cream and caviar. Garnish, if desired. Yield: 8 to 10 servings.

CINNAMON-RAISIN COFFEE CAKE

1½ cups all-purpose flour
1 tablespoon baking powder
½ teaspoon salt
¾ cup sugar
¼ cup shortening
1 large egg, lightly beaten
½ cup milk
1 teaspoon vanilla extract
½ cup firmly packed brown sugar
2 tablespoons all-purpose flour
2 teaspoons ground cinnamon
½ cup raisins or chopped walnuts
2 tablespoons butter or margarine, melted

Combine first 4 ingredients; cut in shortening with a pastry blender until blended. Combine egg, milk, and vanilla; add to flour mixture, stirring until blended. Set batter aside.

Combine brown sugar and next 3 ingredients; stir in butter. Spoon two-thirds of batter into a greased and floured 9-inch round cakepan; sprinkle with brown sugar mixture, and top with remaining batter. Bake at 375° for 25 minutes or until golden. Yield: one 9-inch coffee cake.

ON THE LIGHT SIDE

Scrap The Bacon, Taste The Vegetables

Side meat, fatback, ham hock, and bacon drippings in vegetables are mere memories in the minds of today's health-conscious cooks.

Instead, ingredients are available to enhance, rather than conceal, the flavors of vegetables—without adding excess fat, sodium, or calories. Some of these items may already be in your kitchen: herbs or spices; onion or garlic; lemon or lime juice; white or flavored vinegars; fat-free, low-sodium broths; liquid smoke; mustards; cornstarch; fat-free salad dressings; nonfat sour cream alternative; and fat-free mayonnaise.

Experiment with our recipes to sample these ingredients in action.

BLACK-EYED PEAS

6 cups fresh black-eyed peas *
3 (14½-ounce) cans ready-to-serve, reduced-sodium, fat-free chicken broth
2 teaspoons Creole seasoning
1 teaspoon olive oil
¼ teaspoon hot sauce

Combine all ingredients in a Dutch oven; bring to a boil. Cover, reduce heat, and simmer 45 minutes or until tender, stirring occasionally. Serve with a slotted spoon. Yield: 6 cups (251 calories [7% from fat] per 1-cup serving).

□ 14.8g protein, 2g fat (0.4g saturated), 41.8g carbohydrate, 2.6g fiber, 0mg cholesterol, 111mg sodium, and 42mg calcium.

* 2 (16-ounce) packages frozen black-eyed peas may be substituted for 6 cups fresh black-eyed peas.

LEMON-DILL STEAMED CARROTS

1½ pounds carrots, scraped and cut into thin strips
1½ teaspoons cornstarch
⅓ cup water
1½ tablespoons lemon juice
1 tablespoon chopped fresh dill
1½ teaspoons reduced-calorie margarine
½ teaspoon grated lemon rind
¼ teaspoon salt

Arrange carrots in a steamer basket, and place over boiling water. Cover carrots, and steam 4 minutes or until crisp-tender. Transfer to a serving dish, and keep warm.

Combine cornstarch, water, and lemon juice in a small saucepan, stirring until smooth. Bring to a boil over medium heat, stirring constantly. Boil, stirring constantly, 1 minute. Remove from heat; add dill and remaining ingredients, stirring until margarine melts. Toss with carrots. Yield: 6 servings (58 calories [11% from fat] per ⅔-cup serving).

□ *1.3g protein, 0.7g fat (0.1g saturated), 12.8g carbohydrate, 3.7g fiber, 0mg cholesterol, 150mg sodium, and 41mg calcium.*

CABBAGE WITH CARAWAY

1 teaspoon reduced-calorie margarine
Vegetable cooking spray
8 cups coarsely shredded cabbage (1½ pounds)
1 tablespoon chopped fresh parsley
1 teaspoon sugar
1 teaspoon chicken-flavored bouillon granules
½ teaspoon freshly ground pepper
1 teaspoon caraway seeds

Melt margarine in a large nonstick skillet coated with cooking spray. Add cabbage and next 4 ingredients; cover and cook over medium heat 5 minutes. Sprinkle with caraway seeds; cover and cook 1 minute. Yield: 5 cups (39 calories [23% from fat] per 1-cup serving).

□ *1.6g protein, 1g fat (0.2g saturated), 7.3g carbohydrate, 2.8g fiber, 0mg cholesterol, 194mg sodium, and 58mg calcium.* Mrs. Elmer T. Myers
Maryville, Tennessee

VEGETABLE BUNDLES

Vegetable cooking spray
2 medium-size yellow squash, sliced
1 large onion, cut into 4 slices
1 large tomato, cut into 4 slices
2 tablespoons white wine vinegar
1 tablespoon Dijon mustard
¼ teaspoon salt
¼ teaspoon pepper
2 teaspoons grated Parmesan cheese

Cut 4 (18- x 12-inch) pieces of heavy-duty aluminum foil; coat with cooking spray. Place squash evenly in center of each; top with onion and tomato slices. Combine vinegar and next 3 ingredients; drizzle evenly over vegetable bundles. Sprinkle evenly with cheese, and seal securely; place on a baking sheet. Bake 400° for 20 minutes or until vegetables are tender. Yield: 4 servings (50 calories [18% from fat] per serving).

□ *1.9g protein, 1g fat (0.2g saturated), 8.9g carbohydrate, 2.4g fiber, 1mg cholesterol, 281mg sodium, and 36mg calcium.*

PEPPERY
GREEN BEAN MEDLEY

1 pound fresh green beans
⅔ cup canned, ready-to-serve, reduced-sodium, fat-free chicken broth
2 cloves garlic, minced
¼ teaspoon ground red pepper
1 small sweet red pepper, cut into thin strips
1 small green pepper, cut into thin strips
1 purple onion, sliced and separated into rings
⅛ teaspoon salt
¼ teaspoon pepper

Wash green beans. Trim ends, and remove strings; cut into 1½-inch pieces. Set aside.

Combine chicken broth, garlic, and ground red pepper in a large nonstick

skillet; bring to a boil. Stir in green beans; cover and cook over medium heat 5 minutes. Add pepper strips and onion; cook, uncovered, 5 to 7 minutes or until crisp-tender, stirring often. Gently stir in salt and pepper. Yield: 5 cups (50 calories [1% from fat] per 1-cup serving).

□ *2.3g protein, 0.3g fat (0.1g saturated), 10.9g carbohydrate, 2.9g fiber, 0mg cholesterol, 67mg sodium, and 44mg calcium.* Joy Knight Allard
San Antonio, Texas

Know When and How to Buy

■ Prices of fresh vegetables and fruits change with the seasons. It is best to buy seasonal fresh foods when they are most plentiful and at peak quality.

■ When selecting yellow squash, be sure to look at the stem; it can indicate the quality of the squash. If the stem is hard, dry, shriveled, or darkened, the squash is not fresh.

■ When selecting fresh cabbage, choose heads that are solid and heavy. The cabbage leaves should be fresh, crisp, and free from bruises.

■ When grains, such as rice, are served together with dried beans or peas, the two complement each other, providing a good source of high-quality protein.

■ Remove the tops of carrots before refrigerating. Tops drain the carrots of moisture, making them limp and dry.

Cornbread With Zip

The next time you're craving a taste of the Southwest, try our moist, peppery Mexican Cornbread.

This version was easily slimmed down by replacing the original recipe's Cheddar cheese with a reduced-fat variety of Cheddar, and substituting skim milk for whole milk. We also trimmed fat and cholesterol in this lightened version of cornbread.

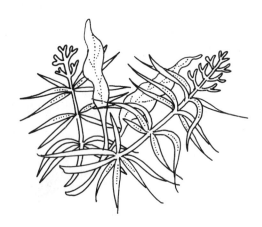

MEXICAN CORNBREAD
(pictured on page 148)

1½ cups yellow cornmeal
½ cup all-purpose flour
1 tablespoon baking powder
¾ teaspoon salt
1 tablespoon sugar
1 cup skim milk
¼ cup egg substitute
3 tablespoons margarine, melted
1 cup frozen whole kernel corn,
  thawed
½ cup (2 ounces) shredded reduced-
  fat sharp Cheddar cheese
1 (4-ounce) can chopped green
  chiles, drained
½ cup finely chopped onion
¼ cup chopped sweet red pepper
Vegetable cooking spray

Combine first 5 ingredients in a large bowl, and make a well in center of mixture. Combine milk and next 7 ingredients; add to dry ingredients, stirring just until moistened. Pour mixture into a 9-inch square pan coated with cooking spray. Bake at 425° for 25 to 30 minutes or until golden. Yield: 16 servings (116 calories [25% from fat] per serving).

□ *3.9g protein, 3.2g fat (0.9g saturated), 18g carbohydrate, 1.2g fiber, 3mg cholesterol, 231mg sodium, and 91mg calcium.*

COMPARE THE NUTRIENTS		
(per serving)		
	Traditional	Light
Calories	138	116
Fat	5.7g	3.2g
Cholesterol	27mg	3mg

The months for summer vegetables never come soon enough. You'll enjoy serving young, tender vegetables sizzled in olive oil in a nonstick skillet and then tossed with fresh herbs.

Here are a few tips to help you enjoy the season's bounty of fresh vegetables, along with a suggestion for an outdoor favorite.

Adding Punch with Garlic

If you enjoy seasoning with the robust flavor of garlic, follow these guidelines. Garlic flavor sweetens with heat, slow cooking, or roasting; used raw, it boasts an intense flavor that can overpower delicate vegetables. Crushing, mincing, or pressing cloves releases essential oils providing a sharp, assertive flavor. The difference in pungency depends on whether the cloves are pressed, crushed, or minced. Pressing a clove with peel left on in a garlic press produces maximum flavor and leaves odor-free hands. Crushed garlic, pounded with a mallet or the flat edge of a chef's knife, peels easily and can be used whole or minced; crushing makes the flavor less pungent than pressing. When minced (finely chopped) or sliced, the flavor is even less intense.

Bundling up Flavor

Make your own bouquet garni to flavor foods while cooking. Tie 3 sprigs fresh parsley, 1 small sprig fresh thyme, and 1 small bay leaf to a celery stalk with string or fruit peel. Suspend the bunch in soups, casseroles, stir-frys, or boiling water for cooking vegetables. Remove the bundle before serving. For flavor variations, add sprigs of fresh sage, marjoram, or savory to poultry or pork, and fresh dill or fennel with orange or lemon peel to seafood. Remember, when cooking stews and soups, it's best to add fresh herbs about 10 to 15 minutes before serving for the finest flavor.

Florida Flash

Patty Mallard, of Jacksonville, Florida, has a suggestion for heating hamburger buns. Place grilled hamburgers or hot dogs immediately in buns; return buns to the package, and seal the bag. Let stand 1 to 2 minutes for soft, steamed buns.

Cooking It Quick—in Nonstick

Fresh vegetables need just a small amount of oil or vegetable cooking spray when stir-fried in a nonstick skillet. To protect the pan's coating and prevent scratching, use plastic or wooden utensils (especially spatulas) for stirring and nonabrasive products for cleanup. To prevent scratches, don't stack skillets with other pans, unless you place paper towels between them. And never heat the skillet without something in it.

Bread for Tea Time

We thought the Lemon Tea Bread that ran on the cover of the May 1993 issue looked delicious, and judging from the number of reader calls, so did you. We asked the homeowner, Sharon Abroms, to share her recipe with us. It's as good as it looks.

LEMON TEA BREAD

¾ cup milk
1 tablespoon chopped fresh lemon
 balm or 1 tablespoon lemon juice
1 tablespoon chopped fresh lemon
 thyme or 1 teaspoon dried thyme
½ cup butter or margarine,
 softened
1 cup sugar
2 large eggs
2 cups all-purpose flour
1½ teaspoons baking powder
¼ teaspoon salt
1 tablespoon grated lemon rind
Lemon Glaze

Combine first 3 ingredients in a small saucepan, and bring to a boil. Remove mixture from heat; cover and let stand 5 minutes. Cool.

Beat butter at medium speed with an electric mixer until creamy, and gradually add sugar, beating mixture well. Add eggs, one at a time, beating after each addition.

Combine flour, baking powder, and salt; add to butter mixture alternately with milk mixture, beginning and ending with flour mixture. Mix after each addition. Stir in lemon rind.

Pour into a greased and floured 9- x 5- x 3-inch loafpan. Bake at 325° for 50 minutes or until a wooden pick inserted in center comes out clean. Cool in pan on a wire rack 10 minutes; remove from pan, and cool completely on wire rack. Pour Lemon Glaze over bread. Yield: 1 loaf.

Lemon Glaze

1 cup sifted powdered sugar
2 tablespoons lemon juice

Combine powdered sugar and lemon juice in a small bowl; stir until smooth. Yield: ⅓ cup.   *Sharon Abroms*
                        Atlanta, Georgia

Fruits And Vegetables — Healthy Choices

Out with the notion that basic food groups are equal: We need more servings of some food groups than others. The fruit and vegetable group is one. Persuading finicky eaters—particularly kids—to meet their daily quota of five or more servings takes planning.

Presentation makes a big impact, and most children prefer raw fruits and vegetables to cooked. Try threading colorful, lightly steamed vegetables on wooden skewers or cocktail straws. At breakfast do the same with fruits. Or add dried and fresh fruit faces on top of hot cereal.

Combine fruits or vegetables in one-dish recipes to provide a variety of nutrients. Some main dishes, such as Vegetable Frittata and Minestrone Stew, contain so many vegetables that the only thing you need to add is a whole-grain bread or pasta to complete the meal.

VEGETABLE FRITTATA

1 clove garlic, minced
3 tablespoons butter or margarine,
 melted
1½ cups sliced fresh mushrooms
1½ cups chopped zucchini
1 cup chopped sweet red pepper
1 cup sliced green onions
1 cup frozen whole kernel corn
1 (8-ounce) package cream cheese,
 softened
¼ cup milk
6 large eggs
1½ cups (6 ounces) shredded
 Cheddar cheese
3 slices white bread, cut into cubes
¾ teaspoon salt
¼ to ½ teaspoon pepper
1 medium tomato, cut into wedges

Cook garlic in butter in a large skillet over medium-high heat, stirring constantly, until tender. Add mushrooms and next 3 ingredients; cook, stirring constantly, 8 to 10 minutes, or until vegetables are tender and excess liquid evaporates. Stir in corn, and remove from heat; set aside.

Beat cream cheese and milk at medium speed with an electric mixer until smooth. Add eggs, one at a time, beating after each addition; fold in vegetable mixture, Cheddar cheese, and next 3 ingredients. Pour into a lightly greased 10-inch springform pan. Bake at 350° for 45 to 50 minutes or until center is set. Cool in pan 10 minutes; carefully remove sides. Arrange tomato wedges on top. Yield: 8 servings.

MINESTRONE STEW

3 large potatoes, peeled and cut
 into cubes
2 small onions, chopped
6 carrots, scraped and cut into
 chunks
1 small zucchini, cut into chunks
2 cloves garlic, minced
1 (10-ounce) package frozen
 chopped spinach
2 cups rotini
6 cups water
1 (18-ounce) can tomato paste
1 cup water
1 (15-ounce) can red kidney beans,
 undrained
1 (8-ounce) can cut green beans,
 undrained
1 (8½-ounce) can English peas,
 undrained
1½ to 2 teaspoons dried oregano
1 teaspoon dried basil
½ teaspoon dried tarragon
½ teaspoon dried thyme
1 bay leaf
Grated Parmesan cheese

Combine first 8 ingredients in a large
Dutch oven; bring to a boil. Cover, reduce heat, and simmer 10 minutes or
until potatoes are tender. Stir tomato
paste and 1 cup water into potato mixture. Add kidney beans and next 7 ingredients; simmer 5 minutes. Remove
and discard bay leaf. Sprinkle each
serving with Parmesan cheese. Yield:
5 quarts.   *Linda Kirkpatrick*
                  Westminster, Maryland

One Recommended Serving

- A whole fruit, such as a medium apple, banana, or orange
- Grapefruit half
- Melon wedge
- ¾ cup juice
- ½ cup berries
- ½ cup cooked or canned fruit
- ¼ cup dried fruit
- ½ cup cooked vegetables
- ½ cup chopped raw vegetables
- 1 cup leafy, raw vegetables

GARDEN VEGETABLE SPREAD

1 (8-ounce) container whipped
 cream cheese
½ cup shredded carrot
½ cup shredded zucchini
1 tablespoon chopped fresh parsley
¼ teaspoon garlic salt
Dash of pepper

Combine all ingredients in a bowl;
cover and chill at least 1 hour. Serve
on party bread or celery stalks. Yield:
1½ cups.   *DeLea Lonadier*
                  Montgomery, Louisiana

ROASTED VEGETABLES AND PASTA
(pictured on page 225)

6 ounces rigatoni, uncooked
1 (1-ounce) package onion soup mix
2 teaspoons dried thyme
½ cup olive oil, divided
2 carrots, cut into 1-inch slices
1 medium zucchini, cut into 1-inch
 slices
1 eggplant, cut into 1-inch pieces
½ pound fresh mushrooms, halved
¼ cup white wine vinegar
⅓ cup pine nuts, toasted
Freshly ground pepper

Cook pasta according to package directions, omitting salt and fat. Drain.
Rinse and drain again; place in a large
bowl, and set aside.
 Combine onion soup mix and
thyme; stir in ¼ cup olive oil. Add carrots and next 3 ingredients, tossing to
coat. Spread evenly into a 15- x 10- x
1-inch jellyroll pan. Bake at 450° for
25 minutes, stirring after 15 minutes.
Stir into pasta.
 Combine remaining ¼ cup olive oil,
white wine vinegar, and pine nuts.
Pour over pasta mixture, tossing to
coat; sprinkle with pepper. Serve immediately. Yield: 4 to 6 servings.

HONEY-BUTTERNUT STIR-FRY

2 tablespoons vegetable oil
1 teaspoon sesame oil
1 small butternut squash, peeled,
 seeded, and cut into ¼-inch slices
 (about 1 pound)
1 cup sliced celery
1 cup broccoli flowerets
½ small onion, thinly sliced and
 separated into rings
1 clove garlic, minced
½ teaspoon grated fresh gingerroot
1 tablespoon lemon juice
2 teaspoons honey
2 tablespoons sunflower kernels

Heat oils in a large skillet; add squash
and next 5 ingredients, and stir-fry 5
minutes. Cover and cook 5 minutes or
until crisp-tender. Combine lemon
juice and honey; pour over vegetables, tossing to coat. Sprinkle with
sunflower kernels, and serve immediately. Yield: 4 cups.   *Edith Askins*
                      Greenville, Texas

MULTI-FRUIT SALAD

1 pint strawberries, halved
2 bananas, peeled and sliced
2 pears, unpeeled and sliced
2 kiwifruit, peeled and sliced
2 cups seedless grapes
1 (15¼-ounce) can pineapple
 chunks, drained
Fruit Salad Dressing

Combine first 6 ingredients in a large
bowl; add Fruit Salad Dressing, stirring mixture to coat well. Yield: 10
servings.

Fruit Salad Dressing

1 (0.9-ounce) package sugar-free
 vanilla instant pudding mix
2¼ cups pineapple juice, chilled

Combine pudding mix and pineapple
juice; mix with a wire whisk or electric
mixer until well blended. Cover and
chill 30 minutes. Yield: 2¼ cups.
                      Corinne Jones
                  Hamilton, Alabama

Mandarin oranges, walnuts, and curry add interesting flavor to Double-Filled Party Sandwiches (recipe, page 159).

*(From left) Shrimp-and-Cucumber
Canapés, Hot Turnip Green Dip With
Jalapeño-Corn Muffins, Black-Eyed
Pea Salsa with tortilla chips, and
Buttermilk-Pecan Chicken Fingers
make a uniquely Southern reception
menu. (Recipes begin on page 164.)*

Serve Southern favorites Pineapple Tea and Mint Julep Brownies with pride (recipes, page 165).

AUGUST

Cooling salads served as side dishes or main-dish meals are summertime favorites. Our light-yet-hearty marinated, grilled, or mixed salads zing with fruit-flavored or herb-spiked vinegars. Discover delicious vine-ripened tomatoes in a trio of quick, no-cook pasta sauces. The easy-to-prepare sauces accent the flavors of the Southwest, Caribbean, and Italy. As summer winds down, enjoy activities with the kids and prepare for the upcoming school year, too, using our food and fun ideas in "For The Kids" special section. We give you the "A-B-Cs" for making that last summer fling memorable and those back-to-school blues bearable.

Light Salads Dressed To Chill

Ward off sultry summer weather and enliven your menu with cool, delicious side-dish and main-dish salads that will enhance any meal. And the best news is that these refreshing salads are light enough for the health-conscious, yet filled with flavor and flair.

These salads let you experience the pizzazz that a splash of flavored vinegar or other seasonings can add. For an extra treat, top your salad with our flavorful croutons made from a bagel, cornbread, or pita bread. (See page 192 for recipes.)

MARINATED CHICKEN-RASPBERRY SALAD

¼ cup stone-ground mustard
2 tablespoons brown sugar
3 tablespoons water
1 tablespoon Raspberry Wine Vinegar (recipe on page 191) *
1 teaspoon olive oil
2 cloves garlic, minced
¼ teaspoon pepper
4 (4-ounce) skinned and boned chicken breast halves
Vegetable cooking spray
¼ cup commercial oil-free salad dressing
¼ cup Raspberry Wine Vinegar *
6 cups mixed salad greens
¼ cup fresh or frozen raspberries, thawed

Combine first 7 ingredients. Place chicken in a shallow dish, and spread marinade evenly over chicken. Cover and refrigerate about 2 hours. Place chicken on a baking sheet coated with cooking spray. Broil 6 inches from heat (with electric oven door partially opened) 5 minutes on each side.

Remove chicken from oven, and let cool. Cut chicken into thin strips, and set aside.

Combine salad dressing and ¼ cup Raspberry Wine Vinegar; pour over salad greens, tossing gently. Place 1½ cups salad greens on each plate; top each with 3 ounces chicken strips, and sprinkle with 1 tablespoon raspberries. Yield: 4 servings (213 calories [22% from fat] per serving).

□ *27.8g protein, 5.3g fat (1.2g saturated), 12.2g carbohydrate, 1.6g fiber, 72mg cholesterol, 306mg sodium, and 22mg calcium.*

* Commercial raspberry wine vinegar may be substituted.

MARINATED BLACK-EYED PEA SALAD
(pictured on pages 222 and 223)

1½ cups water
1 medium onion, halved
½ teaspoon salt
½ teaspoon dried crushed red pepper
⅛ teaspoon hickory-flavored liquid smoke
1 (16-ounce) package frozen black-eyed peas
½ cup Raspberry Wine Vinegar (recipe on page 191) *
¼ cup water
3 tablespoons chopped fresh parsley
1 clove garlic, minced
1 teaspoon olive oil
¼ teaspoon salt
¼ teaspoon freshly ground pepper
½ cup chopped sweet red pepper
⅓ cup small purple onion rings
Leaf lettuce

Combine first 5 ingredients in a medium saucepan; bring to a boil. Add peas; return to a boil. Cover, reduce heat, and simmer 40 to 45 minutes or until peas are tender. Remove and discard onion; drain. Rinse with cold water, and drain. Place in a medium bowl; set aside.

Combine Raspberry Wine Vinegar and next 7 ingredients. Pour over peas, tossing to coat. Cover; refrigerate 8 hours, stirring occasionally. Stir in purple onion. Using a slotted spoon, serve on lettuce-lined plates. Yield: 5 servings. (154 calories [7% from fat] per ¾-cup serving).

□ *8.6g protein, 1.2g fat (0.3g saturated), 27.8g carbohydrate, 2.4g fiber, 0mg cholesterol, 323mg sodium, and 35mg calcium.*

* ½ cup commercial raspberry wine vinegar may be substituted.

WILD RICE SALAD

1 (6-ounce) package long-grain and
  wild rice mix
1 (11-ounce) can white corn,
  drained
¼ cup chopped fresh parsley
3 green onions, chopped
2 carrots, coarsely chopped
1 cucumber, seeded and chopped
¼ cup lemon juice
2 cloves garlic, minced
1 tablespoon olive oil
½ teaspoon dried dillweed
¼ teaspoon pepper
¼ teaspoon dry mustard
3 tablespoons dry-roasted sunflower
  kernels
Leaf lettuce

Prepare rice according to package directions, omitting fat. Combine rice
and next 5 ingredients; set aside.

Combine lemon juice and next 5 ingredients; pour over rice mixture,
tossing gently. Cover and refrigerate
8 hours. Before serving, sprinkle with
sunflower kernels. Serve on lettuce
leaves. Yield: 14 servings (88 calories
[24% from fat] per ½-cup serving).

□ 2.7g protein, 2.3g fat (0.3g saturated), 15.1g carbohydrate, 1.3g fiber,
0mg cholesterol, 256mg sodium, and
26mg calcium.
                    Sue Stephens McWhorter
                        Huntsville, Alabama

GREEN BEANS WITH CREAMY TARRAGON DRESSING
(pictured on pages 222 and 223)

1½ pounds fresh green beans
1 cup fat-free mayonnaise
⅓ cup chopped fresh parsley
¼ cup chopped onion
¼ cup 1% low-fat cottage cheese
3 tablespoons Shallot-Tarragon-
  Garlic Vinegar (recipe on this
  page) *
2 tablespoons skim milk
1½ teaspoons lemon juice
½ teaspoon anchovy paste
Belgian endive, sliced

Wash beans; trim ends, if desired, and
remove strings. Arrange beans in a
steamer basket, and place over boiling
water. Cover and steam 12 minutes or
until crisp-tender. Remove beans, and
plunge into ice water to stop the cooking process. Drain; cover and chill.

Position knife blade in food processor bowl; add mayonnaise and next 7
ingredients. Process 1 minute or until
smooth, stopping once to scrape down
sides. Cover and chill at least 1 hour.

Arrange endive on individual plates;
evenly place beans in center of plates,
and top each serving with 3 tablespoons dressing. Yield: 6 servings (84
calories [4% from fat] per serving).

□ 3.9g protein, 0.4g fat (0.1g saturated), 18g carbohydrate, 2.7g fiber,
0mg cholesterol, 615mg sodium, and
65mg calcium.   Trudy Dunn
                        Dallas, Texas

* 3 tablespoons commercial tarragon
vinegar may be substituted.

Note: When preparing young, tender
green beans, trim the stem end only,
leaving the pointed end of beans on to
enhance the appearance and fiber content of the salad.

SHALLOT-TARRAGON-GARLIC VINEGAR

1 cup fresh tarragon sprigs
10 cloves garlic, divided
4 shallots, divided
2 (17-ounce) bottles white wine
  vinegar
Additional fresh tarragon sprigs
  (optional)

Combine tarragon, 6 garlic cloves, 3
shallots, and vinegar in a large jar;
cover securely. Let stand in bright
light 1 to 2 weeks.

Pour into a large saucepan, and
bring to a boil. Pour through a large
wire-mesh strainer into a decorative
jar or bottle, discarding solids.

Cut remaining shallot into 4 pieces;
alternate pieces with remaining 4 garlic cloves on a wooden skewer. Place

skewer in vinegar; add additional tarragon sprigs, if desired. Cover and
store in a cool, dark place. Yield: 3½
cups (2 calories [0% from fat] per
tablespoon).

□ 0g protein, 0g fat (0g saturated), 0g
carbohydrate, 0g fiber, 0mg cholesterol,
2mg sodium, and 0mg calcium.
                         Trudy Dunn
                        Dallas, Texas

RASPBERRY WINE VINEGAR

3 cups fresh or frozen raspberries
2 (17-ounce) bottles white wine
  vinegar
1 cup sugar

Combine all ingredients in a large
saucepan; bring to a boil. Cover, reduce heat, and simmer 10 minutes.
Pour through a wire-mesh strainer,
discarding pulp. Pour into decorative
jars or bottles; cover. Store in refrigerator. Yield: 5 cups (13 calories [0%
from fat] per tablespoon).

□ 0g protein, 0g fat (0g saturated), 3g
carbohydrate, 0.3g fiber, 0mg cholesterol, 1mg sodium, and 1mg calcium.
                       Nancy Strother
                Fredericksburg, Virginia

Salad Success

■ Remove wilted leaves before
storing lettuce in refrigerator.

■ Be sure lettuce is cold, crisp,
and dry. Tear, don't cut, lettuce
into bite-size pieces. Add salad
dressing just before serving.

■ Add marinated vegetable salads
to your next dinner party. They
can be prepared in advance and
chilled until serving time—an
important time-saver for today's
busy cook.

Spike Salads with Croutons

Give your salad extra crunch and creativity with homemade croutons. Try our recipes, and transform your favorite bread into a tasty salad topper.

CORNBREAD CROUTONS
(pictured on pages 222 and 223)

½ cup yellow cornmeal
½ cup all-purpose flour
½ teaspoon baking soda
¼ teaspoon salt
½ cup nonfat buttermilk
¼ cup egg substitute
1 tablespoon reduced-calorie
   margarine, melted
Butter-flavored cooking spray

Combine first 4 ingredients in a small bowl, and make a well in center of mixture. Combine buttermilk, egg substitute, and margarine, and add to dry ingredients, stirring just until moistened.

Spread batter into an 8-inch square pan coated with cooking spray. Bake at 450° for 10 to 12 minutes or until lightly browned. Let cool. Cut into ½-inch cubes, and arrange in a single layer in a 15- x 10- x 1-inch jellyroll pan. Coat cubes with cooking spray, and bake at 350° for 12 to 15 minutes or until lightly browned. Serve warm. Yield: 2¾ cups (59 calories [18% from fat] per ¼-cup serving).

□ *2.1g protein, 1.2g fat (0.1g saturated), 9.9g carbohydrate, 0.5g fiber, 0mg cholesterol, 121mg sodium, and 24mg calcium.*

 PITA CROUTONS

1 (6-inch) whole wheat pita bread
   round
Butter-flavored cooking spray
½ teaspoon garlic powder

Separate pita bread into 2 rounds; cut each round into 8 wedges. Cut each wedge into 4 small triangles.

Coat a baking sheet with cooking spray; arrange triangles in a single layer, and coat triangles with cooking spray. Sprinkle with garlic powder. Bake at 350° for 5 minutes or until crisp. Let cool on baking sheet. Store triangles in an airtight container. Yield: 64 croutons (35 calories [18% from fat] per 8 croutons).

□ *0.6g protein, 0.7g fat (0g saturated), 6.1g carbohydrate, 1.1g fiber, 0mg cholesterol, 27mg sodium, and 10mg calcium.*

 BAGEL CROUTONS

1 unsliced caraway or pumpernickel
   bagel
Butter-flavored cooking spray

Cut bagel vertically into ⅛-inch round slices. Arrange in a single layer on a baking sheet; coat slices lightly with cooking spray. Bake at 350° for 8 to 10 minutes or until crisp. Let cool on baking sheet. Store in an airtight container. Yield: 30 croutons (34 calories [16% from fat] per 5 croutons).

□ *1g protein, 0.6g fat (0g saturated), 6g carbohydrate, 0g fiber, 0mg cholesterol, 63mg sodium, and 7mg calcium.*

Restaurant Brisket, Backyard Style

In Texas, no one cooks barbecue quite the same. Some smoke it, building a fire just to the side of the pit that allows the smoke and indirect heat to slowly cook the meat and infuse it with flavor. Others believe in using direct heat by cooking over a carefully regulated bed of coals.

Kevin Farris is an energetic pit cook at County Line (On the Lake) in Austin, Texas. He grew up in Huntsville, Alabama, but is a true Texas convert who sings the praises of beef barbecue. Although Kevin can't divulge too many cooking secrets of this chain of restaurants, he said the secret to good brisket is slow cooking.

Here's How

Kevin doesn't trim the brisket before he puts it on the smoker. He waits until it is completely cooked before trimming.

He seasons the brisket with salt, freshly ground pepper, or perhaps a little garlic powder before placing it on the pit. For smoking the meat, he uses oak wood.

We tested Kevin's recipe for brisket in a backyard smoker and found eight hours adequate for a 6-pound brisket; 1 to 1½ hours per pound of meat is a good rule of thumb to follow.

If you try this recipe at home, monitor the temperature of the smoker, keeping it around 175° to 200°. Add wood as needed to keep the temperature constant for the entire cooking time. Kevin occasionally throws in mesquite along with the oak. For a sweeter flavor, he adds a stick or two of pecan.

SMOKE-AT-HOME BRISKET

Mesquite chips
1 (5- to 6-pound) beef brisket
2 teaspoons salt
1½ teaspoons freshly ground
   pepper

Soak mesquite chips in water 4 hours. Prepare oak-wood or charcoal fire in smoker; let burn 1 hour or until flames disappear. Place mesquite on fire. Place water pan in smoker, and fill with water. Sprinkle brisket with salt and pepper; place on food rack. Cover with smoker lid; cook 8 to 9 hours or until meat thermometer registers 180°, adding additional wood or charcoal and water as needed. Yield: 15 to 18 servings.

FOR THE KIDS

Pets On Parade

That new birthday party idea you've been looking for is right in your own backyard. Instead of hauling the gang to a pizza place, invite kids and their furry friends over for an affordable afternoon of fun and feasting.

Take a small group of children and their well-loved pooches, felines, and other creatures. Add some marching music, party horns, and American flags, and you have "Pets on Parade." After a few laps around the yard (goldfish and hamsters may prefer watching from a nearby table), both two-legged and four-legged marchers will enjoy our creative birthday feast.

FEAST WITH THE BEASTS
FOR TWELVE

Spider Sandwiches
Critter Crackers
Fishin'-For-Fun Birthday Cake
Pineapple Lemonade

SPIDER SANDWICHES

24 slices wheat sandwich bread
1½ cups creamy peanut butter
24 raisins
1 (6.5-ounce) can cheese curls

With a 2½-inch round cookie cutter, cut a circle from each bread slice. Spread about 2 tablespoons peanut butter on half of bread rounds; top with remaining bread rounds. Make 2 small indentations on top of sandwiches for "eyes." Using peanut butter as "glue," push 1 raisin into each indentation. Place sandwiches in a shallow container, and cover with plastic wrap; top with a dampened dish towel, and refrigerate.

Just before serving, place sandwiches on a large plate, and arrange 8 cheese curls around each sandwich for "legs," inserting cheese curls between top and bottom bread rounds. Yield: 1 dozen. *Gayle Nicholas Scott*
Chesapeake, Virginia

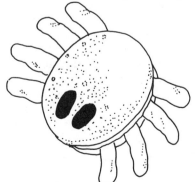

CRITTER CRACKERS

3 cups miniature round buttery crackers
3 cups animal-shaped crackers
2 cups goldfish-shaped crackers
2 cups mini pretzel twists
1 cup honey-roasted peanuts
1 (4.5-ounce) package sesame sticks
⅓ cup butter or margarine, melted

Combine first 6 ingredients in a large roasting pan. Pour butter evenly over mixture, tossing gently to coat. Bake at 250° for 1½ hours, stirring every 15 minutes. Cool; store in an airtight container. Yield: 14 cups.

Helping Hands

To make your party something special for the whole family, let your kids pitch in with the preparations. The little ones can help with these tasks.
■ Cut circles from bread slices with a round cutter; spread peanut butter on half of circles, and add raisins and cheese curls to make Spider Sandwiches.
■ Measure all ingredients except butter, and stir together in a large roasting pan for Critter Crackers.
■ Frost and decorate Fishin'-For-Fun Birthday Cake.
■ Stir together Pineapple Lemonade once you've measured the ingredients.

Dream a Theme

Racking your brain for a party idea for your birthday boy or girl? Almost any topic can become a great theme with a little imagination. Use your child's current interests to spark an idea, or try one of these creative ideas.

Friday Night at the Movies—Older kids would love the excitement of a trip to the theater, but budget-conscious parents might opt for the cheaper video-at-home idea. Vicki Overstreet made a good compromise for her son Will's 12th birthday. She rented a video, and transformed her Jackson, Mississippi, home into a theater for the evening.

For admission, guests presented their ticket-shaped invitations at the door and were issued play money to use at the kitchen-turned-concession stand. Moviegoers "purchased" popcorn, candy bars, suckers, and soft drinks, then headed to the family room to find a seat among the rows of chairs to await showtime.

While waiting on the feature presentation, they perused the old "coming attraction" posters Vicki had gotten from her local video store and scattered on the walls for the occasion.

I've Been Working on the Railroad—All aboard! The Fun Express is headed for a celebration. Celeste Stough of Marietta, Georgia, set the theme for her son's third birthday party with the invitation—a "ticket" to ride the rails with James. She greeted guests with red bandannas to wear around their necks and made them train engineers for an afternoon in keeping with the theme.

Each partygoer decorated his own "boxcar." Before the party, Celeste had gathered large cardboard boxes, cut out the tops and bottoms, and attached two strings to the top, making shoulder straps. She then added "wheels" cut from black construction paper. After coloring the boxes, the kids slipped them on, formed a line, and set the "train" in motion. A bakery cake decorated with a tiny track and windup train completed the party theme.

Here Comes the Bride—Some people are waiting longer to marry these days, but not Ivey London of Birmingham, Alabama. She had a "wedding" for her third birthday. Her mom, Eve, who does calligraphy, penned formal invitations on ecru cards, inviting 25 of her friends to attend.

Guests were seated in chairs set up in rows and decorated with huge pink bows. Ivey was escorted down the aisle by her brothers to the recorded strains of "The Wedding March." The "ceremony" uniting Ivey and her special friend, Richard Baugh, was performed by Ivey's uncle, who also doubled as "minister" and party magician for the occasion. The memorable event was captured on a keepsake video.

After the happy couple exchanged vows, everyone nibbled wedding cake (complete with a miniature bride and bridegroom) and sipped lemon-lime carbonated beverage from plastic champagne glasses. Each guest took home a bag of pastel mints and a tiny ring bearer's pillow with play wedding bands as party favors.

FISHIN'-FOR-FUN BIRTHDAY CAKE

1 (18.25-ounce) package chocolate
    morsel cake mix with pudding
1 (16-ounce) container
    ready-to-spread cream cheese
    frosting
Candy sprinkles
Construction paper
Glue
Party candles

Prepare cake mix according to package directions; spoon batter into 2 greased and floured 8-inch round cakepans. Bake according to package directions. Cool in pans on wire racks 10 minutes; remove from pans, and let cool completely on wire racks.

Spread frosting between layers and on top and sides of cake. Decorate top with candy sprinkles. Cut construction paper into desired animal shapes, and glue 2 cutouts around each candle, matching paper edges; place in cake. Use additional undecorated candles for lighting. Yield: one 8-inch cake.

PINEAPPLE LEMONADE

1 (46-ounce) can unsweetened
    pineapple juice
4 cups water
2 cups fresh lemon juice (about 12
    lemons)
1⅓ cups sugar

Combine all ingredients, stirring until sugar dissolves. Chill; serve over ice. Yield: 3 quarts.   *Marcia Jeffries*
Oklahoma City, Oklahoma

The Bus Stops Here

The best remedy for the school's-starting, summer's-over blues? A breakfast party for the neighborhood gang—right at the bus stop. Set up a fun breakfast "cafe" on your front porch, driveway, or corner of the yard with card tables and folding chairs, and choose one of our kid-tailored menus for the occasion.

These recipes are easy enough for one parent to handle, but if you have a large group, ask a neighbor or two to pitch in. And if you want to skip the tables and chairs, just use lap trays and let kids sit on the ground. Take a few snapshots for the photo album; these are sure to beat the usual first-day-of-school poses.

Mix-and-Match Menus

We did our math and came up with a number of ways to combine these recipes into menus that add up to fun.

Wacky Waffles
Breakfast Delight
or bacon
Quick Banana-Pineapple
Smoothie
(Serves Eight)

WACKY WAFFLES

2 cups all-purpose flour
1 tablespoon baking powder
½ teaspoon salt
2 tablespoons sugar
3 large eggs, separated
1½ cups milk
⅓ cup butter or margarine, melted

Combine first 4 ingredients in a large bowl. Combine egg yolks, milk, and butter; add to flour mixture, stirring just until moistened.

Beat egg whites at high speed with an electric mixer until soft peaks form; gently fold into batter. Bake in preheated, oiled waffle iron until golden. Serve with butter and syrup. Yield: 8 mouse-shaped waffles or 12 (4-inch) waffles.

Note: Check kitchen shops or the housewares section of department stores for a Mickey Mouse-shaped waffle iron. *Minnie Mason*
Richland Hills, Texas

BREAKFAST DELIGHT

1 (16-ounce) package brown-and-serve sausage links
2 (20-ounce) cans sliced apples, drained
⅔ cup honey
½ teaspoon ground cinnamon

Cook sausage according to package directions in a large skillet; drain well. Return sausage to skillet, and add apples and remaining ingredients; cook over medium heat, about 5 minutes, or until liquid is absorbed, stirring often. Serve immediately. Yield: 8 servings. *Jodie McCoy*
Tulsa, Oklahoma

QUICK BANANA-PINEAPPLE SMOOTHIE

4 medium bananas, chilled
4 (8-ounce) cartons pineapple low-fat yogurt
2 (8-ounce) cans crushed pineapple, undrained
Ice cubes

Combine half of first 3 ingredients in container of an electric blender, and process until smooth, stopping once to scrape down sides. Add enough ice to bring mixture to 4-cup level; process 1 minute or until smooth. Repeat procedure with other half of ingredients. Yield: 8 cups. *Erma Jackson*
Huntsville, Alabama

Easy Oven-Baked French Toast
Breakfast Delight *
or fresh fruit
Quick Banana-Pineapple
Smoothie *
(Serves 15)
* make 2 batches for 15 or 16 servings

EASY OVEN-BAKED FRENCH TOAST

16 slices white sandwich bread, cut into 1-inch cubes
1 (8-ounce) package cream cheese, softened
12 large eggs
2 cups whipping cream
½ cup maple syrup
½ teaspoon maple flavoring
Maple syrup

Place bread cubes in a lightly greased 13- x 9- x 2-inch baking dish, and set aside.

Beat cream cheese at medium speed with an electric mixer until smooth; add eggs and next 3 ingredients, beating until blended. Pour over bread cubes; cover and refrigerate 8 hours or overnight.

Remove from refrigerator; let stand at room temperature 30 minutes. Bake at 375° for 40 to 50 minutes or until set, covering with foil after 25 minutes. Serve with additional syrup. Yield: 15 servings. *Becky Sparrow*
Valrico, Florida

**Overnight Refrigerator
Pancakes
Breakfast Delight
or sausage
Quick Banana-Pineapple
Smoothie
(Serves Eight)**

OVERNIGHT REFRIGERATOR PANCAKES

1 package active dry yeast
¼ cup warm water (105° to 115°)
4 cups all-purpose flour
2 tablespoons baking powder
2 teaspoons baking soda
1 teaspoon salt
2 teaspoons sugar
6 large eggs
1 quart buttermilk
¼ cup vegetable oil

Combine yeast and warm water in a 1-cup liquid measuring cup; let stand 5 minutes.

Combine flour and next 4 ingredients in a large bowl; make a well in center.

Combine eggs, buttermilk, and oil; add to flour mixture, stirring just until dry ingredients are moistened. Stir in yeast mixture. Cover and refrigerate 8 hours or overnight.

Remove from refrigerator; stir batter well. For each pancake, pour about ¼ cup batter into a heavy skillet over medium heat. Cook pancakes until tops are covered with bubbles and edges look cooked; turn and cook other side. Yield: 2½ dozen.

Note: Pancake batter may be stored in refrigerator up to one week. To freeze pancakes, prepare according to directions; cool. Place a piece of plastic wrap between each pancake; store in a freezer container. Label and freeze. To serve, remove 2 pancakes; cover with paper towels. Microwave on HIGH 1 to 2 minutes.

Pancakes may be made in the shape of your child's initials by pouring from a measuring cup or using a plastic squeeze bottle with a large tip to "write" with the batter.

*Dolores Thielermeir
Maynard, Arkansas*

**Pancake-Sausage Wedges
Strawberries, grapes, oranges
Quick Banana-Pineapple
Smoothie *
(Serves 12)
* make 1½ batches for 12
servings**

PANCAKE-SAUSAGE WEDGES

12 brown-and-serve sausage links
1½ cups all-purpose flour
2 teaspoons baking powder
½ teaspoon salt
2 large eggs
1 cup milk
3 tablespoons vegetable oil

Cook sausage according to package directions; drain well, pressing between paper towels. Place sausage, spoke fashion, in a lightly greased 9-inch quiche dish; set aside.

Combine flour, baking powder, and salt in a large bowl; make a well in center. Combine eggs, milk, and oil; add to flour mixture, stirring just until dry ingredients are moistened. Spoon over sausages. Bake at 350° for 45 minutes or until golden. Cut into wedges, and serve with butter and syrup. Yield: 12 servings.

*Clairiece Gilbert Humphrey
Charlottesville, Virginia*

Back-To-School Lunch Bunch

You're probably dreading those fast-approaching school mornings when you madly search the pantry for something—*anything*—your child won't trade at the lunch table. Try these kid-friendly, make-ahead recipes that ease nutritional worries and fit into hectic schedules.

Picking Your Packing

Your kids might think the biggest decision in picking a lunchbox is to get one featuring the cartoon character they like best. But that's really not the case. Convenience, food safety, durability, and easy cleaning are all important for you to consider—even if they aren't for your kids.

When shopping for a lunchbox, buy one that's easy for smaller hands to carry, has sturdy handles and hinges, and opens and closes easily.

Our *Southern Living* Test Kitchens staff offers these additional tips:
■ Pick a box that's easy to clean. Avoid those with a lot of crevices.
■ Ask if the box is dishwasher-safe. Many are fine in the top rack, but lesser quality lunchboxes can melt.
■ Make every effort to keep cold foods chilled and hot ones hot:

Prepackaged juice boxes are excellent when frozen and put into a lunchbox to keep other foods cool. By lunchtime, juices will be thawed enough to drink. (Thawing items will sweat through a paper lunch bag.)

You can do the same with frozen fruits, putting them into reusable plastic containers or zip-top plastic bags.

Plain or fruit-flavored yogurt can also be frozen. As it thaws there'll be a little separation, but just stir well.

Keeping lunchbox contents cool until lunchtime is particularly important if you pack items that spoil easily, such as meats, eggs, tuna, chicken, milk, and any dishes made from them.

It's not as easy to keep hot foods at safe temperatures. Store soups, stews, or similar recipes in an insulated thermos or container that will keep food at 140° or above until lunchtime. Test this at home by setting aside a sealed container of hot food for several hours, then inserting a thermometer in the food. (Pouring boiling water into an insulated container, letting the water stand a few minutes, then discarding it before adding food may help keep food hotter.)

GRANOLA

2½ cups regular oats, uncooked
2½ cups whole wheat flake cereal
1 cup flaked coconut
½ cup wheat germ
½ cup sesame seeds
½ cup sunflower kernels
½ cup dry-roasted peanuts
½ cup butter or margarine
½ cup firmly packed brown sugar
½ cup honey
1 teaspoon vanilla extract

Combine first 7 ingredients in a large bowl; set aside. Combine butter, brown sugar, and honey in a small saucepan; cook over medium heat, stirring constantly until butter melts and mixture is thoroughly heated. Stir in vanilla, and pour over oats mixture, stirring to coat evenly.

Spoon into a lightly greased 15- x 10- x 1-inch jellyroll pan. Bake at 275° for 1 hour and 15 minutes or until golden, stirring every 15 minutes. Remove from oven; stir occasionally as mixture cools. Store in an airtight container. Yield: 10 cups.
Valerie Stutsman
Norfolk, Virginia

Note: For whole wheat flake cereal, we used Wheaties.

TORTILLA SOUP

2 (10½-ounce) cans chicken-and-rice soup, undiluted
1 cup canned chopped tomatoes with juice
2 tablespoons canned chopped green chiles
1 cup (4 ounces) shredded Cheddar cheese
2 cups crushed lightly salted tortilla chips

Combine first 3 ingredients; refrigerate overnight. Before packing in lunch, place mixture in a medium saucepan; bring just to a boil. Immediately spoon into insulated containers; seal. To serve, sprinkle with cheese and chips. Yield: about 4 cups.

Note: Pack cheese and chips in separate plastic bags or resealable, reusable containers.

CRACKER SNACKERS

⅓ cup vegetable oil
1 clove garlic, thinly sliced
1 (11-ounce) package oyster crackers
1 (0.7-ounce) envelope Italian salad dressing mix
1 teaspoon dillweed
⅛ teaspoon garlic powder

Combine oil and garlic; let stand 30 minutes. Remove and discard garlic. Place crackers in a medium bowl; sprinkle with oil. Combine salad dressing mix and remaining ingredients; sprinkle over crackers, stirring mixture well. Let stand 30 minutes, stirring every 10 minutes. Store in an airtight container. Yield: 5 cups.
Pat Smith
Palm Harbor, Florida

FROZEN FRUIT CUPS

1 (10-ounce) package frozen strawberries, thawed and halved
1 (6-ounce) can frozen orange juice concentrate, thawed and undiluted
1 (8-ounce) can pineapple tidbits, undrained
1 (11-ounce) can mandarin oranges, undrained
3 bananas, sliced
3 tablespoons lemon juice

Combine all ingredients; pour into ½-cup freezer containers. Freeze 8 hours. Place in lunchboxes. Fruit will thaw by lunchtime. Yield: 11 servings.
Kitten Moser
Monroe, North Carolina

CHOCOLATE-DIPPED HORNS

¼ cup creamy peanut butter
2 cups corn snacks
3 (2-ounce) squares chocolate-flavored candy coating, melted

Spoon peanut butter into a small plastic bag; snip a small hole in corner of bag. Squeeze a small amount of peanut butter into each corn snack; dip each into chocolate coating, and place on wax paper to dry. Store in an airtight container. Yield: about 3½ dozen.
Nancy Moore
Memphis, Tennessee

Note: For 2 cups corn snacks, we used Bugles.

Tip: *Peanut butter will keep its quality longer and taste fresher if stored in the refrigerator.*

Backyard Bravery

You can keep an eye on your brave campers from the kitchen window as you round up a meal hearty enough to get the youngsters through a night in the "wilderness."

While mom or dad grills the hamburgers or hot dogs out back with the gang, another adult can ready the condiments, prepare Chuck Wagon Bean Casserole, and cut up crunchy raw veggies. Serve Peanut Butter Cookie Ice Cream Sandwiches or Oatmeal Crispy Ice Cream Sandwiches for dessert or as a midnight snack.

Coat grill rack with cooking spray; place rack on grill over medium-hot coals (350° to 400°). Place patties on rack, and cook without grill lid, 5 minutes on each side or until patties are done. Serve on buns with lettuce. Yield: 8 to 10 servings.

Note: To create a "space monster" or funny animal, decorate hamburgers with olives (for eyes) and whole small pickles (for ears). *Judy Grimes Brandon, Mississippi*

SURVIVAL SUPPER FOR EIGHT

Hot Diggity Dog Sauce
Over frankfurters
or
Grilled Hamburgers
Chuck Wagon Bean Casserole
Raw veggies
Citrus Slush
Peanut Butter Cookie Ice Cream Sandwiches
or
Oatmeal Crispy Ice Cream Sandwiches

HOT DIGGITY DOG SAUCE

1 pound lean ground beef
½ cup chopped onion
1 clove garlic, minced
1 (15-ounce) can tomato sauce
½ cup water
½ teaspoon chili powder
¼ teaspoon salt

Brown ground beef in a Dutch oven, stirring until it crumbles; drain. Add onion and remaining ingredients. Bring to a boil; cover, reduce heat, and simmer 10 minutes, stirring occasionally. Serve over frankfurters in buns. Yield: 8 to 10 servings.

GRILLED HAMBURGERS

¼ cup milk
2 large eggs, lightly beaten
3 slices white sandwich bread, torn into small pieces
2 pounds lean ground beef
1 (1-ounce) envelope dry onion soup mix
¼ cup grated Parmesan cheese
2 tablespoons dried parsley flakes
¼ teaspoon pepper
Vegetable cooking spray
8 to 10 hamburger buns
Lettuce leaves

Combine milk and eggs in a large bowl; stir in bread, and let mixture stand 5 minutes. Add ground beef and next 4 ingredients; mix well. Shape into 8 to 10 patties.

CHUCK WAGON BEAN CASSEROLE

2 (16-ounce) cans pork and beans
½ cup finely chopped onion
½ cup (2 ounces) shredded sharp Cheddar cheese
1 tablespoon chili powder
2 tablespoons Worcestershire sauce
2 tablespoons molasses
1 tablespoon white vinegar
4 slices bacon, cooked and crumbled

Combine first 7 ingredients in a lightly greased 2-quart shallow baking dish. Bake at 350° for 1 hour, stirring once. Sprinkle with crumbled bacon. Yield: 8 servings. *Lula Bell Hawks Newport, Arkansas*

CITRUS SLUSH

1 (48-ounce) bottle pink grapefruit juice cocktail
1 (12-ounce) can frozen pine-orange-banana juice concentrate, thawed and undiluted
1 (5-ounce) package sweetened lemonade-flavored drink mix
4 cups water
½ cup sugar
2 (1-liter) bottles ginger ale

Combine first 5 ingredients; stir until drink mix and sugar dissolve. Divide into 2 gallon-size, heavy-duty, zip-top plastic bags; freeze.

Remove bags from freezer 1 hour before serving. Place contents of each into a large pitcher, and break into chunks. Add 1 bottle ginger ale to each pitcher; stir until slushy. Yield: 1½ gallons or 3 quarts per bag of mixture.
Shellie Smith
Oklahoma City, Oklahoma

cutter, quickly cut 2 rounds out of each slice. (Reserve remaining ice cream for another use.) Place rounds of ice cream on half of cookies, and top with remaining cookies. Wrap each with plastic wrap, and freeze. Yield: 11 ice cream sandwiches.

Note: Cookies may also be served without ice cream filling. Yield: 22 cookies.
Trenda Leigh
Richmond, Virginia

rounds of ice cream on half of cookies, and top with remaining cookies. Wrap each with plastic wrap, and freeze. Yield: 19 ice cream sandwiches.

Note: Cookies may also be served without ice cream filling. Yield: 38 cookies.
Teenya Blanchard
Arlington, Texas

PEANUT BUTTER COOKIE ICE CREAM SANDWICHES

½ cup butter or margarine, softened
½ cup creamy peanut butter
½ cup sugar
½ cup firmly packed brown sugar
1 large egg
½ teaspoon vanilla extract
¼ teaspoon almond extract
1¼ cups all-purpose flour
¾ teaspoon baking soda
¼ teaspoon salt
1 (½-gallon) carton vanilla or rocky road ice cream

Beat butter and peanut butter at medium speed with an electric mixer until mixture is creamy; gradually add sugars, beating well. Add egg and flavorings, mixing well.

Combine flour, soda, and salt; gradually add to butter mixture, mixing well. Cover and chill 1 hour. Shape dough into 22 (1½-inch) balls, and place 3 inches apart on ungreased cookie sheets. Dip a flat-bottomed glass in flour, and flatten each ball to a 2½-inch circle. Bake at 375° for 8 to 10 minutes. Let stand 1 minute on cookie sheets; transfer to wire racks, and cool completely.

Remove ice cream from carton; quickly cut ice cream into 6 (½-inch-thick) slices. Using a 2½-inch round

OATMEAL CRISPY ICE CREAM SANDWICHES

1 cup shortening
1 cup firmly packed brown sugar
1 cup sugar
2 large eggs
1 teaspoon vanilla extract
1½ cups all-purpose flour
1 teaspoon baking soda
3 cups quick-cooking oats, uncooked
½ cup chopped pecans
1 (½-gallon) carton chocolate or rocky road ice cream

Beat shortening at medium speed with an electric mixer until fluffy; gradually add sugars, beating well. Add eggs and vanilla, mixing well.

Combine flour, soda, and oats; gradually add to shortening mixture, mixing well. Stir in pecans. Cover and chill 1 hour. Shape dough into 38 (1½-inch) balls, and place 3 inches apart on lightly greased cookie sheets. Dip a flat-bottomed glass in flour, and flatten each ball to a 2½-inch circle. Bake at 350° for 12 to 14 minutes; transfer to wire racks to cool.

Remove ice cream from carton; quickly cut ice cream into 10 (¼-inch-thick) slices. Using a 2½-inch round cutter, quickly cut 2 rounds out of each slice. (Reserve remaining ice cream for another use.) Place

Helping Hands

If the kids aren't too busy setting up the "campsite," they may want to help prepare the evening's feast.
■ Let the campers measure and combine ingredients for Chuck Wagon Bean Casserole before you bake it.
■ Kids can shape hamburger patties or put frankfurters into the grilling basket before an adult grills them.
■ Take frozen punch mix out of the freezer an hour before serving. When the kids get thirsty, let them add the ginger ale and watch it fizz into Citrus Slush.
■ A day or two before the campout, get your kids in the mood by letting them help you bake cookies for the ice cream sandwiches.

Have A Tart

There are only a few luscious bites in individual dessert tarts, reason enough to savor every spoonful.

These delicious tart dazzlers show off the brilliant color palette of summer fruits. The recipe for creamy Blackberry Pudding Tarts is "a family heirloom," writes Jean King of Walnut Hill, Florida. Intense in both color and flavor, the tart was a favorite in our Test Kitchens.

Either of these easy-to-make tart recipes will make the perfect ending to a summer meal.

BOWL-ME-OVER
FRESH FRUIT TARTS
(pictured on back cover)

1 (15-ounce) package refrigerated
   piecrusts
1 cup fresh raspberries
1 cup fresh blackberries
1 cup fresh whole strawberries
1 cup fresh or canned apricots,
   halved
2 kiwifruits, peeled and sliced
1 tablespoon sugar (optional)
Lemon Cream Sauce

Unfold 1 piecrust, and roll into a 13-inch circle on a lightly floured surface; carefully tear 3 (5½-inch) circles, leaving jagged edges. Repeat procedure with remaining piecrust. Place 6 (6-ounce) custard cups upside down on a 15- x 10- x 1-inch jellyroll pan; lightly grease bottom and sides of cups. Drape a pastry circle over each cup; pinch dough to make 6 pleats, conforming pastry to shape of cup. Prick bottom and sides with a fork. Bake at 425° for 10 minutes or until lightly browned. Remove to wire racks; cool 5 minutes. Carefully remove pastry from cups; turn right side up, and cool completely on wire racks.

Combine fruit in a large bowl, and sugar, if desired; refrigerate up to 2 hours before serving. Spoon about ¾ cup fruit mixture into each tart shell. Serve with Lemon Cream Sauce. Yield: 6 servings.

Lemon Cream Sauce

1 (11¼-ounce) jar lemon curd
1 cup whipping cream

Combine lemon curd and whipping cream, beating with a wire whisk until smooth. Refrigerate up to 24 hours before serving. Yield: 2 cups.

Note: Lemon curd, a creamy, cooked mixture of lemon juice, sugar, butter, and egg yolks, may be purchased at specialty food shops and large supermarkets. Serve any extra sauce over pound cake.

BLACKBERRY
PUDDING TARTS

1 (15-ounce) package refrigerated
   piecrusts
2 quarts fresh or frozen
   blackberries, thawed
1 cup water
1½ cups sugar
½ cup self-rising flour
¼ cup butter or margarine
2 teaspoons vanilla extract
Whipped cream

Unfold 1 piecrust, and roll into a 15-inch circle on a lightly floured surface; cut into 5 (5½-inch) circles. Fit each circle into a 5-inch round tart pan with removable bottom, and place pans on a baking sheet. Prick bottom and sides with a fork. Repeat procedure with remaining piecrust. Bake at 450° for 8 minutes or until lightly browned. Remove to wire racks; cool.

Combine blackberries and water in a large saucepan; bring to a boil. Reduce heat, and simmer, uncovered, 5 minutes or until blackberries are soft. Mash berries with a fork; pour through a large wire-mesh strainer into a 4-cup liquid measuring cup, discarding pulp and seeds. Measurement should be 2 cups blackberry juice. (If necessary, boil berry juice to reduce to 2 cups.)

Combine sugar and flour in a medium saucepan; gradually add juice, stirring constantly until smooth. Bring to a boil over medium heat, stirring constantly. Reduce heat, and simmer, uncovered, 3 minutes or until slightly thickened. Remove from heat; stir in butter and vanilla. Spoon about ¼ cup mixture into each prepared tart shell. Cool; top with a dollop of whipped cream. Yield: 10 tarts.   *Jean King*
Walnut Hill, Florida

Tip: *Compare costs of fresh, frozen, canned, and dried foods. To compute the best buy, divide the price by the number of servings. The lower price per serving will be the thriftiest buy.*

Savor Summer's Best Sauces

It's too hot to cook. That thought, as well as summer's explosion of vine-ripened tomatoes, inspired us to come up with this trio of quick, no-cook pasta sauces. Each is a regional variation on a winning theme: tomatoes at their flavorful best with generous amounts of fresh herbs and spices and a splash of olive oil.

Get a jump on the heat by cooking pasta early. Then drain, store in a zip-top plastic bag, and refrigerate. Just reheat in the microwave when you're ready to eat. Since each version serves two, grab a loaf of bread, a jug of tea, and your best friend. Then sit down to a special treat.

CARIBBEAN TOMATO PASTA

3 large vine-ripened tomatoes
¾ cup canned black beans, drained
   and rinsed
2 tablespoons extra-virgin olive oil
3 cloves garlic, minced
2 tablespoons chopped fresh
   cilantro
1 tablespoon chopped fresh chives
1 tablespoon fresh lime juice
½ teaspoon ground cumin
¼ teaspoon ground red pepper
¼ teaspoon salt
¼ teaspoon black pepper
4 ounces vermicelli, uncooked
½ cup (2 ounces) shredded
   Monterey Jack cheese

Peel tomatoes, and coarsely chop over a medium bowl, reserving juice. Combine chopped tomatoes, reserved juice, beans, and next 9 ingredients; cover and let stand at room temperature at least 1 hour.

Cook pasta according to package directions; drain. Serve tomato mixture over pasta, and sprinkle with cheese. Yield: 2 servings.

SOUTHWESTERN TOMATO PASTA

3 small vine-ripened tomatoes
2 tablespoons extra-virgin olive oil
3 cloves garlic, minced
1 jalapeño pepper, seeded and
   finely chopped
3 tablespoons chopped fresh
   cilantro
1 tablespoon fresh lime juice
½ teaspoon chili powder
¼ teaspoon salt
¼ teaspoon ground white pepper
4 ounces angel hair pasta,
   uncooked
4 ounces goat cheese, crumbled
2 tablespoons pine nuts, toasted

Peel tomatoes, and coarsely chop over a medium bowl, reserving juice. Combine chopped tomatoes, reserved juice, olive oil, and next 7 ingredients; cover and let stand at room temperature 1 hour.

Cook pasta according to package directions; drain. Serve tomato mixture over pasta; top with cheese and pine nuts. Yield: 2 servings.

ITALIAN TOMATO PASTA

3 large vine-ripened tomatoes
2 tablespoons extra-virgin olive oil
3 cloves garlic, minced
¼ cup sliced ripe olives
1 tablespoon chopped fresh basil
1 tablespoon chopped fresh parsley
¼ teaspoon salt
¼ teaspoon pepper
4 ounces spaghetti, uncooked
4 ounces mozzarella cheese, cut
   into cubes

Peel tomatoes; coarsely chop over a medium bowl, reserving juice. Combine tomatoes, reserved juice, olive oil, and next 6 ingredients; cover and let stand at room temperature 1 hour.

Cook pasta according to package directions; drain. Serve tomato mixture over pasta, and top with cheese. Yield: 2 servings.

Inventory Your Herb Rack

Don't use the same herb time and again. Next time take a new look, and you might rediscover flavors that lead to creative cooking.

While you are looking over your herb rack, check for freshness. Dried herbs retain their best flavor for only six to 12 months.

Here is a quick test: Open the container, and bring it to your nose. If you cannot immediately detect an aroma, the herb has passed its prime.

The chart on page 202 will be useful in reviewing your herbs. When fresh herbs are available in your garden, dry them and resupply your jars. Store the jars in a cool place away from the cooktop, oven, or bright sunlight.

Cooking dried herbs for a long period of time causes them to lose their flavor and aroma. Adding them during the last 10 to 15 minutes of cooking is generally best. For cold foods, add herbs at least one hour before serving to allow flavors to blend.

GRILLED BASIL CHICKEN

3 tablespoons lemon juice
2 teaspoons dried basil
1 clove garlic, minced
¼ cup olive oil
4 chicken breast halves, skinned *

Combine first 3 ingredients in container of an electric blender; process 30 seconds. With motor running, gradually add oil in a slow, steady stream. Reserve ¼ cup basil mixture.

Brush chicken with remaining basil mixture; cover and refrigerate 30 minutes. Cook chicken covered with grill lid over medium coals (300° to 350°) 30 minutes or until done, basting twice with reserved basil mixture. Yield: 4 servings.

* 8 chicken thighs, skinned, may be substituted.
John Floyd
Birmingham, Alabama

How to Use Dried Herbs

Herb	Flavor	Uses
Basil	fragrantly sweet	Italian dishes, beef stew, lamb, poultry, omelets and egg dishes, potato salads, salad dressings, tomatoes, mozzarella cheese, yellow squash, and zucchini
Bay leaves	aromatic, pungent	soups, stews, chowders, custards, tomato sauces, aspics, water for boiling/poaching fish, shellfish, and vegetables (remove bay leaves and discard before serving)
Cilantro	distinctive, pungent	salsas, chutneys, guacamole, bean dips; Mexican, Middle Eastern, and Asian dishes
Dillweed	fresh, sweet	cucumbers, chicken salad, egg dishes, soups, salad dressings, dips and spreads, vegetables, breads, sauces, fish, and shellfish
Marjoram	earthy, mild, resembling oregano	beef, poultry, fish, pork, lamb, egg and cheese dishes, vegetables, and sauces
Oregano	spicy, pungent	Italian, Mexican, and Greek dishes; pasta sauces, chili con carne, salad dressings, vegetable soups, egg and cheese dishes, beef, pork, lamb, chicken, and fish
Rosemary	pinelike, bittersweet	lamb, poultry, pork, potatoes, cauliflower, turnips, barbecued meats, marinades, and vegetable soups
Sage	strong, warm	stuffings and dressings, beef, veal, lamb, pork, chicken, sausage, eggplant, sauces, tomatoes, and bean soups
Tarragon	licoricelike	salad dressings, fish and shellfish, veal and poultry, egg dishes, vinegar, soups, mushrooms, beets, green beans, asparagus, and sauces
Thyme	sweet, pleasantly pungent	soups, chowders, egg and cheese dishes, roasted meats and poultry, Creole dishes, stuffings and dressings, and tomatoes

Advice on Drying Herbs

If you have fresh herbs in your garden, here's how to dry them.
■ Gather herbs at midmorning, using garden shears. Cut them just before they begin flowering to capture them at their peak flavor.
■ Swish the herbs briefly in a sink full of clean water. Shake off excess moisture, and blot dry between paper towels.
■ Group long-stemmed herbs, such as rosemary or thyme, in bunches of 10 to 15 stalks. Tie them with string to suspend in air.

For herbs with larger leaves, such as basil or cilantro, cut the leaves from the washed and dried stalks. Arrange the leaves in a single layer on a paper towel-lined, large screen or a piece of corrugated cardboard. Place prepared herbs in a hot, dry room

with good circulation. Attics, sheds, or garages are usually ideal places for drying herbs.
■ Be sure herbs are thoroughly dry before you store them (that can take anywhere from two to five days.) Strip the leaves from the stalks, and place them in a small bowl. Use kitchen shears to snip them into tiny pieces, or gently crumble with your hands.
■ Place the dried herbs in airtight, labeled jars, and store in a cool, dark place.

ROSEMARY MARINATED LAMB KABOBS

½ cup orange juice
¼ cup lime juice
¼ cup soy sauce
2 tablespoons teriyaki sauce
¼ cup finely chopped green onions
2 teaspoons dried rosemary
1 teaspoon minced garlic
5 to 7 black peppercorns
1 pound lean lamb, cut into 1-inch cubes
2 to 4 green peppers, quartered
1 large purple onion, cut into 8 slices
1 orange, cut into 8 slices
Hot cooked rice

Combine first 8 ingredients in a shallow container or heavy-duty, zip-top plastic bag. Add lamb; cover or seal, and refrigerate 8 hours, turning once.

Drain lamb, discarding marinade. Arrange lamb on skewers. Place green pepper and onion in a grilling basket. Cook lamb and vegetables covered with grill lid over hot coals (400° to 500°) 10 minutes, turning often. Place orange slices on grill rack, and cook just until thoroughly heated, turning once. Serve lamb, vegetables, and orange slices over rice. Yield: 4 servings.
Alex Saied
Hoover, Alabama

FRESH CORN AND BACON CHOWDER

8 ears fresh corn
4 slices bacon
½ cup finely chopped onion
½ cup thinly sliced celery
1 cup water
2 cups milk, divided
1 teaspoon sugar
1 teaspoon dried thyme
½ teaspoon salt
¼ teaspoon pepper
2 teaspoons cornstarch

Cut off tips of corn kernels into a large bowl; scrape milk and remaining pulp from cob with a paring knife, and set aside.

Cook bacon in a large Dutch oven until crisp; remove bacon, reserving 2 tablespoons drippings in Dutch oven. Crumble bacon, and set aside. Cook onion and celery in reserved bacon drippings over medium-high heat, stirring constantly, until tender. Stir in corn and water. Bring to a boil; cover, reduce heat, and simmer 10 minutes, stirring occasionally. Stir in 1½ cups milk and next 4 ingredients.

Combine cornstarch and remaining ½ cup milk; stir until smooth. Gradually add to corn mixture, stirring constantly. Cover and cook 10 minutes until thickened and bubbly, stirring often. Sprinkle with crumbled bacon. Yield: 5½ cups.
Louise Crawford
Coldwater, Mississippi

CUCUMBERS AND SOUR CREAM

1 medium cucumber, thinly sliced
1 teaspoon salt
3 tablespoons sour cream
1 teaspoon sugar
1 teaspoon cider vinegar
½ teaspoon dried dillweed

Place cucumber slices in a large bowl. Sprinkle with salt; cover with water, and let stand 45 minutes. Drain; place on paper towels, and pat dry. Combine sour cream and remaining ingredients in a bowl; add cucumber slices, tossing to coat. Cover and chill at least 1 hour. Yield: 2 to 4 servings.
Mrs. George Evans
Silver Springs, Florida

Tip: *Make a special topping for cooked vegetables or casseroles by crushing ½ cup herb-seasoned stuffing mix and combining it with 2 tablespoons melted butter or margarine; top the dish with this mixture, and then sprinkle with 1 cup shredded cheese.*

QUICK & EASY

New Twists On Tostadas

Mexican food lovers know the tostada is one of the simplest snacks of all. And if you're short on time, the tostada can also be a delicious answer to "What's for dinner?"

Traditionally, a tostada consists of a fried tortilla with meat, lettuce, and cheese. These recipes introduce some new flavor combinations: chicken spiced with tomato salsa; black beans teamed with shrimp; and lump crabmeat blended with Cheddar and cream cheeses.

CRAB TOSTADAS

6 (6-inch) flour tortillas
Vegetable cooking spray
1 (6-ounce) can lump crabmeat, drained and rinsed
1 (3-ounce) package cream cheese, softened
¾ cup (3 ounces) shredded sharp Cheddar cheese
2 tablespoons chopped green onions
1 tablespoon finely chopped pickled jalapeño peppers
1 clove garlic, minced
2 teaspoons chopped fresh cilantro
Garnish: sliced ripe olives

Arrange tortillas in a single layer on baking sheets; coat with cooking spray. Bake at 375° for 8 to 10 minutes or until lightly golden.

Combine crabmeat and next 6 ingredients; spread ¼ cup evenly onto each tortilla. Bake at 375° for 5 minutes or until puffed and bubbly. Cut into wedges with a pizza cutter, and garnish, if desired. Yield: 6 servings.

SHRIMP-AND-BLACK BEAN TOSTADAS

1 small onion, finely chopped
2 cloves garlic, minced
2 tablespoons olive oil
1 (16-ounce) can black beans, drained and rinsed
⅓ cup water
1 teaspoon ground cumin
¼ teaspoon salt
½ teaspoon pepper
4 (8-inch) flour tortillas
Vegetable cooking spray
1½ cups coarsely chopped cooked shrimp (about 1 pound unpeeled medium-size fresh shrimp)
2 tablespoons chopped fresh cilantro
2 cups (8 ounces) shredded Monterey Jack cheese
2 tablespoons sliced pickled jalapeño peppers
Commercial guacamole dip (optional)
Commercial salsa (optional)

Cook onion and garlic in olive oil in a medium skillet over medium-high heat, stirring constantly, until tender.

Combine beans and next 4 ingredients in an electric blender or food processor; process until smooth, stopping once to scrape down sides. Add to onion mixture, and cook over medium heat about 3 minutes or until thickened, stirring occasionally.

Arrange tortillas in a single layer on baking sheets. Coat with cooking spray, and bake at 350° about 10 minutes or until lightly browned.

Spread one-fourth of bean mixture onto each tortilla; top evenly with shrimp and next 3 ingredients. Bake at 375° for 5 minutes or until hot and bubbly. If desired, serve with guacamole and salsa. Yield: 4 servings.

Note: To serve as an appetizer, cut each tortilla into 6 wedges. Yield: 8 to 12 appetizer servings.

CHICKEN TOSTADAS

4 skinned and boned chicken breast halves, cut into ¼-inch-wide strips
¼ cup chopped onion
2 tablespoons butter or margarine, melted
1 (16-ounce) jar salsa
1 (1¼-ounce) package taco seasoning mix
1 (16-ounce) can refried beans
1 (4½-ounce) package tostada shells
2 cups shredded lettuce
1 cup (4 ounces) shredded Cheddar cheese
2 small tomatoes, chopped

Cook half each of chicken strips and onion in 1 tablespoon butter in a large skillet over medium-high heat 2 to 3 minutes, stirring often. Remove chicken mixture, and set aside. Repeat procedure with remaining chicken strips, onion, and butter. Return chicken mixture to skillet; add salsa and taco seasoning mix. Cook mixture over low heat 10 minutes, stirring occasionally.

Heat refried beans in a small saucepan; set aside.

Place tostada shells on a baking sheet, slightly overlapping. Bake at 350° for 5 minutes. Spread about 2 tablespoons refried beans on each tostada; top evenly with chicken mixture, lettuce, cheese, and tomatoes. Yield: 6 servings.
Brenda Byrd
Columbia, South Carolina

Tip: *Fresh meat, poultry, and fish should be loosely wrapped and refrigerated; use in a few days. Loosely wrap fresh ground meat, liver, and kidneys; use in one or two days. Frankfurters, bacon, and sliced sandwich meats can be stored in original wrappings in the refrigerator. Remember to always store all meat in the coldest part of the refrigerator.*

Relax — Eat Outdoors

There's no better place to enjoy the remaining days of summer than outdoors. Wake up to Italian Cinnamon Sticks, fresh fruit, and morning coffee served on the front porch or back terrace. Later, invite friends over for dreamy Almond-Fudge Ice Cream and Ginger Icebox Cookies. And make a date for a family get-together on the patio Saturday afternoon. Kids will love Berry Delicious Lemonade, while adults cool off with Apricot Slush. To complete the party, offer Shrimp Spread on crackers and Apple Dip with apple and pear wedges.

ITALIAN CINNAMON STICKS

¾ cup sugar
½ cup walnuts, ground
1 teaspoon ground cinnamon
1 cup butter or margarine, softened
1 (8-ounce) package cream cheese, softened
2½ cups all-purpose flour
1 large egg, lightly beaten

Combine first 3 ingredients in a small bowl; set aside.

Beat butter and cream cheese at medium speed with an electric mixer until creamy; gradually add flour, mixing until well blended. Shape dough into a ball; wrap in plastic wrap, and chill 30 minutes.

Divide dough in half; place 1 portion between 2 sheets of lightly floured wax paper, and roll into a 10-inch square (about ⅛ inch thick). Brush with egg; sprinkle with half of sugar mixture. Cut into 5- x ½-inch strips; twist strips, and place on ungreased baking sheets. Repeat procedure with remaining dough and sugar mixture.

Bake at 350° for 10 to 12 minutes or until golden. Remove to wire racks to cool. Yield: about 6½ dozen.
Ellie Wells
Lakeland, Florida

ALMOND-FUDGE ICE CREAM

1½ cups sugar
½ cup cocoa
¼ teaspoon salt
1 quart milk, divided
2 large eggs, lightly beaten
3 cups whipping cream
¾ cup slivered almonds, toasted
  and chopped
¼ to ½ teaspoon almond extract
Garnish: slivered almonds, toasted

Combine first 3 ingredients in a large, heavy saucepan. Combine 2 cups milk and eggs; stir into sugar mixture. Cook over medium heat, stirring constantly, until mixture thickens and coats a metal spoon (about 10 minutes). Stir in remaining 2 cups milk; cool chocolate mixture completely.

Combine chocolate mixture, whipping cream, almonds, and almond extract in freezer container of a 1-gallon hand-turned or electric freezer. Freeze according to manufacturer's instructions. Spoon into a 13- x 9- x 2-inch pan; cover and freeze. Garnish, if desired. Yield: about 2 quarts.

Rublelene Singleton
Scotts Hill, Tennessee

GINGER ICEBOX COOKIES

1 cup butter or margarine, softened
1 cup sugar
4½ cups all-purpose flour
1 teaspoon baking soda
1 teaspoon ground ginger
1 teaspoon ground cinnamon
1 cup molasses
¼ cup water

Beat butter at medium speed with an electric mixer until creamy; gradually add sugar, beating well. Combine flour and next 3 ingredients; add to butter mixture alternately with molasses and water. (Dough will be very soft.) Cover and chill 2 hours.

Divide dough into 4 equal portions; shape into 9-inch rolls, and wrap each in wax paper. Freeze at least 2 hours.

Cut dough into ¼-inch-thick slices, and place on lightly greased cookie sheets. Bake at 350° for 10 to 12 minutes. Cool 3 minutes on cookie sheets. Transfer to wire racks to cool completely. Yield: 10 dozen.

Joy Knight Allard
San Antonio, Texas

BERRY DELICIOUS LEMONADE

1 to 1½ cups strawberries,
  sliced
1 cup fresh lemon juice (about 6
  lemons)
1 to 1¼ cups sugar
4 cups cold water
Ice cubes
1 lemon, sliced (optional)

Combine first 3 ingredients in container of an electric blender; process until smooth. Pour strawberry mixture into a large pitcher; stir in cold water, ice, and lemon slices, if desired. Yield: 7 cups.

Peggy Fowler Revels
Woodruff, South Carolina

APRICOT SLUSH

1 (46-ounce) can apricot nectar
1 (46-ounce) can unsweetened
  pineapple juice
1 (6-ounce) can frozen orange
  juice concentrate, thawed and
  undiluted
1 (6-ounce) can frozen lemonade
  concentrate, thawed and
  undiluted
1 cup vodka
1 cup apricot brandy
2 (2-liter) bottles lemon-lime
  carbonated beverage, chilled

Combine first 6 ingredients in a 4-quart plastic container; freeze.

To serve, spoon about 1 cup frozen mixture into each large glass; add 1 cup carbonated beverage to each glass, and stir gently. Yield: 16 servings.

Teenya Blanchard
Arlington, Texas

APPLE DIP

1 (8-ounce) package cream cheese,
  softened
⅓ cup firmly packed brown sugar
¼ cup sugar
1 teaspoon vanilla extract
1 (6-ounce) package almond brickle
  chips

Combine cream cheese and brown sugar, mixing well; let stand 15 minutes. Stir in sugar, vanilla, and almond brickle chips. Cover and chill up to 8 hours. Serve with apple and pear wedges. Yield: 2½ cups.

Everette Milford
Commerce, Georgia

SHRIMP SPREAD

1 (8-ounce) package cream cheese,
  softened
1 (4¼-ounce) can shrimp, drained
  and chopped
6 pimiento-stuffed olives, chopped
2 tablespoons finely chopped onion
2 tablespoons mayonnaise or salad
  dressing
1 teaspoon lemon juice
¼ teaspoon Worcestershire sauce
¼ teaspoon hot sauce
⅛ teaspoon garlic powder

Combine all ingredients; spread on bread or crackers. Yield: 1⅔ cups.

DeLea Lonadier
Montgomery, Louisiana

Tip: *When preparing a recipe, always try to follow directions carefully. Avoid substituting items; for example, don't use soft margarine for butter or margarine, or whipped cream cheese for cream cheese.*

Garden-Fresh Fare

If you've ever tended a vegetable garden, you know the joy of eating the fruits of your labor. Any gardener will tell you that there's nothing finer than homegrown vegetables savored within hours of harvesting. Take advantage of the seasonal bounty with our crop of recipes.

GREEN SALAD WITH MARINATED CHEESE DRESSING

½ cup olive oil
¼ cup red wine vinegar
1 clove garlic, minced
1 teaspoon dried thyme
½ teaspoon salt
¼ teaspoon pepper
1 (8-ounce) package mozzarella cheese, cubed
4 cups mixed salad greens
4 green onions, sliced
3 small tomatoes, cut into wedges
1 cucumber, sliced
1 small sweet red pepper, cut into thin strips
½ cup chopped fresh basil

Combine first 6 ingredients in a 1-quart jar; cover tightly, and shake vigorously. Add mozzarella cheese, and shake; refrigerate 8 hours. Just before serving, drain cheese, reserving dressing.
Combine salad greens and remaining ingredients in a large salad bowl; drizzle with reserved dressing, and add cheese, tossing gently. Yield: 6 servings.

ZUCCHINI-TOMATO SKILLET

1 onion, chopped
¼ cup butter or margarine, melted
4 medium zucchini, sliced (about 1¾ pounds)
¼ pound fresh mushrooms, sliced
3 medium tomatoes, sliced (about 1 pound)
3 tablespoons chopped fresh parsley
¼ cup grated Parmesan cheese
1½ teaspoons chopped fresh basil or ½ teaspoon dried basil
¼ teaspoon salt
¼ teaspoon pepper
⅛ teaspoon garlic powder
1 cup (4 ounces) shredded Cheddar cheese

Cook onion in butter in a large skillet over medium-high heat, stirring constantly, until tender. Add zucchini and mushrooms; cook 5 minutes or until crisp-tender, stirring often. Add tomatoes; cook 1 minute, stirring often. Drain vegetables, and return to skillet; gently stir in parsley and next 5 ingredients. Cook 1 minute or until thoroughly heated. Remove skillet from heat. Sprinkle with cheese; cover and let stand 3 to 5 minutes or until cheese melts. Serve immediately. Yield: 6 servings.

Mary Lanning
Spring, Texas

GREEN BEANS IN SHERRIED MUSHROOM SAUCE

2 pounds fresh green beans
1 cup water
2 tablespoons butter or margarine
¼ cup finely chopped onion
1 clove garlic, minced
½ pound fresh mushrooms, thinly sliced
2 tablespoons all-purpose flour
1 teaspoon salt
¼ teaspoon pepper
½ cup beef broth
½ cup whipping cream
2 tablespoons dry sherry

Wash beans, and remove ends. Bring 1 cup water to a boil in a large saucepan; add beans. Cover, reduce heat, and cook 8 minutes or until tender. Drain and keep warm.
Melt butter in a medium saucepan over medium heat; add onion and garlic, and cook, stirring constantly, 5 minutes. Add mushrooms, and cook until tender, stirring often. Stir in flour, salt, and pepper; cook, stirring constantly, 1 minute. Gradually add beef broth and whipping cream; cook, stirring constantly, until mixture thickens. Add sherry; cook 2 minutes. Add beans, tossing to coat. Serve immediately. Yield: 8 servings.

Mrs. Robert W. Meyer
Seminole, Florida

Get the Most from Your Vegetables

■ Freshen wilted vegetables by letting them stand 10 minutes in cold water to which a few drops of lemon juice have been added; drain. Store the vegetables in a zip-top plastic bag in refrigerator.

■ Use leftover vegetables in a cream sauce served over a plain omelet, in fritter batter, or tossed with French dressing for a delicious salad.

STIR-FRIED SWEET PEPPERS
WITH TOMATOES

4 green peppers, coarsely chopped
⅓ cup olive oil
4 cloves garlic, sliced
3 large tomatoes, peeled and
     coarsely chopped
½ teaspoon salt
½ teaspoon pepper

Cook green peppers in olive oil in a large skillet over medium heat 10 minutes or until lightly browned, stirring often. Add garlic; cook 1 minute. Stir in tomatoes, salt, and pepper; cook 15 minutes or until slightly thickened, stirring often. Yield: 4 servings.

Barbara Carson
Tifton, Georgia

From Our Kitchen To Yours

Determining the percentage of fat in food products can be confusing. If you experience this same frustration and are confused by misleading nutrition labels, take heart. The Food and Drug Administration has come to our rescue. Revised, more informative, and easier-to-read nutrition labels are beginning to show up on many food products. This new information will be required on almost all packaged foods by May 1994.

As you look over this sample nutrition panel, you'll notice the FDA's new labeling requirements address today's health concerns by listing "daily values" for nutrients such as fat, cholesterol, sodium, fiber, and sugars. These percentages show how a particular food fits into your daily diet, especially if you're counting fat grams or watching your cholesterol and sodium.

The food labels also give standardized serving sizes and consistent definitions for terms such as "light," "low fat," "low calorie," "lean," and "high fiber."

The New Food Label at a Glance

The new food label will carry an up-to-date, easier-to-use nutrition information guide, to be required on almost all packaged foods (compared to about 60 percent of products up till now). The guide will serve as a key to help in planning a healthy diet.*

Serving sizes are now more consistent across product lines, stated in both household and metric measures, and reflect the amounts people actually eat.

New title signals that the label contains the newly required information.

Calories from fat are now shown on the label to help consumers meet dietary guidelines that recommend people get no more than 30 percent of their calories from fat.

Nutrition Facts

Serving Size ½ cup (114g)
Servings Per Container 4

Amount Per Serving

Calories 90   Calories from Fat 30

	% Daily Value*
Total Fat 3g	5%
Saturated Fat 0g	0%
Cholesterol 0mg	0%
Sodium 300mg	13%
Total Carbohydrate 13g	4%
Dietary Fiber 3g	12%
Sugars 3g	
Protein 3g	

Vitamin A	80%	Vitamin C	60%
Calcium	4%	Iron	4%

* Percent Daily Values are based on a 2,000 calorie diet. Your daily values may be higher or lower depending on your calorie needs:

		Calories	2,000	2,500
Total Fat	Less than		65g	80g
Sat Fat	Less than		20g	25g
Cholesterol	Less than		300mg	300mg
Sodium	Less than		2,400mg	2,400mg
Total Carbohydrate			300g	375g
Fiber			25g	30g

Calories per gram:
Fat 9   •   Carbohydrate 4   •   Protein 4

% Daily Value shows how a food fits into the overall daily diet.

Daily Values are also something new. Some are maximums, as with fat (65 grams <u>or</u> <u>less</u>); others are minimums, as with carbohydrate (300 grams <u>or more</u>). The daily values for a 2,000- and 2,500-calorie diet must be listed on the label of larger packages. Individuals should adjust the values to fit their own calorie intake.

The **list of nutrients** covers those most important to the health of today's consumers, most of whom need to worry about getting <u>too much</u> of certain items (fat, for example), rather than too few vitamins or minerals, as in the past.

The label of larger packages must now tell the number of calories per gram of fat, carbohydrate, and protein.

* This label is only a sample. Exact specifications are in the final rules.
Source: Food and Drug Administration 1993

Descriptors: While descriptive terms like "low," "good source," and "free" have long been used on food labels, their meaning — and their usefulness in helping consumers plan a healthy diet — have been murky. Now FDA has set specific definitions for these terms, assuring shoppers that they can believe what they read on the package:
•free   •high
•light   •low
•more   •reduced
•good source •less
For fish, meat and poultry:
•lean
•extra lean

Ingredients still will be listed in descending order by weight, and now the list will be required on almost all foods, even standardized ones like mayonnaise and bread.

Health claim message referred to on the front panel is shown here.

Health Claims: For the first time, food labels will be allowed to carry information about the link between certain nutrients and specific diseases. For such a "health claim" to be made on a package, FDA must first determine that the diet-disease link is supported by scientific evidence. At this time, FDA is allowing seven specific claims about the relationships between:

•fat and cancer risk
•saturated fat and cholesterol and heart disease risk
•calcium and osteoporosis risk
•sodium and hypertension risk
•fruits, vegetables and grains that contain soluble fiber and heart disease risk
•fiber-containing grain products, fruits and vegetables and cancer risk
•fruits and vegetables and cancer risk

FROZEN MIXED VEGETABLES
— IN SAUCE —

Low Fat
• Cholesterol Free
• Good Source of Fiber
See back panel for nutrition information.

[See back panel for message on saturated fat and cholesterol and heart disease.]

NET WT. 8.9 oz. (252 g)

Ingredients: Broccoli, carrots, green beans, water chestnuts, soybean oil, milk solids, modified cornstarch, salt, spices.

"While many factors affect heart disease, diets low in saturated fat and cholesterol may reduce the risk of this disease."

Source: Food and Drug Administration 1993

You Bring The Entrée, I'll Do The Rest

Remember when having someone over for dinner was so easy? Family and close friends would bring their own steaks for grilling. The host or hostess would prepare the salad and a side dish to complete the meal.

Today's version of that carefree cookout often features chicken, pork, turkey, or seafood. And the side dishes and salads may be a little fancier. These salads are drizzled with homemade vinaigrettes, and dressed up with sweet red peppers or feta cheese and olives. The potatoes are mashed and seasoned with lemon and herbs. But the dinner is still a breeze.

PARMESAN PEPPER TOSS

1 small sweet red pepper, cut into thin strips
1 small green pepper, cut into thin strips
1 small purple onion, thinly sliced and separated into rings
¼ pound fresh mushrooms, sliced
1 cup thinly sliced celery
¼ cup olive oil
2 tablespoons chopped fresh parsley
2 tablespoons red wine vinegar
½ teaspoon minced garlic
¼ teaspoon salt
¼ teaspoon freshly ground pepper
Leaf lettuce
½ cup freshly grated Parmesan cheese

Combine first 5 ingredients in a large bowl; set aside. Combine olive oil and next 5 ingredients; pour over vegetables, tossing gently. Serve in a lettuce-lined dish, and sprinkle with Parmesan cheese. Yield: 4 to 6 servings.
Sue-Sue Hartstern
Louisville, Kentucky

GREEK SALAD

3 large cucumbers, peeled, seeded, and cubed
3 large tomatoes, cut into thin wedges
1 large onion, chopped
1 (10-ounce) jar peperoncini salad peppers, drained
1 (7-ounce) package feta cheese, crumbled
10 to 15 Greek black olives
½ cup olive oil
½ teaspoon dried oregano
¼ teaspoon salt
¼ teaspoon freshly ground pepper
1 large head romaine lettuce, torn

Combine first 10 ingredients; cover and chill at least 1 hour. Just before serving, toss vegetable mixture with romaine. Yield: 6 to 8 servings.
Barbara Buell
Richmond, Virginia

HERBED LEMON MASHED POTATOES

4 large baking potatoes, peeled and sliced (about 2¾ pounds)
1 tablespoon butter or margarine
⅓ cup chopped onion
1 clove garlic, minced
¾ cup sour cream
1 teaspoon grated lemon rind
1 tablespoon lemon juice
1¼ teaspoons salt
1 teaspoon dried dillweed
¼ teaspoon ground red pepper
Paprika

Cook potatoes in boiling water to cover 10 minutes or until tender; drain and mash.

Melt butter in a small skillet. Add onion and garlic, and cook over medium heat, stirring constantly, until tender. Stir onion mixture, sour cream, and next 5 ingredients into potatoes. Spoon into a lightly greased 2-quart shallow casserole; sprinkle with paprika. Cover and chill up to 8 hours. To serve, let stand at room temperature 30 minutes; bake at 350° for 25 minutes or until thoroughly heated. Yield: 4 to 6 servings.
Sandi Pichon
Slidell, Louisiana

STUFFED GREEN CHILES

2 (4-ounce) cans whole green chiles
1 cup (4 ounces) shredded sharp Cheddar cheese, divided
1 large egg
¼ cup milk
Dash of dry mustard

Carefully slit chiles lengthwise; wash and remove seeds. Drain on paper towels. Spoon 1 to 2 tablespoons cheese into each chile; arrange, spoke-fashion, in a lightly greased 9-inch pieplate. Combine egg, milk, and mustard; pour over chiles. Bake at 350° for 15 minutes; add remaining cheese, and bake an additional 5 minutes or until set. Yield: 6 servings.
Denise T. Raney
Albany, Georgia

SEPTEMBER

Fall is truly a golden time in the South. Kicking off this special season is football and that signals food and fun. And what comes into play more than food fit for tailgating — and railgating, a new twist on the theme. Our recipes for pregame and postgame festivities are sure to win fans. We know how well peanuts score as a snack, so in this chapter we offer recipes featuring the versatile nut as a serious ingredient in a marinade, slaw, and yeast bread. Fruit desserts are the stars of autumn. We encase apples and pears in delicate, flaky pastry and bake them to a rich golden hue. On a lighter note, our flavor-filled, no-cholesterol cobbler with raspberries and cherries just may be better than Grandma's.

The Whole Fruit

Fall is the time for apples and pears. Whether hanging from a bough or piled high in baskets and bushels at the produce stand, these are some of autumn's most prized fruits.

And what versatile ones they are. Bite into a ripe apple and the crunch echoes in your ears; when baked or poached, it becomes pudding in a skin. And the shape of a roly-poly pear certainly belies its fragile flavor.

The wide variety of apples and pears perfectly mirrors the many hues of autumn. Some selections are more suitable for cooking than others, so choose your fruits with care.

Take advantage of abundant fall fruit, and try these eye-popping dishes that only *look* extravagant. They're inexpensive and easy to make—and they'll leave you filled with old-fashioned contentment.

PEARS EN CROÛTE
(pictured on page 226)

2 (15-ounce) packages refrigerated
  piecrusts
5 or 6 firm ripe pears, unpeeled
  (about 2 pounds)
1 egg yolk
1 tablespoon water
Caramel Sauce
Garnish: fresh mint leaves

Unfold piecrusts, one at a time; place on a lightly floured surface, and roll each into a 10-inch square. Cut each square into 1-inch strips. Starting at bottom of pear, carefully begin wrapping with 1 pastry strip, overlapping strip ¼ inch as you cover pear. Continue wrapping by moistening ends of strips with water and joining to previous strip until pear is completely covered. Repeat procedure with remaining pears and pastry strips. Place pears on a baking sheet. Combine egg yolk and water; brush evenly on pastry. Bake at 350° for 1 hour or until tender.

Spoon 2 to 3 tablespoons Caramel Sauce onto each dessert plate; top with a pear. Garnish, if desired. Yield: 5 or 6 servings.

Note: To make ahead, wrap pears in pastry; cover tightly with plastic wrap, and refrigerate 8 hours. Remove plastic wrap; brush with egg yolk mixture, and bake as directed.

Caramel Sauce

1 (12-ounce) jar caramel ice cream
  topping
1 (14-ounce) can sweetened
  condensed milk
2 tablespoons lemon juice
¼ cup Cointreau or other orange-
  flavored liqueur

Combine caramel topping and milk in top of a double boiler; bring water to a boil. Reduce heat to low; cook, stirring constantly, until smooth. Stir in lemon juice and Cointreau. Yield: 2½ cups.   *Jane Micol Schatzman*
Winston-Salem, North Carolina

SUGAR-CRUSTED APPLES IN WALNUT-PHYLLO BASKETS
(pictured on page 227)

¼ cup lemon juice
2 cups water
6 large Granny Smith apples,
  peeled and cored
⅔ cup sugar
⅓ cup all-purpose flour
½ teaspoon ground cinnamon
⅓ cup butter or margarine
1 large egg, lightly beaten
1¼ to 1½ cups orange juice,
  divided
Walnut-Phyllo Baskets
Sifted powdered sugar
Garnish: fresh mint leaves

Combine lemon juice and water in a large bowl; add apples, tossing to coat well, and set aside.

Combine sugar, flour, and cinnamon; cut in butter with a pastry blender until mixture is crumbly.

Drain apples, and pat dry. Brush top half of each apple with egg, and dredge in sugar mixture; place apples in a lightly greased 13- x 9- x 2-inch baking dish.

Spoon remaining sugar mixture into apple cavities. Pour ¾ cup orange juice over apples. Bake at 350° for 1 hour or until tender. Remove apples, reserving pan drippings in baking dish. Place each apple in a Walnut-Phyllo Basket. Gradually add enough of remaining ½ to ¾ cup orange juice to pan drippings, stirring constantly, until sauce is desired consistency; spoon over apples. Sprinkle with sifted powdered sugar, and garnish, if desired. Serve immediately. Yield: 6 servings.

Walnut-Phyllo Baskets

1¼ cups finely chopped walnuts
⅓ cup sugar
1¼ teaspoons grated lemon rind
1 teaspoon ground cinnamon
12 sheets frozen phyllo pastry,
  thawed
Vegetable cooking spray

Combine first 4 ingredients in a small bowl; set aside.

Place phyllo sheets on a damp towel. Using kitchen shears, cut phyllo lengthwise in half, and cut each portion crosswise in half, forming 48 rectangles. Place rectangles on a damp towel. (Keep remaining phyllo covered with a damp towel.) Spray 6 rectangles with cooking spray, and place 1 rectangle in each lightly greased 10-ounce custard cup. Repeat procedure 3 times, placing each rectangle at alternating angles.

Spoon about 1½ tablespoons walnut mixture into each shell; top each with 2 phyllo rectangles coated with cooking spray, alternating angles. Repeat procedure with remaining walnut mixture and phyllo rectangles. Bake at 350° for 20 to 25 minutes or until golden. Gently remove shells from custard cups, and cool on wire racks. Yield: 6 baskets.

Note: To store any leftover thawed phyllo, wrap phyllo sheets in plastic wrap, and place in an airtight container; refreeze.   *Linda Magers*
Clemmons, North Carolina

Praise The Peanut

The peanut is one of the most versatile plants on earth. From nut to shell, every part is put to use. Its shells are compressed to form fireplace logs and wallboard; its oil is used in creams and medicinal salves. But the finest use, few would argue, is as the answer to a nibbler's prayer.

Peanuts are the traditional snack in circus tents, at baseball and football games, and on airplane flights. And in the form of peanut butter, they are the base of most children's first and favorite sandwich.

Passion for the peanut runs deep in the South, where eight states combine to grow 99% of the U.S. peanut crop. "Peanuts are the heartbeat of the Southern soil," says Pat Cook of the National Peanut Festival's Board of Directors in Dothan, Alabama. "We celebrate the peanut here."

The peanut probably has more aliases than any other vegetable. But whether you call it the goober, groundnut pea, or guinea seed, the peanut is a powerhouse of protein, containing a whopping 26%.

Today the peanut takes its place as a serious cooking ingredient. In creative American dishes, as well as foreign foods, peanuts add distinctive flavor and texture to an endless variety of recipes.

So crack open that shell and take a fresh look at this modest little legume.

PEANUT LOVER'S BREAD
(pictured on page 225)

1 package active dry yeast
¼ cup warm water (105° to 115°)
¾ cup buttermilk
3 cups all-purpose flour, divided
¾ teaspoon baking powder
¼ teaspoon baking soda
¾ teaspoon salt
¼ cup sugar
¼ cup peanut oil
¼ cup butter or margarine, softened
Peanut Filling
Butter-flavored cooking spray

Combine yeast and warm water in a 1-cup liquid measuring cup; let stand 5 minutes. Heat buttermilk in a small saucepan; cool to 105° to 115°. Combine 2 cups flour and next 5 ingredients in a large bowl. Add yeast mixture and buttermilk; beat at medium speed with an electric mixer 1 to 2 minutes. Stir in remaining 1 cup flour. Place dough in a greased bowl, turning to grease top. Cover and refrigerate 8 hours.

Punch dough down; turn out onto a floured surface, and knead until smooth and elastic (about 5 minutes). Roll dough into a 16- x 12-inch rectangle; spread with butter, and sprinkle with Peanut Filling, lightly pressing into dough. Cut into 3 (4- x 16-inch) pieces; fold each portion lengthwise in half over filling, pinching seams together to form ropes. Place ropes, seam side down, on a greased

baking sheet (do not stretch); pinch rope ends together at one end to seal. Braid ropes; pinch loose ends to seal, and tuck under. Lightly spray braid with cooking spray. Cover and let rise in a warm place (85°), free from drafts, 45 to 60 minutes or until dough is doubled in bulk. Bake at 375° for 20 to 25 minutes or until golden. Yield: 1 loaf.

Peanut Filling

¾ cup finely chopped unsalted peanuts
⅓ cup crushed commercial French fried onions
3 tablespoons commercial real bacon bits
2 teaspoons poppy seeds
2 tablespoons grated Parmesan cheese
¼ teaspoon garlic powder
1 egg white, lightly beaten

Combine all ingredients, stirring well. Yield: 1¼ cups.   *June Kilgore*
Dothan, Alabama

HOT INDONESIAN PEANUT SAUCE

2 cloves garlic, chopped
2 tablespoons peanut oil
2 tablespoons soy sauce
2 tablespoons water
1½ tablespoons lemon juice
½ cup creamy peanut butter
1 tablespoon brown sugar
2¼ teaspoons cornstarch
1 teaspoon crushed red pepper
¼ teaspoon ground cumin
¼ teaspoon ground ginger

Combine all ingredients in container of an electric blender; process until smooth, stopping once to scrape down sides. Pour over chicken or beef, and refrigerate 1 hour before grilling. Yield: 1 cup.

SPINACH-PEANUT PESTO AND PASTA

2 cups tightly packed fresh spinach, coarsely chopped
1 cup dry-roasted peanuts
2 cloves garlic, halved
¼ teaspoon salt
¼ teaspoon freshly ground pepper
½ cup peanut oil
½ cup water
16 ounces linguine, uncooked
¼ cup coarsely chopped dry-roasted peanuts

Position knife blade in food processor bowl; add first 5 ingredients, and process until smooth, stopping once to scrape down sides. With processor running, gradually add peanut oil and water through food chute in a slow, steady stream; process pesto mixture until smooth.

Cook linguine according to package directions; drain. Spoon pesto mixture over linguine; toss gently, and sprinkle with chopped peanuts. Serve immediately. Yield: 8 servings.

SWEET POTATOES WITH PEANUT CRUST

2 medium sweet potatoes (about 1½ pounds)
½ cup orange juice
2 tablespoons honey
1 teaspoon finely chopped fresh gingerroot
½ teaspoon salt
¼ teaspoon ground red pepper
½ cup finely chopped salted peanuts
¼ cup coarsely chopped fresh parsley
1 tablespoon sesame seeds
Garnishes: orange rind strips, fresh parsley sprigs

Bake sweet potatoes at 400° for 30 minutes. Let cool to touch; peel potatoes, and slice ½ inch thick.

Combine orange juice and next 4 ingredients in a shallow dish; set aside. Combine peanuts, parsley, and sesame seeds in a shallow dish. Dip sweet potato slices into orange juice mixture, and dredge lightly in peanut mixture. Place in a single layer on a lightly greased baking sheet; bake at 375° for 15 to 20 minutes or until tender. Garnish, if desired. Yield: 4 servings.
Steven Petusevsky
Coral Springs, Florida

CHINESE PEANUT SLAW

1 (3-ounce) package chicken-flavored Ramen noodles
⅓ cup peanut oil
3 tablespoons rice wine vinegar
2 tablespoons sugar
1 small cabbage, shredded (about 1½ pounds)
½ cup sliced green onions
1 cup dry-roasted peanuts
¼ cup sesame seeds, toasted

Remove seasoning packet from noodles; set aside. Break noodles into pieces; place in a shallow baking pan. Bake at 400° for 5 minutes or until golden, stirring once; set aside.

Combine seasoning packet, peanut oil, vinegar, and sugar in a small bowl; beat with a wire whisk until well blended. Cover and chill.

Just before serving, combine dressing, cabbage, and remaining ingredients, tossing well. Sprinkle with toasted noodles. Yield: 8 to 10 servings.
Mary Catherine Crowe
Birmingham, Alabama

PEANUT TRUFFLE COOKIES

1 cup peanut butter morsels
½ cup semisweet chocolate morsels
¼ cup sifted powdered sugar
¼ cup finely chopped salted peanuts
3 cups all-purpose flour
1¼ cups butter or margarine, softened
1 tablespoon vanilla extract
1 cup sifted powdered sugar

Combine peanut butter and chocolate morsels in top of a double boiler; bring water to a boil. Reduce heat to low; cook until morsels melt. Remove from heat, and stir in ¼ cup powdered sugar and peanuts. Let stand at room temperature 30 minutes or until mixture is firm enough to make into balls. (Do not refrigerate.) Make into ¾-inch balls, and let stand until firm.

Combine flour, butter, and vanilla in a large mixing bowl; beat at medium speed with an electric mixer until blended. Shape dough into a 10-inch log; cut into ¼-inch slices. Gently press a dough slice around each ball; place on ungreased cookie sheets. Bake at 375° for 18 minutes or until cookies are lightly browned. Remove to wire racks to cool slightly. Roll in 1 cup powdered sugar, and cool completely on wire racks. Yield: about 3 dozen.
Zita Wilensky
Miami Shores, Florida

Drink To Your Health

If your body thirsts for quick refreshment after a strenuous exercise session, try one of our fruity drinks. They take less than five minutes to prepare; so drink up, and feel your energy revive.

TROPICAL SHAKE

1 mango, peeled and chopped
1 banana, peeled and sliced
⅓ cup water
2 ice cubes

Freeze fruit 1 hour. Combine all ingredients in container of an electric blender; process until smooth, stopping once to scrape down sides. Serve immediately. Yield: 2 cups.

FROZEN STRAWBERRY REFRESHER

1 (10-ounce) can frozen strawberry
  daiquiri mix
1 cup orange juice
Ice cubes

Combine daiquiri mix and orange juice in container of an electric blender; add enough ice to bring mixture to 5-cup level. Process until mixture is slushy. Serve immediately. Yield: 5 cups.

Delana Smith
Birmingham, Alabama

JOGGER'S SUNRISE

1 cup orange juice
¼ cup lime juice
2 tablespoons honey
⅛ teaspoon coconut
  extract
Ice cubes

Combine orange juice, lime juice, honey, and coconut extract in container of an electric blender; process until smooth. Add enough ice cubes to bring mixture to 2½-cup level; process until smooth, stopping once to scrape down sides. Serve immediately. Yield: 2½ cups.

Labor Day Easy Grillin'

Relax, Labor Day is a holiday in honor of working people. Here's a menu to celebrate this day of leisure. The layered coleslaw, marinated chicken breasts, and frozen dessert can be prepared in advance. All you have to do is cut, season, and wrap the potatoes; then head out to the grill. While the potatoes and chicken cook, sit back, sip on a tall, cool glass of lemonade, and chat with friends.

LABOR DAY MENU FOR SIX

Commercial chips and salsa
Grilled Jalapeño Chicken
Grilled Sweet Potatoes
Layered Slaw
Caramel-Toffee Bombe
Commercial rolls
Iced tea

GRILLED JALAPEÑO CHICKEN

6 chicken breast halves,
  skinned
½ cup freshly squeezed lime
  juice (about 4 limes)
¼ cup honey
2 tablespoons fresh cilantro
  leaves
3 jalapeño peppers, unseeded
  and sliced
2 tablespoons soy sauce
3 cloves garlic, chopped
¼ teaspoon salt
¼ teaspoon pepper

Place chicken in a 13- x 9- x 2-inch dish, and set aside.

Combine lime juice and remaining ingredients in container of an electric blender; process until smooth. Reserve ¼ cup marinade, and pour remaining amount over chicken, turning to coat. Cover and refrigerate reserved marinade and chicken 8 hours.

Prepare charcoal fire in one end of grill; let burn 15 to 20 minutes or until flames disappear. Place a pan of water opposite the coals. Drain chicken, and place on food rack over pan of water; cook, with grill lid closed, 30 minutes. Turn chicken, and brush with reserved marinade; cook an additional 25 to 30 minutes or until done. Yield: 6 servings.

GRILLED SWEET POTATOES

3 medium sweet potatoes (about
  2¼ pounds)
⅓ cup butter or margarine
¼ cup firmly packed brown sugar
1 tablespoon ground cinnamon

Wash potatoes, and pat dry; cut in half lengthwise. Place each half in center of a 12- x 10-inch piece of aluminum foil; dot evenly with butter. Combine brown sugar and cinnamon; sprinkle evenly over potatoes. Wrap well, and place on food rack. Cook, without grill lid, over hot coals (400° to 500°) for 25 to 30 minutes or until done, turning foil packets once. Yield: 6 servings.

Bill Duke
Atlanta, Georgia

Make It Even Easier

■ Replace Grilled Sweet Potatoes with plain baked potatoes—either sweet or Irish.
■ Serve commercial cookies and ice cream topped with caramel sauce and toasted nuts instead of Caramel-Toffee Bombe.
■ Substitute a commercial slaw mixture and vinaigrette dressing for Layered Slaw.
■ Buy thinly shredded cabbage available at most grocery store produce departments. Use to make "homemade" slaw.
■ Keep the mood casual; serve on paper plates.

LAYERED SLAW

1 medium sweet onion, sliced
1 small cabbage, shredded
2 tomatoes, cut into thin
   wedges
1 cucumber, halved and sliced
1 small yellow pepper, cut into
   thin strips
1 (4-ounce) can sliced ripe olives,
   drained
¾ cup crumbled feta cheese
⅔ cup olive oil
⅓ cup red wine vinegar
2 cloves garlic, minced
1 teaspoon ground cumin
½ teaspoon salt
¼ teaspoon pepper

Cut each onion slice in half, and separate into half rings. Layer onion and next 6 ingredients in a large bowl; set aside. Combine olive oil and remaining ingredients in a jar. Cover tightly, and shake vigorously; pour over salad. Cover and refrigerate 8 hours. Toss and serve with a slotted spoon. Yield: 6 to 8 servings.

CARAMEL-TOFFEE BOMBE

1⅓ cups gingersnap cookie
   crumbs (about 20 cookies)
¼ cup butter or margarine,
   melted
1 quart vanilla ice cream,
   softened
4 (1.4-ounce) English toffee-
   flavored candy bars, crushed
Praline Sauce

Line a 2-quart bowl with heavy-duty plastic wrap. Set aside.
   Combine cookie crumbs and butter; press mixture into prepared bowl. Combine ice cream and crushed candy, and spoon into bowl. Cover and freeze at least 8 hours. To serve, let bowl stand at room temperature 5 minutes; invert onto a serving plate. Carefully remove bowl and plastic wrap. Cut into wedges, and serve immediately with warm Praline Sauce. Yield: 10 to 12 servings.

Praline Sauce

½ cup firmly packed brown
   sugar
½ cup half-and-half
¼ cup butter or margarine
¼ cup slivered almonds, toasted
   and chopped
1 teaspoon vanilla extract

Combine first 3 ingredients in a small saucepan; bring mixture to a boil over medium heat, stirring occasionally. Boil 2 minutes, stirring occasionally. Remove from heat; stir in almonds and vanilla. Yield: 1 cup.

Paula McCollum
Springtown, Texas

Railgating & Tailgating: USC Style

You just *think* you've seen it all. Diehard football fans flock to stadium parking lots weekend after weekend—setting up camp as though they'll never leave. They make themselves comfortable in vans, trailers, RVs, and even limos—but would you believe *railcars?* Ed Robinson sure did, and he was on the right track.
   Over the years of tailgating at Gamecock football at the University of South Carolina, the Columbia, South Carolina, developer grew weary of an abandoned rail spur near the stadium. He came across an article on cabooses headed for scrap piles, and he began to put two and two together. Now there are 22 refurbished "Cockabooses," stationary on the track.
   So how has this changed Gamecock football feasts? Ed's wife, Cathy, and other railgaters, still make favorite recipes from their tailgating days. No matter where you host your pregame or postgame festivities, their party spread is sure to bring cheers.

■ Mix beverage a day ahead, and chill. Transport in an ice chest or an insulated beverage container.

GAME-COCKTAILS

1½ cups red grapefruit juice drink
1½ cups apple-raspberry juice
½ to ¾ cup vodka
2 tablespoons grenadine

Combine all ingredients; chill. Serve over ice. Yield: 3½ cups.

■ Prepare recipe a day ahead; refrigerate. Transport, still in mold, in an ice chest. Pack asparagus and shrimp in separate zip-top plastic bags; keep cold in an ice chest. Unmold and assemble at serving time.

SHRIMP MOLD WITH ASPARAGUS

8 cups water
2½ pounds unpeeled medium-size
   fresh shrimp
1 pound fresh asparagus
1½ tablespoons unflavored
   gelatin
¼ cup cold water
1 (10¾-ounce) can cream of tomato
   soup, undiluted
1 (8-ounce) package cream cheese,
   softened
1 cup mayonnaise
¾ cup finely chopped green
   onions
¾ cup finely chopped celery
2 tablespoons lemon juice
¼ teaspoon salt
¼ teaspoon ground white pepper
Lettuce leaves

Bring 8 cups water to a boil; add shrimp, and cook 3 to 5 minutes or until shrimp turn pink. Drain and rinse with cold water. Peel and devein shrimp. Set aside 1 pound whole shrimp; cover and chill. Chop remaining shrimp; cover and refrigerate.
   Snap off tough ends of asparagus. Remove scales from stalks with a vegetable peeler, if desired. Cook asparagus, covered, in a small amount of

boiling water 6 minutes or until crisp-tender. Drain and plunge into cold water; drain. Cover and refrigerate.

Sprinkle gelatin over ¼ cup cold water in a large saucepan; let stand 1 minute. Cook over low heat; stir until gelatin dissolves (about 2 minutes). Add soup and cream cheese, stirring constantly until blended. Remove from heat; stir in mayonnaise. Chill until consistency of unbeaten egg white; fold in chopped shrimp, green onions, and next 4 ingredients.

Spoon into a lightly oiled 5-cup ring mold; cover and refrigerate 8 hours. Unmold onto a lettuce-lined tray; fill center of mold with asparagus and whole shrimp. Serve with crackers. Yield: 30 appetizer servings.

■ Make Gazpacho a day or two ahead; chill. Transport in an ice chest or an insulated beverage container.

GAZPACHO

6 medium tomatoes, peeled and chopped (3 cups)
1 cup chopped green pepper
1 cup peeled, seeded, and chopped cucumber
½ cup canned sliced or chopped beets
½ cup chopped celery
¼ cup chopped onion
2 cloves garlic, minced
1 cup beef consommé, undiluted
¼ cup red wine vinegar
¼ cup olive oil
2 tablespoons paprika
2 teaspoons salt
1 teaspoon dried basil
¼ teaspoon hot sauce

Place half of tomatoes in container of an electric blender; process until smooth, stopping once to scrape down sides. Gradually add half each of green pepper and next 5 ingredients; process until smooth. Add half each of consommé and next 6 ingredients; process until smooth. Transfer to a bowl. Repeat procedure with remaining ingredients. Cover and chill 8 hours. Yield: 9 cups.

■ Prepare chicken drumsticks the day before, and chill. Transport in an ice chest; serve cold.

LEMON BARBECUED CHICKEN

20 chicken drumsticks (about 3 pounds)
1½ cups vegetable oil
1 cup lemon juice
1½ tablespoons onion powder
1½ tablespoons dried basil
1 tablespoon salt
2 teaspoons paprika
1 teaspoon dried thyme
2 cloves garlic, pressed

Place chicken drumsticks in a heavy-duty, zip-top plastic bag; set aside. Combine oil and remaining ingredients in a jar. Cover and shake vigorously. Pour 2 cups over drumsticks; refrigerate remaining ½ cup mixture. Seal bag, and refrigerate 4 hours, turning occasionally.

Remove drumsticks from marinade, discarding marinade. Cook, covered with grill lid, over medium coals (300° to 350°) 15 minutes on each side, basting occasionally with reserved marinade. Yield: 8 to 10 servings.

Packing Pointers

■ Use an insulated cooler, and avoid transporting it in the trunk.

■ Include a cold source in the cooler. Use ice, commercial ice packs, frozen water or juice; seal in heavy-duty, zip-top plastic bags to avoid spillage.

■ Label each container to avoid confusion upon arrival.

■ Secure screw-top jars and bottles (for dressings and condiments) with tape.

■ Pack sealed containers on the bottom of the cooler, putting heavier items in first. Secure smaller items such as bottles and jars to prevent breakage.

■ Prepare tenderloin and sauce a day ahead; chill. Slice beef, and pack in an ice chest; serve cold. Slice French bread at serving time.

MARINATED BEEF TENDERLOIN

1 (5- to 6-pound) beef tenderloin, trimmed
2 (16-ounce) bottles zesty Italian salad dressing
⅓ cup Allegro meat and vegetable marinade or soy sauce
⅓ cup Burgundy or other dry red wine
1 teaspoon soy sauce
1 clove garlic, minced
½ teaspoon lemon-pepper marinade or lemon-pepper seasoning
Lettuce leaves
Horseradish Sauce

Place meat in a large shallow dish or heavy-duty, zip-top plastic bag. Combine salad dressing and next 5 ingredients, and pour over meat. Cover or seal, and refrigerate 8 hours, turning occasionally.

Drain, discarding marinade. Cook (on a gas grill), covered with grill lid, over high heat 3 minutes; turn and cook 3 minutes. Reduce heat to low, and cook, covered, 12 minutes or until a meat thermometer inserted in thickest portion registers 140° (rare). Let stand 15 minutes before slicing.

Place tenderloin on a lettuce-lined tray. Surround with Broccoli-Stuffed Tomatoes, if desired. Serve tenderloin with Horseradish Sauce and sliced French bread. Yield: 20 to 24 appetizer servings.

Horseradish Sauce

1 cup mayonnaise
1½ tablespoons prepared horseradish

Combine mayonnaise and horseradish. Serve in radicchio leaves with baby carrots, if desired. Yield: 1 cup.

■ Prepare and assemble stuffed tomatoes the day before, and transport in an ice chest. A time-saver: Instead of stuffing tomatoes, serve the filling warm as a dip for crackers, chips, or vegetables. Heat the dip in a fondue pot or chafing dish.

BROCCOLI-STUFFED TOMATOES

2 (10-ounce) packages frozen chopped broccoli, thawed and drained
1 (10¾-ounce) can cream of mushroom soup, undiluted
1 cup mayonnaise
1 cup (4 ounces) shredded sharp Cheddar cheese
2 large eggs, lightly beaten
1 tablespoon grated onion
6½ dozen cherry tomatoes

Combine first 6 ingredients; spoon into a greased 8-inch square baking dish. Bake at 350° for 50 minutes.
Slice top off each tomato; scoop out pulp with a melonballer or small spoon. Invert tomato shells on paper towels to drain. Spoon broccoli mixture into tomato shells. Serve warm or chilled. Yield: 6½ dozen.

■ Make brownies the day before; refrigerate. Transport in an ice chest to keep frosting from melting.

SOUTHERN CHOCOLATE-MINT BROWNIES
(pictured on page 228)

4 large eggs
2 cups sugar
1 cup all-purpose flour
1 cup cocoa
1 cup butter or margarine, melted
1 teaspoon vanilla extract
½ teaspoon peppermint extract
Mint Cream Frosting
3 (1-ounce) squares unsweetened chocolate
3 tablespoons butter or margarine

Beat eggs lightly with a wire whisk in a large bowl. Add sugar, and stir well.

Combine flour and cocoa; gradually stir into egg mixture. Stir in 1 cup butter and flavorings. Pour into a greased 15- x 10- x 1-inch jellyroll pan; bake at 350° for 15 to 18 minutes or until a wooden pick inserted in center comes out clean. Cool in pan on a wire rack.
Spread Mint Cream Frosting over brownie layer; freeze 15 minutes. Melt chocolate squares and 3 tablespoons butter in a heavy saucepan over low heat, stirring constantly, until melted. Spread over frosting with a pastry brush. Refrigerate until firm; cut into squares. Store in refrigerator. Yield: 2 dozen.

Mint Cream Frosting

¼ cup butter or margarine, softened
2¾ cups sifted powdered sugar
2 to 3 tablespoons milk
½ teaspoon peppermint extract
3 or 4 drops of green food coloring

Beat butter at medium speed with an electric mixer; gradually add powdered sugar, beating mixture after each addition. Add milk, and beat until mixture is spreading consistency. Stir in peppermint extract and food coloring. Yield: about 2 cups.

■ Make Chocolate Chewies a day ahead; store in an airtight container.

CHOCOLATE CHEWIES

1 teaspoon instant coffee granules
1 teaspoon hot water
3 egg whites
½ teaspoon vanilla extract
3 cups sifted powdered sugar
⅔ cup cocoa
2 tablespoons all-purpose flour
⅛ teaspoon salt
2 cups finely chopped pecans

Dissolve coffee granules in hot water in a small bowl; stir in egg whites and vanilla.
Combine powdered sugar and next 3 ingredients in a large mixing bowl.

Add egg white mixture, and beat at medium speed with an electric mixer until blended. Stir in pecans. Drop by rounded teaspoonfuls 1-inch apart onto greased and floured cookie sheets. Bake at 350° for 12 to 15 minutes. Remove to wire racks to cool. Yield: 4 dozen.

Seasoning Shortcuts Come In Packets

Need to find time to relax and read a best-seller or take a brisk walk? These recipes will help you sneak leisure time into busy days and still give your family a home-cooked meal. The secret for speeding through supper preparations is in thin envelopes filled with special seasoning blends. These mixes make recipes short on ingredients—not on flavor.

■ With this special blend of seasonings, you can create many variations with only one recipe. Substitute canned shrimp, crabmeat, or tuna for the canned chicken. For added flavor, you can stir in chopped onion or chopped dried tomatoes.

CHICKEN-CHEESE BALL

1 (5-ounce) can chunk chicken, drained
1 (0.4-ounce) envelope original Ranch-style salad dressing mix
2 (8-ounce) packages cream cheese, softened
1 cup pecans, chopped and toasted (optional)

Combine first 3 ingredients in a large mixing bowl; beat at medium speed with an electric mixer until blended. Shape into a ball, and roll in pecans, if desired. Cover and chill. Yield: 1 (4-inch) cheese ball. *Sharon McClatchey Muskogee, Oklahoma*

■ For a one-dish meal, add onions, sliced or quartered potatoes, and carrots to roast in the last 30 minutes of baking. Shred leftover beef for tacos, or roll in flour tortillas for burritos.

EASY RUMP ROAST

1 (4½-pound) boneless rump
  roast
1 (1-ounce) envelope onion soup
  mix
1 cup Burgundy or other dry red
  wine *

Place roast in a Dutch oven; sprinkle with soup mix, and pour in wine. Cover and bake at 325° for 2 hours or until tender. Yield: 8 to 10 servings.

* 1 cup beef broth may be substituted for Burgundy. *Sharron Kay Johnston Fort Worth, Texas*

■ Give the all-time favorite hamburger an extra boost with chili seasoning mix. For added ease, mix ground beef and seasonings, shape into patties, and freeze.

HAMBURGERS MEXICALI

2 pounds lean ground beef
1 tablespoon freeze-dried
  chives
1 (1¾-ounce) envelope chili
  seasoning mix
1 ripe avocado, peeled and
  cut into 16 slices (optional)

Combine first 3 ingredients; shape into 8 patties. Place patties on a lightly greased rack; place rack in broiler pan. Broil 4 inches from heat (with electric oven door partially opened) 10 to 12 minutes, turning once. Top each with 2 avocado slices, if desired, and serve immediately. Yield: 8 servings. *Velma Kestner Berwind, West Virginia*

■ Serve Potatoes au Gratin with Easy Rump Roast, a green salad, and some hot bread. To cook both dishes in the same oven, reduce baking temperature to 325°, and increase the potatoes' baking time to 45 minutes to 1 hour or until tender.

POTATOES AU GRATIN

4 medium potatoes, peeled and
  thinly sliced (about 1½ pounds)
1 teaspoon dried rosemary
¼ teaspoon pepper
1½ cups milk
1 (15/16-ounce) envelope chicken
  gravy mix
3 tablespoons grated Parmesan
  cheese

Place potatoes in a lightly greased 11- x 7- x 1½-inch baking dish. Sprinkle with rosemary and pepper. Combine milk and gravy mix; pour over potatoes. Sprinkle with Parmesan cheese. Bake at 400° for 30 minutes or until tender. Yield: 6 servings.

■ If you keep the ingredients for Hamburgers Mexicali and Skillet Barbecued Beans on hand, supper can be ready in 30 minutes.

SKILLET BARBECUED BEANS

½ pound ground pork sausage
½ cup chopped onion
¼ cup chopped green pepper
1 (28-ounce) can pork and
  beans
1 (3½-ounce) envelope barbecue-
  flavored seasoning and coating
  mix for pork

Cook first 3 ingredients in a large skillet until sausage browns, stirring until it crumbles; drain. Stir in beans and seasoning mix; cook over low heat 15 minutes, stirring occasionally. Yield: 6 servings.

Note: For barbecue-flavored seasoning and coating mix for pork, we used Shake-and-Bake. *Linda Tompkins Birmingham, Alabama*

Hold The Pickles, Hold The Onion

Nothing's quite as enticing as the aroma of a charcoal fire. One whiff and you have all the motivation needed to host a cookout. Whether you lean toward a carefully orchestrated occasion or something more spontaneous, a backyard burger bar is the perfect menu choice.

Instead of familiar condiments, treat your guests and yourself to some fresh flavor combinations: no-fuss vegetable relish, guacamole spiked with peppers and cilantro, or mushrooms simmered in Burgundy. These easy recipes are destined to become new favorites. Make a double batch of each, and you *might* have enough to enjoy later.

CREAMY RELISH SPREAD

1 (8-ounce) package cream cheese,
  softened
¼ cup catsup
¼ cup sweet pickle relish
¼ teaspoon salt

Combine all ingredients. Cover and chill. Yield: 1½ cups.
Sue-Sue Hartstern Louisville, Kentucky

SPICY GUACAMOLE

2 ripe avocados, peeled and
  chopped
3 tablespoons lemon juice
2 green onions, finely chopped
1 medium tomato, peeled and finely
  chopped
¼ cup chopped fresh cilantro
½ teaspoon garlic salt
¼ teaspoon Worcestershire sauce
⅛ teaspoon hot sauce
2 or 3 pickled jalapeño peppers,
  seeded and finely chopped
  (optional)
½ cup (2 ounces) shredded Cheddar
  cheese (optional)

Combine avocado and lemon juice,
stirring to coat; add green onions and
next 5 ingredients. Mash mixture with
a fork until blended (mixture will be
lumpy). If desired, stir in jalapeño
peppers and cheese. Yield: 1½ cups.
Suzy Thompson
Fort Worth, Texas

CARROT CHOWCHOW

3 cups finely chopped carrots
1 cup water
½ cup finely chopped green pepper
½ cup finely chopped sweet red
  pepper
¼ cup finely chopped onion
¼ cup red wine vinegar
3 tablespoons honey
¼ cup sugar
1 tablespoon all-purpose flour
½ teaspoon salt
¼ teaspoon dry mustard
¼ teaspoon celery salt

Combine carrots and water in a medium saucepan. Bring to a boil; cover,
reduce heat, and simmer 5 minutes or
until crisp-tender. Drain and return
carrots to saucepan. Add green pepper and next 4 ingredients.
  Combine sugar and remaining ingredients, and stir into carrot mixture.
Bring to a boil; cover, reduce heat,
and simmer 5 minutes. Cover and
chill. Yield: 3 cups.   *Leslie Genszler*
Roswell, Georgia

BLUE CHEESE
BURGER TOPPING

1 (4-ounce) package crumbled blue
  cheese
1 clove garlic, minced
1 tablespoon mayonnaise or salad
  dressing
1 tablespoon bourbon

Combine all ingredients; cover and
chill. Yield: ⅔ cup.

ZESTY MUSHROOMS

½ pound fresh mushrooms, sliced
½ medium-size green pepper, cut
  into strips
½ cup coarsely chopped onion
2 tablespoons butter or margarine,
  melted
½ cup Burgundy or other dry red
  wine
1½ tablespoons brown sugar
1½ tablespoons Dijon mustard
1 tablespoon Worcestershire sauce
⅛ teaspoon salt
Pinch of coarsely ground pepper

Cook first 3 ingredients in butter in a
large skillet over medium heat, stirring constantly, 6 minutes. Remove
vegetables from heat, and drain. Set
vegetables aside.
  Combine Burgundy and remaining
ingredients in skillet; bring to a boil
over medium heat. Cook until Burgundy mixture is reduced to ½ cup
(about 5 minutes), stirring occasionally. Stir in vegetables; cook 3 to 5
minutes or until thoroughly heated,
stirring occasionally. Serve warm.
Yield: about 2 cups.

Tip: *After buying fresh mushrooms,*
refrigerate in their original container.
If mushrooms are in a plastic bag,
make a few holes in the bag for venti-
lation. Depending on the condition
when purchased, fresh mushrooms can
be refrigerated 7 to 10 days.

Infuse Vinegar
With Basil

Snip the last of summer's basil, and
steep it in wine vinegar to add a jolt of
flavor to recipes calling for plain vinegar. The enhanced flavor can perk up
everything from vinaigrettes, slaws,
and salsas, to marinades and sauces.
Sprinkle the liquid on sliced fresh tomatoes, hot turnip greens, or green
beans; blend it with oil or mayonnaise,
and toss with chicken or seafood for a
main-dish salad.
  You can use any variety of fresh basil. Aroma and flavor range from peppery and robust to sweet and spicy.
For a color surprise, try one of the
red varieties of basil, such as purple
ruffle or dark opal.

BASIL VINEGAR

⅔ cup loosely packed fresh basil
  leaves
1 (17-ounce) bottle champagne wine
  vinegar or white wine vinegar
Fresh basil sprig (optional)

Slighty crush basil with back of spoon,
and place in a 1-quart jar. Bring vinegar to a boil, and pour over basil.
Cover and let stand at room temperature 1 to 2 weeks.
  Pour through a wire-mesh strainer
into a 2-cup liquid measuring cup, discarding basil. Transfer to a decorative
bottle or jar; add a fresh basil sprig, if
desired. Seal bottle with a cork or
other airtight lid. Store in a cool, dark
place up to 6 months. Yield: 2 cups.

Recipes And Reminiscences Of New Orleans

Talk about a fund-raiser. . . . Since 1971, sales of *Recipes and Reminiscences of New Orleans* have netted about $1 million for the Parent's Club of Ursuline Academy in New Orleans.

Filled with Cajun and Creole recipes, the cookbook also includes historical information, an extensive glossary of regional terms, and suggestions on how to be a Creole cook.

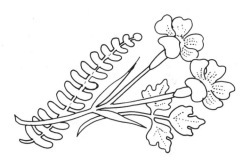

HOT DIRTY RICE

2 cups long-grain rice, uncooked
1 quart water
5 chicken wings (about ¾ pound)
5 chicken gizzards (about ¼ pound)
5 chicken hearts (about 1 ounce)
5 chicken livers (about ¼ pound)
2 pounds ground hot pork sausage
¼ cup butter or margarine
1 large onion, chopped
¾ cup chopped green pepper
2 stalks celery, chopped
½ cup sliced green onions
½ cup chopped cooked ham
1 tablespoon dried parsley flakes

Cook rice according to package directions; set aside.

Combine water and next 3 ingredients in a Dutch oven; bring to a boil. Cover, reduce heat, and simmer 20 minutes; add chicken livers, and cook 10 minutes or until tender. Drain, reserving ¾ cup liquid. Remove meat from wings; coarsely chop wing meat, gizzards, hearts, and livers. Set chopped meat aside.

Brown sausage in Dutch oven, stirring until it crumbles. Drain sausage, and set aside.

Melt butter in Dutch oven; add onion, pepper, and celery. Cook over medium heat 5 minutes or until tender, stirring often. Add green onions, and cook 2 minutes. Add ham, sausage, chopped meat, and reserved liquid. Bring to a boil; cover, reduce heat, and simmer 15 minutes. Stir in cooked rice and parsley. Serve warm. Yield: 10 to 12 servings.

PETIT BRÛLÉ

2 navel oranges
4 sugar cubes
4 whole cloves
½ cup brandy
2 (3-inch) sticks cinnamon

Remove a small slice from top of each orange; scoop out pulp. (Reserve pulp for another use.) Place 2 sugar cubes and 2 cloves in each orange shell, and set aside.

Place brandy in a small, long-handled saucepan; heat until warm (do not boil). Remove from heat. Ignite with a long match, and pour into orange shells. Place a cinnamon stick in each, and serve immediately after flames die down. Yield: 2 servings.

FRENCH MARKET BEIGNETS

1 cup milk
2 tablespoons margarine or shortening
1 tablespoon brown sugar
1 tablespoon sugar
1 package active dry yeast
1 large egg
3 cups all-purpose flour
1 teaspoon salt
1 teaspoon ground nutmeg
Vegetable oil
Sifted powdered sugar

Combine first 4 ingredients in a small saucepan; cook over low heat until margarine melts, stirring often. Cool to 105° to 115°. Transfer to a large mixing bowl. Stir in yeast; let stand 5 minutes. Stir in egg.

Combine flour, salt, and nutmeg; add 1½ cups to yeast mixture. Beat at medium speed with an electric mixer until smooth (about 1 minute). Stir in enough of remaining flour mixture to make a soft dough.

Place dough in a well-greased bowl, turning to grease top. Cover and let rise in a warm place (85°), free from drafts, about 1 hour or until dough is doubled in bulk.

Punch dough down; turn out onto a lightly floured surface, and knead 4 or 5 times. Roll dough into a 15- x 12-inch rectangle; cut into 20 (3-inch) squares. Cut each square in half diagonally, forming triangles. Place on a floured surface; cover and let rise in a warm place (85°), free from drafts, 30 minutes or until doubled in bulk.

Pour oil to depth of 3 inches in a Dutch oven; heat to 375°. Fry beignets, 4 or 5 at a time, in hot oil about 1 minute on each side or until golden brown. Drain well on paper towels; sprinkle with powdered sugar. Serve warm. Yield: 40 beignets.

From Our Kitchen To Yours

For the first-time cook, choosing among the array of pots and pans and other essentials needed to stock a kitchen is intimidating. To keep from buying things you really don't need, make a list of the basics.

Prices for cookware can be a shock. Advising someone to invest in quality and choose a few pieces of cookware at a time is easy—stretching the budget to buy them isn't.

For beginning cooks, here are a few tips on buying cookware.

Ask Yourself

■ Why is quality important? Buying the best cookware that you can afford pays off in the long run. The gauge or thickness determines the quality—the heavier the cookware, the better. Inexpensive pieces can warp, dent, and develop hot spots.

■ What are you paying for? Cookware prices are based on the quality of material, gauge or thickness, workmanship, and fittings. Special colors and trimmings add to the price and care—not to the efficiency or durability. Lower-priced pieces are usually made with lightweight material and less durable fittings, handles, and covers, and are assembled with shortcuts in workmanship.

■ What kind of cooking do you plan to do—quick and easy, gourmet, or a combination? Will you cook for company? Do you enjoy spending time in the kitchen, or do you plan to microwave your meals? No matter what your lifestyle, you don't need to begin with everything all at once.

■ Should you buy a matched starter set? Starter sets, which generally include the basics, offer savings over individual pieces. If you're interested in cookware of one material, starter sets can be a wise investment. However, consider the pieces in the set and how often each piece will be used. One advantage of purchasing pieces individually is that each one can be selected in the type of material that is best suited for its particular purpose.

What Are the Basics?

Start with two different-size saucepans with lids, one Dutch oven, and one skillet. Because these pieces are included in starter sets, compare prices for the best buy.

After deciding on the necessities, make another list to add more flexibility. Include items such as baking dishes and pans, a shallow roasting pan, and a cookie sheet.

Shopping Tips

■ Collect brochures from cookware departments, and carefully read the information on construction, use, and care. Be sure that the care instructions meet your lifestyle (not all cookware is dishwasher-safe), and check the guarantee.

■ Shop for cookware that conducts heat without hot spots, has an interior surface that prevents excessive sticking, and that has flat bottoms and snug-fitting lids.

■ Select cookware made of a material that won't be affected by the acids or salts in foods.

■ Be sure handles and knobs on cookware are sturdy, attached securely, and easy to grasp; the handle should be strong enough to support the weight of the filled piece of cookware. It helps to have handles that stay cool when on the cooktop.

■ Look for easy-to-clean pieces.

■ Consider cookware that is ovenproof and versatile. For example, a double boiler may be converted into two saucepans and a deep skillet with a lid may serve as a small Dutch oven.

■ Keep storage in mind; choose utensils that stack or can be hung.

■ Take advantage of sales and special offers. Most companies offer a pan (usually a small skillet) at a good price to get you to try their product.

Best Choice—Your Choice

The variety of cookware available offers something for everyone. Each type of cookware has advantages and disadvantages. Here's what we found. (Brand names of cookware are listed in parentheses.)

■ *Enameled cast-iron cookware* (Le Creuset)
Pros: oven-to-table
Cons: heavy, some pieces not recommended for dishwasher, metal utensils may scratch surface

■ *Enamel-on-steel cookware* (Chantal)
Pros: dishwasher-safe, glass lids, oven-to-table, heats quickly
Cons: foods can burn when cooked at high temperatures

■ *Hard-anodized or fully anodized aluminum cookware* (Calphalon, Anolon, and Circulon)
Pros: scratch-resistant, some with nonstick finishes
Cons: heavy, all handles are not heat-resistant, and not recommended for dishwasher

■ *Porcelain-on-aluminum* (T-fal)
Pros: nonstick finish
Cons: stirring with metal utensils may scratch surface

■ *Stainless-steel cookware* (Revere Ware, Farberware, Cuisinart, and All-Clad)
Pros: dishwasher-safe
Cons: acidic or salty foods shouldn't remain in cookware long; lighter-weight brands cannot be used on high heat, copper bottoms tarnish easily

Cost

Costs vary. However, a basic seven-piece starter set will cost less than cookware purchased individually.

Nothing tops French baguette rounds like elegant Goat Cheese With Sun-Dried Tomatoes and Rosemary (recipe, page 175).

Enliven your summer menu with
Marinated Black-Eyed Pea Salad with
Cornbread Croutons or Green Beans
With Creamy Tarragon Dressing.
(Recipes begin on page 190.)

Above: *Chopped peanuts and bacon bits are among the ingredients sprinkled inside Peanut Lover's Bread (recipe, page 211).*

Far left: *Hopping John With Grilled Pork Medaillons (recipe, page 229) is an upscale, lower-fat version of a classic Southern dish.*

Left: *Made with rigatoni pasta (and pine nuts for added crunch), Roasted Vegetables and Pasta (recipe, page 184) is easy for everyday meals, yet different enough for company.*

Autumn's abundance dresses up for dinner in dazzling Pears en Croûte (recipe, page 210). But don't let the look of extravagance fool you—this spectacular dessert has only three main ingredients.

For best results, select firm cooking apples such as Granny Smith when you make showy Sugar-Crusted Apples in Walnut-Phyllo Baskets (recipe, page 210).

When tailgating with friends, show your hospitality with Southern Chocolate-Mint Brownies (page 216).

ON THE LIGHT SIDE

Beans Go Upscale

Though once thought of as a humble food, beans are considered healthful and fashionable today. A peek at the menus of some of the South's trendiest restaurants is proof that beans are tickling the culinary fancies of talented chefs. And they're not the only ones coming up with new ideas; we've created a few of our own. Try them and see how great beans can be.

HOPPING JOHN WITH GRILLED PORK MEDAILLONS
(pictured on page 224)

¾ cup chopped onion
½ cup chopped celery
1 teaspoon olive oil
2 (16-ounce) cans ready-to-serve, reduced-sodium, fat-free chicken broth
1 teaspoon dried thyme
½ cup wild rice, uncooked
1 cup frozen black-eyed peas
½ cup long-grain rice, uncooked
¾ cup chopped tomato
2 teaspoons lemon juice
2 tablespoons chopped fresh parsley
½ teaspoon salt
¼ teaspoon ground red pepper
¼ teaspoon freshly ground black pepper
Grilled Pork Medaillons
1 Red Delicious apple, cut into 12 wedges
Garnish: fresh thyme sprig

Cook onion and celery in olive oil in a large saucepan over medium heat, stirring constantly, until tender. Add chicken broth and dried thyme; bring mixture to a boil.

Rinse wild rice in three changes of hot water; drain. Add wild rice to broth mixture. Cover, reduce heat, and cook 30 minutes.

Add black-eyed peas and next 7 ingredients; cover and cook 20 minutes or until rice is tender. Serve with Grilled Pork Medaillons and apple wedges. Garnish, if desired. Yield: 4 servings (403 calories [16% from fat] per 1¼ cups Hopping John with 3 pork medaillons and 3 apple wedges).

□ *30.5g protein, 5.2g fat (1.4g saturated), 55.7g carbohydrate, 4.5g fiber, 59mg cholesterol, 845mg sodium, and 56mg calcium.*

Grilled Pork Medaillons

¼ cup lemon juice
2 tablespoons reduced-sodium soy sauce
2 cloves garlic, pressed
1 (¾-pound) pork tenderloin, trimmed
Vegetable cooking spray

Combine first 3 ingredients in a shallow container or a large, heavy-duty, zip-top plastic bag. Add tenderloin; cover or seal, and refrigerate 8 hours, turning occasionally.

Remove tenderloin from marinade, discarding marinade. Coat food rack with cooking spray; place rack on grill over medium-hot coals (350° to 400°). Place tenderloin on rack, and cook, covered with grill lid, 12 minutes on each side or until a meat thermometer inserted in thickest portion registers 160°. Cut into 12 slices. Yield: 4 servings (107 calories [26% from fat] per serving).

□ *18.4g protein, 3.1g fat (1.1g saturated), 0g carbohydrate, 0g fiber, 59mg cholesterol, 59mg sodium, and 7mg calcium.*

WHITE BEAN RELISH

1 (16-ounce) can navy beans, drained and rinsed
1 cup finely chopped tomato
¾ cup finely chopped sweet red pepper
¾ cup sliced green onions
½ cup finely chopped celery
2 tablespoons chopped fresh cilantro or parsley
1 jalapeño pepper, seeded and chopped
1 clove garlic, minced
1 (0.7-ounce) envelope Italian salad dressing mix
½ cup water
¼ cup cider vinegar
1 tablespoon olive oil

Combine first 8 ingredients; set relish mixture aside.

Combine dressing mix and remaining ingredients in a jar. Cover jar tightly, and shake vigorously. Pour dressing over relish mixture, and toss gently. Cover and refrigerate. Toss before serving. Using a slotted spoon, serve relish with grilled fish, pork, hamburgers, or vegetables. Yield: 8 servings (65 calories [6% from fat] per ¼-cup serving).

□ *3.5g protein, 0.4g fat (0.1g saturated), 18.6g carbohydrate, 2.3g fiber, 0mg cholesterol, 158mg sodium, and 31mg calcium.*

BLACK BEAN TERRINE WITH FRESH TOMATO COULIS AND JALAPEÑO SAUCE

3 (16-ounce) cans black beans, drained and rinsed
⅓ cup egg substitute
1½ teaspoons salt-free, extra-spicy herb and spice blend
1½ teaspoons ground cumin
¼ teaspoon freshly ground pepper
Vegetable cooking spray
Fresh Tomato Coulis
Jalapeño Sauce

Position knife blade in food processor bowl; add first 5 ingredients, and process until smooth, stopping occasionally to scrape down sides. Pack bean mixture into an 8½- x 4½- x 3-inch loafpan coated with cooking spray. Cover with aluminum foil, and place in a large, shallow pan. Add hot water to pan to depth of 1 inch. Bake at 350° for 55 to 60 minutes or until a knife inserted in center comes out clean.

Remove pan from water, and place a small weight on top of bean mixture; cover and refrigerate 8 hours. Cut into 16 (½-inch) slices, and serve with Fresh Tomato Coulis and Jalapeño Sauce. Yield: 16 servings (136 calories [6% from fat] per 1 slice, 2 tablespoons Fresh Tomato Coulis, and 1 tablespoon Jalapeño Sauce).

□ *9.3g protein, 0.9g fat (0.1g saturated), 24.5g carbohydrate, 4.4g fiber, 0mg cholesterol, 289mg sodium, and 57mg calcium.*

Note: For salt-free, extra-spicy herb and spice blend, we used extra-spicy Mrs. Dash.

Fresh Tomato Coulis

4 medium-to-large tomatoes, peeled and seeded
1 clove garlic, halved
3 tablespoons chopped fresh cilantro
2 tablespoons rice wine vinegar
1 teaspoon dried thyme
1 teaspoon freshly ground pepper

Place tomatoes in container of an electric blender; process until smooth. Set puree aside. Place colander in a large bowl; line colander with 2 layers of cheesecloth or a coffee filter. Pour puree into colander; cover loosely with plastic wrap, and refrigerate 24 hours. Discard liquid in bowl.

Combine puree, garlic, and remaining ingredients in container of an electric blender; process until smooth. Yield: 1½ cups (12 calories [15% from fat] per 1½ tablespoons).

□ *0.5g protein, 0.2g fat (0g saturated), 2.6g carbohydrate, 0.7g fiber, 0mg cholesterol, 5mg sodium, and 6mg calcium.*

Jalapeño Sauce

¾ cup plain nonfat yogurt
1 clove garlic, minced
¼ cup seeded and chopped jalapeño peppers
¼ cup chopped fresh cilantro
1 teaspoon frozen unsweetened orange juice concentrate, thawed
½ teaspoon ground cumin
¼ teaspoon salt

Combine all ingredients in a small bowl. Yield: 1 cup (8 calories [0% from fat] per tablespoon).

□ *0.7g protein, 0g fat (0g saturated), 1.3g carbohydrate, 0.1g fiber, 0mg cholesterol, 45mg sodium, and 24mg calcium.*

Tomato Tips

■ If you're faced with peeling a large quantity of tomatoes, try this method: Dip the tomatoes into boiling water for 1 minute; then plunge them into cold water. The skins will then slip off easily.

■ When you are out of canned tomatoes for a recipe, try substituting 1 (6-ounce) can tomato paste plus 1 cup water. It will make very little difference in most recipes.

LIGHT FAVORITE

Cozy Up To Fruit Cobbler

Just when you thought nothing could beat Grandma's steamy fruit cobbler, we present its competition: Raspberry-Cherry Cobbler. Our version has none of the cholesterol and only a fourth of the fat of the original, yet it's filled with flavor.

A total of 8.5 grams of fat was eliminated from the recipe by substituting reduced-calorie margarine for butter, nonfat yogurt for sour cream, and evaporated skimmed milk for heavy cream. Eliminating ½ cup of sugar from the fruit mixture reduces calories, while retaining sweetness.

RASPBERRY-CHERRY COBBLER

1 (16-ounce) package frozen unsweetened raspberries, thawed
1 (16-ounce) package frozen no-sugar-added pitted dark sweet cherries, thawed
1 cup sugar
¼ cup all-purpose flour
1 tablespoon lemon juice
⅛ teaspoon ground cinnamon
Vegetable cooking spray
2 cups all-purpose flour
1 tablespoon baking powder
1 teaspoon baking soda
1 teaspoon salt
2 tablespoons sugar
¼ cup reduced-calorie margarine
¾ cup plain nonfat yogurt
¼ cup evaporated skimmed milk

Combine first 6 ingredients; spoon into an 11- x 7- x 1½-inch baking dish coated with cooking spray.

Combine 2 cups flour and next 4 ingredients in a large bowl; cut in margarine with a pastry blender until mixture is crumbly. Add yogurt and milk, stirring with a fork until dry ingredients are moistened. Turn dough out onto a lightly floured surface, and knead about 10 times.

Roll dough to ½-inch thickness; cut 12 rounds using a 2-inch cutter. Cut 6 diamonds from remaining dough.

Arrange rounds and diamond shapes on top of fruit mixture. Bake at 425° for 20 to 25 minutes or until bubbly and golden brown. Remove from oven; lightly coat each biscuit with cooking spray. Yield: 12 servings (225 calories [11% from fat] per serving).

□ *4.4g protein, 2.7g fat (0.4g saturated), 47.1g carbohydrate, 3.6g fiber, 0mg cholesterol, 403mg sodium, and 125mg calcium.*

COMPARE THE NUTRIENTS
(per serving)

	Traditional	Light
Calories	319	225
Fat	11.2g	2.7g
Cholesterol	29mg	0mg

See The Light With Black Beans

For centuries a staple in Central and South American meals, black beans are now the rage in North America. Low in cost and high in protein, black beans go upscale or down-home. But the traditional way to serve them is in soup. The wine gives ours a slight flavor variation; if you don't want to use wine, substitute chicken broth.

BLACK BEAN SOUP

1 pound dried black beans
7 cups water
1½ teaspoons salt
1 cup chopped onion
1 cup chopped green pepper
1 cup chopped cooked ham
½ cup Burgundy or other dry red wine
¼ cup tomato paste
2 teaspoons pepper
1 teaspoon ground cumin
4 bay leaves
Garnish: sliced green onions

Sort and wash beans; place in a large Dutch oven. Cover with water 2 inches above beans; let soak 8 hours. Drain well, and return beans to Dutch oven. Add 7 cups water and salt; bring to a boil. Cover, reduce heat, and simmer 1½ hours.

Stir in onion and next 7 ingredients; cover and simmer 1 hour or until beans are tender. Remove and discard bay leaves. Pour 4 cups mixture into container of an electric blender; process until smooth, stopping once to scrape down sides. Stir into remaining soup. Garnish, if desired. Yield: about 10 cups.
La Juan Coward
Jasper, Texas

Enhance Flavors

■ For new flavor, experiment with wine in your cooking. The alcohol evaporates during cooking, leaving behind flavor and few calories.

■ Bring out the flavor of lower-fat foods such as chicken, fish, and lean pork, as well as vegetables, with savory marinades. For marinade ideas, see our recipes beginning on page 101.

Bread Also Rises — In A Machine

Can a bread machine really mix, knead, rise, and bake bread in one pan . . . in approximately four hours? Because each brand of bread machine has its own recommended recipes, we selected some of our favorite *Southern Living* recipes made the old-fashioned way and tried them in Hitachi, Panasonic, and Zojirushi bread machines. Whether made by hand or in a bread machine, there was very little difference.

PARMESAN BREAD

For large loaf:
1 cup water
1 large egg
¼ cup butter or margarine, cut into small pieces
3 cups bread flour
⅓ cup grated Parmesan cheese
2 tablespoons sugar
2 teaspoons dried onion flakes
1 teaspoon salt
½ teaspoon garlic salt
1 package active dry yeast

For regular loaf:
½ cup water
2 tablespoons egg substitute
2 tablespoons butter or margarine, cut into small pieces
1½ cups bread flour
2½ tablespoons Parmesan cheese
1 tablespoon sugar
1 teaspoon dried onion flakes
½ teaspoon salt
¼ teaspoon garlic salt
2 teaspoons active dry yeast

Combine all ingredients in bread machine according to manufacturer's instructions. Process in regular bake cycle. Remove from baking pan, and cool on a wire rack. Yield: 1 loaf.

■ We tried Honey-Oat Bread in both size bread-making machines—regular and large—because the recipe didn't work when halved. In the regular-size machine, the bread overbrowned in several places on top; however, the flavor and texture was the same in both machines.

HONEY-OAT BREAD

¾ cup plus 2 tablespoons water
¼ cup vegetable oil
¼ cup honey
¼ cup egg substitute
1¼ cups whole wheat flour
1 cup bread flour
½ cup unprocessed oat bran
¾ teaspoon salt
1 tablespoon active dry yeast

Combine all ingredients in bread machine according to manufacturer's instructions. Process in regular bake cycle. Remove from baking pan, and cool on a wire rack. Yield: 1 loaf.

■ When company comes and homemade rolls are on the menu, make Sour Cream Yeast Rolls. We tried the recipe in different machines, and found that it worked only in the regular (1-pound loaf) machine. Because the flavor is our favorite, we used the dough as a base for Cinnamon Rolls.

SOUR CREAM YEAST ROLLS

¼ cup water
¼ cup sour cream
¼ cup butter or margarine, cut into
   small pieces
1 large egg
2 cups bread flour
¼ cup sugar
½ teaspoon salt
1 package active dry yeast

Combine all ingredients in bread machine according to manufacturer's instructions. Process in dough cycle. Turn dough out onto a lightly floured surface, and knead 4 or 5 times; divide in half. Shape each portion into 9 rolls, and place in an 8-inch round pan.

Cover and let rise in a warm place (85°), free from drafts, 40 minutes or until doubled in bulk. Bake at 375° for 10 to 12 minutes. Yield: 1½ dozen.

To make Cinnamon Rolls, roll each half into a 12-inch square; brush with 2 tablespoons melted butter, and sprinkle with ⅓ cup firmly packed brown sugar and 2 teaspoons ground cinnamon. Starting with long side, roll dough, jellyroll fashion; pinch seams to seal. Cut into 12 (1-inch) slices; place, cut side down, in two lightly greased 8-inch square pans. Cover and let rise in a warm place (85°), free from drafts, 40 minutes. Bake at 375° for 12 to 15 minutes or until done. Combine ¾ cup sifted powdered sugar, 1½ tablespoons milk, and ¼ teaspoon vanilla extract; drizzle over warm rolls. Yield: 2 dozen.

Best Bread-Machine Baking

Here are tips for experimenting with your favorite recipes.

■ Several factors will influence the success of each recipe. Varying amounts of ingredients are called for in different machine brands and models. Baking pans vary in size, shape, and capacity; blades vary in design and mixing action.

■ Bread machines typically use about 2 cups of flour for a regular 1-pound loaf or about 3 cups of flour for a 1½-pound loaf. When selecting a recipe, make sure it's the right size for your machine; it won't properly mix smaller or larger amounts.

■ Substitute an equal amount of bread flour for all-purpose flour.

■ Recipes yielding two loaves can often be halved to make one loaf.

■ It's easier to use egg substitute than to divide one egg—2 tablespoons equals one-half egg.

■ For consistent results, keep your machine in one place and maintain even room temperature and humidity.

■ A mismeasured tablespoon of water or teaspoon of salt can make a big difference in a bread-making recipe and the finished product.

■ Many bread-baking disasters occur because ingredients were left out or added twice. To avoid a mishap, assemble all ingredients in order of use. Carefully measure ingredients into pan; then recheck the list to be sure you used each ingredient.

■ Promptly remove baked bread; it will become soggy if you leave it in the warm pan.

OCTOBER

The warm golden colors of fall are inspiring, and that's why our ideas for delicious October recipes range from pumpkins to pecans. As an ingredient, pumpkin can't be beat for its versatility. It's perfect in our recipes for creamy soup, cookies, and cakes, all accented with aromatic spices. But how about pumpkin as a base for stuffed pasta shells with a Southwest flavor? And speaking of pumpkins, the growing popularity of Halloween with the young and young-at-heart inspired us to create wholesome goodies. Try our health-ful savory and sweet treats; they won't play tricks on you.

If pecan pie is your autumn passion, you'll love the surprising variations of this Southern classic. Our pie recipes range from the traditional version to exotic variations.

Where's The Pumpkin?

Here, we salute pumpkin for its versatility as an ingredient. (All of our recipes use canned pumpkin, a form most busy cooks prefer today.) In cream soup to cookies, pumpkin brings a depth of flavor as rich as its color. And it harmonizes with a multitude of seasonings—from cinnamon to *salsa*. If you think teaming pumpkin and pasta is odd culinary casting, wait until you try our stuffed shells. We predict many encore performances.

CREAM OF PUMPKIN SOUP
(pictured on pages 262 and 263)

1 tablespoon butter or margarine
1 large onion, chopped
2 (14½-ounce) cans ready-to-serve chicken broth, divided
1 (16-ounce) can pumpkin
1 teaspoon salt
¼ teaspoon ground cinnamon
¼ teaspoon ground nutmeg
⅛ teaspoon ground ginger
⅛ teaspoon pepper
1½ cups milk
1 cup half-and-half
Bourbon Croutons
Garnish: fresh chives with flowers

Melt butter in a Dutch oven over medium-high heat; add onion, and cook, stirring constantly, until tender (about 5 minutes). Add 1 can chicken broth; bring mixture to a boil over medium heat. Cover, reduce heat, and simmer 15 minutes.

Pour into container of an electric blender; process until smooth (about 1 minute). Return to Dutch oven; stir in remaining 1 can broth, pumpkin, and next 5 ingredients. Bring to a boil over medium heat. Cover, reduce heat, and simmer 10 minutes. Add milk and half-and-half; cook over low heat, stirring constantly, until thoroughly heated. Serve with Bourbon Croutons, and garnish, if desired. Yield: 7 cups.

Bourbon Croutons

⅓ cup butter or margarine, softened
2 tablespoons brown sugar
2 tablespoons bourbon
8 slices white sandwich bread

Combine butter and brown sugar; gradually add bourbon, and set aside.

Remove crusts from bread. Spread half of mixture on one side of bread slices; cut into 1½-inch triangles, and place, buttered side up, on a baking sheet. Bake at 300° for 15 minutes. Turn triangles over, and spread with remaining butter mixture. Bake an additional 10 to 15 minutes or until golden brown. Yield: 2½ cups.

Velma Kestner
Berwind, West Virginia

SOUTHWESTERN STUFFED SHELLS
(pictured on pages 262 and 263)

18 jumbo pasta shells, uncooked
1 (16-ounce) can pumpkin
1 large egg
½ cup Italian-seasoned breadcrumbs
½ cup (2 ounces) shredded Parmesan cheese
½ teaspoon ground nutmeg
1 (16-ounce) jar picante sauce or salsa, divided
1 cup (4 ounces) shredded Monterey Jack cheese with peppers
2 tablespoons chopped fresh parsley
Garnish: fresh parsley sprigs

Cook pasta shells according to package directions; drain, and set aside.

Combine pumpkin and next 4 ingredients; stuff each shell with mixture.

Spread 1 cup picante sauce into a 13- x 9- x 2-inch baking dish. Place filled shells on sauce; top with remaining sauce. Cover and bake at 350° for 35 minutes. Sprinkle with Monterey Jack cheese and parsley. Garnish, if desired. Yield: 3 to 4 servings.

Janice Elder
Charlotte, North Carolina

EASY PUMPKIN SWIRL
(pictured on page 264)

3 large eggs
1 cup sugar
⅔ cup canned pumpkin
¾ cup biscuit mix
2 teaspoons ground cinnamon
1 teaspoon pumpkin pie spice
1 cup chopped pecans
2 to 3 tablespoons powdered sugar
1 (8-ounce) package cream cheese, softened
⅓ cup butter or margarine, softened
1 cup sifted powdered sugar
1 teaspoon vanilla extract

Grease bottom and sides of a 15- x 10- x 1-inch jellyroll pan; line with wax paper, and grease wax paper. Set aside.

Beat eggs at high speed with an electric mixer until thick and pale. Gradually add 1 cup sugar, beating until soft peaks form and sugar dissolves (2 to 4 minutes). Fold in pumpkin.

Combine biscuit mix and spices; fold into pumpkin mixture, and spread evenly into prepared pan. Sprinkle with chopped pecans. Bake at 375° for 13 to 15 minutes.

Sift 2 to 3 tablespoons powdered sugar in a 15- x 10-inch rectangle on a cloth towel. When cake is done, immediately loosen from sides of pan, and turn out onto sugared towel. Carefully peel off wax paper. Starting at narrow end, roll up cake and towel together, and cool completely on a wire rack, seam side down.

Beat cream cheese and butter at medium speed with an electric mixer until creamy; add 1 cup powdered sugar and vanilla, beating well. Unroll cake; spread with cream cheese mixture, and reroll without towel. Place on a serving plate, seam side down; chill at least 2 hours. Yield: 12 servings.
Ernestine Jones
Gore Springs, Mississippi

PUMPKIN GINGERBREAD WITH CARAMEL SAUCE

2¼ cups all-purpose flour
½ cup sugar
⅔ cup butter or margarine
¾ cup chopped pecans
¾ cup buttermilk
½ cup canned pumpkin
½ cup molasses
1 large egg
1½ teaspoons ground ginger
1 teaspoon baking soda
½ teaspoon ground cinnamon
¼ teaspoon salt
¼ teaspoon ground cloves
Caramel Sauce
Vanilla ice cream

Combine flour and sugar; cut in butter with a pastry blender until mixture is crumbly. Stir in pecans. Press 1¼ cups mixture into bottom of an ungreased 9-inch square pan; set aside.

Combine remaining crumb mixture, buttermilk, and next 8 ingredients; beat at low speed with an electric mixer until blended. Pour over crumb mixture, and bake at 350° for 40 minutes or until a wooden pick inserted in center comes out clean. Cool in pan on a wire rack. Cut into squares, and serve with Caramel Sauce and ice cream. Yield: 12 servings.

Caramel Sauce

½ cup butter or margarine
1¼ cups firmly packed brown sugar
2 tablespoons light corn syrup
½ cup whipping cream

Melt butter in a small heavy saucepan over low heat; add brown sugar and corn syrup. Bring to a boil; cook, stirring constantly, 1 minute or until sugar dissolves. Gradually add whipping cream; return mixture to a boil. Remove from heat. Yield: 2 cups.
Linda Magers
Clemmons, North Carolina

PUMPKIN-CHOCOLATE CHIP COOKIES
(pictured on pages 262 and 263)

1 cup shortening
1 cup sugar
1 large egg
1 cup canned pumpkin
2 cups all-purpose flour
1 teaspoon baking soda
1 teaspoon baking powder
½ teaspoon salt
1 teaspoon ground cinnamon
1 teaspoon vanilla extract
1 (6-ounce) package semisweet chocolate morsels (1 cup)
½ cup chopped pecans

Beat shortening at medium speed with an electric mixer until fluffy; gradually add sugar, beating well. Add egg and pumpkin, mixing well. Combine flour and next 4 ingredients; add to pumpkin mixture. Stir in vanilla, chocolate morsels, and pecans.

Drop dough by tablespoonfuls onto lightly greased cookie sheets. Bake at 350° for 13 minutes. Remove to wire racks to cool completely. Yield: 5½ dozen.
Kathy Stanger
Morgantown, West Virginia

From Our Kitchen To Yours

The culinary detectives are on the scene in the Test Kitchens. The evidence sits in the center of the taste-testing table—tough muffins and a curdled sauce. Looking for clues by tearing apart a muffin and peering closely at the sauce, we discuss solutions. Sometimes the answers are easy. Methods and techniques can be responsible for a recipe gone awry—overbeating or underbeating, or the wrong temperature and time. However, there are a few instances when the problem remains a mystery. As food sleuths, it is our responsibility to investigate.

Are the muffins tough because the vegetable oil was omitted and applesauce substituted? Did the sauce reach the boiling point, causing the separation? Rapid-fire opinions from around the table offer possible answers. After reaching a conclusion, the recipe is retested.

To help track down solutions for kitchen dilemmas at your house, check product labels on food packages for toll-free consumer hotlines. The consumer specialists answering the calls offer invaluable advice and possible solutions.

Smoky Mountain Reunion

College roommates Chip Smith of Houston, Texas, and Paul Frederick of Huntsville, Alabama, first staked out their Cades Cove spot in 1973 for a simple wine-and-cheese lunch with their dates. Over the past two decades, the lunch date has evolved into an elaborate picnic celebrating fall's harvest, crisp mountain air, and dear friends.

The meal highlights an annual four-day respite from reality. They retreat to a Gatlinburg, Tennessee, condominium big enough for Chip and Paul, a few buddies they've added over the years, and their spouses and children. The group treasures hiking excursions up Mount LeConte and cozy evenings catching up in front of the fireplace. But the feast in a specific Cades Cove meadow makes the trip—and the memories.

Food for the picnic arrives in antique wicker baskets, ice chests, and plastic containers, but when the feast is laid out, it's restaurant elegance. Serving platters, wine glasses, silverware, and even fresh flowers and garnishes grace the gathering.

After the leisurely lunch of wild game, vegetable salads, and simple autumn desserts, these old college friends relax, recline, and reminisce until it's time to pack up the baskets. As they gather up their belongings after another memory-filled picnic, they're already renewing their promises of "same time—and same spot— next year."

SMOKED QUAIL

10 quail (about 4 pounds)
1 (12-ounce) bottle white wine
   marinade
Mesquite chips
Vegetable cooking spray
Garnish: crabapples

Place quail in a shallow dish; pour marinade over quail. Cover and refrigerate 8 hours. Drain quail, reserving marinade.

Soak mesquite chips in water at least 15 minutes. Prepare charcoal fire in smoker, and let burn 15 to 20 minutes. Place mesquite chips on hot coals. Place water pan in smoker; add reserved marinade to water pan, and fill with hot water. Coat food rack with cooking spray, and place in smoker.

Place quail on food rack. Cover with smoker lid, and cook 2 hours or until done. Garnish, if desired. Yield: 10 servings.

Note: For white wine marinade, we used Mr. Marinade.

HONEY-MUSTARD MARINATED VEGETABLES

2 cups broccoli flowerets
2 cups cauliflower flowerets
6 large fresh mushrooms, sliced
1 small onion, sliced
¼ cup sliced celery
½ cup commercial honey-mustard
   salad dressing
¼ cup white vinegar
1 tablespoon poppy seeds
½ teaspoon salt

Combine first 5 ingredients in a large bowl. Combine salad dressing and remaining ingredients; pour over vegetables, tossing to coat. Cover and chill 3 hours, stirring occasionally. Serve with a slotted spoon, if desired. Yield: 4 to 6 servings.

Note: For salad dressing, we used Fogcutter Honey-Mustard Salad Dressing.

Tip: *Wipe mushrooms clean with a damp paper towel or quickly rinse them in a colander before using; never immerse mushrooms in water.*

CORN-IN-THE-SHUCK SALAD

7 to 8 ears fresh corn
½ cup apple cider vinegar
1 tablespoon sugar
2 tablespoons molasses
½ cup chopped green pepper
½ cup chopped sweet red pepper
1½ tablespoons dry mustard
1½ tablespoons lime juice
1 teaspoon celery salt
½ teaspoon turmeric
Slaw Silks
Garnishes: lemon half, red grapes,
   crabapples

Remove husks and silks from corn, reserving husks. Cut off tips of kernels; measure 4 cups, and set aside.

Combine vinegar, sugar, and molasses in a medium saucepan; bring to a boil. Add green pepper and next 5 ingredients. Bring to a boil; reduce heat, and simmer, 5 minutes, stirring often. Add corn, and return to a boil; reduce heat, and simmer 4 minutes, stirring often. Cool. Cover and refrigerate at least 3 hours.

To serve, stack 2 or 3 corn husks together; spoon about ⅓ cup corn mixture into each. Top with about 3 tablespoons Slaw Silks, letting mixture spill out of end of husks. Garnish, if desired. Yield: 10 servings.

Slaw Silks

2 cups long thinly shredded cabbage
½ Granny Smith apple, cut into
   very thin strips
2½ tablespoons commercial
   chowchow
1 tablespoon Dijon mustard
2¼ teaspoons mayonnaise or salad
   dressing

Combine cabbage and apple in a bowl. Combine chowchow, mustard, and mayonnaise; stir into cabbage mixture. Cover and refrigerate at least 3 hours. Yield: 2½ cups.

WILD RICE-AND-MUSHROOM QUICHES

4 slices bacon
⅔ cup wild rice, uncooked
2 cups water
1½ cups (6 ounces) shredded Swiss cheese
½ cup finely chopped green onions
1 cup chopped shiitake mushrooms
1 cup peeled, chopped tomatoes, drained
1 teaspoon salt
1 teaspoon ground black pepper
½ teaspoon ground red pepper
4 large eggs
2 cups whipping cream
16 unbaked (3-inch) frozen pastry shells

Cook bacon in a large skillet until crisp; remove bacon, reserving 1 tablespoon drippings. Crumble bacon, and set aside.

Wash wild rice in 3 changes of hot water; drain. Combine rice, 2 cups water, and reserved bacon drippings in a heavy saucepan. Bring to a boil; cover, reduce heat, and simmer 50 to 60 minutes or until tender. Drain, if necessary. Combine cooked rice, crumbled bacon, cheese, and next 6 ingredients; set aside.

Combine eggs and whipping cream in a large bowl; beat at high speed with an electric mixer 2 minutes. Stir in rice mixture. Spoon into pastry shells. Place on a baking sheet, and bake at 375° for 25 to 30 minutes. Yield: 16 (3-inch) quiches.

Note: Wild rice-and-mushroom mixture may be divided and baked in 2 (9-inch) pastry-lined quiche dishes. Bake on lower rack of oven at 375° for 45 minutes, covering loosely with aluminum foil to prevent excessive browning, if necessary.

■ After years of testing, our kitchens have established a tried-and-true standard procedure for pound cakes. But we just had to test this recipe's unusual mixing method. We worried as we watched this extremely thick batter challenge our mixers; then we shook our heads in disbelief at the spectacular baking results. Because a hand-held mixer (and less adventuresome cooks) probably won't stand up to this batter, we offer our standard method as well. We're pleased with the results of both methods.

SMOOTHEST SOUTHERN POUND CAKE

1 cup butter or margarine, softened
3 cups sugar
3 cups sifted cake flour
¼ teaspoon baking soda
6 large eggs
1 (8-ounce) carton sour cream
1 teaspoon vanilla extract

Beat butter at medium speed with an electric mixer (not a hand-held one) about 2 minutes or until creamy. Gradually add sugar, beating at medium speed 5 to 7 minutes. Combine cake flour and baking soda, and add to butter mixture one cup at a time. (Batter will be extremely thick.)

Separate eggs; add yolks to batter, and mix well. Stir in sour cream and vanilla. Beat egg whites until stiff, and fold into batter.

Spoon batter into a greased and floured Bundt or 10-inch tube pan. Bake at 300° for 2 hours or until a wooden pick inserted in center of cake comes out clean. (You may also spoon batter into two 9- x 5- x 3-inch loafpans, and bake at 300° for 1½ hours or until a wooden pick inserted in center comes out clean.) Cool in pan on a wire rack 10 to 15 minutes; remove from pan, and cool completely on a wire rack. Yield: one 10-inch cake or two loaves.

Note: Standard Mixing Method: If you are using a hand-held mixer or prefer a more conventional pound cake method, here's the procedure that we suggest.

Beat butter at medium speed with an electric mixer about 2 minutes or until creamy. Gradually add 3 cups sugar, beating at medium speed 5 to 7 minutes. Add eggs, one at time, beating just until yellow disappears.

Combine cake flour and baking soda; add to butter mixture alternately with sour cream, beginning and ending with flour mixture. Mix at lowest speed just until mixture is blended after each addition. Stir in vanilla. Bake as directed.

■ We used store-bought pears for this pie, but it's named for the "backyard pears" Harriet Frederick's mother uses in her recipe. In some ways, you never grow up; Harriet's mom baked this pie and sent it along with her daughter to share with the whole gang at their annual picnic.

BACKYARD PEAR PIE

4 large pears, peeled, cored, and thinly sliced
¼ to ⅓ cup lemon juice
3 tablespoons butter or margarine
½ cup firmly packed brown sugar
½ cup sugar
1 teaspoon ground cinnamon
½ teaspoon salt
½ teaspoon ground nutmeg
2 tablespoons all-purpose flour
1 (15-ounce) package refrigerated piecrusts
1 teaspoon all-purpose flour

Combine first 8 ingredients in a large saucepan; cook over medium heat about 12 minutes or until pears are tender, stirring occasionally. Gradually sprinkle in 2 tablespoons flour, stirring constantly; cook, stirring constantly, about 2 minutes or until slightly thickened.

Unfold 1 piecrust, and press out fold lines; sprinkle with 1 teaspoon flour, spreading over surface. Place crust, floured side down, in a 9-inch pieplate; spoon in pear mixture. Roll remaining piecrust on a lightly floured surface to press out fold lines; place over pear mixture. Fold edges under, and crimp. Cut slits in top crust for steam to escape. Bake at 350° for 45 minutes. Yield: one 9-inch pie.

A Victorian Victory Feast

Sybil Hudson of Columbia, South Carolina, recalls her surprise the day her husband, Jim, casually mentioned he had bought one of the unfinished "Cockabooses" from Ed Robinson, also of Columbia. Unfamiliar with the project and not a football fan of the University of South Carolina Gamecocks, she was skeptical.

However, after much remodeling and decorating, Sybil and her designers had transformed the railcar into a pleasant place. Sybil carries the railcar's Victorian theme into her entertaining, using delicate plates and serving pieces and a bouquet of roses finished with a lace bow.

Like the decor, some of the recipes also reach into the past. Sybil always serves old family favorites such as Mother's Brownies and Mama Hudson's Chicken Salad.

SHRIMP SALAD

7½ cups water
1½ teaspoons salt, divided
2½ pounds unpeeled medium-size
  fresh shrimp
1½ cups long-grain rice, uncooked
1 small onion, finely chopped
1 small green pepper, finely
  chopped
1 cup chopped cauliflower
1 (3-ounce) jar pimiento-stuffed
  olives, drained and chopped
1 cup mayonnaise or salad dressing
½ teaspoon pepper
Lettuce leaves

Bring water and 1 teaspoon salt to a boil; add shrimp, and cook 3 to 5 minutes or until shrimp turn pink. Drain well; rinse with cold water. Peel, devein, and chop shrimp; set aside.

Cook rice according to package directions. Combine rice, shrimp, remaining ½ teaspoon salt, onion, and next 5 ingredients; cover and chill. Serve in a lettuce-lined bowl with crackers. Yield: 10 cups.

SAUSAGE PINWHEELS

2 cups self-rising flour
¼ cup shortening
⅔ cup milk
¾ pound bulk hot pork
  sausage

Place flour in a medium bowl; cut in shortening with a pastry blender until mixture is crumbly. Add milk, stirring with a fork until dry ingredients are moistened. Turn dough out onto a lightly floured surface; knead lightly 3 or 4 times.

Roll dough into a 12- x 9-inch rectangle. Spread uncooked sausage (at room temperature) over dough, leaving a ½-inch border. Roll up, jellyroll fashion, starting at long side; pinch seam to seal. Wrap in plastic wrap, and refrigerate several hours.

Unwrap and cut roll into ¼-inch slices, and place 1 inch apart on lightly greased baking sheets. Bake at 450° for 12 to 14 minutes or until golden brown. Serve warm or at room temperature. Yield: about 3½ dozen.

MAMA HUDSON'S CHICKEN SALAD

1 (3½-pound) broiler-fryer
2 quarts water
1 teaspoon salt
⅓ cup coarsely chopped celery
4 large hard-cooked eggs, finely
  chopped
½ cup sweet pickle cubes
¾ cup mayonnaise or salad
  dressing
½ teaspoon salt
¼ teaspoon pepper
Lettuce leaves

Combine first 3 ingredients in a Dutch oven; bring to a boil. Cover, reduce heat, and simmer 1 hour or until chicken is tender; remove chicken. (Reserve broth for another use.) Let cool; skin and bone chicken.

Position knife blade in food processor bowl; add half of chicken. Pulse several times or until chicken is finely chopped, stopping once to scrape down sides; transfer to a large bowl. Repeat procedure with remaining chicken. With knife blade in position, add celery; pulse 2 or 3 times or until finely chopped.

Combine chicken, celery, eggs, and next 4 ingredients. Cover and chill at least 2 hours; spoon into a lettuce-lined bowl, and serve with crackers. Yield: 2¾ cups.

TRAWLER CRAB DIP

1¼ cups mayonnaise or salad
  dressing
1 cup fresh crabmeat, drained and
  flaked *
¼ cup commercial French salad
  dressing
½ cup (2 ounces) finely shredded
  Cheddar cheese
1 teaspoon prepared horseradish

Combine all ingredients; cover and refrigerate. Serve dip with crackers. Yield: 2 cups.

* 1 (4¼-ounce) can lump crabmeat, drained, may be substituted for 1 cup fresh crabmeat.

HOT TACO DIP

1 pound lean ground beef
1 medium onion, chopped
1 (16-ounce) can spicy chili beans,
  undrained
1 (4-ounce) can mushroom stems
  and pieces, undrained
1 (1¼-ounce) envelope taco
  seasoning mix
1 to 2 tablespoons chili powder
½ teaspoon garlic salt
1 cup (4 ounces) shredded Cheddar
  cheese

Combine beef and onion in a Dutch oven; cook until beef is browned, stirring until it crumbles. Drain. Add beans and next 4 ingredients; cover, reduce heat, and simmer 15 minutes, stirring occasionally. Serve immediately or refrigerate. To serve, spoon into a chafing dish, and heat; sprinkle with cheese. Serve with corn chips. Yield: 3⅔ cups.

MYSTERY BARS

1 cup all-purpose flour
1½ cups firmly packed brown sugar, divided
½ cup butter or margarine, softened
2 large eggs
2 tablespoons all-purpose flour
½ teaspoon baking powder
¼ teaspoon salt
1 cup chopped pecans
½ cup flaked coconut
1 teaspoon vanilla extract

Combine 1 cup flour and ½ cup brown sugar; cut in butter with pastry blender until mixture is crumbly. Press into bottom of a 9-inch square pan. Bake at 350° for 15 minutes.

Beat eggs at medium speed with an electric mixer about 2 minutes or until thick and pale. Stir in remaining 1 cup sugar, 2 tablespoons flour, baking powder, and salt; add pecans, coconut, and vanilla, mixing well. Spoon into pan. Bake at 350° for 30 minutes. Cut into bars. Yield: 16 bars.

MOTHER'S BROWNIES

½ cup butter or margarine, melted
1 cup sugar
2 large eggs
1 teaspoon vanilla extract
⅔ cup all-purpose flour
¼ cup cocoa
⅛ teaspoon salt
1 cup chopped pecans
Chocolate Frosting

Combine butter and sugar in a large bowl; stir in eggs and vanilla. Combine

flour, cocoa, and salt; stir into butter mixture. Stir in pecans. Pour into a greased and floured 8-inch square pan. Bake at 325° for 25 to 30 minutes or until a wooden pick inserted in center comes out clean. Cool in pan on a wire rack. Spread Chocolate Frosting over top. Cut into squares. Yield: 16 brownies.

Chocolate Frosting

1 cup sifted powdered sugar
2½ tablespoons cocoa
2 tablespoons butter or margarine, melted
1 to 1½ tablespoons half-and-half
1 teaspoon vanilla extract

Combine first 3 ingredients in a small mixing bowl; beat at low speed with an electric mixer until blended. Add half-and-half and vanilla; beat at high speed until spreading consistency. Yield: about 1 cup.

STRAWBERRIES JAMAICA

1 (16-ounce) carton nonfat sour cream alternative
½ cup fat-free cream cheese
½ cup firmly packed brown sugar
2 tablespoons Grand Marnier or other orange-flavored liqueur
1½ to 2 quarts fresh strawberries

Combine first 4 ingredients; cover and chill. Serve with strawberries. Yield: 2⅓ cups.

Recipes That Cut The Mustard

We're all familiar with the bright-yellow (often called "prepared") mustard on hot dogs. And most of us have used Dijon mustard, the French version made from brown mustard seeds. But don't stop there.

Take a look at today's grocery shelf. The yellow plastic squeeze bottle is surrounded by jars of designer mustards. We've used a variety of these mustards to give zing to the following recipes. And if you want to make your own, see the recipes for mustard on page 240.

TURKEY CUTLETS WITH TARRAGON-MUSTARD SAUCE

4 turkey cutlets
1 teaspoon garlic salt
¼ teaspoon pepper
2 tablespoons olive oil
½ cup plain yogurt
2 tablespoons Dijon mustard
¼ teaspoon dried tarragon
¼ teaspoon sugar
⅛ teaspoon hot sauce

Sprinkle turkey with garlic salt and pepper. Cook in hot olive oil in a large skillet over medium-high heat 2 minutes on each side. Remove turkey, and keep warm. Combine yogurt and remaining ingredients in skillet; cook over low heat until thoroughly heated. Serve over turkey. Yield: 4 servings.
Cathy Darling
Grafton, West Virginia

MUSTARD CHICKEN

4 skinned and boned chicken breast halves
1 (8-ounce) jar sweet brown mustard
1 teaspoon mustard seeds

Place chicken on a lightly greased rack; place rack in a broiler pan. Combine mustard and mustard seeds; brush on chicken breasts. Broil 5½ inches from heat (with electric oven door partially opened) 15 to 20 minutes or until done. Yield: 4 servings.

Note: For sweet brown mustard, we used Honeycup prepared mustard.
Alice Pahl
Raleigh, North Carolina

SHRIMP WITH MUSTARD-VINEGAR SAUCE

6 cups water
2 pounds unpeeled medium-size
    fresh shrimp
¼ cup tarragon vinegar
2 tablespoons commercial
    horseradish mustard
1 tablespoon catsup
¼ cup chopped green onions
¼ cup chopped celery
1 small clove garlic, minced
1½ teaspoons paprika
¼ teaspoon salt
¼ teaspoon ground red pepper
½ cup vegetable oil
Lettuce leaves

Bring water to a boil; add shrimp, and cook 3 to 5 minutes or until shrimp turn pink. Drain well; rinse with cold water. Chill; peel and devein shrimp.

Combine vinegar and next 8 ingredients in container of an electric blender; process until smooth, stopping once to scrape down sides. With blender on high, slowly add oil. Arrange shrimp on lettuce, and drizzle with mustard-vinegar mixture. Yield: 4 to 6 servings.   *Sandy Pichon*
Slidell, Louisiana

POTATO STIR-FRY

1½ pounds new potatoes, unpeeled
    and cut into wedges
1½ teaspoons dried rosemary
3 tablespoons vegetable oil
1 large sweet red pepper, cut into
    thin strips
1 (10-ounce) package frozen
    English peas, thawed *
2 tablespoons prepared mustard
½ teaspoon salt

Cook potatoes and rosemary in oil in a large skillet over medium-high heat 7 to 8 minutes, stirring constantly, until potatoes are crisp-tender and lightly browned. Add red pepper strips; cook, stirring constantly, 3 minutes. Add peas, mustard, and salt; cook over medium heat 2 minutes or until

peas are thoroughly heated. Yield: 6 to 8 servings.

* ¾ pound Sugar Snap peas, shelled, may be substituted; cook with sweet red pepper strips.   *Nora Henshaw*
Okemah, Oklahoma

HOT MUSTARD SAUCE

2 tablespoons dry hot mustard
1 tablespoon teriyaki sauce
1 tablespoon white vinegar
⅔ cup sour cream
⅔ cup mayonnaise

Combine first 3 ingredients, stirring until smooth; stir in sour cream and mayonnaise. Cover and chill. Serve with vegetables or as a sandwich spread. Yield: 1½ cups.

CREAMY MUSTARD SAUCE

⅓ cup whipping cream
½ cup sour cream
3 tablespoons Dijon mustard
2 tablespoons prepared horseradish
2 teaspoons lemon juice
½ teaspoon salt
½ teaspoon ground white pepper
2 tablespoons vegetable oil

Beat whipping cream at medium speed with an electric mixer until soft peaks form. Add sour cream and next 5 ingredients, beating until blended. Gradually add oil, a few drops at a time, beating just until blended. Cover and chill. Serve with pork, beef, corned beef, or vegetables. Yield: 1⅓ cups.   *Millie Givens*
Savannah, Georgia

■ Try these quick, easy recipes for making your own designer mustards—Horseradish, Jalapeño, Bourbon, and Hot Honey.

HORSERADISH MUSTARD

½ cup Dijon mustard
¼ cup sour cream
3 tablespoons prepared horseradish

Combine all ingredients; cover and refrigerate at least 2 hours. Serve with beef. Yield: about 1 cup.

JALAPEÑO MUSTARD

½ cup prepared mustard
1 to 2 tablespoons pickled jalapeño
    peppers, seeded and finely
    chopped

Combine mustard and jalapeño peppers; cover and refrigerate at least 2 hours. Serve with hamburgers, hot dogs, or as a sandwich spread. Yield: ½ cup.

BOURBON MUSTARD

½ cup Dijon or stone-ground
    mustard
3 tablespoons bourbon

Combine mustard and bourbon; cover and refrigerate at least 2 hours. Serve with pork or beef. Yield: ½ cup.

HOT HONEY MUSTARD

½ cup Dijon mustard
¼ cup honey

Combine mustard and honey; cover and refrigerate at least 2 hours. Serve with ham or as a sandwich spread. Yield: ¾ cup.

A Plate Tailored For Fall

If summer's end leaves you feeling a little blue, take heart. We'd like to prescribe this fall vegetable plate to raise your spirits.

It's a meal of sweet, earthy combinations. Just try our salad of apples and mixed greens drizzled with a dressing of vinegar, brown sugar, and bacon drippings. Breadcrumbs and rosemary coat the sweet potato rounds. They're baked rather than fried and served on a bed of chutney. The menu even includes the stubby turnip, cut into cubes and sautéed with sweet red pepper and carrots, and seasoned with mace.

Finally, what gathering of vegetables would be complete without corn sticks? Thyme and garlic jazz up this version. If you're running short on time, just stir them into your favorite cornbread mix.

OVEN-FRIED SWEET POTATOES WITH CHUTNEY

3 large sweet potatoes, unpeeled (about 2 pounds)
⅔ cup fine, dry breadcrumbs
¾ teaspoon dried rosemary
⅓ cup milk
Vegetable cooking spray
Commercial mango chutney

Scrub potatoes; cut crosswise into ⅜-inch slices.

Combine breadcrumbs and rosemary; dip each potato slice in milk, and dredge in breadcrumb mixture. Place on a lightly greased baking sheet, and coat potatoes with cooking spray. Bake at 450° for 15 minutes; turn potatoes, and bake 10 to 15 minutes or until tender. Serve with mango chutney. Yield: 6 servings.

CARROT-TURNIP SAUTÉ

2 large turnips, peeled (about 1 pound)
3 medium carrots, scraped
3 tablespoons butter or margarine
¼ teaspoon salt
¼ teaspoon pepper
1 small sweet red pepper, finely chopped
½ teaspoon ground mace

Cut turnips and carrots into ½-inch cubes; set aside. Melt butter in a skillet over medium-high heat. Add turnips, carrots, salt, and pepper; cook, stirring constantly, over medium-high heat 5 minutes. Add chopped sweet red pepper; cook, stirring constantly, 2 minutes or until vegetables are tender. Sprinkle with mace, and stir once. Yield: 6 servings.

SALAD GREENS WITH APPLE AND BRIE

1 Red Delicious apple, cut into thin wedges
Apple cider
4 slices bacon
¼ cup apple cider
¼ cup balsamic vinegar
1 tablespoon brown sugar
6 cups mixed salad greens, torn
Walnut-Baked Brie

Dip apple wedges in cider to prevent browning; set aside.

Cook bacon in a small skillet until crisp; remove bacon, reserving 1 tablespoon drippings in skillet. Crumble bacon, and set aside. Add ¼ cup apple cider, balsamic vinegar, and brown sugar to drippings; cook dressing over medium heat, stirring constantly, until sugar dissolves.

Just before serving, arrange greens, apple slices, and Walnut-Baked Brie on plates. Drizzle with dressing, and sprinkle with crumbled bacon. Yield: 6 servings.

Walnut-Baked Brie

1 (8-ounce) round Brie
2 tablespoons brown sugar
¼ cup walnuts, toasted and coarsely chopped

Remove top rind from Brie. Cut cheese into 6 wedges; place on a lightly greased baking sheet. Sprinkle cheese with brown sugar and walnuts. Bake at 450° for 2 to 3 minutes or just until soft. Serve immediately. Yield: 6 servings.

Tip: *Deep green, yellow, and orange fruit and vegetables are good sources of vitamin A. Common sources of vitamin C are citrus fruit, deep green vegetables, and potatoes.*

GARLIC-THYME CORN STICKS

1¼ cups yellow cornmeal
¾ cup all-purpose flour
1 tablespoon sugar
1 tablespoon plus 1 teaspoon
 baking powder
¾ teaspoon salt
¾ teaspoon garlic powder
1 tablespoon chopped fresh thyme
 or 1 teaspoon dried thyme
2 large eggs, lightly beaten
1 cup milk
¼ cup vegetable oil

Heat well-greased, cast-iron corn stick pans in a 425° oven for 3 minutes or until hot. Combine first 7 ingredients in a large bowl; make a well in center of mixture. Combine eggs, milk, and oil; add to dry ingredients, stirring just until moistened.

Remove pans from oven; spoon batter into pans, filling two-thirds full. Bake at 425° for 12 minutes or until lightly browned. Yield: 1½ dozen.

Frozen Assets

Wouldn't it be great to open your freezer and find a terrific meal that could be ready in minutes? If you're in the market for some make-ahead ideas, try these blue-chip reader recipes. Sample them individually or together in our menus. You'll soon be convinced that cooking ahead and freezing pays handsome dividends.

Because each main-dish recipe generously serves eight, you may want to package servings for two or four in each freezer container. Remember to choose containers that are similar in size to the amount of food being frozen. Leave about ½ inch of space at the top, because foods will expand during freezing. More than ½ inch of space allows too much extra air, causing large ice crystals to form. This results in freezer burn, which damages the taste and texture of food. Make

sure you seal freezer containers tightly and label them clearly.

Before packing and freezing, quickly cool foods, uncovered in the refrigerator, stirring occasionally. Cooling at room temperature can create food safety problems.

For best results, use airtight, moisture-proof packaging materials, including microwave-safe, rigid plastic containers and heavy-duty plastic storage bags designed for freezing. When you are ready to reheat, simply use the microwave, or thaw overnight in the refrigerator and reheat in a conventional oven.

MEXICAN FIESTA

Grapefruit Freeze
Chili Cheese Spread
With crackers
Mexican Chicken Rolls
Commercial Spanish rice
Praline Brownies
Commercial vanilla ice cream

GRAPEFRUIT FREEZE

1½ cups sugar
1 cup water
½ cup chopped mint leaves
1 (46-ounce) can unsweetened
 grapefruit juice
Garnish: fresh mint sprigs

Combine sugar and water in a medium saucepan; bring to a boil. Add mint; cover and let stand 5 minutes. Pour mixture through a wire-mesh strainer into an 8-cup container; discard mint. Add grapefruit juice. Divide mixture into two 1-quart freezer containers; cover and freeze. Remove from freezer 2 hours before serving. Stir until slushy. Garnish, if desired. Yield: about 2 quarts.   *Regina Axtell*
Buffalo, Texas

CHILI CHEESE SPREAD

1 (8-ounce) package cream cheese,
 softened
1 (1¾-ounce) envelope chili
 seasoning mix
3 tablespoons commercial salsa
1 cup chopped pecans
2 cups (8 ounces) finely shredded
 Monterey Jack cheese, divided
Garnish: fresh parsley sprigs,
 jalapeño pepper

Combine first 3 ingredients; beat at medium speed with an electric mixer until smooth. Stir in pecans and 1 cup cheese. Divide mixture in half; shape each portion into a cheese log or cheese ball. Roll each log in remaining cheese. Wrap each in plastic wrap; cover with aluminum foil, and freeze up to 3 months. Thaw at room temperature just before serving. Garnish, if desired, and serve with crackers. Yield: 3 cups.   *Bunny Campbell*
Gainesville, Florida

MEXICAN·CHICKEN ROLLS

½ cup fine, dry breadcrumbs
¼ cup grated Parmesan cheese
1 teaspoon chili powder
¼ teaspoon ground cumin
¼ teaspoon pepper
8 skinned and boned chicken breast
 halves
1 (8-ounce) package Monterey Jack
 cheese with peppers, cut
 crosswise into 8 equal slices
⅓ cup butter or margarine, melted

Combine first 5 ingredients in a shallow dish; set aside.

Place each chicken breast between 2 sheets of wax paper; flatten to ¼-inch thickness using a meat mallet or rolling pin. Place a slice of cheese on each chicken breast. Roll up from short side, and secure with wooden picks. Dip chicken rolls in butter, and dredge in breadcrumb mixture. Place rolls, seam side down, on a baking sheet. Cover and freeze until firm; transfer to a large heavy-duty plastic freezer bag and return to freezer. Freeze up to 6 months.

To serve, place frozen chicken rolls in a lightly greased 11- x 7- x 1½-inch baking dish; bake at 400° for 30 minutes. Yield: 8 servings.

Valynda Kingsley
Woodbridge, Virginia

PRALINE BROWNIES

1 (21.5-ounce) package fudge
 brownie mix
¾ cup firmly packed brown sugar
¾ cup chopped pecans
3 tablespoons butter or margarine,
 melted

Prepare brownie mix according to package directions; spoon batter into a 13- x 9- x 2-inch pan. Combine brown sugar and remaining ingredients, and sprinkle over batter. Bake at 350° for 30 to 35 minutes. Cool in pan on a wire rack. Cut into squares. Wrap each square in heavy-duty plastic wrap, and place in an airtight container; freeze up to 6 months. Thaw at room temperature 2 hours before serving. Yield: 2 dozen.

Kathy Alexander
Spartanburg, South Carolina

Freezing Facts

■ Select containers for freezing that will hold only enough of a fruit or vegetable for one meal.

■ For the quickest freezing, leave a little space between freezer containers so that air can circulate freely. Place containers closer together after they are frozen.

WEEKNIGHT DELIGHT

Commercial vegetable juice
Turkey Noodle Bake
Mixed greens with
Vinaigrette dressing
Commercial garlic bread
Vanilla Almond Crunch

TURKEY NOODLE BAKE

2 pounds ground turkey or beef
2 cups chopped celery
¼ cup chopped green pepper
¼ cup chopped onion
2 tablespoons olive oil
1 (10¾-ounce) can cream of
 mushroom soup, undiluted
¼ cup soy sauce
1 (8-ounce) can sliced water
 chestnuts, drained
1 (4.5-ounce) jar sliced mushrooms,
 drained
1 (4-ounce) jar chopped pimiento,
 drained
1 teaspoon salt
½ teaspoon lemon-pepper
 seasoning
1 (5-ounce) package egg noodles
1 (8-ounce) container sour cream
¼ cup sliced almonds, toasted
Garnish: celery leaves

Line two 2-quart shallow baking dishes with aluminum foil. Set aside.

Cook first 4 ingredients in olive oil in a Dutch oven over medium heat until meat crumbles, stirring often. Drain. Stir in mushroom soup and next 6 ingredients. Bring turkey mixture to a boil; cover, reduce heat, and simmer 20 minutes, stirring often.

Cook noodles according to package directions; drain. Stir noodles and sour cream into turkey mixture; divide in half. Spoon into prepared dishes, and freeze. Frozen casseroles may be removed from baking dishes. Wrap in foil or place in large heavy-duty plastic freezer bags; freeze up to 6 months.

To serve one or both casseroles, remove foil, and place frozen casserole in a lightly greased 2-quart shallow

baking dish. Cover and bake at 350° for 1 hour and 30 minutes or until thoroughly heated. Sprinkle with almonds, and garnish, if desired. Yield: 4 servings per casserole.

Note: To omit freezing, immediately bake assembled casserole in a lightly greased 2-quart baking dish at 350° for 20 minutes or until heated.

Jane Maloy
Wilmington, North Carolina

VANILLA ALMOND CRUNCH

¼ cup butter or margarine
1½ cups flaked coconut
1 (3-ounce) package slivered
 almonds
1 (5.1-ounce) package instant
 vanilla pudding mix
1 teaspoon almond extract
2½ cups milk
1 (2.6-ounce) package whipped
 topping mix
1 cup milk
1 teaspoon vanilla extract

Combine first 3 ingredients in a 13- x 9- x 2-inch pan. Bake at 350° for 10 minutes, stirring every 3 minutes. Cool. Reserve ½ cup coconut mixture for topping; spread remaining coconut mixture evenly in pan.

Combine pudding mix, almond extract, and 2½ cups milk in a large mixing bowl; beat at low speed with an electric mixer 2 minutes or until smooth. Transfer to a large bowl.

Combine 2 envelopes whipped topping mix, 1 cup milk, and vanilla in large mixing bowl. Beat at high speed about 4 minutes or until mixture thickens and forms peaks; fold into pudding mixture. Spoon over coconut mixture, and sprinkle with reserved ½ cup coconut mixture. Freeze until firm. Cover with plastic wrap and aluminum foil; freeze up to 1 month.

Remove from freezer; let stand 10 minutes before serving. Yield: 12 to 15 servings. *Mrs. Clifford Davis*
Fort Smith, Arkansas

A Halloween Party You'll Love At First Bite

If you're haunted by thoughts of giving traditional goodies this Halloween, consider this wholesome class party menu that serves 30. Kids will love Monster Mash Dip with fresh vegetable dippers, Black Widow Snack Cake, Buzzard's Nests, Caramel-Peanut Apples, and Popcorn With Pizzazz—all washed down with a tingling glass of Witch's Brew.

Except for the punch, these quick and simple recipes can be made a day in advance. If the party is not held at home, carry beverage ingredients, dip, and vegetables on ice and then transfer them to a refrigerator or freezer until serving time.

For added ease, use Halloween-themed paper plates, plastic tumblers, and serving trays.

WITCH'S BREW

3 (12-ounce) containers frozen unsweetened apple juice concentrate, thawed and undiluted
9 cups water
½ cup lime juice
½ gallon lime sherbet, softened
9 cups club soda, chilled

Combine apple juice, water, and lime juice in a large bowl; cover mixture and chill. Just before serving, spoon sherbet into a large punch bowl; slowly pour apple juice mixture and club soda over sherbet, stirring gently. Yield: 28 cups (92 calories [5% from fat] per ¾-cup serving).

□ *0.6g protein, 0.5g fat (0g saturated), 21.9g carbohydrate, 0g fiber, 0mg cholesterol, 47mg sodium, and 25mg calcium.*

MONSTER MASH DIP

4½ cups 1% low-fat cottage cheese
⅓ cup fat-free mayonnaise or salad dressing
3 tablespoons white vinegar
3 tablespoons grated Parmesan cheese
3 tablespoons finely chopped onion
1 tablespoon chopped fresh or frozen chives
¼ teaspoon dried dillweed
¼ teaspoon pepper

Position knife blade in food processor bowl; add all ingredients. Process until smooth. Cover and refrigerate at least 1 hour; serve with assorted fresh vegetables. Yield: 4 cups (28 calories [15% from fat] per 2 tablespoons dip).

□ *4.2g protein, 0.5g fat (0.3g saturated), 1.6g carbohydrate, 0g fiber, 2mg cholesterol, 173mg sodium, and 26mg calcium.*

CARAMEL-PEANUT APPLES

10 medium apples
10 wooden craft sticks
1 (14-ounce) package caramels
2 tablespoons water
⅔ cup honey-roasted peanuts, finely chopped
Vegetable cooking spray

Wash and dry apples; insert craft sticks into stem end of each apple. Set aside. Combine caramels and water in a medium bowl; microwave at HIGH 3½ to 4½ minutes or until smooth, stirring after each minute.

Dip two-thirds of each apple into hot caramel sauce, turning to coat. Scrape excess sauce from bottom of apples; roll coated bottoms in peanuts. Place on wax paper coated with cooking spray. Store in refrigerator. Let stand at room temperature 15 minutes before serving to allow caramel to soften. Yield: 10 servings (279 calories [19% from fat] per apple).

□ *3.7g protein, 5.8g fat (3.2g saturated), 55.1g carbohydrate, 4.8g fiber, 3mg cholesterol, 135mg sodium, and 64mg calcium.*

Note: For 30 Caramel-Peanut Apples, make the recipe three times. Do not triple; three packages of caramels are difficult to work with at one time.

BUZZARD'S NESTS

2 egg whites
⅛ teaspoon cream of tartar
½ teaspoon ground cinnamon
¾ teaspoon vanilla extract
Dash of salt
⅔ cup sugar
½ (10-ounce) package large shredded whole wheat cereal biscuits, crushed
1 (12-ounce) package candy-coated chocolate-covered peanuts

Combine first 5 ingredients in a small mixing bowl; beat at high speed with an electric mixer until soft peaks form.

Gradually add sugar, 1 tablespoon at a time, beating until stiff peaks form and sugar dissolves; stir in crushed cereal. Drop by level tablespoonfuls onto lightly greased baking sheets; make an indentation in center of each with the back of a teaspoon. Place 3 peanut candies in each indentation; bake at 275° for 30 minutes or until set. Immediately remove to wire racks to cool. Store in an airtight container. Yield: 3 dozen (78 calories [29% from fat] per cookie).

□ *1.6g protein, 2.5g fat (1g saturated), 12.5g carbohydrate, 0.4g fiber, 0mg cholesterol, 14mg sodium, and 10mg calcium.*

POPCORN WITH PIZZAZZ

¾ teaspoon salt
½ teaspoon onion powder
½ teaspoon garlic powder
½ teaspoon chili powder
½ teaspoon paprika
½ teaspoon ground thyme
2½ teaspoons grated Parmesan
   cheese
15 cups popped corn (popped
   without fat or salt)
Butter-flavored cooking spray

Combine first 7 ingredients. Coat popped corn lightly with cooking spray; sprinkle with about one-third of seasoning mixture, and toss. Repeat procedure twice; serve immediately. Yield: 15 cups (100 calories [13% from fat] per 3-cup serving).

□ *3.4g protein, 1.5g fat (0.3g saturated), 19.5g carbohydrate, 3.8g fiber, 1mg cholesterol, 371mg sodium, and 21mg calcium.)*

Note: For party setting where numerous foods are served, allow ½ cup popcorn for each child.

BLACK WIDOW SNACK CAKE

1 (18.5-ounce) package low-fat
   devil's food cake mix
Vegetable cooking spray
4 cups sifted powdered sugar
5 to 7 tablespoons skim milk
1 cup sifted powdered sugar
¼ cup unsweetened cocoa
2 tablespoons skim milk
Garnish: plastic spider

Prepare cake mix according to package directions, using 3 egg whites. Pour into two 8-inch square aluminum foil pans coated with cooking spray; bake at 350° for 30 to 35 minutes or until a wooden pick inserted in center comes out clean. Cool in pans on a wire rack.

Combine 4 cups powdered sugar and 5 to 7 tablespoons milk in a large bowl; spread a thin layer of mixture evenly over each cake.

Combine 1 cup powdered sugar, cocoa, and 2 tablespoons milk; spoon into a small zip-top plastic bag. Close bag securely, and snip a tiny hole in bottom corner of bag; carefully pipe concentric circles onto each cake. Pipe straight lines at intervals from the inner circle through the outside circle, forming a web design. Garnish, if desired. Yield: 32 servings (141 calories [11% from fat] per serving).

□ *1.4g protein, 1.7g fat (0.4g saturated), 31.9g carbohydrate, 0g fiber, 0mg cholesterol, 134mg sodium, and 43mg calcium.*

Outsmart the Halloween Diet Demons

■ Limit the number of houses your kids visit and the amount of candy they collect.

■ Allow candy only after mealtime, and control portions.

■ Form a pact with your neighbors to pass out only nutritious treats to children on their rounds. Develop a master list of choices and have everyone commit to something different for variety.

■ Design your own Halloween party with a healthful menu.

■ Who says treats have to be edible? Pencils, erasers, cups, straws in funny shapes, or balloons with Halloween themes are alternatives that won't send little goblins to the dentist.

■ Focus on fun instead of food. Have a howling contest or stage a showy costume parade.

Indulge In French Onion Soup

Nothing beats a good bowl of hot soup, especially when you treat yourself to this lighter version of French Onion Soup. Our recipe has 28 fewer grams of fat, less than half the calories, and only a fraction of the cholesterol of its heftier counterpart.

The original recipe called for ½ pound of butter, but we shaved it down to 2 tablespoons, drastically cutting fat while salvaging satisfying flavor. By replacing a portion of beef consommé with canned, no-salt-added, fat-free beef broth and water, we also reduced the sodium content from 1,878 milligrams per serving to 798. A small amount of Chablis and freshly ground pepper add flavor.

FRENCH ONION SOUP

Vegetable cooking spray
2 tablespoons butter
6 large onions, thinly sliced (3 pounds)
2 (10½-ounce) cans beef consommé, undiluted
1 (13¾-ounce) can ready-to-serve, no-salt-added, fat-free beef-flavored broth
1⅓ cups water
¼ cup Chablis or other dry white wine
¼ teaspoon freshly ground pepper
7 (1-inch-thick) slices French bread
¼ cup grated Parmesan cheese

Melt butter in a Dutch oven coated with cooking spray. Add onion, and cook over medium heat, 5 minutes, stirring often. Add 1 can of beef consommé; cook over low heat 30 minutes. Gradually add remaining beef consommé, and next 4 ingredients; bring to a boil, reduce heat, and simmer 10 minutes.

Place bread slices on a baking sheet; sprinkle with Parmesan cheese. Broil 6 inches from heat (with electric oven door partially opened) until cheese is golden brown. Ladle soup into serving bowls, and top each with a toasted bread slice. Yield: 7 servings (219 calories [22% from fat] per 1-cup serving).

□ *9.4g protein, 5.3g fat (2.8g saturated), 33.5g carbohydrate, 4g fiber, 28mg cholesterol, 798mg sodium, and 91mg calcium.*

COMPARE THE NUTRIENTS (per serving)		
	Traditional	Light
Calories	475	219
Fat	33.2g	5.3g
Cholesterol	116mg	28mg

A New Slant On Slaw

Shred your old ideas of coleslaw; there's no cabbage allowed in this innovative collection. Instead, we've dug into the bountiful harvest of fall fruits and vegetables for some surprising new flavor combinations. These recipes still have the same make-ahead advantage of traditional cabbage versions. And for Zesty Broccoli Slaw you can use a preshredded, bagged broccoli mixture found in many produce sections.

SWEET POTATO-CURRANT SLAW

1 cup water
1 large sweet potato, peeled and shredded (about 1 pound)
1 Red Delicious apple, unpeeled and shredded
¼ cup currants or golden raisins
½ cup vanilla low-fat yogurt
2 tablespoons orange juice
1 tablespoon honey
Lettuce leaves
½ cup chopped pecans, toasted

Bring water to a boil in a large saucepan; add sweet potato. Cover and cook 1 minute; drain immediately. Place sweet potato in ice water; let stand 5 minutes. Drain well, and pat dry with paper towels.

Combine sweet potato and next 5 ingredients, tossing to coat. Cover and refrigerate 2 to 3 hours. To serve, spoon onto lettuce leaves, and sprinkle with pecans. Yield: 4 to 6 servings.

ZESTY BROCCOLI SLAW

1½ pounds fresh broccoli *
¾ cup cider vinegar
¾ cup vegetable oil
1 clove garlic, pressed
2 teaspoons dried dillweed
¾ teaspoon salt

Remove broccoli leaves, and cut off tough ends of lower stalks; discard. Wash broccoli. Remove flowerets. (Reserve flowerets for another use.) Cut stems into thin strips; place in a medium bowl.

Combine vinegar and remaining ingredients; pour mixture over broccoli, stirring gently to coat. Cover and chill at least 2 hours. Drain before serving, or serve with a slotted spoon. Yield: 6 servings.

* 1 (16-ounce) package fresh broccoli, carrot, and red cabbage slaw mix may be substituted for fresh broccoli.

Gwen Louer
Roswell, Georgia

These Rings Lighten Up

Remember the old-fashioned drive-in restaurant where you enjoyed many a fried onion ring? Now you can make this favorite treat at home, with almost no fat and only a fraction of the calories in the original.

CRISPY BAKED ONION RINGS

2 large sweet onions
1 (7-ounce) package corn flakes
  cereal, crushed
1 teaspoon seasoned salt
2 teaspoons sugar
1 teaspoon paprika
1 cup egg substitute
Vegetable cooking spray

Cut each onion into 4 thick slices; separate into rings. (Reserve small rings for another use.) Set aside.

Combine cereal and next 3 ingredients; divide in half, and set aside.

Beat egg substitute at high speed with an electric mixer until soft peaks form. Dip half of onion rings in egg substitute; dredge in half of crumb mixture. Place in a single layer on baking sheets coated with cooking spray. Repeat procedure with remaining onion rings, egg substitute, and crumb mixture. Bake at 375° for 15 minutes or until crisp; serve warm. Yield: 4 servings (254 calories [2% from fat] per serving).

□ 10.8g protein, 0.5g fat (0.1g saturated), 50.6g carbohydrate, 2.2g fiber, 0mg cholesterol, 1,178mg sodium, and 39mg calcium.

Mega Meat Loaves

Who would have guessed it could happen? The humble meat loaf—a weeknight staple—has gone fancy on us—in looks and taste, that is.

Our well-rounded meat loaves bring unconventional flavors to this traditional main dish. Minted Lamb Meat Loaf is seasoned with herbs common in Greek cooking. Canned tomatoes with green chiles fire up Southwestern Meat Loaf.

It's always been a difficult choice: Finish the meat loaf at supper or save some for sandwiches later. With these three delicious recipes, the decision just got harder.

■ Serve leftover Blue Cheese Meat Loaf Roll on French bread spread with a commercial creamy mustard blend.

BLUE CHEESE MEAT LOAF ROLL

8 slices white bread, torn into
  small pieces
¼ cup milk
1 (4-ounce) package blue cheese,
  crumbled
1 large egg, lightly beaten
1 pound lean ground beef
½ pound ground pork
2 cups soft breadcrumbs (about
  5 slices white bread)
½ cup chopped onion
2 teaspoons salt
⅛ teaspoon pepper
3 tablespoons chopped fresh parsley
3 tablespoons catsup
1 tablespoon Worcestershire sauce
2 large eggs, lightly beaten
Garnish: fresh parsley

Combine bread and milk; stir in cheese and 1 egg. Set aside.

Combine ground beef and next 9 ingredients. Shape into a 15- x 12-inch rectangle on heavy-duty plastic wrap. Spread blue cheese mixture on top, leaving a 1-inch margin around edges. Starting at the short side and using plastic wrap to lift, roll up jellyroll fashion. Press edges and ends to seal. Place, seam side down, on a lightly greased rack; place rack in broiler pan. Bake at 375° for 1 hour. Garnish, if desired. Yield: 6 to 8 servings.

Judith Hartley
Signal Mountain, Tennessee

Tip: *Lightly mix and shape ground meat or meat loaf mixtures. Excessive handling of the meat results in a compact mixture.*

■ Fold up leftover Southwestern Meat Loaf in flour tortillas, and drizzle with commercial salsa.

SOUTHWESTERN MEAT LOAF

4 slices whole wheat bread
1 large onion, chopped
½ green pepper, chopped
1 pound lean ground beef
½ pound ground pork
2 large eggs, lightly beaten
1 (10-ounce) can tomatoes with green chiles
¾ teaspoon salt

Position knife blade in food processor bowl; add bread and process about 15 seconds or until reduced to fine crumbs. Transfer to a large bowl, and set aside.

Cook onion and green pepper in a nonstick skillet, stirring constantly, until tender. Stir onion and green pepper into breadcrumbs; add ground beef and remaining ingredients, mixing well. (Mixture will be soft.) Shape into a 12-inch loaf, and place on a lightly greased rack; place rack in broiler pan. Cover loosely with aluminum foil. Bake at 375° for 1 hour; remove foil, and bake an additional 20 minutes. Let stand 5 minutes. Yield: 6 servings.   *Amber Louise Jenkins*
Buckhannon, West Virginia

■ Serve leftover Minted Lamb Meat Loaf in halved pita bread rounds spread with plain yogurt. Tuck in thin slivers of cucumber for a cool crunch.

MINTED LAMB MEAT LOAF

2½ pounds lean ground lamb
1 large onion, finely chopped
1 medium-size green pepper, finely chopped
2 cloves garlic, minced
1 (8-ounce) can tomato sauce
½ cup fine, dry breadcrumbs
2 large eggs, lightly beaten
½ cup loosely packed fresh mint leaves, finely chopped
2 teaspoons dried oregano
2 teaspoons dried basil
2 teaspoons pepper
1 teaspoon dried rosemary, crushed
½ teaspoon salt

Combine all ingredients in a large bowl. Firmly press into a lightly greased 9- x 5- x 3-inch loafpan. Bake, uncovered, at 350° for 1½ hours or until done. Drain off juices, and remove from pan. Yield: 8 to 10 servings.   *Lorraine Brownell*
Salisbury, North Carolina

If you favor other cheeses, substitute them in Creamy Macaroni and Cheese; it's basic enough to accommodate most cheese flavors. By using new low-fat products on the market, you can lighten that same recipe considerably. The traditional macaroni and cheese still tasted best, but we thought the lightened version gave it a *good* run for the money.

MACARONI AND BLUE CHEESE

2 quarts water
1 teaspoon salt
1 (8-ounce) package elbow macaroni
¼ cup butter or margarine
¼ cup all-purpose flour
2 cups milk
1 (4-ounce) package crumbled blue cheese
1 egg, lightly beaten
1 (2-ounce) jar diced pimiento, drained
½ cup soft breadcrumbs
½ cup walnuts, finely chopped
Garnish: fresh parsley sprig

Bring water and salt to a boil in a large Dutch oven; stir in macaroni. Return to a rapid boil, and cook 8 to 10 minutes or until tender; drain. Rinse with cold water; drain.

Melt butter in Dutch oven over low heat; add flour, stirring until mixture is smooth. Cook, stirring constantly, 1 minute. Gradually add milk; cook over medium heat, stirring constantly, until mixture is thickened. Add blue cheese, stirring until melted. Stir about one-fourth of hot cheese mixture into egg; add to remaining hot mixture, stirring constantly.

Stir in macaroni and pimiento; spoon into a lightly greased 2-quart shallow baking dish. Sprinkle with breadcrumbs and walnuts. Bake at 350° for 35 minutes. Garnish, if desired. Yield: 6 servings.

Note: For blue cheese lovers, increase blue cheese to 2 (4-ounce) packages.

Let's Do The Twist: Macaroni, That Is

If Yankee Doodle could spoon into these surprising macaroni dishes, he'd pronounce them dandy. Every one is worth the time it takes to make *real* macaroni and cheese from scratch.

With so many cheeses readily available at the supermarket, we decided to experiment by adding blue cheese, Monterey Jack with peppers, and even Jarlsberg—a type of Swiss cheese. The toppings are different, too, from cheese crackers to breadcrumbs to chili powder.

CREAMY MACARONI AND CHEESE

2 quarts water
1 teaspoon salt
1 (8-ounce) package elbow
  macaroni
4 cups (16 ounces) shredded
  Cheddar or Jarlsberg cheese
1 (8-ounce) carton sour cream
1 cup mayonnaise or salad dressing
2 tablespoons chopped onions
1 cup cheese crackers, crushed
Garnish: green onion fan

Bring water and salt to a boil in a large Dutch oven; stir in macaroni. Return to a rapid boil, and cook 8 to 10 minutes or until tender; drain. Rinse with cold water; drain.

Combine macaroni and next 4 ingredients. Spoon into a lightly greased 11- x 7- x 1½-inch baking dish; sprinkle with crackers. Bake at 325° for 30 to 35 minutes. Garnish, if desired. Yield: 6 to 8 servings.

Note: To cut fat and calories, substitute nonfat sour cream alternative, fat-free mayonnaise, and reduced-fat Cheddar cheese.
Nat Holland
Columbia, South Carolina

JACK-IN-THE-MACARONI BAKE

2 quarts water
1 teaspoon salt
1 (8-ounce) package elbow
  macaroni
2 tablespoons butter or margarine
¼ cup chopped onion
¼ cup chopped sweet red pepper
2 cups (8 ounces) shredded
  Monterey Jack cheese with
  peppers
1 (10¾-ounce) can cream of celery
  soup, undiluted
½ cup sour cream
Chili powder
Garnish: celery leaves

Bring water and salt to a boil in a large Dutch oven; stir in macaroni. Return

to a rapid boil, and cook 8 to 10 minutes or until tender; drain. Rinse with cold water; drain.

Melt butter in a Dutch oven; add onion and sweet red pepper. Cook over medium heat, stirring constantly, until vegetables are crisp-tender. Remove from heat. Stir in shredded cheese, soup, and sour cream. Stir in macaroni; spoon into a shallow 2-quart casserole. Sprinkle with chili powder. Bake at 350° for 30 minutes. Garnish, if desired. Yield: 6 servings.

Spinach With A Flourish

Try these different and delightful recipes for new ways to serve spinach. They're so good, even the kids will want more.

Fresh spinach is available year-round. It can be used raw in salads, cooked and used as a vegetable, or as part of a dish.

SPINACH STRUDELS

1½ pounds fresh spinach
2 tablespoons butter or margarine
6 shallots, chopped
1 (8-ounce) package cream cheese,
  softened
1 (6-ounce) package Gorgonzola
  cheese, crumbled
1 large egg, lightly beaten
¼ teaspoon pepper
15 sheets frozen phyllo pastry,
  thawed
Butter-flavored cooking spray
½ cup fine, dry breadcrumbs,
  divided

Remove stems from spinach; wash leaves thoroughly. Arrange spinach in a steamer basket; place over boiling water. Cover and steam 5 minutes or just until wilted. Remove spinach; finely chop. Drain well.

Melt butter in a large skillet; add shallots, and cook over medium-high heat, stirring constantly, until tender (about 3 minutes). Add spinach, and cook until all moisture evaporates (about 8 minutes) stirring occasionally. Remove from heat; stir in cheeses, egg, and pepper. Cool.

Unfold phyllo, and cover with a slightly damp towel to prevent pastry from drying out. Place 1 sheet of phyllo on a flat surface; spray evenly with cooking spray, and sprinkle with 1½ teaspoons breadcrumbs. Place 2 additional phyllo sheets on top, and repeat procedure with cooking spray and breadcrumbs. Cut stacked sheets lengthwise into 3 (4-inch) strips.

Place about 3 tablespoons spinach mixture at base of each strip; fold the right bottom corner over to form a triangle. Continue folding back and forth into a triangle, gently pressing corners together, to end of strip. Repeat procedure 4 times with remaining phyllo sheets, breadcrumbs, and spinach mixture.

Spray triangles with cooking spray, and place, seam side down, on greased baking sheets. Bake at 325° for 30 minutes or until golden. Serve as a side dish, a sandwich, or as a seated appetizer with a cream sauce. Yield: 15 servings.
Martha Haller
Gadsden, Alabama

SAUTÉED SPINACH

1 (10-ounce) package fresh spinach
3 tablespoons butter or margarine
1 green onion, chopped
¼ teaspoon sugar
¼ teaspoon salt
Lemon wedges (optional)

Remove stems from spinach; wash leaves thoroughly, and pat dry. Set spinach aside.

Melt butter in a large skillet over medium heat; add green onion, and cook, stirring constantly, until tender. Add spinach, sugar, and salt; cover and cook 3 to 5 minutes or until spinach is wilted and tender, stirring once. Drain; serve immediately with lemon wedges, if desired. Yield: 3 servings.

Charlotte Pierce
Greensburg, Kentucky

SPINACH AND SUN-DRIED TOMATO SALAD

1 (3-ounce) package sun-dried tomatoes
1 cup boiling water
1 cucumber
8 cups torn fresh spinach
1 small purple onion, sliced and separated into rings
1 cup sliced fresh mushrooms
¼ cup freshly grated Parmesan cheese
Spinach Salad Dressing

Place tomatoes in a small bowl; add boiling water, and let stand 10 minutes. Drain and set aside. Cut cucumber in half lengthwise, and scoop out seeds with a spoon; cut cucumber into thin slices. Combine tomatoes, cucumber and next 4 ingredients. Toss with Spinach Salad Dressing. Yield: 8 to 10 servings.

Spinach Salad Dressing

½ cup olive oil
¼ cup red wine vinegar
1 teaspoon Dijon mustard
½ teaspoon salt
¼ teaspoon pepper

Combine all ingredients in a jar. Cover tightly, and shake vigorously to blend. Yield: ¾ cup.

A Passion For Pecans

Meet Charles Wallace of Austin, Texas. He's quick to tell you that his favorite dessert is pecan pie, prepared any one of 70 different ways. Talk with him a little longer, and you'll soon discover that the native Texan's interest in his state's official nut is nothing short of passionate.

The no-frills collection of 70-plus recipes in his cookbook, *Nuttin' 'Cept Pecan Pies*, ranges from the traditional version Charles's mom used to make, Old Pecan Street Special, to the more exotic Turtle Pecan Pie and Chocolate-Pecan Chess Pie variations.

TURTLE PECAN PIE

3 cups chocolate wafer crumbs
½ cup butter or margarine, melted
1¼ cups semisweet chocolate morsels
1 cup evaporated milk
1 cup miniature marshmallows
⅛ teaspoon salt
1 quart vanilla ice cream, divided
1 cup pecan halves, toasted

Spinach Tips

Selection: Look for crisp, dark-green smaller leaves; avoid leaves that are wilted, yellowed, or bruised, as well as those with thick central stems. You can also purchase 10-ounce bags of pre-washed spinach.
Storage: If prepackaged bags are purchased, sort and discard wilted leaves. Place unwashed spinach in plastic bags in the refrigerator's vegetable bin up to three days.
Preparation: To wash away the sandy soil that clings to the leaves, place the spinach in a large basin of water, and gently agitate.

Change the water three times or until there are no traces of grit. Even bags of prewashed spinach need a rinse to remove grit.

If the spinach is to be cooked, use hot water once to relax the crinkles in the leaves and release the sand.
Cooking: Quickly steam or sauté fresh spinach *just until* limp (about 3 to 5 minutes). Then enhance the rich flavor with a squeeze of fresh lemon juice and basil, pepper, Parmesan cheese, chives, garlic, onion, oregano, parsley, rosemary, or thyme.

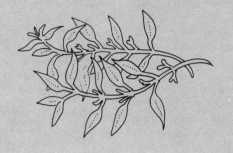

Combine chocolate crumbs and butter; firmly press into a 9-inch, deep-dish pieplate, and freeze 15 minutes.

Combine chocolate morsels and next 3 ingredients in a heavy saucepan. Cook over low heat, stirring constantly, until thickened and smooth. Remove from heat, and set aside.

Spread 2 cups ice cream into prepared pieplate; cover and freeze 30 minutes. Pour half of chocolate mixture over ice cream layer; cover and freeze 30 minutes. Spread remaining ice cream over chocolate mixture; cover and freeze 30 minutes. Spread remaining chocolate mixture over ice cream, and top with pecans. Cover and freeze. Yield: one 9-inch pie.

OLD PECAN STREET SPECIAL

4 large eggs, lightly beaten
1 cup light corn syrup
⅔ cup sugar
3 tablespoons butter or margarine, melted
1 tablespoon vanilla extract
1½ cups coarsely chopped pecans
1 unbaked 9-inch deep-dish pastry shell

Combine first 5 ingredients; stir in chopped pecans, and pour into pastry shell. Bake at 350° for 50 to 55 minutes. Cool on a wire rack. Yield: one 9-inch pie.

LEMON-PECAN PIE

1 unbaked 9-inch deep-dish pastry shell
4 large eggs, lightly beaten
6 tablespoons butter or margarine, softened
1 cup light corn syrup
½ cup firmly packed brown sugar
2 teaspoons grated lemon rind
¼ cup lemon juice
3 tablespoons all-purpose flour
1¼ cups coarsely chopped pecans
Whipped cream

Bake pastry shell at 450° for 5 to 7 minutes. Remove from oven, and cool crust completely.

Combine eggs and next 6 ingredients; stir in pecans and pour into prepared crust. Bake at 350° for 40 minutes, shielding edges with strips of aluminum foil after 25 minutes to prevent excessive browning. Cool on a wire rack. Serve with whipped cream. Yield: one 9-inch pie.

CHOCOLATE-PECAN CHESS PIE

1¼ cups sugar
¼ cup cocoa
1 tablespoon all-purpose flour
1 tablespoon cornmeal
Pinch of salt
¾ cup chopped pecans
4 large eggs, lightly beaten
½ cup milk
1 tablespoon vanilla extract
1 unbaked 9-inch deep-dish pastry shell

Combine first 6 ingredients in a medium bowl. Combine eggs, milk, and vanilla, and stir into sugar mixture; pour into pastry shell. Bake at 350° for 45 minutes or until set. Cool on a wire rack. Yield: one 9-inch pie.

QUICK & EASY

Jammin' It Up

Fall has officially arrived. Summer's only remnants are faded suntans and vacation memories. Days are shorter and cooler—so chances are you're finding the kitchen more inviting.

Even so, you may be stumped for ideas as you jump back into the season's mealtime mainstream. Take a look at jams, jellies, and preserves for some sweet inspiration. The spreads pack a wallop of flavor in quick sauces, glazes, and fillings.

JELLY-GLAZED CORNISH HENS

3 (1½-pound) Cornish hens, split
½ teaspoon salt
¼ teaspoon pepper
1 (10½-ounce) jar jalapeño jelly
2 teaspoons grated lime rind
⅓ cup lime juice
¼ cup vegetable oil
1 tablespoon chopped fresh cilantro

Sprinkle hens with salt and pepper, and place, cut side down, in a large, shallow dish; set aside.

Melt jelly in a small saucepan over low heat; add lime rind and remaining ingredients. Pour jalapeño marinade over hens; cover and refrigerate 3 hours, turning occasionally.

For a charcoal grill, prepare fire, and let burn until coals are white. Rake coals to opposite sides of grill, and place a drip pan between coals. For a gas grill, light one burner, placing drip pan on opposite side.

Drain hens, reserving jalapeño marinade. Arrange hens on food rack over drip pan. Cook, covered with grill lid, over medium-hot coals (350° to 400°) 35 minutes. Brush with jalapeño marinade; cook an additional 40 minutes. Yield: 6 servings.

Tip: *For a fast and easy way to perk up leftovers, spoon commercial jelly, preserves, or chutney over chicken, fish, ham, pork, or other meats before reheating. The toppings will add new flavor to leftovers and keep them moist during reheating.*

APRICOT-GLAZED HAM SLICE

½ cup apricot preserves
¼ cup catsup
2 tablespoons finely chopped onion
1 tablespoon vegetable oil
1 tablespoon prepared mustard
1 teaspoon Worcestershire sauce
1 (1½- to 2-pound) boneless, fully cooked ham slice *

Combine first 6 ingredients in a small saucepan; cook over low heat 5 minutes, stirring occasionally. Divide mixture in half; set aside.

Cut slashes about 3 inches apart around edge of ham slice to avoid curling. Cook, with grill lid opened, over medium-hot coals (350° to 400°) 5 minutes on each side or until ham is done, basting often with one portion of apricot glaze; discard any remaining basting apricot glaze. Serve with reserved half of glaze. Yield: 4 servings.

* 1½-pounds boneless chicken breast halves may be substituted for ham. Sprinkle with ½ teaspoon salt, and brush on glaze during the last 5 minutes of cooking.   *Eugenia W. Bell*
Lexington, Kentucky

CURRIED APPLES

4 cooking apples (about 2½ pounds), peeled, cored, and cut into ½-inch slices
2 tablespoons butter or margarine
¾ cup orange marmalade
¾ cup commercial chutney
1 teaspoon ground cinnamon
½ teaspoon curry powder

Arrange sliced apples in a lightly greased 11- x 7- x 1½-inch baking dish; set aside.

Melt butter in a medium saucepan; add marmalade and remaining ingredients. Bring to a boil over medium heat, stirring constantly; pour over apples. Bake at 400° for 35 minutes or until apples are tender. Serve with ham or pork. Yield: 6 to 8 servings.

RASPBERRY BRIE IN RYE

2 (7-inch-round) loaves rye bread
1 (15-ounce) round Brie
½ cup seedless raspberry jam
¼ cup sliced almonds

Using a large serrated knife, slice off about ½ inch from top of one bread loaf. Reserve top of loaf.

Place Brie on top of bread; trace around outer edge of cheese with knife. Remove cheese, and set aside.

Using traced mark as a guide, cut bread vertically 2 inches deep; remove bread, leaving a 5- x 2-inch cavity. Cut bread top, trimmings, and remaining loaf into 1- to 1½-inch cubes; set aside.

Remove rind from top of cheese. Place cheese in bread cavity; spread with jam, and sprinkle with almonds. Bake at 325° for 15 to 20 minutes or just until soft. Serve immediately with bread cubes. Yield: 6 servings.

Mary Dempsey
Silver Spring, Maryland

Give Napkins a Ring

The dining experience has come a long way since the Middle Ages. Back then there were no permanent dining tables or individual chairs, and, instead of plates, diners were handed thick, square slices of old bread. No forks, no spoons—just fingers and the bread.

But by the 19th century, things were downright elegant. So much so that, in 1869, a patent for napkin rings was granted. The ring was used to mark each person's napkin, as it was hard to wash linens daily.

With today's strong emphasis on recycling, many people are coming back to cloth napkins, and along with them come some unique napkin rings.

Facts That Ring True

■ In rural areas, bamboo was cut into pieces to be used as napkin rings in the early 1900s.
■ Many people buy antique silver napkin rings and split them in half to be worn as bracelets.
■ If you are a guest at someone's home, it is not proper to put your napkin back into the ring after the meal is over; napkins are returned to the ring only if you are a frequent visitor to that table.

Napkin Rings You Can Make

■ A 15-inch piece of fresh ivy can be woven into a 3-inch ring for any occasion.
■ White cotton rope, available at most hardware stores, knotted at each end and then tied into a square knot, makes a simple napkin ring for casual events. For color, use multicolored rappelling rope from an outdoor equipment store. Allow ½ to ⅔ yard of rope to make each napkin ring.
■ Plastic toy watches found in variety stores are not only fun for children as party favors, but they can serve as napkin rings, too.

NOVEMBER

Create a memorable holiday season for your family and friends using our "Holiday Dinners" special section as a blueprint for entertaining with ease and elegance. For impresssive holiday parties, we present a variety of festive ideas, tips, menus, and recipes—ranging from traditional to trendy. Turkey still reigns supreme at a time-honored celebration, but for a new idea, serve it with a dressing made from grits or cornbread peppered with fiery green chiles. For a fanciful finale, choose from a wide array of international-inspired desserts including delicious Scandinavian and Italian cookies and sweet baked breads, or beautiful French petits fours, the crown jewels of your holiday table.

Sweet Little Endings

No one's in a hurry to leave the dinner table when you bring out petits fours—those sweet little gems.

Make a wide selection of petits fours for your dinner party, or arrange only one or two varieties on a large serving tray. They're *all* beautiful, and the Raspberry Jellyrolls, Lemon Cream Puffs, and Crème de Menthe Squares are particularly easy to make.

Because they're so pretty, petits fours have earned a la-di-da reputation. But as the dessert tray passes around the table for the third or fourth time, you'll find petits fours take on a very cozy air.

COFFEE MERINGUES WITH BUTTERSCOTCH MOUSSE
(pictured on page 299)

3 egg whites
1 teaspoon instant coffee granules
¼ teaspoon cream of tartar
1 cup sugar
Butterscotch Mousse
Garnish: chocolate-covered coffee beans

Combine first 3 ingredients in a large mixing bowl; beat at high speed with an electric mixer until foamy. Gradually add sugar, 1 tablespoon at a time, beating mixture until stiff peaks form.

Drop mixture by rounded teaspoonfuls onto baking sheets lined with unglazed brown paper. (Do not use recycled paper.) Make an indentation in center of each with back of a spoon. Bake at 225° for 1 hour and 15 minutes; turn oven off, and let cool in oven 2 hours or overnight. Carefully remove meringues from paper; store in an airtight container up to 1 week. Just before serving, spoon Butterscotch Mousse into each meringue. Garnish, if desired. Yield: 4½ dozen.

Butterscotch Mousse

1 cup butterscotch morsels
3 tablespoons butter or margarine
1 tablespoon instant coffee granules
3 tablespoons water
1 large egg, lightly beaten
1 cup whipping cream, whipped

Combine first 4 ingredients in a heavy saucepan; cook over low heat, stirring constantly, until morsels and butter melt. Gradually stir about one-fourth of hot mixture into egg; add to remaining hot mixture, stirring constantly. Cook over medium heat, stirring constantly, 1 minute. Remove from heat, and cool to room temperature. Fold in whipped cream. Cover and refrigerate 8 hours or overnight, if desired. Yield: 2⅔ cups.

Mike Singleton
Memphis, Tennessee

LEMON CREAM PUFFS
(pictured on page 299)

½ cup water
¼ cup butter or margarine
½ cup all-purpose flour
Dash of salt
2 large eggs
1 (12-ounce) jar lemon curd
1 tablespoon grated lemon rind
1 cup whipping cream, whipped
Garnishes: lemon wedges, fresh mint sprigs

Combine water and butter in a medium saucepan; bring to a boil. Add flour and salt, all at once, stirring vigorously over medium-high heat until mixture leaves sides of pan and forms a smooth ball. Remove from heat, and cool 4 to 5 minutes.

Add eggs, one at a time, beating with a wooden spoon after each addition; beat until batter is smooth. Drop batter by slightly rounded teaspoonfuls onto lightly greased baking sheets. Bake at 425° for 12 minutes. Reduce temperature to 350°, and bake an additional 10 minutes. Remove cream puffs from oven; pierce side of each with a small sharp knife. Turn oven off. Return cream puffs to oven, leaving door open, and let stand 10 minutes. Remove from oven; cool. Cut off tops, and discard. Store in an airtight container in refrigerator up to 2 days, if desired.

Beat lemon curd at medium speed with an electric mixer until smooth. Fold in lemon rind and whipped cream. Pipe about 1½ tablespoons lemon filling into each cream puff; garnish, if desired. Yield: 2½ dozen.

MERINGUES WITH CRAN-APPLE MOUSSE FILLING
(pictured on page 299)

2 egg whites
Pinch of salt
¼ teaspoon cream of tartar
⅓ cup superfine sugar
1 teaspoon vanilla extract
Cran-apple Mousse
Garnish: fresh cranberries

Combine first 3 ingredients in a medium mixing bowl; beat at high speed with an electric mixer until foamy. Gradually add sugar, beating until stiff peaks form. Stir in vanilla.

Drop 24 level teaspoons of meringue mixture onto a baking sheet lined with unglazed brown paper. (Do not use recycled paper.) Using a flat spatula, spread each small mound into a 1-inch circle to form a base. Fit a star-shaped tip with a ¼-inch opening into a decorating bag; spoon remaining meringue mixture into bag. Pipe a circle around edge of each base. Bake at 225° for 1 hour and 15 minutes; turn oven off, and let cool in oven 2 hours or overnight. Carefully remove meringues from paper; store in an airtight container up to 1 week.

Just before serving, pipe Cran-apple Mousse into each meringue. Garnish, if desired. Yield: 2 dozen.

Cran-apple Mousse

1 cup cran-apple juice drink
½ cup sugar
1 cup whipping cream, whipped
2 or 3 drops of red food coloring
    (optional)

Combine juice drink and sugar in a small heavy saucepan; cook over low heat, stirring until sugar dissolves. Cook over medium heat, without stirring, until mixture reaches 230° (about 10 minutes). Remove from heat, and cool to room temperature. Fold mixture into whipped cream. Stir in food coloring, if desired. Cover and refrigerate up to 4 hours. Yield: 2 cups.

Note: If you don't have a decorating bag and tip, drop meringue mixture by rounded teaspoonfuls onto a baking sheet lined with unglazed brown paper. (Do not use recycled paper.) Make an indentation in center of each mixture with back of a spoon. Bake according to recipe directions, and spoon mousse into each meringue; garnish, if desired.

RASPBERRY JELLYROLLS
(pictured on pages 298 and 299)

1 (10½-ounce) loaf angel food cake
1 tablespoon brandy
¼ to ⅓ cup seedless raspberry
    jam
Sifted powdered sugar
Garnishes: fresh or frozen
    raspberries, fresh mint leaves

Trim crust from cake with an electric knife. Cut cake lengthwise into 7 slices (about ⅓ inch thick). Place each slice on a sheet of wax paper; roll to ⅛-inch thickness with a rolling pin. Cover with wax paper; microwave at HIGH 8 seconds. Remove top sheet of wax paper; starting at narrow end, immediately roll up cake and wax paper together. Place, seam side down, on a wire rack; let cool completely.

Unroll each slice. Brush with brandy, and spread with 2 teaspoons jam; carefully reroll (without wax paper). Cut each roll in half crosswise. Store in an airtight container in refrigerator up to 2 days. Sprinkle with powdered sugar, and garnish, if desired. Yield: 14 jellyrolls.

CHOCOLATE-ALMOND PETITS FOURS
(pictured on pages 298 and 299)

¾ cup butter or margarine,
    softened
2 (8-ounce) cans almond paste
1½ cups sugar
8 large eggs
1½ cups all-purpose flour
1 (12-ounce) can apricot filling *
Chocolate Ganache
6 ounces white chocolate, melted
    (optional)

Grease bottom and sides of two 15- x 10- x 1-inch jellyroll pans, and line with wax paper; grease and flour wax paper. Set aside.

Beat butter and almond paste at medium speed with an electric mixer until creamy. Gradually add sugar, beating well. Add eggs, one at a time, beating after each addition. Stir in

flour. Spread batter evenly into prepared pans. Bake at 400° for 8 to 10 minutes. Cool in pans on wire racks.

Turn one cake out onto a flat surface; remove wax paper, and spread with apricot filling. Top with remaining cake, and cut with a 1½-inch round cutter.

Place small cakes on a wire rack in a large, shallow pan. Using a squeeze bottle, coat top and sides with warm Chocolate Ganache. (Spoon up excess frosting that drips through rack; reheat and refill bottle, and use to continue frosting cakes.) Chill cakes 10 minutes. Pipe dots on frosted cakes with white chocolate, if desired. Yield: 3½ dozen.

* 1 (10-ounce) jar apricot spreadable fruit may be substituted.

Chocolate Ganache

1½ cups whipping cream
24 (1-ounce) squares semisweet
    chocolate, chopped

Heat whipping cream in a heavy saucepan over low heat. Add chocolate, stirring until smooth. (Mixture thickens as it cools; reheat over low heat, if necessary.) Yield: 3 cups.

Note: Chocolate-Almond Petits Fours may be frozen up to three months.
Shannon Stansell-Boykin
Birmingham, Alabama

Kitchen Hints

■ Use shiny cookie sheets, baking sheets, and cakepans for baking. Dark pans absorb more heat and may cause baked products to overbrown.
■ Here's a quick garnish: Use a vegetable peeler to make chocolate curls. Just pull the peeler firmly down the flat surface of a chocolate bar.

CRÈME DE MENTHE SQUARES
(pictured on pages 298 and 299)

2 cups all-purpose flour
2 teaspoons baking soda
2 cups sugar
1 cup butter or margarine
1 cup water
¼ cup cocoa
⅔ cup buttermilk
2 large eggs
1 teaspoon vanilla extract
Crème de Menthe Frosting
1 (1-ounce) square unsweetened
   chocolate, melted

Combine first 3 ingredients in a large bowl; set aside. Combine butter, water, and cocoa in a small saucepan; bring to a boil. Pour mixture over dry ingredients, stirring until blended. Stir in buttermilk, eggs, and vanilla. Pour batter into a greased and floured 15- x 10- x 1-inch jellyroll pan. Bake at 350° for 20 minutes or until a wooden pick inserted in center comes out clean. Cool on a wire rack. Spread with Crème de Menthe Frosting; cover and refrigerate until frosting is firm. Cut into 1-inch squares; drizzle with chocolate. Yield: 12 dozen.

Crème de Menthe Frosting

½ cup butter or margarine,
   softened
1 (3-ounce) package cream cheese,
   softened
2 tablespoons vanilla instant
   pudding mix
2 cups sifted powdered sugar
1½ tablespoons green crème de
   menthe

Beat butter and cream cheese at medium speed with an electric mixer until smooth. Add pudding mix, beating well. Gradually add powdered sugar, beating mixture until light and fluffy. Stir in crème de menthe. Yield: about 1½ cups.
Connie Smith
Jasper, Missouri

Tip: *For best results with cake baking, let butter reach room temperature before mixing.*

Gobblers For Gobbling

Thanksgiving turkey doesn't need to come out of the oven. At least that's the way it is for Elizabeth Yarborough of Birmingham, Alabama. She shares her holiday recipe for making these sweet turkey-shaped treats.

This tasty project is a great way to get the kids involved in preparing for a holiday party, a November birthday, or the big Thanksgiving feast itself. All they will need is a little help separating the cookies.

TURKEY TREATS

1 (16-ounce) package cream-filled
   chocolate sandwich cookies
¼ cup red cinnamon candies
1¼ cups malted milk balls
1 (16-ounce) container
   ready-to-spread chocolate
   frosting
1 (9½-ounce) package candy
   corn

Carefully separate each cookie, leaving cream filling on one side; set cookie halves without filling aside.
   To make a turkey body, attach or "glue" a cinnamon candy (for turkey head) to each malted milk ball (turkey body) with a dab of chocolate frosting. Attach a turkey body to center of each cookie half with cream filling using a dab of chocolate frosting.
   Spread chocolate frosting on the inside of each cookie half that does not have cream filling. For the turkey tail, arrange candy corn on chocolate-frosting cookies with wide end of candy along outer edge. Attach each turkey tail behind a turkey body using chocolate frosting. Store assembled turkeys in the refrigerator. Yield: 42 cookies.

Holiday Dinners

Wine & Dine The Wives

When these Raleigh, North Carolina, men entertain their wives, it's beyond burgers, and no pot or pan is left unturned. However, it's not as altruistic as it sounds. These six friends—calling themselves "Men's Gourmet"—banded together against the idea that only their wives could plan memorable social evenings and dinner menus to match.

Their egos on the line, they established some strict standards. No per chance, potluck gatherings allowed. Instead, their events would be more like dining in a fine restaurant.

The wives are never allowed behind the scenes. From their "front-row seats," they would never guess the disarray and chaos that sometimes lurks backstage.

Host Tom Andrus shows the beginnings of Oysters Bienville to Rick Wathern. "Does that look like yours? I followed your recipe." Rick shrugs his shoulders and laughs.

Andrus spies the limo, sent earlier to pick up their wives, and issues the alert, "It's showtime!" They all scramble out of aprons, pull on their suit coats, and head to the front door to greet their wives.

Their theme is "An Evening at the Lodge," and they're all about to enjoy an "After the Hunt" menu of wild game and seafood.

So ladies, sit back and relax. For the next few hours, the only thing you'll need to lift is your fork.

AFTER THE HUNT: AN EVENING AT THE LODGE FOR TWELVE

Oysters Bienville
Southern Shellfish Boil
Splendid Stalks
Pepper Feet
Samurai 'Shrooms
Mussel Soup
Blackened Duck Breasts
Green Beans With Roasted Red Peppers and Pearl Onions
Pear-Macadamia Pie

OYSTERS BIENVILLE

3 cups water
¾ pound unpeeled medium-size fresh shrimp
3 pounds rock salt
⅓ cup butter or margarine
⅔ cup chopped scallions or green onions
3 tablespoons finely chopped fresh parsley
2 cloves garlic, minced
⅓ cup all-purpose flour
1¼ cups milk
⅓ cup half-and-half
2 egg yolks, lightly beaten
3 tablespoons sherry
1 teaspoon salt
½ teaspoon ground white pepper
¼ to ½ teaspoon ground red pepper
⅔ cup chopped fresh mushrooms
3 dozen fresh oysters (in the shell)
¼ cup grated Parmesan cheese
¼ cup soft breadcrumbs
¼ teaspoon paprika
Garnishes: lemon wedges, fresh parsley sprigs

Bring water to a boil; add shrimp, and cook 3 to 5 minutes or until shrimp turn pink. Drain well; rinse with cold water. Chill; peel, devein, and chop shrimp. Set aside.

Sprinkle rock salt in two 15- x 10- x 1-inch jellyroll pans; set aside.

Melt butter in a large skillet; add scallions, chopped parsley, and garlic. Cook over medium-high heat, stirring constantly, until tender. Add flour, stirring until smooth. Cook, stirring constantly, 1 minute. Gradually add milk and half-and-half; cook over medium heat, stirring constantly, until thickened. Gradually stir about one-fourth of hot mixture into yolks; add to remaining hot mixture, stirring constantly. Stir in sherry and next 4 ingredients; cook, stirring constantly, 2 minutes. Stir in shrimp.

Scrub and open oyster shells. Discard tops; arrange bottoms (containing oysters) over rock salt. Spoon shrimp mixture evenly over oysters. Combine Parmesan cheese, breadcrumbs, and paprika; sprinkle over oysters. Bake at 350° for 15 to 20 minutes or until lightly browned. Garnish, if desired. Yield: 36 appetizers.

SOUTHERN SHELLFISH BOIL

5 quarts water
¼ cup cider vinegar
1 large onion, quartered
5 cloves garlic, peeled
¼ cup fresh thyme sprigs
¼ cup fresh rosemary sprigs
¼ cup fresh sage leaves
1 teaspoon dillseeds
1 teaspoon celery seeds
1 pound unpeeled cooked crawfish *
1 pound unpeeled medium-size
  fresh shrimp

Combine first 9 ingredients in a large Dutch oven; bring to a boil. Add crawfish and shrimp; cook 3 to 5 minutes or until shrimp turn pink. (Do not overcook.) Drain and serve immediately, or refrigerate and serve chilled. Yield: 4 to 6 servings.

* One additional pound unpeeled medium-size fresh shrimp may be substituted if crawfish is not available.

■ This whimsical recipe title refers to stuffed celery sticks. You can use a heavy duty, zip-top plastic bag with one corner cut out to pipe cheese filling into celery, but the guys have their own trick—a battery-operated cookie gun with a piping attachment. (Be sure to blend the filling mixture well, to avoid clogging the hole.)

SPLENDID STALKS

8 ounces Gruyère cheese, shredded
  and divided
½ cup firmly packed fresh basil
  leaves
3 tablespoons pine nuts
2 tablespoons white wine vinegar
¼ to ⅓ cup olive oil
1 bunch celery, cut into 3-inch
  pieces
Garnish: fresh parsley sprigs

Position knife blade in food processor bowl; add ½ cup cheese and next 3 ingredients. Process until smooth; remove food pusher. With processor running, slowly pour olive oil through food chute, blending just until mixture is smooth.

Transfer mixture to a bowl; stir in remaining cheese. Spoon into a heavy-duty, zip-top plastic bag; cut a small hole in one corner of bag, and pipe mixture into celery pieces. Arrange on a serving platter, and garnish, if desired. Yield: about 3 dozen.

■ Yes, this appetizer recipe is peppery, and the quail it's made from have feet, but they're not actually included in this dish. The guys are just pulling your leg, as usual. To crack whole peppercorns, put them in a zip-top plastic bag and pound lightly with a rolling pin or hammer.

PEPPER FEET

4 quail, quartered
⅓ cup catsup
2 tablespoons olive oil
1 tablespoon cider vinegar
1 to 2 tablespoons cracked black
  pepper

Rinse quail thoroughly with cold water; pat dry. Place in an 11- x 7- x 1½-inch dish. Combine catsup and remaining ingredients; pour over quail, turning to coat. Cover and let stand 30 minutes. Cook, without grill lid, over hot coals (400° to 500°) 2 to 3 minutes on each side or until done. Yield: 16 appetizer servings.

■ These stuffed mushrooms contain Tom Andrus's homemade Teriyaki Sauce, which he bottles and gives as Christmas gifts. One of the sauce's ingredients is sake (SAH-kee), a Japanese rice wine used in cooking. It's available at some grocery stores.

SAMURAI 'SHROOMS

24 large fresh mushrooms (about 1
  pound)
½ pound orange roughy
1 egg white
2½ tablespoons Teriyaki Sauce *
2 tablespoons whipping cream
Ground red pepper
Garnishes: lemon slices, fresh
  parsley sprigs

Clean mushrooms with damp paper towels; remove stems. (Reserve for another use.) Place caps, stem side up, on a wire rack on a baking sheet, and set aside.

Position knife blade in food processor bowl; add orange roughy. Process until smooth. Remove food pusher. With processor running, slowly pour egg white, Teriyaki Sauce, and whipping cream through food chute, stopping once to scrape down sides and blending just until smooth. Spoon about 2 teaspoons mixture into each mushroom cap. Sprinkle with red pepper. Bake at 325° for 20 minutes. Garnish, if desired. Yield: 24 appetizers.

* 2½ tablespoons commercial teriyaki sauce may be substituted.

Teriyaki Sauce

2 cups soy sauce
1 cup cider vinegar
¾ cup sake
1½ cups sugar
⅓ cup grated fresh gingerroot

Combine all ingredients in a large saucepan. Bring to a boil; reduce heat, and simmer, uncovered, 45 minutes.

Pour mixture through a wire-mesh strainer into a 4-cup liquid measuring cup, discarding gingerroot. Pour into decorative bottles; refrigerate up to one month. Yield: 2¾ cups.

■ Look for mussels in your grocer's fresh seafood department. Be sure all shells are tightly closed, and thoroughly scrub them with a brush before cooking. (The "beard" or silklike threads attached to the shell should come off while scrubbing.) Shells should open during cooking; discard any that don't.

MUSSEL SOUP

3 pounds mussels
4 cups Chardonnay or other dry white wine
¾ cup butter or margarine
2 large onions, chopped
½ cup chopped fresh parsley
4 bay leaves
1½ tablespoons dried thyme
2 to 3 teaspoons salt
½ to 1 teaspoon pepper
2 quarts whipping cream

Scrub shells well with a brush, removing beards. Discard any opened or cracked mussels.

Combine mussels and next 8 ingredients in a large Dutch oven; bring mixture to a boil. Cover, reduce heat, and simmer 8 to 10 minutes. (Mussels should open during cooking.) Pour wine mixture through a large wire-mesh strainer into a small Dutch oven. Discard any unopened mussels and other solids, reserving opened mussels.

Bring wine mixture to a boil; gradually add whipping cream, stirring constantly. Cook over medium heat until thoroughly heated (do not boil). Garnish each serving with a mussel. (Reserve remaining mussels for another use.) Yield: 14 cups.

■ The blackening in this recipe is best done outdoors on a propane cooker due to the heavy smoke produced. If you haven't been duck hunting lately or can't find duck breast, use 12 skinned and boned chicken breast halves, instead. It's almost as good.

BLACKENED DUCK BREASTS

3 (7-ounce) packages long-grain and wild rice mix *
2 (0.9-ounce) envelopes béarnaise sauce mix
12 duck breast halves, skinned and boned
⅓ cup butter or margarine, melted
3 tablespoons Cajun blackened seasoning
2 (14-ounce) cans artichoke hearts, drained
½ pound fresh mushrooms, sliced
1 cup Chablis or other dry white wine
2 cloves garlic, crushed
Garnishes: lemon slices, fresh parsley sprigs

Prepare rice mix according to package directions; keep warm.

Prepare béarnaise sauce mix according to package directions, and keep warm.

Place a large, greased cast-iron skillet over an outdoor propane cooker until very hot (about 10 minutes), following manufacturer's instructions. Brush duck with butter; sprinkle with seasoning, and cook in hot skillet about 4 minutes on each side or until done. Remove from skillet, and keep warm.

Combine artichokes and next 3 ingredients in a heavy saucepan; cook until mushrooms are tender. To serve, slice duck breast into thin strips, and place on a bed of cooked rice mix. Using a slotted spoon, pour artichoke mixture evenly over duck. Top with béarnaise sauce. Garnish, if desired. Yield: 12 servings.

* 12 ounces angel hair pasta, cooked according to package directions, may be substituted for rice mix.

What Goes with Game?

■ Choose an appropriate bread to accompany game. Include biscuits, French bread, garlic bread, cornbread, corn muffins, cornpone, or homemade rolls.

■ Be sure to offer tangy relishes or chutneys with game.

■ Consider other classic game accompaniments: cabbage, turnips, chestnuts, mushrooms, onions, grits, or rice.

■ Serve brandied fruits as an elegant side dish with wild duck and other types of game.

GREEN BEANS WITH ROASTED RED PEPPERS AND PEARL ONIONS

2 sweet red peppers
3 cups water
1¼ pounds pearl onions, unpeeled
¼ cup balsamic vinegar
¼ cup olive oil
½ teaspoon pepper
¼ teaspoon salt
3 pounds fresh green beans
3 cups water
¼ cup balsamic vinegar
3 tablespoons olive oil
1 tablespoon Dijon mustard
1 teaspoon dried thyme
½ teaspoon salt
½ teaspoon pepper

Wash and dry sweet red peppers; place on an aluminum foil-lined baking sheet. Bake at 500° for 20 to 25 minutes or until blistered. Place in a heavy-duty, zip-top plastic bag; seal and let stand 10 minutes to loosen skins; peel peppers. Split peppers, if necessary, and remove and discard membranes and seeds. Cut peppers into ⅓-inch strips; set aside.

Bring 3 cups water to a boil in a Dutch oven. Add pearl onions; cook 1 minute. Drain. Plunge onions into ice water, and drain. Peel onions, and set aside.

Combine ¼ cup balsamic vinegar and next 3 ingredients; pour over onions, tossing to coat. Place onions in a 15- x 10- x 1-inch jellyroll pan. Bake at 400° for 40 minutes, stirring at 10-minute intervals. Set aside.

Wash green beans, and trim ends. Bring 3 cups water to a boil in a Dutch oven. Add beans; cover, reduce heat, and cook 6 minutes, stirring occasionally. Drain and plunge beans into ice water. Drain. Combine beans, onions, and pepper strips in a large bowl; set aside.

Combine ¼ cup balsamic vinegar and remaining ingredients; pour over vegetable mixture, tossing gently.

Place vegetables in a 13- x 9- x 2-inch baking dish. Cover and bake at 350° for 25 to 30 minutes or until thoroughly heated. Yield: 12 servings.

Note: To make ahead, assemble ingredients in baking dish as directed; cover and refrigerate 8 hours. To serve, remove from refrigerator; let stand at room temperature 30 minutes. Bake as directed.

■ If you don't want to make the fellows' pastry laced with lemon rind, take the easy way out with a commercial refrigerated piecrust. Unlike the frozen type in the foil pan, this one fits into your own pieplate and could fool even Grandma.

PEAR-MACADAMIA PIE

Hint-of-Citrus Pastry *
½ cup pear preserves
2 tablespoons Frangelico or other hazelnut-flavored liqueur
⅔ cup macadamia nuts
½ cup sugar
1½ tablespoons all-purpose flour
¼ cup butter or margarine, softened
1 large egg
2½ pounds ripe cooking pears, peeled, cored, and thinly sliced

Prepare pastry; set aside, keeping warm. Combine preserves and Frangelico in a small heavy saucepan; cook over medium heat, stirring constantly, until warm. Pour mixture through a wire-mesh strainer, discarding solids. Gently brush a thin layer of glaze over warm pastry, reserving remaining glaze.

Position knife blade in food processor bowl; add nuts, sugar, and flour. Process until finely ground. Add butter and egg; process until smooth. Spread mixture evenly over pastry, and freeze 15 minutes.

Arrange pear slices over nut mixture; bake at 350° for 30 minutes. Cover loosely with aluminum foil, and bake an additional 40 minutes or until pears are tender and golden brown. Remove from oven; immediately brush pears with reserved glaze. Cool. Yield: one 10-inch pie.

Hint-of-Citrus Pastry

1½ cups all-purpose flour
¼ cup sugar
1 teaspoon grated lemon rind
⅛ teaspoon salt
3 tablespoons butter
3 tablespoons shortening
6 to 7 tablespoons cold water

Combine first 4 ingredients in a bowl; cut in butter and shortening with a pastry blender until mixture is crumbly. Sprinkle cold water, 1 tablespoon at a time, evenly over surface; stir with a fork until dry ingredients are moistened. Shape into a ball; chill.

Roll pastry to ⅛-inch thickness on a lightly floured surface. Gently place in a 10-inch pieplate; trim off excess pastry along edges. Fold edges under, and crimp; bake at 350° for 5 minutes. Yield: one 10-inch pastry shell.

* One-half of a 15-ounce package refrigerated piecrusts may be substituted, if desired. Unfold 1 piecrust, and lightly roll to fit a 10-inch pieplate. Sprinkle with 1 teaspoon all-purpose flour, spreading over surface. Place piecrust, floured side down, in a 10-inch pieplate; fold edges under, and crimp. Bake as directed.

Enjoy a taste of the holidays without all the calories and fat. Sit down to a cup of your favorite coffee and a slice of Pumpkin Cake (recipe, page 303) topped with reduced-calorie whipped topping.

Showcase a fall favorite—pumpkin— in (left to right) Southwestern Stuffed Shells, Cream of Pumpkin Soup, and Pumpkin-Chocolate Chip Cookies. (Recipes begin on page 234.)

Delight your dinner guests with the spicy taste of cinnamon in Easy Pumpkin Swirl (recipe, page 234).

A Foreign Affair

After a hard day's work, some unwind by exercising, reading, or watching television. This time of year, Jim and Sandra Kolka of Marietta, Georgia, bake . . . and bake . . . and bake. Their friends reap the benefits at a December open house featuring the couple's array of international breads, pastries, and cookies.

Jim is the third generation of his Scandinavian family to bake breads. Sandra learned to bake cookies at her Italian mother's side.

A peek at the couple's kitchen shows they're serious: More than 1,100 cookbooks, cookware of every shape and size imaginable, and a butcher block island perfect for kneading doughs are at the ready.

As November turns into December, their freezers and guest list grow ever fuller. By staggering the times on invitations, Jim and Sandra have no trouble accommodating a few hundred friends, clients, and associates over Saturday and Sunday afternoons.

■ This Swiss recipe is not as hard as it looks. Once you get the dough mixed, it's just a matter of making the bread figures.

GRITTIBANZ (SWISS BREAD FIGURE)

1¼ cups milk
½ cup butter or margarine
½ cup sugar
1 teaspoon salt
1 teaspoon grated orange rind
1 teaspoon vanilla extract
1 package active dry yeast
½ teaspoon sugar
¼ cup warm water (105° to 115°)
2 large eggs
5½ to 7 cups bread flour, divided
1 teaspoon ground cardamom
Milk
Whole almonds or hazelnuts
Candied cherries, raisins, or
  crystallized ginger
1 large egg
1 tablespoon milk

Combine 1¼ cups milk and butter in a medium saucepan; heat until butter melts, stirring occasionally. Stir in ½ cup sugar and next 3 ingredients. Cool to 105° to 115°.

Combine yeast, ½ teaspoon sugar, and warm water in a 1-cup measuring cup; let stand 5 minutes. Combine yeast mixture, milk mixture, 2 eggs, 3 cups flour, and cardamom in a large mixing bowl; beat at medium speed with an electric mixer until blended. Gradually stir in enough remaining flour to make a soft dough.

Turn dough out onto a heavily floured surface; knead until smooth and elastic (about 10 minutes). Place dough in a well-greased bowl, turning to grease top. Cover and let rise in a warm place (85°), free from drafts, 1½ hours or until dough is doubled in bulk.

Punch dough down; turn out onto a lightly floured surface, and knead lightly 4 or 5 times. Cover dough, and let rest 10 minutes.

Place two baking sheets together to form a large 16-inch square; cover with heavy-duty aluminum foil. Grease foil; set aside.

Set aside one-third of dough; shape remaining two-thirds into a 12- x 9-inch oval for body, and place on prepared baking sheets. Divide reserved one-third into 3 pieces. Shape 1 piece into a ball for head, and place on baking sheet; pat into a circle. Using kitchen shears dipped in flour, snip dough at 1-inch intervals (about 6 times) to resemble hair. Cut each remaining piece in half. (You will have 4 equal parts.)

Shape 1 part of dough into a 12-inch log; cut into 2 (6-inch) logs for arms, and attach to body. Shape second part into a 20-inch log; cut into 2 (3-inch) strips of dough for sleeve cuffs and 2 (7-inch) strips for necklace and apron. Brush large oval body with milk, and attach strips on arms and body. Cut remaining 2 parts in half; roll each half into a 9-inch strip. Twist 2 strips of dough together, and place at waistline for belt. Repeat procedure with remaining 2 strips of dough.

Gently push nuts and fruits into dough for eyes, nose, mouth, buttons, cuffs, and hem.

Combine 1 egg and 1 tablespoon milk in a small bowl; brush mixture over dough. Cover and let rise in a warm place (85°), free from drafts, 20 minutes. Bake at 350° for 35 to 40 minutes or until bread sounds hollow when tapped. (Cover loosely with foil after 20 minutes to prevent overbrowning, if necessary.) Cool 5 minutes on baking sheet; remove bread to a wire rack, and cool completely. Yield: 1 loaf.

Note: To make a boy figure, make a 5- to 6-inch slice in oval with kitchen shears; separate legs, placing 5 inches apart. Do not cut slits for hair. Shape logs for belt and tie by twisting 2 strips of dough together; add fruits and nuts for decorations.

■ This recipe makes a novel serving bowl for cookies. Weave a ribbon through the cutouts for color.

CHRISTMAS GINGERBREAD BOWL

1 cup butter or margarine, softened
¾ cup firmly packed dark brown sugar
½ cup sugar
3 large eggs
¾ cup dark corn syrup
⅓ cup molasses
2 teaspoons vanilla extract
1 teaspoon orange extract
8½ cups all-purpose flour
1 tablespoon baking soda
1 teaspoon salt
1 tablespoon ground cinnamon
2 teaspoons ground cloves
2 teaspoons ground ginger
1 teaspoon ground allspice
½ teaspoon freshly ground pepper
Vegetable cooking spray

Beat butter at medium speed with an electric mixer until creamy; gradually add sugars, beating well. Add eggs, one at a time, beating mixture after each addition. Stir in corn syrup and next 3 ingredients.

Combine flour and next 7 ingredients. Gradually add to butter mixture. (Dough will be stiff.) Divide dough into fourths; wrap each portion in plastic wrap, and refrigerate 8 hours.

Invert a 1½-quart, ovenproof glass bowl with a lipped edge on a cookie sheet; cover with aluminum foil, wrapping foil around and under lipped edge. Smooth foil with a rubber spatula, and coat with cooking spray. Set aside.

Roll 1 portion of dough to ¼-inch thickness on a lightly floured surface. Carefully lift dough, and press over outside of bowl, molding firmly to bowl shape. (Do not stretch dough.) Trim edges; with a small cookie cutter, make decorative cutouts around edge of bowl, if desired. Cover and refrigerate 1 hour.

Remove from refrigerator, and bake at 350° for 20 to 30 minutes or until lightly browned. Let cool completely on bowl. Carefully loosen foil; lift foil and gingerbread shell off bowl, and peel off foil. Store shell in a dry place. Repeat procedure with second portion of dough.

Roll remaining portions of dough to ¼-inch thickness on lightly greased cookie sheets; cut cookies close together with 5-inch gingerbread cutters. Remove excess dough from cookie sheets. Bake at 350° for 8 to 10 minutes or until lightly browned. Cool 2 minutes on cookie sheets; transfer to wire racks to cool completely. Decorate cookies as desired. Yield: 2 gingerbread bowls and about 1½ dozen cookies.

■ A traditional Italian Christmas yeast bread, Panettone is baked in a 2-quart soufflé dish or can be baked in an ordinary round baking dish with straight sides.

PANETTONE

2 packages active dry yeast
1 cup warm water (105° to 115°)
½ cup butter or margarine, softened
½ cup sugar
2 large eggs, beaten
3 egg yolks, beaten
2 teaspoons salt
2 teaspoons grated lemon rind
1 teaspoon vanilla extract
5 to 6 cups bread flour, divided
1 cup chopped candied citron
1 cup currants
2 tablespoons butter or margarine, melted

Combine yeast and warm water in a 2-cup liquid measuring cup; let stand 5 minutes. Combine yeast mixture, ½ cup butter, and next 6 ingredients in a large bowl, stirring with a wooden spoon until blended. Gradually stir in 3 cups flour, mixing well. Stir in citron and currants. Gradually stir in enough remaining flour to make a soft dough.

Turn dough out onto a lightly floured surface, and knead until smooth and elastic (about 2 minutes). Place in a well-greased bowl, turning to grease top. Cover and let rise in a warm place (85°), free from drafts, 1½ hours or until doubled in bulk.

Punch dough down, and place in a greased 2-quart soufflé dish; brush with melted butter. Cover and let rise in a warm place (85°), free from drafts, 1 hour or until almost doubled in bulk. Using a sharp knife, cut a deep X in top of bread. Bake on lower rack of oven at 350° for 8 minutes. Reduce temperature to 325°, and bake 1 hour or until bread sounds hollow when tapped. (Cover loosely with aluminum foil after 45 minutes to prevent overbrowning, if necessary.) Remove from dish immediately; cool on a wire rack. Yield: 1 loaf.

ALMOND-ANISE BISCOTTI

½ cup butter or margarine, softened
¼ cup canola or vegetable oil
1¼ cups sugar
6 large eggs
1 teaspoon anise oil
½ teaspoon vanilla extract
6 to 7 cups all-purpose flour, divided
1 teaspoon baking powder
2 cups whole blanched almonds, toasted
1¼ cups sifted powdered sugar
2 tablespoons milk
Nonpareils

Beat first 3 ingredients at medium speed with an electric mixer until well blended. Add eggs, one at a time, beating after each addition. Stir in anise oil and vanilla.

Combine 6 cups flour and baking powder; add to butter mixture. Gradually stir in enough remaining flour to make a stiff dough. Stir in almonds. Lightly flour hands, and divide dough into 5 portions. Shape each portion into an 8-inch log, and place on lightly greased cookie sheets. Bake at 350° for 35 minutes or until lightly browned; cool on wire racks.

Using a serrated knife, carefully cut each log crosswise into ½-inch slices. Place on ungreased cookie sheets; bake at 350° for 10 minutes on each side. Cool on wire racks.

Combine powdered sugar and milk; spread over top of biscotti, and sprinkle with nonpareils. Yield: about 5½ dozen.

Note: You can find anise oil at drugstores or cake decorating supply stores.

■ Perhaps the easiest recipe in the collection, these cookies are mixed mostly in a food processor, rolled into balls, pinched, and baked.

BRUTTI MA BUONI (UGLY BUT GOOD)

8 ounces slivered almonds (1⅓ cups)
1⅓ cups sifted powdered sugar
Pinch of salt
¼ teaspoon vanilla extract
¼ teaspoon almond extract
1 egg white
⅓ cup coarsely chopped walnuts
3 tablespoons finely chopped dried apricots

Position knife blade in food processor bowl; add almonds. Process 2 to 3 minutes or until almonds form a fine powder that begins to hold together, stopping occasionally to scrape down sides. Add powdered sugar and next 3

ingredients; process until blended. With processor running, add egg white, blending just until mixture forms a ball. Transfer to a bowl, and stir in walnuts and apricots. Shape dough into 1-inch balls, and pinch into irregular shapes. Place 1 inch apart on a lightly greased cookie sheet. Bake at 350° for 10 to 12 minutes. Cool on a wire rack. Store in an airtight container. Yield: 2 dozen.

■ This classic Italian bread is traditionally baked in a tall, star-shaped pan. If you can't find one, use an 8-inch springform pan instead. "Sponge" takes on a new meaning in this recipe; it's a yeast mixture used like a starter for this bread.

PANDORO

"Sponge" (recipe on this page)
1 teaspoon active dry yeast
1 tablespoon warm water (105° to 115°)
6½ cups bread flour, divided
¼ cup sugar
2 large eggs
¼ cup butter or margarine, softened and cut into pieces
4 large eggs
2 egg yolks
1 cup sugar
1 teaspoon salt
2 teaspoons vanilla extract
1½ tablespoons grated lemon rind
1¼ cups butter or margarine, softened and cut into pieces
½ cup chopped candied citron
¼ to ½ cup bread flour
Butter-flavored cooking spray

Prepare "Sponge" according to recipe, and set aside.

Combine yeast and warm water in a 1-cup liquid measuring cup; let stand 5 minutes. Stir yeast mixture, 2½ cups flour, ¼ cup sugar, and 2 eggs into "Sponge"; stir vigorously with a

wooden spoon until blended. Gradually stir in ¼ cup butter. Cover and let rise in a warm place (85°), free from drafts, 45 minutes or until dough is doubled in bulk.

Add 4 eggs and next 5 ingredients; beat at medium speed with an electric mixer until smooth. Gradually add 2 cups flour, beating until blended. Stir in remaining 2 cups flour with a wooden spoon. Gradually stir in 1¼ cups butter and citron.

Turn dough out onto a heavily floured surface, and knead until smooth and elastic (about 5 minutes), adding an additional ¼ to ½ cup flour, if needed. Place in a well-greased bowl, turning to grease top. Cover and let rise in a warm place 1½ hours or until doubled in bulk.

Punch dough down, and divide in half; place in two Pandoro pans or 8-inch springform pans coated with cooking spray. Cover and let rise in a warm place (85°), free from drafts, 1½ hours or until doubled in bulk. Bake at 350° for 30 minutes. Cover with aluminum foil, and reduce heat to 300°; bake an additional 20 minutes. Yield: 2 loaves.

"Sponge"

2 packages active dry yeast
½ cup warm water (105° to 115°)
1 large egg
2 tablespoons sugar
¾ cup bread flour

Combine yeast and warm water in a 1-cup measuring cup; let stand 5 minutes. Combine yeast mixture and remaining ingredients in a large mixing bowl; beat at medium speed with an electric mixer until mixture is smooth. Cover "Sponge," and let rise in a warm place (85°), free from drafts, 30 minutes or until doubled in bulk. Yield: about 1½ cups.

BISCOTTI CIOCCOLATA

1 cup whole natural almonds, toasted
1¾ cups all-purpose flour
1 teaspoon baking soda
¼ teaspoon salt
⅓ cup unsweetened cocoa
1 cup sugar
2 tablespoons instant espresso or coffee granules
4 ounces bittersweet chocolate, chopped
3 large eggs
1 teaspoon vanilla extract
½ teaspoon almond extract
Vegetable cooking spray
4 (1-ounce) squares semisweet chocolate
1 teaspoon shortening

Position knife blade in food processor bowl; add almonds. Process until coarsely chopped. Remove from bowl, and set aside.

Add flour and next 6 ingredients to food processor bowl; process mixture 20 to 30 seconds or until chocolate is finely chopped, stopping once to scrape down sides.

Beat eggs and flavorings at medium speed with an electric mixer until thick and pale; gradually add flour mixture, beating at low speed (mixture will be stiff). Stir in almonds. Place dough on a lightly floured surface, and divide in half. Lightly flour hands, and shape each portion into a 12-inch log; place logs on a cookie sheet coated with cooking spray. Bake at 300° for 50 minutes; cool on wire racks.

Using a serrated knife, carefully cut each log crosswise into ½-inch slices. Place slices on cookie sheets, and bake at 300° for 40 minutes, turning slices over after 15 minutes. Cool on wire racks.

Melt semisweet chocolate and shortening in a heavy saucepan over low heat, stirring mixture until smooth; spread on top of biscotti. Cool. Yield: 3½ dozen.

Bah Humbug—
A Crabby Christmas!

It's a match made in heaven . . . literally. Nancy and Claxton "Clack" Walker of Baltimore, Maryland, were both born on July 11 under the astrological sign of the crab, and they've been collecting crab recipes for more than 20 years.

This time, they're celebrating a holiday evening with the family, which is no small affair. The Walkers are expecting most of their 10 grown children and spouses, as well as several close friends.

Clack, who frequently challenges nearby Chesapeake Bay in his sailboat, *The Stormy Petrel,* tends bar. He sets out fresh raw oysters, horseradish sauce, vodka, and shot glasses, then demonstrates Oyster Shooters for squeamish onlookers. "Down the hatch!" he commands.

He also offers Bay Bloodies, a twist on Bloody Marys, with Old Bay seasoning on the glass rims. And then there's his signature Stormy Petrel Rum Thunder Punch.

Meanwhile, in the galley, a feast Nancy calls "Maryland's Bounty" is about to set sail. The hostess brings out Hot Crab Dip and Chesapeake Nuts for appetizers. The crowd helps themselves to the buffet, enjoying Angel Biscuits and Sotterley Plantation Country Ham (named for the nearby historic home that sells them) served on Nancy's antique ham rack. And her Easy Crab Casserole with crab-shaped Toast Points stands out as a favorite. As if that's not enough, a luscious, creamy dessert of raspberry mousse and chocolate awaits in the next room.

BAY BLOODIES

Lime wedges
Old Bay seasoning
4 cups commercial Bloody Mary mix
1 cup vodka
½ cup Worcestershire sauce
2 tablespoons prepared horseradish
2 tablespoons lime juice

Rub rims of glasses with lime wedges. Place Old Bay seasoning in a saucer, and spin rim of each glass in seasoning to coat. Set prepared glasses aside.

Combine Bloody Mary mix and remaining ingredients. Serve over ice in prepared glasses. Yield: 6 cups.

STORMY PETREL RUM THUNDER PUNCH

4½ cups spiced rum
3 cups sweet vermouth
2½ cups commercial daiquiri mix
1½ cups Triple Sec or other orange-flavored liqueur
⅔ cup apple brandy or brandy
2 tablespoons bitters
4 (12-ounce) cans cherry-flavored lemon-lime carbonated beverage or lemon-lime carbonated beverage, chilled
Lime and lemon slices

Combine first 6 ingredients; add carbonated beverage and fruit slices. Serve in a punch bowl. Yield: about 5 quarts.

Note: If punch is too strong for your tastes, add additional carbonated beverage to dilute mixture.

HOT CRAB DIP

1 (8-ounce) package cream cheese
1 cup mayonnaise or salad dressing
2 tablespoons lemon juice
1 teaspoon Worcestershire sauce
¼ to ½ teaspoon Old Bay seasoning
1 pound fresh lump crabmeat, drained
Garnishes: sweet red pepper strips, parsley sprigs

Cook cream cheese in a heavy saucepan over low heat, stirring constantly, until cheese melts. Stir in mayonnaise and next 3 ingredients. Add crabmeat, and cook over low heat until thoroughly heated. Transfer to a chafing dish, and keep warm. Serve with crackers, and garnish, if desired. Yield: 2¾ cups.

CHESAPEAKE NUTS

1½ cups raw shelled peanuts (about ½ pound)
2 cups pecan halves
1½ tablespoons vegetable oil
1 tablespoon Old Bay seasoning

Spread peanuts in a 15- x 10- x 1-inch jellyroll pan. Bake at 350° for 5 minutes. Add pecan halves; drizzle with oil, and sprinkle with seasoning, tossing to coat. Bake an additional 10 minutes, stirring after 5 minutes. Yield: 3½ cups.

BAKED OYSTERS ON THE HALF SHELL

Rock salt
½ cup butter, divided
¼ cup chopped green onions
¼ cup chopped celery
1 tablespoon dried chervil
1 tablespoon dried parsley flakes
1 cup loosely packed fresh watercress leaves
⅓ cup soft breadcrumbs
⅛ teaspoon salt
Pinch of ground black pepper
Pinch of ground red pepper
1 (10-ounce) package frozen chopped spinach, thawed
⅓ cup Pernod or other licorice-flavored liqueur
2 dozen fresh oysters (in the shell) *
½ cup freshly grated Parmesan cheese
Garnish: watercress sprigs

Sprinkle a layer of rock salt in two 15- x 10- x 1-inch jellyroll pans; set pans aside.

Melt ¼ cup butter in a large skillet over medium heat; add green onions and next 3 ingredients, and cook, stirring constantly, until tender. Add watercress; stir until wilted, and remove from heat. Pour mixture into container of an electric blender; process 1 minute, stopping once to scrape down sides. Stir in breadcrumbs and next 3 ingredients.

Drain spinach well, and press between paper towels to remove excess moisture. Melt remaining ¼ cup butter in skillet over medium heat, add spinach, and cook, stirring constantly, 3 minutes; stir in watercress mixture and Pernod.

Scrub oyster shells, and open, discarding tops. Arrange shell bottoms (containing oysters) over rock salt. Spoon 2 teaspoons watercress mixture over each oyster; sprinkle with grated Parmesan cheese. Bake at 450° for 6 to 8 minutes or until oysters begin to curl. Garnish, if desired. Yield: 2 dozen.

* Shelled fresh oysters sold in plastic tubs may be substituted for fresh ones. Prepare recipe in shell-shaped baking dishes found at gourmet kitchen shops.

Serving Seafood

■ Count on 2 servings per ½ to 1 pound of shucked or shelled crab, lobsters, scallops, oysters, and shrimp.

■ The terms Select and Standard refer to oyster sizes. Select oysters are medium size; Standard oysters are small.

EASY CRAB CASSEROLE

1 pound fresh lump crabmeat,
  drained
1 cup chopped onion
1 cup chopped celery
1 cup herb-seasoned stuffing mix
1 cup mayonnaise or salad dressing
1 cup half-and-half
1 (3-ounce) jar capers, drained
1 teaspoon Old Bay seasoning
Garnish: sweet red pepper strips
Toast Points

Combine first 6 ingredients in a large bowl; spoon into an 11- x 7- x 1½-inch baking dish. Sprinkle with capers and Old Bay seasoning. Bake at 350° for 35 minutes. Garnish, if desired, and serve with Toast Points. Yield: 24 appetizer servings or 4 to 6 main-dish servings.

Toast Points

12 slices day-old white bread
Melted butter or margarine

Roll bread slices with a rolling pin to flatten; brush with butter. Cut bread slices in half diagonally, and place on a baking sheet. Bake at 225° for 4 minutes or until lightly toasted. Yield: 24 servings.

Note: You may also use a crab-shaped cutter to cut out bread.

ANGEL BISCUITS

1 package active dry yeast
½ cup warm water (105° to 115°)
5 cups all-purpose flour
1 tablespoon baking powder
1 teaspoon baking soda
1 teaspoon salt
3 tablespoons sugar
1 cup shortening
1¾ cups buttermilk

Combine yeast and warm water in a 1-cup liquid measuring cup; let stand 5 minutes. Combine flour and next 4 ingredients in a large bowl; cut in shortening with a pastry blender until mixture is crumbly. Add yeast mixture and buttermilk; stir just until dry ingredients are moistened.

Turn dough out onto a lightly floured surface; knead 6 to 10 times. Roll dough to ½-inch thickness. Cut with a 2-inch round cutter; place on lightly greased baking sheets. Bake at 400° for 12 minutes or until lightly browned. Serve with ham and various commercial spreads. Yield: 5 dozen.

Note: Biscuits may be baked for 5 minutes and frozen up to three months. To serve, remove from freezer, and place on lightly greased baking sheets. Bake at 400° for 10 minutes or until lightly browned.

SOTTERLEY PLANTATION COUNTRY HAM

1 (14- to 16-pound) uncooked
  country ham
7 cups apple juice
1½ cups firmly packed brown sugar
1 tablespoon white vinegar
2 teaspoons prepared mustard
1 teaspoon ground cloves
Whole cloves

Place ham in a very large container; cover with water, and soak 8 hours. Pour off water. Scrub ham with warm water using a stiff brush, and rinse well. Place ham in a large roasting pan; pour apple juice over ham. Cover and bake at 325° for 2½ to 3 hours.

Carefully remove ham from pan, reserving 1 tablespoon pan juices; discard remaining juices. Remove skin. Return ham to pan, fat side up. Combine reserved pan juices, brown sugar, and next 3 ingredients; coat exposed portion of ham with brown sugar mixture. Stud with whole cloves. Insert meat thermometer into ham, making sure it does not touch fat or bone. Bake ham, uncovered, 20 minutes or until thermometer registers 142°. Yield: 24 to 26 servings.

RASPBERRY MOUSSE IN CHOCOLATE CRINKLE CUPS

1 pint fresh raspberries
1 cup sugar
1 envelope unflavored gelatin
3 tablespoons cold water
3 tablespoons boiling water
1 tablespoon lemon juice
1 cup whipping cream, whipped
Chocolate Crinkle Cups *

Wash raspberries; set aside 24 raspberries for garnish.

Position knife blade in food processor bowl, add remaining raspberries and sugar. Process until smooth; pour mixture through a fine wire-mesh strainer into a bowl; discarding seeds. Set aside.

Sprinkle gelatin over 3 tablespoons cold water; stir and let stand 1 minute. Add boiling water, stirring until gelatin dissolves. Stir in lemon juice. Stir into raspberry mixture; chill until consistency of unbeaten egg white. Fold in whipped cream, and chill until set. To serve, spoon evenly into Chocolate Crinkle Cups. Garnish each with a reserved raspberry. Yield: 3½ cups.

* Commercial chocolate cups may be substituted.

Chocolate Crinkle Cups

1 (6-ounce) package semisweet
  chocolate morsels
1 teaspoon shortening
3 (1-ounce) squares
  chocolate-flavored candy
  coating

Combine chocolate morsels and shortening in top of a double boiler; bring water to a boil, stirring until chocolate melts and mixture is smooth. Spoon into a small bowl, and set aside.

Melt candy coating in top of double boiler, stirring until smooth. Using a small artist brush, paint about a ⅛-inch layer of candy coating on inside of miniature foil baking cups. Chill 10 minutes.

Paint a thick layer of melted chocolate morsels over candy coating. Chill at least 1 hour. Carefully peel off foil cups. Store in an airtight container in refrigerator until ready to serve. Yield: 1½ to 2 dozen.

Tropical Holiday Elegance

Abby and Bill Myers love to host parties throughout the year in their Jacksonville, Florida, home. But come the holiday season, this lively couple pulls out all the stops with an annual black-tie dinner. This time, they're serving a taste of the tropics with Orange-Ginger Marinated Swordfish Steaks.

The Myers plan all their parties together. "Bill can remember every dinner, every menu," says Abby. "He reminds me when I've served too many chocolate desserts. I like to tell people I married my party planner."

Does formal attire bring a stately mood to this couple's convivial dinner table? "The tuxedo matches my cow apron," Bill says, showing off a black-and-white holstein print. "Laughter is kind of the password around here. If you wear a tux to dinner at our house, you need to be sure you have an adjustable cummerbund."

TROPICAL HOLIDAY ELEGANCE FOR TEN

Artichoke-and-Shrimp Appetizer
Orange-Ginger Marinated Swordfish Steaks
Tricolor Pasta With Clam Sauce
Steamed broccoli
Spinach Salad With Dried Tomato Vinaigrette
Sabayon

ARTICHOKE-AND-SHRIMP APPETIZER

1 large artichoke
3 tablespoons lemon juice
3 cups water
30 unpeeled large fresh shrimp
1 teaspoon butter or margarine
2¼ teaspoons finely chopped shallots
½ teaspoon minced garlic
½ (8-ounce) package light cream cheese, softened
1 tablespoon chopped green onions
1 tablespoon nonfat plain yogurt
½ teaspoon dried savory
⅛ teaspoon Nature's seasoning blend *
⅛ teaspoon pepper
Dash of hot sauce
Garnishes: fresh parsley sprigs, pitted ripe olives, paprika
Lettuce leaves

Wash artichoke by plunging up and down in cold water. Cut off stem end, and trim about ½ inch from top. Remove loose bottom leaves. Place artichoke in a Dutch oven; cover with water, and add lemon juice. Bring to a boil; cover, reduce heat, and simmer 30 to 35 minutes or until lower leaves pull out easily. Drain; cool. Pull apart 30 leaves, and arrange on serving dish; set aside. (Reserve heart for another use.)

Bring 3 cups water to a boil; add shrimp. Cook 3 to 5 minutes or until

shrimp turn pink. Drain and rinse with cold water. Peel and devein shrimp; refrigerate.

Melt butter in a large skillet; add shallots and garlic. Cook over medium-high heat, stirring constantly, until tender. Stir in cream cheese and next 6 ingredients; remove from heat. Cover and refrigerate.

Just before serving, spoon about 1 teaspoon cream cheese mixture onto each artichoke leaf, and top with a shrimp. Garnish, if desired. Serve on a lettuce-lined tray. Yield: 30 appetizers.

* For Nature's seasoning blend, we used Morton's Nature's Seasons.

ORANGE-GINGER MARINATED SWORDFISH STEAKS

10 (8-ounce) swordfish steaks (about 1 inch thick)
1½ cups tomato-based barbecue sauce
1 cup white wine
2 tablespoons grated orange rind
1 cup orange juice
¼ cup soy sauce
2 tablespoons finely chopped fresh gingerroot
4 cloves garlic, minced
Vegetable cooking spray
Garnishes: parsley sprigs, orange slices

Arrange fish in a large shallow dish. Combine barbecue sauce and next 6 ingredients; pour marinade over fish. Cover and refrigerate 2 to 24 hours, turning occasionally.

Remove fish from marinade, discarding marinade. Place fish in grill baskets that have been coated with cooking spray. Cook, covered with grill lid, over medium coals (300° to 350°) 10 minutes on each side. Garnish, if desired, and serve immediately. Yield: 10 servings.

TRICOLOR PASTA WITH CLAM SAUCE

6 (6½-ounce) cans chopped clams, undrained
2 tablespoons butter or margarine
1½ tablespoons olive oil
¼ cup finely chopped onion
4 cloves garlic, minced
½ cup Chablis or other dry white wine
¼ cup chopped fresh parsley
1 tablespoon spaghetti seasoning mix
1 tablespoon dried Italian seasoning
2 tablespoons lemon juice
1 (8-ounce) package squid ink-flavored angel hair pasta *
1 (8-ounce) package tomato-flavored angel hair pasta *
1 (8-ounce) package spinach-flavored angel hair pasta *
2 tablespoons grated Parmesan cheese

Drain clams, reserving 1 cup liquid; set aside.

Melt butter in a large skillet; add olive oil, onion, and garlic. Cook over medium heat, stirring constantly, until tender. Stir in wine; cook until liquid is reduced to ¼ cup, stirring occasionally. Add clams, reserved liquid, parsley, and next 3 ingredients; cook about 30 minutes or until sauce consistency, stirring occasionally.

Combine pastas, and cook according to package directions; drain. Transfer to a large serving platter; spoon clam sauce over pasta, and sprinkle with Parmesan cheese. Yield: 10 to 12 servings.

Note: Spaghetti seasoning mix is sold in envelope packets. (Reserve unused portion for another use.)

* You can substitute 8 ounces of regular angel hair pasta for any of the three kinds of flavored pasta.

SPINACH SALAD WITH DRIED TOMATO VINAIGRETTE

1 pound fresh spinach *
1 (14.4-ounce) can hearts of palm, drained and cut into ½-inch slices
1 pound fresh mushrooms, sliced
2 ripe avocados, cubed
1 medium sweet onion, sliced and separated into rings
½ cup unsalted sunflower kernels, toasted
Dried Tomato Vinaigrette

Remove stems from spinach; wash leaves thoroughly, and pat dry. Tear into bite-size pieces. Combine spinach and next 5 ingredients; toss with Dried Tomato Vinaigrette. Serve immediately. Yield: 10 servings.

* One (10-ounce) package fresh spinach may be substituted.

Dried Tomato Vinaigrette

1 (7-ounce) jar oil-packed sun-dried tomatoes
⅔ cup loosely packed fresh basil leaves
2 tablespoons chopped shallots
1 clove garlic, chopped
¼ teaspoon salt
⅛ teaspoon pepper
¼ cup red wine vinegar
Olive oil

Drain tomatoes, reserving oil; set oil aside.

Position knife blade in food processor bowl; add tomatoes, and pulse 3 or 4 times. Add basil and next 5 ingredients; process tomato mixture until smooth, stopping once to scrape down sides.

Add enough olive oil to reserved oil from tomatoes to equal ½ cup. With processor running, pour oil mixture through food chute in a slow, steady stream, processing until blended. Yield: 1 cup.

SABAYON
(pictured on page 297)

15 egg yolks
½ cup sugar
3 tablespoons Marsala wine
2 cups fresh or frozen raspberries, thawed
2 cups fresh or frozen blueberries, thawed
2 cups fresh or frozen blackberries, thawed
Sweetened whipped cream
Garnish: fresh mint sprigs

Bring water to a boil in bottom of a double boiler. Place egg yolks in top of double boiler on countertop; beat at high speed with a hand-held electric mixer until foamy. Gradually add sugar, 1 tablespoon at a time, beating until thick and pale. Gradually add Marsala, beating mixture well. Place over boiling water, and cook, stirring constantly with a wire whisk, 10 minutes or until mixture reaches 160°. Remove top of double boiler from heat, and place in a large bowl of ice water, stirring with whisk until mixture is cold.

Arrange fruit in compotes or individual serving dishes; immediately spoon sauce over fruit. Dollop with whipped cream, and garnish, if desired. Serve immediately. Yield: 10 servings.

Note: Although the name is French, this cooked custard is a classic Italian dessert. (The Italians refer to it as "zabaglione.")

Feliz Navidad

It's a few nights before Christmas, and Libby and Jim Collet of Dallas, Texas, and the other members of their supper club are meeting for an annual holiday celebration.

"We all have varied careers and outside interests," says Jim. "We hail from various parts of the country—South, East Coast, and Midwest—so there's a multiregional flavor to many of our dinners."

Inspired by their love of the Southwest, the group looks to Mexico to come up with a Mexican fiesta menu for their celebration.

FIESTA GRANDE FOR TEN

Margaritas
Fiesta Cheesecake
Tortilla chips
Tortilla Soup
Chicken Enchiladas Verde
Havarti-and-Corn-Stuffed
Chiles Rellenos With
Walnut Cream Sauce
Cinnamon Ice Cream Sombreros
Coffee
Suggested Wines:
Cabernet
Chardonnay

■ Andy Hughes's version of this favorite Southwestern refreshment requires just four ingredients. And an electric blender makes preparation even easier.

MARGARITAS

2 (6-ounce) cans frozen limeade
  concentrate, undiluted
1½ cups tequila
⅔ cup Triple Sec
Ice

Combine half of first 3 ingredients in container of an electric blender; add enough ice to bring mixture to 5-cup level. Process until smooth. Add additional ice, and continue processing, until 5-cup level is reached. Repeat procedure with remaining ingredients. Yield: 2½ quarts.

■ To avoid a last-minute rush, Libby Collet normally bakes and chills the cheesecake one or two days before serving. A few hours before serving, she unmolds the cheesecake onto a bed of fresh cilantro or parsley; then she tops it off with a decorative arrangement of peppers, green onions, tomato, and ripe olives.

FIESTA CHEESECAKE

1½ cups finely crushed tortilla
  chips
¼ cup butter or margarine, melted
2 (8-ounce) packages cream cheese,
  softened
1 (3-ounce) package cream cheese,
  softened
2 large eggs
2½ cups (10 ounces) shredded
  Monterey Jack cheese with
  peppers
1 (4-ounce) can chopped green
  chiles, drained
¼ teaspoon ground red pepper
1 (8-ounce) carton sour cream
½ cup chopped green pepper
½ cup chopped sweet yellow pepper
½ cup chopped sweet red pepper
½ cup chopped green onions
1 medium tomato, chopped
2 tablespoons finely chopped ripe
  olives
2 bunches fresh cilantro or parsley
  (optional)

Combine tortilla chips and butter; press onto bottom of a lightly greased 9-inch springform pan. Bake at 325° for 15 minutes. Cool on a wire rack.

Beat cream cheese at medium speed with an electric mixer 3 minutes or until fluffy; add eggs, one at a time, beating after each addition. Stir in shredded cheese, chiles, and ground red pepper. Pour into prepared pan, and bake at 325° for 30 minutes. Cool 10 minutes on a wire rack. Gently run a knife around edge of pan to release sides; carefully remove sides of pan. Let cool completely. Spread sour cream evenly over top; cover and chill. Arrange green pepper and remaining ingredients on top as desired. Place on a bed of fresh cilantro or parsley, if desired. Serve with tortilla chips. Yield: one 9-inch cheesecake or 25 appetizer servings.

Say Cheese!

■ Brush oil on a grater before shredding cheese for an easy cleanup.

■ Shred Cheddar or Swiss cheese and freeze; whenever you need some for cooking, just measure and use.

■ Do not throw away cheese that has dried out or any small leftover pieces. Grate the cheese; cover and freeze for use in casseroles or to top baked potatoes or toast.

■ This soup recipe is long on ingredients, but the effort you'll spend yields a richly seasoned, versatile stock. The flavor is best if the soup is made ahead and frozen.

TORTILLA SOUP

16 medium tomatoes, unpeeled
  (about 8½ pounds)
2 large onions, peeled and
  quartered
½ cup vegetable oil, divided
2 poblano chile peppers
3 cloves garlic, minced
24 (6-inch) corn tortillas, cut into
  thin strips and divided
1 tablespoon ground cumin
1 teaspoon chili powder
1 bay leaf
5 (14-ounce) cans ready-to-serve
  chicken broth
4 (14-ounce) cans ready-to-serve
  beef broth
1 (8-ounce) can tomato sauce
½ teaspoon salt
¼ teaspoon ground red pepper
¼ teaspoon ground black pepper
Mesquite chips
8 (4-ounce) skinned, boned chicken
  breast halves
2 cups (8 ounces) shredded Colby-
  Monterey Jack cheese blend
1 avocado, peeled and sliced
Garnish: fresh cilantro sprigs

Combine tomatoes, onions, and 3 tablespoons vegetable oil, tossing to coat; place in a shallow roasting pan. Broil 5 inches from heat (with electric oven door partially opened) until tomatoes look blistered, stirring often. Position knife blade in food processor bowl; add about one-third of tomato mixture. Process until smooth. Transfer mixture to a large Dutch oven. Repeat process twice with remaining tomato mixture; set aside.
  Wash and dry peppers; place on an aluminum foil-lined baking sheet; broil 5 inches from heat (with electric oven door partially opened) about 5 minutes

on each side or until peppers look blistered, turning once. Immediately place in a heavy-duty, zip-top plastic bag; seal and let stand 10 minutes to loosen skins. Peel peppers, and remove seeds; chop. Cook chopped peppers and garlic in 2 tablespoons oil in a small skillet over medium heat, stirring constantly, 3 minutes.
  Add pepper mixture, half of tortilla strips, and next 6 ingredients to tomato mixture, and bring to a boil. Cover, reduce heat to low, and simmer mixture 30 minutes. Stir in salt, red pepper, and black pepper. Pour mixture through a large wire-mesh strainer into a large container, discarding solids.
  For a charcoal grill, soak mesquite chips in water 1 to 24 hours; drain. (Do not soak chips if using a gas grill.) Wrap chips in heavy-duty aluminum foil; punch several holes in top of foil. Place on medium-hot coals or lava rocks (350° to 400°). Cook chicken, covered with grill lid, 15 minutes or until done, turning once. Cut chicken into strips, and keep warm.
  Pour remaining 3 tablespoons oil into a large skillet. Fry remaining tortilla strips in hot oil over high heat until crisp. Drain on paper towels.
  To serve, place small amounts of crisp tortilla strips, chicken, cheese, and avocado into individual bowls; ladle soup into bowls. Garnish, if desired. Yield: 22 cups.

Note: To make ahead, prepare soup with first 15 ingredients; cover and refrigerate up to three days or freeze up to three months. Thaw soup in refrigerator. Prepare chicken and remaining tortilla strips; reheat soup. Serve according to directions.

■ You can prepare this hearty entrée over several days, if necessary, to streamline your party-day schedule. This is also a perfect dish for two compadres to make. Many hands make light work of roasting and peeling poblano chile peppers and shucking tomatillos for Verde Sauce.
  Prepare Verde Sauce and Red Pepper Puree one or two days ahead; cover and refrigerate until needed. Assemble enchiladas one or two days ahead; cover and refrigerate until ready to bake.

CHICKEN ENCHILADAS VERDE

14 chicken breast halves, skinned
  (about 7 pounds)
3 quarts water
2 tablespoons ground red pepper
1 tablespoon salt
14 fresh tomatillos
1½ cups chopped onion
3 cloves garlic, minced
2 tablespoons vegetable oil
1 teaspoon salt
¼ cup chopped fresh cilantro
4 cups (16 ounces) shredded
  Monterey Jack cheese, divided
1 cup vegetable oil
20 corn tortillas
Verde Sauce
8 ounces feta cheese, crumbled
Red Pepper Puree
Garnish: fresh cilantro leaves

Combine first 4 ingredients in a large Dutch oven; bring to a boil. Cover, reduce heat, and simmer 35 minutes or until tender. Remove chicken, discarding broth; cool. Bone and shred chicken; set aside.
  Remove husks from tomatillos, and cook in a saucepan in boiling water to cover 5 minutes; drain and set aside.
  Cook onion and garlic in 2 tablespoons oil in Dutch oven over medium-high heat until tender, stirring often. Add tomatillos and 1 teaspoon salt. Bring to a boil; reduce heat, and simmer 5 minutes. Add

chicken and cilantro; cook 10 minutes. Stir in 1 cup Monterey Jack cheese.

Heat 1 cup vegetable oil in a medium skillet. Fry tortillas, one at a time, 3 or 4 seconds on each side; drain on paper towels. Dip each tortilla in Verde Sauce, coating well. Place about ½ cup chicken mixture down center of each tortilla, and roll up. Repeat procedure with each tortilla. Place, seam side down, into two 13- x 9- x 2-inch baking dishes; top with remaining sauce, spreading to cover ends of tortillas. Sprinkle with remaining Monterey Jack and feta cheeses. Cover and bake at 425° for 20 to 30 minutes or until thoroughly heated. Serve with Red Pepper Puree. Garnish, if desired. Yield: 20 enchiladas.

Verde Sauce

8 poblano chile peppers
32 fresh tomatillos
3 cups chicken broth, divided
1 medium onion, chopped
4 cloves garlic, minced
6 romaine lettuce leaves, torn
½ cup chopped fresh cilantro
2½ teaspoons salt

Wash and dry peppers; place on an aluminum foil-lined baking sheet. Broil peppers 5 inches from heat (with electric oven door partially opened) about 5 minutes on each side or until peppers look blistered, turning once. Immediately place in a heavy-duty, zip-top plastic bag; seal and let stand 10 minutes to loosen skins. Peel peppers, and remove seeds; set aside.

Remove husks from tomatillos, and cook in a Dutch oven in boiling water to cover 5 minutes; drain. Position knife blade in food processor bowl. Add peppers, tomatillos, 1 cup chicken broth, and remaining ingredients; process 20 to 30 seconds or until smooth, stopping once to scrape down sides. Transfer to a Dutch oven, and cook, over medium heat, stirring constantly, 5 minutes. Slowly stir in remaining chicken broth, and simmer until thickened (about 10 to 12 minutes). Yield: 6 cups.

Red Pepper Puree

5 sweet red peppers
1 teaspoon salt

Wash and dry peppers; place on an aluminum foil-lined baking sheet. Broil peppers 5 inches from heat (with electric oven door partially opened) about 5 minutes on each side or until peppers look blistered, turning once. Immediately place peppers in a heavy-duty, zip-top plastic bag; seal and let stand 10 minutes to loosen skins. Peel peppers, and remove seeds. Position knife blade in food processor bowl. Add peppers and salt; process until smooth, stopping once to scrape down sides. Cover and chill, if desired. Yield: 2 cups.

■ Mild poblano chile peppers that are baked, not fried, are a cooling counterpoint to the menu's spicy enchiladas. Fill peppers with cheese-and-corn stuffing several hours ahead; cover and refrigerate. Prepare Walnut Cream Sauce ahead, and reheat while peppers bake.

HAVARTI-AND-CORN-STUFFED CHILES RELLENOS WITH WALNUT CREAM SAUCE

10 large poblano chile peppers
    (about 2 pounds)
6 medium ears fresh corn
2 cups (8 ounces) shredded Havarti
    cheese
2 cups (8 ounces) shredded
    Monterey Jack cheese
Walnut Cream Sauce

Wash and dry peppers; place on an aluminum foil-lined baking sheet. Broil peppers 5 inches from heat (with electric oven door partially opened) about 5 minutes on each side or until peppers look blistered, turning once. Immediately place in a heavy-duty, zip-top plastic bag; seal and let stand 10 minutes to loosen skins. Peel peppers, keeping stems intact; split one side of peppers, if necessary. Remove and discard membranes and seeds. Set aside.

Remove husks and silks from corn, and wrap each ear in wax paper. Microwave at HIGH 12 to 14 minutes or until done, rearranging every 4 minutes. Cool. Cut corn from cob, reserving ¼ cup.

Combine corn and cheeses; spoon mixture down center of each pepper, and fold together to close. Arrange peppers on a lightly greased baking sheet. Bake at 350° for 10 minutes or until thoroughly heated. Arrange on each plate; top with Walnut Cream Sauce, and sprinkle with reserved corn. Yield: 10 servings.

Walnut Cream Sauce

1 (8-ounce) package cream cheese,
    softened
⅓ cup milk
½ cup chopped walnuts, toasted

Position knife blade in food processor bowl; add cream cheese. Process until smooth. Add milk; process mixture until blended. Add walnuts; process 20 seconds or until walnuts are finely chopped.

Transfer mixture to a small saucepan. Cook over low heat until thoroughly heated, stirring occasionally, (do not boil). Yield: 1½ cups.

■ You can prepare each element of this elaborate-looking dessert, including garnishes, well ahead of serving; then assemble at the last minute. We suggest preparing and freezing both cornmeal crêpes and ice cream several days before serving. No more than four hours before assembling desserts, fry the crêpes to form "sombreros."

CINNAMON ICE CREAM SOMBREROS

4 cups milk
1 teaspoon vanilla extract
¼ cup ground cinnamon
1⅓ cups sugar
12 egg yolks
1 cup whipping cream
1 (8-ounce) package semisweet chocolate
8 ounces white chocolate
Chocolate Sauce
Cornmeal Sombreros
Garnish: fresh strawberry "fans"

Combine first 3 ingredients in a saucepan; bring to a boil over medium heat,

stirring occasionally. Remove from heat; cover and let stand 15 minutes.

Combine sugar and egg yolks in a large mixing bowl; beat at high speed with an electric mixer 3 minutes or until thick and pale. Gradually stir about one-fourth of hot mixture into yolks; add to remaining hot mixture, stirring constantly. Cook over low heat until mixture reaches 185° (about 3 minutes). Remove from heat; set saucepan in ice. Stir in whipping cream; cover and chill.

Pour mixture into freezer container of a 1-gallon, hand-turned or electric freezer. Freeze according to manufacturer's instructions. Spoon ice cream into a 13- x 9- x 2-inch pan; cover and freeze 8 hours.

One hour before assembling sombreros, scoop ice cream into 10 balls, and place on a baking sheet. Cover with plastic wrap, and immediately return to freezer.

Melt semisweet chocolate in a small saucepan over low heat, stirring until smooth. Place a 14- x 10-inch piece of wax paper on a cloth towel, and spread melted chocolate evenly into a

12- x 8-inch rectangle. Make "waves" of chocolate by loosely gathering towel crosswise under wax paper. Let chocolate harden; peel off wax paper. Break or cut chocolate into 3- x 2-inch pieces, and freeze until ready to serve. Repeat procedure with white chocolate. To serve, spoon warm Chocolate Sauce evenly onto dessert plates. Place Cornmeal Sombreros on sauce, and fill with Cinnamon Ice Cream balls. Position chocolate pieces around ice cream. Garnish, if desired. Yield: 10 servings.

Chocolate Sauce

1 cup whipping cream
2½ cups semisweet chocolate morsels
¼ cup butter or margarine
2 tablespoons sugar
1 teaspoon vanilla extract

Place whipping cream in a saucepan; bring to a boil over medium heat. Remove from heat; add chocolate morsels and remaining ingredients, stirring until chocolate melts and mixture

Christmas Gift Exchange

These Dallas supper club members look forward to their annual gift exchange as another way of sharing holiday spirit and fun. Each member brings an inexpensive, wrapped gift that's usually entertainment related. Tradition gets a twist, however, when group members turn the usual present swap into a game called Chinese Gift Exchange. Here are the rules of play.
■ To determine the order of play for the game, have each person draw a number.

■ The person drawing number one selects and opens a gift.
■ Player 2 then either chooses another unopened gift or takes the gift Player 1 has opened. If the opened gift is taken, Player 1 then selects another unopened gift.
■ Player 3 then either selects a new unopened gift or chooses

from the two opened gifts, and so on as the swap continues.
■ As players' gifts are taken, they re-enter the game and have the option of selecting an unopened gift or taking already opened gifts from other players.
■ Players cannot immediately reclaim a gift that has just been lost; they must wait until another turn.
■ A player may select the same gift twice.
■ The game reaches an end when the last player selects the last unopened gift.

is smooth. Cover and refrigerate. Just before serving, cook over low heat until warm. Yield: 2½ cups.

Cornmeal Sombreros

¾ cup all-purpose flour
⅓ cup yellow cornmeal
3 tablespoons sugar
1 teaspoon salt
¾ cup milk
½ cup water
3 large eggs
1 tablespoon butter or margarine, melted
Vegetable cooking spray
8 cups vegetable oil

Combine first 4 ingredients in container of an electric blender; process 1 minute. Add milk and next 3 ingredients; process 25 seconds, stopping once to scrape down sides. Transfer batter to a bowl; cover and refrigerate at least 1 hour or overnight.

Coat bottom of a 5-inch crêpe pan or small nonstick skillet with cooking spray; place over medium heat until just hot, not smoking. Pour 3 tablespoons batter into pan, and quickly tilt pan in all directions so batter covers pan in a thin film. Cook about 1 minute or until crêpe can be shaken loose from pan. Flip crêpe, and cook about 30 seconds.

Place crêpes on a towel to cool. Stack between layers of wax paper to prevent sticking. Repeat until all batter is used. Freeze crêpes, if desired. (Thaw crêpes before frying.)

Pour oil into a Dutch oven; heat to 375°. Spray a tortilla or "bird's nest" frying basket with cooking spray. Arrange 1 crêpe in bottom basket; place smaller basket on top, and secure with clip. Completely immerse basket in hot oil; fry crêpe until golden (about 1 minute). Remove from oil, and unclip frying basket. Gently turn out sombrero onto paper towels. Repeat procedure with remaining crêpes. Yield: 15 sombreros.

A Plantation Christmas

Any excuse will do, but the holiday season prompts a gathering of three Mississippi hostesses. Sisters Ruth Ellen Calhoun and Ethel Banta and their friend Daisye Howell—all owners and residents of historic Mississippi homes—put their heads and hearts together for a reunion rich with traditional feasts and memories.

Forest Home

Playful deer scamper among the trees lining the driveway to Daisye and Boatner Howell's retreat, a peaceful place called Forest Home outside Natchez, Mississippi.

True to the old Southern ways, Daisye has selected the menu from some favorite family recipes, and her cook, Molly Griffin, is tending to details. Daisye joins her guests in the parlor, serving china mugs of creamy, chilled Sweet Pepper Soup for sipping before the main course. What follows is a grand meal served buffet style and a cozy evening of reminiscing together.

FOREST HOME DINNER
FOR TWELVE

Sweet Pepper Soup
Grilled Venison Roast
Herbed Rice
Stuffed Mirlitons
Dilled Green Beans
Lemon Solid

SWEET PEPPER SOUP

4 large sweet red peppers, coarsely chopped (about 2¾ pounds)
2 large sweet yellow peppers, coarsely chopped (about 1¼ pounds)
1 bunch green onions, chopped
2 tablespoons olive oil
4 (14½-ounce) cans ready-to-serve chicken broth, divided
2 teaspoons salt
1½ teaspoons curry powder
1 quart buttermilk

Cook first 3 ingredients in olive oil in a large Dutch oven over medium-high heat, stirring constantly, until tender. Cool slightly. Place about one-fourth of mixture into container of an electric blender or food processor; add about ½ cup broth, and process until smooth. Pour mixture through a large wire-mesh strainer into a large bowl, discarding pulp. Repeat procedure 3 times with remaining pepper mixture and 1½ cups broth.

Return pepper mixture, remaining broth, salt, and curry powder to Dutch oven; bring to a boil over medium heat. Reduce heat to low, and simmer 15 minutes; cool. Using a wire whisk, stir in buttermilk. Cover and chill. Serve cold. Yield: 12 cups.

■ Molly Griffin's recipe for venison roast is served with a thin gravy made with juniper berries, a common flavor accompaniment for wild game. You'll find these in small jars in the spice section, but you can substitute gin (which is made from the berries) if they're unavailable.

GRILLED VENISON ROAST

8½ pounds bone-in venison saddle, trimmed
2 cloves garlic, halved
½ cup Worcestershire sauce
2 tablespoons soy sauce
2 teaspoons garlic powder
2 teaspoons lemon-pepper seasoning
Hickory chips
Juniper Sauce
Garnishes: fresh bay leaves, kumquats

Place venison in a roasting pan. Cut 4 slits in venison, and insert garlic halves. Combine Worcestershire sauce and soy sauce, and pour over venison; sprinkle all sides with garlic powder and lemon-pepper seasoning. Cover and refrigerate 2 hours.

Soak hickory chips in water 30 minutes. Prepare charcoal fire on sides of grill around a drip pan; let burn 30 minutes. Place venison on grill rack over pan. Cook, covered with grill lid,

over low coals (250°) 3 hours or until meat thermometer inserted in thickest portion of meat registers 140° or desired degree of doneness. Carefully remove drip pan, and reserve 2 tablespoons drippings to use in Juniper Sauce. Serve venison with Juniper Sauce, and garnish, if desired. Yield: 12 servings.

Juniper Sauce

4 (14½-ounce) cans ready-to-serve chicken broth
1 (10-ounce) jar red currant jelly
½ cup bourbon
2 tablespoons dried juniper berries, coarsely crushed *
2 tablespoons black peppercorns
¼ teaspoon dried thyme
2 tablespoons reserved pan drippings

Combine first 6 ingredients in a saucepan; bring to a boil over high heat. Reduce heat, and simmer about 1 hour or until liquid is reduced to 4 cups. Pour mixture through a large wire-mesh strainer into a 4-cup liquid measuring cup, discarding seeds. Stir in 2 tablespoons reserved pan drippings. Yield: 4 cups.

* 1 tablespoon gin may be substituted for juniper berries.

HERBED RICE

½ pound fresh mushrooms, sliced
Vegetable cooking spray
1 tablespoon beef-flavored bouillon granules
½ cup hot water
6 cups cooked long-grain rice
1 teaspoon salt
½ teaspoon dried rosemary
½ teaspoon dried thyme
½ teaspoon dried savory

Cook mushrooms in a large skillet coated with cooking spray over medium-high heat until tender; set aside. Dissolve bouillon granules in water. Combine bouillon, mushrooms, rice, and remaining ingredients. Spoon mixture into a 13- x 9- x 2-inch baking dish; cover and bake at 350° for 20 minutes or until thoroughly heated. Yield: 12 servings.

■ Daisye Howell learned to cook this recipe from her mother-in-law, who Daisye says was a "superb Creole cook." After tasting this dish, we agree. A mirliton (mihr-lih-ton) is a mild Louisiana winter squash resembling a pear. (They're also grown in California and Florida, where they're called chayote squash instead.)

STUFFED MIRLITONS

6 mirlitons or chayotes, cut in half and seeded
1 pound unpeeled medium-size fresh shrimp
½ cup butter or margarine
1 bunch green onions, chopped
2 to 3 cloves garlic, minced
1 pound fresh crabmeat, drained and flaked
¼ cup soft breadcrumbs
1 teaspoon salt
¼ teaspoon ground red pepper
¼ cup butter or margarine, melted
1 cup soft breadcrumbs
Garnish: fresh thyme sprigs

Cook mirlitons in boiling water to cover 10 minutes; drain. Let cool to touch. Using a melon baller or spoon, carefully scoop out pulp, leaving shells intact; set shells aside. Chop pulp, and drain; set aside.

Peel and devein shrimp; coarsely chop. Set aside. Melt ½ cup butter

---

Savory Sauces

■ Allow about ½ cup of marinade for every pound of meat to be marinated.

■ To mix up a quick and easy sauce to serve with game, stir 2 tablespoons horseradish and ½ teaspoon dry mustard into ½ cup currant jelly.

in a large skillet over medium-high heat; add green onions and garlic, and cook, stirring constantly, until tender. Add shrimp, and cook over medium heat 3 minutes or until shrimp turn pink. Gently stir in mirliton pulp, crabmeat, and next 3 ingredients; cook over medium heat until thoroughly heated, stirring occasionally.

Spoon shrimp mixture into shells. Combine ¼ cup butter and 1 cup breadcrumbs; spoon evenly over shrimp mixture. Bake at 350° for 40 minutes or until thoroughly heated and lightly browned. Garnish, if desired. Yield: 12 servings.

DILLED GREEN BEANS

3 pounds fresh green beans
1½ cups water
3 tablespoons olive oil
4 cloves garlic
1 tablespoon dried dillweed
½ teaspoon salt
¼ teaspoon pepper

Wash beans; remove ends. Bring water to a boil in a Dutch oven; add beans. Cover, reduce heat to medium, and cook 10 minutes, stirring occasionally. Drain; plunge into ice water to stop cooking, and drain.

Heat olive oil in a wok or 2 large skillets; add garlic, and cook, stirring constantly, until lightly browned. Remove garlic; add beans, and cook, stirring constantly, until thoroughly heated. Add dillweed, salt, and pepper, tossing well. Serve immediately. Yield: 12 servings.

■ The name for this congealed dessert is English, and a friend shared the recipe with Daisye Howell after a trip to England. It settles into two distinct layers, one transparent and one more opaque, or "solid."

LEMON SOLID

2 envelopes unflavored gelatin
4 cups milk
1½ cups sugar
3 tablespoons grated lemon rind
⅔ cup fresh lemon juice
Sliced fresh strawberries
Sliced kiwifruit

Sprinkle gelatin over milk in a medium saucepan; let stand 1 minute. Stir in sugar; cook over low heat, stirring until gelatin and sugar dissolve (about 2 minutes). Remove from heat; stir in lemon rind and juice (mixture will curdle). Pour into a lightly oiled 6-cup ring mold; cover and refrigerate until firm. Unmold onto a platter. Serve with fruit. Yield: 12 servings.

Dinner at Elgin

Instead of the predictable turkey and dressing, Mississippi quail stuffed with cornbread dressing heads the menu at Ruth Ellen Calhoun's Elgin home. The mustard greens she grows go into smooth-as-silk Cream of Mustard Green Soup. Ruth Ellen makes her own basil vinegar, which she uses in her Crabmeat Rémoulade appetizer. Several ribboned bottles wait under the Christmas tree in the parlor as gifts for visitors. Lizzie Davis, who has helped Ruth Ellen cook for years, whips up her special Elgin Biscuits, which they like to serve with homemade wild plum jelly. The plums came from the Calhoun's yard.

Expectant faces greet Thelma Jones as she serves dessert in Ruth Ellen's elegant Old Paris china pots de crème set. The dishes are certainly traditional, but the Easy Pots de Crème recipe is not. Ruth Ellen simplified the custard (usually baked) by using vanilla instant pudding mix laced with sherry.

DINING AT ELGIN
FOR TWELVE

Spicy Pecans
Crabmeat Rémoulade
Bacon-Wrapped Crackers
Cream of Mustard Green Soup
Quail Stuffed With Cornbread
Dressing
Spinach-Stuffed Tomatoes
Elgin Biscuits
Easy Pots de Crème

SPICY PECANS

2 cups pecan halves
2 tablespoons vegetable oil
⅛ teaspoon hot sauce
6 small bay leaves
½ teaspoon salt
½ teaspoon curry powder
½ teaspoon chili powder
¼ teaspoon garlic powder
¼ teaspoon ground cardamom
¼ teaspoon ground cinnamon
Garnish: fresh bay leaves

Combine first 3 ingredients in a large, heavy-duty, zip-top plastic bag; shake well. Add 6 bay leaves and next 6 ingredients, shaking well.

Spread pecan mixture evenly into a 15- x 10- x 1-inch jellyroll pan. Bake at 325° for 30 minutes, stirring pecan mixture every 5 minutes. Remove from oven, and let cool completely. Remove and discard bay leaves. Store pecans in an airtight container. Garnish, if desired. Yield: 2 cups.

CRABMEAT RÉMOULADE

1 (10½-ounce) French baguette
⅓ cup butter or margarine, melted
Lettuce leaves
6 cups shredded leaf lettuce
Rémoulade Sauce
1 pound fresh lump crabmeat, drained
Garnish: fresh dill sprigs

Slice baguette into ¼-inch-thick rounds. Brush with melted butter; place on baking sheets. Bake at 350° for 10 minutes; turn and bake an additional 5 minutes. Cool on wire racks.

To serve, line salad plates with lettuce leaves. Top each lettuce-lined plate with ½ cup shredded lettuce, ¼ cup Rémoulade Sauce, and 3 tablespoons crabmeat; garnish, if desired. Serve with toasted bread slices. Yield: 12 appetizer servings.

Rémoulade Sauce

¼ cup Creole mustard
¼ cup basil vinegar *
2 cups olive oil
2 tablespoons paprika
2 teaspoons minced garlic
⅛ teaspoon hot sauce
¼ cup anchovy paste
2 tablespoons prepared horseradish
1 cup chopped celery
2 cups chopped green onions

Position knife blade in food processor bowl; add mustard and vinegar. Process 20 seconds, stopping once to scrape down sides. With processor running, slowly pour oil through food chute. Add paprika and next 6 ingredients; process until smooth. Add 2 to 4 tablespoons water, if necessary, and process until smooth. Cover and chill. Yield: 3½ cups.

* ¼ cup white wine vinegar may be substituted.

BACON-WRAPPED CRACKERS

12 slices bacon, cut in half
24 saltine crackers

Wrap a half slice of bacon around each cracker, overlapping ends. Place, seam side down, on a rack in a shallow roasting pan; bake at 350° for 30 minutes or until bacon is crisp. Serve immediately. Yield: 2 dozen.

■ Ruth Ellen Calhoun makes good ol' "country" greens positively elegant in this delectable soup. Even if you aren't crazy about mustard greens, you'll *love* this recipe. Trust us.

CREAM OF MUSTARD GREEN SOUP

1 (1-pound) center-cut ham slice with bone
8 cups water
1 large bunch fresh mustard greens, washed and finely chopped (about 4½ pounds)
¼ cup butter or margarine
2 cups chopped green onions
2 cups chopped celery
1 cup chopped onion
⅓ cup butter or margarine
⅓ cup all-purpose flour
5 cups half-and-half
½ teaspoon salt
⅛ teaspoon hot sauce

Combine ham and water in a Dutch oven; bring to a boil. Cover, reduce heat, and simmer 3 hours. Remove ham, leaving liquid in Dutch oven. (Reserve ham for another use.) Add mustard greens to Dutch oven, and cook, uncovered, 1 hour, stirring occasionally. Set aside.

Melt ¼ cup butter in a large skillet over medium heat; add green onions, celery, and onion, and cook, stirring constantly, until tender. Remove from

heat. Position knife blade in food processor bowl; add onion mixture. Process onion mixture until smooth, stopping occasionally to scrape down sides. Set aside.

Melt ⅓ cup butter in Dutch oven over low heat; gradually add flour, stirring until smooth. Cook, stirring constantly, 1 minute. Gradually add half-and-half; cook over medium heat, stirring constantly, until thickened and bubbly. Stir in mustard green mixture, pureed vegetables, salt, and hot sauce. Cook just until thoroughly heated (do not boil). Yield: 10 cups.

QUAIL STUFFED WITH CORNBREAD DRESSING

2½ cups water
½ cup butter or margarine
1 (16-ounce) package cornbread stuffing mix
24 quail
1 teaspoon salt
½ teaspoon pepper
1 (6-ounce) can frozen orange juice concentrate, thawed and undiluted
¾ cup Chablis or other dry white wine
Lettuce leaves
Garnishes: orange slices, mint sprigs

Combine water and butter in a saucepan; bring to a boil. Remove from heat, and stir in cornbread stuffing mix. Spoon about 2 tablespoons mixture into each quail. Tie legs together with heavy string. Sprinkle quail with salt and pepper; place on a lightly greased rack in a broiler pan.

Combine orange juice concentrate and wine, and brush over quail; reserve remaining orange juice mixture. Broil quail on middle rack of oven (with electric oven door partially opened) 3 to 5 minutes or until quail is browned. Baste again with reserved orange juice mixture; cover with aluminum foil, and bake at 350° for 1 hour, basting every 20 minutes. Remove and discard string. Serve quail on lettuce leaves and garnish, if desired. Yield: 12 servings.

SPINACH-STUFFED TOMATOES

2 tablespoons butter or
  margarine
1 cup chopped onion
4 stalks celery, chopped
1 cup chopped fresh parsley
1 cup chopped green onions
4 (10-ounce) packages frozen
  chopped spinach, thawed and well
  drained
½ cup soft breadcrumbs
2 tablespoons Worcestershire sauce
2 tablespoons Pernod or other
  licorice-flavored liqueur
1 teaspoon salt
1 teaspoon hot sauce
2 teaspoons anchovy paste
12 medium tomatoes
½ cup soft breadcrumbs
½ cup freshly grated Parmesan
  cheese
¼ cup butter or margarine,
  melted

Melt 2 tablespoons butter in a saucepan over medium-high heat; add onion and next 3 ingredients, and cook, stirring constantly, 5 minutes or until tender. Remove from heat. Stir in spinach and next 6 ingredients.

Slice off top of each tomato, and carefully scoop out pulp, leaving a ¼-inch shell. (Reserve pulp for another use.) Spoon spinach mixture evenly into tomatoes; place on a baking sheet. Bake at 350° for 15 minutes.

Combine ½ cup breadcrumbs and Parmesan cheese; sprinkle evenly over tomatoes. Drizzle with butter; bake 5 to 10 minutes or until cheese is lightly browned. Yield: 12 servings.

■ Lizzie Davis's biscuits are best served with homemade plum jelly. But you can use a commercial jelly for ease, or even eat these biscuits plain. They're that good.

ELGIN BISCUITS

2 cups self-rising flour
1 teaspoon baking powder
2 teaspoons sugar
¾ cup butter-flavored
  shortening
¾ cup evaporated milk

Combine first 3 ingredients in a large bowl; cut in shortening with a pastry blender until mixture is crumbly. Add milk, stirring with a fork until dry ingredients are moistened. (Dough will be sticky.) Turn dough out onto a heavily floured surface, and knead lightly 4 or 5 times.

Roll dough to ½-inch thickness; cut with a 2-inch round cutter, and place on a lightly greased baking sheet. Bake at 425° for 10 to 12 minutes or until lightly browned. Serve with butter and jelly. Yield: 1½ dozen.

EASY POTS DE CRÈME

1 quart milk
1 cup cream sherry
2 teaspoons vanilla extract
2 (5.1-ounce) packages vanilla
  instant pudding mix
Whipped cream

Combine first 3 ingredients in a large mixing bowl. Add pudding mix, and beat with a wire whisk or at low speed with an electric mixer 1 to 2 minutes or until mixture is well blended. Spoon into 12 pots de crème or 6-ounce custard cups; cover and chill. To serve, dollop with whipped cream. Yield: 12 servings.

Butter—
Shaped For Show

Making butter curls and molds are two of the easiest and prettiest ways to shape butter or margarine. These particular designs require only a little preparation and a few simple tools that can be found at most large department stores or kitchen specialty shops. Once you complete your butter designs, cover and chill them until ready to serve. Remember that butter will soften and lose its shape rapidly at room temperature. Serve shaped butter in an icer, on a bed of crushed ice if you want it to hold its shape longer, or on a serving dish.

Butter Curls

For making butter curls, use a hook-shaped implement called a butter curler. Work with a stick of butter at refrigerator temperature. Place the butter on a flat surface, and pull the butter curler, ridged side down, length-wise down the stick. The butter will curl up and over the curler. One stick yields about two dozen curls.

Butter Molds

For molding butter, we found that rubber, plastic, or porcelain molds unmold more easily than wooden ones. The molds come in both large and pat-size designs. To make butter molds, first soften the butter. Spread butter into cavity of the mold, scraping the back surface of the butter to level it. Freeze 30 minutes or until the butter is firm. Then invert the mold, and pop the butter out. Yields for butter molds vary.

Hope Farm

After the delicious dinners at Daisye Howell's and Ruth Ellen Calhoun's, Ethel Banta offers the weekend grand finale with Sunday brunch, starting with cheese wafers, champagne, and orange juice served on the back porch. Then guests move inside for a warm meal of Shrimp Creole over Saffron Rice served with Herbed French Bread.

Ethel's cooks, Inez Granger and Mary Green, keep the delicious food coming while she keeps her guests in stitches with stories. The afternoon and the reunion slowly wind down, but these friends have added volumes to their "remember when" stash . . . for next time.

BRUNCH
AT HOPE FARM
FOR TWELVE

Hope Farm Cheese Wafers
Shrimp Creole over Saffron Rice
Avocado-Grapefruit Salad
Herbed French Bread

■ Sisters Ethel Banta and Ruth Ellen Calhoun both use this recipe for entertaining. They serve the wafers as a sweet appetizer or bite-size dessert dusted with powdered sugar.

HOPE FARM CHEESE WAFERS

1 cup (4 ounces) shredded sharp
 Cheddar cheese
½ cup butter or margarine,
 softened
1 cup all-purpose flour
¼ teaspoon salt
½ teaspoon ground red pepper
32 pecan halves

Beat cheese and butter at medium speed with an electric mixer about 2 minutes or until creamy. Combine flour, salt, and red pepper; gradually add to cheese mixture, mixing at low speed just until blended. Divide in half; shape each portion into an 8- x 1-inch log, and wrap in plastic wrap. Chill at least 2 hours.

Cut each log into ½-inch-thick slices, and place 2 inches apart on ungreased baking sheets. Place a pecan half on each wafer; bake at 375° for 11 to 13 minutes. Remove to wire racks to cool. Yield: 2½ dozen.

Note: You may freeze 8- x 1-inch dough logs up to one week. Let dough stand 15 minutes before slicing into wafers; bake as directed.

SHRIMP CREOLE

¼ cup vegetable oil or bacon
 drippings
¼ cup all-purpose flour
1½ cups chopped onion
1 cup chopped green onions
1 cup chopped celery
1 cup chopped green pepper
2 cloves garlic, minced
1 (16-ounce) can chopped tomatoes,
 undrained
1 (8-ounce) can tomato sauce
1 (6-ounce) can tomato paste
1 cup water
1½ teaspoons salt
1 teaspoon black pepper
½ teaspoon ground red pepper
2 or 3 bay leaves
1 tablespoon lemon juice
1 teaspoon Worcestershire sauce
⅛ teaspoon hot sauce
5 pounds unpeeled jumbo fresh
 shrimp
Saffron Rice
½ cup finely chopped fresh parsley
Garnish: fresh parsley sprigs

Combine oil and flour in a cast-iron skillet; cook over medium heat, stirring constantly, 15 minutes or until roux is chocolate colored. Stir in onion and next 4 ingredients; cook 15 minutes, stirring often. Transfer mixture to a large Dutch oven; add tomatoes and next 10 ingredients. Bring to a boil; cover, reduce heat, and simmer 1 hour, stirring occasionally.

Peel and devein shrimp; add to tomato mixture, and simmer 10 to 15 minutes or until shrimp turn pink. Remove and discard bay leaves. Sprinkle with finely chopped parsley; serve over Saffron Rice. Garnish, if desired. Yield: 14 cups.

Saffron Rice

7 cups water
2 tablespoons butter or margarine
2 (10-ounce) packages saffron
 yellow rice mix

Bring water and butter to a boil in a large saucepan; stir in rice mix. Cover, reduce heat, and simmer 20 minutes or until rice is tender and water is absorbed. Garnish, if desired. Yield: 8 cups.

Note: Shrimp Creole can be made one day in advance and refrigerated. To serve, reheat over medium heat, stirring occasionally (do not boil).

AVOCADO-GRAPEFRUIT
SALAD

4 grapefruit *
3 medium avocados
8 cups torn leaf lettuce
½ cup olive oil
¾ cup white wine vinegar
¼ teaspoon salt
⅛ teaspoon pepper

Peel grapefruit; section and seed over a bowl, reserving juice. Peel and slice avocados. Immediately combine juice, grapefruit sections, and avocado slices in bowl; toss gently. Cover and refrigerate up to 2 hours. Drain and toss with lettuce in a serving bowl.

Combine olive oil and remaining ingredients in a jar. Cover tightly; shake vigorously. Serve with salad. Yield: 10 to 12 servings.

* You may substitute 2 (26-ounce) jars, drained, for 4 fresh grapefruit.

HERBED FRENCH BREAD

½ cup butter or margarine, softened
2 tablespoons salt-free garlic-and-herb seasoning
1 (16-ounce) loaf unsliced French bread, cut into 1-inch slices

Combine butter and seasoning; spread between bread slices, and place loaf on a baking sheet. Bake at 350° for 10 to 15 minutes or until thoroughly heated. Yield: 1 loaf.

Note: For salt-free garlic-and-herb seasoning, we used McCormick's Salt-Free Garlic-and-Herb Seasoning.

Christmas For The Birds

Just in back of Cathy and Terril Nell's house in Gainesville, Florida, there's a lot of chirping in the air. Dinner is about to be served: Pretzel Garlands, Bread Stars, Orange Baskets, Cranberry Hearts, Snowy Doughnuts, and

Peanut Butter-Suet Pinecones. *Suet?* Why yes. It's Christmas for the birds, and they're all singing for their supper at this merry party.

The Nells' party theme delights daughters Emily, 7, and Amanda, 10, as well as the cardinals, woodpeckers, and black-capped chickadees living in the nearby woods.

The morning of the party, the Nells string popcorn garlands and tie red bows on the birds' outdoor tree; then they set up the children's party table inside. At party time, the kids swoop up Cathy's delicious treats as quickly as blue jays down popcorn kernels. (Her eye-popping Birdhouse Cake is an architectural marvel—see our "Blueprint for a Birdhouse Cake" for building tips on page 285.)

GINGERBIRDS

1 cup molasses
½ cup sugar
½ cup firmly packed brown sugar
1 tablespoon ground ginger
1 tablespoon ground cinnamon
½ teaspoon ground cloves
2¼ teaspoons baking soda
1 cup butter or margarine, softened
2 large eggs
6 cups all-purpose flour
Yellow Decorator Frosting
Nonpareils

Combine first 6 ingredients in top of double boiler; place over boiling water, and cook, stirring constantly, until sugar melts. Stir in soda; remove top pot from heat.

Place butter in a large mixing bowl; add hot molasses mixture, and beat at low speed with an electric mixer until butter melts. Let cool 10 minutes. Add eggs; beat at low speed until blended. Gradually add flour, mixing after each addition. Divide dough in

half; wrap each portion in plastic wrap, and chill 30 minutes.

Roll each portion to ¼-inch thickness on a lightly floured surface. Cut with a 4- or 5-inch, bird-shaped cutter, and place on lightly greased cookie sheets. Bake at 325° for 12 minutes or until firm to touch. Transfer to wire racks to cool.

Spread a thin layer of Yellow Decorator Frosting on cookies; add nonpareils for eyes. Let dry. Store in an airtight container. Yield: 6 dozen (4-inch) or 3½ dozen (5-inch) cookies.

Yellow Decorator Frosting

4 cups sifted powdered sugar
3 tablespoons lemon juice
3 tablespoons water
Yellow paste food coloring

Combine first 3 ingredients; stir until smooth. Stir in desired amount of food coloring. Yield: 1½ cups.

NECTAR PUNCH

2 (12-ounce) cans apricot nectar
1 (6-ounce) can frozen lemonade concentrate, thawed and undiluted
1½ cups water
1 (12-ounce) bottle club soda, chilled

Combine first 3 ingredients. Just before serving, stir in club soda. Serve over ice. Yield: 1½ quarts.

MERINGUE ACORNS

4 egg whites
¼ teaspoon cream of tartar
¾ cup sugar
½ teaspoon almond extract
1 (6-ounce) package semisweet
   chocolate morsels (1 cup) *
1 cup finely chopped pecans

Cathy's Party Tips

■ Be prepared: This party is merry but *messy!* It's best to prepare the birds' feast outside to ensure a successful—and smudge-free—party.
■ Serve the children *before* the birds. "The birds' pretzels and doughnuts will never make it to the tree if the kids are hungry," says Cathy.
■ Pop the corn for garlands several days before you plan to string it. It's easier to thread if it's stale and soft.
■ If the tree you plan to decorate is in a container, be sure it is well weighted. The kids will pull on the boughs as they reach up to hang their ornaments.
■ Even the little ones want to decorate high boughs. Place a stool near the tree—and have an adult offer a helping hand.
■ Cover the party tables with a vinyl or paper tablecloth, and shake the excess crumbs from the feast into the yard.
■ Keep several rolls of damp paper towels on the party tables. "Peanut butter and suet is a gooey combination," Cathy says.
■ "The hardest thing," Cathy laughs, "is transporting the kids back and forth to the bathroom without touching the walls." Be forewarned.

Beat egg whites and cream of tartar in a large mixing bowl at high speed with an electric mixer until foamy. Gradually add sugar, 1 tablespoon at a time, beating until stiff peaks form. Stir in almond extract.

Spoon mixture into a decorating bag fitted with a large round tip. Pipe into chocolate kiss shapes, onto greased and floured cookie sheets. Bake at 200° for 2 hours. Turn oven off, and leave meringues in oven overnight.

Melt chocolate morsels in a heavy saucepan over low heat. Dip bottom of meringues in chocolate; dip chocolate-covered bottom in pecans. Cool on waxed paper. Yield: 8 dozen.

* 6 ounces chocolate-flavored candy coating can be substituted, if desired.

Note: Meringues may be piped using a large heavy-duty, zip-top plastic bag. Spoon mixture into plastic bag; snip ½ inch off corner of bag, and follow directions.

BIRD'S NEST COOKIES

2 cups butter or margarine,
   softened
1½ teaspoons vanilla extract
3 cups all-purpose flour
1½ cups sifted powdered sugar
½ cup cornstarch
2 to 3 cups flaked coconut
1 cup small gourmet jelly beans

Beat butter and vanilla at medium speed with an electric mixer until creamy. Combine flour, sugar, and cornstarch; gradually add to butter mixture, beating well. To firm up dough, cover and chill 1 hour, if necessary. Shape into 1-inch balls; roll in coconut. Place 1 inch apart on ungreased cookie sheets; flatten slightly with bottom of a glass, gently press 2 or 3 jelly beans into each cookie. Bake

at 300° for 25 minutes or until coconut is golden. Yield: 5 dozen.

Note: Use gourmet jelly beans because the ordinary type will melt during baking.

BIRDHOUSE CAKE

2 (18.25-ounce) packages yellow
   cake mix
Buttercream Frosting
8 plastic drinking straws
1 (7½-inch) square heavy cardboard
Decorator Frosting
1 chocolate wafer
1 peppermint stick
1 plastic bird (optional)

Prepare cake mix according to package directions. Pour 3½ cups batter into a greased and floured 8-inch square pan; pour remaining 7½ cups batter into a greased and floured 15- x 10- x 1-inch jellyroll pan. Bake at 375° for 30 to 35 minutes or until a wooden pick inserted in center comes out clean. Cool in pans on wire racks 10 minutes; remove from pans, and let cool completely on wire racks. Wrap in plastic wrap, and freeze 1 hour or until firm. (Cake is easier to assemble with frozen layers.)

Trim and discard rounded tops from cakes using a long serrated knife. Cut large cake into 3 (10- x 5-inch) rectangles. Stack 3 rectangles on a serving plate spreading about ½ cup red Buttercream Frosting between each layer and on top. Vertically insert 5 drinking straws through layers, spacing evenly to give support; trim and discard excess straws.

To assemble roof section, spread one side of cardboard square with a thin layer of red frosting. Diagonally cut square cake in an X pattern to form 4 equal triangles. Place cake triangles on cardboard base, longest side down, and point up, spreading red frosting between each triangle. Trim off cardboard edges, if necessary. Horizontally insert 3 drinking straws through layers; trim and discard excess straws.

Place roof section onto rectangular cake, trimming ends, if necessary. Spread sides of house with remaining red frosting; spread top of roof with green Buttercream Frosting. Decorate rooftop with Decorator Frosting. Position chocolate wafer for an entrance hole and a peppermint stick for a perch. Attach plastic bird, if desired.

Buttercream Frosting

3 (16-ounce) packages powdered
   sugar, sifted
½ cup plus 1 tablespoon butter or
   margarine
½ cup plus 1 tablespoon shortening
½ cup plus 1 tablespoon milk
1½ tablespoons vanilla extract
Red and green paste food coloring

Combine half each of first 5 ingredients in a large mixing bowl; beat at low speed with an electric mixer until blended. (Mixer and bowl can't handle whole recipe; it must be made in batches.) Beat at high speed 5 minutes or until light and fluffy. Transfer to a bowl, and repeat procedure. Remove 2 cups frosting; stir in desired amount of green food coloring. Stir desired amount of red food coloring into remaining frosting. Yield: 6 cups.

Decorator Frosting

3 tablespoons meringue powder
1 (16-ounce) package powdered
   sugar, sifted
¼ cup plus 2 tablespoons warm
   water

Combine all ingredients in a mixing bowl; beat at high speed with an electric mixer 7 to 10 minutes or until stiff peaks form. Cover with a damp cloth to prevent drying. Yield: 3 cups.

Blueprint for a Birdhouse Cake

The Birdhouse Cake recipe beginning on facing page is easy, but construction takes patience. Helpful hint: Think of the plastic straws used in the cake as support beams. With our birdhouse "blueprints," building your own cake should proceed without a hitch.
■ Cut frozen cake layers into triangles and rectangles as illustrated.
■ Stack three rectangles on a serving plate, spreading with frosting as directed. Insert five drinking straws through layers as shown. Trim excess straws level with cake top.
■ Spread red frosting on cardboard square. Place cake triangles on cardboard as shown. Insert three drinking straws through layers; trim excess straws level with cake top.
■ Place roof section (triangles on cardboard square) onto rectangle cake. Frost and decorate as directed.

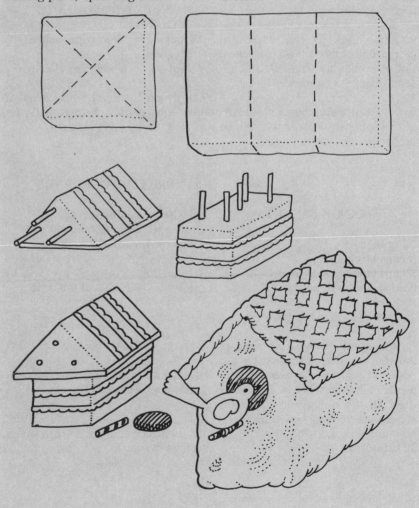

Bird Tree Ornaments

PEANUT BUTTER-SUET PINECONES

6 yards 18-gauge florist wire
12 pinecones
3 pounds peanut butter
1½ pounds suet
10 pounds birdseed

Before guests arrive, twist an 18-inch length of florist wire around big end of each pinecone, making a large hook at end of wire.

Mix peanut butter and suet. Using small handfuls, let children spread peanut butter mixture on pinecones. Roll pinecones in a large bowl of bird-seed. Yield: 12 pinecones.

Note: Suet is available at supermarket meat departments. Ask that it be ground fine for easier mixing.

ORANGE BASKETS

12 oranges
3 cups birdseed
3 cups suet (ground fine)
3 cups sunflower seeds
3 cups raisins
12 feet ½-inch-wide ribbon

Before guests arrive, cut oranges into basket shapes and scoop out pulp. Put birdseed and next 3 ingredients in individual bowls. Have children fill the orange baskets with ingredients from the bowls. Loop ribbon through basket "handles." Yield: 12 ornaments.

CRANBERRY HEARTS

6 yards 22-gauge florist wire
2 pounds fresh cranberries

Cut florist wire into 18-inch lengths. Thread cranberries onto wires; bend each into a heart shape. Yield: 12 ornaments.

SNOWY DOUGHNUTS

12 small powdered sugar-coated doughnuts
4 yards ¼-inch-wide red ribbon

Cut ribbon into 12 (12-inch) lengths. Loop ribbon through doughnuts; tie in knot. Yield: 12 ornaments.

PRETZEL GARLANDS

Unsalted miniature pretzels
¼-inch-wide red ribbon, cut to desired length of garland

Weave ribbon through pretzels to make an edible garland for birds.

BREAD STARS

1 loaf stale white sandwich bread
Christmas ornament hangers

Using a star-shaped cookie cutter, cut each slice of bread. Attach an ornament hanger to each shape.

CHRISTMAS TREE COOKIES

½ cup butter or margarine, softened
½ cup sugar
1 large egg
1 tablespoon lemon juice
2¼ cups all-purpose flour
¼ teaspoon baking soda
¼ teaspoon salt
Green Decorator Frosting
1 (4¼-ounce) tube white decorating frosting (optional)
1 (4¼-ounce) tube red decorating frosting (optional)

Beat butter at medium speed with an electric mixer until creamy; gradually add sugar, beating well. Add egg and lemon juice; mix well. Combine flour, soda, and salt; add to butter mixture, mixing well. Divide dough in half; wrap each portion in plastic wrap, and chill at least 1 hour or until firm enough to handle. Roll each portion to ⅛-inch thickness on a lightly floured surface. Cut with a 5-inch, tree-shaped cookie cutter; place on lightly greased cookie sheets. Bake at 375° for 8 minutes or until lightly browned. Transfer to wire racks to cool.

Spread Green Decorator Frosting on cookies; let dry. If desired, drizzle white decorating frosting on cookies. To make a small bird shape, place two small dots of red decorating frosting side by side; pull a wooden pick upward through one dot to make bird's tail. Yield: 2 dozen (5-inch) cookies.

Green Decorator Frosting

3 cups sifted powdered sugar
1½ tablespoons lemon juice
2 to 3 tablespoons water
Green paste food coloring

Combine sugar, lemon juice and 2 tablespoons water, stirring well. Stir in desired amount of food coloring. Add additional water for desired consistency, if necessary. Yield: 1 cup.

Old Friends Cheer The New Year

Circumstance brought four families together in 1977 on an isolated American government base near England's Yorkshire moors. "It was friendship out of necessity, at first," says Beth Snelson of Warrenton, Virginia.

Beth and her husband, Ron, soon shared every holiday with their extended family: May and Paul Edwards, now of Mayo, Maryland; Pat and Wendell Lucas of Hot Springs, Virginia; and Jean and Bill Reichert of Mount Airy, Maryland.

Over time, the families returned to the United States. And just as they did in England, they continue celebrating their friendship, and visit each others' homes on holidays.

NEW YEAR'S EVE MENU FOR EIGHT

Terrine of Pork and Veal
Broiled Crab Meltaways
Pinecone Cheese Ball
Cream of Peanut Soup
Beef Wellington
Duchess Potatoes
Peas and Celery
Sherried Cherries
White Christmas Pie
English Trifle

TERRINE OF PORK AND VEAL

2 tablespoons butter or margarine
1 medium onion, finely chopped
1 clove garlic, minced
1½ pounds ground pork
1 pound ground veal
⅔ cup Chablis or other dry white wine
1 large egg, lightly beaten
2 teaspoons salt
½ teaspoon dried thyme
¼ teaspoon freshly ground pepper
¼ teaspoon allspice
1 pound lean bacon
Lettuce leaves
Garnishes: cherry tomatoes, sweet gherkins

Melt butter in a small skillet; add onion and garlic, and cook over medium-high heat, stirring constantly, until tender. Transfer mixture to a large bowl. Add ground pork and next 7 ingredients, mixing well.

Line bottom and sides of a 9- x 5- x 3-inch loafpan with two-thirds of bacon. Press pork mixture into pan, and cover with remaining bacon slices. Cover tightly with aluminum foil, and place loafpan in a 13- x 9- x 2-inch pan. Add hot water to larger pan to depth of 1 inch. Bake at 350° for approximately 2 hours or until a wooden pick inserted in center comes out clean.

Remove from oven, and cool, draining off pan drippings as terrine cools.

Cover with aluminum foil; place a slightly smaller pan on top of terrine, and fill with pie weights, dried beans, or unopened cans. (Weighting will compact it for the shape and texture characteristic of this dish.) Chill at least 8 hours.

Discard foil wrap. Run a knife around pan to loosen the bacon lining from sides, if the terrine has not shrunk. After wiping off the gelatin that has formed, invert terrine onto a lettuce-lined platter. Garnish, if desired. Serve with melba rounds. Yield: 18 to 20 servings.

BROILED CRAB MELTAWAYS

1 (7-ounce) jar sharp process cheese spread
1 (4½-ounce) can lump crabmeat, drained
¼ cup butter or margarine, softened
2 tablespoons mayonnaise or salad dressing
⅛ teaspoon garlic powder
Dash of seasoned salt
6 English muffins, split

Combine first 6 ingredients; spread about 2 tablespoons on cut side of each muffin half. Cut each half into 4 pieces, and place on baking sheets; freeze at least 30 minutes. (May be frozen up to 2 months.)

To serve, broil 6 inches from heat (with electric oven door partially opened) 3 minutes or until puffed and bubbly. Yield: 4 dozen.

PINECONE CHEESE BALL

1¼ to 1½ cups blanched whole
  almonds
1 (8-ounce) package cream cheese,
  softened
1 cup (4 ounces) shredded Cheddar
  cheese
½ cup mayonnaise or salad
  dressing
5 slices bacon, cooked and
  crumbled
1 tablespoon diced pimiento
1 tablespoon chopped green onions
½ teaspoon dried dillweed
⅛ teaspoon pepper
Garnish: fresh parsley sprigs

Place almonds in a 9-inch square pan; bake at 300° for 20 to 25 minutes or until lightly browned, stirring occasionally. Cool and set aside.

Combine cream cheese and next 7 ingredients; cover and refrigerate at least 2 hours.

Divide mixture in half; form each half into a pinecone shape, and place on a serving dish. Holding the narrow end of each almond, start at the narrow end of cheese ball, pressing almonds into mixture at slight angles and forming overlapping rows. Continue until each cheese ball is covered completely and resembles a pinecone. Garnish, if desired. Serve with assorted crackers. Yield: 2 cheese balls.

CREAM OF PEANUT SOUP

½ cup butter or margarine
4 celery stalks, chopped
1 large onion, chopped
¼ cup all-purpose flour
2 (14½-ounce) cans chicken broth
1½ cups creamy peanut butter
¼ to ½ teaspoon pepper
½ teaspoon paprika
¼ teaspoon salt
2 cups milk
2 cups half-and-half

Melt butter in a large saucepan; add celery and onion, and cook over medium heat, stirring constantly, 5 minutes or until tender. Add flour, stirring until smooth; cook, stirring constantly, 1 minute. Gradually add chicken broth; cook over low heat 30 minutes, stirring occasionally.

Remove from heat; pour mixture through a large wire-mesh strainer into a bowl, discarding vegetables. Return to saucepan; stir in peanut butter and next 3 ingredients. Gradually add milk and half-and-half, stirring constantly; cook over low heat 5 minutes or until thoroughly heated (do not boil). Yield: 7 cups.

BEEF WELLINGTON

1 (2½-pound) trimmed beef
  tenderloin
1 tablespoon freshly ground pepper
¼ cup butter or margarine, divided
1 cup fresh sliced mushrooms
1 teaspoon chopped fresh parsley
½ teaspoon dried basil
½ teaspoon dried tarragon
½ teaspoon dried thyme
½ (17¼-ounce) package frozen puff
  pastry sheets, thawed
1 large egg, lightly beaten
Garnish: fresh parsley sprigs

Evenly shape tenderloin by tucking small end underneath; tie with string. Sprinkle beef with pepper.

Melt 2 tablespoons butter in a large skillet; add beef, and cook on all sides over medium-high heat until browned. Reduce heat to medium, and cook 30 minutes, turning occasionally. Remove from pan; cover and chill. Wipe out skillet.

Melt remaining butter in skillet; add mushrooms, and cook over medium-high heat 2 minutes. Stir in parsley and next 3 ingredients; cook over medium heat until all liquid evaporates.

Roll pastry into a 16- x 14-inch rectangle. Spoon mushroom mixture down center. Remove string from beef, and place beef lengthwise in middle of pastry. Bring sides of pastry up, and overlap slightly to form a seam; trim off excess pastry. Reserve all pastry trimmings. Trim ends of pastry to make even; fold over, and seal. Place roast, seam side down, onto a lightly greased baking sheet; brush with beaten egg.

Roll out reserved pastry trimmings; cut into decorative shapes, and arrange on top of pastry, as desired. Brush pastry shapes with remaining beaten egg.

Cover and refrigerate 2 hours. Remove from refrigerator, and let stand at room temperature 30 minutes. Bake at 400° for 20 to 25 minutes or until golden brown. Garnish, if desired. Yield: 8 servings.

DUCHESS POTATOES

10 medium baking potatoes, peeled
  and cut into eighths (about 2½
  pounds)
¼ cup butter or margarine
¼ cup milk
¾ teaspoon salt
¼ teaspoon pepper
2 large eggs, lightly beaten
2 tablespoons butter or margarine,
  melted
Paprika

Cook potatoes in boiling water to cover, 15 minutes or until tender; drain and mash. Stir in butter and next 3 ingredients. Let cool 10 minutes. Stir in eggs. Spoon mixture into a large decorating bag fitted with a large star tip. Pipe 14 (2-inch) rosettes onto a lightly greased baking sheet. Drizzle with melted butter, and sprinkle with paprika. Bake at 350° for 15 minutes or until lightly browned around the edges. Yield: 14 rosettes.

Note: To make ahead, pipe potatoes into rosettes; cover and refrigerate up to 3 hours. Let potatoes stand at room temperature 30 minutes; bake as directed.

PEAS AND CELERY

¼ cup butter or margarine
1 cup diagonally sliced celery
¼ cup finely chopped onion
1 (6-ounce) jar sliced mushrooms, drained
1 (2-ounce) jar diced pimiento, drained
1 teaspoon salt
¼ to ½ teaspoon dried savory (optional)
2 (10-ounce) packages frozen English peas, thawed

Melt butter in a large skillet; add celery and next 4 ingredients. Stir in savory, if desired. Cook over medium heat 5 to 7 minutes or until celery is crisp-tender, stirring often. Add peas, and cook until thoroughly heated. Yield: 8 servings.

SHERRIED CHERRIES

1 (16-ounce) can tart red pitted cherries, undrained
¾ cup dry sherry
½ cup red currant jelly
1 (3-ounce) package cherry-flavored gelatin
¼ cup lemon juice

Drain cherries, reserving ¾ cup juice; set cherries aside. Combine reserved juice, sherry, and jelly in a saucepan; bring to a boil. Remove from heat; add gelatin, stirring until gelatin dissolves. Stir in lemon juice. Pour into a 4-cup serving bowl, and chill until the consistency of unbeaten egg white. Fold in cherries, and refrigerate until firm. Yield: 8 servings.

WHITE CHRISTMAS PIE

1 envelope plus 1 teaspoon unflavored gelatin
¼ cup cold water
¼ cup sugar
¼ cup all-purpose flour
¼ teaspoon salt
1½ cups milk
1 teaspoon vanilla extract
¼ teaspoon almond extract
½ to ¾ cup mixed candied fruit, finely chopped
1 tablespoon powdered sugar
1½ cups whipping cream
¼ cup sugar
1 (3½-ounce) can flaked coconut, divided
Pastry Shell

Sprinkle gelatin over cold water in a medium saucepan, and let stand 1 minute. Add ¼ cup sugar and next 3 ingredients; cook mixture over low heat, stirring until gelatin dissolves and mixture is hot. Remove from heat, and chill until consistency of unbeaten egg white.

Add vanilla and almond extracts; beat mixture at medium speed with an electric mixer until smooth.

Combine fruit and powdered sugar, tossing to coat; set aside.

Beat whipping cream until foamy; gradually add ¼ cup sugar, beating until soft peaks form. Fold fruit mixture, whipped cream, and 1 cup coconut into gelatin mixture. Spoon into Pastry Shell; sprinkle with remaining coconut. Chill 8 hours. Yield: one 9-inch pie.

Pastry Shell

1¼ cups all-purpose flour
½ teaspoon salt
½ cup shortening
3 tablespoons cold water

Combine flour and salt; cut in shortening with a pastry blender until mixture is crumbly. Sprinkle cold water (1 tablespoon at a time) evenly over surface; stir with a fork until dry ingredients are moistened. Shape into a ball; cover and chill 5 minutes.

Roll pastry to about ¼-inch thickness on a lightly floured surface. Place pastry in a 9-inch pieplate; trim off excess pastry along edges. Fold edges under, and crimp. Prick sides and bottom of pastry with a fork. Bake at 450° for 10 to 12 minutes or until lightly browned. Cool on a wire rack. Yield: one 9-inch crust.

ENGLISH TRIFLE

1 (4.6-ounce) package vanilla pudding mix
3 cups milk
1 (16-ounce) frozen pound cake loaf, thawed and crumbled
⅓ cup cream sherry
1 (16-ounce) can fruit cocktail, drained
½ cup seedless raspberry preserves
1 cup whipping cream, whipped
Nonpareils

Combine pudding mix and milk in a saucepan; bring to a boil over medium heat, stirring constantly. Remove from heat, and let cool 10 minutes.

Place crumbled cake in a 3-quart trifle bowl; drizzle with sherry. Layer fruit cocktail and pudding over cake. Spread preserves over pudding. Cover and chill at least 8 hours. Top with whipped cream and nonpareils. Yield: 8 to 10 servings.

Dinners From The Diners

Thank goodness you can find a diner in just about any Southern town. We've found many in our travels, but three stand out. At any one of them, you can order home cooking as plain as you like it. But a few items on their menus caught our eye, raised our eyebrows . . . and a few questions.

Did you say veal meat loaf? Flavored with fresh herbs? And your version of chips and dip is fried sweet potatoes and blue cheese dressing? Hmmm. The diner decor—and several menu choices—say "yesteryear." But these new creations swing flavors right into the nineties.

■ You just have to love a place with a motto that promises: "Everything's OK—24 Hours a Day." No matter when you drop in, these folks make sure you have a good time and a great meal. Like a typical diner, the OK Cafe in Atlanta, Georgia, offers booths or stools at the counter, laminated menus, a vegetable plate, and pie for dessert.

But you'll also discover a funky art collection and some adventuresome dishes. We passed up the tofu burger, but dove right into Sweet Potato Chips With Blue Cheese. It's packed with calories, but we won't tell; it's OK—24 hours a day.

Pour oil to depth of 2 inches into a Dutch oven; heat to 350°. Fry potatoes (in batches) 1 to 2 minutes or until golden and crisp, removing chips as they brown. Drain on paper towels. Spoon dressing evenly into a large soup bowl. Top with chips; sprinkle with blue cheese. Serve immediately. Yield: 4 to 6 appetizer servings.

SWEET POTATO CHIPS WITH BLUE CHEESE

Vegetable oil
2 sweet potatoes, peeled and very thinly sliced (about 2 pounds)
½ cup commercial blue cheese dressing
2 ounces crumbled blue cheese (about ½ cup)

FRIED CHICKEN GINGER SALAD

1 carrot, scraped and cut into thin strips
½ cup fresh or frozen Sugar Snap peas, cut in half
½ pound commercial fresh or frozen chicken nuggets or chicken fingers
4 cups mixed salad greens
¼ cup Ginger Dressing, divided
½ cup shredded red cabbage
½ cup sliced fresh mushrooms
1 tablespoon sliced almonds, toasted
Commercial cheese straws (optional)

Arrange carrot and Sugar Snap peas in a steamer basket; place over boiling water. Cover and steam 1 minute. Remove vegetables, and plunge into ice water to stop cooking process. Drain vegetables, and set aside.

Fry or bake chicken nuggets according to package directions. Drain on paper towels, and set aside.

Combine salad greens and 2 tablespoons Ginger Dressing, tossing to coat; arrange greens evenly on 2 serving plates. Combine carrot, peas, cabbage, mushrooms, and remaining 2 tablespoons dressing; spoon on top of greens. Top with chicken nuggets, and sprinkle with toasted almonds. Serve with cheese straws, if desired. Yield: 2 servings.

Ginger Dressing

¼ cup rice wine vinegar
¼ cup peanut oil
¼ cup soy sauce
¼ cup hoisin sauce
1 to 2 tablespoons grated fresh gingerroot
½ teaspoon sugar
½ teaspoon dry mustard
¼ teaspoon Chinese five-spice powder
¼ teaspoon minced garlic
¼ teaspoon chili oil

Combine all ingredients; let stand at room temperature 2 hours. Pour dressing through a fine wire-mesh strainer into a jar, discarding ginger and garlic. Yield: 1 cup.

Note: You can purchase hoisin sauce in the ethnic foods section of most large supermarkets.

■ In the heart of Cajun country in Lafayette, Louisiana, you can step back in time at the Hub City Diner.

As lunchtime rolls around, so does the business crowd. Blue-suited bankers break for a blue plate special—including local favorites such as red beans and rice or gumbo. At night, it's families enjoying the specials.

Whether you can remember the decades of diners or not, you'll love Hub City. Go for the Cajun specialties, such as Catfish Louisiana and the Pain-Perdu Po-boy. In this neck of the woods, "pain perdu" is French for "lost bread," meaning stale French bread. But all is not lost if you make French toast with it as the locals do. The diner layers it with ham, and you have a po-boy. Pass the cane syrup, please.

CATFISH LOUISIANA

Shrimp Topping
2 large eggs, lightly beaten
½ cup milk
½ cup buttermilk
¼ teaspoon hot sauce
1 tablespoon seasoned salt,
   divided
1½ cups all-purpose flour
4 (6-ounce) farm-raised catfish
   fillets
1 cup vegetable oil
Garnishes: chopped fresh parsley,
   green onions
Hot cooked rice

Prepare Shrimp Topping, and keep warm. Combine eggs and next 3 ingredients; add 1½ teaspoons seasoned salt, and set aside.

Combine flour and remaining seasoned salt in a shallow dish. Dredge each fillet in flour mixture; dip in egg mixture, and dredge in flour mixture. Pour oil into a large heavy skillet. Fry half of fillets in hot oil over medium-high heat 5 minutes on each side or until golden. Remove from skillet, and drain on paper towels. Repeat procedure with remaining fillets. Immediately spoon warm Shrimp Topping over catfish, and garnish, if desired. Serve with rice. Yield: 4 servings.

Shrimp Topping

¼ pound unpeeled small fresh
   shrimp
3 tablespoons vegetable oil, divided
2 tablespoons all-purpose flour
¼ cup chopped celery
¼ cup chopped green pepper
¼ cup chopped onion
1 clove garlic, minced
1 cup hot water
¼ cup Chablis or other dry white
   wine
1 teaspoon chicken-flavored
   bouillon granules
¼ teaspoon seasoned salt
¼ teaspoon paprika
½ teaspoon hot sauce

Peel and devein shrimp; set aside.

Combine 2 tablespoons oil and flour with a wire whisk in a small heavy skillet; cook over medium heat, stirring constantly, until roux is caramel colored. Set mixture aside.

Cook celery, green pepper, and onion in remaining 1 tablespoon oil in a heavy saucepan over medium-high heat, stirring constantly, 1 minute. Add shrimp and garlic; cook, stirring constantly, 1 minute. Stir in water and remaining ingredients. Gradually add reserved flour mixture, stirring until smooth, and cook until thoroughly heated. Remove from heat; keep warm. Yield: 1⅓ cups.

PAIN-PERDU PO-BOY

½ cup sugar
1½ teaspoons ground cinnamon
¾ teaspoon ground nutmeg
4 large eggs
2 cups milk
¼ cup butter or margarine, divided
1 pound sliced ham
1 (16-ounce) loaf French bread
Sifted powdered sugar

Combine first 3 ingredients. Add eggs and milk; stir with a wire whisk until frothy and sugar dissolves.

Melt 1 tablespoon butter in a large skillet; add ham, and cook until browned on both sides. Remove from skillet, and set aside.

Cut bread loaf diagonally into ten ¾-inch-thick slices. Dip slices in milk mixture, turning to coat. Melt 1 tablespoon butter in skillet; add 3 slices bread, and cook over medium heat about 1 minute on each side or until golden brown. Remove from pan; keep warm. Repeat procedure twice, cooking 4 slices the last time. Arrange ham slices on half of bread; top with remaining bread slices, and cut in half. Sprinkle with powdered sugar, and serve immediately with cane syrup. Yield: 5 servings.

Gift Wrap From The Pantry

Here's a creative new approach to gift wrapping using items from your kitchen. Dried fruits, herbs, and spices teamed with kraft paper and ribbon or twine can easily turn your holiday packages into something special and original.

To dry fruit, slice oranges and apples, and arrange on a baking sheet. Bake at 200° for 8 to 10 hours with electric oven door partially opened. Wrap boxes in kraft paper, and attach the dried fruits and cinnamon sticks with fabric ribbon or hot glue. (Fruit will last a couple of months, and you can store it in a tin until you're ready to use it.)

For a Christmas tree design, use a glue gun to attach bay leaves in a tree shape. Attach cinnamon sticks beneath leaves for the "trunk."

Finish the package with a festive plaid Christmas ribbon.

■ If you're planning a Disney vacation, make sure to schedule a meal at the 50's Prime Time Cafe at Disney MGM Studios in Lake Buena Vista, Florida. This is a diner like *no* other.

This diner is the home of that veal meat loaf (we offer an equally wonderful pork option for the budget-conscious), and a sinfully thick Peanut Butter and Jelly Shake. (You'll never miss the bread.)

Yes, the chili recipe at the diner has more than 20 ingredients, but they're all canned, or are things you likely have on hand. It's basically a matter of chop, dump, stir, and wait. Or you can just head to Florida, and let Prime Time make it.

VEAL MEAT LOAF

2 pounds ground veal *
½ cup soft breadcrumbs
⅓ to ½ cup finely chopped green or sweet red pepper
3 large eggs
1½ teaspoons salt
¼ teaspoon finely chopped fresh thyme or ⅛ teaspoon dried thyme
¼ teaspoon finely chopped fresh or dried rosemary
¼ teaspoon pepper
1¼ cups sliced fresh mushrooms (4½ ounces)
Vegetable cooking spray

Combine first 8 ingredients; stir in mushrooms. Divide mixture into 6 portions; place each portion in a 4- x 2½- x 1½-inch loafpan coated with cooking spray. Place pans in a shallow baking pan. Bake at 350° for 25 to 30 minutes or until done. Let stand 5 minutes. Yield: 6 servings.

* 2 pounds ground pork may be substituted for ground veal.

Note: For 1 large loaf, place meat mixture in a 7½- x 3- x 2-inch loafpan coated with cooking spray. Bake at 350° for 1 hour and 5 minutes.

MOM'S CHILI

1½ cups chopped green pepper or sweet red pepper
¾ cup chopped celery
¾ cup chopped onion
¾ cup chopped carrot
¾ cup sliced mushrooms
2 to 3 tablespoons minced garlic
¼ cup olive oil
1½ tablespoons chili powder
¾ teaspoon dried thyme
¾ teaspoon dried oregano
¾ teaspoon ground cumin
¾ teaspoon cracked black pepper
¼ to ½ teaspoon ground red pepper
3 (14½-ounce) cans ready-to-serve chicken broth
2 (6-ounce) cans tomato paste
1 (15-ounce) can black beans, drained and rinsed
1 (15-ounce) can red kidney beans, drained and rinsed
1 (15.8-ounce) can Great Northern beans, drained and rinsed
1 (16-ounce) can pinto beans, drained and rinsed
1 (17-ounce) can whole kernel corn, drained and rinsed
3 (14½-ounce) cans whole tomatoes, drained and chopped
½ cup ripe olives, quartered
3 jalapeño peppers, seeded and finely chopped
2 to 2½ tablespoons cornstarch
3 tablespoons water
12 ounces angel hair pasta or thin spaghetti, uncooked
Garnishes: tortilla chips, watercress

Cook first 6 ingredients in olive oil in a large Dutch oven over medium-high heat, stirring constantly, until tender (about 5 minutes). Add chili powder and next 5 ingredients; cook 2 minutes, stirring occasionally. Add chicken broth, and bring to a boil. Stir in tomato paste and next 8 ingredients. Bring to a boil over medium heat; reduce heat, and simmer, uncovered, 10 minutes.

Combine cornstarch and water, stirring until smooth; add to chili, stirring constantly. Bring to a boil, and boil 1 minute.

Cook pasta according to package directions; drain. Serve with chili. Garnish, if desired. Yield: 12 servings.

PBJ SHAKE

¼ cup creamy peanut butter
3 tablespoons grape jelly
¼ cup milk
3 cups vanilla ice cream, softened

Combine peanut butter and jelly in a small bowl, mixing well. Combine milk, ice cream, and peanut butter mixture in container of an electric blender; process mixture until smooth, stopping once to scrape down sides. Yield: 3¾ cups.

QUICK & EASY

Saucy Secrets

Any of these entrées can be ready in less than an hour. No one will guess that each recipe starts with a jar of commercial tomato-based sauce you probably have in your pantry.

ANGEL HAIR PASTA WITH TOMATO CREAM SAUCE

1 (27-ounce) can garlic-and-herb spaghetti sauce
1 cup half-and-half
1 clove garlic, pressed
½ teaspoon salt
¼ teaspoon freshly ground pepper
⅛ teaspoon ground nutmeg
8 ounces angel hair pasta
2 tablespoons finely chopped fresh basil
¼ cup freshly grated Parmesan cheese

Combine first 6 ingredients in a medium saucepan, stirring with a wire whisk until blended. Cook over very low heat until thoroughly heated (do not boil).

Cook pasta according to package directions; drain and return to pan. Add cream sauce, basil, and Parmesan cheese; toss gently. Yield: 4 main-dish servings or 8 side-dish servings.

CHICKEN-AND-BEAN TACOS

8 (8-inch) flour tortillas
2/3 cup chopped onion
1/3 cup chopped green pepper
2 tablespoons vegetable oil
2 cups shredded cooked chicken
1 (16-ounce) jar taco sauce
1 teaspoon sugar
1½ teaspoons chili powder
1 (15-ounce) can refried beans
8 taco shells
2 cups shredded lettuce
1 cup chopped tomato
1 cup (4 ounces) shredded Cheddar
  cheese

Heat tortillas according to package directions; set aside.

Cook onion and green pepper in oil in a heavy saucepan over medium heat, stirring constantly, until tender. Stir in chicken and next 3 ingredients; cook until thoroughly heated.

Cook refried beans in a small saucepan over medium-low heat until thoroughly heated. Place about 2 tablespoons refried beans on each tortilla, spreading refried beans to within ½ inch of edge. Place a taco shell in center of each tortilla, pressing tortilla up and onto sides of taco shell. Fill each taco shell with about 1/3 cup chicken mixture, ¼ cup shredded lettuce, 2 tablespoons chopped tomato, and 2 tablespoons shredded Cheddar cheese. Serve tacos immediately. Yield: 8 tacos.

Tip: *Tortillas, translated "little cakes," are flat, unleavened rounds made from either corn flour or wheat flour and baked on a griddle. Versatile and economical, tortillas are available at supermarkets and usually come in packages of eight or 10. Tortillas may be eaten plain, stuffed, rolled, layered, or used as a base for ingredients as varied as cheese, beef, tomatoes, chicken, beans, and chiles.*

HEAVENLY EGGPLANT

1 medium eggplant, peeled and cut
  into ½-inch slices
2 large eggs, lightly beaten
1 cup Italian-seasoned breadcrumbs
¼ cup olive oil
1 (15-ounce) carton ricotta cheese
1 teaspoon dried Italian seasoning
½ cup grated Parmesan cheese,
  divided
1 (14-ounce) jar spaghetti sauce
1 (6-ounce) package mozzarella
  cheese slices

Dip each eggplant slice in egg, and dredge in breadcrumbs. Fry eggplant in hot olive oil over medium-high heat until golden brown on each side. Drain on paper towels.

Arrange eggplant in a lightly greased, shallow 2-quart baking dish. Spread ricotta cheese over eggplant; sprinkle with Italian seasoning and ¼ cup Parmesan cheese. Top with spaghetti sauce and remaining Parmesan cheese. Bake at 350° for 20 minutes. Arrange mozzarella cheese slices on top; bake an additional 5 minutes. Yield: 4 servings.   *DeLea Lonadier*
Montgomery, Louisiana

SPICY VEGETABLE SOUP

1 pound ground beef
1 cup chopped onion
2 cloves garlic, pressed
1 (30-ounce) jar chunky
  garden-style spaghetti sauce with
  mushrooms and peppers
1 (10½-ounce) can beef broth,
  undiluted
2 cups water
1 cup sliced celery
1 teaspoon sugar
1 teaspoon salt
½ teaspoon freshly ground pepper
1 (10-ounce) can diced tomatoes
  and green chiles
1 (16-ounce) package frozen mixed
  vegetables

Cook first 3 ingredients in a large Dutch oven over medium heat until meat is browned, stirring to crumble. Drain and return meat to Dutch oven.

Add spaghetti sauce and next 6 ingredients. Bring to a boil; cover, reduce heat, and simmer 20 minutes, stirring occasionally. Stir in tomatoes and vegetables; return to a boil. Cover and simmer 10 to 12 minutes or until vegetables are tender. Yield: 12 cups.
Jan Downs
Shreveport, Louisiana

A Taste Of Aloha

Yearning for the flavors of the tropics? Then this cookbook is for you. *A Taste of Aloha* provides typical Hawaiian recipes and gives suggestions for planning a luau, or Hawaiian feast. And if you have questions about the regional seafood, produce, and other foods called for, don't worry. There's an extensive glossary to help.

Since it was first produced by The Junior League of Honolulu, Hawaii, in 1983, 100,000 copies have been printed. Funds from the sale of the cookbooks go toward supporting community projects.

■ Since most people aren't used to measuring in ounces, we changed the measurements in this beverage recipe to cups and tablespoons.

PINK PALACE

½ cup pineapple juice
3 tablespoons cream of coconut
2 tablespoons half-and-half
2 tablespoons Grand Marnier or
  other orange-flavored liqueur
1½ teaspoons lemon juice
Dash of grenadine
Crushed ice

Combine first 6 ingredients in container of an electric blender; process until smooth, stopping once to scrape down sides. Serve over crushed ice. Yield: about ¾ cup.

■ This recipe is slightly different from the *A Taste of Aloha* original. As with many recipes we test, we reduced the butter and salt.

ALII ARTICHOKE CASSEROLE

1 (8-ounce) package cream cheese
¼ cup butter or margarine
3 (10-ounce) packages frozen, chopped spinach, thawed and well drained
2 tablespoons Worcestershire sauce
¾ teaspoon salt
½ teaspoon garlic powder
½ teaspoon ground black pepper
⅛ teaspoon ground red pepper
⅛ teaspoon hot sauce
1 tablespoon lemon juice
2 (14-ounce) cans artichoke hearts, drained and cut in half
¼ to ½ cup Italian-seasoned breadcrumbs

Combine cream cheese and butter in a large saucepan; cook over low heat, stirring constantly, until mixture melts. Stir in spinach and next 7 ingredients. Set aside.

Place half of artichokes in a lightly greased shallow 2-quart baking dish; top with half of spinach mixture. Repeat layers. Sprinkle with breadcrumbs. Bake at 350° for 30 minutes. Yield: 8 servings.

COCONUT CHICKEN WITH FRESH FRUIT

2 tablespoons butter or margarine
8 skinned and boned chicken breast halves
1 tablespoon finely chopped fresh gingerroot *
½ teaspoon salt
⅓ cup flaked coconut, toasted and divided
1 cup whipping cream
2 to 3 bananas, quartered
1 large papaya, peeled, seeded, and sliced
Garnishes: lime wedges, Italian parsley

Melt butter in a large skillet over medium-high heat; add chicken, and cook 4 minutes on each side or until lightly browned. Sprinkle with gingerroot, salt, and 3 tablespoons coconut; add whipping cream. Cover and cook over low heat 10 minutes. Arrange chicken, bananas, and papaya on a large serving platter. Pour warm sauce over chicken, and sprinkle with remaining coconut. Garnish, if desired. Yield: 8 servings.

* ¾ teaspoon ground ginger may be substituted, if desired.

Never Too Much Citrus

Remember finding an orange in the toe of your stocking on Christmas morning? Today, Southerners continue to give citrus as holiday gifts. So if you have more oranges or grapefruit than you know what to do with, try these tangy citrus recipes that use plenty of juice or pulp.

ORANGE-GRAPEFRUIT SALAD

2 tablespoons sugar
¼ teaspoon salt
2 tablespoons malt vinegar
2 tablespoons vegetable oil
⅛ teaspoon almond extract
6 cups torn salad greens
3 medium oranges, peeled, seeded, and sectioned
1 medium grapefruit, peeled, seeded, and sectioned
½ cup thinly sliced celery
2 tablespoons sliced green onions

Combine first 5 ingredients in a jar; cover tightly, and shake vigorously. Set aside.

Just before serving, combine salad greens and remaining ingredients; drizzle with dressing, and toss gently. Yield: 6 servings.

BURGUNDY-SPICED ORANGE SLICES

6 large oranges
1 cup Burgundy or other dry red wine
2 tablespoons white wine vinegar
3 (2-inch) sticks cinnamon
15 whole cloves
¾ cup sugar

Peel oranges; cut each into 4 slices, cutting across sections; discard seeds. Place in a shallow 2-quart container; set aside. Combine Burgundy and remaining ingredients in a saucepan; cook over medium heat 10 minutes. Pour over oranges; cover and let stand until cooled. Serve hot or cold. Yield: 6 servings. *Bunny Campbell Gainesville, Florida*

Citrus Section

■ Citrus fruit keeps one to two weeks at room temperature. For longer storage, refrigerate in a plastic bag or vegetable crisper drawer.
■ Don't throw away those citrus rinds. Grate rinds; then freeze them in zip-top plastic bags. Thaw rinds as needed, and use as you would fresh.
■ Fresh orange equivalents:
2 to 4 medium oranges = 1 cup orange juice
2 medium oranges = 1 cup bite-size pieces
1 medium orange = 10 to 12 sections
1 medium orange = 4 teaspoons grated rind
■ Fresh grapefruit equivalents:
1 medium grapefruit = ⅔ cup grapefruit juice
1 medium grapefruit = 10 to 12 sections
1 medium grapefruit = 3 to 4 tablespoons grated rind

KIWI-AND-ORANGE DESSERT

4 kiwifruit, peeled and sliced
4 large oranges, peeled, seeded, and sectioned
¼ cup fresh orange juice
¼ cup sugar
1½ teaspoons Grand Marnier or other orange-flavored liqueur (optional)
Sweetened whipped cream

Combine fruit in a medium bowl. Combine orange juice, sugar, and liqueur, if desired, stirring until sugar dissolves; pour over fruit mixture, tossing lightly. Cover and chill at least 1 hour. Serve in individual bowls with whipped cream. Yield: 4 servings.
Carrie Treichel
Johnson City, Tennessee

ORANGE CHIFFON DESSERT

2 (3-ounce) packages ladyfingers
3 to 4 tablespoons Grand Marnier or other orange-flavored liqueur
3 envelopes unflavored gelatin
1¾ cups cold water, divided
1 cup sugar
3 oranges, peeled, seeded, and sectioned
1 tablespoon grated orange rind
1¾ cups fresh orange juice
2 tablespoons fresh lemon juice
1¾ cups whipping cream
¾ cup miniature marshmallows
¼ cup chopped pecans, toasted
Garnishes: orange sections, fresh mint leaves

Cut a 30- x 3-inch strip of wax paper; line sides of a 9-inch springform pan with strip. Split ladyfingers in half lengthwise; line sides and bottom of pan with ladyfingers. Brush ladyfingers with liqueur. Set aside.
Sprinkle gelatin over ¾ cup cold water; stir and let stand 1 minute. Combine remaining 1 cup water and sugar in a saucepan; bring to a boil, stirring until sugar dissolves. Add gelatin, stirring until it dissolves. Chop orange sections; drain on paper towels. Stir oranges and next 3 ingredients into gelatin mixture. Chill until consistency of unbeaten egg white (about 30 minutes).
Beat whipping cream until soft peaks form. Fold whipped cream and marshmallows into orange mixture. Spoon into prepared pan, and sprinkle with pecans. Cover and chill 8 hours. Remove ring from springform pan; remove wax paper. Place on serving plate, and garnish, if desired. Yield: 10 to 12 servings.
Eloise W. Terry
Huntsville, Alabama

SUNNY MORNING

2 cups fresh orange juice, chilled
½ cup Grand Marnier or other orange-flavored liqueur, chilled
Ice
2 cups champagne, chilled
Garnishes: orange slices and strawberries

Combine orange juice and liqueur in container of an electric blender. Add enough ice to bring to 3½-cup level; process until smooth, stopping once to scrape down sides. Transfer to a pitcher, and stir in champagne. Garnish, if desired. Yield: 5½ cups.
Sandra J. Enwright
Winter Park, Florida

CHRISTMAS WASSAIL

½ gallon apple cider
4 cups fresh orange juice (about 9 oranges)
⅓ cup fresh lemon juice (about 2 lemons)
½ cup honey
4 (3-inch) sticks cinnamon
¼ teaspoon ground nutmeg

Combine all ingredients in a large Dutch oven. Bring mixture to a boil over medium heat; reduce heat, and simmer 10 minutes. Remove and discard cinnamon sticks; serve hot. Yield: 14 cups.
Louise W. Mayer
Richmond, Virginia

Curls: Curling a strip of citrus rind before dropping it into your favorite drink or using it as a garnish releases its fragrant oils.

Slivered Rind: Without cutting pulp, cut rind of a whole citrus fruit into quarters. Carefully remove with fingers. Use the tip of a spoon to scrape most of the white membrane from the rind. Stack two or three pieces at one time; cut into thin strips.

Stand-up Twists: Cut citrus crosswise into ⅜-inch slices. Make a cut from the center of the slice through the outer rind. Twist the ends in opposite directions; gently place twist in position.

Baskets: Cut a citrus fruit halfway down, slightly off center. Make a horizontal cut towards the base of first cut; repeat on other side. Lift out wedges. Cut away pulp under handle; scoop out of base. Decorate "handle" with a raffia bow.

Simply Chocolate

Chocolate is the predominant flavor in these easy dessert recipes with the exception of Chocolate-Pecan Tart With Caramel Sauce. We included it because you get excellent returns from the short time invested; there's no crust to handle, and the Caramel Sauce requires only three ingredients.

Chocolate Pots de Crème is a recipe whose name belies its easy preparation. Those little lids with the pots de crème cups prevent surface skin from forming on the cooked custard inside. If you don't have a pots de crème set, simply use custard cups, covered with plastic wrap.

CHOCOLATE-PECAN TART WITH CARAMEL SAUCE

2 cups pecan pieces
¼ cup firmly packed brown sugar
¼ teaspoon ground cinnamon
2 tablespoons butter or margarine, softened
1 (12-ounce) package semisweet chocolate morsels
½ cup half-and-half
Caramel Sauce

Position knife blade in food processor bowl; add pecans, and pulse 5 or 6 times or until finely chopped. Add brown sugar, cinnamon, and butter; process 30 seconds, stopping once to scrape down sides. Press mixture evenly onto bottom and ½ inch up sides of a 9-inch tart pan. Bake at 325° for 28 minutes; set aside.

Combine chocolate morsels and half-and-half in a large saucepan; cook over medium heat, stirring constantly, until chocolate melts and mixture is smooth. Pour mixture into tart shell. Cover and chill at least 2 hours. Serve with warm Caramel Sauce. Yield: one 9-inch tart.

Caramel Sauce

½ cup butter or margarine
1¼ cups sugar
2 cups half-and-half

Melt butter in a heavy saucepan over medium heat; add sugar, and cook, stirring constantly with a whisk, about 10 minutes or until mixture is a deep, golden brown. Add half-and-half (mixture will lump); cook, stirring constantly, until mixture is smooth and reduced to 2¼ cups (about 10 minutes). Yield: 2¼ cups.

Louise Bodziony
Gladstone, Missouri

DARK CHOCOLATE SAUCE

¾ cup cocoa
½ cup sugar
½ cup light corn syrup
¼ cup vegetable oil
¼ cup butter or margarine
¼ cup water
1 teaspoon vanilla extract

Combine cocoa and sugar in a medium saucepan; stir in corn syrup and oil. Cook over low heat 8 to 10 minutes, stirring constantly, or until sugar dissolves. Add butter, water, and vanilla; cook, stirring constantly, just until butter melts. Serve over ice cream. Yield: 1⅔ cups.

Note: Sauce may be reheated.

Anne Fowler Newell
Johnsonville, South Carolina

EASY CHOCOLATE CHEWIES

1 (18.25-ounce) package devil's food cake mix
½ cup vegetable shortening
2 large eggs, lightly beaten
1 tablespoon water
½ cup sifted powdered sugar

Combine first 4 ingredients in a large bowl, stirring until smooth. Shape dough into 1-inch balls, and roll in powdered sugar. Place 2 inches apart on lightly greased cookie sheets. Bake at 375° for 10 minutes. Cool 10 minutes on cookie sheets; remove to wire racks to cool completely. Yield: 4 dozen.

Mrs. Chris Bryant
Johnson City, Tennessee

CHOCOLATE POTS DE CRÈME

1 (6-ounce) package semisweet chocolate morsels
1 cup whipping cream
½ cup half-and-half
2 egg yolks

Combine first 3 ingredients in a heavy saucepan; cook over low heat, stirring constantly, until chocolate melts. Beat egg yolks until thick and pale. Gradually stir about one-fourth of hot mixture into yolks; add to remaining hot mixture, stirring constantly. Cook over low heat, stirring constantly, 2 minutes or until mixture thickens slightly. Spoon into individual serving containers; cover and chill. Yield: 4 to 6 servings.

Mrs. C. M. Conklin II
Dallas, Texas

Choose fresh or frozen raspberries, blueberries, and blackberries to accent exotic Sabayon (recipe, page 272).

Above: *Create your own conversation piece for tea with (left to right) Chocolate-Almond Petits Fours, Crème de Menthe Squares, and Raspberry Jellyrolls. (Recipes begin on page 255.)*

Right: *An after-dinner sweet to sigh for: Crème de Menthe Squares (recipe, page 256) are easy to make by the dozens.*

Stand back and wait for the raves when you present petits fours elegant enough for any French pâtisserie. (Recipes begin on page 254.)

'Tis the season to indulge! And luscious Chocolate Trifle (recipe, page 326) rises to the occasion.

Holiday Nuts

Whether featured as appetizers or tempting gifts, nuts appreciate in flavor and crunch when toasted.

Nippy Nuts is a mixture of almonds and pecans coated with spices and sautéed before toasting. Curry powder complements the subtly sweet flavor of hazelnuts in Curried Hazelnuts.

CURRIED HAZELNUTS

¼ cup butter or margarine
2 teaspoons curry powder
2 cups hazelnuts
¼ teaspoon salt

Melt butter in a skillet over medium heat; stir in curry powder. Add hazelnuts; cook, stirring constantly, about 5 minutes or until hazelnuts begin to brown. Drain on paper towels; sprinkle with salt. Yield: 2 cups.

NIPPY NUTS

2 tablespoons olive oil
½ teaspoon garlic salt
½ teaspoon ground cumin
½ teaspoon chili powder
¼ teaspoon ground cinnamon
¼ teaspoon ground ginger
¼ teaspoon curry powder
¼ teaspoon ground red pepper
2 cups blanched whole almonds
2 cups pecan halves

Heat olive oil in a large skillet over medium heat; stir in garlic salt and next 6 ingredients. Add almonds; cook, stirring constantly, 4 minutes. Add pecans, stirring until coated. Spread in a 15- x 10- x 1-inch jellyroll pan. Bake at 325° for 15 minutes, stirring every 5 minutes. Remove from oven; cool. Yield: 4 cups.

Tip: *Delight your friends with a gift from your kitchen. Be sure to include information such as storing, shelf life, freezing, and instructions for any further cooking that may be needed.*

Make It Easy; Make A Casserole

No matter how you dish it up, nothing beats a light casserole to simplify life for busy cooks. Made in advance and frozen, or served steaming hot right out of the oven, these casseroles offer homemade food that's fast but not fatty. So skip the frozen commercial choices for a while, and pair any of these with a crusty bread and a salad to make a meal.

LENTILS-AND-RICE CASSEROLE

1 cup dried lentils
1 teaspoon reduced-calorie margarine
1 cup chopped onion
1 cup chopped green pepper
2 cloves garlic, minced
1 (14½-ounce) can whole tomatoes, chopped and undrained
1 teaspoon paprika
¼ teaspoon salt
½ teaspoon black pepper
½ teaspoon ground red pepper
2 cups cooked brown rice (cooked without salt or fat)
Vegetable cooking spray
1½ cups (6 ounces) shredded fat-free Cheddar cheese

Cook lentils according to package directions, omitting salt. Drain lentils, and set aside.

Melt margarine in a large nonstick skillet over medium heat; add onion, green pepper, and garlic, and cook until tender, stirring often. Stir in lentils, tomatoes, and next 4 ingredients; cover, reduce heat, and simmer 20 minutes, stirring occasionally.

Spoon brown rice into a 2-quart baking dish coated with cooking spray; pour lentil mixture over rice. Bake at 325° for 15 minutes; sprinkle with cheese, and coat with cooking spray. Bake an additional 5 minutes. Yield: 5 servings (311 calories [6% from fat] per serving).

□ *25.2g protein, 2.1g fat (0.3g saturated), 50g carbohydrate, 7.6g fiber, 6mg cholesterol, 511mg sodium, and 362mg calcium.* Lisa Kessler
Carrboro, North Carolina

MEDITERRANEAN RAVIOLI

Vegetable cooking spray
2 teaspoons olive oil
½ pound eggplant, peeled and cut into ½-inch cubes
1 cup chopped onion
2 cloves garlic, minced
1 (15-ounce) package refrigerated light chunky tomato sauce
2 tablespoons sliced ripe olives
1 tablespoon balsamic vinegar
1 teaspoon dried thyme
1 (9-ounce) package refrigerated, light cheese-filled ravioli, uncooked
3 tablespoons grated Parmesan cheese

Coat a large nonstick skillet with cooking spray; add olive oil, and place skillet over medium-high heat. Add eggplant, onion, and garlic; cook, stirring constantly, 5 minutes or until tender. Stir in tomato sauce and next 3 ingredients; remove skillet from heat.

Cook ravioli according to package directions; drain. Rinse with cold water, and drain. Toss with vegetable mixture, and place in a 1½-quart shallow baking dish coated with cooking spray. Sprinkle with cheese. Bake at 350° for 30 minutes. Yield: 4 servings (288 calories [25% from fat] per serving).

□ *14.1g protein, 7.9g fat (2.6g saturated), 40g carbohydrate, 1.9g fiber, 44.3mg cholesterol, 771mg sodium, and 129mg calcium.*

HAM-POTATO-PINEAPPLE BAKE

1 (1¼-pound) lean, reduced-sodium, center-cut ham steak
Vegetable cooking spray
1 (16-ounce) can sweet potatoes, drained and sliced
1 (16-ounce) can unsweetened pineapple slices, drained
¼ cup apple cider vinegar
1 cup firmly packed brown sugar
1 teaspoon dry mustard
¼ teaspoon ground cloves

Trim excess fat from ham. Place in an 11- x 7- x 1½-inch baking dish coated with cooking spray; arrange potatoes and pineapple over ham. Set aside. Combine vinegar and remaining ingredients in a heavy saucepan; cook over medium heat until hot. Pour over ham. Cover and bake at 325° for 45 minutes. Yield: 4 servings (359 calories [20% from fat] per serving).

□ 27.2g protein, 7.8g fat (0.1g saturated), 47.8g carbohydrate, 3.8g fiber, 69mg cholesterol, 1,114mg sodium, and 36mg calcium.

Wendy Leigh Rurka
Owings Mills, Maryland

CHICKEN CHILI BAKE

½ cup brown rice, uncooked
1¾ cups ready-to-serve, fat-free, reduced-sodium chicken broth
2 cups chopped, cooked chicken breast (skinned before cooking and cooked without salt)
1 (12-ounce) jar medium salsa (1½ cups)
1 (10¾-ounce) can reduced-sodium, fat-free cream of chicken soup, undiluted
1 cup frozen whole kernel corn, thawed
½ cup finely chopped onion
1 tablespoon reduced-sodium Worcestershire sauce
2 teaspoons chili powder
1 teaspoon dried oregano
½ teaspoon curry powder
¼ teaspoon pepper
Vegetable cooking spray

Combine rice and chicken broth in a medium saucepan; bring to a boil. Cover, reduce heat, and simmer 50 minutes or until rice is tender and liquid is absorbed.

Combine chicken and next 9 ingredients in a bowl; stir in rice. Spoon mixture into a 2-quart casserole coated with cooking spray. Bake at 350° for 30 minutes or until bubbly. Yield: 5 servings (263 calories [16% from fat] per 1-cup serving).

□ 20.6g protein, 4.6g fat (0.9g saturated), 34.8g carbohydrate, 3.2g fiber, 49mg cholesterol, 338mg sodium, and 34mg calcium.

Stephanie Mosca Bolden
Newport News, Virginia

LIGHT FAVORITE

Old-Fashioned Chicken And Dumplings

Nothing warms the heart and soothes the soul like a hearty pot of chicken and dumplings. This recipe has less fat and a fraction of the sodium of grandma's version, yet plenty of nostalgic taste.

OLD-FASHIONED CHICKEN AND DUMPLINGS

1 (3½-pound) broiler-fryer, cut up and skinned
1 stalk celery, cut into thirds
1 medium onion, quartered
2 quarts water
1 teaspoon salt
½ teaspoon pepper
2 cups all-purpose flour
½ teaspoon baking soda
½ teaspoon salt
3 tablespoons margarine, softened
2 tablespoons chopped fresh parsley
¾ cup nonfat buttermilk

Combine first 5 ingredients in a Dutch oven; bring to a boil. Cover, reduce heat, and simmer 1 hour or until chicken is tender. Remove chicken, reserving broth in Dutch oven; discard vegetables. Let chicken and broth cool. Bone and cut chicken into bite-size pieces. Place in separate containers; cover and refrigerate 8 hours. Remove fat from broth; bring to a boil, and add pepper.

Combine flour, soda, and ½ teaspoon salt; cut in margarine with a pastry blender until mixture is crumbly. Add parsley and buttermilk, stirring with a fork until dry ingredients are moistened. Turn dough out onto a heavily floured surface, and knead lightly 4 or 5 times. Pat dough to ¼-inch thickness. Pinch off 1½-inch pieces, and drop into boiling broth. Add chicken. Reduce heat to medium-low, and cook 8 to 10 minutes, stirring occasionally. Yield: 8 servings (283 calories [27% from fat] per 1-cup serving).

□ 20.6g protein, 8.5g fat (1.3g saturated), 26.8g carbohydrate, 1g fiber, 50mg cholesterol, 613mg sodium, and 57mg calcium.

Note: For a hearty yet lightened version of chicken and dumplings, we eliminated an egg to drop the cholesterol content by 181 milligrams. Also, nonfat buttermilk replaced whole milk, further trimming the fat.

This recipe uses the whole chicken for its succulent meat and savory broth that stews dumplings to tender perfection. The broth must be chilled and the fat skimmed to leave behind flavorful broth that's virtually fat-free.

COMPARE THE NUTRIENTS (per serving)		
	Traditional	Light
Calories	947	283
Fat	46.6g	8.5g
Cholesterol	231mg	50mg

LIGHT MENU

Ward Off Holiday Pounds

Take a break from the rich menu circuit, and treat yourself to a lighter plate. This menu falls below 560 calories and has only 11 grams of fat. Rating high on the flavor scale, it's guaranteed to hold your interest and keep your waistline in place.

WAIST-WISE MENU FOR FOUR

**Shrimp With Peanut Sauce
Steamed Herbed Vegetables
Pumpkin Cake**

SHRIMP WITH PEANUT SAUCE

2 tablespoons sliced green onions
2 cloves garlic, minced
Vegetable cooking spray
¾ cup ready-to-serve, no-salt-added chicken broth
3 tablespoons creamy peanut butter
1 tablespoon reduced-sodium soy sauce
1 tablespoon lemon juice
1 teaspoon chili powder
1 teaspoon brown sugar
½ teaspoon ground ginger
1 pound unpeeled large fresh shrimp

Cook green onions and garlic in a skillet coated with cooking spray over medium heat, stirring constantly, about 3 minutes. Add chicken broth and next 6 ingredients, stirring until smooth. Reduce heat, and simmer 10 minutes, stirring often. Remove from heat; cool.

Peel and devein shrimp, leaving tails attached. Place shrimp in sauce; turn to coat. Cover and refrigerate 1 hour. Remove from sauce; discard sauce. Thread shrimp onto skewers.

Broil 6 inches from heat (with electric oven door partially opened) 5 minutes on each side or until shrimp turn pink. Yield: 4 servings (146 calories [28% from fat] per serving).

□ *22.6g protein, 4.5g fat (0.8g saturated), 3g carbohydrate, 1.1g fiber, 156mg cholesterol, 231mg sodium, and 59mg calcium.* Caryl A. Lambert
Memphis, Tennessee

STEAMED HERBED VEGETABLES

1 cup broccoli flowerets
1 cup diagonally cut, 2-inch-long asparagus pieces
½ cup (2- x ½-inch) pieces sweet red pepper
½ cup (2- x ½-inch) pieces sweet yellow pepper
½ cup sliced fresh mushrooms
1 tablespoon chopped fresh marjoram
1 teaspoon chopped fresh oregano or ¼ teaspoon dried oregano
½ teaspoon chopped fresh rosemary
¼ teaspoon salt
⅛ teaspoon pepper
1 tablespoon water
1 tablespoon reduced-calorie margarine

Combine all ingredients in a 1½-quart microwave-safe casserole. Cover tightly with heavy-duty plastic wrap; fold back a small edge (or corner) of wrap to allow steam to escape. Microwave at HIGH 3½ minutes or until crisp-tender, stirring once. Yield: 4 servings (42 calories [39% from fat] per ⅔-cup serving).

□ *2.4g protein, 1.8g fat (0.3g saturated), 5.6g carbohydrate, 1.9g fiber, 0mg cholesterol, 194mg sodium, and 27mg calcium.* Nita Hamilton
Columbia, Tennessee

Tip: *Revive the flavor of long-dried herbs by soaking them for 10 minutes in lemon juice.*

PUMPKIN CAKE
(pictured on page 261)

2¾ cups all-purpose flour
1 teaspoon baking soda
½ teaspoon baking powder
¼ teaspoon salt
1 teaspoon ground nutmeg
1 teaspoon ground cloves
1 teaspoon ground cinnamon
3 large eggs, lightly beaten
2 cups sugar
1 cup unsweetened applesauce
1 (16-ounce) can pumpkin
1 cup raisins, chopped
½ cup chopped pecans
Vegetable cooking spray
1 teaspoon sifted powdered sugar
1 cup reduced-calorie frozen whipped topping, thawed

Combine first 7 ingredients in a large bowl; make a well in center of mixture. Combine eggs and next 3 ingredients; add to dry ingredients, stirring just until moistened. Fold in raisins and pecans. Spoon into a 12-cup Bundt pan coated with cooking spray. Bake at 350° for 1 hour and 10 minutes or until a wooden pick inserted in center comes out clean. Cool in pan on a wire rack 10 minutes; remove from pan, and cool completely on wire rack. Sprinkle with powdered sugar. Dollop 1 tablespoon whipped topping on each slice. Yield: 16 servings (269 calories [15% from fat] per serving).

□ *4.5g protein, 4.5g fat (0.6g saturated), 54.8g carbohydrate, 2g fiber, 41mg cholesterol, 98mg sodium, and 45mg calcium.* Judy Trang
Homewood, Alabama

Celebrate Earth's Bounty

Thanksgiving is a celebration of the harvest's bounty, and these side-dish recipes remind us that fall's cornucopia is reason to give thanks.

Ranging from simple to simply terrific, these recipes are the perfect complement to a holiday feast. Choose classic green beans sautéed with fresh rosemary, apples and carrots baked in a light orange sauce, or a savory squash puree. Each recipe can be assembled a day ahead and then reheated just before serving, leaving you some time to relax before dinner.

APPLE-CARROT BAKE

1 pound carrots, scraped and sliced
   diagonally
½ cup water
¼ cup sugar
2 tablespoons all-purpose flour
4 medium cooking apples, peeled,
   cored, and sliced
¼ cup butter or margarine, divided
¾ cup orange juice

Combine carrots and ½ cup water in a saucepan. Bring to a boil; cover, reduce heat, and simmer 5 minutes or until crisp-tender. Drain carrots, and set aside.

Combine sugar and flour; set aside.

Layer half each of carrots and apples in a lightly greased, shallow 2-quart baking dish; sprinkle with half of flour mixture, and dot with 2 tablespoons butter. Repeat procedure. Drizzle with orange juice. Bake at 350° for 45 minutes. Toss before serving. Yield: 8 servings.

Debbie E. Ipock
Charlotte, North Carolina

FOUR ONION BAKE

2 large leeks (about 4½ pounds)
3 tablespoons butter or margarine
½ pound shallots, peeled and
   chopped
1 large yellow onion, halved
   lengthwise and thinly sliced
2 cloves garlic, minced
1 (16-ounce) package frozen small
   white onions
2 cups whipping cream
¼ cup chopped fresh parsley
¾ teaspoon salt
¼ teaspoon pepper
1 tablespoon fine, dry
   breadcrumbs

Remove roots, tough outer leaves, and tops from leeks. Split leeks in half lengthwise; wash well. Cut into ¼-inch slices. Melt butter in a large skillet; add leeks, shallots, yellow onion, and garlic. Cook over medium heat, stirring constantly, until tender (about 5 minutes). Add small onions, and cook 6 to 8 minutes or until tender. Drain and set aside.

Cook whipping cream in a large heavy saucepan, over medium heat, stirring often, until reduced to about 1½ cups (about 15 minutes). Stir in onion mixture, parsley, salt, and pepper. Spoon mixture into a lightly greased 11- x 7- x 1½-inch baking dish; sprinkle with breadcrumbs. Bake at 425° for 15 to 18 minutes. Yield: 8 to 10 servings.

Note: To make this side dish ahead, assemble Four Onion Bake; cover and refrigerate up to three hours. Remove from refrigerator, and let stand at room temperature 30 minutes. Bake as directed.

LEMON-WALNUT GREEN BEANS

⅓ cup chopped walnuts
2 pounds fresh green beans
¼ teaspoon salt
3 tablespoons butter or
   margarine
⅓ cup sliced green onions
1 tablespoon finely chopped fresh
   rosemary or dried rosemary
1 tablespoon lemon juice
1 tablespoon grated lemon rind
Garnishes: lemon slice, fresh
   rosemary sprigs

Spread walnuts on an ungreased baking sheet; bake at 300° for 10 minutes. Set aside.

Wash beans, and remove ends. Cut in half, and sprinkle with salt. Arrange beans in a steamer basket, and place over boiling water. Cover and steam 8 to 12 minutes or until crisp-tender. Plunge green beans into cold water to stop cooking process; drain and set aside.

Melt butter in a large skillet over medium heat; add green onions, and cook, stirring constantly, about 3 minutes. Add green beans, walnuts, rosemary, and lemon juice; cook, stirring constantly, until mixture is thoroughly heated. Sprinkle with lemon rind, and garnish, if desired. Serve immediately. Yield: 8 servings.

ACORN SQUASH-MUSHROOM PUREE

5 acorn squash
⅓ cup butter or margarine, melted
2 tablespoons brown sugar
½ teaspoon salt
¼ teaspoon ground nutmeg
⅛ teaspoon freshly ground pepper
¼ cup butter or margarine
½ pound sliced fresh mushrooms
Ground nutmeg

Cut squash in half crosswise; remove seeds. Place squash, cut side down, on a lightly greased baking sheet. Bake at 375° for 45 minutes or until very tender.

Scoop out pulp, leaving a ¼-inch shell on 6 halves; discard remaining shells. Place pulp in a blender or food processor; add ⅓ cup butter and next 4 ingredients. Process until smooth.

Melt ¼ cup butter in a skillet; add mushrooms, and cook over low heat 5 to 8 minutes, stirring occasionally. Drain. Combine mushrooms and squash mixture. Spoon into reserved shells; place on a baking sheet. Sprinkle with additional nutmeg. Bake at 350° for 15 minutes or until thoroughly heated. Yield: 6 servings.

Making the Most of Mushrooms

■ For best results, sauté fresh sliced or chopped mushrooms before freezing them. Thaw mushrooms and add to recipe.

■ To retain white color of fresh mushrooms, slice just before using or dip in lemon juice.

■ To slice mushrooms quickly and uniformly, use an egg slicer.

Please Pass The Dressing

For many, cornbread dressing is the soul of Thanksgiving dinner. Rich with butter and broth, made fragrant with onions and herbs, this side dish stands out among holiday pleasures. Whether moist or dry, cornbread- or white bread-based, dressing is often the most popular part of the feast. We took the tradition a step further, using grits, apples, and even green chiles.

Our dishes are perfect partners for traditional roast turkey, but they would also be a great match for baked chicken, crown of roast pork, tenderloin of beef, Cornish hens, or wild game. If dressing is the hands-down favorite at your Thanksgiving table, surprise your guests with a couple of these treats.

Each of these recipes is *dressing,* not a stuffing. The dressings are baked separately from the turkey in a casserole dish. For safety's sake, we recommend this method.

SAUSAGE-APPLE DRESSING

1 (1-pound) loaf thick-sliced bread, cut into 1-inch cubes
1 pound bulk mild pork sausage
6 slices bacon, chopped
1 large onion, chopped
1 cup chopped celery
1 (8-ounce) package fresh mushrooms, sliced
2 Granny Smith apples, peeled, cored, and chopped
2 cups chicken broth
1 cup chopped fresh parsley
1 teaspoon rubbed sage
1 teaspoon dried thyme
½ teaspoon pepper
¼ teaspoon salt

Place bread cubes on a baking sheet. Bake at 225° for 1 hour, stirring occasionally. Set aside.

Cook sausage and bacon in a Dutch oven, stirring until sausage crumbles; drain, reserving 3 tablespoons drippings in Dutch oven. Cook onion and next 3 ingredients in drippings over medium-high heat, stirring constantly, until tender (about 5 minutes). Combine sausage mixture, bread cubes, chicken broth, and remaining ingredients in a large bowl; spoon into a lightly greased 13- x 9- x 2-inch baking dish. Cover with aluminum foil; bake at 350° for 30 minutes. Uncover; bake an additional 30 minutes. Yield: 8 to 10 servings. *Marguerite Morgan*
Horse Shoe, North Carolina

GREEN CHILE-CORNBREAD DRESSING

¼ cup butter or margarine
2 cups chopped onion
1 cup sliced celery
1 (14½-ounce) can ready-to-serve chicken broth
1 (17-ounce) can whole kernel corn, drained
2 (4-ounce) cans chopped green chiles, drained
3 tablespoons chopped fresh parsley
½ teaspoon poultry seasoning
½ teaspoon salt
¼ teaspoon dried oregano
¼ teaspoon pepper
6 cups cornbread crumbs
½ cup chopped pecans, toasted

Melt butter in a large Dutch oven; add onion and celery, and cook over medium-high heat, stirring constantly, until tender. Stir in broth and next 7 ingredients. Add cornbread crumbs and pecans, tossing until crumbs are moistened; spoon into a lightly greased 13- x 9- x 2-inch baking dish. Cover and bake at 350° for 30 minutes or until thoroughly heated. Yield: 8 to 10 servings.   *Charlotte Pierce*
Greensburg, Kentucky

GRITS DRESSING

3 cups regular grits, uncooked
1 cup all-purpose flour
1 teaspoon baking powder
¼ teaspoon baking soda
2 large eggs
4 cups buttermilk
2 tablespoons vegetable oil
1 large onion, chopped
1 cup chopped celery
2 to 4 tablespoons leaf sage, crumbled
1 teaspoon baking powder
2 large eggs, lightly beaten
1 (12-ounce) can evaporated milk
2 (14½-ounce) cans ready-to-serve chicken broth

Heat a well-greased, 10-inch cast-iron skillet in a 325° oven 5 minutes or until hot. Combine first 4 ingredients in a large bowl; make a well in center of mixture. Combine 2 eggs, buttermilk, and vegetable oil; add to dry ingredients, stirring mixture just until moistened.

Remove skillet from oven, and pour batter into skillet. Bake at 325° for 1 hour or until firm in center, but not browned. Cool and crumble.

Combine crumbled bread, onion, and remaining ingredients; pour into a lightly greased 13- x 9- x 2-inch baking dish. Bake at 325° for 50 minutes or until firm. Yield: 10 servings.

Time-Saver Turkey

Here's a good idea. This year, buy a turkey that's a few pounds bigger than you need. Why? Because you can use the leftover meat in this terrific open-faced turkey sandwich recipe.

Be sure to remove all the meat from the bone, and refrigerate leftovers within two hours after cooking. Freezing the leftovers in heavy-duty freezer bags will extend the storage life of the turkey. Just package it in meal-sized portions.

HOT TURKEY SANDWICH

2 tablespoons butter or margarine
¼ cup all-purpose flour
2 cups milk
1 cup (4 ounces) shredded sharp Cheddar cheese
1 teaspoon Worcestershire sauce
1 teaspoon prepared mustard
¼ teaspoon salt
⅛ teaspoon ground red pepper
½ pound thinly sliced smoked turkey
8 bread slices, toasted and sliced diagonally
4 tomato slices
8 slices bacon, cooked
¼ cup grated Parmesan cheese
Paprika

Melt butter in a heavy saucepan over low heat; add flour. Cook, stirring constantly, 1 minute. Gradually stir in milk; cook over medium heat, stirring constantly, until mixture is thickened and bubbly. Stir in Cheddar cheese and next 4 ingredients, stirring until cheese melts. Set aside.

Arrange turkey slices evenly on 4 toast slices; cover with cheese sauce, and top with tomato and bacon slices. Sprinkle with Parmesan cheese and paprika; serve immediately. Yield: 4 servings.   *Geri McSwain*
Salem, South Carolina

From Our Kitchen To Yours

With the first cut into the Thanksgiving turkey, the time-honored technique of carving begins. You may think carving a turkey is complicated, but it's actually simple. Whether you'll be using an antique sterling silver carving set or a stainless steel knife and fork, follow these easy steps.

Carve with Confidence

Step 1. Place turkey, breast side up, on a large platter. To remove drumstick and thigh, pull the leg (thigh and drumstick) away from the body, and slice through skin between the leg and body. Cut down to the joint where the thigh connects to the back. Push on the leg to open joint, and cut through joint.

Step 2. To sever the joint between drumstick and thigh of the turkey, feel for a small indentation and cut through it, bending the drumstick back gently while cutting.

Step 3. To cut off wings, roll turkey on its side, and pull the wing away from body. Cut into the hollow between wing and body. Pulling wing away from the body, ang cut around wing joint. Bend wing back, exposing the joint, and cut through it.

Step 4. To slice breast meat, make a deep horizontal cut into breast above where wing was attached. Beginning at the outer edge of one side of breast, cut thin, even slices from the top down to the base cut.

Step 5. If you're serving a large crowd, repeat procedure on the other side of turkey, and slice meat from drumstick and thigh, cutting parallel to the bones. For fewer guests, carve enough for the first helping; arrange sliced meat in front of the carved side, and fill in the sides and back of the platter with parsley or watercress and seasonal fruit.

Turkey Tidbits

■ Remove turkey from the oven, and let stand 20 minutes before carving. This resting time makes slicing easier, prevents shredding, and keeps the juices from running all over the serving platter.

■ Put turkey on a serving platter big enough to also hold the carved meat.

■ Remove stuffing with a long-handled spoon to a service plate or bowl, if necessary.

■ Select carving tools that provide easy handling. Use a sharp carving knife and a two-pronged fork.

■ Carve across the grain of the turkey, keeping the knife at the same angle to ensure uniform and even slices.

■ Plan a practice carving session before Thanksgiving: Roast a whole chicken and practice carving it.

Basting Instincts

Does the thought of a well-basted golden-roasted turkey sitting in the center of the table make you nostalgic for Thanksgiving at Grandma's? But are you a little afraid of preparing one yourself? Relax. Our step-by-step instructions show you how.

Buy Enough

Buy the right amount. The following amounts should allow ample turkey for Thanksgiving day, plus leftovers to enjoy later.

Buying Guide

Up to 12 pounds* ..1 pound per person
Over 12 pounds* ..¾ pound per person
Bone-in Breast.....½ pound per person
Boneless Breast
   or Roll ....⅓ pound per person
* For prestuffed turkeys, add an extra ¼ pound per person.

Store It Right

Frozen turkey will keep up to one year in a freezer set at 0°. Store fresh turkeys in the refrigerator and use within two days of purchase, or by the sell-by date if one is given.

Thawing Takes Time

When thawing a turkey, check it frequently, so you know when it thaws. Then cook it promptly, or store in the refrigerator and cook within 24 hours. Never thaw frozen, prestuffed turkeys. They should be cooked according to package directions, while still frozen.

Refrigerator thawing is safest. Place the frozen turkey in its original wrapper in a pan to catch any drips.

Refrigerator Thawing Guide

6 to 8 pounds..............1 to 1¾ days
8 to 12 pounds...............1 to 2 days
12 to 16 pounds ....2 to 3 days
16 to 20 pounds ....3 to 4 days
Bone-in Breast ....1 to 2 days
Boneless Breast
   or Roll ....1½ to 2 days

Cold-water thawing is quicker. Check the wrapping on the turkey to be sure there are no punctures or tears. Place the bird in its unopened wrapper in the sink, and cover with cold water. If the bag has any punctures, tightly seal the turkey in another plastic bag before placing it in the water.

Change the water frequently (about every 30 minutes). The water must stay cold to prevent the outside of the turkey from getting warm before the inside thaws. If the surface of the turkey becomes warm, bacteria can grow and produce toxins that cannot be killed during cooking.

Cold-Water Thawing Guide

6 to 8 pounds...............3 to 4 hours
8 to 12 pounds.............4 to 6 hours
12 to 16 pounds...........6 to 8 hours
16 to 20 pounds ....8 to 10 hours
Bone-in Breast.............4 to 8 hours
Boneless Breast or Roll..3 to 5 hours

Get Ready to Cook

Reach inside the body cavity, and pull out the bag containing the neck and giblets. Cook giblets separately.

Rinse the turkey, inside and out, with cold water, and drain. To help prevent spreading harmful bacteria, be sure to wash your hands, utensils, sink, and anything else that comes in contact with the raw turkey with hot, soapy water.

Cook

Place the turkey, breast side up, on a rack in a shallow roasting pan to keep the turkey from cooking in its own juices.

Cook the turkey at 325° for the time given on the wrapping or in the chart on the next page. Because cooking times and ovens vary, begin checking doneness about 1 hour before the shortest estimated cooking time. Watch for excessive browning. If the turkey begins to look too dark, cover it with a large piece of aluminum foil folded to form a loose-fitting tent.

Cooking Guide
(Unstuffed Turkey)

6 to 8 pounds	2¼ to 3¼ hours
8 to 12 pounds	3 to 4 hours
12 to 16 pounds	3½ to 4½ hours
16 to 20 pounds	4 to 5 hours
Bone-in Breast	1½ to 2¼ hours
Boneless Breast or Roll	1¾ to 2½ hours

Is It Done Yet?

Meat thermometers are the most accurate. Regular thermometers are inserted before placing the turkey in the oven, while instant-read are inserted to check the temperature during cooking and then removed. Whichever type you use, insert it into the thickest part of the thigh muscle next to the body. For turkey breasts or rolls, insert it into the thickest area. Make sure the thermometer doesn't touch fat or bone. Cook whole turkeys to 180° and turkey breasts or rolls to 170°.

Don't have a meat thermometer? To check for doneness, press the fleshy part of the thigh with fingers protected by a cloth. When done, the meat feels soft, the leg moves up and down easily, and the hip joint yields readily or breaks. Another test is to pierce the thickest part of the inner thigh with a long-tined fork. If the juices are clear, not pink, the turkey is done.

Serve with Pride

Once the turkey is done, let it stand 15 minutes before carving. (See instructions beginning on page 306.) If the turkey is done before you're ready to eat, keep it moist by covering it with foil (sealing the foil to the edges of the pan), and placing it in an oven set as low as possible. To keep the meat safe, it should not stay at room temperature for more than two hours.

Save the Leftovers

Leftover turkey should be refrigerated or frozen within two hours.

Store turkey in the refrigerator for three or four days, or freeze in airtight containers up to one month.

Well-Bred Breads

Bake one or both of our tempting quick breads, mix up a honey or fruit spread or two, and then indulge. But be warned: These flavorful breads and spreads are so good your friends may hint they'd love a loaf and container of spread, to go. Maybe you should prepare a few extra of both for gift-giving. (Both of the breads may be frozen up to three months.)

CHOCOLATE-ZUCCHINI BREAD

¾ cup butter or margarine,
  softened
2 cups sugar
3 large eggs
2 cups grated zucchini (about 2
  large)
½ cup milk
2 teaspoons vanilla extract
2½ cups all-purpose flour
2½ teaspoons baking powder
1½ teaspoons baking soda
½ teaspoon salt
1 teaspoon ground cinnamon
½ cup cocoa
1 cup chopped pecans

Beat butter at medium speed with an electric mixer until creamy; gradually add sugar, beating well. Add eggs, one at a time, beating mixture after each addition.

Combine zucchini, milk, and vanilla. Combine flour and next 5 ingredients; add to butter mixture alternately with zucchini mixture, beginning and ending with flour mixture. Stir in pecans. Spoon batter into two greased 8½- x 4½- x 3-inch loafpans. Bake at 350° for 50 minutes or until a wooden pick inserted in center comes out clean.

Cool in pans on wire racks 10 minutes; remove from pans, and cool completely on wire racks. Yield: 2 loaves.
Bernadette Colvin
Houston, Texas

BOURBON-PECAN BREAD

¼ cup butter or margarine,
  softened
1 cup sugar
1 large egg
1 cup milk
½ cup bourbon
3 cups all-purpose flour
1 tablespoon baking powder
1½ teaspoons salt
1½ cups chopped pecans,
  divided
2 teaspoons grated orange
  rind
2 tablespoons bourbon

Beat butter at medium speed with an electric mixer until creamy; gradually add sugar, beating well. Add egg, beating well.

Combine milk and ½ cup bourbon. Combine flour, baking powder, and salt; add to butter mixture alternately with milk mixture, beginning and ending with flour mixture. Stir in 1¼ cups pecans and orange rind. Spoon batter into a greased and floured 9- x 5- x 3-inch loafpan. Sprinkle with remaining pecans.

Bake at 350° for 1 hour and 10 minutes or until a wooden pick inserted in center comes out clean. Drizzle with 2 tablespoons bourbon. Cool in pan on a wire rack 10 minutes; remove from pan, and cool completely on wire rack. Yield: 1 loaf.
Trenda Leigh
Richmond, Virginia

Spreads for Bread

We tried to match a spread to each bread, but quickly discovered there wasn't a combination we didn't like. Because these are homemade (without any added preservatives), plan to make only what you know will be used within a week.

HONEY BUTTER

1 cup butter or margarine,
  softened
2 tablespoons honey
¼ teaspoon ground cinnamon

Beat butter at medium speed with an electric mixer until creamy. Stir in honey and cinnamon. Cover and refrigerate. Yield: 1 cup.

Debbie Turner
Douglas, Georgia

CHERRY SPREAD

½ cup cream cheese,
  softened (4 ounces)
¼ cup butter or margarine,
  softened
½ cup cherry preserves
1 tablespoon kirsch or other
  cherry-flavored liqueur
  (optional)

Beat cream cheese and butter at medium speed with an electric mixer until smooth. Stir in preserves and kirsch, if desired. Cover and refrigerate. Yield: 1 cup.

COCONUT-PINEAPPLE SPREAD

1 (8-ounce) container soft
  cream cheese
⅓ cup flaked coconut
2 tablespoons pineapple
  preserves *

Beat cream cheese at medium speed with an electric mixer until smooth. Stir in coconut and preserves. Cover and refrigerate. Yield: 1¼ cups.

* 2 tablespoons apricot or peach preserves may be substituted.

Kay C. Cooper
Madison, Alabama

Buenos Días Brunch

Wake up your taste buds with these zesty Tex-Mex flavors. Soothe the hot, spicy flavors of chile peppers, sausage, and chili powder with the refreshing tastes of fresh fruit and cilantro. (If desired, substitute fresh mint for the cilantro.) A blend of sweetened chocolate, cinnamon, and coffee makes a delicious finale.

MEXICAN BRUNCH MENU FOR SIX

**Mexicali Quiche With
Avocado Topping
Fruit Salad With
Citrus-Cilantro Dressing
Commercial cinnamon rolls
Mexican Coffee**

■ Cook sausage mixture for quiche up to a day ahead, and chill until ready to mix quiche filling.
■ Cut up fruit, except for berries. Prepare dressing for the fruit salad up to a day ahead; chill in separate containers. An hour before serving, mix fruit and berries, and toss with dressing.

MEXICALI QUICHE WITH AVOCADO TOPPING

6 (6-inch) corn tortillas
½ pound bulk hot pork sausage
¼ cup finely chopped onion
1 tablespoon chili powder
1 teaspoon ground cumin
3 large eggs, lightly beaten
1 (4-ounce) can chopped green
  chiles, divided
1½ cups half-and-half
½ teaspoon salt
⅛ teaspoon pepper
1½ cups (6 ounces) shredded
  Monterey Jack cheese, divided
Avocado Topping

Bring 2 inches of water to a boil in a large skillet; remove from heat. Dip each tortilla in water to soften; drain on paper towels. Place tortillas in six lightly greased 10-ounce custard cups; set aside.

Cook sausage and next 3 ingredients in skillet over medium heat until meat is browned, stirring until it crumbles; drain and set aside.

Combine eggs, half of green chiles, and next 3 ingredients in a large bowl; stir in sausage mixture. Spoon half of egg mixture evenly into tortilla shells; sprinkle with half of cheese. Pour remaining egg mixture evenly over cheese. Bake at 350° for 20 minutes. Sprinkle with remaining cheese, and bake an additional 5 minutes. Remove from oven, and let stand 5 minutes. Remove from custard cups, and sprinkle with remaining green chiles.

Serve with Avocado Topping. Yield: 6 servings.

Avocado Topping

1 avocado, peeled and mashed
1 tomato, peeled, seeded, and
  chopped
1 clove garlic, minced
1 to 2 tablespoons lime juice

Combine all ingredients in a small bowl. Yield: 1½ cups.

Note: To make Mexicali Quiche in a 9-inch deep-dish pieplate, soften 8 corn tortillas in boiling water, as directed; place in lightly greased pieplate, overlapping and extending tortillas about ½ inch over edge. Spoon half of egg mixture into shell; sprinkle with half of cheese, and spoon remaining egg mixture over cheese. Bake at 350° for 30 minutes. Sprinkle with remaining cheese, and bake an additional 5 minutes. Remove from oven, and let stand 5 minutes. Serve with Avocado Topping. Yield: one 9-inch quiche.

FRUIT SALAD WITH CITRUS-CILANTRO DRESSING

3 cups fresh pineapple chunks or 1 (20-ounce) can pineapple chunks in juice, drained
2 cups pink grapefruit sections (about 3 grapefruit)
2 cups fresh strawberry slices
1 mango, peeled and sliced
Citrus-Cilantro Dressing
1 tablespoon chopped fresh cilantro

Combine first 4 ingredients in a large bowl; toss with Citrus-Cilantro Dressing, and sprinkle with cilantro. Cover and chill 1 hour. Serve with a slotted spoon. Yield: 6 to 8 servings.

Citrus-Cilantro Dressing

⅓ cup orange juice
⅓ cup fresh lime juice
3 tablespoons chopped fresh cilantro
2 tablespoons honey

Combine first 3 ingredients in a small saucepan. Bring mixture to a boil; reduce heat, and simmer 5 minutes. Pour through a wire-mesh strainer into a bowl; discard cilantro. Stir in honey. Yield: about ½ cup.

MEXICAN COFFEE

½ cup ground dark roast coffee
1 tablespoon ground cinnamon
¼ teaspoon ground nutmeg
5 cups water
¼ cup firmly packed dark brown sugar
⅓ cup chocolate syrup
1 cup milk
1 teaspoon vanilla extract
Sweetened whipped cream
Garnish: ground cinnamon

Place coffee in coffee filter or filter basket; add cinnamon and nutmeg. Add water to coffeemaker, and brew.
  Combine brown sugar, chocolate syrup, and milk in a large heavy saucepan. Cook over low heat, stirring constantly, until brown sugar dissolves. Stir in coffee and vanilla. Serve immediately with a dollop of whipped cream; garnish, if desired. Yield: 6½ cups.

Fruit Tips

■ For an interesting change, use fresh pineapple, cantaloupe, or other shells as containers for dips and spreads. Pineapple halves scooped out are beautiful for serving cheese dips or main-dish salads. Other fruit shells, such as melon, are colorful containers for salads or appetizers.

■ Use canned, not fresh, pineapple in gelatin salads. A natural enzyme in the fresh fruit will prevent the gelatin from setting.

■ Mix liquid from canned fruit in a jar as you acquire it; use it in a gelatin dessert or as a punch.

■ Use the syrup from canned fruit in gelatin salads or fruit desserts for additional flavor and sweetness. Chances are the syrup won't make the dish too sweet, but the best rule is to taste and judge.

■ Use slivered orange or lemon rind to add a tangy taste to stews and other dishes.

■ To ripen cantaloupe or honeydew melons quickly, place them in a brown paper bag, close the top, and let sit at room temperature for a couple of days.

■ For an appetizer, wrap honeydew melon wedges or fresh figs with prosciutto (thinly sliced Italian ham).

■ Remember to hull strawberries after washing so that they won't become mushy.

■ To easily remove the white membrane when peeling citrus fruit, soak the unpeeled fruit in boiling water 5 minutes.

■ If you use a food processor or blender to chop dried fruit, freeze the fruit first. It will be easier to chop and less sticky.

■ For easy chopping of dried fruit by hand, place fruit in freezer 2 hours before chopping. Cut fruit with a knife or kitchen shears dipped frequently in hot water to prevent sticking.

DECEMBER

Visions of sugarplums . . . and pinwheels and coconut shortbread and apricot surprises . . . . These are just a few of the sweets from our dazzling array of holiday confections in this chapter. Quick, easy, and delicious, these cookies are perfect for holiday entertaining, last-minute gifts, and as treats for a busy Santa. As a matter of fact, we already know they're Santa approved. Ask any seasoned hostess her secret to successful entertaining for a crowd and she'll tell you the key ingredients are "make ahead" and "rental." So, using these tips, we came up with a versatile menu that includes dips, a marinated bean salad, fruit casserole, biscuits, pound cake, and rum balls. Now, all that remains is a phone call to your neighborhood rental store.

Menu Fit For A Crowd

Break the rules! Instead of expensive flowers, decorate with clove-studded citrus and raffia-wrapped lemons. Instead of working yourself into a frenzy, serve this simple but sumptuous make-ahead buffet for a crowd of 20 or more.

Ask any caterer. Make-ahead recipes anchor even the flashiest parties. For this menu, Sweet Potato Angel Biscuits, Marinated Bean Salad, Ginger-Orange Baked Fruit, and all the dips and desserts can be made ahead of time.

Once the basics are checked off your list, plan one stunning display for the buffet. Heap assorted vegetables on top of cake stands and platters for a showy arrangement. Tangy dips served inside cabbages or sweet pepper cups lend the crowning accent. Don't be intimidated—if you can cut up vegetables and mix the dip, you can do this.

The KISS (Keep It Simple, Silly) rule applies to entertaining as well as business matters. These foods require only forks and small plates—skip the grand table setting for parties of this size. Use what you have in your cabinets, and rent the rest. For that little splurge, pack a standing champagne bucket with ice and sparkling wine or grape juice. Place it near a table full of glassware and lit candles, and let guests help themselves.

dry ingredients are moistened. Turn dough out onto a lightly floured surface; knead 5 minutes. Place dough in a lightly greased bowl, turning to grease top; cover and refrigerate 8 hours or overnight, if desired.

Roll dough to ½-inch thickness; cut with a 2-inch round cutter. Place on ungreased baking sheets; cover and let rise in a warm place (85°), free from drafts, 20 minutes or until doubled in bulk. Bake at 400° for 10 to 12 minutes or until lightly browned. Yield: 7 dozen.

* 3 cups canned, mashed sweet potatoes may be substituted.

Note: Unbaked biscuits may be frozen up to one month. To serve, let thaw 30 minutes; cover and let rise in a warm place (85°), free from drafts, 20 minutes or until doubled in bulk. Bake as directed.
Therese Reid
Rhodesdale, Maryland

A GATHERING
FOR 20 OR MORE

Sweet Potato Angel Biscuits
Commercially sliced 3- to 3½-pound ham
Marinated Bean Salad
Ginger-Orange Baked Fruit
Vegetable-and-shrimp platter
Featuring
Blue Cheese Dip
Antipasto Dip
Curry-Onion Dip
Marbled Pecan Pound Cake
Rum Balls
Wine

MARINATED BEAN SALAD
(pictured on page 335)

3 (15-ounce) cans red kidney beans, drained and rinsed
3 (15.8-ounce) cans Northern beans, drained and rinsed
2 large green peppers, finely chopped
2 carrots, scraped and sliced
1 bunch green onions, sliced
⅔ cup lemon juice
⅔ cup white wine vinegar
1 cup olive oil
1 (2-ounce) jar diced pimiento, drained
1 to 2 cloves garlic, crushed
1 teaspoon freshly ground pepper
¼ cup finely chopped fresh parsley

Combine first 5 ingredients in a large bowl. Combine lemon juice and next 5 ingredients; pour over bean mixture. Sprinkle with parsley, and stir gently. Cover and refrigerate 8 hours or overnight. Yield: 12 cups.

SWEET POTATO ANGEL BISCUITS
(pictured on page 335)

3 large sweet potatoes *
3 packages active dry yeast
¾ cup warm water (105° to 115°)
7½ cups all-purpose flour
1 tablespoon baking powder
1 tablespoon salt
1½ cups sugar
1½ cups shortening

Wash sweet potatoes; bake at 375° for 1 hour or until done. Let potatoes cool to touch; peel and mash. Set aside 3 cups, and keep warm.

Combine yeast and warm water in a 2-cup liquid measuring cup; let stand 5 minutes.

Combine flour and next 3 ingredients in a large bowl; cut in shortening with a pastry blender or fork until mixture is crumbly. Add yeast mixture and sweet potatoes, stirring until

GINGER-ORANGE
BAKED FRUIT
(pictured on page 335)

6 cups pitted prunes, cut in half
6 cups frozen sliced peaches,
   thawed and drained
1½ cups raisins
3 cups orange juice
1 (18-ounce) jar orange marmalade
1 tablespoon ground ginger
1 (3½-ounce) can flaked coconut,
   toasted

Layer first 3 ingredients in a lightly greased 13- x 9- x 2-inch baking dish. Combine orange juice, marmalade, and ginger; pour over fruit. Bake at 350° for 45 to 50 minutes or until bubbly; sprinkle with coconut. Serve with a slotted spoon. If desired, bake fruit as directed, omitting coconut; spoon into individual compotes, and sprinkle with coconut. Yield: 18 to 20 servings.
Joel Allard
San Antonio, Texas

BLUE CHEESE DIP
(pictured on pages 334 and 335)

1¼ cups crumbled blue cheese,
   divided
1 cup mayonnaise
¼ cup catsup
2 tablespoons sugar
2 tablespoons vegetable oil
2 tablespoons white vinegar
1 teaspoon dry mustard
½ teaspoon salt
½ teaspoon paprika
¼ teaspoon celery seeds (optional)

Combine ¾ cup blue cheese and remaining ingredients in container of an electric blender; process until smooth, stopping once to scrape down sides. Pour mixture into a bowl, and stir in half of remaining blue cheese. Cover and refrigerate 8 hours. Serve in a hollow cabbage head, if desired. Sprinkle with remaining blue cheese. Yield: 2 cups.
Dan McNeely
Bradenton, Florida

ANTIPASTO DIP
(pictured on pages 334 and 335)

1 (14-ounce) can artichoke hearts,
   drained and chopped
2 (4-ounce) cans sliced mushrooms,
   drained and chopped
1 (4-ounce) jar diced pimientos,
   drained
1 cup pimiento-stuffed olives,
   chopped
½ cup chopped green pepper
½ cup chopped celery
½ cup vegetable oil
½ cup finely chopped onion
1 clove garlic, minced
⅔ cup white vinegar
2½ teaspoons Italian seasoning
1 teaspoon seasoning salt
1 teaspoon sugar
½ teaspoon freshly ground pepper

Combine first 6 ingredients in a bowl; set aside. Heat oil in a saucepan over medium heat; add onion and garlic, and cook 3 minutes or until tender. Add vinegar and remaining ingredients; bring to a boil. Pour over vegetables; cover and refrigerate 8 hours or overnight. Serve on fresh endive leaves or with crackers. Yield: 5 cups.
Pam Rappaport
Pembroke Pines, Florida

CURRY-ONION DIP
(pictured on pages 334 and 335)

2 cups mayonnaise or salad
   dressing
2 to 3 tablespoons grated onion
2 tablespoons tarragon vinegar
2 tablespoons chili sauce
1 tablespoon freeze-dried chives
2 teaspoons curry powder
½ teaspoon salt
¼ teaspoon dried thyme
⅛ teaspoon pepper
Garnish: chopped green onion tops

Combine first 9 ingredients; cover and refrigerate 8 hours or overnight. Serve in a pepper cup with vegetables or boiled shrimp. Garnish, if desired. Yield: 2¼ cups.
Linda Walton
Fort Valley, Georgia

MARBLED PECAN
POUND CAKE
(pictured on page 336)

½ cup butter or margarine,
   softened
½ cup shortening
3 cups sugar
5 large eggs
3 cups all-purpose flour
½ teaspoon baking powder
¼ teaspoon salt
1 cup milk
1 teaspoon vanilla extract
1 (1-ounce) square unsweetened
   chocolate
1 tablespoon shortening
½ cup chopped pecans

Beat butter and ½ cup shortening at medium speed with an electric mixer about 2 minutes or until creamy. Gradually add sugar, beating at medium speed 5 to 7 minutes. Add eggs, one at a time, beating just until yellow disappears.

Combine flour, baking powder, and salt; add to butter mixture alternately with milk, beginning and ending with flour mixture. Mix at low speed just until blended after each addition. Stir in vanilla.

Combine chocolate and 1 tablespoon shortening in a small, heavy saucepan; cook over low heat, stirring constantly, until chocolate melts. Remove 2 cups batter, and add chocolate mixture, stirring until blended. Pour one-third of remaining plain batter into a greased and floured 10-inch tube pan; top with half of chocolate batter. Repeat layers, ending with plain batter. Gently swirl batter with a knife to create a marbled effect, and sprinkle with pecans. Bake at 350° for 1 hour and 10 minutes or until a wooden pick inserted in center comes out clean. Cool in pan on a wire rack 10 to 15 minutes; remove from pan, and let cool completely on wire rack. Yield: one 10-inch cake.
Billie Taylor
Wytheville, Virginia

RUM BALLS
(pictured on page 336)

1 (12-ounce) package vanilla
   wafers
1 (16-ounce) package pecan
   pieces
½ cup honey
⅓ cup bourbon
⅓ cup dark rum
Sugar or vanilla wafer crumbs

Position knife blade in food processor bowl; add vanilla wafers. Process until crumbs are fine. Transfer to a large bowl. Place pecans in processor bowl; process until finely chopped. Stir into vanilla wafer crumbs. Stir in honey, bourbon, and rum. Shape into 1-inch balls, and roll in sugar or additional vanilla wafer crumbs. Place in an airtight container, and store in refrigerator up to one month. Yield: 6 dozen.

Lela H. Coggins
Brevard, North Carolina

Honey Tips

■ Honey is available in several forms, the most common being liquid and chunk. Chunk honey contains a piece of the honeycomb. Creamed honey, similar to a buttery spread and sold in refrigerated cases, is not as widely available as liquid or chunk honey.
■ There are recipes created especially for honey as the sweetener. But if you want to substitute honey for sugar in other recipes, try replacing 1 cup of granulated sugar with ⅔ or ¾ cup of honey, depending on desired sweetness. For every cup of sugar replaced by honey, reduce the total liquid by ¼ cup. Also reduce the baking temperature 25 degrees.
■ Too much honey in a recipe may make the dish too brown.

Sweet Dreams

We've gathered an array of goodies that will lend a sweet note to your holidays. You needn't be an experienced cook to create these dazzlers. Each of these confections will still leave you plenty of time for tree trimming, party going, and making merry.

If your holidays just wouldn't be complete without a flour-dusted afternoon of baking, you'll find new inspiration in our selection of cookie recipes. As diverse as the ornaments on a Christmas tree, these recipes are short and sweet—just right for the last hectic days of the year. Enlist the help of your favorite elves, and try several of the cookie recipes early in December and freeze. You'll wind up with some wonderful memories and treats to give later as gifts.

Lighter-than-air mousses provide a festive ending to a holiday feast. Layered as parfaits or presented in a sack of chocolate, they'll top off an evening in splendid fashion. Now all that's left is a long winter's nap.

SMALL CHOCOLATE SACK
(pictured on cover and page 333)

1 (7¾- x 4- x 2½-inch) paper bag
2 wooden picks
1 (6-inch) wooden or metal skewer
2 (2-ounce) squares vanilla-flavored
   or chocolate-flavored candy
   coating

Cut 3 inches from top of bag with pinking shears. Place picks on outside base, parallel to short edges of bag, tucking ends under diagonal folds. Insert skewer through center fold and under picks. Set aside.

Place candy coating in top of a double boiler, and bring water to a boil. Reduce heat to low; cook until candy coating melts. Remove from heat; cool to 100°. Pour about half of candy coating into bag, and tilt bag to coat interior. Shake bag over double boiler to remove excess candy coating. Suspend bag between two cans, supporting bag with wooden skewer; let stand until firm.

Remelt candy coating in double boiler; cool to 100°. Hold bag to light to find any thin places. Using a pastry brush, coat thin places, corners, and creases with candy coating; let stand until firm.

Remelt candy coating; cool to 100°. Pour into bag, tilting to coat interior and shaking to remove excess. Suspend and let stand until firm. Carefully peel paper bag from candy coating. Store in a cool, dry place. Yield: 1 (4¾- x 4- x 2½-inch) sack.

Large Chocolate Sack: Use a 10¾- x 5⅛- x 3⅛-inch brown lunch bag. Cut 3 inches from top. Position two 6-inch wooden skewers trimmed to width of bag in place of wooden picks, and insert a 12-inch wooden or metal skewer under picks. Repeat melting and pouring procedure using 4 (2-ounce) squares candy coating three times, brushing thin places, corners, and creases twice. Yield: 1 (7¾- x 5⅛- x 3⅛-inch) sack.

Note: For vanilla-flavored and chocolate-flavored candy coating, we used Plymouth Pantry or Borden products. For more detailed instructions, see From Our Kitchen to Yours on page 317.

WHITE CHOCOLATE MOUSSE
(pictured on cover)

1 cup white chocolate morsels
¼ cup whipping cream
1 tablespoon Raspberry Sauce
1 drop of liquid red food coloring
1½ cups whipping cream, whipped
Garnishes: fresh raspberries, fresh
  mint leaves

Combine white chocolate morsels and ¼ cup whipping cream in a heavy saucepan; cook over low heat, stirring constantly, until chocolate melts. Cool. Stir in Raspberry Sauce and food coloring; fold in whipped cream. To serve, pipe or spoon into serving dishes or chocolate sacks. Serve with

---

In the Bag
■ To assemble our elegant dessert for two, spoon 2 to 3 tablespoons of Raspberry Sauce onto center of 10- to 12-inch china dinner plate.
■ Position Small Chocolate Sack diagonally across pool of sauce.
■ Pipe or spoon about ¾ cup White Chocolate Mousse into open end of sack; allow mousse to spill out onto sauce.
■ Scatter fresh raspberries over mousse and sauce. Garnish with mint leaves, if desired.
■ Make a bow from gold lamé organza ribbon, leaving ends of ribbon long. Place bow on top of chocolate sack.

---

remaining Raspberry Sauce. Garnish, if desired. Yield: 3 cups.

Note: For white chocolate morsels, we used Ghirardelli Classic White Chips.

Raspberry Sauce

1 (10-ounce) package frozen
  raspberries, thawed
2 tablespoons sugar
2 tablespoons Cointreau or other
  orange-flavored liqueur

Place raspberries in container of an electric blender; process until pureed. Pour mixture through a fine wire-mesh strainer into a small bowl, discarding seeds. Add sugar and Cointreau to puree, stirring until sugar dissolves. Yield: 1 cup.

White Chocolate-Raspberry Swirl Parfait: Layer White Chocolate Mousse and Raspberry Sauce into six (4-ounce) parfait glasses. Gently swirl mixtures with a wooden skewer. Cover and freeze at least 1 hour or up to 2 days. Let stand 10 to 15 minutes before serving. If desired, top with fresh raspberries and mint leaves. Yield: 6 servings.

PEPPERMINT MOUSSE

1 (5-ounce) can evaporated milk
1 (10-ounce) package
  marshmallows
½ cup milk
1½ cups whipping cream, whipped
½ teaspoon clear peppermint
  extract
2 drops of liquid red food coloring

Combine evaporated milk and marshmallows in a heavy saucepan; cook over low heat, stirring constantly, until marshmallows melt. Remove from heat; let stand 10 minutes. Stir in ½ cup milk; cover and chill until thickened, stirring occasionally. Fold in whipped cream, peppermint extract,

---

and food coloring; cover and chill at least 4 hours. Spoon or pipe into serving dishes or chocolate sacks. Yield: 4¼ cups.

Peppermint Parfait: (pictured on page 333). Layer Peppermint Mousse and 1 cup chocolate wafer crumbs into 10 (4-ounce) parfait glasses. Cover and freeze at least 1 hour or up to 2 days. Let stand 10 to 15 minutes before serving. If desired, top with whipped cream and crushed hard peppermint candies. Yield: 10 servings.

SNOWBALL SURPRISES
(pictured on page 333)

1 cup butter or margarine,
  softened
½ cup sugar
1 teaspoon vanilla extract
2 cups all-purpose flour
1 cup finely chopped pecans
10 chocolate-coated peppermint
  patties, quartered
Sifted powdered sugar

Beat butter at medium speed with an electric mixer until creamy; gradually add sugar, beating mixture well. Stir in vanilla. Gradually stir in flour and pecans, mixing well; cover and chill at least 1 hour.

Press 1 tablespoon dough around each candy piece, forming a ball. Place on ungreased cookie sheets; bake at 350° for 12 minutes. (Cookies will not brown.) Let cool 5 minutes on cookie sheets, and roll in powdered sugar. Place on wire racks to cool. Yield: 40 cookies.

Note: Cookies may be frozen in an airtight container up to one month.
Nellie H. Leech
Lexington, Virginia

APRICOT WONDERS
(pictured on page 333)

1½ cups shortening
1½ cups sugar
2 large eggs
1 tablespoon grated orange rind
1 teaspoon vanilla extract
4 cups all-purpose flour
1 tablespoon baking powder
½ teaspoon salt
2 to 3 tablespoons milk
Apricot Filling

Beat shortening at medium speed with an electric mixer until fluffy; gradually add sugar, beating mixture well. Add eggs, one at a time, beating mixture after each addition. Stir in orange rind and vanilla.

Combine flour, baking powder, and salt; add to shortening mixture alternately with milk, mixing well after each addition. Cover mixture and chill, if necessary.

Roll dough to ⅛-inch thickness on a lightly floured surface. Cut with a 3-inch star-shaped cookie cutter, and place on lightly greased cookie sheets. Use a ½-inch star-shaped cutter to cut out a star in half of cookies. Bake at 350° for 8 minutes. Remove to wire racks to cool. Spread each solid cookie with about 1 teaspoon Apricot Filling, and top with a cutout cookie. Yield: 4½ dozen.

Apricot Filling

1 (6-ounce) package dried
  apricots
½ cup sugar
½ cup water

Combine all ingredients in a small saucepan; bring to a boil over medium heat. Reduce heat, and simmer about 15 minutes or until tender. Spoon into container of an electric blender or food processor; process until smooth. Yield: 1 cup.

Note: Cookies and Apricot Filling may be frozen separately up to six months. To serve, thaw cookies and filling, and assemble as directed.
Mary Cunningham
Cleveland, Tennessee

COCONUT SHORTBREAD COOKIES
(pictured on page 333)

¾ cup butter or margarine,
  softened
⅓ cup sugar
1½ teaspoons vanilla extract
1¾ cups all-purpose flour
½ teaspoon baking powder
¼ teaspoon salt
1 cup flaked coconut
1 (6-ounce) package semisweet
  chocolate morsels
2 teaspoons shortening
Flaked coconut, toasted

Beat butter at medium speed with an electric mixer until creamy; gradually add sugar, beating well. Stir in vanilla. Combine flour, baking powder, and salt; gradually add to butter mixture, mixing well. Stir in 1 cup coconut. Cover and chill 1 hour, if necessary.

Roll dough to ¼-inch thickness on a lightly floured surface. Cut dough into desired shapes with 2-inch cookie cutters, and place on lightly greased cookie sheets. Bake at 300° for 25 to 30 minutes or until edges are lightly browned. Remove cookies to wire racks to cool.

Melt chocolate morsels and shortening in a small, heavy saucepan over medium-low heat. Dip edges of cookies in chocolate mixture; then dip in toasted coconut. Place on cookie sheets lined with wax paper. Chill 10 minutes. Yield: 2 dozen.

Note: Cookies may be frozen up to six months.
Evelyn I. Randall
Spartanburg, South Carolina

PINWHEEL COOKIES
(pictured on page 333)

½ cup butter or margarine,
  softened
1 cup firmly packed brown sugar
1 large egg
1 teaspoon vanilla extract
2 cups all-purpose flour
1 teaspoon baking powder
¼ teaspoon salt
2 tablespoons cocoa

Beat butter at medium speed with an electric mixer until creamy; gradually add brown sugar, beating well. Add egg and vanilla, beating well. Combine flour, baking powder, and salt; gradually add to butter mixture, mixing well. Divide dough in half; stir cocoa into one portion.

Roll each portion into a 12- x 9-inch rectangle on wax paper. Invert chocolate dough onto plain dough; peel off wax paper, and press chocolate dough firmly onto plain dough with a rolling pin. Roll up jellyroll fashion starting with long side; cover and chill 8 hours.

Cut dough with an electric knife into ¼-inch-thick slices; place on lightly greased cookie sheets. Bake at 350° for 6 to 8 minutes. Remove to wire racks to cool. Yield: about 4 dozen.

Note: Unbaked cookie dough may be frozen up to three weeks. Before baking, thaw in the refrigerator; slice and bake as directed.
Mildred Bickley
Bristol, Virginia

CHOCOLATE-ALMOND MOUSSE

1 (6-ounce) package milk chocolate
  morsels
2 tablespoons water
2 to 3 tablespoons amaretto or
  other almond-flavored liqueur
1½ cups whipping cream, whipped
Garnishes: toasted almonds,
  whipped cream

Combine chocolate and water in a saucepan; cook over low heat, stirring constantly, until chocolate melts. Cool. Stir in amaretto. Fold in whipping cream. To serve, pipe or spoon into serving dishes or chocolate sacks. Garnish, if desired. Yield: 3 cups.

From Our Kitchen To Yours

While experimenting with the chocolate sack recipe on page 314, we had at least 50 bags scattered on any vacant spot in the Test Kitchens.

Trying to find the easiest way to make the chocolate sacks, we first painted the outside of a few paper bags; however, removing them from the candy coating was tedious and many broke. We tried brushing the bag first with oil, but the coating wouldn't adhere. The biggest breakthrough was pouring the candy coating *into* the bag.

Retaining the shape of the bag was another obstacle. The solution: Suspend the candy-coated bag between two cans of equal height, letting the excess candy coating drip while the sack dries.

Making a chocolate sack is time-consuming but not difficult. Follow these steps and tips to create a sweet memory at your table.

Helpful Hints

■ We used Plymouth Pantry and Borden products for chocolate-flavored or vanilla-flavored candy coating.
■ Use gift bags or inexpensive brown or white paper bags; 13-ounce coffee bags also work.
■ Be sure to cool melted candy coating to 100°; hot coating will melt the first layer.
■ If you don't have a double boiler, melt the candy coating in a saucepan or microwave candy coating according to package directions.
■ Avoid refrigerating the chocolate sacks to speed drying process; any moisture forming on the chocolate sacks softens the coating.
■ Remove excess chocolate from pinked edges with a wooden skewer or pick while coating is soft, if a more defined look is desired.
■ Use tweezers and kitchen shears to assist in removing the paper bag from the candy coating.

■ Avoid overhandling the chocolate sacks; the warmth from your hands softens the candy coating.

■ Melt any candy sack if dissatisfied; coating can be remelted and repoured many times.

How to Make a Chocolate Sack

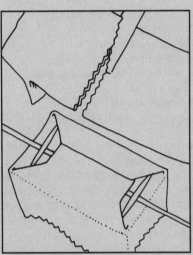

Step 1: *Cut 3 inches from top of bag with pinking shears. Place wooden picks on outside base, parallel to short edges of bag, tucking ends under diagonal folds. Insert wooden skewer through center fold and under wooden picks.*

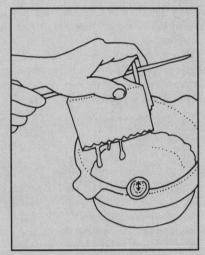

Step 2: *Melt candy coating in top of a double boiler, and cool to 100°. Pour about half into bag, tilting to coat interior. Shake bag over double boiler to remove excess candy coating. Suspend bag between two cans.*

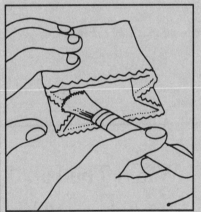

Step 3: *Remelt candy coating; cool to 100°. Hold bag to light to find any thinly coated places. Using a pastry brush, reinforce thin places, corners, and creases with candy coating; let stand until firm. Repeat pouring and tilting step.*

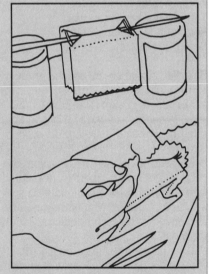

Step 4: *Carefully peel paper bag away from chocolate sack. Store chocolate sack in a cool, dry place.*

Light Velvet

Dazzle your guests with a lavish Red Velvet Cake but don't mention you've left out almost all the fat—they'll never know.

Using a small amount of butter along with a fat-free cream cheese product ensure flavor and moistness in this version of Red Velvet Cake.

RED VELVET CAKE

½ cup butter, softened
4 ounces fat-free cream cheese
  product, softened
1½ cups sugar
½ cup egg substitute
2 (1-ounce) bottles liquid red food
  coloring
2¼ cups sifted cake flour
2 tablespoons unsweetened cocoa
1 teaspoon baking soda
¼ teaspoon salt
1 cup nonfat buttermilk
1 teaspoon vanilla extract
Vegetable cooking spray
Boiled Frosting

Beat butter and cream cheese product at medium speed with an electric mixer until creamy; gradually add sugar, beating well. Gradually add egg substitute, beating well. Stir in food coloring.

Combine flour and next 3 ingredients; add to butter mixture alternately with buttermilk, beginning and ending with flour mixture. Mix batter just until blended after each addition. Stir in vanilla.

Pour batter into three 9-inch round cakepans coated with cooking spray. Bake at 350° for 20 to 25 minutes. Cool in pans on wire racks 10 minutes; remove from pans; cool completely on wire racks. Spread Boiled Frosting between layers and on top

and sides of cake. Yield: 16 servings (278 calories [20% from fat] per serving).

□ *4.2g protein, 6.1g fat (3.7g saturated), 52.1g carbohydrate, 0g fiber, 17mg cholesterol, 243mg sodium, and 57mg calcium.*

Boiled Frosting

1½ cups sugar, divided
¾ cup water
1 tablespoon light corn syrup
2 egg whites
⅛ teaspoon salt
1 teaspoon vanilla extract

Reserve 2 tablespoons sugar. Combine remaining sugar, water, and corn syrup in a heavy pan. Cook over medium heat, stirring constantly, until sugar dissolves and mixture is clear. Cook, without stirring, to soft ball stage (240°). Remove from heat.

Quickly beat egg whites and salt until soft peaks form; gradually add reserved sugar; beat until blended. Continue to beat, slowly adding syrup mixture. Add vanilla, and beat until stiff peaks form and frosting is thick. Yield: 4 cups (79 calories [0% from fat] per ¼-cup serving).

□ *0.4g protein, 0g fat, 19.8g carbohydrate, 0g fiber, 0mg cholesterol, 26mg sodium, and 1mg calcium.*

LIGHT MENU

Watch The Fat, Not The Pot

Make this simple, low-fat meal to give your family a break from holiday fare—and yourself a break from the kitchen. Who wouldn't welcome Bean-and-Turkey Soup, Light and Creamy

Coleslaw, and flavor-packed Parsley-Garlic Rolls on a cool evening? Plan ahead, and the meal can be ready when you get home.

SOUP SUPPER
FOR SIX

**Light and Creamy Coleslaw
Bean-and-Turkey Soup
Parsley-Garlic Rolls**

LIGHT AND CREAMY
COLESLAW

6 cups shredded cabbage
¼ cup chopped green onions
Creamy Dressing
Lettuce leaves
Garnish: green onion fans

Combine cabbage and green onions in a large bowl; stir in Creamy Dressing. Cover and chill at least 1 hour. Spoon onto lettuce-lined plates; garnish, if desired. Yield: 6 servings (36 calories [7% from fat] per 1-cup serving).

□ *1.8g protein, 0.3g fat, (0g saturated), 7.5g carbohydrate, 2g fiber, 0mg cholesterol, 172mg sodium, and 61mg calcium.*

Creamy Dressing

¼ cup nonfat yogurt
¼ cup fat-free mayonnaise
2 tablespoons rice wine
  vinegar
2 teaspoons spicy brown
  mustard

Combine all ingredients, mixing well. Yield: ⅔ cup (8 calories [7% from fat] per tablespoon).

□ *0.4g protein, 0.1g fat, (0g saturated), 1.7g carbohydrate, 0g fiber, 0mg cholesterol, 85mg sodium, and 11mg calcium.*

BEAN-AND-TURKEY SOUP

2 cups chopped cooked turkey
   breast
2 cups peeled, chopped tomatoes
1 cup canned red kidney beans,
   drained and rinsed
1 cup canned pinto beans, drained
   and rinsed
1 cup canned black beans, drained
   and rinsed
1 cup canned garbanzo beans,
   drained and rinsed
1 cup frozen whole kernel corn
1 cup chopped onion
2 jalapeño peppers, seeded and
   chopped
2 cloves garlic, minced
2 (16-ounce) cans ready-to-serve,
   fat-free, reduced-sodium chicken
   broth
1 (12-ounce) can light beer
3 tablespoons chili powder
2 tablespoons curry powder
1 teaspoon dried basil
1 teaspoon dried oregano
1 teaspoon dried thyme
¼ teaspoon pepper
3 tablespoons reduced-sodium soy
   sauce
2 tablespoons Worcestershire sauce

Combine all ingredients in a large Dutch oven; bring to a boil over medium heat. Reduce heat, and simmer, uncovered, 2 hours, stirring occasionally. Yield: 9½ cups (251 calories [11% from fat] per 1⅓-cup serving).

□ *20.5g protein, 3.1g fat (0.7g saturated), 36.6g carbohydrate, 5.7g fiber, 24mg cholesterol, 555mg sodium, and 83mg calcium.*

Note: Bean-and-Turkey Soup may be frozen up to six months. To serve, thaw in refrigerator 8 hours; cook over medium heat until thoroughly heated. *Stephanie Mosca Bolden*
Newport News, Virginia

Tip: *Use leftover liquid from canned or cooked vegetables in gelatin molds, soups, stews, sauces, or casseroles for additional flavor.*

PARSLEY-GARLIC ROLLS

2 tablespoons reduced-calorie
   margarine, melted
2 cloves garlic, crushed
1 (16-ounce) loaf frozen bread
   dough, thawed
1 tablespoon chopped fresh
   parsley
Vegetable cooking spray

Combine margarine and garlic; set mixture aside.

Cut bread dough crosswise into 6 even portions with kitchen shears; cut portions in half crosswise. Roll each half to ¼-inch thickness on a lightly floured surface; brush with margarine mixture, and sprinkle with parsley. Roll each piece of dough, jellyroll fashion, and place, swirled side down, in muffin pans coated with cooking spray. Cover and let rise in a warm place (85°), free from drafts, 1 hour or until doubled in bulk. Bake at 400° for 10 to 12 minutes. Serve immediately. Yield: 1 dozen (97 calories [20% from fat] per roll).

□ *3g protein, 2.2g fat (0.2g saturated), 16.1g carbohydrate, 0g fiber, 0mg cholesterol, 196mg sodium, and 21mg calcium.*   *Hilda Marshall*
Front Royal, Virginia

QUICK & EASY

Vegetarian Entrées

Some nights supper has to be ready fast. These quick, all-in-one main dishes combine vegetables with grains, beans, pasta, or cheese.

Serve these meatless main dishes with a fruit or green salad and bread, and you have a meal so flavorful and satisfying no one will miss the meat.

■ Vegetarian Burritos are ready in 35 minutes.

VEGETARIAN BURRITOS

8 (10-inch) flour tortillas
1 tablespoon olive oil
1 medium carrot, scraped and
   shredded
1 small onion, chopped
1 clove garlic, pressed
1 (8-ounce) can tomato sauce
1 (10-ounce) package frozen
   chopped broccoli, thawed and
   well drained
1 (10-ounce) package frozen whole
   kernel corn, thawed and drained
1 (15-ounce) can black beans,
   drained and rinsed
1 tablespoon chili powder
½ teaspoon salt
¼ teaspoon ground cumin
Dash of hot sauce
1 (8-ounce) package shredded
   Cheddar cheese
Commercial salsa
Commercial guacamole

Heat tortillas according to package directions; keep warm.

Heat olive oil in a large skillet. Add carrot, onion, and garlic; cook over low heat, stirring constantly, 2 minutes. Stir in tomato sauce and next 7 ingredients; cover and simmer 5 minutes. Spoon about ½ cup vegetable mixture evenly down center of each tortilla; sprinkle evenly with ¼ cup Cheddar cheese. Fold opposite sides over filling, securing with a wooden pick, if necessary. Serve immediately with commercial salsa and guacamole. Yield: 4 servings.

■ The fennel flavor in Vegetable Lasagna tricked us; you'll think there is Italian sausage in this dish, too. Although it may take a little longer (preparation time 35 minutes and baking time 35 minutes), you'll have two casseroles—one to serve for supper and one to freeze for use later.

VEGETABLE LASAGNA

12 lasagna noodles, uncooked
2 cups sliced mushrooms
1 cup shredded carrots (about 5 medium carrots)
½ cup chopped onion
1 tablespoon vegetable oil
1 (18-ounce) can tomato paste
1 (15-ounce) can tomato sauce
1 (4-ounce) can sliced ripe olives, drained
1½ teaspoons dried oregano
1 teaspoon dried fennel
2 cups cottage cheese, divided
1 (10-ounce) package frozen chopped spinach, thawed and well drained
2 (8-ounce) packages sliced mozzarella cheese, divided
Grated Parmesan cheese

Cook noodles according to package directions; drain and set aside.

Cook mushrooms, carrots, and onion in oil in a large skillet over medium heat until tender. Stir in tomato paste and next 4 ingredients; bring to a boil. Remove from heat.

Lightly grease two 8-inch baking dishes; arrange 3 noodles in each dish. Top each with one-fourth each of cottage cheese, spinach, vegetable mixture, and mozzarella. Repeat layers with remaining noodles, cottage cheese, spinach, and vegetable mixture. Cover and freeze one casserole up to six months. Bake remaining casserole at 375° for 30 minutes. Add half of remaining mozzarella slices, and bake an additional 5 minutes. Let casserole stand 10 minutes; serve with Parmesan cheese. Yield: 4 servings per casserole.

Note: To serve frozen casserole, thaw in refrigerator 24 hours. Bake at 375° for 45 minutes; add remaining mozzarella cheese slices, and bake an additional 5 minutes. Serve with Parmesan cheese.

Note: Vegetable Lasagna may be prepared in a 13- x 9- x 2-inch baking dish. Bake at 375° for 40 minutes; top with mozzarella cheese slices, and bake an additional 5 minutes.

Sunny Tiedemann
Bartlesville, Oklahoma

■ For a quick-to-assemble supper of Marinara on Beds of Spinach and Orzo, top spinach with orzo (rice-shaped pasta) and a commercial marinara sauce. Ready in 30 minutes.

MARINARA ON BEDS OF SPINACH AND ORZO

½ cup orzo, uncooked
1 (10-ounce) package frozen leaf spinach, thawed and well drained
1 tablespoon olive oil
¼ teaspoon pepper
1 (12-ounce) jar marinara sauce
½ cup grated Parmesan cheese

Cook orzo according to package directions; keep warm.

Cook spinach in olive oil in a skillet over medium heat, stirring constantly, until thoroughly heated. Sprinkle with pepper, tossing well. Spoon evenly onto two individual plates; set aside.

Cook marinara sauce in skillet over medium-high heat, stirring constantly, until thoroughly heated.

Spoon orzo onto spinach; top with marinara sauce, and sprinkle with Parmesan cheese. Yield: 2 servings.

Tip: *Drain pasta immediately after cooking, and transfer to a warmed serving bowl. No rinsing is necessary unless specifically stated in the recipe or unless preparing a cold pasta salad. Slightly undercook any pasta to be used as part of a recipe requiring further cooking.*

Let The Salad Be The Star

During the holidays, we tend to indulge more and eat heavy foods. For those evenings when you want something lighter, try our new and refreshing main-dish salads.

TURKEY CAESAR SALAD

2 cloves garlic
2 tablespoons red wine vinegar
1 tablespoon Dijon mustard
½ teaspoon salt
½ teaspoon pepper
½ cup olive oil
1 pound turkey cutlets
1 head romaine, torn
½ cup cherry tomatoes, halved
½ sweet red pepper, cut into thin strips
¼ cup Greek calamata olives
1½ teaspoons anchovy paste
¼ cup freshly grated Parmesan cheese

Combine first 5 ingredients in container of an electric blender; process 10 seconds. With blender on high, gradually add olive oil in a slow, steady stream; reserve ¼ cup dressing. Place turkey cutlets in a heavy-duty, zip-top plastic bag. Pour remaining dressing over turkey cutlets; refrigerate 1 hour.

Drain cutlets, discarding marinade. Cook cutlets in a large skillet over medium-high heat 2 minutes on each side. Remove from skillet, and cut into ½-inch strips. Keep warm.

Combine romaine and next 3 ingredients in a large bowl. Add anchovy paste to reserved ¼ cup dressing, mixing well; pour over salad, tossing well. Arrange on individual plates; top with turkey strips, and sprinkle with cheese. Yield: 4 servings.

WESTERN-STYLE BEEF SALAD

6 cups shredded lettuce
½ pound cooked roast beef, cut into thin strips
1 (8-ounce) package Monterey Jack cheese, cut into thin strips
2 medium tomatoes, cut into wedges
½ cup pitted ripe olives
1 small onion, cut into thin slices and separated into rings
½ cup commercial French salad dressing
1 (8-ounce) carton sour cream
1 teaspoon chili powder
Tortilla chips

Arrange lettuce on a large platter; arrange next 5 ingredients on lettuce. Combine dressing, sour cream, and chili powder in a small bowl; spoon mixture evenly over salad. Serve with tortilla chips. Yield: 4 to 6 servings.

Ethel C. Jernegan
Savannah, Georgia

MARINATED SHRIMP SALAD

6 cups water
1 (3-ounce) package dry shrimp-and-crab boil
1 teaspoon salt
2 pounds unpeeled medium-size fresh shrimp
1 cucumber
1 small onion, cut into thin slices and separated into rings
2 shallots, finely chopped
1 sweet red pepper, coarsely chopped
¼ cup chopped fresh parsley
Dressing
Mixed baby lettuces
2 avocados, peeled and sliced

Combine first 3 ingredients in a large Dutch oven; bring to a boil, and cook 5 minutes. Add shrimp; cook 3 to 5 minutes or until shrimp turn pink. Drain well; rinse with cold water. Peel and devein shrimp; chill.

Peel cucumber, and cut in half lengthwise. Scoop out seeds with a spoon; cut cucumber into ¼-inch slices. Combine shrimp, cucumber, and next 4 ingredients in a bowl. Add Dressing, tossing well; cover and refrigerate 8 hours. Drain salad; spoon onto a lettuce-lined plate. Top with avocado slices. Yield: 4 to 6 servings.

Dressing

½ cup olive oil
½ cup white wine vinegar
2 tablespoons lemon juice
1 tablespoon Worcestershire sauce
½ teaspoon salt
¼ teaspoon dry mustard
¼ teaspoon pepper
½ teaspoon hot sauce

Combine all ingredients in a jar; cover tightly, and shake vigorously. Yield: about 1¼ cups.

Go For The Bold!

In these appetizers, cooks across the South have adopted the bold flavors and varied textures that characterize the Southwest's spicy heritage. A sampling yields a menu as diverse as the ethnic groups who have settled in the region.

SOUTH-OF-THE-BORDER QUICHE

½ pound chorizo sausage *
Pastry for 9-inch pie
2 tablespoons cornmeal
¾ cup (3 ounces) shredded Monterey Jack cheese with jalapeño peppers
¾ cup (3 ounces) shredded Cheddar cheese
5 large eggs, lightly beaten
1 (10¾-ounce) can cream of mushroom soup, undiluted

Remove sausage from casing; brown sausage in a skillet, stirring until it crumbles. Drain well.

Line a 9-inch tart pan or a 9-inch deep-dish pieplate with pastry; trim excess pastry around edges. Prick bottom and sides with a fork. Bake at 425° for 8 to 10 minutes or until lightly browned; cool.

Sprinkle cornmeal in bottom of crust; layer sausage and cheeses over cornmeal. Combine eggs and soup; pour mixture over cheese. Bake at 375° for 40 to 45 minutes or until a knife inserted in center comes out clean. Let cool 10 minutes. Cut quiche into wedges. Yield: 16 appetizer servings.

* A mixture of ½ pound bulk pork sausage, 1½ teaspoons chopped fresh cilantro, 1 teaspoon chili powder, and 1 tablespoon white vinegar may be substituted for chorizo sausage.

Joan Powell
Dallas, Texas

SOUTH TEXAS NACHOS

2 cups water
½ pound unpeeled medium-size fresh shrimp
1 (4-ounce) can diced green chiles, drained
1 (2¼-ounce) can sliced pitted ripe olives, drained
1½ cups (6 ounces) shredded Cheddar cheese
½ cup sliced green onions
½ cup mayonnaise or salad dressing
8 dozen round tortilla chips

Bring water to a boil; add shrimp, and cook 3 to 5 minutes or until shrimp turn pink. Drain well; rinse with cold water. Peel and devein shrimp; coarsely chop. Combine shrimp and next 5 ingredients.

Place tortilla chips on baking sheets; top each with 1½ teaspoons shrimp mixture. Bake at 350° for 5 minutes or until cheese melts. Yield: 8 dozen.

Carol Barclay
Portland, Texas

SPICY CORN SALSA

2 (17-ounce) cans whole kernel
  corn, rinsed and drained
1 (4-ounce) can chopped green
  chiles, drained
1 (2¼-ounce) can sliced pitted ripe
  olives, drained
1 large tomato, chopped
2 to 3 jalapeño peppers, seeded and
  finely chopped
3 tablespoons white vinegar
⅓ cup olive oil or vegetable oil
½ teaspoon salt
1 tablespoon chopped fresh cilantro
  (optional)

Combine first 8 ingredients in a non-
aluminum bowl; add cilantro, if desired. Cover and chill at least 2 hours,
stirring often. Serve with tortilla chips
or as a relish with grilled beef or
chicken. Yield: 6 cups.

Joellyn Beckham
Birmingham, Alabama

QUESO BLANCO

1 cup mayonnaise or salad dressing
1½ cups grated Parmesan cheese
1 cup (4 ounces) shredded Monterey
  Jack cheese
2 (4-ounce) cans chopped green
  chiles, undrained
¼ teaspoon ground cumin
⅛ teaspoon chili powder

Combine all ingredients, and spoon
into a 1-quart baking dish. Bake at
350° for 20 minutes. Serve hot with
tortilla chips. Yield: 3 cups.

Mary Bonny
Sterling, Virginia

Six Courses Made Simple

"He'd never fixed anything but a cup
of instant coffee," Joan Yearwood of
Nashville, Tennessee, explains. She
still sounds surprised that her husband, Randall, has just prepared a full
six-course meal.

When Randall retired as an archi-
tect, he started cooking . . . *really*
cooking. His first culinary inspiration
came from New York chefs he noticed
on a television show. He ordered the
cookbook mentioned on the show
and started trying the recipes. Soon,
he was serving elegant dinners to
their friends.

Not all of his meals turn out perfectly, however. "We've had two evenings that weren't fun," Randall
explains in good humor. "I didn't time
things right."

After several successful evenings,
including a black-tie benefit dinner,
Randall knows the secret to great entertaining. "My main tip is this: Don't
get lost in the details. Plan the details,
but keep your mind on the great
evening ahead. If you get uptight, you
lose it, and errors compound on you.
It makes everybody else unhappy if
you are."

SIX COURSES, WITH EASE
FOR SIX

Make-Ahead Tomato-Basil Bisque
Liver Pâté With Madeira Sauce
Endive-Tomato Starburst Salad
Merlot Ice
Chicken Provolone
Rice and Asparagus
Fruit, Cheese, and Nuts

■ A true bisque is strained and free of
chunks. To make your own crème fraîche for the garnish, combine one cup
sour cream and one cup whipping
cream. Wine: champagne.

MAKE-AHEAD
TOMATO-BASIL BISQUE

½ pound leeks, finely chopped
1 stalk celery, chopped
2 to 3 cloves garlic, crushed
2 tablespoons olive oil
2 (14½-ounce) cans Italian-style
  tomatoes, undrained and chopped
12 fresh basil leaves
1 (14½-ounce) can ready-to-serve
  chicken broth
¼ teaspoon salt
¼ teaspoon white pepper
1 cup whipping cream
Crème fraîche (optional)

Cook first 3 ingredients in olive oil in a
Dutch oven over low heat, stirring
constantly, 10 to 12 minutes (do not
brown). Add tomatoes and basil; cook
over medium heat 10 minutes, stirring
occasionally. Add broth, salt, and pepper; bring to a boil. Reduce heat, and
simmer, uncovered, 1 hour, stirring
occasionally. Cool; cover and refrigerate 2 hours.

Position knife blade in food processor bowl, and add tomato mixture.
Process until smooth. (If a finer texture is desired, pour mixture through
a fine wire-mesh strainer into a
2-quart container, discarding pulp.)
Cover mixture and chill at least 1 hour
or overnight.

To serve, stir in whipping cream,
and spoon into individual bowls. If desired, pipe crème fraîche on top in a
design or initial. Yield: 5¼ cups.

■ Randall sometimes uses foie gras (goose liver) for this recipe in place of the liver pâté. To use the foie gras, brown it in a skillet before placing it on the lettuce leaves.

LIVER PÂTÉ WITH MADEIRA SAUCE

1 cup Madeira
¾ cup chicken broth
⅓ cup golden raisins
2 tablespoons capers, drained
Leaf lettuce
3 (⅜-inch-thick) slices commercial liver pâté, cut into halves
Garnish: edible flowers

Bring wine to a boil in a saucepan; cook until reduced to ¼ cup. Remove from heat, and stir in broth, raisins, and capers; let stand 1 hour.

Arrange lettuce on individual salad plates; top each with a slice of pâté and about 2 tablespoons sauce. Garnish, if desired. Serve immediately. Yield: 6 appetizer servings.

■ The flashy presentation for this endive and tomato salad belies its easy preparation.

ENDIVE-TOMATO STARBURST SALAD

8 Roma tomatoes, peeled
6 heads Belgian endive
Tangy Mustard Dressing

Place tomatoes, stem end down, on a cutting board; cut 3 slices around outside of each. Set slices aside. (Reserve tomato centers for another use.)

Remove 4 outer leaves from each head of endive; set remaining endive aside. Arrange outer leaves on individual plates; place tomato slices, cut side down, between endive. Just before serving, thinly slice remaining endive; place in center of each plate. Drizzle with Tangy Mustard Dressing; serve immediately. Yield: 6 servings.

Tangy Mustard Dressing

½ cup olive oil
¼ cup red wine vinegar
¼ cup sherry vinegar
2 tablespoons stone-ground mustard
⅛ teaspoon pepper

Combine all ingredients in a jar; cover dressing tightly, and shake vigorously. Yield: 1 cup.

■ For variety, you can substitute lemon juice, grapefruit juice, or champagne for the Merlot in this refreshing sorbet.

MERLOT ICE

3 cups water
1 cup sugar
1 cup Merlot or other dry red wine
Garnish: rose petals

Combine water and sugar in a saucepan; bring to a boil, stirring until sugar dissolves. Cool. Add wine, and pour into an 8-inch square pan. Freeze until firm, stirring occasionally. Using a melon ball cutter, scoop mixture into small balls, placing 2 to 4 balls in each serving dish. Garnish, if desired. Yield: 4 cups.

■ Serve the chicken breast on the plate with the Rice and Asparagus. Fan the asparagus spears over the top of the rice, and place the chicken breast just below them. Wine: Chardonnay or Pinot Noir.

CHICKEN PROVOLONE

6 chicken breast halves, skinned and boned
6 slices prosciutto
6 ounces provolone cheese, shredded
Garnish: purple basil leaf or fresh rosemary sprig

Grill chicken, without grill lid, over medium coals (300° to 350°) 15 to 20 minutes, turning once.

Place chicken on a baking sheet; top each breast with a prosciutto slice, and sprinkle evenly with cheese. Bake at 300° for 6 minutes. Garnish, if desired. Yield: 6 servings.

Tips from Randall

For this menu, Randall Yearwood starts the tomato bisque and Merlot Ice two days in advance. He prepares the other foods the afternoon before a dinner. He doesn't spend time agonizing over garnishes, and he likes simple ones, such as edible flowers or herbs. He's always on the lookout for new food ideas from restaurants, and then adjusts for his preferences.

Randall keeps his recipes fairly simple. You'll notice that several of them are short on ingredients but long on flavor. He insists on making his own broth, and says cutting fresh herbs with kitchen shears or scissors is more efficient and better for flavor than chopping them.

If you don't want to tackle an entire six-course meal, just pare down the courses. Simply serve the Make-Ahead Tomato-Basil Bisque, Chicken Provolone, and Rice and Asparagus; end the meal with Merlot Ice.

■ Cooking rice in broth adds extra flavor with little effort.

RICE AND ASPARAGUS

1 medium onion, chopped
2 tablespoons olive oil
3½ cups chicken broth, divided
½ teaspoon salt
¼ teaspoon pepper
1 cup long-grain rice, uncooked
1 sprig fresh rosemary
1½ pounds fresh asparagus

Cook onion in oil in a medium saucepan over medium-high heat, stirring constantly, 3 minutes or until tender. Add 2 cups broth, salt, and pepper; bring to a boil. Stir in rice and rosemary. Cover, reduce heat, and simmer 20 minutes or until rice is tender and liquid is absorbed. Remove from heat, and keep warm. Remove and discard rosemary before serving.

Snap off tough ends of asparagus. Remove scales from stalks with a knife or vegetable peeler, if desired. Combine asparagus and remaining broth in a large saucepan; cook, uncovered, over medium-high heat 6 to 8 minutes or until crisp-tender. Drain. Spoon rice onto individual plates; fan asparagus on top. Yield: 6 servings.

■ Randall decided on this as his dessert course after sampling similar pairings while traveling in France. Serve this dessert with Tawny Port (a sweet fortified wine).

FRUIT, CHEESE, AND NUTS

¾ pound seedless red grapes
¾ pound seedless green grapes
6 (½-ounce) slices Stilton cheese
6 (½-ounce) slices goat cheese
1½ cups walnuts

Arrange first 4 ingredients evenly on 6 salad plates; set aside.

Place walnuts in an 8-inch square pan; bake at 350° for 10 to 12 minutes or until lightly toasted. Add ¼ cup walnuts to each plate; serve immediately. Yield: 6 servings.

Homespun Hospitality

Twin chimneys and a wide front porch grace the large, sunshine-colored house just off Main Street in Arkadelphia, Arkansas.

In the 20 years since Snookie and Bill Dixon acquired the house, they have restored the 19th-century structure to its original grandeur. A host of common interests—including cooking and decorating—have earned them a reputation for dispensing a special brand of homespun hospitality.

With their active careers—Snookie serves as Minister of Education for a local church, and Bill is Dean of Students at nearby Ouachita University—the couple often provides a home away from home for students.

HOLIDAY FEAST
FOR EIGHT

Hot Vegetable Juice Appetizer
Spinach Dip
Fresh vegetables
Make-Ahead Cheese Spread
Assorted crackers
Broccoli-Mandarin Salad
Herb-Seasoned Chicken Breasts
Sweet Potato Soufflé
Christmas Corn
Buffet Green Beans
Dinner Rolls
Chocolate Trifle

HOT VEGETABLE JUICE
APPETIZER

1 (46-ounce) can vegetable juice
2 tablespoons lemon juice
2 tablespoons Worcestershire sauce
¼ teaspoon garlic powder
¼ teaspoon onion powder
¼ teaspoon hot sauce

Combine all ingredients in a heavy saucepan; cook over medium heat until thoroughly heated. Serve hot. Yield: 5⅔ cups.

SPINACH DIP

1 (10-ounce) package frozen chopped spinach, thawed
1 (8-ounce) can water chestnuts, drained and chopped
1 (16-ounce) carton nonfat sour cream alternative
½ cup fat-free salad dressing or mayonnaise
1 (0.9-ounce) envelope vegetable soup mix
½ teaspoon lemon juice

Drain spinach on paper towels. Combine spinach and remaining ingredients; cover mixture, and chill. Serve with assorted fresh vegetables. Yield: 3 cups.

MAKE-AHEAD CHEESE
SPREAD

1 (16-ounce) loaf light process cheese spread, cut into small pieces
1 (3-ounce) package cream cheese, softened
1 cup butter or margarine, softened
⅓ cup prepared horseradish
½ teaspoon hot sauce
⅛ to ¼ teaspoon paprika

Combine first 3 ingredients in a heavy saucepan; cook over low heat until cheese mixture melts, stirring occasionally. Spoon into a mixing bowl; add horseradish, hot sauce, and paprika. Beat at medium speed with an electric mixer until smooth and creamy (about 3 minutes). Spoon into an airtight container; refrigerate up to 3 weeks. Yield: 3½ cups.

BROCCOLI-MANDARIN SALAD

1 large egg
1 egg yolk
½ cup sugar
1½ teaspoons cornstarch
1 teaspoon dry mustard
¼ cup tarragon wine vinegar
¼ cup water
½ cup mayonnaise
3 tablespoons butter or margarine, softened
4 cups fresh broccoli flowerets
2 cups sliced fresh mushrooms
1 small purple onion, sliced
1 (11-ounce) can mandarin oranges, drained
6 slices bacon, cooked and crumbled
½ cup raisins
½ cup slivered almonds, toasted

Combine first 5 ingredients in a non-aluminum saucepan; gradually add vinegar and water, stirring constantly with a wire whisk. Cook over medium heat, stirring constantly, 5 minutes or until mixture thickens. Remove from heat; stir in mayonnaise and butter. Cover dressing, and chill.

Combine broccoli and remaining ingredients; add dressing, tossing to coat. Serve immediately. Yield: 8 to 10 servings.

HERB-SEASONED CHICKEN BREASTS

8 skinned and boned chicken breast halves
1½ cups herb-seasoned stuffing mix
1 tablespoon butter or margarine, melted
¼ cup orange juice
Hot cooked wild rice
Sweet Orange Sauce

Arrange chicken in a lightly greased 13- x 9- x 2-inch baking dish. Sprinkle with stuffing mix; drizzle with butter. Pour orange juice over chicken; cover and bake at 350° for 1 hour. Serve over wild rice with Sweet Orange Sauce. Yield: 8 servings.

Sweet Orange Sauce

1 (6-ounce) can frozen orange juice concentrate, thawed and undiluted
½ cup orange marmalade
2 tablespoons steak sauce

Combine all ingredients in a microwave-safe container. Microwave on HIGH 6 minutes or until hot and bubbly, stirring once. Yield: 1⅓ cups.

SWEET POTATO SOUFFLÉ

2 large sweet potatoes (about 2½ pounds)
1 cup sugar
½ cup evaporated milk
⅓ cup butter or margarine, softened
2 large eggs
1 tablespoon frozen orange juice concentrate, thawed
¼ teaspoon salt
1 cup firmly packed brown sugar
1 cup chopped pecans
⅓ cup all-purpose flour
⅓ cup butter or margarine, melted

Cook sweet potatoes in boiling water to cover 30 minutes or until tender. Let cool to touch; peel and mash potatoes. Combine potatoes and next 6 ingredients; spoon evenly into two lightly greased 9-inch pieplates. Combine brown sugar, pecans, and flour; sprinkle evenly over potato mixture. Drizzle evenly with ⅓ cup butter. Bake at 350° for 25 to 30 minutes. Yield: 8 servings.

CHRISTMAS CORN

2 (16-ounce) cans whole kernel corn, undrained
1 (4-ounce) jar diced pimiento, drained
1 (4-ounce) can whole mushrooms, drained
1½ teaspoons dried parsley flakes

Combine all ingredients in a large saucepan; cook over medium heat until thoroughly heated. Serve with a slotted spoon. Yield: 8 servings.

BUFFET GREEN BEANS

8 slices bacon, chopped
1 large onion, sliced
½ cup white vinegar
¼ cup sugar
3 (16-ounce) cans whole green beans, drained

Cook bacon and onion in a large skillet over medium heat, stirring often, until bacon is crisp. Remove bacon and onion with a slotted spoon, reserving ¼ cup drippings in skillet; drain bacon and onion on paper towels, and set mixture aside.

Combine vinegar and sugar, and pour into reserved drippings; bring to a boil. Add beans; cook over medium heat until thoroughly heated, stirring occasionally. Spoon into a serving dish; top with bacon and onion. Yield: 8 servings.

Cookware Basics

■ Bent or dented measuring utensils give inaccurate measures. Use only standard measuring cups and spoons that are in good condition.

■ Always try to match pan size with the burner size.

■ Sprinkle burnt pans liberally with baking soda, adding just enough water to moisten. Let stand for several hours, and lift burned portions out of pans.

■ Always turn saucepan and skillet handles toward back of range to prevent accidents.

DINNER ROLLS

½ cup butter or margarine
1 cup water
1 package active dry yeast
½ cup warm water (105° to 115°)
½ cup sugar
¾ teaspoon salt
2 large eggs, lightly beaten
1 cup whole wheat flour
4 cups all-purpose flour
2 tablespoons butter or margarine, melted

Combine ½ cup butter and 1 cup water in a large glass mixing bowl. Microwave at HIGH 2 to 3 minutes; stir until butter melts. Cool mixture to 105° to 115°.

Combine yeast and ½ cup warm water in a 1-cup liquid measuring cup; let stand 5 minutes. Add yeast mixture, sugar, salt, and eggs to butter mixture, stirring well. Gradually stir in whole wheat flour. Stir in enough all-purpose flour to make a soft dough. Cover and refrigerate at least 8 hours.

Turn dough out onto a lightly floured surface, and knead 2 or 3 times. Roll to ¾-inch thickness; cut with a 2-inch round cutter, and place on lightly greased baking sheets. Cover and let rise in a warm place (85°), free from drafts, about 40 minutes or until doubled in bulk. Bake at 350° for 15 minutes or until golden brown. Brush with butter. Yield: about 3 dozen.

Note: Instead of microwaving, you may combine ½ cup butter and 1 cup water in a small saucepan; cook over medium heat until butter melts, stirring occasionally. Cool to 105° to 115°. Pour into a large bowl, and proceed as directed.

CHOCOLATE TRIFLE
(pictured on page 300)

1 (19.8-ounce) package fudge brownie mix
½ cup Kahlúa or other coffee-flavored liqueur *
3 (3.9-ounce) packages chocolate instant pudding mix
1 (12-ounce) container frozen whipped topping, thawed
6 (1.4-ounce) English toffee-flavored candy bars, crushed

Prepare brownie mix, and bake according to package directions in a 13- x 9- x 2-inch pan. Prick top of warm brownies at 1-inch intervals using a fork; drizzle with Kahlúa. Let cool, and crumble.

Prepare pudding mix according to package directions, omitting chilling. Place one-third of crumbled brownies in bottom of a 3-quart trifle dish. Top with one-third each of pudding, whipped topping, and crushed candy bars. Repeat layers twice with remaining ingredients, ending with crushed candy bars. Chill 8 hours. Yield: 16 to 18 servings.

* 4 tablespoons strong brewed coffee and 1 teaspoon sugar may be substituted for Kahlúa.

Chili From The Pantry

Start with a basic chili recipe; then add a few more ingredients to create these exciting variations. Want to add another choice to the menu? Serve any of these chilis on top of cornbread, nachos, baked potatoes, spaghetti noodles, or taco salad. They'd also be good in burritos or tacos. You're likely to have most of the ingredients on hand, so it's easy to turn a chilly night into a *chili* night.

BASIC CHILI

1 pound ground beef
1 medium onion, chopped
½ to 1 cup water
1 (16-ounce) can crushed tomatoes, undrained
1 (15-ounce) can light red kidney beans, undrained
1 (8-ounce) can tomato sauce
1 (6-ounce) can tomato paste
2 to 4 tablespoons chili powder

Cook ground beef and onion in a Dutch oven until meat is browned, stirring until it crumbles; drain. Add ½ cup water and remaining ingredients. Bring to a boil; reduce heat, and simmer, uncovered, stirring occasionally, 10 minutes. (Add additional water, if necessary.) Yield: 7 cups.

Cyndy Hinton
Franklin, Tennessee

BASIC CHILI GOES SOUTHWEST

Basic Chili ingredients (see recipe above)
½ pound bulk hot pork sausage
1 (15-ounce) can black beans, drained and rinsed
1 (8-ounce) can whole kernel corn, drained
1 (4-ounce) can diced green chiles
½ cup water
1 tablespoon cocoa powder
1 teaspoon ground cumin
¼ to ½ teaspoon ground red pepper

Cook sausage with ground beef and onion for Basic Chili, stirring until meat crumbles; drain. Add 1 cup water and remaining ingredients for Basic Chili. Stir in black beans and remaining ingredients. Bring to a boil; reduce heat, and simmer, uncovered, 10 minutes, stirring occasionally. Yield: about 10 cups.

BASIC CHILI EMBELLISHED

Basic Chili (see recipe on page 326)
⅓ to ½ cup beer
1 clove garlic, minced
1 tablespoon dried green pepper
  flakes
1½ teaspoons dehydrated parsley
1 teaspoon Worcestershire sauce
1 bay leaf

Prepare Basic Chili using 1 cup water. Add beer and remaining ingredients. Bring to a boil; reduce heat, and simmer, uncovered, 10 minutes, stirring occasionally. Remove and discard bay leaf. Yield: about 8 cups.

Shopping Smart

■ Update your file of coupons twice a year. Many coupons expire in the summer months and at the end of the year.

■ Plan your menus for the week, but stay flexible enough to substitute good buys when you spot them. By planning ahead, you can use leftovers in another day's meal.

■ Check foods closely as you are shopping to be sure they are not spoiled. Do not buy cans that are leaking, bulging at the ends, or badly dented. Do not select packages with broken seals.

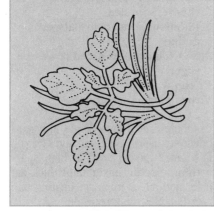

On Your Mark . . .
Get Set . . . Eat

Here are breakfast foods guaranteed to get your family off to a good start. To save preparation time in the morning, measure the wet and dry ingredients separately for the muffins or quick bread the night before. (Store liquid ingredients in the refrigerator.) Even if your family members have time only to grab a napkin-wrapped piece of bread or Country Breakfast Pie and dash out the door, they'll have the ammunition for a great day.

MORNING GLORY MUFFINS

2 cups all-purpose flour
1⅓ cups sugar
2 teaspoons baking soda
1 teaspoon ground cinnamon
½ teaspoon salt
2 cups grated carrot
½ cup raisins
½ cup coconut
½ cup chopped pecans
1 (8-ounce) can crushed pineapple,
  drained
1 cup vegetable oil
3 large eggs, lightly beaten
2 teaspoons vanilla extract

Combine first 5 ingredients in a mixing bowl; stir in carrot and next 4 ingredients. Make a well in center of mixture. Combine vegetable oil and remaining ingredients; add to flour mixture, stirring just until moistened. Place paper baking cups in muffin pans. Spoon batter into paper cups, filling two-thirds full; bake at 350° for 25 minutes or until golden brown. Remove from pans immediately. Yield: 22 muffins.
Sandy Bell
Little Rock, Arkansas

CRUNCHY BREAKFAST BREAD

1¾ cups all-purpose flour
2½ teaspoons baking powder
½ teaspoon salt
1 cup sugar
¾ cup nutlike cereal nuggets
½ cup raisins
2 tablespoons grated orange rind
1 large egg, lightly beaten
1 cup milk
¼ cup vegetable oil

Combine first 7 ingredients in a large bowl; make a well in center of mixture. Combine egg and remaining ingredients; add to dry ingredients, stirring just until moistened. Spoon into a greased and floured 8½- x 4½- x 3-inch loafpan. Bake at 350° for 1 hour or until a wooden pick inserted in center comes out clean. Cool in pan on a wire rack 10 minutes; remove from pan, and cool on wire rack. Yield: 1 loaf.
Jodie McCoy
Tulsa, Oklahoma

COUNTRY BREAKFAST PIE

4 slices bacon, cut in half
2 cups frozen hash brown potatoes
  with onions and green peppers *
6 large eggs, lightly beaten
¼ cup milk
½ teaspoon salt
⅛ teaspoon pepper
1 cup (4 ounces) shredded Cheddar
  cheese

Place bacon in a 9-inch pieplate, and cover with paper towels. Microwave at HIGH 3 to 4 minutes or until bacon is crisp; remove bacon, reserving drippings in pieplate. Crumble bacon, and set aside.

Spread potatoes in pieplate; microwave, uncovered, at HIGH 6 to 7 minutes. Combine eggs and next 3 ingredients; pour over potato mixture. Cover with heavy-duty plastic wrap; fold back a small edge of wrap to allow steam to escape. Microwave potato mixture at HIGH 6 to 7 minutes, giving dish a quarter-turn after 3 minutes. Sprinkle with cheese and crumbled bacon; cover and microwave at HIGH 1 to 2 minutes. Let stand 5 minutes; cut into wedges. Yield: 6 servings.

* 2 cups frozen hash brown potatoes, ¼ cup chopped green pepper, and ¼ cup chopped onion may be substituted.
Diane Logan
Bowie, Texas

Oh! Gratins

By their very name, "au gratin" dishes conjure up warmth. Topped with breadcrumbs mixed with a bit of butter, grated cheese, or cookie crumbs, golden gratins beautifully capture the intense flavors and rich juices beneath their crusts.

Foods cooked gratiné are best served in the dishes in which they were cooked. Use shallow dishes so that each portion gets a share of that crunchy top.

DUAL POTATO GRATIN

Garlic Mashed Potatoes *
3 tablespoons butter or margarine
3 large baking potatoes, peeled and
  cut into ⅛-inch slices
Butter-flavored cooking spray
2 tablespoons grated Parmesan
  cheese
Garnish: fresh chives

Spoon Garlic Mashed Potatoes evenly into four lightly greased, 4-inch gratin dishes, reserving ¾ cup mashed potatoes; set aside.

Melt butter in a large saucepan; add half of sliced potatoes in a single layer, and cook 2 minutes on each side or until tender. Drain on paper towels. Repeat procedure with remaining sliced potatoes.

Layer potato slices around outside edges of mashed potatoes forming circles. Pipe reserved mashed potatoes in center of each dish, or roll mixture into balls, placing in center. Coat gratins with cooking spray, and sprinkle evenly with Parmesan cheese. Bake at 400° for 10 minutes or until lightly browned. Garnish, if desired. Yield: 4 servings.

* 3 cups leftover mashed potatoes may be substituted.

Garlic Mashed Potatoes

3 large baking potatoes
1 teaspoon vegetable oil
2 tablespoons butter or margarine
¼ cup sour cream
2 cloves garlic, crushed
½ teaspoon salt
¼ teaspoon pepper

Scrub potatoes, and rub evenly with vegetable oil. Bake at 400° for 1 hour or until done. Cut potatoes in half; scoop out pulp, discarding skin. Combine potato pulp, butter, and remaining ingredients in a mixing bowl, and beat at medium speed with an electric mixer until fluffy. Yield: 3 cups.
Jean Carriger
Lakeland, Florida

PINEAPPLE GRATIN

1 (20-ounce) can pineapple chunks
  in juice, undrained
⅓ cup sugar
3 tablespoons all-purpose flour
1 cup (4 ounces) shredded sharp
  Cheddar cheese
½ cup round buttery cracker
  crumbs
2 tablespoons butter or margarine,
  melted

Drain pineapple, reserving 3 tablespoons juice. Combine reserved pineapple juice, sugar, and flour; stir in pineapple and cheese. Spoon into a lightly greased, shallow 2-cup baking dish. Combine cracker crumbs and butter; sprinkle evenly over pineapple mixture. Bake at 350° for 25 minutes or until bubbly. Serve as an accompaniment to turkey, ham, pork, or chicken. Yield: 4 servings.
Sheryl Jennings
Uvalde, Texas

PEAR-BLUE CHEESE GRATIN

¼ cup sugar
1 tablespoon all-purpose flour
1 teaspoon cornstarch
1 large egg
1 egg yolk
1 cup half-and-half
2 tablespoons butter or
  margarine
½ teaspoon vanilla extract
2 tablespoons cream cheese,
  softened
3 tablespoons crumbled blue
  cheese, softened
1 (8.5-ounce) can pear halves,
  drained
2 to 3 tablespoons sifted powdered
  sugar
¼ cup walnuts, chopped
¼ cup gingersnap crumbs

Combine first 3 ingredients in a small bowl; set aside. Beat egg and egg yolk in a small mixing bowl at high speed with an electric mixer until thick and pale; add sugar mixture, beating until blended. Set mixture aside.

Heat half-and-half in a small saucepan (do not boil). Gradually stir about one-fourth of hot liquid into egg mixture; add to remaining hot mixture, stirring constantly with a wire whisk. Cook over low heat, stirring constantly, until thickened. Remove from heat; stir 1 minute. Transfer to a bowl; stir in butter and vanilla. Cover and chill at least 2 hours or overnight.

Combine cream cheese and blue cheese; beat at medium speed with an electric mixer until smooth. Fold into chilled mixture; spoon evenly into four lightly greased, 4-inch gratin dishes or 10-ounce custard cups. Place an inverted pear half in each; sprinkle with powdered sugar. Place gratins in a 9-inch square pan; broil 4 to 5 inches from heat (with electric oven door partially opened) for 1½ minutes or until gratins are lightly browned. Combine walnuts and gingersnap crumbs; sprinkle evenly over gratins. Broil 30 to 40 seconds. Serve warm. Yield: 4 servings.

Goodies To Give

Now here's a great holiday gift idea from Holly Fondots of Birmingham, Alabama. Give your friends an assortment of frozen appetizers with directions for baking.

You can prepare them to the point of baking and divide them among zip-top plastic bags. Then slip them into gift bags for several of *your* closest—and busiest—friends.

CHEESE BITES

½ cup butter or margarine, softened
2 cups (8 ounces) shredded Cheddar cheese
1¼ cups all-purpose flour
¼ teaspoon salt
¼ teaspoon ground red pepper

Beat butter at medium speed with an electric mixer until creamy; gradually add cheese, beating well. Combine flour, salt, and red pepper; gradually add to cheese mixture, mixing well. Cover and chill 1 hour. Roll dough into ¾-inch balls; place on baking sheets, and freeze until firm. Place in an airtight container; label and return to freezer.

To serve, place frozen cheese balls on a baking sheet; bake at 400° for 12 to 14 minutes. Yield: 3 dozen.

PHYLLO CHEESE TRIANGLES

2 cups (8 ounces) shredded Muenster cheese
1 cup (4 ounces) shredded extra-sharp Cheddar cheese
¼ cup chopped fresh parsley
1 large egg, lightly beaten
Dash of ground red pepper
½ (16-ounce) package frozen phyllo pastry, thawed
1 cup butter or margarine, melted *

Combine first 5 ingredients; set aside. Unfold phyllo, and cover with a slightly damp towel to prevent pastry from drying out. Place one sheet of phyllo on a flat surface; brush with butter. Cut lengthwise into 1½-inch strips. Place about ½ teaspoon cheese mixture at base of each strip; fold the right bottom corner over to form a triangle. Continue folding back and forth into a triangle, gently pressing corners together.

Repeat procedure with remaining phyllo sheets, butter, and cheese mixture. Brush triangles with remaining butter, and place seam side down on baking sheets; freeze until firm. Place in an airtight container; label and return to freezer.

To serve, place frozen triangles on a baking sheet; bake at 400° for 20 minutes. Yield: 5 dozen.

* Butter-flavored cooking spray may be substituted.

HOT ASPARAGUS ROLLS

50 fresh asparagus spears *
1 (8-ounce) package cream cheese, softened
1 (4-ounce) package crumbled blue cheese
1 large egg
25 slices thin sandwich bread
⅓ cup butter or margarine, melted

Snap off tough ends of asparagus. Remove scales with a vegetable peeler or knife, if desired. Arrange half of asparagus in a steamer basket; place over boiling water. Cover and steam 6 to 8 minutes or until crisp-tender. Remove from steamer, and place in a single layer on paper towels to cool. Repeat procedure.

Combine cheeses and egg in a small mixing bowl; beat at medium speed with an electric mixer until blended.

Trim crust from bread; roll each slice with a rolling pin to flatten. Spread cheese mixture on bread. Place 2 asparagus spears, tips pointing toward opposite edges, on one end of each bread slice; roll up, and secure with two wooden picks. Brush with butter. Place on a lightly greased baking sheet, and freeze until firm.

Place in an airtight container; label and return to freezer. To serve, thaw and cut in half. Place on a baking sheet; bake at 400° for 12 to 15 minutes. Yield: 50 appetizers.

* Canned or frozen asparagus may be substituted; do not steam.

Tip: *To make use of thick asparagus stalks, peel the lower part up to the tender part with a vegetable peeler or knife. Use stalks in casseroles, stews, or pureed for dips or cream soups.*

BACON ROLLS

¼ cup butter or margarine
½ cup water
1½ cups herb-seasoned stuffing mix
¼ pound bulk pork sausage
1 large egg, lightly beaten
12 slices bacon, cut in half

Melt butter in a medium saucepan; add water, and bring to a boil. Remove from heat; stir in stuffing mix. Add sausage and egg; mix well. Cover and chill 30 minutes.

Shape into 24 (2- x ¾-inch) logs; wrap a piece of bacon around each log, and secure with wooden picks. Place on a rack in a broiler pan; bake at 375° for 20 minutes. Turn logs, and bake an additional 15 minutes or until lightly browned. Drain on paper towels, and cool. Place in an airtight container; label and return to freezer.

To serve, thaw rolls; place on a baking sheet, and cover with aluminum foil. Bake at 375° for 10 minutes or until heated. Yield: 2 dozen.

Note: Bacon Rolls may be assembled and frozen unbaked. To serve, thaw and place on a baking sheet; bake at 375° for 30 to 35 minutes or until browned. Drain on paper towels.

Give a Gift from Your Kitchen

■ Line a painted wooden box with tissue paper or fabric before placing the food in it.

■ Be sure to label each food gift, saying what it is and the date it was prepared.

■ Use brightly colored gift bags as containers for wrapped foods.

Ornaments And Hors D'Oeuvres

At Barbara Ritchie's house in Waynesboro, Virginia, there are handmade Christmas ornaments *everywhere!* For 19 years, Barbara has invited friends to an ornament swap and hors d'oeuvre party on the first Friday in December.

"The first year there were just five of us," recalls Barbara, "and I still remember the ornaments we gave each other." This time, 30 women gather in Barbara's cozy home, admiring each other's handiwork and nibbling on a variety of appetizers—Beef Sticks, Kissy Cookies, Dill Dip, and Brown Sugar Shortbread.

Each woman gives a copy of her hors d'oeuvre recipe and a hand-crafted ornament to each guest.

"I leave the party with 30 new ornaments, 30 new recipes, and many new friends," says Barbara Gough of Greenville, Virginia.

"These ornaments are made of ingenuity," says hostess Barbara, showing off a sweet gum ball turned into a golden "star." (See instructions on facing page.)

"Every decoration on my tree represents a memory," Barbara says with a smile. "And our buffet gets bigger every year."

NACHO DIP

1 (8-ounce) package cream cheese
1 (15-ounce) can chili without beans
1 (4-ounce) can chopped green chiles, drained
1½ cups (6 ounces) shredded sharp Cheddar cheese

Place cream cheese in a 9-inch deep-dish pieplate. Microwave at MEDIUM LOW (30% power) 1½ to 2 minutes or until softened; spread evenly over bottom of pieplate. Spread chili evenly over cream cheese; cover tightly with heavy-duty plastic wrap, folding back a small edge to allow steam to escape.

Microwave at HIGH 1 to 2 minutes. Sprinkle with chiles and Cheddar cheese; cover and microwave at HIGH 2 to 3 minutes. Serve dip with tortilla chips. Yield: 3½ cups.

DILL DIP

⅔ cup mayonnaise or salad dressing
⅔ cup sour cream
1 tablespoon dried dillweed
1 tablespoon grated onion
1 teaspoon Beau Monde seasoning

Combine all ingredients. Serve immediately, or cover and refrigerate up to 2 days. Serve in hollowed cabbage or bowl with assorted fresh vegetables. Yield: 1⅓ cups.

Note: If Beau Monde seasoning is not available at a grocery or specialty store in your area, combine 1½ teaspoons ground celery seeds, ¾ teaspoon onion powder, and ¾ teaspoon salt. Use 1 teaspoon in dip, and store remaining mixture in an airtight container. Yield: 1 tablespoon.

BEEF STICKS

5 pounds ground beef
1 pound bulk pork sausage
3 tablespoons meat-cure mix
2½ teaspoons coarsely ground
 pepper
2½ teaspoons garlic powder
2½ teaspoons mustard seeds
2½ teaspoons hickory-flavored
 liquid smoke
Garnish: fresh parsley sprigs

Combine first 7 ingredients; cover and refrigerate 8 hours. Divide mixture into 8 portions, and shape each portion into an 8-inch log. Place logs on a wire rack; place rack in a shallow baking pan. Bake at 225° for 6 hours, turning occasionally. Drain on paper towels; cool. Wrap individually, and refrigerate up to 3 weeks or freeze up to 2 months. Slice and serve with commercial onion mustard and party pumpernickel bread slices. Garnish, if desired. Yield: 8 (8-inch) logs.

Note: For meat-cure mix, we used Morton's Tender Quick.

JEZEBEL SAUCE

½ cup prepared horseradish
1 cup pineapple preserves
1 cup apple jelly
2 tablespoons dry mustard
Garnishes: lemon rind curls, fresh
 parsley sprigs

Drain horseradish well by pressing between layers of paper towels. Combine horseradish and next 3 ingredients; cover and refrigerate at least 2 hours. Store in refrigerator. Serve over cream cheese with crackers. Garnish, if desired. Yield: 2¼ cups.

KISSY COOKIES

1 (20-ounce) package refrigerated,
 sliceable sugar cookie dough
52 milk chocolate kisses,
 unwrapped

Cut cookie dough into 13 even slices; cut each slice into quarters. Place paper baking cups into miniature (1¾-inch) muffin pans. Place 1 dough quarter into each cup. Bake at 375° for 8 minutes or until lightly browned. (Do not overbake.) Remove from oven, and immediately press a chocolate kiss into center of each cookie. Let cool in pan. Store in airtight containers. Yield: 52 cookies.

BROWN SUGAR SHORTBREAD

1 cup butter or margarine, softened
¾ cup firmly packed dark brown
 sugar
2 cups all-purpose flour
2 egg whites, divided
Red paste food coloring
Green paste food coloring

Beat butter at medium speed with an electric mixer until creamy; gradually add brown sugar, beating until light and fluffy. Stir in flour. (Dough will be stiff.) Firmly press dough into a lightly greased and floured 9-inch cookie mold or cakepan. Bake at 300° for 1 hour to 1 hour and 5 minutes. Invert shortbread onto a cookie sheet.

Combine 1 egg white and red food coloring in a small bowl. Combine remaining egg white and green food coloring in another small bowl. Using a small, clean paintbrush, paint design onto hot shortbread as desired. Return to oven, and bake an additional 5 minutes. Cool. Cut into wedges. Yield: 1 (9-inch) cookie.

WINE PUNCH

1 (3-liter) bottle rosé, chilled
1 (12-ounce) can frozen lemonade
 concentrate, thawed and
 undiluted
1 (2-liter) bottle lemon-lime
 carbonated beverage, chilled

Combine all ingredients, and serve immediately. Yield: 5½ quarts.

Starburst Ornament

Materials:
Sweet gum balls
All-purpose white glue
**Wooden picks (square or
 round)**
Gold metallic spray paint
Gold spray glitter
Gold narrow, flat braid
Hot-glue gun

Collect sweet gum balls from sweet gum tree after they are fully dry and have fallen to the ground. Select large balls with firm points. Remove stems from balls.

 Place a drop of all-purpose white glue into an opening of each ball. Push a wooden pick firmly into glue. Work around entire ball, gluing a wooden pick in approximately every other hole so that the ornament looks symmetrical. (Use approximately 25 wooden picks per ball.) Let balls dry for 24 hours.

 Spray entire ball with gold metallic spray paint. Use two coats for good coverage, letting balls dry between coats. Let dry, and spray painted balls with gold glitter (found in most crafts stores).

 Cut 6-inch lengths of gold narrow, flat braid for hangers. After ball is completely dry, place a dab of hot glue where the stem was attached to ball. Double braid to form a loop, and attach by pushing cut ends into hot glue using wooden pick until loop seems to hold. Let balls dry.

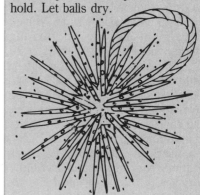

Very Merry Cranberries

Too often the sparkling little cranberry appears as a canned condiment—a round, jellied slice brightening the holiday plate.

But these winning recipes turn the cranberry into a well-rounded ingredient. Its tangy flavor perfectly enhances Oven-Barbecued Cranberry Chicken. And in our Cranberry Salsa recipe, the shiny, scarlet berry takes a sassy, contemporary twist.

More than half of the fresh cranberry crop comes to market during November and December. Consider freezing a supply of fresh cranberries for use throughout the year to add ruby richness to dressings, pies, quick breads, and relishes.

OVEN-BARBECUED CRANBERRY CHICKEN

1 (2½- to 3-pound) broiler-fryer, cut up and skinned
¼ cup vegetable oil
¼ teaspoon salt
¼ teaspoon pepper
½ cup chopped onion
¼ cup chopped celery
1 cup whole-berry cranberry sauce
½ cup catsup
1 tablespoon brown sugar
2 tablespoons lemon juice
1 tablespoon Worcestershire sauce
1 tablespoon prepared mustard
1 tablespoon red wine vinegar

Cook chicken in a large skillet in hot oil over medium-high heat until lightly browned on all sides. Drain on paper towels, discarding oil. Arrange chicken in a lightly greased 11- x 7- x 1½-inch baking dish; sprinkle with salt and pepper. Cook onion and celery in skillet over medium heat until tender, stirring often. Stir in cranberry sauce and remaining ingredients. Bring to a boil; remove from heat, and spoon over chicken. Bake at 325° for 1 hour, basting every 15 minutes. Yield: 4 servings.
Mildred T. Hurst
Mathews, Virginia

CRANBERRY SALSA WITH SWEET POTATO CHIPS

1 orange, unpeeled, quartered, and seeded
2 cups fresh or frozen cranberries, thawed
⅔ cup sugar
⅛ teaspoon salt
½ medium-size green pepper, chopped
1 to 2 jalapeño peppers, seeded and finely chopped
3 tablespoons chopped fresh cilantro
¼ cup chopped pecans, toasted
Sweet Potato Chips

Position knife blade in food processor bowl; add orange quarters. Process until coarsely chopped, stopping once to scrape down sides.

Add cranberries, sugar, and salt; pulse 2 or 3 times or until cranberries are coarsely chopped. Transfer mixture to a bowl, and stir in green pepper, jalapeño pepper, cilantro, and chopped pecans.

Cover mixture, and chill at least 2 hours. Serve salsa with Sweet Potato Chips or as a spread for turkey sandwiches. Yield: 3 cups.

Sweet Potato Chips

1 (8-ounce) sweet potato, peeled
Vegetable cooking spray
¼ teaspoon salt

Using a very sharp knife or vegetable cutter, slice sweet potato crosswise into ⅛-inch slices; arrange in a single layer on baking sheets coated with cooking spray. Coat sweet potato slices with cooking spray. Bake at 325° for 15 to 25 minutes or until crisp. Remove chips from baking sheet as they begin to brown. Cool. Sprinkle with salt. Store in an airtight container. Yield: 3 dozen.

CRANBERRY-COCONUT COFFEE CAKE

1 (18.25-ounce) package yellow cake mix
1 (3.4-ounce) package vanilla instant pudding mix
5 large eggs
½ cup bourbon
½ cup milk
½ cup vegetable oil
2 cups fresh or frozen cranberries, thawed and chopped
1 cup chopped pecans
1 cup flaked coconut
Sifted powdered sugar

Combine first 6 ingredients in a large mixing bowl; beat at low speed with an electric mixer until smooth. Beat at high speed 3 minutes. Fold in cranberries, pecans, and coconut. Pour mixture into a greased and floured Bundt pan. Bake at 350° for 55 minutes or until a wooden pick inserted in center of cake comes out clean. Cool in pan on a wire rack 10 minutes; remove from pan, and let cool on a wire rack. Sprinkle with powdered sugar. Yield: one 10-inch cake.
Carol Barclay
Portland, Texas

Cool Peppermint Parfait accompanies holiday baking at its best: (from left to right) Coconut Shortbread Cookies, Snowball Surprises, Small Chocolate Sack, Pinwheel Cookies, and Apricot Wonders. (Recipes begin on page 314.)

Above: *Fill your plate with delicious recipes from a festive buffet: (clockwise from top) Ginger-Orange Baked Fruit, Marinated Bean Salad, chilled shrimp, Sweet Potato Angel Biscuits, assorted vegetables, and endive stuffed with Antipasto Dip. (Recipes begin on page 312.)*

Left: *Transform an ordinary buffet into an extraordinary presentation without a lot of time or fuss. Begin with a cake stand atop a slab of marble; pour Blue Cheese Dip into a hollowed cabbage, and place it on the cake stand. Spoon Antipasto Dip into a pepper cup and onto endive leaves. Add Curry-Onion Dip to another pepper cup, and then place them on the slab. Fill in with the stuffed endive leaves and vegetables. Add chilled shrimp near the Curry-Onion Dip just before guests arrive. (Recipes for dips are on page 313.)*

Entertaining for a crowd is easy with make-ahead Marbled Pecan Pound Cake (page 313) and Rum Balls (page 314).

Cake Fit For A King

Imagine biting into a piece of cake and finding a bean or pea. It's not cause for alarm, but cause for celebration—a Twelfth Night celebration. This holiday, 12 days after Christmas, marks the arrival of the Wise Men to the manger. You can celebrate the holiday and create a new tradition by baking your own Twelfth Night Cake.

We updated this old recipe, making it lighter in texture and easier for today's cook. Just before you place the cake in the oven, drop a dried bean in the batter on one side of one cake layer, and a dried pea in the other. When serving the cake, cut it into equal slices, giving pieces from the bean side to your male guests, and from the pea side to female guests.

Following tradition, the man who finds the bean becomes King of the Feast with the privilege of choosing games and songs at your party. The woman with the pea reigns as queen. If you want to carry it further, have the king host next year's Twelfth Night festivities, while the queen prepares the next cake.

TWELFTH NIGHT CAKE

2 cups butter or margarine,
  softened
1 (16-ounce) package brown sugar
8 large eggs
3¼ cups all-purpose flour, divided
1 teaspoon baking soda
2 teaspoons ground mace
1 teaspoon ground cinnamon
2 (2-ounce) packages slivered
  almonds
1 (15-ounce) package raisins
1 (10-ounce) package currants
½ cup chopped candied citron
½ cup chopped candied lemon peel
1 dried bean (optional)
1 dried pea (optional)
1 (12-ounce) can apricot filling
White Buttercream Frosting

Beat butter at medium speed with an electric mixer until creamy; gradually add brown sugar, beating well. Add eggs, one at a time, beating after each addition.

Combine 3 cups flour and next 3 ingredients; gradually add to butter mixture. Mix at low speed just until blended after each addition. Combine remaining ¼ cup flour, almonds, and next 4 ingredients; stir into batter.

Spoon batter into 3 greased and wax paper-lined 9-inch round cakepans. If desired, drop dried bean in batter on one side of a cake layer and a dried pea on opposite side. Bake at 325° for 30 to 35 minutes or until a wooden pick inserted in center comes out clean. Cool in pans on wire racks 10 minutes; remove from pans, and let cool completely on wire racks. Spread apricot filling between cake layers. Spread White Buttercream Frosting on top and sides of cake. Decorate, if desired. Yield: one 3-layer cake.

White Buttercream Frosting

⅔ cup water
¼ cup commercial meringue
  powder
3 (16-ounce) packages powdered
  sugar, sifted
1¼ cups shortening
¾ teaspoon salt
½ teaspoon vanilla extract
¼ teaspoon butter flavoring

Combine water and meringue powder in a large bowl; beat at high speed with a heavy-duty electric mixer until soft peaks form. Add 4 cups powdered sugar, 1 cup at a time, beating at low speed after each addition. Add remaining sugar alternately with shortening, beating after each addition. Stir in salt and flavorings. Yield: 7 cups.

The Plate As Canvas

Chefs have come into their own as artists. And from the looks of things, a few take that title literally—treating the dinner plate like a canvas.

We found four in our recent travels who frame their culinary creations with striking palette-to-palate rim garnishes. The good news? They're much easier than they look. These chefs share the secrets of their masterpieces with you.

Chef Doug Shook

From the Key West, Florida, kitchen at Louie's Backyard (see page 30), Doug Shook enhances the tropical flavors of his recipes with eye-catching garnishes.

"We try not to get too complicated. People should have fun in the kitchen," he says. "It's so pretty just to put a few leaves or sprigs of herbs in a repeating pattern on the rim." He grows a lot of his own herbs; you can buy small bunches of cut ones from the market.

Chef Norman Van Aken

This chef, cookbook author, and consultant confesses to occasionally serving pizza at home—but not without the special touches that he's known for at a Mano's in Miami. He and his family eat it by the glow of candles, not television. And so goes his theory on garnishing: "It makes an everyday meal festive."

When Norman Van Aken serves even a simple dessert, it looks like there's a party on the plate. Armed with a plastic catsup or mustard bottle filled with raspberry sauce, this chef splashes the rim with color.

"I literally decided to paint the plate," says Van Aken. He then sprinkles a "confetti" of minced pansies (or other edible flowers) over the haphazard lines of sauce. Drawing a variety of geometric shapes with savory sauces enhances entrées.

This is so easy, a child could do it. In fact, he encourages it. "Let your kids put dots of catsup on the plate with their fries. It'll build their creative interests."

Chef Emeril Lagasse

Known for his evolution of New Orleans cooking, it's not surprising that Emeril Lagasse reaches for a Creole ingredient in this garnish. Bright-orange Creole seasoning offsets sliced green onions.

"I think it's creative to make the plate pop visually, whether you're eating at home or in a restaurant," he says. "There are simple ways of doing that," he says.

The only tool you need for this technique is your hand. Just reach into a bowl of each ingredient and alternately lay "pinches" of both around the plate. He sometimes uses chives or other chopped herbs and a rainbow of diced sweet peppers.

Look for Creole seasoning at your supermarket, or substitute other dried herbs or spices.

Chef Allen Susser

Desserts at Chef Allen's in Miami can be wild and whimsical. The master at work tints powdered sugar with powdered food coloring; then dusts the plate rim in patches, making a feathery rainbow to showcase his confections. Place a saucer or smaller plate upside down in the center of the dessert plate (to keep color on the rim only), and remove after sprinkling.

Mix the coloring (available at kitchen, crafts, and cake decorating shops) with the sugar by shaking them together in a jar or a coffee cup covered with plastic wrap and secured with a rubberband. For best results, mix in a food processor.

You can achieve a similar effect with ingredients you have on hand—cinnamon and cocoa. "The cinnamon sparkles against the flat color of cocoa," Susser explains. This version would be good for chocolate, nut, or spice desserts while the "rainbow" look would be pretty with white or pastel desserts.

An Apple Treat A Day

Here's the secret to flavorful cooked apples: The cooking time should be short enough for the apples to hold their shape and flavor, but long enough to tenderize them. Times will differ with varieties, but 15 minutes is just about right. Choose apples with firm flesh to make sure they do not collapse when simmered or baked. McIntosh, Rome Beauty, Jonathan, Granny Smith, Winesap, and Golden Delicious apples are good selections with distinctive tastes.

COOKED APPLES

10 cooking apples, peeled and
    sliced (about 4½ pounds)
2 cups sugar
½ cup water
¼ cup frozen orange juice
    concentrate, thawed and
    undiluted
1 tablespoon lemon juice

Combine all ingredients in a 4-quart Dutch oven, and bring to a boil over medium-high heat. Reduce heat and simmer, uncovered, 10 minutes, stirring occasionally. Yield: about 5½ cups.
Mrs. Thomas Byrd
Nashville, Tennessee

PARMESAN PORK CHOPS WITH APPLES

1 large egg, lightly beaten
¼ cup milk
1 cup all-purpose flour
½ cup grated Parmesan cheese
6 (½-inch-thick) boneless pork
    chops
¼ teaspoon salt
¼ teaspoon freshly ground pepper
2 tablespoons olive oil
1 cup Cooked Apples (see recipe)
Ground cinnamon

Combine egg and milk; set aside. Combine flour and Parmesan cheese; set aside. Dip pork chops into egg mixture, and sprinkle evenly with salt and pepper; dredge in flour mixture. Heat oil in a large nonstick skillet over medium-high heat; add pork chops and brown on both sides. Transfer to a lightly greased 13- x 9- x 2-inch baking dish; top with Cooked Apples. Cover with aluminum foil; bake at 350° for 45 minutes. Sprinkle with cinnamon. Yield: 6 servings.

BAKED APPLE TURNOVERS

1 (15-ounce) package refrigerated
    piecrusts
¾ cup Cooked Apples (see recipe)
2 tablespoons sugar
½ teaspoon ground cinnamon

Cut pastry into eight 4½-inch circles. Spoon 1½ tablespoons Cooked Apples on one half of each circle. Moisten edges with water; fold dough over apple mixture, pressing edges to seal.

Crimp edges with a fork. Place on a lightly greased baking sheet, and bake at 425° for 13 to 15 minutes. Combine sugar and cinnamon; sprinkle over turnovers. Yield: 8 turnovers.

APPLE-TOPPED PANCAKES

2 cups milk
3 tablespoons butter or margarine
1 package active dry yeast
¼ cup warm water (105° to 115°)
2 large eggs, lightly beaten
1½ cups all-purpose flour
1 cup cornmeal
¼ teaspoon salt
2 cups Cooked Apples (see recipe)
Cooked crumbled bacon
Shredded sharp Cheddar cheese

Combine milk and butter in a saucepan; cook over medium heat until butter melts. Remove from heat; cool to 105° to 115°. Combine yeast and warm water in a 1-cup liquid measuring cup; let stand 5 minutes. Combine yeast mixture, milk mixture, eggs, and next 3 ingredients in a large bowl. Cover and chill 8 hours. Remove from refrigerator, and stir to blend.

For each pancake, pour ¼ cup batter onto a moderately hot, lightly greased griddle. Turn pancakes when tops are covered with bubbles and edges look cooked. Serve each with 2 tablespoons Cooked Apples; top with crumbled bacon and Cheddar cheese. Yield: 16 pancakes.

Tip: *To loosen bacon slices before cooking, roll a package of bacon into a tube before opening. This will relax the slices and keep them from sticking together.*

Recipes With "A-Peel"

Cake, pudding, and muffins—you'll go bananas for these new recipes.

Bananas are perfect in desserts and quick breads. They add flavor and nutrients, and help keep baked goods moist.

JUMBO BANANA-CHOCOLATE CHIP MUFFINS

1 cup butter or margarine, softened
¾ cup firmly packed brown sugar
3 cups mashed banana (about 6 medium)
½ cup milk
4 large eggs
1 teaspoon vanilla extract
3 cups all-purpose flour
2 teaspoons baking powder
2 teaspoons baking soda
½ teaspoon salt
1 cup chopped pecans
1 cup semisweet chocolate morsels
Additional chocolate morsels, melted (optional)

Beat butter at medium speed with an electric mixer until creamy; gradually add sugar, beating well. Add mashed banana and next 3 ingredients, beating until well blended. Combine flour and next 3 ingredients; add to butter mixture, stirring just until blended. Stir in pecans and 1 cup chocolate morsels. Spoon into greased jumbo (3¼-inch) muffin pans, filling half full. Bake at 375° for 25 minutes or until a wooden pick inserted in center comes out clean. Cool in pans 5 minutes; remove from pans immediately, and let cool completely on a wire rack. Drizzle with melted chocolate morsels, if desired. Yield: 1½ dozen.

Note: To bake muffins in regular (2½-inch) muffin pans, fill each muffin cup with 3 tablespoons batter, and bake at 375° for 15 to 18 minutes. Remove from pans immediately. Yield: 2 dozen.
Beth Donaldson
Northport, Alabama

BANANAS FOSTER CRUNCH CAKE

½ cup butter or margarine, softened
1½ cups sugar
2 large eggs
2 cups mashed banana (about 4 medium)
¼ cup light rum
1 teaspoon vanilla extract
1½ cups all-purpose flour
¾ cup cornmeal
1½ teaspoons baking powder
½ teaspoon baking soda
½ teaspoon salt
½ cup all-purpose flour
⅓ cup chopped pecans
¼ cup firmly packed brown sugar
¼ cup butter or margarine, melted

Beat butter at medium speed with an electric mixer until creamy; gradually add sugar, beating well. Add eggs, one at a time, beating after each addition. Stir in mashed banana, rum, and vanilla. Combine 1½ cups flour and next 4 ingredients; add to butter mixture, mixing until blended. Pour into a greased and floured 10-inch tube pan; set aside.

Combine ½ cup flour and remaining ingredients; sprinkle over batter. Bake at 350° for 55 minutes or until a wooden pick inserted in center of cake comes out clean.

Cool in pan on a wire rack 10 to 15 minutes; remove from pan, and let cool completely on wire rack. Yield: one 10-inch cake.
Mrs. J. David Stearns
Mobile, Alabama

PEANUT BUTTER-BANANA PUDDING

1 cup sugar
3 tablespoons all-purpose flour
⅛ teaspoon salt
2 large eggs, lightly beaten
3 cups milk
1 teaspoon vanilla extract
½ cup creamy peanut butter
1 (12-ounce) package vanilla wafers
6 medium bananas, sliced
1 (8-ounce) container frozen whipped topping, thawed
½ cup unsalted roasted peanuts, chopped

Combine first 3 ingredients in a heavy saucepan; add eggs and milk, mixing well. Cook over low heat, stirring constantly, 25 minutes or until thickened. Remove from heat, and stir in vanilla.

Spread about ½ teaspoon peanut butter between 2 vanilla wafers forming a sandwich; repeat procedure with remaining peanut butter and vanilla wafers. Layer one-third of peanut butter-wafer sandwiches in bottom of a 3-quart bowl; top with one-third of bananas. Pour one-third of custard over bananas. Repeat layers twice. Cover and chill. Spread with whipped topping; sprinkle with peanuts. Yield: 8 to 10 servings.   *Mary Jensen*
Bessemer, Alabama

Banana "A-peel"

■ Ripe bananas can be refrigerated to keep them an additional three to five days. Or peel, mash, and freeze bananas, and store in airtight containers for use in baking.

■ Bananas that have passed their prime are still useful. Remove any brown portions, and puree the rest to make banana cake, banana bread, or banana muffins.

Cheers For The Holidays

The cheer you create for family and friends can be even brighter with our collection of holiday refreshers. Why not begin, or end, a gathering with something to sip?

■ A frozen version of the classic cocktail, this spirited concoction will brighten up the chilliest night. Because the recipe makes a generous amount, it's a great one to mix ahead and have waiting in the freezer when friends drop in.

OLD-FASHIONED SLUSH

2 cups boiling water
4 regular-size tea bags
1½ cups sugar
6 cups water
2 cups bourbon
1 (12-ounce) can frozen orange juice concentrate, thawed and undiluted
1 (12-ounce) can frozen lemonade concentrate, thawed and undiluted
8 (12-ounce) bottles lemon-lime carbonated beverage, chilled
Garnishes: lemon rind curls, maraschino cherries

Pour boiling water over tea bags; cover and let stand 5 minutes. Remove tea bags, squeezing gently; add sugar, stirring until it dissolves. Stir in 6 cups water and next 3 ingredients. Cover and freeze at least 8 hours. To serve, spoon ½ cup bourbon mixture into each glass, and add ½ cup carbonated beverage to each. Garnish, if desired. Yield: 6 quarts.   *Janice Risoya*
Louisville, Kentucky

■ Sparkling white grape juice lends a festive tingle to this nonalcoholic brew. An ice ring will keep the bowlful of cheer chilled. To make the ring, fill a small ring mold with additional ginger ale or distilled water, and freeze.

MOCK CHAMPAGNE PUNCH

2 (25.4-ounce) bottles nonalcoholic sparkling white grape juice, chilled
2 (2-liter) bottles ginger ale, chilled
1 (32-ounce) bottle white grape juice, chilled
1 (6-ounce) can frozen lemonade concentrate, thawed and undiluted
Ice ring (optional)

Combine all ingredients in a large punch bowl; add an ice ring, if desired. Yield: 6½ quarts.   *Regina Axtell*
Buffalo, Texas

■ Eggnog is a traditional holiday treat. This new rendition combines the flavors of eggnog and Irish coffee. It would also be a fitting finish for a special holiday meal.

IRISH COFFEE NOG

3 tablespoons instant coffee granules
1 cup Irish whiskey or bourbon
2 quarts eggnog
⅓ cup firmly packed brown sugar
½ teaspoon ground cinnamon
½ teaspoon ground nutmeg
1 quart coffee ice cream

Dissolve coffee in whiskey in a large bowl; add eggnog and next 3 ingredients. Beat at low speed with an electric mixer until smooth. Cover and chill at least 1 hour. Pour into a punch bowl, and top with scoops of ice cream. Yield: 3½ quarts.

Note: For individual servings, pour eggnog mixture into mugs, and top each with a scoop of ice cream.
Beverly Sabathier
Oakton, Virginia

■ Bring the season to life faster than you can say "Ho! Ho! Ho!" All you'll need is this recipe, a handful of ingredients, and a blender.

BLENDER EGGNOG

1½ cups egg substitute
1⅓ cups whipping cream
¼ cup sugar
¼ cup spiced rum
Ice cubes
Grated nutmeg

Combine first 4 ingredients in container of an electric blender; process 5 seconds. Add enough ice to bring mixture to 2½-cup level; process until smooth, stopping once to scrape down sides. Sprinkle each serving with nutmeg, and serve immediately. Yield: 2½ cups.
Judi Grigoraci
Charleston, West Virginia

■ If hot cocoa is your favorite winter warm-up, you'll want to try this jazzy version. A microwave oven makes preparation fast and easy. If a more potent cup is your pleasure, just add a generous splash of coffee-flavored liqueur.

MEXICAN MOCHA

3 cups milk
1 (12-ounce) can evaporated milk
⅓ cup chocolate syrup
1 tablespoon instant coffee granules
6 (3-inch) sticks cinnamon
1½ cups frozen whipped topping, thawed

Combine first 4 ingredients in a 2-quart glass measuring cup. Cover tightly with plastic wrap; fold back a small edge of wrap to allow steam to escape. Microwave at MEDIUM (50% power) 4 to 8 minutes or until steaming, stirring once. To serve, pour into six individual mugs; add a cinnamon stick. Top each serving with ¼ cup whipped topping. Yield: 5 cups.
Louise E. Ellis
Talbott, Tennessee

Make A Quick Jelly

The flavor of sangría is easy to preserve, and a jar of this jelly makes a quick appetizer when spread on a round of Brie cheese. Stirring in liquid pectin quickly gels the ingredients. Remember these tips when preparing the jelly: Do not double the recipe, and a *full rolling boil* is one that doesn't stop when stirred.

You can make the jelly in less than 30 minutes and store jars in the refrigerator. For longer storage, place filled jars on a rack in a large pot of boiling water; return water to a full rolling boil, and process for 5 minutes. Remove from water, cool, and store in a cool, dry place up to one year.

SANGRÍA JELLY

3 cups sugar
1½ cups Burgundy or other dry red wine
1 tablespoon grated orange rind
¼ cup orange juice
2 teaspoons Cointreau or other orange-flavored liqueur
1 (3-ounce) package liquid pectin

Combine first 5 ingredients in a large Dutch oven; bring to a full rolling boil. Boil 1 to 2 minutes, stirring often. Remove from heat.

Stir in pectin, and skim off foam with a metal spoon.

Quickly pour jelly into hot sterilized jars, filling to ¼ inch from top; wipe jar rims. Cover at once with metal lids, and screw on bands.

Process in boiling water bath 5 minutes; or let cool, and store in the refrigerator up to three months. Yield: 4 half pints.

Share The Season's Spirit

We've created two terrific packaging ideas for your special homemade goodies. And if you need some suggestions on what to put in these clever containers, don't forget our cookie recipes in "Sweet Dreams" beginning on page 314.

Gifts of the Magi. *To make cookie purses, cut an 18-inch circle of heavy tapestry fabric. Glue braid onto edges with a hot-glue gun. Pack cookies in zip-top plastic bags, and place in center of fabric circle. Gather fabric into pouch shape, and tie with tassel and ornament.*

Bucketful of Stars. *Enamel sand buckets purchased from a variety store and lined with a bandana are great for children. After the cookies are gone, the children can use the bucket to collect seashells and other treasures.*

Glossary

à la King—Food prepared in a creamy white sauce containing mushrooms and sweet red and/or green peppers

à la Mode—Dessert that is served with ice cream

al Dente—The point in the cooking of pasta at which it is still fairly firm to the tooth; that is, very slightly undercooked

Aspic—A jellied meat juice or a liquid held together with gelatin

au Gratin—Food served crusted with breadcrumbs and/or shredded cheese

au Jus—Meat served in its own juice

Bake—To cook any food in an oven by dry heat

Barbecue—To roast meat slowly over coals on a spit or framework, or to roast in an oven, basting intermittently with a special kind of sauce

Batter—A mixture of flour and liquid that is thin enough to pour

Baste—To spoon pan liquid and/or a sauce over meats while they are roasting to prevent surface from drying

Beat—To mix vigorously with a brisk motion with spoon, fork, egg beater, or electric mixer

Béchamel—A white sauce of butter, flour, cream (not milk), and seasonings

Bisque—A thick, creamy soup usually of shellfish, but sometimes made of pureed vegetables

Blanch—To dip food briefly into boiling water

Blend—To stir two or more ingredients together until well mixed

Blintz—A cooked crêpe stuffed with cheese or other filling

Boil—To cook food in boiling water or liquid that is mostly water (at 212°F. at sea level) in which bubbles constantly rise to the surface and burst

Boiling water-bath canning method—Used for processing acid foods, such as fruit, tomatoes, pickled vegetables, and sauerkraut. These acid foods are canned safely at boiling temperatures in a water-bath canner

Borscht—Soup containing beets and other vegetables; it is usually made with a meat stock base

Bouillabaisse—A highly seasoned fish soup or chowder containing two or more kinds of fish

Bouillon—Clear soup made by boiling meat in water

Bouquet Garni—Herbs tied in cheese-cloth which are cooked in a mixture and removed before serving

Bourguignon—Name applied to dishes containing Burgundy and often braised onions and mushrooms

Braise—To cook slowly with a small amount of liquid in a covered utensil (less tender cuts of meat may be browned slowly first on all sides in a small amount of shortening; then the meat is seasoned, and water is added)

Bread, to—To coat with plain or seasoned crumbs, usually in combination with egg or other binder

Broil—To cook by direct heat, either under the heat of a broiler, over hot coals, or between two hot surfaces

Broth—A thin soup or a liquid in which meat, fish, or vegetables have been cooked

Brown—To cook in a skillet or oven or under a broiler until brown

Bruise—To partially crush an ingredient, such as herbs, to release flavor for seasoning food

Capers—Buds from a Mediterranean plant, usually packed in brine and used as a condiment in dressings or sauces

Caramelize—To cook white sugar in a skillet over medium heat, stirring constantly, until the sugar forms a golden-brown syrup

Casserole—An ovenproof baking dish, usually with a cover; also the food cooked inside it

Charlotte—A molded dessert containing gelatin, usually formed in a glass dish or a pan that is lined with ladyfingers or pieces of cake

Clarified butter—Butter that has been melted and chilled. The solid is then lifted away from the liquid and discarded. Clarification raises the smoke point of butter. Clarified butter will stay fresh in the refrigerator for at least two months

Coat—To cover completely, as in "coat with flour"

Cocktail—An appetizer; either a beverage or a light, highly seasoned food served before a meal

Coddle—To gently poach in barely simmering water

Compote—Mixed fruit, raw or cooked, usually served in "compote" dishes

Condiments—Seasonings that enhance the flavor of foods with which they are served

Consommé—Clear broth that is made from meat

Cool—To let food stand at room temperature until not warm to the touch

Court Bouillon—A highly seasoned broth made with water and meat, fish or vegetables, and seasonings

Cream, whipped—Cream that has been whipped until it is stiff

Crème de Cacao—A chocolate-flavored liqueur

Crème de Café—A coffee-flavored liqueur, sometimes used in cooking

Crêpes—Paper-thin pancakes used for savory or dessert fillings

Crimp—To seal pastry edges together by pinching

Croquette—Minced food, shaped like a ball, patty, cone, or log, bound with a heavy sauce, breaded, and fried

Croutons—Cubes of bread, toasted or fried, served with soups or salads

Cruller—A doughnut of twisted shape; very light in texture

Cube, to—To cut food into cube-shaped pieces; larger than diced

Curaçao—An orange-flavored liqueur

Cut in, to—To incorporate by cutting or chopping motions, as in cutting shortening into flour for pastry

Demitasse—A small cup of coffee served after dinner

Devil, to—To prepare with spicy seasoning or sauce

Dice—To cut into tiny cubes

Dissolve—To mix a dry substance with liquid until the dry substance becomes a part of the solution

Dot—To scatter small bits of an ingredient over another food

Dust—To lightly sprinkle with a dry ingredient, such as flour or sugar

Dredge—To coat with something, usually flour or sugar

En Croûte—Sweet or savory food that is wrapped in pastry and baked

Filé—Powder made of sassafras leaves used to season and thicken foods

Fillet—Boneless piece of meat or fish

Flambé—To flame, using alcohol as the burning agent; flame causes caramelization, enhancing flavor

Flan—In France, a filled pastry; in Spain, a custard

Florentine—A food containing or placed upon spinach

Flour—To coat with flour

Flute—To make a decorative edge on pastry

Fold—To add a whipped ingredient, such as cream or egg white, to another ingredient by very gentle over-and-under movement

Frappé—A drink whipped with ice to make a thick, frosty consistency

Fricassee—A stew, usually of poultry or veal

Fritter—Vegetable or fruit dipped into, or combined with, batter and fried

Fry—To cook in hot shortening

Garnish—A decorative, edible accompaniment to a food or a drink

Glaze (To make a shiny surface)—In meat preparation, a jelled broth applied to meat surface; in breads and pastries, a wash of egg or syrup; for doughnuts and cakes, a sugar preparation for coating

Grate—To obtain small particles of food by rubbing on a grater or shredder

Grill—To broil under or over a source of direct heat

Grits—Coarsely ground dried corn, served boiled, or boiled and then fried

Gumbo—Roux-based soup or stew made with vegetables, meats, and shellfish

Herb—Aromatic plant used for seasoning and garnishing foods

Hollandaise—A sauce made of butter, egg, and lemon juice or vinegar

Jardinière—Vegetables in a savory sauce or soup

Julienne, to—To cut foods into ⅛-inch-thick matchstick pieces

Kahlúa—A coffee-flavored liqueur

Kirsch—A cherry-flavored brandy

Knead—To work a food (usually dough) by hand, using a folding-back and pressing-forward motion

Marinade—A seasoned liquid in which food is soaked

Marinate, to—To soak food in a seasoned liquid

Meringue—Egg white-sugar preparations including pie topping, poached meringue used to top custard, crisp meringue dessert shells, and divinity candy

Mince—To chop into very fine pieces

Mornay—White sauce with egg, cream, and cheese added

Mousse—A molded dish based on meat or sweet whipped cream stiffened with egg white and/or gelatin (if mousse contains ice cream, it is called bombe)

Panbroil—To cook over direct heat in an uncovered skillet containing little or no shortening

Panfry—To cook in an uncovered skillet in small amount of shortening

Parboil—To partially cook in boiling water before final cooking

Pare—To shave away the skins of fruits or vegetables

Pasta—A large family of flour paste products, such as spaghetti, macaroni, and noodles

Pâté (French for paste)—A paste made of liver or meat

Petits Fours—A small cake, which has been frosted and decorated

Pilau or pilaf—A dish of the Middle East consisting of rice and meat or vegetables in a seasoned stock

Pipe—To squeeze a smooth, shapeable mixture through a decorating bag to make decorative shapes

Poach—To cook in liquid held below the boiling point

Preheat—To turn on oven so that desired temperature will be reached before food is inserted for baking

Puree—A thick sauce or paste made by forcing cooked food through a sieve

Reduce—To boil down, evaporating liquid from a cooked dish

Rémoulade—A rich mayonnaise-based sauce containing anchovy paste, capers, herbs, and mustard

Render—To melt fat away from surrounding meat

Rind—Outer shell or peel of fruit

Roast, to—To cook in oven by dry heat (usually refers to meats)

Roux—A mixture of butter and flour used to thicken gravies and sauces; it may be white or brown, if mixture is browned before liquid is added

Sauté—To fry food lightly over fairly high heat in a small amount of fat in a shallow, open pan

Scald—To heat milk just below the boiling point; to dip certain foods into boiling water before freezing them (procedure is also called blanching)

Scallop—A bivalve mollusk of which only the muscle hinge is eaten; to bake food in a sauce topped with crumbs

Score—To cut shallow gashes on surface of food, as in scoring fat on ham before glazing

Sear—To brown surface of meat over high heat to seal in juices

Set—Term used to describe the consistency of gelatin when it has jelled enough to unmold

Shred—Break into thread-like or stringy pieces, usually by rubbing over the surface of a vegetable shredder

Simmer—To cook gently at a temperature below boiling point

Soufflé—A spongy hot dish, made from a sweet or savory mixture (often milk or cheese), lightened by stiffly beaten egg whites or whipped cream

Steam—To cook food with steam either in a pressure cooker, on a platform in a covered pan, or in a special steamer

Steam-pressure canning method—Used for processing low-acid foods, such as meats, fish, poultry, and most vegetables. A temperature higher than a boiling temperature is required to can these foods safely. The food is processed in a steam-pressure canner at 10 pounds' pressure (240°) to ensure that all of the spoilage microorganisms are destroyed

Steep—To let food, such as tea, stand in not quite boiling water until the flavor is extracted

Stew—A mixture of meat or fish and vegetables cooked by simmering in its own juices along with other liquid, such as water and/or wine

Stir-fry—To cook quickly in oil over high heat, using light tossing and stirring motions to preserve shape of food

Stock—The broth in which meat, poultry, fish, or vegetables has been cooked

Syrupy—Thickened to about the consistency of egg white

Toast, to—To brown by direct heat, as in a toaster or under broiler

Torte—A round cake, sometimes made with breadcrumbs instead of flour

Tortilla—A Mexican flat bread made of corn flour or wheat flour

Toss—To mix together with light tossing motions, in order not to bruise delicate food, such as salad greens

Triple Sec—An orange-flavored liqueur

Truss, to—To tie or secure with string or skewers the legs and wings of poultry or game in order to make the bird easier to manage during cooking

Veal—Flesh of milk-fed calf up to 14 weeks of age

Velouté—White sauce made of flour, butter, and a chicken or veal stock, instead of milk

Vinaigrette—A cold sauce of oil and vinegar flavored with parsley, finely chopped onions, and other seasonings; served with cold meats or vegetables or as a dressing with salad greens

Whip—To beat rapidly to increase air and increase volume

Wok—A round bowl-shaped metal cooking utensil of Chinese origin used for stir-frying and steaming (with rack inserted) of various foods

Zest—Gratings of the colored portion of citrus skin

Recipe Title Index

An alphabetical listing of every recipe by exact title
All microwave recipe page numbers are preceded by an "M."

Acorn Squash-Mushroom Puree, 305
Alii Artichoke Casserole, 294
All-American Meat Loaf, 46
Almond-Anise Biscotti, 266
Almond-Fudge Ice Cream, 205
Amaretto-Cinnamon Sauce, 171
Amaretto Crème on Fresh Fruit, 176
Amaretto-Lime Veal, 54
American Steakhouse Beef, 15
Angel Biscuits, 270
Angel Cake Surprise, 86
Angel Hair Pasta with Tomato
   Cream Sauce, 292
Anise-Whole Wheat Bread, 36
Antipasto Dip, 313
Apple-Berry Sparkler, 104
Apple-Carrot Bake, 304
Apple-Cinnamon Sauce, 42
Apple Dip, 205
Apple-Nut Topping, 162
Apple-Topped Pancakes, 339
Apricot-Almond Coffee Cake, 26
Apricot Filling, 316
Apricot-Glazed Ham Slice, 252
Apricot Slush, 205
Apricot Wonders, 316
Artichoke-and-Shrimp Appetizer, 271
Artichoke Bread, 140
Artichoke Dip in a Bread Basket, 13
Asparagus-and-Mushroom Sauté, 115
Asparagus Vinaigrette, 174
Asparagus with Goat Cheese Sauce, 116
Avocado-Fruit Salad with Honey-Yogurt
   Dressing, 172
Avocado-Grapefruit Salad, 282
Avocado Topping, 309

Baby Lettuces with Mustard Vinaigrette, 67
Baby Squash, 118
Backyard Pear Pie, 237
Bacon Rolls, 330
Bacon-Wrapped Crackers, 280
Bagel Croutons, 192
Baked Apple Turnovers, 338
Baked Beans Quintet, 105
Baked Oysters on the Half Shell, 269
Baked Pleated Potatoes, 54
Banana-Coconut Cake, 154
Banana-Nut Muffins, 140
Banana-Pecan Shortcake, 43
Banana-Raspberry Bisque, 161
Bananas Foster Crunch Cake, 339
Banana Smoothie, 95
Barbecued Lamb Shanks, 113
Barbecued Pork Loin Roast, 34
Barbecue Sauce, 129
Basic Chili, 326
Basic Chili Embellished, 327

Basic Chili Goes Southwest, 326
Basic Pralines, 50
Basil Biscuits, 160
Basil-Brown Butter Sauce, 92
Basil-Tomato Sauce, 25, 48, 65
Basil Vinaigrette, 106
Basil Vinegar, 218
Bay Bloodies, 268
Bean-and-Turkey Soup, 319
Beef and Cauliflower over Rice, 94
Beef-and-Shrimp Stir-Fry, 32
Beef Brisket in Beer, 63
Beef Brisket Pot Roast, 20
Beef Pot Pies with Yorkshire Pudding
   Topping, 45
Beef Sticks, 331
Beef Stroganoff, 18
Beef Wellington, 288
Berry Delicious Lemonade, 205
Birdhouse Cake, 284
Bird's Nest Cookies, 284
Biscotti Cioccolata, 268
Biscuit Pudding, 51
Black Beans, 28
Black Bean Salsa, 155
Black Bean Sauce, 59
Black Bean Soup, 231
Black Bean Terrine with Fresh Tomato
   Coulis and Jalapeño Sauce, 230
Blackberry Pudding Tarts, 200
Blackened Duck Breasts, 259
Black-Eyed Pea Pâté, 97
Black-Eyed Peas, 180
Black-Eyed Pea Salsa, 164
Black Widow Snack Cake, 245
Blender Eggnog, 341
BLT Croissants, 158
BLT in Pita Pockets, 158
Blueberries à la Frederick, 123
Blueberry-Banana Pie, 115
Blue Cheese Burger Topping, 218
Blue Cheese Dip, 313
Blue Cheese Meat Loaf Roll, 247
Blue Cheese Stuffed Eggs, 87
Boiled Frosting, 318
Boston Lettuce and Watercress Salad, 65
Bourbon Croutons, 234
Bourbon Mustard, 240
Bourbon-Pecan Bread, 308
Bourbon Pralines, 51
Bourbon Sauce, 51
Bowl-Me-Over Fresh Fruit Tarts, 200
Braised Belgian Endive and Peas, 22
Brandied Chocolate Fondue, 162
Bread Stars, 286
Breakfast Delight, 195
Breakfast Oatmeal Surprise, 178
Brie Wrapped in Phyllo, 173

Broccoli-Mandarin Salad, 325
Broccoli-Parmesan Fettuccine, 55
Broccoli-Stuffed Tomatoes, 216
Broiled Crab Meltaways, 287
Broiled Marinated Potatoes, 54
Broiled Tuna with Rosemary, 127
Brown Sugar Shortbread, 331
Brutti Ma Buoni (Ugly but Good), 267
Buffet Green Beans, 325
Buñuelos, 29
Burgundy-Spiced Orange Slices, 294
Buttercream Frosting, 53, 285
Buttermilk-Pecan Chicken Fingers, 165
Butterscotch Mousse, 254
Buzzard's Nests, 244

Cabbage with Caraway, 181
Caesar Salad with White Beans, 30
Café au Lait Pralines, 51
Caramel Peaches, 134
Caramel-Peanut Apples, M244
Caramel Sauce, 210, 235, 296
Caramel-Toffee Bombe, 214
Caramel Turtle Truffle Tart, M131
Caribbean Shrimp-and-Black Bean Salad, 143
Caribbean Tomato Pasta, 201
Carne Guisada, 68
Carrot Chowchow, 218
Carrot-Pecan Casserole, 44
Carrot-Turnip Sauté, 241
Catfish Louisiana, 291
Cereal Snack Mix, 129
Champagne Oranges, 83
Charleston Press Club Meatballs, 129
Cheese-and-Orange Filling, 159
Cheese Bites, 329
Cheese Sauce, 48
Cheesy Pita Triangles, 70
Cheesy Sausage Muffins, 144
Cherry Bonbon Cookies, 52
Cherry Glaze, 52
Cherry Spread, 309
Chesapeake Nuts, 269
Chicken Almondette Fingers, 12
Chicken-and-Bean Tacos, 293
Chicken-and-Chiles Casserole, 107
Chicken-Cheese Ball, 216
Chicken Chili Bake, 302
Chicken Chimichangas, 68
Chicken Cordon Bleu, 126
Chicken Enchiladas Verde, 274
Chicken Florentine, 107
Chicken Lasagna, 25
Chicken Provolone, 323
Chicken Tostadas, 204
Chicken with Mole Sauce, 34
Chile-Cheese Deviled Eggs, 87
Chili, 89

Chili Cheese Spread, 242
Chilled Avocado Soup, 108
Chilled Sweet Red Pepper Soup, 69
Chinese Peanut Slaw, 212
Chocolate-Almond Cheesecake, 53
Chocolate-Almond Mousse, 316
Chocolate-Almond Petits Fours, 255
Chocolate-Amaretto Cheesecake, 97
Chocolate Chewies, 216
Chocolate Chip Pound Cake, 105
Chocolate Chip-Pudding Cookies, 21
Chocolate-Cinnamon Cake, 154
Chocolate Crinkle Cups, 270
Chocolate-Dipped Horns, 197
Chocolate Frosting, 239
Chocolate Ganache, 255
Chocolate Glaze, 52
Chocolate-Kahlúa Brownies, 99
Chocolate-Mint Pralines, 51
Chocolate-Mint Sauce, 86
Chocolate-Orange Delights, 52
Chocolate-Peanut Butter Pralines, 51
Chocolate-Peanut Crispies, 80
Chocolate-Pecan Chess Pie, 251
Chocolate-Pecan Tart with Caramel Sauce, 296
Chocolate Pots de Crème, 296
Chocolate Pralines, 51
Chocolate Sauce, 276
Chocolate Trifle, 326
Chocolate-Zucchini Bread, 308
Christmas Corn, 325
Christmas Gingerbread Bowl, 266
Christmas Tree Cookies, 286
Christmas Wassail, 295
Chuck Wagon Bean Casserole, 198
Cinnamon Crisps, 106
Cinnamon Ice Cream Sombreros, 276
Cinnamon Pound Cake Croutons, 161
Cinnamon-Raisin Breakfast Biscuits, 159
Cinnamon-Raisin Coffee Cake, 180
Cinnamon-Soy Marinade, 103
Citrus-Cilantro Dressing, 310
Citrus Cooler, 105
Citrus Custard with Fresh Fruit, 70
Citrus Marinade, 103
Citrus Punch, 99
Citrus Slush, 198
Claret Lemonade, 72
Classic Charleston Breakfast Shrimp, 60
Coconut Chicken with Fresh Fruit, 294
Coconut Pie, 115
Coconut-Pineapple Spread, 309
Coconut Shortbread Cookies, 316
Coffee Meringues with Butterscotch
    Mousse, 254
Cooked Apples, 338
Cornbread, 122
Cornbread Croutons, 192
Cornbread Supreme, 67
Corn Casserole, 141
Corn Dog Bites, 79
Corned Beef and Cabbage, 64
Corn-in-the-Shuck Salad, 236
Cornmeal Sombreros, 277
Corn Pancakes, 43
Cottage Cheese Sun-Dried Tomato Dip, 13
Cottage Potatoes, M92
Country Breakfast Pie, M328
Crab Canapés, 130
Crabmeat Karen, 49
Crabmeat Rémoulade, 280

Crab Spread, 167
Crab Tostadas, 203
Cracker Snackers, 197
Cran-Apple Mousse, 255
Cran-Apple Spice Sorbet, 153
Cranberry-Coconut Coffee Cake, 332
Cranberry Hearts, 286
Cranberry Salsa with Sweet Potato Chips, 332
Cream Cheese Frosting, 20
Cream Cheese Mints, 79
Creamed Crabmeat with Artichoke Hearts, 26
Creamed Sugar Snaps and Carrots, 139
Cream of Mustard Green Soup, 280
Cream of Peanut Soup, 288
Cream of Pumpkin Soup, 234
Cream Sauce, 157
Creamy Dressing, 318
Creamy Enchiladas, 174
Creamy Grits, 60
Creamy Ham Dip, 125
Creamy Lemon-Asparagus Salad, 116
Creamy Macaroni and Cheese, 249
Creamy Mustard Sauce, 240
Creamy Relish Spread, 217
Creamy Tomato Sauce, 71
Creamy Turkey Sauté, 19
Crème de Menthe Frosting, 256
Crème de Menthe Squares, 256
Crème Fraîche Sauce, 135
Creole Rub, 101
Crêpes, 123
Crispy Baked Onion Rings, 247
Crispy Coconut-Oatmeal Cookies, 80
Critter Crackers, 193
Croutons and Croûtes, 30
Crunchy Breakfast Bread, 327
Crunchy Snack Mix, 94
Cucumbers and Sour Cream, 203
Cucumber Spread, 158
Curried Apples, 252
Curried BLT Sandwiches, 158
Curried Deviled Eggs, 87
Curried Green Tomatoes, 138
Curried Hazelnuts, 301
Curry-Onion Dip, 313
Curry Spread, 159

Daiquiri Glaze, 83
Daiquiri Pound Cake, 83
Dark Chocolate Sauce, 296
Decorator Frosting, 285
Deli-Style Roast Beef, 15
Destin Lamb Steak, 113
Deviled Nuts, 118
Dill-and-Sour Cream Potato
    Salad, 105
Dill Dip, 330
Dilled Croutons, 161
Dilled Cucumber Salad, 65
Dilled Green Beans, 279
Dill Green Beans, 136
Dinner Rolls, M326
Double-Filled Party Sandwiches, 159
Down-Home Chicken Drummettes, 157
Dried Tomato Vinaigrette, 272
Dual Potato Gratin, 328
Duchess Potatoes, 288

Easy Chicken à la King, 14
Easy Chocolate Chewies, 296
Easy Crab Casserole, 270

Easy Crab Imperial, 128
Easy Lasagna, M24
Easy Oven-Baked French Toast, 195
Easy Oven Roast, 64
Easy Pots de Crème, 281
Easy Pumpkin Swirl, 234
Easy Rump Roast, 217
Easy Stuffed Eggs, 87
Éclair Cake, 42
Eggplant Casserole, 44
Eggs Baked in Mushroom Sauce, 47
Elgin Biscuits, 281
Endive-Tomato Starburst Salad, 323
Endive-Watercress Salad, 22
Endive with Caviar, 118
English Trifle, 289

Family-Style Meat Loaf, 18
Featherbed Eggs, 122
Fiesta Cheesecake, 273
Firestarter Chili, 34
Fishin'-for-Fun Birthday Cake, 194
Florentine Sauce, 48
Four Onion Bake, 304
French Market Beignets, 219
French Onion Soup, 246
Fresh Corn and Bacon Chowder, 203
Fresh Fruit Tartlets, 96
Fresh Fruit with Lemon-Yogurt
    Dressing, 17
Fresh Mozzarella-Tomato-Basil Salad, 131
Fresh Mushroom Salad, 65
Fresh Okra Muffins, 161
Fresh Raspberry Crêpes with Yogurt
    Filling, 123
Fresh Raspberry Sauce, 120
Fresh Salmon with Mushrooms and Green
    Onions, 180
Fresh Spinach Sauté, 55
Fresh Tomato Coulis, 230
Fresh Tomato Sauce over Basil Pasta, 176
Fresh Vegetable Frittata, 140
Fried Chicken Ginger Salad, 290
Fried Marinated Shrimp with Mango Slaw, 31
Fried Okra and Green Tomatoes, 160
Fried Potato Patties, 54
Frozen Fruit Cups, 197
Frozen Peach Torte, 135
Frozen Strawberry Refresher, 213
Frozen Viennese Torte, 171
Frozen Whiskey Sours, 176
Fruit, Cheese, and Nuts, 324
Fruited Cream Cheese Spread, 79
Fruit Salad Dressing, 184
Fruit Salad with Citrus-Cilantro Dressing, 310
Fruit Salad with Honey-Lemon Dressing, 21

Game-Cocktails, 214
Game Hens with Chutney-Mustard Glaze, 66
Garbanzo Dip, 94
Garden Vegetable Spread, 184
Garlic Broccoli, 35
Garlic-Honey Marinade, 102
Garlic Mashed Potatoes, 328
Garlic Pita Wedges, 98
Garlic-Rolled Lamb Roast, 113
Garlic-Thyme Corn Sticks, 242
Gazpacho, 215
German Chocolate Pie, 129
Gingerbirds, 283
Ginger-Cinnamon Carrots, 168

Ginger Dressing, 290
Ginger-Garlic Appetizer Drummettes, 157
Ginger Icebox Cookies, 205
Ginger-Marmalade Glazed Beets, 35
Ginger-Orange Baked Fruit, 313
Ginger-Pear Pie, 48
Glazed Breakfast Fruit Sandwiches, 178
Goat Cheese with Sun-Dried Tomatoes
   and Rosemary, 175
Granola, 197
Grapefruit Freeze, 242
Grapefruit-Mint Sorbet, 153
Greek Salad, 208
Greek-Style Leg of Lamb, 170
Green Beans in Sherried Mushroom Sauce, 206
Green Beans Vinaigrette, 120
Green Beans with Creamy Tarragon
   Dressing, 191
Green Beans with Mushrooms, 89
Green Beans with Roasted Red Peppers and
   Pearl Onions, 260
Green Chile-Cornbread Dressing, 306
Green Decorator Frosting, 286
Green Fruit Salad with Honey-Lime
   Dressing, 71
Green Salad with Marinated Cheese
   Dressing, 206
Green Tomato Sweet Relish, 136
Grillades and Grits, 62
Grilled Basil Chicken, 201
Grilled Florida Tuna, 128
Grilled Hamburgers, 198
Grilled Herbed Salmon Steaks, 176
Grilled Jalapeño Chicken, 213
Grilled Marinated Beef Roast, 141
Grilled Marinated Turkey Steaks, 170
Grilled Pizzas, 178
Grilled Polenta with Black Bean Salsa, 155
Grilled Pork Medaillons, 229
Grilled Sweet Potatoes, 213
Grilled Vegetable Kabobs, 170
Grilled Venison Roast, 278
Grits Dressing, 306
Grittibanz (Swiss Bread Figure), 265
Guilt-Free Cheese Sauce, M95

Ham-and-Black-Eyed Pea Stew, 20
Ham-and-Cheese Bundles, 63
Ham-and-Cheese Muffins, 144
Ham-and-Eggs Crescent Pizza, 47
Ham Appetillas, 63
Hamburgers Mexicali, 217
Ham Devils, 88
Ham-Potato-Pineapple Bake, 302
Havarti-and-Corn-Stuffed Chiles Rellenos
   with Walnut Cream Sauce, M275
Heavenly Eggplant, 293
Herbed Biscuits, 67
Herbed Cheese Omelet, 47
Herbed French Bread, 283
Herbed Lemon Mashed Potatoes, 208
Herbed Rice, 278
Herbed Vinaigrette, 120
Herb Rub, 102
Herbs-and-Cheese Bread, 56
Herb-Seasoned Chicken Breasts, M325
Herb-Sour Cream Stuffed Eggs, 87
Hint-of-Citrus Pastry, 260
Honey-Baked Pears, 47
Honey Butter, 309
Honey-Butternut Stir-Fry, 184

Honeyed Peaches 'n' Cream, 134
Honey-Lime Dressing, 71
Honey-Mustard Marinade, 103
Honey-Mustard Marinated Vegetables, 236
Honey-Oat Bread, 232
Honey-Poppy Seed Sauce, 13
Honey-Walnut Dressing, 107
Honey-Yogurt Dressing, 172
Hope Farm Cheese Wafers, 282
Hopping John with Grilled Pork Medaillons, 229
Horseradish Mustard, 240
Horseradish Sauce, 215
Hot-and-Light Potato Salad, 90
Hot Asparagus Rolls, 329
Hot Crab Dip, 269
Hot Diggity Dog Sauce, 198
Hot Dirty Rice, 219
Hot Dog Pizzas, 78
Hot Dog Supper, 78
Hot Honey Mustard, 240
Hot Indonesian Peanut Sauce, 211
Hot Laced Marshmallow Chocolate, 53
Hot Mustard Sauce, 240
Hot Spicy Pralines, 51
Hot Taco Dip, 238
Hot Tomatoes, 138
Hot Turkey Sandwich, 306
Hot Turnip Green Dip with Jalapeño-Corn
   Muffins, 164
Hot Vegetable Juice Appetizer, 324
Hot Vegetable Punch, 12
Hungarian Stir-Fry, 64

Irish Coffee Nog, 340
Italian Cheese Terrine, 64
Italian Cinnamon Sticks, 204
Italian-Style Braised Fennel, 56
Italian Tomato Pasta, 201

Jack-in-the-Macaroni Bake, 249
Jalapeño-Corn Muffins, 164
Jalapeño Mustard, 240
Jalapeño Sauce, 230
Jelly-Glazed Cornish Hens, 251
Jerk Rub, 101
Jezebel Sauce, 331
Jogger's Sunrise, 213
Julienne Vegetables, 31
Jumbo Banana-Chocolate Chip Muffins, 339
Juniper Sauce, 278

Kissy Cookies, 331
Kiwi-and-Orange Dessert, 295
Kiwifruit-Onion Chutney, 125

Lamb Shish Kabobs, 70
Large Chocolate Sack, 314
Lasagna Supreme, 24
Layered Slaw, 214
Lazy Day Turkey, 93
Lemon Barbecued Chicken, 215
Lemon Cream Puffs, 254
Lemon Cream Sauce, 200
Lemon-Dill Chicken, 19
Lemon-Dill Steamed Carrots, 180
Lemon-Egg Drop Soup, 81
Lemon Fluff Pie, 46
Lemon Frosting, 81
Lemon Glaze, 154, 183
Lemon Meringue Torte with Raspberry
   Sauce, 82

Lemon-Parsley Sauce, 48
Lemon-Pecan Pie, 251
Lemon-Poppy Seed Cake, 154
Lemon Solid, 279
Lemon Sorbet, 153
Lemon Tea Bread, 183
Lemon Veal, 35
Lemon Vegetables, 83
Lemon-Walnut Green Beans, 304
Lemon-Yogurt Dressing, 17
Lentils-and-Rice Casserole, 301
Light and Creamy Coleslaw, 318
Light Chiles Rellenos, 156
Light Cream of Broccoli Soup, 17
Light Eggs Benedict, M68
Lime Hollandaise Sauce, 121
Lime-Rum Cream, 169
Linguine with Red Pepper Sauce, 127
Lion Benedict, 121
Liver Pâté with Madeira Sauce, 323
Luscious Lemon Cake, 81

Macaroni and Blue Cheese, 248
Make-Ahead Cheese Spread, 324
Make-Ahead Tomato-Basil Bisque, 322
Mama Hudson's Chicken Salad, 238
Mango Slaw, 31
Maple Syrup, 16
Marbled Pecan Pound Cake, 313
Margaritas, 273
Marinara on Beds of Spinach and Orzo, 320
Marinated Bean Salad, 312
Marinated Beef Tenderloin, 215
Marinated Black Beans, 131
Marinated Black-Eyed Pea Salad, 190
Marinated Chicken-Raspberry Salad, 190
Marinated Crab-and-Endive Salad, 22
Marinated Dried Cherry Tomatoes, 23
Marinated Fennel Salad, 56
Marinated Potato Slices, 98
Marinated Sauerbraten Beef, 16
Marinated Shrimp Salad, 321
Marinated Tex-Mex Salad, 106
Meatless Enchiladas, 106
Mediterranean Ravioli, 301
Medium White Sauce, 48
Meringue Acorns, 284
Meringues with Cran-Apple Mousse Filling, 254
Merlot Ice, 323
Mexicali Quiche with Avocado Topping, 309
Mexican Chicken Rolls, 242
Mexican Coffee, 310
Mexican Cornbread, 182
Mexican Franks, 78
Mexican Mocha, M341
Mexican Pinto Beans, 69
Mexican Rub, 102
Mexi-Chicken Casserole, 69
Minestrone Stew, 184
Miniature Cornmeal Muffins, 119
Mint Cream Frosting, 216
Minted Lamb Meat Loaf, 248
Mint Julep Brownies, 165
Mixed Fruit Compote, 123
Mixed Fruit Tzimmes with Brisket, 114
Mocha Pralines, 51
Mock Champagne Punch, 340
Mock Guacamole, 36
Mock Hollandaise Sauce, 68
Mogumbo, 32
Mom's Chili, 292

Monster Mash Dip, 244
Morning Glory Muffins, 327
Mother's Brownies, 239
Multi-Fruit Salad, 184
Mussel Soup, 259
Mustard Chicken, 239
Mustard Sauce, 118
Mystery Bars, 239

Nacho Dip, M330
Nautical Knots, 168
Nectar Punch, 283
Nippy Nuts, 301
No-Bake Cherry Confetti Pie, 114

Oatmeal Crispy Ice Cream Sandwiches, 199
Oatmeal-Raisin Cookies, 127
Okra Goulash, 160
Okra Pilaf, 160
Old-Fashioned Chicken and Dumplings, 302
Old-Fashioned Pound Cake, 120
Old-Fashioned Slush, 340
Old-Fashioned Sweet Coleslaw, 128
Old Pecan Street Special, 251
Olive Bread, 78
Onion-Dill Muffins, 144
Onion Focaccia, 77
Onion Jelly, 135
Orange Baskets, 286
Orange Chiffon Dessert, 295
Orange-Curd Dressing, 22
Orange-Ginger Marinated Swordfish
    Steaks, 271
Orange-Grapefruit Salad, 294
Orange-Pecan Chicken Drummettes, 158
Orange-Pecan Pound Cake, 13
Orange Pralines, 51
Orange-Strawberry Salad with Orange-Curd
    Dressing, 22
Oregano-and-Lemon Skillet Potatoes, 54
Oriental Marinade, 102
Oven-Barbecued Cranberry Chicken, 332
Oven-Fried Chicken, 90
Oven-Fried Sweet Potatoes with Chutney, 241
Overnight Refrigerator Pancakes, 196
Oysters Bienville, 257
Oysters Stewed in Cream, 50

Pain-Perdu Po-Boy, 291
Pancake-Sausage Wedges, 196
Pandoro, 267
Panettone, 266
Pan-Fried Grits, 62
Pan-Fried Grits with Creamed Oysters, 62
Parmesan Bread, 231
Parmesan-Crusted Perch, 91
Parmesan Onions, 170
Parmesan Pepper Toss, 208
Parmesan Pizza Crust, 58
Parmesan Pork Chops with Apples, 338
Parmesan Potatoes, M46
Parmesan-Spinach Spread, 55
Parsley-Garlic Rolls, 319
Pasta Primavera, 168
Pastry Shell, 289
Pâté de Champignon, 171
PBJ Shake, 292
Pea-and-Watercress Soup, 162
Peach Crisp, 134
Peach Ice Cream, 135
Peach Jam, 135

Peach Melba Sundae Shake, 134
Peach Sorbet, 153
Peanut Butter-Banana Pudding, 340
Peanut Butter Bars, 166
Peanut Butter Candy, 166
Peanut Butter Cookie Ice Cream
    Sandwiches, 199
Peanut Butter French Toast, 166
Peanut Butter Lovers' Dip, 162
Peanut Butter Pralines, 51
Peanut Butter-Suet Pinecones, 286
Peanut Filling, 211
Peanut Lover's Bread, 211
Peanut Truffle Cookies, 212
Pear-Blue Cheese Gratin, 328
Pear-Cream Cheese Spread, 80
Pear-Macadamia Pie, 260
Pears en Croûte, 210
Peas and Celery, 289
Peas and Pasta, 139
Peking Pork Tenderloin, 173
Pepper Feet, 258
Peppermint Mousse, 315
Peppermint Parfait, 315
Pepper Pecans, 79
Peppery Chicken in Pita, 62
Peppery Green Bean Medley, 181
Pesto-Stuffed Chicken Rolls, 82
Petit Brûlé, 219
Phyllo Cheese Triangles, 329
Picadillo II, 72
Pickled Carrots, 12
Pickled Jalapeño Peppers, 136
Pickled Yellow Squash, 136
Pineapple Angel Food Trifle, 86
Pineapple Gratin, 328
Pineapple Lemonade, 194
Pineapple Tea, 165
Pinecone Cheese Ball, 288
Pink Palace, 293
Pinwheel Cookies, 316
Pita Croutons, 192
Pizza on a Bagel, M94
Poached Eggs, 121
Polenta with Sausage, 32
Popcorn with Pizzazz, 245
Poppy Seed Dressing, 65, 168
Pork Chops with Baked Beans, 18
Potatoes au Gratin, 90, 217
Potatoes Moussaka, 44
Potato Stir-Fry, 240
Pots de Crème au Chocolate, 53
Praline Brownies, 243
Praline Sauce, 214
Pretzel Garlands, 286
Primavera Salad, 140
Puff Pastry Baskets, 177
Pumpkin Cake, 303
Pumpkin-Chocolate Chip Cookies, 235
Pumpkin Gingerbread with Caramel Sauce, 235

Quail Stuffed with Cornbread Dressing, 280
Queso Blanco, 322
Quick-and-Easy Mashed Potatoes, 41
Quick Apple Shortcake, 42
Quick Banana-Pineapple Smoothie, 195
Quick Chicken and Pasta, 14

Raisin-Whole Wheat Bread, 77
Raspberry-Almond Biscuits, 160
Raspberry Brie in Rye, 252

Raspberry-Cherry Cobbler, 230
Raspberry Jellyrolls, M255
Raspberry Mousse in Chocolate
    Crinkle Cups, 270
Raspberry Sauce, 82, 99, 315
Raspberry Wine Vinegar, 191
Red Chili, 108
Red Hot Sauce, 158
Red Pepper Puree, 275
Red Pepper-Tomato Sauce, 59
Red Potato Salad, 119
Red Velvet Cake, 318
Rémoulade Sauce, 280
Rice and Asparagus, 324
Rice with Black-Eyed Peas, 66
Roast Chicken, 14
Roasted Chicken Salad, 14
Roasted Vegetables and Pasta, 184
Ropa Vieja, 28
Roquefort Dressing, 128
Rosemary-Garlic Yams, 174
Rosemary Marinated Lamb Kabobs, 203
Rum Balls, 314
Rum Sundae Sauce, 162

Sabayon, 272
Saffron Rice, 282
Sage-Pecan Cheese Wafers, 12
Salad Composé, 126
Salad Greens with Apple and Brie, 241
Salmon Fillets with Sweet Corn Relish, 119
Salmon on Mixed Greens with Creamy
    Dill Dressing, 143
Samurai 'shrooms, 258
Sangría Jelly, 341
Sauerbraten Sauce, 16
Sausage-Apple Dressing, 305
Sausage Pinwheels, 238
Sautéed Spinach, 250
Savory Corn Sticks, 33
Scallops with Champagne-Saffron Sauce, 177
Seafood Salad Sussex Shores, 98
Seafood Seasoning Rub, 101
Sea Mist, 167
Seasoned Toast Strips, 98
Secret Gazpacho, 161
Sesame-Soy Dressing, 106
Sesame-Wheat Breadsticks, 114
Shallot-Tarragon-Garlic Vinegar, 191
Sherried Cherries, 289
Shortcut Aioli, 157
Shrimp-and-Black Bean Tostadas, 204
Shrimp-and-Cucumber Canapés, 164
Shrimp Creole, 282
Shrimp Mold with Asparagus, 214
Shrimp, Orange, and Olive Salad with
    Sherry Vinaigrette, 177
Shrimp Salad, 238
Shrimp Scampi, 70
Shrimp Spread, 205
Shrimp Stock, 60
Shrimp Topping, 291
Shrimp with Mustard-Vinegar Sauce, 240
Shrimp with Pasta Primavera, 168
Shrimp with Peanut Sauce, 303
Skillet Barbecued Beans, 217
Skinny Ranch Dip, 96
Slaw Silks, 236
Small Chocolate Sack, 314
Smoke-at-Home Brisket, 192
Smoked Quail, 236

Smoked Vegetable Gazpacho, 156
Smoked Vegetable Puree, 156
Smoothest Southern Pound Cake, 237
Snowball Surprises, 315
Snowy Doughnuts, 286
Sotterley Plantation Country Ham, 270
Sour Cream Coffee Cake, 154
Sour Cream Sauce, 162
Sour Cream Yeast Rolls, 232
Southern Chocolate-Mint Brownies, 216
Southern Shellfish Boil, 258
South-of-the-Border Quiche, 321
South Texas Nachos, 321
Southwestern Chicken Drummettes, 158
Southwestern Grits Cakes, 61
Southwestern Marinade, 102
Southwestern Meat Loaf, 248
Southwestern Stuffed Shells, 234
Southwestern Tomato Pasta, 201
Spaghetti-Ham Pie, 19
Spiced Apples, 123
Spiced Bread Pudding, 52
Spicy Corn Salsa, 322
Spicy Guacamole, 218
Spicy Hot Eggplant Casserole, 92
Spicy Mexican Corn, 90
Spicy New York Strip Roast, 131
Spicy Pecans, 279
Spicy Pepper Soup, 98
Spicy Sauce, 52
Spicy Tortilla Soup, 108
Spicy Vegetable Soup, 293
Spider Cookies, M166
Spider Sandwiches, 193
Spinach and Sun-Dried Tomato Salad, 250
Spinach-Artichoke Casserole, 44
Spinach Dip, 324
Spinach Fantastic, 173
Spinach Parmesan, 72
Spinach Pasta Sauce, 71
Spinach-Peanut Pesto and Pasta, 212
Spinach Pesto Sauce, 59
Spinach Salad, 46, 65
Spinach Salad Dressing, 250
Spinach Salad with Dried Tomato
    Vinaigrette, 272
Spinach Strudels, 249
Spinach-Stuffed Tomatoes, 281
Splendid Stalks, 258
"Sponge," 267
Steak Kabobs, 95
Steak Parmesan, 41
Steamed Fennel with Garlic Butter, 56
Steamed Garden Vegetables, 155
Steamed Herbed Vegetables, M303
Stir-Fried Sweet Peppers with Tomatoes, 207
Stormy Petrel Rum Thunder Punch, 269
Strawberries Arnaud, 50
Strawberries Arnaud Sauce, 50
Strawberries Jamaica, 239
Strawberry Crispy Shortcakes, 42
Strawberry Fudge Balls, 80
Strawberry Sorbet, 153
Strawberry-Spinach Salad, 168
Stuffed Green Chiles, 208
Stuffed Mirlitons, 278

Stuffed Mushrooms, 172
Stuffed Rainbow Trout, 121
Sugar Cookie Crust, 131
Sugar-Crusted Apples in Walnut-Phyllo
    Baskets, 210
Sugar Snap Peas with Basil and Lemon, 66
Sugar Snaps and Peppers, 139
Sugar Syrup, 29
Summer Salad, 179
Sunburst Chicken-and-Walnut Salad, 91
Sunny Morning, 295
Sunrise Smoothie, 139
Surf-and-Sand Parfaits, 169
Sweet Bacon Dressing, 108
Sweet Corn Relish, 119
Sweet Deviled Eggs, 88
Sweetheart Cookies, 53
Sweet Onion Butter, 124
Sweet Onion Relish, 124
Sweet Orange Sauce, M325
Sweet Pepper Soup, 277
Sweet Potato Angel Biscuits, 312
Sweet Potato Chips, 332
Sweet Potato Chips with Blue Cheese, 290
Sweet Potato-Currant Slaw, 246
Sweet Potatoes with Peanut Crust, 212
Sweet Potato Rolls, 172
Sweet Potato Soufflé, 325

Tabbouleh, 70
Taco Sauce, 69
Taco-Topped Potatoes, M18
Tangy Mustard Dressing, 323
Tangy Orange Vinaigrette Dressing, 46
Tennessee Bread Pudding with Bourbon
    Sauce, 51
Teriyaki Marinade, 102
Teriyaki Sauce, 258
Terrine of Pork and Veal, 287
Tex-Mex Corn Muffins, 144
Three Cheese Stuffed French Toast, 122
Three Tomato Salsa, 138
Toast Points, 270
Tocino del Cielo, 29
Toffee Crunch Cookies, 80
Tomato-and-Cucumber Summer Salad, 141
Tomato-Curry-Orange Butter, 159
Tomato Gravy, 18
Tortellini with Parsley-Caper Sauce, 175
Tortilla Soup, 197, 274
Trail Jambalaya, 179
Traveling Linguine with Roasted
    Vegetables, 178
Trawler Crab Dip, 238
Tricolor Pasta with Clam Sauce, 272
Triple Mint Ice-Cream Angel Dessert, 86
Tropical Fruit Tray, 72
Tropical Puff Pastry Baskets, 177
Tropical Shake, 212
Tuna-and-Red Pepper Salad, 143
Turkey Caesar Salad, 320
Turkey Cutlets with Tarragon-Mustard
    Sauce, 239
Turkey-in-the-Orange Salad, 21
Turkey Noodle Bake, 243
Turkey Pot Pie, 45

Turkey Treats, 256
Turtle Candies, M41
Turtle Pecan Pie, 250
Twelfth Night Cake, 337

Vanilla Almond Crunch, 243
Vanilla Pralines, 51
Veal Meat Loaf, 292
Veal Terrine with Mustard Sauce, 118
Vegetable Bundles, 181
Vegetable-Chicken Bake with Sweet
    Bacon Dressing, 108
Vegetable Frittata, 183
Vegetable Lasagna, 320
Vegetable Lasagna Casserole, 25
Vegetable-Rice Pancakes, 43
Vegetables and Rice, 91
Vegetable Soup, 157
Vegetable-Topped Orange Roughy, 67
Vegetarian Burritos, 319
Verde Sauce, 275
Versatile Vinaigrette, 140, 141
Vinaigrette Dressing, 41
Virginia Ham Breakfast Soufflé, 121

Wacky Waffles, 195
Walnut-Baked Brie, 241
Walnut Bread, 77
Walnut Coffee Cake, 124
Walnut Cream Sauce, 275
Walnut-Phyllo Baskets, 210
Warm Curry Vinaigrette, 107
Watercress Mayonnaise, 119
Weeknight Enchiladas, 63
Western-Style Beef Salad, 321
Whipped Cream Frosting, 86
White Bean Relish, 229
White Bean Spread, 30
White Buttercream Frosting, 337
White Chocolate Mousse, 315
White Chocolate-Raspberry Swirl Parfait, 315
White Christmas Pie, 289
White Wine Sauce, 49
Whole Grain Pancakes, 123
Whole Wheat-Oat Pancakes, 16
Whole Wheat Pizza Crust, 58
Wild Rice-and-Mushroom Quiches, 237
Wild Rice Salad, 191
Wilted Spinach Salad, 125
Wine Punch, 331
Wine Vinegar Dressing, 126
Witch's Brew, 244
"Working For Peanuts" Pie, 115

Yellow Decorator Frosting, 283
Yellowtail Snapper with Julienne Vegetables, 31
Yia Yia's Holland Rusk Pudding, 124
Yuca Con Mojo, 29

Zesty Broccoli Slaw, 246
Zesty Mushrooms, 218
Zucchini-Carrot Cake, 20
Zucchini-Mushroom Sauce, 71
Zucchini Pancakes, 43
Zucchini Soup with Cilantro, 130
Zucchini-Tomato Skillet, 206

Month-by-Month Index

*An alphabetical listing within the month of every food article and accompanying recipes
All microwave recipe page numbers are preceded by an "M."*

JANUARY

A Cook's Guide To Weeknight Survival, 18
Beef Stroganoff, 18
Creamy Turkey Sauté, 19
Family-Style Meat Loaf, 18
Lemon-Dill Chicken, 19
Pork Chops with Baked Beans, 18
Spaghetti-Ham Pie, 19
Taco-Topped Potatoes, M18
Cream Of Broccoli Soup, 17
Light Cream of Broccoli Soup, 17
Dive Into Belgian Endive, 22
Braised Belgian Endive and Peas, 22
Endive-Watercress Salad, 22
Marinated Crab-and-Endive Salad, 22
Football, Feasting, And Fun, 12
Artichoke Dip in a Bread Basket, 13
Chicken Almondette Fingers, 12
Cottage Cheese Sun-Dried Tomato Dip, 13
Hot Vegetable Punch, 12
Orange-Pecan Pound Cake, 13
Pickled Carrots, 12
Sage-Pecan Cheese Wafers, 12
From Our Kitchen To Yours, 23
Marinated Dried Cherry Tomatoes, 23
Layer On The Flavor, 24
Chicken Lasagna, 25
Easy Lasagna, M24
Lasagna Supreme, 24
Vegetable Lasagna Casserole, 25
Marinade Magic For Beef, 15
American Steakhouse Beef, 15
Deli-Style Roast Beef, 15
Marinated Sauerbraten Beef, 16
Put The Freeze On Winter Blues, 20
Beef Brisket Pot Roast, 20
Chocolate Chip-Pudding Cookies, 21
Ham-and-Black-Eyed Pea Stew, 20
Zucchini-Carrot Cake, 20
Salads Bloom With Citrus, 21
Fruit Salad with Honey-Lemon Dressing, 21
Orange-Strawberry Salad with Orange-Curd Dressing, 22
Turkey-in-the-Orange Salad, 21
Southern Sideboards, **26**
Apricot-Almond Coffee Cake, 26
Creamed Crabmeat with Artichoke Hearts, 26
Start With Chicken, 14
Easy Chicken à la King, 14
Quick Chicken and Pasta, 14
Roast Chicken, 14
Roasted Chicken Salad, 14
Wake Up Breakfast For A Change, 16
Fresh Fruit with Lemon-Yogurt Dressing, 17
Maple Syrup, 16
Whole Wheat-Oat Pancakes, 16

FEBRUARY

Anise Flavors The Bread, 36
Anise-Whole Wheat Bread, 36
A Taste Of Tradition: Arnaud's 75th, 49
Crabmeat Karen, 49
Oysters Stewed in Cream, 50
Strawberries Arnaud, 50
A Touch Of Almond Flavor, 53
Amaretto-Lime Veal, 54
Chocolate-Almond Cheesecake, 53
Hot Laced Marshmallow Chocolate, 53
Pots de Crème au Chocolate, 53
Baked With You In Mind, 52
Cherry Bonbon Cookies, 52
Chocolate-Orange Delights, 52
Sweetheart Cookies, 53
Batter Up For These Vegetable Pancakes, 43
Corn Pancakes, 43
Vegetable-Rice Pancakes, 43
Zucchini Pancakes, 43
Begin With A White Sauce, 48
Medium White Sauce, 48
Cast Iron: Well Seasoned And Timeless, 32
Beef-and-Shrimp Stir-Fry, 32
Mogumbo, 32
Polenta with Sausage, 32
Savory Corn Sticks, 33
Come Home To Breakfast, 47
Eggs Baked in Mushroom Sauce, 47
Ham-and-Eggs Crescent Pizza, 47
Herbed Cheese Omelet, 47
Cook Valentine's Dinner For Dad, 41
Éclair Cake, 42
Quick-and-Easy Mashed Potatoes, 41
Steak Parmesan, 41
Turtle Candies, M41
Vinaigrette Dressing, 41
Dip Into Mock Guacamole, 36
Mock Guacamole, 36
From Our Kitchen To Yours, 33
How to Season and Care for Cast-Iron Cookware, 33
Ginger And Pears—Wow!, 47
Ginger-Pear Pie, 48
Honey-Baked Pears, 47
Homesick? Try A Pot Pie, 45
Beef Pot Pies with Yorkshire Pudding Topping, 45
Turkey Pot Pie, 45
Not Just Plain Pralines, 50
Basic Pralines, 50
Potatoes Are Versatile Vegetables, 54
Baked Pleated Potatoes, 54
Broiled Marinated Potatoes, 54
Fried Potato Patties, 54
Oregano-and-Lemon Skillet Potatoes, 54

Proof Of The Pudding, 51
Biscuit Pudding, 51
Spiced Bread Pudding, 52
Tennessee Bread Pudding with Bourbon Sauce, 51
Serve A Relaxing Dinner For Two, 35
Garlic Broccoli, 35
Ginger-Marmalade Glazed Beets, 35
Lemon Veal, 35
South Florida Sampler, 28
Black Beans, 28
Buñuelos, 29
Caesar Salad with White Beans, 30
Fried Marinated Shrimp with Mango Slaw, 31
Ropa Vieja, 28
Tocino del Cielo, 29
Yellowtail Snapper with Julienne Vegetables, 31
Yuca Con Mojo, 29
Spruced Up Vegetables, 44
Carrot-Pecan Casserole, 44
Eggplant Casserole, 44
Potatoes Moussaka, 44
Spinach-Artichoke Casserole, 44
Surprise Yourself With Fennel, 56
Italian-Style Braised Fennel, 56
Marinated Fennel Salad, 56
Steamed Fennel with Garlic Butter, 56
The Unexpected Side Of Chocolate, 34
Barbecued Pork Loin Roast, 34
Chicken with Mole Sauce, 34
Firestarter Chili, 34
Try Fresh Parmesan Cheese, 55
Broccoli-Parmesan Fettuccine, 55
Fresh Spinach Sauté, 55
Herbs-and-Cheese Bread, 56
Parmesan-Spinach Spread, 55
Weeknight Family Fare, 46
All-American Meat Loaf, 46
Lemon Fluff Pie, 46
Parmesan Potatoes, M46
Spinach Salad, 46
Winter Shortcakes, 42
Banana-Pecan Shortcake, 43
Quick Apple Shortcake, 42
Strawberry Crispy Shortcakes, 42

MARCH

Add A Fresh Accent To Fish, 67
Baby Lettuces with Mustard Vinaigrette, 67
Cornbread Supreme, 67
Vegetable-Topped Orange Roughy, 67
Amazingly Gracious: Luncheon Is Served, 82
Champagne Oranges, 83
Daiquiri Pound Cake, 83
Lemon Vegetables, 83
Pesto-Stuffed Chicken Rolls, 82

MARCH
(continued)

An Italian-Inspired Terrine, 64
Italian Cheese Terrine, 64
Beef Up Weeknight Meals, 63
Beef Brisket in Beer, 63
Corned Beef and Cabbage, 64
Easy Oven Roast, 64
Hungarian Stir-Fry, 64
Cumin: A Worldly Spice Comes Home, 68
Carne Guisada, 68
Chicken Chimichangas, 68
Mexican Pinto Beans, 69
Mexi-Chicken Casserole, 69
Taco Sauce, 69
Easy But Impressive Spring Fare, 70
Cheesy Pita Triangles, 70
Citrus Custard with Fresh Fruit, 70
Lamb Shish Kabobs, 70
Tabbouleh, 70
Eatin' O' The Green, 71
Green Fruit Salad with Honey-Lime Dressing, 71
Exercising The Need To Knead, 77
Olive Bread, 78
Onion Focaccia, 77
Raisin-Whole Wheat Bread, 77
Walnut Bread, 77
From Our Kitchen To Yours, 83
Freezer Guidelines During a Power Outage, 83
Grits To Write Home About, 60
Classic Charleston Breakfast Shrimp, 60
Grillades and Grits, 62
Pan-Fried Grits with Creamed Oysters, 62
Southwestern Grits Cakes, 61
Healthful Dieting With Flair, 66
Game Hens with Chutney-Mustard Glaze, 66
Herbed Biscuits, 67
Rice with Black-Eyed Peas, 66
Sugar Snap Peas with Basil and Lemon, 66
Hot Dog! Supper's Ready, 78
Corn Dog Bites, 79
Hot Dog Pizzas, 78
Hot Dog Supper, 78
Mexican Franks, 78
Keep Your Cool With Pepper Soup, 69
Chilled Sweet Red Pepper Soup, 69
Make Room For Eggs Benedict, 68
Light Eggs Benedict, M68
Mamma Mia! Pizza With Pizzazz, 58
Black Bean Sauce, 59
Parmesan Pizza Crust, 58
Red Pepper-Tomato Sauce, 59
Spinach Pesto Sauce, 59
Whole Wheat Pizza Crust, 58
Pasta Toppers, 70
Creamy Tomato Sauce, 71
Shrimp Scampi, 70
Spinach Pasta Sauce, 71
Zucchini-Mushroom Sauce, 71
So Glad You Dropped By, 79
Cream Cheese Mints, 79
Fruited Cream Cheese Spread, 79
Pear-Cream Cheese Spread, 80
Pepper Pecans, 79
Strawberry Fudge Balls, 80

Sunshine In Every Bite, 81
Lemon-Egg Drop Soup, 81
Lemon Meringue Torte with Raspberry Sauce, 82
Luscious Lemon Cake, 81
The Gasparilla Cookbook, 72
Claret Lemonade, 72
Picadillo II, 72
Spinach Parmesan, 72
Tropical Fruit Tray, 72
Toss A Spring Medley Of Vegetables, 65
Boston Lettuce and Watercress Salad, 65
Dilled Cucumber Salad, 65
Fresh Mushroom Salad, 65
Spinach Salad, 65
Treats That Travel, 80
Chocolate-Peanut Crispies, 80
Crispy Coconut-Oatmeal Cookies, 80
Toffee Crunch Cookies, 80
Wrapping Up A Meal, 62
Ham-and-Cheese Bundles, 63
Ham Appetillas, 63
Peppery Chicken in Pita, 62
Weeknight Enchiladas, 63

APRIL

Angel Food Spectacular, 86
Angel Cake Surprise, 86
Pineapple Angel Food Trifle, 86
Triple Mint Ice-Cream Angel Dessert, 86
Asparagus: A Delicacy Of Spring, 115
Asparagus-and-Mushroom Sauté, 115
Asparagus with Goat Cheese Sauce, 116
Creamy Lemon-Asparagus Salad, 116
Bring On The Breadsticks, 114
Sesame-Wheat Breadsticks, 114
Chicken Dinners With Real Pluck, 107
Chicken-and-Chiles Casserole, 107
Chicken Florentine, 107
Vegetable-Chicken Bake with Sweet Bacon Dressing, 108
Devilish Ideas For All Those Eggs, 87
Blue Cheese Stuffed Eggs, 87
Chile-Cheese Deviled Eggs, 87
Curried Deviled Eggs, 87
Easy Stuffed Eggs, 87
Ham Devils, 88
Herb-Sour Cream Stuffed Eggs, 87
Sweet Deviled Eggs, 88
Easter At The White House, 88
Traditional Easter Fun, 88
Forecast: Expecting Showers, 104
Apple-Berry Sparkler, 104
Baked Beans Quintet, 105
Chocolate Chip Pound Cake, 105
Cinnamon Crisps, 106
Citrus Cooler, 105
Dill-and-Sour Cream Potato Salad, 105
Marinated Tex-Mex Salad, 106
Meatless Enchiladas, 106
From Our Kitchen To Yours, 103
New and Not-so-New Items Used for Grilling, 103
Let Them Eat Pie, 114
Blueberry-Banana Pie, 115
Coconut Pie, 115
No-Bake Cherry Confetti Pie, 114
"Working For Peanuts" Pie, 115

LIGHT & EASY, 89
Beef Up Lean Red Meat, 94
Beef and Cauliflower over Rice, 94
Steak Kabobs, 95
Don't Be Stingy With Starch, 90
Hot-and-Light Potato Salad, 90
Spicy Mexican Corn, 90
Vegetables and Rice, 91
Is It A "Butter" Substitute?, 92
Basil-Brown Butter Sauce, 92
Cottage Potatoes, M92
Lazy Day Turkey, 93
Light Entrées In A Flash, 91
Parmesan-Crusted Perch, 91
Spicy Hot Eggplant Casserole, 92
Sunburst Chicken-and-Walnut Salad, 91
Simple Ways To Lighten Recipes, 100
Tips for Preparing Healthful Foods, 100
Snack Smart, 93
Crunchy Snack Mix, 94
Garbanzo Dip, 94
Pizza on a Bagel, M94
Tour De John, 97
Black-Eyed Pea Pâté, 97
Chocolate-Kahlúa Brownies, 99
Citrus Punch, 99
Garlic Pita Wedges, 98
Raspberry Sauce, 99
Seafood Salad Sussex Shores, 98
Seasoned Toast Strips, 98
Spicy Pepper Soup, 98
Weed Out Menus For Spring, 89
Chili, 89
Green Beans with Mushrooms, 89
Oven-Fried Chicken, 90
Potatoes au Gratin, 90
What's New In The Dairy Case?, 95
Banana Smoothie, 95
Chocolate-Amaretto Cheesecake, 97
Fresh Fruit Tartlets, 96
Guilt-Free Cheese Sauce, M95
Skinny Ranch Dip, 96

Observe Passover With Tzimmes, 114
Mixed Fruit Tzimmes with Brisket, 114
Oil + Vinegar + Flavoring = Vinaigrette, 106
Basil Vinaigrette, 106
Honey-Walnut Dressing, 107
Sesame-Soy Dressing, 106
Warm Curry Vinaigrette, 107
Olé! Soups, 108
Chilled Avocado Soup, 108
Red Chili, 108
Spicy Tortilla Soup, 108
The New Flavors Of Grilling, 101
Cinnamon-Soy Marinade, 103
Citrus Marinade, 103
Creole Rub, 101
Garlic-Honey Marinade, 102
Herb Rub, 102
Honey-Mustard Marinade, 103
Jerk Rub, 101
Mexican Rub, 102
Oriental Marinade, 102
Seafood Seasoning Rub, 101
Southwestern Marinade, 102
Teriyaki Marinade, 102

Well-Seasoned Lamb, 113
  Barbecued Lamb Shanks, 113
  Destin Lamb Steak, 113
  Garlic-Rolled Lamb Roast, 113

MAY

A Little Dab Will Do You, 128
  Easy Crab Imperial, 128
  Grilled Florida Tuna, 128
  Old-Fashioned Sweet Coleslaw, 128
  Roquefort Dressing, 128
Breakfast—B&B Style, 120
  Blueberries à la Frederick, 123
  Featherbed Eggs, 122
  Fresh Raspberry Crêpes with Yogurt
    Filling, 123
  Lion Benedict, 121
  Mixed Fruit Compote, 123
  Spiced Apples, 123
  Stuffed Rainbow Trout, 121
  Three Cheese Stuffed French Toast, 122
  Virginia Ham Breakfast Soufflé, 121
  Walnut Coffee Cake, 124
  Whole Grain Pancakes, 123
  Yia Yia's Holland Rusk Pudding, 124
Classy Cooking Comes Easy, 130
  Caramel Turtle Truffle Tart, M131
  Crab Canapés, 130
  Fresh Mozzarella-Tomato-Basil Salad, 131
  Marinated Black Beans, 131
  Spicy New York Strip Roast, 131
  Zucchini Soup with Cilantro, 130
Cookies For The Health Conscious, 127
  Oatmeal-Raisin Cookies, 127
From Our Kitchen To Yours, 132
  Definitions of Cooking Terms, 132
Help! The Boss Is Coming To
  Dinner, 125
  Broiled Tuna with Rosemary, 127
  Chicken Cordon Bleu, 126
  Creamy Ham Dip, 125
  Linguine with Red Pepper Sauce, 127
  Salad Composé, 126
  Wilted Spinach Salad, 125
Mountain Measures, 129
  Charleston Press Club Meatballs, 129
  German Chocolate Pie, 129
Picnic At Wolf Trap, 118
  Baby Squash, 118
  Deviled Nuts, 118
  Endive with Caviar, 118
  Fresh Raspberry Sauce, 120
  Green Beans Vinaigrette, 120
  Miniature Cornmeal Muffins, 119
  Old-Fashioned Pound Cake, 120
  Red Potato Salad, 119
  Salmon Fillets with Sweet Corn
    Relish, 119
  Veal Terrine with Mustard Sauce, 118
Shake Up A Cereal Snack, 129
  Cereal Snack Mix, 129
Sweet Onions To Cry For, 124
  Kiwifruit-Onion Chutney, 125
  Sweet Onion Butter, 124
  Sweet Onion Relish, 124

JUNE

Add Flavor With Smoked Vegetable
  Puree, 156
  Smoked Vegetable Gazpacho, 156
  Smoked Vegetable Puree, 156

Bake A Batch Of Savory Muffins, 144
  Cheesy Sausage Muffins, 144
  Ham-and-Cheese Muffins, 144
  Onion-Dill Muffins, 144
  Tex-Mex Corn Muffins, 144
Chicken Takes Wing, 157
  Down-Home Chicken Drummettes, 157
  Ginger-Garlic Appetizer
    Drummettes, 157
  Orange-Pecan Chicken Drummettes, 158
  Southwestern Chicken Drummettes, 158
Come To Tea, 159
  Double-Filled Party Sandwiches, 159
Eat The Peas And The Pod, 138
  Creamed Sugar Snaps and Carrots, 139
  Peas and Pasta, 139
  Sugar Snaps and Peppers, 139
Enchant Guests With
  A Meatless Feast, 155
  Grilled Polenta with Black Bean Salsa, 155
  Steamed Garden Vegetables, 155
Enjoy Summer's Easy Rhythm, 139
  Artichoke Bread, 140
  Banana-Nut Muffins, 140
  Corn Casserole, 141
  Fresh Vegetable Frittata, 140
  Grilled Marinated Beef Roast, 141
  Primavera Salad, 140
  Sunrise Smoothie, 139
  Tomato-and-Cucumber Summer
    Salad, 141
From Our Kitchen To Yours, 136
  Steps and Safety Guidelines for
    Canning, 136
Have Your Cake And Eat It, Too, 154
  Banana-Coconut Cake, 154
  Chocolate-Cinnamon Cake, 154
  Lemon-Poppy Seed Cake, 154
  Sour Cream Coffee Cake, 154
Hooked On Salads, 143
  Caribbean Shrimp-and-Black
    Bean Salad, 143
  Salmon on Mixed Greens with Creamy
    Dill Dressing, 143
  Tuna-and-Red Pepper Salad, 143
Made-In-The-Shade Soups, 161
  Banana-Raspberry Bisque, 161
  Pea-and-Watercress Soup, 162
  Secret Gazpacho, 161
Newfangled Biscuits, 159
  Basil Biscuits, 160
  Cinnamon-Raisin Breakfast
    Biscuits, 159
  Raspberry-Almond Biscuits, 160
Preserve Earth's Bounty, 135
  Dill Green Beans, 136
  Green Tomato Sweet Relish, 136
  Onion Jelly, 135
  Peach Jam, 135
  Pickled Jalapeño Peppers, 136
  Pickled Yellow Squash, 136
Shortcuts To Make Summer
  Living Easy, 142
  Ways to Shorten Kitchen Duty During
    Summer Months, 142
Sorbets—Frozen To Perfection, 153
  Cran-Apple Spice Sorbet, 153
  Grapefruit-Mint Sorbet, 153
  Lemon Sorbet, 153
  Peach Sorbet, 153
  Strawberry Sorbet, 153

The Jewels Of Summer, 134
  Caramel Peaches, 134
  Frozen Peach Torte, 135
  Honeyed Peaches 'n' Cream, 134
  Peach Crisp, 134
  Peach Ice Cream, 135
  Peach Melba Sundae Shake, 134
The Mighty Okra, 160
  Fresh Okra Muffins, 161
  Fried Okra and Green Tomatoes, 160
  Okra Goulash, 160
  Okra Pilaf, 160
Toppings For A Sweet Tooth, 162
  Apple-Nut Topping, 162
  Brandied Chocolate Fondue, 162
  Peanut Butter Lovers' Dip, 162
  Rum Sundae Sauce, 162
  Sour Cream Sauce, 162
When The Time Is Ripe For Green
  Tomatoes, 138
  Curried Green Tomatoes, 138
  Hot Tomatoes, 138
  Three Tomato Salsa, 138
With Mexican Appeal, 156
  Light Chiles Rellenos, 156
Worldly BLTs, 158
  BLT Croissants, 158
  BLT in Pita Pockets, 158
  Curried BLT Sandwiches, 158

JULY

A Taste Of Oregon, 179
  Cinnamon-Raisin Coffee Cake, 180
  Fresh Salmon with Mushrooms and
    Green Onions, 180
  Summer Salad, 179
Cornbread With Zip, 182
  Mexican Cornbread, 182
From Our Kitchen To Yours, 182
  Lemon Tea Bread, 183
Fruits And Vegetables—Healthy
  Choices, 183
  Garden Vegetable Spread, 184
  Honey-Butternut Stir-Fry, 184
  Minestrone Stew, 184
  Multi-Fruit Salad, 184
  Roasted Vegetables and Pasta, 184
  Vegetable Frittata, 183
It's A Southern Affair, 164
  Black-Eyed Pea Salsa, 164
  Buttermilk-Pecan Chicken
    Fingers, 165
  Hot Turnip Green Dip with
    Jalapeño-Corn Muffins, 164
  Mint Julep Brownies, 165
  Pineapple Tea, 165
  Shrimp-and-Cucumber Canapés, 164
Lip-Smacking Peanut Butter
  Treats, 166
  Peanut Butter Bars, 166
  Peanut Butter Candy, 166
  Peanut Butter French Toast, 166
  Spider Cookies, M166
Revamping Camping, 178
  Breakfast Oatmeal Surprise, 178
  Glazed Breakfast Fruit
    Sandwiches, 178
  Grilled Pizzas, 178
  Trail Jambalaya, 179
  Traveling Linguine with Roasted
    Vegetables, 178

JULY
(continued)

Scrap The Bacon, Taste The Vegetables, 180
Black-Eyed Peas, 180
Cabbage with Caraway, 181
Lemon-Dill Steamed Carrots, 180
Peppery Green Bean Medley, 181
Vegetable Bundles, 181

SUMMER SUPPERS, 167
Been Around The Block?, 174
Creamy Enchiladas, 174
Tortellini with Parsley-Caper Sauce, 175
Cool Off By The Pool, 176
Scallops with Champagne-Saffron Sauce, 177
Shrimp, Orange, and Olive Salad with Sherry Vinaigrette, 177
Tropical Puff Pastry Baskets, 177
Dinner On The Deck, 170
Frozen Viennese Torte, 171
Greek-Style Leg of Lamb, 170
Grilled Marinated Turkey Steaks, 170
Grilled Vegetable Kabobs, 170
Parmesan Onions, 170
Going The Distance For Friends, 171
Avocado-Fruit Salad with Honey-Yogurt Dressing, 172
Pâté de Champignon, 171
Stuffed Mushrooms, 172
Sweet Potato Rolls, 172
20,000 Ideas Under The Sea, 167
Crab Spread, 167
Ginger-Cinnamon Carrots, 168
Nautical Knots, 168
Sea Mist, 167
Shrimp with Pasta Primavera, 168
Strawberry-Spinach Salad, 168
Surf-and-Sand Parfaits, 169
Ladies' Night Out, 172
Asparagus Vinaigrette, 174
Brie Wrapped in Phyllo, 173
Peking Pork Tenderloin, 173
Rosemary-Garlic Yams, 174
Spinach Fantastic, 173
Southern Hospitality Isn't Gone With The Wind, 175
Amaretto Crème on Fresh Fruit, 176
Fresh Tomato Sauce over Basil Pasta, 176
Frozen Whiskey Sours, 176
Goat Cheese with Sun-Dried Tomatoes and Rosemary, 175
Grilled Herbed Salmon Steaks, 176

AUGUST
FOR THE KIDS, 193
Back-To-School Lunch Bunch, 196
Chocolate-Dipped Horns, 197
Cracker Snackers, 197
Frozen Fruit Cups, 197
Granola, 197
Tortilla Soup, 197

Backyard Bravery, 198
Chuck Wagon Bean Casserole, 198
Citrus Slush, 198
Grilled Hamburgers, 198
Hot Diggity Dog Sauce, 198
Oatmeal Crispy Ice Cream Sandwiches, 199
Peanut Butter Cookie Ice Cream Sandwiches, 199
Pets On Parade, 193
Critter Crackers, 193
Fishin'-for-Fun Birthday Cake, 194
Pineapple Lemonade, 194
Spider Sandwiches, 193
The Bus Stops Here, 195
Breakfast Delight, 195
Easy Oven-Baked French Toast, 195
Overnight Refrigerator Pancakes, 196
Pancake-Sausage Wedges, 196
Quick Banana-Pineapple Smoothie, 195
Wacky Waffles, 195

From Our Kitchen To Yours, 207
Revised Nutrition Labels, 207
Garden-Fresh Fare, 206
Green Beans in Sherried Mushroom Sauce, 206
Green Salad with Marinated Cheese Dressing, 206
Stir-Fried Sweet Peppers with Tomatoes, 207
Zucchini-Tomato Skillet, 206
Have A Tart, 200
Blackberry Pudding Tarts, 200
Bowl-Me-Over Fresh Fruit Tarts, 200
Inventory Your Herb Rack, 201
Cucumbers and Sour Cream, 203
Fresh Corn and Bacon Chowder, 203
Grilled Basil Chicken, 201
Rosemary Marinated Lamb Kabobs, 203
Light Salads Dressed To Chill, 190
Bagel Croutons, 192
Cornbread Croutons, 192
Green Beans with Creamy Tarragon Dressing, 191
Marinated Black-Eyed Pea Salad, 190
Marinated Chicken-Raspberry Salad, 190
Pita Croutons, 192
Raspberry Wine Vinegar, 191
Shallot-Tarragon-Garlic Vinegar, 191
Wild Rice Salad, 191
New Twists On Tostadas, 203
Chicken Tostadas, 204
Crab Tostadas, 203
Shrimp-and-Black Bean Tostadas, 204
Relax—Eat Outdoors, 204
Almond-Fudge Ice Cream, 205
Apple Dip, 205
Apricot Slush, 205
Berry Delicious Lemonade, 205
Ginger Icebox Cookies, 205
Italian Cinnamon Sticks, 204
Shrimp Spread, 205
Restaurant Brisket, Backyard Style, 192
Smoke-at-Home Brisket, 192
Savor Summer's Best Sauces, 201
Caribbean Tomato Pasta, 201
Italian Tomato Pasta, 201
Southwestern Tomato Pasta, 201

You Bring The Entrée, I'll Do The Rest, 208
Greek Salad, 208
Herbed Lemon Mashed Potatoes, 208
Parmesan Pepper Toss, 208
Stuffed Green Chiles, 208

SEPTEMBER
Beans Go Upscale, 229
Black Bean Terrine with Fresh Tomato Coulis and Jalapeño Sauce, 230
Hopping John with Grilled Pork Medaillons, 229
White Bean Relish, 229
Bread Also Rises—In A Machine, 231
Honey-Oat Bread, 232
Parmesan Bread, 231
Sour Cream Yeast Rolls, 232
Cozy Up To Fruit Cobbler, 230
Raspberry-Cherry Cobbler, 230
Drink To Your Health, 212
Frozen Strawberry Refresher, 213
Jogger's Sunrise, 213
Tropical Shake, 212
From Our Kitchen To Yours, 220
Stocking Your Kitchen, 220
Hold The Pickles, Hold The Onion, 217
Blue Cheese Burger Topping, 218
Carrot Chowchow, 218
Creamy Relish Spread, 217
Spicy Guacamole, 218
Zesty Mushrooms, 218
Infuse Vinegar With Basil, 218
Basil Vinegar, 218
Labor Day Easy Grillin', 213
Caramel-Toffee Bombe, 214
Grilled Jalapeño Chicken, 213
Grilled Sweet Potatoes, 213
Layered Slaw, 214
Praise The Peanut, 211
Chinese Peanut Slaw, 212
Hot Indonesian Peanut Sauce, 211
Peanut Lover's Bread, 211
Peanut Truffle Cookies, 212
Spinach-Peanut Pesto and Pasta, 212
Sweet Potatoes with Peanut Crust, 212
Railgating & Tailgating: USC Style, 214
Broccoli-Stuffed Tomatoes, 216
Chocolate Chewies, 216
Game-Cocktails, 214
Gazpacho, 215
Lemon Barbecued Chicken, 215
Marinated Beef Tenderloin, 215
Shrimp Mold with Asparagus, 214
Southern Chocolate-Mint Brownies, 216
Recipes And Reminiscences Of New Orleans, 219
French Market Beignets, 219
Hot Dirty Rice, 219
Petit Brûlé, 219
Seasoning Shortcuts Come In Packets, 216
Chicken-Cheese Ball, 216
Easy Rump Roast, 217
Hamburgers Mexicali, 217
Potatoes au Gratin, 217
Skillet Barbecued Beans, 217
See The Light With Black Beans, 231
Black Bean Soup, 231

The Whole Fruit, 210
  Pears en Croûte, 210
  Sugar-Crusted Apples in Walnut-Phyllo
    Baskets, 210

OCTOBER

A Halloween Party You'll Love
  At First Bite, 244
  Black Widow Snack Cake, 245
  Buzzard's Nests, 244
  Caramel-Peanut Apples, M244
  Monster Mash Dip, 244
  Popcorn with Pizzazz, 245
  Witch's Brew, 244
A New Slant On Slaw, 246
  Sweet Potato-Currant Slaw, 246
  Zesty Broccoli Slaw, 246
A Passion For Pecans, 250
  Chocolate-Pecan Chess Pie, 251
  Lemon-Pecan Pie, 251
  Old Pecan Street Special, 251
  Turtle Pecan Pie, 250
A Plate Tailored For Fall, 241
  Carrot-Turnip Sauté, 241
  Garlic-Thyme Corn Sticks, 242
  Oven-Fried Sweet Potatoes
    with Chutney, 241
  Salad Greens with Apple and Brie, 241
A Victorian Victory Feast, 238
  Hot Taco Dip, 238
  Mama Hudson's Chicken Salad, 238
  Mother's Brownies, 239
  Mystery Bars, 239
  Sausage Pinwheels, 238
  Shrimp Salad, 238
  Strawberries Jamaica, 239
  Trawler Crab Dip, 238
From Our Kitchen To Yours, 235
  Determining Solutions to Failed
    Recipes, 235
Frozen Assets, 242
  Chili Cheese Spread, 242
  Grapefruit Freeze, 242
  Mexican Chicken Rolls, 242
  Praline Brownies, 243
  Turkey Noodle Bake, 243
  Vanilla Almond Crunch, 243
Give Napkins A Ring, 252
  Creative Ideas for Napkin Rings, 252
Indulge In French Onion Soup, 246
  French Onion Soup, 246
Jammin' It Up, 251
  Apricot-Glazed Ham Slice, 252
  Curried Apples, 252
  Jelly-Glazed Cornish Hens, 251
  Raspberry Brie in Rye, 252
Let's Do The Twist: Macaroni,
  That Is, 248
  Creamy Macaroni and Cheese, 249
  Jack-in-the-Macaroni Bake, 249
  Macaroni and Blue Cheese, 248
Mega Meat Loaves, 247
  Blue Cheese Meat Loaf Roll, 247
  Minted Lamb Meat Loaf, 248
  Southwestern Meat Loaf, 248

Recipes That Cut The Mustard, 239
  Bourbon Mustard, 240
  Creamy Mustard Sauce, 240
  Horseradish Mustard, 240
  Hot Honey Mustard, 240
  Hot Mustard Sauce, 240
  Jalapeño Mustard, 240
  Mustard Chicken, 239
  Potato Stir-Fry, 240
  Shrimp with Mustard-Vinegar
    Sauce, 240
  Turkey Cutlets with Tarragon-Mustard
    Sauce, 239
Smoky Mountain Reunion, 236
  Backyard Pear Pie, 237
  Corn-in-the-Shuck Salad, 236
  Honey-Mustard Marinated
    Vegetables, 236
  Smoked Quail, 236
  Smoothest Southern Pound Cake, 237
  Wild Rice-and-Mushroom Quiches, 237
Spinach With A Flourish, 249
  Sautéed Spinach, 250
  Spinach and Sun-Dried Tomato
    Salad, 250
  Spinach Strudels, 249
These Rings Lighten Up, 247
  Crispy Baked Onion Rings, 247
Where's The Pumpkin?, 234
  Cream of Pumpkin Soup, 234
  Easy Pumpkin Swirl, 234
  Pumpkin-Chocolate Chip Cookies, 235
  Pumpkin Gingerbread with
    Caramel Sauce, 235
  Southwestern Stuffed Shells, 234

NOVEMBER

A Taste Of Aloha, 293
  Alii Artichoke Casserole, 294
  Coconut Chicken with Fresh Fruit, 294
  Pink Palace, 293
Basting Instincts, 307
  Step-by-Step Instructions for Roasting
    a Turkey, 307
Buenos Días Brunch, 309
  Fruit Salad with Citrus-Cilantro
    Dressing, 310
  Mexicali Quiche with Avocado
    Topping, 309
  Mexican Coffee, 310
Celebrate Earth's Bounty, 304
  Acorn Squash-Mushroom Puree, 305
  Apple-Carrot Bake, 304
  Four Onion Bake, 304
  Lemon-Walnut Green Beans, 304
Dinners From The Diners, 290
  Catfish Louisiana, 291
  Fried Chicken Ginger Salad, 290
  Mom's Chili, 292
  Pain-Perdu Po-Boy, 291
  PBJ Shake, 292
  Sweet Potato Chips with Blue Cheese, 290
  Veal Meat Loaf, 292
From Our Kitchen To Yours, 306
  How to Carve a Turkey with
    Confidence, 306
Gift Wrap From The Pantry, 291
  Use Dried Fruits, Herbs, and Spices
    to Decorate Packages, 291
Gobblers For Gobbling, 256
  Turkey Treats, 256

HOLIDAY DINNERS, 257
A Foreign Affair, 265
  Almond-Anise Biscotti, 266
  Biscotti Cioccolata, 268
  Brutti Ma Buoni (Ugly but Good), 267
  Christmas Gingerbread Bowl, 266
  Grittibanz (Swiss Bread Figure), 265
  Pandoro, 267
  Panettone, 266
A Plantation Christmas, 277
  Avocado-Grapefruit Salad, 282
  Bacon-Wrapped Crackers, 280
  Crabmeat Rémoulade, 280
  Cream of Mustard Green Soup, 280
  Dilled Green Beans, 279
  Easy Pots de Crème, 281
  Elgin Biscuits, 281
  Grilled Venison Roast, 278
  Herbed French Bread, 283
  Herbed Rice, 278
  Hope Farm Cheese Wafers, 282
  Lemon Solid, 279
  Quail Stuffed with Cornbread
    Dressing, 280
  Shrimp Creole, 282
  Spicy Pecans, 279
  Spinach-Stuffed Tomatoes, 281
  Stuffed Mirlitons, 278
  Sweet Pepper Soup, 277
Bah Humbug—A Crabby
  Christmas!, 268
  Angel Biscuits, 270
  Baked Oysters on the Half Shell, 269
  Bay Bloodies, 268
  Chesapeake Nuts, 269
  Easy Crab Casserole, 270
  Hot Crab Dip, 269
  Raspberry Mousse in Chocolate
    Crinkle Cups, 270
  Sotterley Plantation Country Ham, 270
  Stormy Petrel Rum Thunder Punch, 269
Christmas For The Birds, 283
  Birdhouse Cake, 284
  Bird's Nest Cookies, 284
  Bread Stars, 286
  Christmas Tree Cookies, 286
  Cranberry Hearts, 286
  Gingerbirds, 283
  Meringue Acorns, 284
  Nectar Punch, 283
  Orange Baskets, 286
  Peanut Butter-Suet Pinecones, 286
  Pretzel Garlands, 286
  Snowy Doughnuts, 286
Feliz Navidad, 273
  Chicken Enchiladas Verde, 274
  Cinnamon Ice Cream Sombreros, 276
  Fiesta Cheesecake, 273
  Havarti-and-Corn-Stuffed Chiles
    Rellenos with Walnut Cream
    Sauce, M275
  Margaritas, 273
  Tortilla Soup, 274

Holiday Dinners
(continued)

Old Friends Cheer The New Year, 287
  Beef Wellington, 288
  Broiled Crab Meltaways, 287
  Cream of Peanut Soup, 288
  Duchess Potatoes, 288
  English Trifle, 289
  Peas and Celery, 289
  Pinecone Cheese Ball, 288
  Sherried Cherries, 289
  Terrine of Pork and Veal, 287
  White Christmas Pie, 289
Tropical Holiday Elegance, 271
  Artichoke-and-Shrimp Appetizer, 271
  Orange-Ginger Marinated Swordfish
    Steaks, 271
  Sabayon, 272
  Spinach Salad with Dried Tomato
    Vinaigrette, 272
  Tricolor Pasta with Clam Sauce, 272
Wine & Dine The Wives, 257
  Blackened Duck Breasts, 259
  Green Beans with Roasted Red Peppers
    and Pearl Onions, 260
  Mussel Soup, 259
  Oysters Bienville, 257
  Pear-Macadamia Pie, 260
  Pepper Feet, 258
  Samurai 'shrooms, 258
  Southern Shellfish Boil, 258
  Splendid Stalks, 258

Holiday Nuts, 301
  Curried Hazelnuts, 301
  Nippy Nuts, 301
**Make It Easy; Make A
Casserole**, 301
  Chicken Chili Bake, 302
  Ham-Potato-Pineapple Bake, 302
  Lentils-and-Rice Casserole, 301
  Mediterranean Ravioli, 301
Never Too Much Citrus, 294
  Burgundy-Spiced Orange Slices, 294
  Christmas Wassail, 295
  Kiwi-and-Orange Dessert, 295
  Orange Chiffon Dessert, 295
  Orange-Grapefruit Salad, 294
  Sunny Morning, 295
**Old-Fashioned Chicken And
Dumplings**, 302
  Old-Fashioned Chicken and
    Dumplings, 302
Please Pass The Dressing, 305
  Green Chile-Cornbread
    Dressing, 306
  Grits Dressing, 306
  Sausage-Apple Dressing, 305
Saucy Secrets, 292
  Angel Hair Pasta with Tomato Cream
    Sauce, 292
  Chicken-and-Bean Tacos, 293
  Heavenly Eggplant, 293
  Spicy Vegetable Soup, 293
Simply Chocolate, 296
  Chocolate-Pecan Tart with Caramel
    Sauce, 296
  Chocolate Pots de Crème, 296
  Dark Chocolate Sauce, 296
  Easy Chocolate Chewies, 296

Sweet Little Endings, 254
  Chocolate-Almond Petits Fours, 255
  Coffee Meringues with Butterscotch
    Mousse, 254
  Crème de Menthe Squares, 256
  Lemon Cream Puffs, 254
  Meringues with Cran-Apple
    Mousse Filling, 254
  Raspberry Jellyrolls, M255
Time-Saver Turkey, 306
  Hot Turkey Sandwich, 306
Ward Off Holiday Pounds, 303
  Pumpkin Cake, 303
  Shrimp with Peanut Sauce, 303
  Steamed Herbed Vegetables, M303
Well-Bred Breads, 308
  Bourbon-Pecan Bread, 308
  Cherry Spread, 309
  Chocolate-Zucchini Bread, 308
  Coconut-Pineapple Spread, 309
  Honey Butter, 309

DECEMBER
An Apple Treat A Day, 338
  Apple-Topped Pancakes, 339
  Baked Apple Turnovers, 338
  Cooked Apples, 338
  Parmesan Pork Chops with
    Apples, 338
Cake Fit For A King, 337
  Twelfth Night Cake, 337
Cheers For The Holidays, 340
  Blender Eggnog, 341
  Irish Coffee Nog, 340
  Mexican Mocha, M341
  Mock Champagne Punch, 340
  Old-Fashioned Slush, 340
Chili From The Pantry, 326
  Basic Chili, 326
  Basic Chili Embellished, 327
  Basic Chili Goes Southwest, 326
From Our Kitchen To Yours, 317
  Making an Edible
    Chocolate Sack, 317
Go For The Bold!, 321
  Queso Blanco, 322
  South-of-the-Border Quiche, 321
  South Texas Nachos, 321
  Spicy Corn Salsa, 322
Goodies To Give, 329
  Bacon Rolls, 330
  Cheese Bites, 329
  Hot Asparagus Rolls, 329
  Phyllo Cheese Triangles, 329
Homespun Hospitality, 324
  Broccoli-Mandarin Salad, 325
  Buffet Green Beans, 325
  Chocolate Trifle, 326
  Christmas Corn, 325
  Dinner Rolls, M326
  Herb-Seasoned Chicken
    Breasts, M325
  Hot Vegetable Juice
    Appetizer, 324
  Make-Ahead Cheese Spread, 324
  Spinach Dip, 324
  Sweet Potato Soufflé, 325
Let The Salad Be The Star, 320
  Marinated Shrimp Salad, 321
  Turkey Caesar Salad, 320
  Western-Style Beef Salad, 321

Light Velvet, 318
  Red Velvet Cake, 318
Make A Quick Jelly, 341
  Sangría Jelly, 341
Menu Fit For A Crowd, 312
  Antipasto Dip, 313
  Blue Cheese Dip, 313
  Curry-Onion Dip, 313
  Ginger-Orange Baked Fruit, 313
  Marbled Pecan Pound Cake, 313
  Marinated Bean Salad, 312
  Rum Balls, 314
  Sweet Potato Angel Biscuits, 312
Oh! Gratins, 328
  Dual Potato Gratin, 328
  Pear-Blue Cheese Gratin, 328
  Pineapple Gratin, 328
On Your Mark . . . Get Set . . . Eat, 327
  Country Breakfast Pie, M328
  Crunchy Breakfast Bread, 327
  Morning Glory Muffins, 327
Ornaments And Hors D'Oeuvres, 330
  Beef Sticks, 331
  Brown Sugar Shortbread, 331
  Dill Dip, 330
  Jezebel Sauce, 331
  Kissy Cookies, 331
  Nacho Dip, M330
  Wine Punch, 331
Recipes With "A-Peel," 339
  Bananas Foster Crunch Cake, 339
  Jumbo Banana-Chocolate Chip
    Muffins, 339
  Peanut Butter-Banana Pudding, 340
Share The Season's Spirit, 341
  Make Pretty Packages for Holiday
    Treats, 341
Six Courses Made Simple, 322
  Chicken Provolone, 323
  Endive-Tomato Starburst Salad, 323
  Fruit, Cheese, and Nuts, 324
  Liver Pâté with Madeira Sauce, 323
  Make-Ahead Tomato-Basil Bisque, 322
  Merlot Ice, 323
  Rice and Asparagus, 324
Sweet Dreams, 314
  Apricot Wonders, 316
  Chocolate-Almond Mousse, 316
  Coconut Shortbread Cookies, 316
  Peppermint Mousse, 315
  Pinwheel Cookies, 316
  Small Chocolate Sack, 314
  Snowball Surprises, 315
  White Chocolate Mousse, 315
The Plate As Canvas, 337
  Suggestions for Attractive Food
    Presentation, 337
Vegetarian Entrées, 319
  Marinara on Beds of Spinach
    and Orzo, 320
  Vegetable Lasagna, 320
  Vegetarian Burritos, 319
Very Merry Cranberries, 332
  Cranberry-Coconut Coffee Cake, 332
  Cranberry Salsa with Sweet
    Potato Chips, 332
  Oven-Barbecued Cranberry Chicken, 332
Watch the Fat, Not the Pot, 318
  Bean-and-Turkey Soup, 319
  Light and Creamy Coleslaw, 318
  Parsley-Garlic Rolls, 319

General Recipe Index

A listing of every recipe by food category and/or major ingredient
All microwave recipe page numbers are preceded by an "M."

Almonds

Biscotti, Almond-Anise, 266
Biscuits, Raspberry-Almond, 160
Cake, Apricot-Almond Coffee, 26
Cheese Ball, Pinecone, 288
Cheesecake, Chocolate-Almond, 53
Chicken Almondette Fingers, 12
Crunch, Vanilla Almond, 243
Ice Cream, Almond-Fudge, 205
Mousse, Chocolate-Almond, 316
Nippy Nuts, 301
Petits Fours, Chocolate-Almond, 255
Praline Sauce, 214

Appetizers

Artichoke-and-Shrimp Appetizer, 271
Asparagus Rolls, Hot, 329
Bacon Rolls, 330
Bacon-Wrapped Crackers, 280
Beef Sticks, 331
Buzzard's Nests, 244
Carrots, Pickled, 12
Cheese
    Ball, Chicken-Cheese, 216
    Ball, Pinecone Cheese, 288
    Bites, Cheese, 329
    Brie Wrapped in Phyllo, 173
    Fiesta Cheesecake, 273
    Goat Cheese with Sun-Dried Tomatoes
      and Rosemary, 175
    Phyllo Cheese Triangles, 329
    Queso Blanco, 322
    Terrine, Italian Cheese, 64
    Wafers, Hope Farm Cheese, 282
    Wafers, Sage-Pecan Cheese, 12
Chicken Almondette Fingers, 12
Chicken Drummettes, Down-Home, 157
Chicken Drummettes, Orange-Pecan, 158
Chicken Drummettes, Southwestern, 158
Chocolate-Dipped Horns, 197
Corn Salsa, Spicy, 322
Crab Canapés, 130
Crab Casserole, Easy, 270
Crabmeat Rémoulade, 280
Crab Meltaways, Broiled, 287
Crackers, Critter, 193
Cracker Snackers, 197
Dips
    Antipasto Dip, 313
    Apple Dip, 205
    Artichoke Dip in a Bread
      Basket, 13
    Blue Cheese Dip, 313
    Cottage Cheese Sun-Dried
      Tomato Dip, 13
    Crab Dip, Hot, 269
    Crab Dip, Trawler, 238
    Curry-Onion Dip, 313
    Dill Dip, 330
    Garbanzo Dip, 94
    Ham Dip, Creamy, 125

    Monster Mash Dip, 244
    Nacho Dip, M330
    Peanut Butter Lovers' Dip, 162
    Ranch Dip, Skinny, 96
    Spinach Dip, 324
    Taco Dip, Hot, 238
    Turnip Green Dip with Jalapeño-Corn
      Muffins, Hot, 164
Drummettes, Ginger-Garlic Appetizer, 157
Endive with Caviar, 118
Granola, 197
Ham Appetillas, 63
Hazelnuts, Curried, 301
Jezebel Sauce, 331
Mix, Cereal Snack, 129
Mix, Crunchy Snack, 94
Mushrooms, Stuffed, 172
Nachos, South Texas, 321
Nuts, Chesapeake, 269
Nuts, Deviled, 118
Nuts, Nippy, 301
Pâtés
    Black-Eyed Pea Pâté, 97
    Champignon, Pâté de, 171
    Liver Pâté with Madeira Sauce, 323
Pecans, Pepper, 79
Pepper Feet, 258
Pita Wedges, Garlic, 98
Popcorn with Pizzazz, 245
Quiche, South-of-the-Border, 321
Samurai 'shrooms, 258
Sandwiches, Double-Filled Party, 159
Sausage Pinwheels, 238
Shrimp-and-Black Bean Tostadas, 204
Shrimp-and-Cucumber Canapés, 164
Shrimp Mold with Asparagus, 214
Spicy Pecans, 279
Spinach Strudels, 249
Spreads and Fillings
    Cheese Spread, Make-Ahead, 324
    Chili Cheese Spread, 242
    Crab Spread, 167
    Shrimp Spread, 205
    Vegetable Spread, Garden, 184
Stalks, Splendid, 258
Sweet Potato Chips, 332
Sweet Potato Chips with Blue Cheese, 290
Toast Points, 270
Toast Strips, Seasoned, 98
Vegetable Juice Appetizer, Hot, 324

Apples

Bake, Apple-Carrot, 304
Breakfast Delight, 195
Caramel-Peanut Apples, M244
Cooked Apples, 338
Curried Apples, 252
Dip, Apple, 205
Dressing, Sausage-Apple, 305
Mousse, Cran-Apple, 255
Pancakes, Apple-Topped, 339

Pork Chops with Apples, Parmesan, 338
Salad Greens with Apple and Brie, 241
Sauce, Apple-Cinnamon, 42
Shortcake, Quick Apple, 42
Sorbet, Cran-Apple Spice, 153
Sparkler, Apple-Berry, 104
Spiced Apples, 123
Sugar-Crusted Apples in Walnut-Phyllo
    Baskets, 210
Topping, Apple-Nut, 162
Turnovers, Baked Apple, 338

Apricots

Cake, Apricot-Almond Coffee, 26
Filling, Apricot, 316
Ham Slice, Apricot-Glazed, 252
Slush, Apricot, 205
Wonders, Apricot, 316

Artichokes

Appetizer, Artichoke-and-Shrimp, 271
Bread, Artichoke, 140
Casserole, Alii Artichoke, 294
Casserole, Spinach-Artichoke, 44
Crabmeat with Artichoke Hearts,
    Creamed, 26
Dip in a Bread Basket, Artichoke, 13

Asparagus

Goat Cheese Sauce, Asparagus with, 116
Guacamole, Mock, 36
Rice and Asparagus, 324
Rolls, Hot Asparagus, 329
Salad, Creamy Lemon-Asparagus, 116
Sauté, Asparagus-and-Mushroom, 115
Shrimp Mold with Asparagus, 214
Vinaigrette, Asparagus, 174

Avocados

Guacamole, Spicy, 218
Salad, Avocado-Grapefruit, 282
Salad with Honey-Yogurt Dressing,
    Avocado-Fruit, 172
Soup, Chilled Avocado, 108
Topping, Avocado, 309

Bacon

Chowder, Fresh Corn and
    Bacon, 203
Crackers, Bacon-Wrapped, 280
Croissants, BLT, 158
Dressing, Sweet Bacon, 108
Pie, Country Breakfast, M328
Pita Pockets, BLT in, 158
Rolls, Bacon, 330
Sandwiches, Curried BLT, 158

Bananas

Bisque, Banana-Raspberry, 161
Cake, Banana-Coconut, 154
Cake, Bananas Foster Crunch, 339
Muffins, Banana-Nut, 140
Muffins, Jumbo Banana-Chocolate Chip, 339
Pie, Blueberry-Banana, 115
Pudding, Peanut Butter-Banana, 340

Bananas
(continued)
Shortcake, Banana-Pecan, 43
Smoothie, Banana, 95
Smoothie, Quick Banana-Pineapple, 195
Barbecue
Beans, Skillet Barbecued, 217
Chicken, Lemon Barbecued, 215
Chicken, Oven-Barbecued Cranberry, 332
Lamb Shanks, Barbecued, 113
Pork Loin Roast, Barbecued, 34
Sauce, Barbecue, 129
Beans. *See also* Lentils.
Baked
    Pork Chops with Baked Beans, 18
    Quintet, Baked Beans, 105
Barbecued Beans, Skillet, 217
Black Beans, 28
Black Bean Salsa, 155
Black Bean Sauce, 59
Black Beans, Marinated, 131
Black Bean Terrine with Fresh Tomato Coulis
    and Jalapeño Sauce, 230
Black Bean Tostadas, Shrimp-and-, 204
Casserole, Chuck Wagon Bean, 198
Chili Goes Southwest, Basic, 326
Chili, Mom's, 292
Garbanzo Dip, 94
Green
    Buffet Green Beans, 325
    Dilled Green Beans, 279
    Dill Green Beans, 136
    Lemon-Walnut Green Beans, 304
    Medley, Peppery Green Bean, 181
    Mushroom Sauce, Green Beans in
        Sherried, 206
    Mushrooms, Green Beans with, 89
    Red Peppers and Pearl Onions, Green
        Beans with Roasted, 260
    Tarragon Dressing, Green Beans with
        Creamy, 191
    Vinaigrette, Green Beans, 120
Mogumbo, 32
Pinto Beans, Mexican, 69
Salads
    Black Bean Salad, Caribbean
        Shrimp-and-, 143
    Marinated Bean Salad, 312
Soup, Bean-and-Turkey, 319
Soup, Black Bean, 231
Tacos, Chicken-and-Bean, 293
White Bean Relish, 229
White Beans, Caesar Salad with, 30
White Bean Spread, 30
Beef
Brisket in Beer, Beef, 63
Brisket, Smoke-at-Home, 192
Carne Guisada, 68
Chili, Firestarter, 34
Chili, Red, 108
Corned Beef and Cabbage, 64
Grillades and Grits, 62
Pot Pies with Yorkshire Pudding Topping,
    Beef, 45
Rice, Beef and Cauliflower over, 94
Roasts
    Deli-Style Roast Beef, 15
    Easy Oven Roast, 64
    Grilled Marinated Beef Roast, 141
    New York Strip Roast, Spicy, 131

    Pot Roast, Beef Brisket, 20
    Rump Roast, Easy, 217
    Sauerbraten Beef, Marinated, 16
Salad, Western-Style Beef, 321
Steaks
    American Steakhouse Beef, 15
    Kabobs, Steak, 95
    Parmesan, Steak, 41
    Ropa Vieja, 28
Stir-Fry, Beef-and-Shrimp, 32
Stir-Fry, Hungarian, 64
Stroganoff, Beef, 18
Tenderloin, Marinated Beef, 215
Tzimmes with Brisket, Mixed Fruit, 114
Wellington, Beef, 288
Beef, Ground
Chili
    Basic Chili, 326
    Basic Chili Embellished, 327
    Basic Chili Goes Southwest, 326
    Chili, 89
Enchiladas, Weeknight, 63
Hamburgers
    Grilled Hamburgers, 198
    Mexicali, Hamburgers, 217
Lasagna, Easy, M24
Lasagna Supreme, 24
Meatballs, Charleston Press Club, 129
Meat Loaf
    All-American Meat Loaf, 46
    Blue Cheese Meat Loaf Roll, 247
    Family-Style Meat Loaf, 18
    Southwestern Meat Loaf, 248
Picadillo II, 72
Potatoes, Taco-Topped, M18
Sticks, Beef, 331
Beets
Glazed Beets, Ginger-Marmalade, 35
Beverages
Alcoholic
    Apricot Slush, 205
    Bay Bloodies, 268
    Chocolate, Hot Laced Marshmallow, 53
    Eggnog, Blender, 341
    Game-Cocktails, 214
    Irish Coffee Nog, 340
    Lemonade, Claret, 72
    Margaritas, 273
    Old-Fashioned Slush, 340
    Pink Palace, 293
    Punch, Stormy Petrel Rum Thunder, 269
    Punch, Wine, 331
    Sea Mist, 167
    Sunny Morning, 295
    Whiskey Sours, Frozen, 176
Apple-Berry Sparkler, 104
Banana-Pineapple Smoothie, Quick, 195
Banana Smoothie, 95
Brew, Witch's, 244
Citrus Cooler, 105
Citrus Slush, 198
Coffee, Mexican, 310
Jogger's Sunrise, 213
Lemonade, Berry Delicious, 205
Lemonade, Pineapple, 194
Mocha, Mexican, M341
Punch. *See also* Beverages/Alcoholic.
    Citrus Punch, 99
    Mock Champagne Punch, 340
    Nectar Punch, 283
    Vegetable Punch, Hot, 12

    Shake, PBJ, 292
    Shake, Peach Melba Sundae, 134
    Shake, Tropical, 212
Strawberry Refresher, Frozen, 213
Sunrise Smoothie, 139
Tea, Pineapple, 165
Wassail, Christmas, 295
Biscuits
Angel Biscuits, 270
Basil Biscuits, 160
Cinnamon-Raisin Breakfast
    Biscuits, 159
Elgin Biscuits, 281
Herbed Biscuits, 67
Pudding, Biscuit, 51
Raspberry-Almond Biscuits, 160
Sweet Potato Angel Biscuits, 312
Blackberries
Tarts, Blackberry Pudding, 200
Blueberries
à la Frederick, Blueberries, 123
Pie, Blueberry-Banana, 115
Breads. *See also* specific types.
Artichoke Bread, 140
Bourbon-Pecan Bread, 308
Breakfast Bread, Crunchy, 327
Chocolate-Zucchini Bread, 308
French Bread, Herbed, 283
Herbs-and-Cheese Bread, 56
Lemon Tea Bread, 183
Nautical Knots, 168
Pita Triangles, Cheesy, 70
Puddings
    Spiced Bread Pudding, 52
    Tennessee Bread Pudding with Bourbon
        Sauce, 51
Stars, Bread, 286
Toast Points, 270
Toast Strips, Seasoned, 98
Yeast
    Beignets, French Market, 219
    Focaccia, Onion, 77
    Grittibanz (Swiss Bread Figure), 265
    Honey-Oat Bread, 232
    Olive Bread, 78
    Pandoro, 267
    Panettone, 266
    Parmesan Bread, 231
    Peanut Lover's Bread, 211
    Raisin-Whole Wheat Bread, 77
    Sesame-Wheat Breadsticks, 114
    "Sponge," 267
    Walnut Bread, 77
    Whole Wheat Bread, Anise-, 36
Broccoli
Fettuccine, Broccoli-Parmesan, 55
Garlic Broccoli, 35
Salad, Broccoli-Mandarin, 325
Slaw, Zesty Broccoli, 246
Soup, Light Cream of Broccoli, 17
Tomatoes, Broccoli-Stuffed, 216
Bulgur
Tabbouleh, 70
Burritos
Vegetarian Burritos, 319
Butter
Honey Butter, 309
Onion Butter, Sweet, 124
Tomato-Curry-Orange Butter, 159
Butterscotch
Mousse, Butterscotch, 254

Cabbage. *See also* Sauerkraut.
Caraway, Cabbage with, 181
Corned Beef and Cabbage, 64
Slaws
    Broccoli Slaw, Zesty, 246
    Layered Slaw, 214
    Light and Creamy Coleslaw, 318
    Old-Fashioned Sweet Coleslaw, 128
    Peanut Slaw, Chinese, 212
    Silks, Slaw, 236
Cakes. *See also* Breads, Cookies.
Angel Food
    Ice-Cream Angel Dessert,
      Triple Mint, 86
    Surprise, Angel Cake, 86
    Trifle, Pineapple Angel Food, 86
Apple Shortcake, Quick, 42
Banana-Coconut Cake, 154
Banana-Pecan Shortcake, 43
Bananas Foster Crunch Cake, 339
Birdhouse Cake, 284
Cheesecakes
    Chocolate-Almond Cheesecake, 53
    Chocolate-Amaretto Cheesecake, 97
    Fiesta Cheesecake, 273
Chocolate
    Birthday Cake, Fishin'-for-Fun, 194
    Cinnamon Cake, Chocolate-, 154
    Snack Cake, Black Widow, 245
Coffee Cakes
    Apricot-Almond Coffee Cake, 26
    Cinnamon-Raisin Coffee Cake, 180
    Cranberry-Coconut Coffee Cake, 332
    Sour Cream Coffee Cake, 154
    Walnut Coffee Cake, 124
Éclair Cake, 42
Gingerbread with Caramel Sauce,
  Pumpkin, 235
Lemon Cake, Luscious, 81
Lemon Meringue Torte with Raspberry
  Sauce, 82
Lemon-Poppy Seed Cake, 154
Petits Fours, Chocolate-Almond, 255
Pound
    Chocolate Chip Pound Cake, 105
    Croutons, Cinnamon Pound Cake, 161
    Daiquiri Pound Cake, 83
    Marbled Pecan Pound Cake, 313
    Old-Fashioned Pound Cake, 120
    Orange-Pecan Pound Cake, 13
    Southern Pound Cake,
      Smoothest, 237
Pumpkin Cake, 303
Red Velvet Cake, 318
Strawberry Crispy Shortcakes, 42
Twelfth Night Cake, 337
Zucchini-Carrot Cake, 20
Candies
Fudge Balls, Strawberry, 80
Mints, Cream Cheese, 79
Peanut Butter Candy, 166
Rum Balls, 314
Turtle Candies, M41
Canning. *See also* Pickles and Relishes.
Green Beans, Dill, 136
Caramel
Apples, Caramel-Peanut, M244
Bombe, Caramel-Toffee, 214
Peaches, Caramel, 134
Sauce, Caramel, 210, 235, 296
Tart, Caramel Turtle Truffle, M131

Carrots
Bake, Apple-Carrot, 304
Cake, Zucchini-Carrot, 20
Casserole, Carrot-Pecan, 44
Chowchow, Carrot, 218
Ginger-Cinnamon Carrots, 168
Muffins, Morning Glory, 327
Pickled Carrots, 12
Sauté, Carrot-Turnip, 241
Steamed Carrots, Lemon-Dill, 180
Sugar Snaps and Carrots, Creamed, 139
Casseroles
Bean Casserole, Chuck Wagon, 198
Franks, Mexican, 78
Lentils-and-Rice Casserole, 301
Macaroni and Blue Cheese, 248
Macaroni and Cheese, Creamy, 249
Macaroni Bake, Jack-in-the-, 249
Poultry
    Chicken-and-Chiles Casserole, 107
    Chicken Bake with Sweet Bacon
      Dressing, Vegetable- 108
    Chicken Casserole, Mexi-, 69
    Chicken Chili Bake, 302
    Chicken Chimichangas, 68
    Chicken Florentine, 107
    Turkey Noodle Bake, 243
Ravioli, Mediterranean, 301
Seafood
    Crab Casserole, Easy, 270
    Crabmeat with Artichoke Hearts,
      Creamed, 26
Shells, Southwestern Stuffed, 234
Vegetable
    Artichoke Casserole, Alii, 294
    Carrot-Pecan Casserole, 44
    Corn Casserole, 141
    Eggplant Casserole, 44
    Eggplant Casserole, Spicy Hot, 92
    Eggplant, Heavenly, 293
    Lasagna Casserole, Vegetable, 25
    Onion Bake, Four, 304
    Potatoes Moussaka, 44
    Spinach-Artichoke Casserole, 44
    Spinach Fantastic, 173
    Spinach Parmesan, 72
Cauliflower
Beef and Cauliflower over Rice, 94
Caviar
Endive with Caviar, 118
Celery
Peas and Celery, 289
Splendid Stalks, 258
Cheese. *See also* Appetizers/Cheese.
Breads
    Herbs-and-Cheese Bread, 56
    Muffins, Cheesy Sausage, 144
    Muffins, Ham-and-Cheese, 144
    Parmesan Bread, 231
    Pita Triangles, Cheesy, 70
Casseroles
    Jack-in-the-Macaroni Bake, 249
    Macaroni and Blue Cheese, 248
    Macaroni and Cheese, Creamy, 249
Cheesecake. *See* Cakes/Cheesecakes.
Chicken Provolone, 323
Crust, Parmesan Pizza, 58
Dressing, Roquefort, 128
Eggs, Blue Cheese Stuffed, 87
Eggs, Chile-Cheese Deviled, 87
Enchiladas, Meatless, 106

Fettuccine, Broccoli-Parmesan, 55
French Toast, Three Cheese Stuffed, 122
Frosting, Cream Cheese, 20
Fruit, Cheese, and Nuts, 324
Gratin, Pear-Blue Cheese, 328
Ham-and-Cheese Bundles, 63
Meat Loaf Roll, Blue Cheese, 247
Mints, Cream Cheese, 79
Omelet, Herbed Cheese, 47
Perch, Parmesan-Crusted, 91
Pineapple Gratin, 328
Pork Chops with Apples, Parmesan, 338
Quiche, South-of-the-Border, 321
Raspberry Brie in Rye, 252
Salad, Fresh Mozzarella-Tomato-Basil, 131
Sauces
    Cheese Sauce, 48
    Goat Cheese Sauce, Asparagus
      with, 116
    Guilt-Free Cheese Sauce, M95
Spreads and Fillings
    Chili Cheese Spread, 242
    Cream Cheese Spread, Fruited, 79
    Cream Cheese Spread, Pear-, 80
    Make-Ahead Cheese Spread, 324
    Orange Filling, Cheese-and-, 159
    Parmesan-Spinach Spread, 55
Steak Parmesan, 41
Stuffed Chiles Rellenos with Walnut Cream
  Sauce, Havarti-and-Corn-, M275
Sweet Potato Chips with Blue Cheese, 290
Terrine, Italian Cheese, 64
Topping, Blue Cheese Burger, 218
Vegetables
    Onions, Parmesan, 170
    Pepper Toss, Parmesan, 208
    Potatoes au Gratin, 90, 217
    Potatoes, Parmesan, M46
    Potato Gratin, Dual, 328
    Spinach Parmesan, 72
    Stalks, Splendid, 258
Wafers, Hope Farm Cheese, 282
Wafers, Sage-Pecan Cheese, 12
Walnut-Baked Brie, 241
Cheesecakes. *See* Cakes/Cheesecakes.
Cherries
Cobbler, Raspberry-Cherry, 230
Cookies, Cherry Bonbon, 52
Glaze, Cherry, 52
Pie, No-Bake Cherry Confetti, 114
Sherried Cherries, 289
Spread, Cherry, 309
Chicken
à la King, Easy Chicken, 14
Bake, Chicken Chili, 302
Bake with Sweet Bacon Dressing,
  Vegetable-Chicken, 108
Ball, Chicken-Cheese, 216
Barbecued
    Lemon Barbecued Chicken, 215
    Oven-Barbecued Cranberry
      Chicken, 332
Casserole, Chicken-and-Chiles, 107
Casserole, Mexi-Chicken, 69
Chimichangas, Chicken, 68
Coconut Chicken with Fresh Fruit, 294
Cordon Bleu, Chicken, 126
Drummettes, Down-Home Chicken, 157
Drummettes, Ginger-Garlic
  Appetizer, 157
Drummettes, Orange-Pecan Chicken, 158

Chicken
(continued)

Drummettes, Southwestern Chicken, 158
Dumplings, Old-Fashioned Chicken and, 302
Enchiladas, Creamy, 174
Enchiladas Verde, Chicken, 274
Fingers, Buttermilk-Pecan Chicken, 165
Florentine, Chicken, 107
Fried
    Fingers, Chicken Almondette, 12
    Oven-Fried Chicken, 90
Grilled Basil Chicken, 201
Grilled Jalapeño Chicken, 213
Herb-Seasoned Chicken Breasts, M325
Lasagna, Chicken, 25
Lemon-Dill Chicken, 19
Mole Sauce, Chicken with, 34
Mustard Chicken, 239
Pasta, Quick Chicken and, 14
Pita, Peppery Chicken in, 62
Provolone, Chicken, 323
Roast Chicken, 14
Rolls, Mexican Chicken, 242
Rolls, Pesto-Stuffed Chicken, 82
Salads
    Ginger Salad, Fried Chicken, 290
    Mama Hudson's Chicken Salad, 238
    Marinated Chicken-Raspberry Salad, 190
    Roasted Chicken Salad, 14
    Walnut Salad, Sunburst Chicken-and-, 91
Tacos, Chicken-and-Bean, 293
Tostadas, Chicken, 204

Chili
Basic Chili, 326
Basic Chili Embellished, 327
Basic Chili Goes Southwest, 326
Chili, 89
Firestarter Chili, 34
Mom's Chili, 292
Red Chili, 108

Chocolate
Bars and Cookies
    Biscotti Cioccolata, 268
    Brownies, Chocolate-Kahlúa, 99
    Brownies, Mint Julep, 165
    Brownies, Mother's, 239
    Brownies, Southern Chocolate-Mint, 216
    Brownies, Praline, 243
    Chewies, Chocolate, 216
    Chewies, Easy Chocolate, 296
    Crème de Menthe Squares, 256
    Crispies, Chocolate-Peanut, 80
    Kissy Cookies, 331
    Orange Delights, Chocolate-, 52
    Pinwheel Cookies, 316
    Pudding Cookies, Chocolate Chip-, 21
    Pumpkin-Chocolate Chip Cookies, 235
Beverages
    Coffee, Mexican, 310
    Marshmallow Chocolate, Hot Laced, 53
    Mocha, Mexican, M341
Bread, Chocolate-Zucchini, 308
Cakes and Tortes
    Birthday Cake, Fishin'-for-Fun, 194
    Cheesecake, Chocolate-Almond, 53
    Cheesecake, Chocolate-Amaretto, 97
    Cinnamon Cake, Chocolate-, 154

Petits Fours, Chocolate-Almond, 255
Pound Cake, Chocolate Chip, 105
Pound Cake, Marbled Pecan, 313
Snack Cake, Black Widow, 245
Candies
    Fudge Balls, Strawberry, 80
    Pralines, Chocolate, 51
    Pralines, Chocolate-Mint, 51
    Pralines, Chocolate-Peanut Butter, 51
    Pralines, Mocha, 51
    Turtle Candies, M41
Cups, Chocolate Crinkle, 270
Fondue, Brandied Chocolate, 162
Frostings, Fillings, and Toppings
    Chocolate Frosting, 239
    Ganache, Chocolate, 255
    Glaze, Chocolate, 52
Horns, Chocolate-Dipped, 197
Ice Cream, Almond-Fudge, 205
Meringue Acorns, 284
Mousse, Chocolate-Almond, 316
Mousse, White Chocolate, 315
Muffins, Jumbo Banana-Chocolate Chip, 339
Parfait, White Chocolate-Raspberry Swirl, 315
Pies and Tarts
    Caramel Turtle Truffle Tart, M131
    German Chocolate Pie, 129
    Pecan Chess Pie, Chocolate-, 251
    Pecan Tart with Caramel Sauce, Chocolate-, 296
    Turtle Pecan Pie, 250
Pots de Crème au Chocolate, 53
Pots de Crème, Chocolate, 296
Sack, Large Chocolate, 314
Sack, Small Chocolate, 314
Sauces
    Chocolate Sauce, 276
    Dark Chocolate Sauce, 296
    Mint Sauce, Chocolate-, 86
Torte, Frozen Viennese, 171
Trifle, Chocolate, 326

Chowder
Corn and Bacon Chowder, Fresh, 203

Christmas. *See also* Cookies/Christmas.
Bread Stars, 286
Cookies, Christmas Tree, 286
Corn, Christmas, 325
Cranberry Hearts, 286
Doughnuts, Snowy, 286
Gingerbread Bowl, Christmas, 266
Grittibanz (Swiss Bread Figure), 265
Orange Baskets, 286
Pandoro, 267
Panettone, 266
Pie, White Christmas, 289
Pinecones, Peanut Butter-Suet, 286
Pretzel Garlands, 286
Wassail, Christmas, 295

Clams
Sauce, Tricolor Pasta with Clam, 272

Coconut
Cake, Banana-Coconut, 154
Cake, Cranberry-Coconut Coffee, 332
Chicken with Fresh Fruit, Coconut, 294
Cookies, Coconut Shortbread, 316
Cookies, Crispy Coconut-Oatmeal, 80
Pie, Coconut, 115
Spread, Coconut-Pineapple, 309

Coffee
Meringues with Butterscotch Mousse, Coffee, 254
Mexican Coffee, 310
Mocha, Mexican, M341
Mocha Pralines, 51
Pralines, Café au Lait, 51
Coleslaw. *See* Cabbage or Salads.
Cookies
Almond-Anise Biscotti, 266
Bars and Squares
    Brownies, Chocolate-Kahlúa, 99
    Brownies, Mint Julep, 165
    Brownies, Mother's, 239
    Brownies, Southern Chocolate-Mint, 216
    Brownies, Praline, 243
    Chocolate-Peanut Crispies, 80
    Crème de Menthe Squares, 256
    Mystery Bars, 239
    Peanut Butter Bars, 166
Bird's Nest Cookies, 284
Biscotti Cioccolata, 268
Brutti Ma Buoni (Ugly but Good), 267
Cherry Bonbon Cookies, 52
Chocolate Chewies, Easy, 296
Christmas
    Gingerbread Bowl, Christmas, 266
    Tree Cookies, Christmas, 286
Cinnamon Sticks, Italian, 204
Coconut-Oatmeal Cookies, Crispy, 80
Drop
    Chocolate Chewies, 216
    Chocolate Chip-Pudding Cookies, 21
    Chocolate-Orange Delights, 52
    Oatmeal-Raisin Cookies, 127
    Pumpkin-Chocolate Chip Cookies, 235
    Toffee Crunch Cookies, 80
Kissy Cookies, 331
Peanut Truffle Cookies, 212
Refrigerator
    Cheese Wafers, Hope Farm, 282
    Gingerbirds, 283
    Ginger Icebox Cookies, 205
    Peanut Butter Cookie Ice Cream Sandwiches, 199
    Pinwheel Cookies, 316
    Snowball Surprises, 315
Rolled
    Apricot Wonders, 316
    Shortbread Cookies, Coconut, 316
    Sweetheart Cookies, 53
Shortbread, Brown Sugar, 331
Spider Cookies, M166
Turkey Treats, 256
Cooking Light. *See* On The Light Side.
Corn
Casserole, Corn, 141
Chowder, Fresh Corn and Bacon, 203
Christmas Corn, 325
Mexican Corn, Spicy, 90
Muffins, Tex-Mex Corn, 144
Pancakes, Corn, 43
Relish, Sweet Corn, 119
Salad, Corn-in-the-Shuck, 236
Salsa, Spicy Corn, 322
Stuffed Chiles Rellenos with Walnut Cream Sauce, Havarti-and-Corn-, M275
Cornbreads
Cornbread, 122
Croutons, Cornbread, 192

Dressing, Green Chile-Cornbread, 306
Dressing, Quail Stuffed with Cornbread, 280
Mexican Cornbread, 182
Muffins, Jalapeño-Corn, 164
Muffins, Miniature Cornmeal, 119
Muffins, Tex-Mex Corn, 144
Sticks, Garlic-Thyme Corn, 242
Sticks, Savory Corn, 33
Supreme, Cornbread, 67

Cornish Hens
Chutney-Mustard Glaze, Game Hens with, 66
Glazed Cornish Hens, Jelly-, 251

Crab
Benedict, Lion, 121
Broiled Crab Meltaways, 287
Canapés, Crab, 130
Casserole, Easy Crab, 270
Creamed Crabmeat with Artichoke
    Hearts, 26
Dip, Hot Crab, 269
Dip, Trawler Crab, 238
Imperial, Easy Crab, 128
Karen, Crabmeat, 49
Rémoulade, Crabmeat, 280
Salad, Marinated Crab-and-Endive, 22
Spread, Crab, 167
Tostadas, Crab, 203

Crackers
Bacon-Wrapped Crackers, 280
Snackers, Cracker, 197

Cranberries
Cake, Cranberry-Coconut Coffee, 332
Chicken, Oven-Barbecued Cranberry, 332
Hearts, Cranberry, 286
Mousse, Cran-Apple, 255
Salsa with Sweet Potato Chips, Cranberry, 332
Sparkler, Apple-Berry, 104

Crème Fraîche
Sauce, Crème Fraîche, 135

Crêpes
Cornmeal Sombreros, 277
Crêpes, 123
Raspberry Crêpes with Yogurt
    Filling, Fresh, 123

Croutons
Bagel Croutons, 192
Bourbon Croutons, 234
Cinnamon Pound Cake Croutons, 161
Cornbread Croutons, 192
Croûtes, Croutons and, 30
Dilled Croutons, 161
Pita Croutons, 192

Cucumbers
Canapés, Shrimp-and-Cucumber, 164
Salad, Dilled Cucumber, 65
Salad, Tomato-and-Cucumber Summer, 141
Sour Cream, Cucumbers and, 203
Spread, Cucumber, 158

Curry
Apples, Curried, 252
Butter, Tomato-Curry-Orange, 159
Dip, Curry-Onion, 313
Eggs, Curried Deviled, 87
Hazelnuts, Curried, 301
Sandwiches, Curried BLT, 158
Spread, Curry, 159
Tomatoes, Curried Green, 138
Vinaigrette, Warm Curry, 107

Custards
Citrus Custard with Fresh Fruit, 70
Tocino del Cielo, 29

Desserts. *See also* specific types.
Apples, Cooked, 338
Brûlé, Petit, 219
Cherries, Sherried, 289
Chocolate
    Cups, Chocolate Crinkle, 270
    Pots de Crème au Chocolate, 53
    Pots de Crème, Chocolate, 296
    Sack, Large Chocolate, 314
    Sack, Small Chocolate, 314
    Trifle, Chocolate, 326
Cinnamon Crisps, 106
Éclair Cake, 42
Frozen
    Caramel-Toffee Bombe, 214
    Cinnamon Ice Cream
        Sombreros, 276
    Fruit Cups, Frozen, 197
    Grapefruit Freeze, 242
    Ice-Cream Angel Dessert,
        Triple Mint, 86
    Peach Torte, Frozen, 135
    Torte, Frozen Viennese, 171
    Vanilla Almond Crunch, 243
Fruit. *See also* specific types.
    Amaretto Crème on Fresh
        Fruit, 176
    Cheese, and Nuts, Fruit, 324
    Compote, Mixed Fruit, 123
Kiwi-and-Orange Dessert, 295
Lemon Solid, 279
Orange Chiffon Dessert, 295
Oranges, Champagne, 83
Orange Slices, Burgundy-Spiced, 294
Parfaits
    Peppermint Parfait, 315
    Surf-and-Sand Parfaits, 169
    White Chocolate-Raspberry Swirl
        Parfait, 315
Peaches, Caramel, 134
Peaches 'n' Cream, Honeyed, 134
Pear-Blue Cheese Gratin, 328
Pots de Crème, Easy, 281
Pumpkin Swirl, Easy, 234
Raspberry Jellyrolls, M255
Rum Balls, 314
Sabayon, 272
Sauces
    Amaretto-Cinnamon Sauce, 171
    Apple-Cinnamon Sauce, 42
    Bourbon Sauce, 51
    Caramel Sauce, 210, 235, 296
    Chocolate-Mint Sauce, 86
    Chocolate Sauce, 276
    Chocolate Sauce, Dark, 296
    Crème Fraîche Sauce, 135
    Lemon Cream Sauce, 200
    Praline Sauce, 214
    Raspberry Sauce, 82, 99, 315
    Raspberry Sauce, Fresh, 120
    Rum Sundae Sauce, 162
    Spicy Sauce, 52
    Strawberries Arnaud
        Sauce, 50
Strawberries Arnaud, 50
Strawberries Jamaica, 239
Trifle, English, 289
Trifle, Pineapple Angel Food, 86

Doughnuts
Snowy Doughnuts, 286

Dressings. *See* Stuffings and Dressings.

Duck
Blackened Duck Breasts, 259

Dumplings
Chicken and Dumplings, Old-Fashioned, 302

Eggnog
Blender Eggnog, 341
Irish Coffee Nog, 340

Eggplant
Casserole, Eggplant, 44
Casserole, Spicy Hot Eggplant, 92
Heavenly Eggplant, 293
Moussaka, Potatoes, 44

Eggs
Baked in Mushroom Sauce, Eggs, 47
Benedict, Light Eggs, M68
Benedict, Lion, 121
Featherbed Eggs, 122
Frittata, Fresh Vegetable, 140
Frittata, Vegetable, 183
Omelet, Herbed Cheese, 47
Pie, Country Breakfast, M328
Pizza, Ham-and-Eggs Crescent, 47
Poached Eggs, 121
Soup, Lemon-Egg Drop, 81
Stuffed
    Blue Cheese Stuffed Eggs, 87
    Deviled Eggs, Chile-Cheese, 87
    Deviled Eggs, Curried, 87
    Deviled Eggs, Sweet, 88
    Ham Devils, 88
    Herb-Sour Cream Stuffed Eggs, 87
    Stuffed Eggs, Easy, 87

Enchiladas
Chicken Enchiladas Verde, 274
Creamy Enchiladas, 174
Meatless Enchiladas, 106
Weeknight Enchiladas, 63

Endive
Braised Belgian Endive and Peas, 22
Salad, Endive-Watercress, 22
Salad, Marinated Crab-and-Endive, 22

Fettuccine
Broccoli-Parmesan Fettuccine, 55

Fillings. *See* Frostings.

Fish. *See also* specific types and Seafood.
Catfish Louisiana, 291
Orange Roughy, Vegetable-Topped, 67
Perch, Parmesan-Crusted, 91
Snapper with Julienne Vegetables,
    Yellowtail, 31
Swordfish Steaks, Orange-Ginger
    Marinated, 271
Trout, Stuffed Rainbow, 121

Frankfurters
Corn Dog Bites, 79
Mexican Franks, 78
Pizzas, Hot Dog, 78
Sauce, Hot Diggity Dog, 198
Supper, Hot Dog, 78

French Toast
Oven-Baked French Toast, Easy, 195
Pain-Perdu Po-Boy, 291
Peanut Butter French Toast, 166
Stuffed French Toast, Three Cheese, 122

Fritters
Buñuelos, 29

Frostings, Fillings, and Toppings
Apple-Nut Topping, 162
Apples, Cooked, 338

Frostings, Fillings, and Toppings
(continued)

Apricot Filling, 316
Avocado Topping, 309
Blue Cheese Burger Topping, 218
Boiled Frosting, 318
Buttercream Frosting, 53, 285
Cheese-and-Orange Filling, 159
Cherry Glaze, 52
Chocolate Frosting, 239
Chocolate Ganache, 255
Chocolate Glaze, 52
Cran-Apple Mousse, 255
Cream Cheese Frosting, 20
Crème de Menthe Frosting, 256
Daiquiri Glaze, 83
Decorator Frosting, 285
Decorator Frosting, Green, 286
Decorator Frosting, Yellow, 283
Lemon Frosting, 81
Lemon Glaze, 154, 183
Lime-Rum Cream, 169
Mint Cream Frosting, 216
Peanut Filling, 211
Red Pepper Puree, 275
Shrimp Topping, 291
Whipped Cream Frosting, 86
White Buttercream Frosting, 337
Fruit. *See also* specific types.
Amaretto Crème on Fresh Fruit, 176
Baked Fruit, Ginger-Orange, 313
Cheese, and Nuts, Fruit, 324
Chicken with Fresh Fruit,
    Coconut, 294
Compote, Mixed Fruit, 123
Custard with Fresh Fruit, Citrus, 70
Dressing, Fruit Salad, 184
Fresh Fruit with Lemon-Yogurt
    Dressing, 17
Frozen Fruit Cups, 197
Puff Pastry Baskets, Tropical, 177
Salads
    Avocado-Fruit Salad with Honey-Yogurt
        Dressing, 172
    Citrus-Cilantro Dressing, Fruit Salad
        with, 310
    Green Fruit Salad with Honey-Lime
        Dressing, 71
    Honey-Lemon Dressing, Fruit Salad
        with, 21
    Multi-Fruit Salad, 184
Sandwiches, Glazed Breakfast Fruit, 178
Shake, Tropical, 212
Spread, Fruited Cream Cheese, 79
Tartlets, Fresh Fruit, 96
Tarts, Bowl-Me-Over Fresh Fruit, 200
Tropical Fruit Tray, 72
Tzimmes with Brisket, Mixed Fruit, 114

Game. *See also* specific types.
Pepper Feet, 258
Quail, Smoked, 236
Quail Stuffed with Cornbread Dressing, 280
Venison Roast, Grilled, 278
Garnishes
Chocolate Crinkle Cups, 270
Chocolate Sack, Large, 314
Chocolate Sack, Small, 314
Granola
Granola, 197

Grapefruit
Freeze, Grapefruit, 242
Salad, Avocado-Grapefruit, 282
Salad, Orange-Grapefruit, 294
Sorbet, Grapefruit-Mint, 153
Greens. *See also* specific types.
Mustard Green Soup, Cream of, 280
Turnip Green Dip with Jalapeño-Corn
    Muffins, Hot, 164
Grits
Cakes, Southwestern Grits, 61
Creamy Grits, 60
Dressing, Grits, 306
Grillades and Grits, 62
Pan-Fried Grits, 62
Gumbo
Mogumbo, 32

Ham. *See also* Pork.
Appetillas, Ham, 63
Bake, Ham-Potato-Pineapple, 302
Bundles, Ham-and-Cheese, 63
Cordon Bleu, Chicken, 126
Country Ham, Sotterley Plantation, 270
Devils, Ham, 88
Dip, Creamy Ham, 125
Glazed Ham Slice, Apricot-, 252
Muffins, Ham-and-Cheese, 144
Pain-Perdu Po-Boy, 291
Pie, Spaghetti-Ham, 19
Pizza, Ham-and-Eggs Crescent, 47
Soufflé, Virginia Ham Breakfast, 121
Stew, Ham-and-Black-Eyed Pea, 20
Honey
Bread, Honey-Oat, 232
Butter, Honey, 309
Dressing, Fruit Salad with Honey-
    Lemon, 21
Dressing, Honey-Lime, 71
Dressing, Honey-Walnut, 107
Dressing, Honey-Yogurt, 172
Marinade, Garlic-Honey, 102
Marinade, Honey-Mustard, 103
Mustard, Hot Honey, 240
Peaches 'n' Cream, Honeyed, 134
Pears, Honey-Baked, 47
Sauce, Honey-Poppy Seed, 13
Stir-Fry, Honey-Butternut, 184
Vegetables, Honey-Mustard
    Marinated, 236
Hors D'Oeuvres. *See* Appetizers.
Hot Dogs. *See* Frankfurters.

Ice Creams and Sherbets
Almond-Fudge Ice Cream, 205
Cinnamon Ice Cream Sombreros, 276
Cran-Apple Spice Sorbet, 153
Grapefruit-Mint Sorbet, 153
Lemon Sorbet, 153
Merlot Ice, 323
Mint Ice-Cream Angel Dessert, Triple, 86
Peach Ice Cream, 135
Peach Sorbet, 153
Sandwiches, Oatmeal Crispy Ice
    Cream, 199
Sandwiches, Peanut Butter Cookie Ice
    Cream, 199
Strawberry Sorbet, 153

Jams and Jellies
Onion Jelly, 135
Peach Jam, 135
Sangría Jelly, 341
Kabobs
Lamb Kabobs, Rosemary Marinated, 203
Lamb Shish Kabobs, 70
Steak Kabobs, 95
Vegetable Kabobs, Grilled, 170
Kiwifruit
Chutney, Kiwifruit-Onion, 125
Dessert, Kiwi-and-Orange, 295

Lamb
Kabobs, Lamb Shish, 70
Kabobs, Rosemary Marinated
    Lamb, 203
Leg of Lamb, Greek-Style, 170
Meat Loaf, Minted Lamb, 248
Roast, Garlic-Rolled Lamb, 113
Shanks, Barbecued Lamb, 113
Steak, Destin Lamb, 113
Lasagna
Chicken Lasagna, 25
Easy Lasagna, M24
Supreme, Lasagna, 24
Vegetable Lasagna, 320
Vegetable Lasagna Casserole, 25
Lemon
Beverages
    Berry Delicious Lemonade, 205
    Claret Lemonade, 72
    Pineapple Lemonade, 194
Bread, Lemon Tea, 183
Carrots, Lemon-Dill Steamed, 180
Chicken, Lemon Barbecued, 215
Chicken, Lemon-Dill, 19
Desserts
    Cake, Lemon-Poppy Seed, 154
    Cake, Luscious Lemon, 81
    Cream Puffs, Lemon, 254
    Frosting, Lemon, 81
    Glaze, Lemon, 154
    Pie, Lemon Fluff, 46
    Pie, Lemon-Pecan, 251
    Sauce, Lemon Cream, 200
    Solid, Lemon, 279
    Sorbet, Lemon, 153
    Torte with Raspberry Sauce, Lemon
        Meringue, 82
Dressing, Fruit Salad with Honey-Lemon, 21
Dressing, Lemon-Yogurt, 17
Glaze, Lemon, 183
Green Beans, Lemon-Walnut, 304
Potatoes, Herbed Lemon Mashed, 208
Potatoes, Oregano-and-Lemon Skillet, 54
Salad, Creamy Lemon-Asparagus, 116
Sauce, Lemon-Parsley, 48
Soup, Lemon-Egg Drop, 81
Sugar Snap Peas with Basil and Lemon, 66
Veal, Lemon, 35
Vegetables, Lemon, 83
Lentils
Casserole, Lentils-and-Rice, 301
Lettuce
Baby Lettuces with Mustard
    Vinaigrette, 67
Croissants, BLT, 158
Pita Pockets, BLT in, 158
Sandwiches, Curried BLT, 158

Lime
Cream, Lime-Rum, 169
Dressing, Honey-Lime, 71
Parfaits, Surf-and-Sand, 169
Sauce, Lime Hollandaise, 121
Veal, Amaretto-Lime, 54
Linguine
Red Pepper Sauce, Linguine with, 127
Vegetables, Traveling Linguine
with Roasted, 178
Liver
Pâté with Madeira Sauce, Liver, 323

Macaroni
Bake, Jack-in-the-Macaroni, 249
Blue Cheese, Macaroni and, 248
Cheese, Creamy Macaroni and, 249
Mangoes
Slaw, Mango, 31
Marinades. *See* Sauces.
Marshmallows
Chocolate, Hot Laced Marshmallow, 53
Mayonnaise
Watercress Mayonnaise, 119
Meatballs
Charleston Press Club Meatballs, 129
Meat Loaf. *See* Beef, Ground/Meat Loaf.
Meringues
Acorns, Meringue, 284
Coffee Meringues with Butterscotch
Mousse, 254
Meringues with Cran-Apple Mousse
Filling, 254
Microwave
Apples, Caramel-Peanut, M244
Candies, Turtle, M41
Chicken Breasts, Herb-Seasoned, M325
Chiles Rellenos with Walnut Cream Sauce,
Havarti-and-Corn-Stuffed, M275
Cookies, Spider, M166
Dip, Nacho, M330
Eggs Benedict, Light, M68
Jellyrolls, Raspberry, M255
Lasagna, Easy, M24
Mocha, Mexican, M341
Pie, Country Breakfast, M328
Pizza on a Bagel, M94
Potatoes, Cottage, M92
Potatoes, Parmesan, M46
Potatoes, Taco-Topped, M18
Rolls, Dinner, M326
Sauce, Guilt-Free Cheese, M95
Sauce, Sweet Orange, M325
Tart, Caramel Turtle Truffle, M131
Vegetables, Steamed Herbed, M303
Mousses
Butterscotch Mousse, 254
Chocolate-Almond Mousse, 316
Cran-Apple Mousse, 255
Peppermint Mousse, 315
Raspberry Mousse in Chocolate
Crinkle Cups, 270
White Chocolate Mousse, 315
Muffins
Banana-Chocolate Chip Muffins, Jumbo, 339
Banana-Nut Muffins, 140
Cornmeal Muffins, Miniature, 119
Corn Muffins, Jalapeño-, 164
Corn Muffins, Tex-Mex, 144
Ham-and-Cheese Muffins, 144
Morning Glory Muffins, 327

Okra Muffins, Fresh, 161
Onion-Dill Muffins, 144
Sausage Muffins, Cheesy, 144
Mushrooms
Acorn Squash-Mushroom Puree, 305
Green Beans with Mushrooms, 89
Pâté de Champignon, 171
Quiches, Wild Rice-and-Mushroom, 237
Salad, Fresh Mushroom, 65
Salmon with Mushrooms and Green Onions,
Fresh, 180
Samurai'shrooms, 258
Sauce, Eggs Baked in Mushroom, 47
Sauce, Green Beans in Sherried
Mushroom, 206
Sauce, Zucchini-Mushroom, 71
Sauté, Asparagus-and-Mushroom, 115
Stuffed Mushrooms, 172
Zesty Mushrooms, 218
Mustard
Bourbon Mustard, 240
Chicken, Mustard, 239
Dressing, Tangy Mustard, 323
Glaze, Game Hens with
Chutney-Mustard, 66
Honey Mustard, Hot, 240
Horseradish Mustard, 240
Jalapeño Mustard, 240
Marinade, Honey-Mustard, 103
Sauce, Creamy Mustard, 240
Sauce, Hot Mustard, 240
Sauce, Mustard, 118
Sauce, Shrimp with Mustard-Vinegar, 240
Sauce, Turkey Cutlets with
Tarragon-Mustard, 239
Vegetables, Honey-Mustard Marinated, 236
Vinaigrette, Baby Lettuces
with Mustard, 67

Noodles
Bake, Turkey Noodle, 243

Oatmeal
Breakfast Oatmeal Surprise, 178
Cookies, Crispy Coconut-Oatmeal, 80
Cookies, Oatmeal-Raisin, 127
Ice Cream Sandwiches, Oatmeal
Crispy, 199
Pancakes, Whole Wheat-Oat, 16
Okra
Fried Okra and Green Tomatoes, 160
Goulash, Okra, 160
Muffins, Fresh Okra, 161
Pilaf, Okra, 160
Olives
Bread, Olive, 78
Salad with Sherry Vinaigrette, Shrimp,
Orange, and Olive, 177
Onions
Bake, Four Onion, 304
Butter, Sweet Onion, 124
Chutney, Kiwifruit-Onion, 125
Dip, Curry-Onion, 313
Focaccia, Onion, 77
Green Beans with Roasted Red Peppers and
Pearl Onions, 260
Jelly, Onion, 135
Muffins, Onion-Dill, 144
Parmesan Onions, 170
Relish, Sweet Onion, 124
Rings, Crispy Baked Onion, 247

Salmon with Mushrooms and Green Onions,
Fresh, 180
Soup, French Onion, 246
On The Light Side
Appetizers
Buzzard's Nests, 244
Dip, Creamy Ham, 125
Dip, Garbanzo, 94
Dip, Monster Mash, 244
Dip, Skinny Ranch, 96
Mix, Crunchy Snack, 94
Pâté, Black-Eyed Pea, 97
Pita Wedges, Garlic, 98
Popcorn with Pizzazz, 245
Beverages
Banana Smoothie, 95
Brew, Witch's, 244
Punch, Citrus, 99
Breads
Biscuits, Herbed, 67
Cornbread, Mexican, 182
Cornbread Supreme, 67
Rolls, Parsley-Garlic, 319
Toast Strips, Seasoned, 98
Croutons, Bagel, 192
Croutons, Cornbread, 192
Croutons, Pita, 192
Desserts
Apples, Caramel-Peanut, M244
Brownies, Chocolate-Kahlúa, 99
Cake, Banana-Coconut, 154
Cake, Black Widow Snack, 245
Cake, Chocolate-Cinnamon, 154
Cake, Lemon-Poppy Seed, 154
Cake, Pumpkin, 303
Cake, Red Velvet, 318
Cheesecake, Chocolate-Amaretto, 97
Cobbler, Raspberry-Cherry, 230
Coffee Cake, Sour Cream, 154
Cookies, Oatmeal-Raisin, 127
Frosting, Boiled, 318
Fruit Tartlets, Fresh, 96
Glaze, Lemon, 154
Eggs Benedict, Light, M68
Fruit with Lemon-Yogurt Dressing, Fresh, 17
Guacamole, Mock, 36
Linguine with Red Pepper Sauce, 127
Main Dishes
Beef, American Steakhouse, 15
Beef and Cauliflower over Rice, 94
Beef, Marinated Sauerbraten, 16
Chicken and Dumplings,
Old-Fashioned, 302
Chicken Chili Bake, 302
Chicken Cordon Bleu, 126
Chicken, Oven-Fried, 90
Chicken with Mole Sauce, 34
Chiles Rellenos, Light, 156
Chili, 89
Chili, Firestarter, 34
Game Hens with Chutney-Mustard
Glaze, 66
Ham-Potato-Pineapple Bake, 302
Hopping John with Grilled Pork
Medaillons, 229
Lentils-and-Rice Casserole, 301
Orange Roughy, Vegetable-Topped, 67
Perch, Parmesan-Crusted, 91
Polenta with Black Bean Salsa, Grilled, 155
Pork Loin Roast, Barbecued, 34
Pork Medaillons, Grilled, 229

On The Light Side, Main Dishes
(continued)

Ravioli, Mediterranean, 301
Roast Beef, Deli-Style, 15
Shrimp with Peanut Sauce, 303
Steak Kabobs, 95
Tuna with Rosemary,
    Broiled, 127
Turkey, Lazy Day, 93
Veal, Lemon, 35
Pancakes, Whole Wheat-Oat, 16
Pizza on a Bagel, M94
Relish, White Bean, 229
Rice with Black-Eyed Peas, 66
Salad Dressings
    Creamy Dressing, 318
    Lemon-Yogurt Dressing, 17
    Wine Vinegar Dressing, 126
Salads
    Black-Eyed Pea Salad, Marinated, 190
    Chicken-and-Walnut Salad,
        Sunburst, 91
    Chicken-Raspberry Salad,
        Marinated, 190
    Coleslaw, Light and Creamy, 318
    Composé, Salad, 126
    Green Beans with Creamy Tarragon
        Dressing, 191
    Lettuces with Mustard Vinaigrette,
        Baby, 67
    Potato Salad, Hot-and-Light, 90
    Potato Slices, Marinated, 98
    Seafood Salad Sussex Shores, 98
    Spinach Salad, Wilted, 125
    Wild Rice Salad, 191
Sauces
    Basil-Brown Butter Sauce, 92
    Cheese Sauce, Guilt-Free, M95
    Hollandaise Sauce, Mock, 68
    Jalapeño Sauce, 230
    Raspberry Sauce, 99
    Salsa, Black Bean, 155
    Sauerbraten Sauce, 16
Soups
    Bean-and-Turkey Soup, 319
    Broccoli Soup, Light Cream of, 17
    Pepper Soup, Spicy, 98
Syrup, Maple, 16
Vegetables
    Beets, Ginger-Marmalade Glazed, 35
    Black Bean Terrine with Fresh Tomato
        Coulis and Jalapeño Sauce, 230
    Black-Eyed Peas, 180
    Bundles, Vegetable, 181
    Cabbage with Caraway, 181
    Carrots, Lemon-Dill Steamed, 180
    Corn, Spicy Mexican, 90
    Eggplant Casserole, Spicy Hot, 92
    Garlic Broccoli, 35
    Green Bean Medley, Peppery, 181
    Green Beans with Mushrooms, 89
    Onion Rings, Crispy Baked, 247
    Potatoes au Gratin, 90
    Potatoes, Cottage, M92
    Rice, Vegetables and, 91
    Steamed Garden Vegetables, 155
    Steamed Herbed Vegetables, M303
    Sugar Snap Peas with Basil
        and Lemon, 66
    Tomato Coulis, Fresh, 230

Vinegar, Raspberry Wine, 191
Vinegar, Shallot-Tarragon-Garlic, 191
Oranges
Baked Fruit, Ginger-Orange, 313
Baskets, Orange, 286
Beverage
    Jogger's Sunrise, 213
Butter, Tomato-Curry-Orange, 159
Chicken Drummettes, Orange-Pecan, 158
Desserts
    Cake, Orange-Pecan Pound, 13
    Champagne Oranges, 83
    Chiffon Dessert, Orange, 295
    Chocolate-Orange Delights, 52
    Kiwi-and-Orange Dessert, 295
    Pralines, Orange, 51
    Slices, Burgundy-Spiced Orange, 294
Dressing, Orange-Curd, 22
Filling, Cheese-and-Orange, 159
Salads
    Grapefruit Salad, Orange-, 294
    Mandarin Salad, Broccoli-, 325
    Shrimp, Orange, and Olive Salad with
        Sherry Vinaigrette, 177
    Strawberry Salad with Orange-Curd
        Dressing, Orange-, 22
    Turkey-in-the-Orange Salad, 21
Sauce, Sweet Orange, M325
Swordfish Steaks, Orange-Ginger
    Marinated, 271
Vinaigrette Dressing, Tangy Orange, 46
Orzo
Marinara on Beds of Spinach and Orzo, 320
Oysters
Baked Oysters on the Half Shell, 269
Bienville, Oysters, 257
Creamed Oysters, Pan-Fried Grits with, 62
Stewed in Cream, Oysters, 50

Pancakes
Apple-Topped Pancakes, 339
Corn Pancakes, 43
Pancakes, Whole Wheat-Oat, 16
Refrigerator Pancakes, Overnight, 196
Sausage Wedges, Pancake-, 196
Vegetable-Rice Pancakes, 43
Whole Grain Pancakes, 123
Zucchini Pancakes, 43
Pastas. *See also* specific types.
Angel Hair Pasta with Tomato
    Cream Sauce, 292
Basil Pasta, Fresh Tomato Sauce over, 176
Chicken and Pasta, Quick, 14
Peas and Pasta, 139
Primavera, Pasta, 168
Ravioli, Mediterranean, 301
Shells, Southwestern Stuffed, 234
Spinach-Peanut Pesto and Pasta, 212
Tomato Pasta, Caribbean, 201
Tomato Pasta, Italian, 201
Tomato Pasta, Southwestern, 201
Tortellini with Parsley-Caper Sauce, 175
Tricolor Pasta with Clam Sauce, 272
Vegetables and Pasta, Roasted, 184
Pâtés. *See* Appetizers/Pâtés.
Peaches
Caramel Peaches, 134
Cream, Honeyed Peaches 'n', 134
Crisp, Peach, 134
Ice Cream, Peach, 135
Jam, Peach, 135

Shake, Peach Melba Sundae, 134
Sorbet, Peach, 153
Torte, Frozen Peach, 135
Peanut Butter
Bars, Peanut Butter, 166
Candy, Peanut Butter, 166
Cookies, Peanut Truffle, 212
Dip, Peanut Butter Lovers', 162
French Toast, Peanut Butter, 166
Ice Cream Sandwiches, Peanut Butter
    Cookie, 199
Pie, "Working for Peanuts," 115
Pinecones, Peanut Butter-Suet, 286
Pralines, Chocolate-Peanut Butter, 51
Pralines, Peanut Butter, 51
Pudding, Peanut Butter-Banana, 340
Sandwiches, Spider, 193
Shake, PBJ, 292
Soup, Cream of Peanut, 288
Peanuts
Apples, Caramel-Peanut, M244
Bread, Peanut Lover's, 211
Chesapeake Nuts, 269
Chocolate-Peanut Crispies, 80
Crust, Sweet Potatoes with Peanut, 212
Filling, Peanut, 211
Pesto and Pasta, Spinach-Peanut, 212
Pie, "Working for Peanuts," 115
Sauce, Hot Indonesian Peanut, 211
Sauce, Shrimp with Peanut, 303
Slaw, Chinese Peanut, 212
Pears
Baked Pears, Honey-, 47
en Croûte, Pears, 210
Gratin, Pear-Blue Cheese, 328
Pie, Backyard Pear, 237
Pie, Ginger-Pear, 48
Pie, Pear-Macadamia, 260
Spread, Pear-Cream Cheese, 80
Peas
Black-Eyed
    Hopping John with Grilled Pork
        Medaillons, 229
    Pâté, Black-Eyed Pea, 97
    Peas, Black-Eyed, 180
    Rice with Black-Eyed Peas, 66
    Salad, Marinated Black-Eyed Pea, 190
    Salsa, Black-Eyed Pea, 164
    Stew, Ham-and-Black-Eyed Pea, 20
English
    Braised Belgian Endive and Peas, 22
    Celery, Peas and, 289
    Pasta, Peas and, 139
    Soup, Pea-and-Watercress, 162
    Sugar Snap Peas with Basil and Lemon, 66
    Sugar Snaps and Carrots, Creamed, 139
    Sugar Snaps and Peppers, 139
Pecans
Bread, Bourbon-Pecan, 308
Cake, Marbled Pecan Pound, 313
Cake, Orange-Pecan Pound, 13
Casserole, Carrot-Pecan, 44
Chesapeake Nuts, 269
Chicken Drummettes, Orange-Pecan, 158
Chicken Fingers, Buttermilk-Pecan, 165
Deviled Nuts, 118
Muffins, Banana-Nut, 140
Nippy Nuts, 301
Pepper Pecans, 79
Pie, Chocolate-Pecan Chess, 251
Pie, Lemon-Pecan, 251

Pie, Turtle Pecan, 250
Praline Brownies, 243
Pralines, Basic, 50
Pralines, Bourbon, 51
Pralines, Café au Lait, 51
Pralines, Chocolate, 51
Pralines, Chocolate-Mint, 51
Pralines, Chocolate-Peanut Butter, 51
Pralines, Hot Spicy, 51
Pralines, Mocha, 51
Pralines, Orange, 51
Pralines, Peanut Butter, 51
Pralines, Vanilla, 51
Shortcake, Banana-Pecan, 43
Special, Old Pecan Street, 251
Spicy Pecans, 279
Tart with Caramel Sauce, Chocolate-Pecan, 296
Topping, Apple-Nut, 162
Wafers, Sage-Pecan Cheese, 12

Peppermint
Brownies, Southern Chocolate-Mint, 216
Dessert, Triple Mint Ice-Cream Angel, 86
Frosting, Mint Cream, 216
Mousse, Peppermint, 315
Parfait, Peppermint, 315
Pralines, Chocolate-Mint, 51
Snowball Surprises, 315

Peppers
Chile
    Green Chile-Cornbread Dressing, 306
    Havarti-and-Corn-Stuffed Chiles
        Rellenos with Walnut Cream
        Sauce, M275
    Sauce, Verde, 275
    Stuffed Green Chiles, 208
Jalapeño
    Chicken, Grilled Jalapeño, 213
    Muffins, Jalapeño-Corn, 164
    Mustard, Jalapeño, 240
    Pickled Jalapeño Peppers, 136
    Sauce, Jalapeño, 230
Parmesan Pepper Toss, 208
Red Pepper Puree, 275
Red Peppers and Pearl Onions, Green Beans
    with Roasted, 260
Red Pepper Salad, Tuna-and-, 143
Red Pepper Sauce, Linguine with, 127
Red Pepper Soup, Chilled Sweet, 69
Soup, Spicy Pepper, 98
Soup, Sweet Pepper, 277
Sugar Snaps and Peppers, 139
Sweet Peppers with Tomatoes, Stir-
    Fried, 207

Pickles and Relishes
Carrots, Pickled, 12
Chutney, Kiwifruit-Onion, 125
Corn Relish, Sweet, 119
Jalapeño Peppers, Pickled, 136
Onion Relish, Sweet, 124
Salsa, Spicy Corn, 322
Squash, Pickled Yellow, 136
Tomato Sweet Relish, Green, 136
White Bean Relish, 229

Pies and Pastries
Blueberry-Banana Pie, 115
Cherry Confetti Pie, No-Bake, 114
Chocolate Pie, German, 129
Christmas Pie, White, 289
Cobblers
    Peach Crisp, 134
    Raspberry-Cherry Cobbler, 230

Coconut Pie, 115
Cream Puffs, Lemon, 254
Lemon Fluff Pie, 46
Main Dish
    Beef Pot Pies with Yorkshire Pudding
        Topping, 45
    Breakfast Pie, Country, M328
    Spaghetti-Ham Pie, 19
    Turkey Pot Pie, 45
Pastries and Crusts
    Citrus Pastry, Hint-of-, 260
    Pastry Shell, 289
    Phyllo Baskets, Walnut-, 210
    Puff Pastry Baskets, 177
    Sugar Cookie Crust, 131
Peanuts" Pie, "Working for, 115
Pear-Macadamia Pie, 260
Pear Pie, Backyard, 237
Pear Pie, Ginger-, 48
Pears en Croûte, 210
Pecan
    Chocolate-Pecan Chess Pie, 251
    Lemon-Pecan Pie, 251
    Special, Old Pecan Street, 251
    Turtle Pecan Pie, 250
Puff Pastry Baskets, Tropical, 177
Strudels, Spinach, 249
Tarts
    Blackberry Pudding Tarts, 200
    Caramel Turtle Truffle Tart, M131
    Chocolate-Pecan Tart with Caramel
        Sauce, 296
    Fruit Tartlets, Fresh, 96
    Fruit Tarts, Bowl-Me-Over Fresh, 200
Turnovers, Baked Apple, 338

Pineapple
Bake, Ham-Potato-Pineapple, 302
Gratin, Pineapple, 328
Lemonade, Pineapple, 194
Muffins, Morning Glory, 327
Smoothie, Quick Banana-Pineapple, 195
Spread, Coconut-Pineapple, 309
Tea, Pineapple, 165
Trifle, Pineapple Angel Food, 86

Pizza
Bagel, Pizza on a, M94
Crust, Parmesan Pizza, 58
Crust, Whole Wheat Pizza, 58
Grilled Pizzas, 178
Ham-and-Eggs Crescent Pizza, 47
Hot Dog Pizzas, 78

Popcorn
Pizzazz, Popcorn with, 245

Pork. See also Bacon, Ham, Sausage.
Chops
    Beans, Pork Chops with Baked, 18
    Parmesan Pork Chops with Apples, 338
Meat Loaf
    Family-Style Meat Loaf, 18
    Veal Meat Loaf, 292
Picadillo II, 72
Roast, Barbecued Pork Loin, 34
Tenderloin
    Medaillons, Grilled Pork, 229
    Peking Pork Tenderloin, 173
Terrine of Pork and Veal, 287

Potatoes
au Gratin, Potatoes, 90, 217
Baked
    Pleated Potatoes, Baked, 54
    Taco-Topped Potatoes, M18

Bake, Ham-Potato-Pineapple, 302
Broiled Marinated Potatoes, 54
Cottage Potatoes, M92
Duchess Potatoes, 288
Fried Potato Patties, 54
Gratin, Dual Potato, 328
Mashed Potatoes, Garlic, 328
Mashed Potatoes, Herbed Lemon, 208
Mashed Potatoes, Quick-and-Easy, 41
Moussaka, Potatoes, 44
Parmesan Potatoes, M46
Pie, Country Breakfast, M328
Salads
    Dill-and-Sour Cream Potato Salad, 105
    Hot-and-Light Potato Salad, 90
    Marinated Potato Slices, 98
    Red Potato Salad, 119
Skillet Potatoes, Oregano-and-Lemon, 54
Stir-Fry, Potato, 240

Potatoes, Sweet
Biscuits, Sweet Potato Angel, 312
Chips, Sweet Potato, 332
Chips with Blue Cheese, Sweet Potato, 290
Grilled Sweet Potatoes, 213
Oven-Fried Sweet Potatoes
    with Chutney, 241
Peanut Crust, Sweet Potatoes with, 212
Rolls, Sweet Potato, 172
Slaw, Sweet Potato-Currant, 246
Soufflé, Sweet Potato, 325
Yams, Rosemary-Garlic, 174

Pralines
Basic Pralines, 50
Bourbon Pralines, 51
Brownies, Praline, 243
Café au Lait Pralines, 51
Chocolate-Mint Pralines, 51
Chocolate-Peanut Butter Pralines, 51
Chocolate Pralines, 51
Hot Spicy Pralines, 51
Mocha Pralines, 51
Orange Pralines, 51
Peanut Butter Pralines, 51
Vanilla Pralines, 51
Sauce, Praline, 214

Pretzels
Garlands, Pretzel, 286

Puddings. See also Custards.
Biscuit Pudding, 51
Blackberry Pudding Tarts, 200
Bread Pudding, Spiced, 52
Bread Pudding with Bourbon Sauce,
    Tennessee, 51
Holland Rusk Pudding, Yia Yia's, 124
Peanut Butter-Banana Pudding, 340

Pumpkin
Cake, Pumpkin, 303
Cookies, Pumpkin-Chocolate Chip, 235
Gingerbread with Caramel Sauce,
    Pumpkin, 235
Soup, Cream of Pumpkin, 234
Swirl, Easy Pumpkin, 234

Quail
Pepper Feet, 258
Smoked Quail, 236
Stuffed with Cornbread Dressing, Quail, 280

Quiches
Mexicali Quiche with Avocado Topping, 309
South-of-the-Border Quiche, 321
Wild Rice-and-Mushroom Quiches, 237

Raisins
Biscuits, Cinnamon-Raisin Breakfast, 159
Bread, Raisin-Whole Wheat, 77
Cake, Cinnamon-Raisin Coffee, 180
Cookies, Oatmeal-Raisin, 127
Slaw, Sweet Potato-Currant, 246

Raspberries
Biscuits, Raspberry-Almond, 160
Bisque, Banana-Raspberry, 161
Brie in Rye, Raspberry, 252
Cobbler, Raspberry-Cherry, 230
Crêpes with Yogurt Filling, Fresh
    Raspberry, 123
Jellyrolls, Raspberry, M255
Mousse in Chocolate Crinkle Cups,
    Raspberry, 270
Parfait, White Chocolate-Raspberry
    Swirl, 315
Salad, Marinated Chicken-Raspberry, 190
Sauce, Fresh Raspberry, 120
Sauce, Raspberry, 82, 99, 315
Shake, Peach Melba Sundae, 134
Vinegar, Raspberry Wine, 191

Relishes. *See* Pickles and Relishes.

Rice
Asparagus, Rice and, 324
Beef and Cauliflower over Rice, 94
Black-Eyed Peas, Rice with, 66
Casserole, Lentils-and-Rice, 301
Dirty Rice, Hot, 219
Herbed Rice, 278
Pancakes, Vegetable-Rice, 43
Pilaf, Okra, 160
Saffron Rice, 282
Vegetables and Rice, 91
Wild Rice
    Quiches, Wild Rice-and-Mushroom, 237
    Salad, Wild Rice, 191

Rolls and Buns. *See also* Breads.
Dinner Rolls, M326
Parsley-Garlic Rolls, 319
Sour Cream Yeast Rolls, 232
Sweet Potato Rolls, 172

Salad Dressings
Basil Vinaigrette, 106
Citrus-Cilantro Dressing, 310
Creamy Dressing, 318
Curry Vinaigrette, Warm, 107
Dried Tomato Vinaigrette, 272
Fruit Salad Dressing, 184
Ginger Dressing, 290
Honey-Lemon Dressing, Fruit Salad with, 21
Honey-Lime Dressing, 71
Honey-Walnut Dressing, 107
Honey-Yogurt Dressing, 172
Lemon-Yogurt Dressing, 17
Mustard Dressing, Tangy, 323
Mustard Vinaigrette, Baby Lettuces with, 67
Orange-Curd Dressing, 22
Orange Vinaigrette Dressing, Tangy, 46
Poppy Seed Dressing, 65, 168
Roquefort Dressing, 128
Sesame-Soy Dressing, 106
Spinach Salad Dressing, 250
Vinaigrette Dressing, 41
Vinaigrette, Herbed, 120
Vinaigrette, Versatile, 140
Wine Vinegar Dressing, 126

Salads
Avocado-Grapefruit Salad, 282
Bean Salad, Marinated, 312
Beef Salad, Western-Style, 321
Black-Eyed Pea Salad, Marinated, 190
Broccoli-Mandarin Salad, 325
Caesar Salad, Turkey, 320
Caesar Salad with White Beans, 30
Chicken
    Fried Chicken Ginger Salad, 290
    Mama Hudson's Chicken Salad, 238
    Marinated Chicken-Raspberry
        Salad, 190
    Roasted Chicken Salad, 14
    Walnut Salad, Sunburst Chicken-and-, 91
Congealed
    Asparagus Salad, Creamy Lemon-, 116
Corn-in-the-Shuck Salad, 236
Crab-and-Endive Salad, Marinated, 22
Cucumber Salad, Dilled, 65
Endive-Tomato Starburst Salad, 323
Fennel Salad, Marinated, 56
Fruit. *See also* Salads/Congealed.
    Avocado-Fruit Salad with Honey-Yogurt
        Dressing, 172
    Citrus-Cilantro Dressing, Fruit Salad
        with, 310
    Green Fruit Salad with Honey-Lime
        Dressing, 71
    Honey-Lemon Dressing, Fruit Salad
        with, 21
    Multi-Fruit Salad, 184
Greek Salad, 208
Green. *See also* Salads/Spinach.
    Apple and Brie, Salad Greens with, 241
    Boston Lettuce and Watercress
        Salad, 65
    Endive-Watercress Salad, 22
    Lettuces with Mustard Vinaigrette,
        Baby, 67
    Marinated Cheese Dressing, Green
        Salad with, 206
Mozzarella-Tomato-Basil Salad, Fresh, 131
Mushroom Salad, Fresh, 65
Orange-Grapefruit Salad, 294
Orange-Strawberry Salad with Orange-Curd
    Dressing, 22
Potato
    Dill-and-Sour Cream Potato Salad, 105
    Hot-and-Light Potato Salad, 90
    Marinated Potato Slices, 98
    Red Potato Salad, 119
Rice Salad, Wild, 191
Salmon on Mixed Greens with Creamy Dill
    Dressing, 143
Seafood Salad Sussex Shores, 98
Shrimp-and-Black Bean Salad,
    Caribbean, 143
Shrimp, Orange, and Olive Salad with Sherry
    Vinaigrette, 177
Shrimp Salad, 238
Shrimp Salad, Marinated, 321
Slaws
    Broccoli Slaw, Zesty, 246
    Layered Slaw, 214
    Light and Creamy Coleslaw, 318
    Mango Slaw, 31
    Old-Fashioned Sweet Coleslaw, 128
    Peanut Slaw, Chinese, 212
    Silks, Slaw, 236
    Sweet Potato-Currant Slaw, 246

Spinach and Sun-Dried Tomato Salad, 250
Spinach Salad, 46, 65
Spinach Salad, Strawberry-, 168
Spinach Salad, Wilted, 125
Spinach Salad with Dried Tomato
    Vinaigrette, 272
Summer Salad, 179
Tabbouleh, 70
Tex-Mex Salad, Marinated, 106
Tomato-and-Cucumber Summer Salad, 141
Tuna-and-Red Pepper Salad, 143
Turkey-in-the-Orange Salad, 21
Vegetable. *See also* Salads/Congealed.
    Composé, Salad, 126
    Primavera Salad, 140

Salmon
Fillets with Sweet Corn Relish, Salmon, 119
Mixed Greens with Creamy Dill Dressing,
    Salmon on, 143
Mushrooms and Green Onions, Fresh Salmon
    with, 180
Steaks, Grilled Herbed Salmon, 176

Sandwiches
BLT Croissants, 158
BLT in Pita Pockets, 158
BLT Sandwiches, Curried, 158
Fruit Sandwiches, Glazed Breakfast, 178
Ice Cream Sandwiches, Oatmeal Crispy, 199
Ice Cream Sandwiches, Peanut Butter
    Cookie, 199
Party Sandwiches, Double-Filled, 159
Po-Boy, Pain-Perdu, 291
Spider Sandwiches, 193
Turkey Sandwich, Hot, 306

Sauces. *See also* Desserts/Sauces.
Barbecue Sauce, 129
Basil-Brown Butter Sauce, 92
Black Bean Sauce, 59
Champagne-Saffron Sauce,
    Scallops with, 177
Cheese Sauce, 48
Cheese Sauce, Guilt-Free, M95
Clam Sauce, Tricolor Pasta with, 272
Cream Sauce, 157
Florentine Sauce, 48
Goat Cheese Sauce, Asparagus with, 116
Hollandaise Sauce, Lime, 121
Hollandaise Sauce, Mock, 68
Honey-Poppy Seed Sauce, 13
Horseradish Sauce, 215
Hot Diggity Dog Sauce, 198
Jezebel Sauce, 331
Juniper Sauce, 278
Lemon-Parsley Sauce, 48
Marinade, Cinnamon-Soy, 103
Marinade, Citrus, 103
Marinade, Garlic-Honey, 102
Marinade, Honey-Mustard, 103
Marinade, Oriental, 102
Marinade, Southwestern, 102
Marinade, Teriyaki, 102
Mushroom Sauce, Eggs Baked in, 47
Mustard Sauce, 118
Mustard Sauce, Creamy, 240
Mustard Sauce, Hot, 240
Mustard-Vinegar Sauce, Shrimp with, 240
Orange Sauce, Sweet, M325
Parsley-Caper Sauce, Tortellini with, 175
Peanut Sauce, Hot Indonesian, 211
Peanut Sauce, Shrimp with, 303
Pesto and Pasta, Spinach-Peanut, 212

Red Hot Sauce, 158
Rémoulade Sauce, 280
Salsa, Black Bean, 155
Salsa, Black-Eyed Pea, 164
Salsa, Three Tomato, 138
Sauerbraten Sauce, 16
Sour Cream Sauce, 162
Spinach Pasta Sauce, 71
Spinach Pesto Sauce, 59
Taco Sauce, 69
Tarragon-Mustard Sauce, Turkey Cutlets
  with, 239
Teriyaki Sauce, 258
Tomato Cream Sauce, Angel Hair
  Pasta with, 292
Tomato Sauce, Basil-, 25, 48, 65
Tomato Sauce, Creamy, 71
Tomato Sauce over Basil Pasta, Fresh, 176
Tomato Sauce, Red Pepper-, 59
Verde Sauce, 275
Vinaigrette, Versatile, 141
Walnut Cream Sauce, 275
White Sauce, Medium, 48
Wine Sauce, White, 49
Zucchini-Mushroom Sauce, 71

Sausage
Breakfast Delight, 195
Chili Goes Southwest, Basic, 326
Dressing, Sausage-Apple, 305
Jambalaya, Trail, 179
Muffins, Cheesy Sausage, 144
Pancake-Sausage Wedges, 196
Pinwheels, Sausage, 238
Polenta with Sausage, 32
Quiche, South-of-the-Border, 321
Quiche with Avocado Topping,
  Mexicali, 309
Sticks, Beef, 331

Scallops
Champagne-Saffron Sauce,
  Scallops with, 177

Seafood. *See also* specific types and Fish.
Boil, Southern Shellfish, 258
Mussel Soup, 259
Salad Sussex Shores, Seafood, 98
Seasoning Rub, Seafood, 101

Seasonings
Creole Rub, 101
Herb Rub, 102
Jerk Rub, 101
Mexican Rub, 102
Seafood Seasoning Rub, 101

Shrimp
Appetizer, Artichoke-and-Shrimp, 271
Boil, Southern Shellfish, 258
Breakfast Shrimp, Classic Charleston, 60
Canapés, Shrimp-and-Cucumber, 164
Creole, Shrimp, 282
Fried Marinated Shrimp with Mango Slaw, 31
Mold with Asparagus, Shrimp, 214
Mustard-Vinegar Sauce, Shrimp with, 240
Pasta Primavera, Shrimp with, 168
Peanut Sauce, Shrimp with, 303
Salad, Caribbean Shrimp-and-Black
  Bean, 143
Salad, Marinated Shrimp, 321
Salad, Shrimp, 238
Salad with Sherry Vinaigrette, Shrimp,
  Orange, and Olive, 177
Scampi, Shrimp, 70
Spread, Shrimp, 205

Stir-Fry, Beef-and-Shrimp, 32
Stock, Shrimp, 60
Topping, Shrimp, 291
Tostadas, Shrimp-and-Black Bean, 204

Soufflés
Ham Breakfast Soufflé, Virginia, 121
Sweet Potato Soufflé, 325

Soups. *See also* Chili, Chowder, Gumbo, Stews.
Avocado Soup, Chilled, 108
Bean-and-Turkey Soup, 319
Bisque, Banana-Raspberry, 161
Bisque, Make-Ahead Tomato-Basil, 322
Black Bean Soup, 231
Broccoli Soup, Light Cream of, 17
Gazpacho, 215
Gazpacho, Secret, 161
Gazpacho, Smoked Vegetable, 156
Jambalaya, Trail, 179
Lemon-Egg Drop Soup, 81
Mussel Soup, 259
Mustard Green Soup, Cream of, 280
Onion Soup, French, 246
Pea-and-Watercress Soup, 162
Peanut Soup, Cream of, 288
Pepper Soup, Spicy, 98
Pepper Soup, Sweet, 277
Pumpkin Soup, Cream of, 234
Red Pepper Soup, Chilled Sweet, 69
Tortilla Soup, 197, 274
Tortilla Soup, Spicy, 108
Vegetable Soup, 157
Vegetable Soup, Spicy, 293
Zucchini Soup with Cilantro, 130

Spaghetti
Pie, Spaghetti-Ham, 19

Spinach
Casserole, Spinach-Artichoke, 44
Dip, Spinach, 324
Fantastic, Spinach, 173
Florentine, Chicken, 107
Florentine Sauce, 48
Marinara on Beds of Spinach and Orzo, 320
Parmesan, Spinach, 72
Pesto and Pasta, Spinach-Peanut, 212
Salad Dressing, Spinach, 250
Salads
  Dried Tomato Vinaigrette, Spinach
    Salad with, 272
  Spinach Salad, 46, 65
  Strawberry-Spinach Salad, 168
  Sun-Dried Tomato Salad,
    Spinach and, 250
Salad, Wilted Spinach, 125
Sauce, Spinach Pasta, 71
Sauce, Spinach Pesto, 59
Sautéed Spinach, 250
Sauté, Fresh Spinach, 55
Spread, Parmesan-Spinach, 55
Strudels, Spinach, 249
Tomatoes, Spinach-Stuffed, 281

Spreads. *See also* Appetizers/Spreads.
Aioli, Shortcut, 157
Cheese Spread, Make-Ahead, 324
Cherry Spread, 309
Chili Cheese Spread, 242
Coconut-Pineapple Spread, 309
Crab Spread, 167
Cranberry Salsa with Sweet
  Potato Chips, 332
Cucumber Spread, 158
Curry Spread, 159

Pear-Cream Cheese Spread, 80
Relish Spread, Creamy, 217
Shrimp Spread, 205
White Bean Spread, 30

Squash. *See also* Zucchini.
Acorn Squash-Mushroom Puree, 305
Baby Squash, 118
Butternut Stir-Fry, Honey-, 184
Mirlitons, Stuffed, 278
Yellow Squash, Pickled, 136

Stews. *See also* Chili, Gumbo, Soups.
Ham-and-Black-Eyed Pea Stew, 20
Minestrone Stew, 184
Shrimp Creole, 282
Tzimmes with Brisket, Mixed Fruit, 114

Strawberries
Arnaud, Strawberries, 50
Frozen Strawberry Refresher, 213
Fudge Balls, Strawberry, 80
Jamaica, Strawberries, 239
Lemonade, Berry Delicious, 205
Salad, Strawberry-Spinach, 168
Salad with Orange-Curd Dressing,
  Orange-Strawberry, 22
Sauce, Strawberries Arnaud, 50
Shortcakes, Strawberry Crispy, 42
Sorbet, Strawberry, 153

Stroganoff
Beef Stroganoff, 18

Stuffings and Dressings
Cornbread Dressing, Green Chile-, 306
Cornbread Dressing, Quail Stuffed with, 280
Grits Dressing, 306
Sausage-Apple Dressing, 305

Syrups
Maple Syrup, 16
Sugar Syrup, 29

Tacos
Chicken-and-Bean Tacos, 293
Dip, Hot Taco, 238
Potatoes, Taco-Topped, M18
Sauce, Taco, 69

Terrines
Black Bean Terrine with Fresh Tomato Coulis
  and Jalapeño Sauce, 230
Cheese Terrine, Italian, 64
Pork and Veal, Terrine of, 287
Veal Terrine with Mustard Sauce, 118

Tomatoes
Bisque, Make-Ahead Tomato-Basil, 322
Butter, Tomato-Curry-Orange, 159
Cherry Tomatoes, Marinated Dried, 23
Coulis, Fresh Tomato, 230
Croissants, BLT, 158
Dip, Cottage Cheese Sun-Dried Tomato, 13
Dried Tomato Vinaigrette, 272
Gravy, Tomato, 18
Green Tomatoes, Curried, 138
Green Tomatoes, Fried Okra and, 160
Green Tomato Sweet Relish, 136
Hot Tomatoes, 138
Pasta, Caribbean Tomato, 201
Pasta, Italian Tomato, 201
Pasta, Southwestern Tomato, 201
Pita Pockets, BLT in, 158
Salad, Endive-Tomato Starburst, 323
Salad, Fresh Mozzarella-Tomato-Basil, 131
Salad, Tomato-and-Cucumber Summer, 141
Salsa, Three Tomato, 138
Sandwiches, Curried BLT, 158

Tomatoes
(continued)

Sauce, Angel Hair Pasta with Tomato
   Cream, 292
Sauce, Basil-Tomato, 25, 48, 65
Sauce, Creamy Tomato, 71
Sauce over Basil Pasta, Fresh Tomato, 176
Sauce, Red Pepper-Tomato, 59
Skillet, Zucchini-Tomato, 206
Stir-Fried Sweet Peppers with
   Tomatoes, 207
Stuffed Tomatoes, Broccoli-, 216
Stuffed Tomatoes, Spinach-, 281
Sun-Dried Tomatoes and Rosemary, Goat
   Cheese with, 175
Sun-Dried Tomato Salad, Spinach and, 250
Tortillas. *See also* Burritos, Enchiladas,
   Tacos.
Chicken Tostadas, 204
Franks, Mexican, 78
Ham Appetillas, 63
Soup, Spicy Tortilla, 108
Soup, Tortilla, 197, 274
Tostadas, Crab, 203
Tostadas, Shrimp-and-Black Bean, 204
Tuna
Broiled Tuna with Rosemary, 127
Grilled Florida Tuna, 128
Salad, Tuna-and-Red Pepper, 143
Turkey
Bake, Turkey Noodle, 243
Cutlets with Tarragon-Mustard Sauce,
   Turkey, 239
Lasagna, Easy, M24
Lazy Day Turkey, 93
Pot Pie, Turkey, 45
Salad, Turkey Caesar, 320
Salad, Turkey-in-the-Orange, 21
Sandwich, Hot Turkey, 306
Sauté, Creamy Turkey, 19
Soup, Bean-and-Turkey, 319
Steaks, Grilled Marinated Turkey, 170
Treats, Turkey, 256
Turnips
Sauté, Carrot-Turnip, 241

Vanilla
Almond Crunch, Vanilla, 243
Pralines, Vanilla, 51
Veal
Amaretto-Lime Veal, 54
Lemon Veal, 35
Meat Loaf, Veal, 292
Terrine of Pork and Veal, 287
Terrine with Mustard Sauce, Veal, 118
Vegetables. *See also* specific types and
   Canning.
Appetizer, Hot Vegetable Juice, 324
Bake with Sweet Bacon Dressing,
   Vegetable-Chicken, 108
Bundles, Vegetable, 181
Buñuelos, 29
Burritos, Vegetarian, 319
Chili, Mom's, 292
Enchiladas, Meatless, 106
Fennel, Italian-Style Braised, 56
Fennel with Garlic Butter,
   Steamed, 56
Frittata, Fresh Vegetable, 140
Frittata, Vegetable, 183
Gazpacho, Smoked Vegetable, 156
Julienne Vegetables, 31
Kabobs, Grilled Vegetable, 170
Lasagna Casserole, Vegetable, 25
Lasagna, Vegetable, 320
Lemon Vegetables, 83
Marinated Vegetables, Honey-Mustard, 236
Orange Roughy, Vegetable-Topped, 67
Pancakes, Vegetable-Rice, 43
Primavera, Pasta, 168
Punch, Hot Vegetable, 12
Puree, Smoked Vegetable, 156
Rice, Vegetables and, 91
Roasted Vegetables and Pasta, 184
Roasted Vegetables, Traveling Linguine
   with, 178
Salads
   Composé, Salad, 126
   Fennel Salad, Marinated, 56
   Greek Salad, 208
   Primavera Salad, 140
   Slaw, Layered, 214

Soups
   Spicy Vegetable Soup, 293
   Vegetable Soup, 157
Spread, Garden Vegetable, 184
Steamed Garden Vegetables, 155
Steamed Herbed Vegetables, M303
Stew, Minestrone, 184
Yuca Con Mojo, 29
Venison
Roast, Grilled Venison, 278
Vinegars
Basil Vinegar, 218
Shallot-Tarragon-Garlic Vinegar, 191

Waffles
Wacky Waffles, 195
Walnuts
Bread, Walnut, 77
Brie, Walnut-Baked, 241
Cake, Walnut Coffee, 124
Chicken-and-Walnut Salad,
   Sunburst, 91
Dressing, Honey-Walnut, 107
Fruit, Cheese, and Nuts, 324
Green Beans, Lemon-Walnut, 304
Phyllo Baskets, Walnut-, 210
Sauce, Walnut Cream, 275
Wild Rice. *See* Rice/Wild Rice.
Wok Cooking
Beef-and-Shrimp Stir-Fry, 32
Hungarian Stir-Fry, 64

Yogurt
Dressing, Honey-Yogurt, 172
Dressing, Lemon-Yogurt, 17
Filling, Fresh Raspberry Crêpes
   with Yogurt, 123

Zucchini
Bread, Chocolate-Zucchini, 308
Cake, Zucchini-Carrot, 20
Pancakes, Zucchini, 43
Sauce, Zucchini-Mushroom, 71
Skillet, Zucchini-Tomato, 206
Soup with Cilantro,
   Zucchini, 130

Favorite Recipes

Record your favorite recipes below for quick and handy reference.

Recipe	Source/Page	Remarks

Recipe	Source/Page	Remarks